THE PURPOSE of this volume is to
☐ present and pote   ad'r'
                'irect

TIMOTHY W. COSTELLO holds a Ph.D.
from Fordham University and is Professor of Psychology and Management
in the Graduate School of Business
Administration of New York University. He is a consultant in management
development to business and to several governmental agencies. He is currently engaged in research on the
behavioral consequences of organizational change.

SHELDON S. ZALKIND holds a Ph.D.
from New York University. He is the
co-author of a previous volume on
developing people in industry, and has
done consulting and research with
major organizations. He is Associate
Professor of Psychology at the Bernard
M. Baruch School of Business and
Public Administration, The City College of The City University of New
York.

Both authors are members of the
American Psychological Association.

Psychology
in
Administration
A Research Orientation

Text with Integrated Readings

TIMOTHY W. COSTELLO

*Professor of Psychology and Management
Graduate School of Business Administration, New York University*

SHELDON S. ZALKIND

*Associate Professor of Psychology, Bernard
M. Baruch School of Business and Public
Administration, The City College of The
City University of New York*

PRENTICE-HALL, Inc., *Englewood Cliffs, N.J.*

Behavioral Sciences in Business Series
Herbert A. Simon, *Editor*

TO FORMER MENTORS TO WHOM WE OWE MUCH
Joseph F. Kubis and Louis D. Cohen
and
Douglas H. Fryer

Current printing (last digit):
13   12   11   10   9   8   7   6   5   4

PRENTICE-HALL INTERNATIONAL, INC.,   *London*
PRENTICE-HALL OF AUSTRALIA, PTY., LTD.,   *Sydney*
PRENTICE-HALL OF CANADA, LTD.,   *Toronto*
PRENTICE-HALL OF INDIA (PRIVATE) LTD.,   *New Delhi*
PRENTICE-HALL OF JAPAN, INC.,   *Tokyo*

C 73286

Foreword

When a human being goes to work for an organization, he brings with him all the characteristics of a whole man—motivations and emotions, knowledge, and intellectual capacities. Although placed in a different environment, he is the same man whom the individual psychologist has been studying in the laboratory. We should expect the same laws to govern his behavior.

This observation, so obvious by hindsight, has been a major guiding force in our recent rapid progress toward an understanding of administration and organizations. We have learned, step by step, to recognize in the complex behavior that we observe in organizations the same basic mechanisms that have emerged in the simpler conditions of the laboratory.

The route from psychology to administration is a two-way street. Going in one direction, we interpret administrative behavior in terms of psychological laws. Going the other way, we use organizational settings as social environments where psychological laws can be tested, and where ideas may be generated for their development and improvement. Thus, it becomes more and more essential for students of administration to have a good basic understanding of psychology, and for psychologists to know something about human behavior as it is observed in organizations.

This book is aimed at facilitating the passage between administration and psychology for those who start at either end of the route. It is organized in terms of categories that are familiar to the psychologist: perception, motivation, emotion, learning, attitude, and thinking. Each section starts with a discussion of basic psychological laws and knowledge that apply to the mechanisms under consideration. It proceeds toward examples of how these mechanisms operate in organizational situations.

A student of administration who works thoughtfully through the text and readings should find himself prepared to approach the professional literature of psychology, and to extract its implications for administrative behavior. Like Moliere's hero, he will realize that he has been speaking prose all his life—that only the vocabulary of traditional administrative theory has concealed its concern with human motivation and thinking.

A student of psychology can find herein some answers to questions about human behavior, but perhaps more interesting, suggestions of dozens of new questions calling for investigation—enough for several lifetimes of doctoral dissertations and research. Since World War II, psychology has taken new courage in exploring complex aspects of human behavior. Theory and technique have advanced to the point where it no longer seems hopeless to study problem solving, for example, in the laboratory, or even in organizational settings. The psychologist need no longer take the vow of poverty, eschewing the fascination and practical importance of behavior in organizations for the austerity of the memory drum or animal maze.

In sum, the organization of this book expresses confidence that we have reached a stage in the behavioral sciences where administration and psychology can cooperate closely with genuine advantage to both. The book's content gives some of the reasons for that confidence.

HERBERT A. SIMON
Carnegie Institute of Technology

Preface

This book is designed to bring present and potential administrators, and students into first-hand contact with the writings, theories, experiments, and problem-solving efforts of today's behavioral scientists. It makes available for modern management one means of meeting the growing pressure to find more scientific approaches toward the solution of organizational problems.

The book also has been developed for readers who seek answers to the question: "What should I know about the behavior of the individual in order to carry out more effectively the administrative phase of management?" Readers, curious about the answer to such a question, will be found at four levels: those already in managerial positions who wish to keep abreast of current scientific developments; participants in both formal and informal management development programs; graduate business students who are taking courses in administration; and advanced, undergraduate students in business administration programs. Although knowledge alone is not enough to develop administrative skill, it can provide a useful foundation on which skill can be built.

We ourselves are also certain that psychologists teaching various courses will find that many parts of this book may be appropriately assigned to students —but then, of course, we may be biased.

Each chapter contains both original text and selected readings. The readings have been embedded in textual material to provide both comprehensive and systematic coverage of major areas of psychological study. Our aim is to have each chapter provide both an overview and significant details of an aspect of human behavior relevant to administration.

The readings we have selected meet several criteria: (1) they concern aspects of behavior relevant to the administrative process; (2) they draw conclusions based principally on actual research rather than on armchair speculation or even experienced reminiscence; (3) they have been originally published within the past ten years or have achieved classical status in their influence on current thinking; (4) their language largely avoids the technical jargon that can make some professional writing overly difficult to understand.

Occasionally, the readings overlap in citing some of the same research findings. We have not deleted such material where we felt that to do so would interfere with the development of the author's own ideas. In the readings, we have adhered to the style of footnotes and bibliographic referencing as originally published, except where stated.

Some experienced administrators, looking at the research results included here, may be inclined to say that many findings only seem to verify "common sense." Two relevant comments can be made: sometimes "common sense" is supported by evidence from carefully controlled research and sometimes it is not. Without the research, we can't know which hunch is the correct one. Second, we sometimes have mutually contradictory, "after-the-fact" bits of "common sense," as shown in such old proverbs as "Out of sight, out of mind" versus "Absence makes the heart grow fonder." It may be that we all ought to keep in mind Stuart Chase's definition of common sense: that which assures us that the world is flat.

Our major expression of gratitude must go to the authors whose readings we have used. We hope they will find agreeable the setting in which we have placed their work and thank them for permission to use their writing. We are, in addition, particularly indebted to the many researchers whose findings we have cited in our research summaries.

Herbert A. Simon, Editor of the Prentice-Hall Behavioral Sciences in Business Series, has been especially helpful in his careful reading of our manuscript and in the many suggestions he made for its improvement. The structuring of Part Three and several aspects of Part Six have particularly benefitted from his helpful comments. We would like to hold him responsible for the shortcomings that remain, but alas, we cannot.

As every author knows, a book comes to completion only through the help of many people who contribute their ideas, time, and special skills. We have tried to indicate our appreciation to each of them by using the improvements they made possible. Here, we can mention only a few by name: Dr. Ronald Schwartz, for generously providing many bibliographic items in the area of person perception; Theodore Schwartz, for his assistance in the final verifying of bibliographic items; Doris Jacques, for generously providing skillful assistance in many areas, especially in "over-seeing" the typing of the manuscript and in the preparation of the index; David Sortor, for painstaking care in typing parts of the manuscript and bibliography; Robert Walters of the Prentice-Hall editorial staff for effective assistance in converting a manuscript into a book. Arlene Giulio, Veronica Ferrariola, and Marie Nasca were helpful in typing earlier parts of the manuscript. We express a very personal note of thanks to our students and others who, during the past year, have "understood" when we were not immediately available as they sought conferences, grades, or special assistance.

We gratefully acknowledge permissions to reprint copyrighted material granted by the following: American Psychological Association; *Human Relations;* American Psychiatric Association; Foundation for Research on Human Behavior; American Medical Association; *Personnel Administration; Administrative Science Quarterly; The Journal of Conflict Resolution; Saturday Review;* McGraw-Hill Book Company, Inc.; Scott Foresman & Company; University of Nebraska Press; American Personnel and Guidance Association; *Human Organization; Personnel Psychology, Industrial Management Review; Annual Review of Psychology;* American Association for the Advancement of Science; and Fund for the Republic.

We also acknowledge copyright permissions from: Harper & Row Publishers; Holt, Rinehart & Winston, Inc.; D. C. Heath & Company; The Macmillan Company; The Ronald Press Company; *The Journal of Business; The Public Opinion Quarterly; Industrial and Labor Relations Review; Sociometry;* and Stanford University Press.

TIMOTHY W. COSTELLO

SHELDON S. ZALKIND

Contents

PART ONE

Perceiving
People
and
Situations

Introduction

Significant interaction between two or more people would seem to be the very heart of administrative action. In these human relationships, perceiving plays an important, if sometimes subtle and intangible part.

Literally hundreds of times during the day, the administrator is perceived and his behavior interpreted by people around him. He, in turn, perceives others and interprets their behavior. This perceiving is not usually a slow and deliberate process of observation. Often, such activities are fleeting and barely conscious but they help to make up the human atmosphere in which the person lives and functions and moreover, are crucial for administrative success. For instance, the way an administrator is perceived as a conference leader can determine how often others participate and how well they accept his ideas. His own perceptions of the group will, in part, determine what he does as the leader. Also, when planning, he takes into account either explicitly or implicitly, the people who are involved in and affected by the planning. The success of his planning will depend to some extent on how he, as well as the plan, is perceived. His very ability to plan depends upon a complex sensory and perceptual process of which he is only dimly aware. His knowledge of the organization, his department, and company; the kinds of controls he decides to set up; and the way he directs the work effort of his group are all dependent upon a perceptual background that has accumulated over a lifetime.

That perceiving is not simply an accurate registering of "the outside," that it may, as a matter of fact, be considerably distorted, is suggested by a study of Likert's (1961),* summarized in Figure 1-1.

It is not possible to say who is "right." It is certain that the subordinates and supervisors are not "seeing" the same situation. Failure to communicate—in the sense of no communication—may be part of the reason; failure to communicate accurately—through perceptual distortion—is another important part.

---

* Bibliographic references are listed in the Bibliography at the end of the book, arranged alphabetically for each major part of the book. Where two or more references have the same author the date of each reference is indicated in the text; otherwise, only the author's name is given, either in the body of the text or in parenthesis at the end of the relevant sentence.

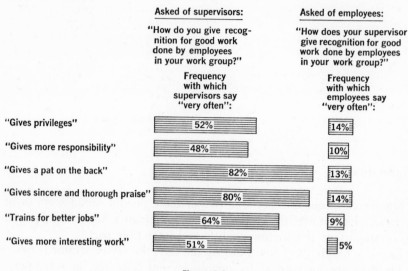

	Asked of supervisors: "How do you give recognition for good work done by employees in your work group?" Frequency with which supervisors say "very often":	Asked of employees: "How does your supervisor give recognition for good work done by employees in your work group?" Frequency with which employees say "very often":
"Gives privileges"	52%	14%
"Gives more responsibility"	48%	10%
"Gives a pat on the back"	82%	13%
"Gives sincere and thorough praise"	80%	14%
"Trains for better jobs"	64%	9%
"Gives more interesting work"	51%	5%

Figure 1-1

Comparison of Supervisors' Description of Their Behavior With Employees' Description of Their Experience. (R. Likert, *New Patterns in Management,* New York: McGraw-Hill Book Company, Inc., 1961, p. 91.)

Preview of Part One

Keeping in mind the ever-present function of perceiving in the administrative day, as well as the likelihood and importance of perceptual error, we turn our attention in Part One to some facts about perception developed through both laboratory and organizational research.

The earliest work in perception and judgment differed from the later research in two ways: (1) it dealt with the judgment of objects, not of people, and (2) it examined the influence of cues from the outside environment rather than subjective influences from within the individual. Emphasis gradually shifted from the objective to the subjective, and in 1958 Bruner, citing a series of researches, described the "New Look" in perception as one in which personal behavioral determinants of the perceptual process—need, values, cultural background—were being stressed. Taguiri, in the same year, edited a volume of research on perception of persons.

In one of the readings that follow, Bruner summarizes some of the earliest work on subjective influences on the perceptual process, and in his concept of "perceptual readiness" describes the importance of the framework or category system that the perceiver himself brings to the perceiving process. Tapping a different vein of research, Cantril describes perceiving as a "transaction" between the perceiver and the perceived, a process of negotiation in which the perceptual end-product is a result both of influences within the perceiver and of characteristics of the perceived. His work provides another perspective on the sizing up process.

The apparently simple process of forming impressions of others has been revealed as, in fact, a complex one. Because we may size up people quickly does not mean that the process is simple. The summary of work by Dailey illustrates one facet of this complexity—drawing premature conclusions—and how this affects our image of the other person.

There has been sufficient research on interpersonal perception for us to be able to identify some systematic errors that creep into the process. These are stereotyping, projection, the halo effect, and perceptual defense. Selections by Haire and by Haire and Grunes, as well as summaries of other research, describe the operation of these distorting influences.

Of particular relevance to administrative practice is the influence on perception of the characteristics of the perceiver, of the perceived, and of the situation. We summarize the research to highlight some conclusions that emerge from it. Along comparable lines, Dearborn and Simon illustrate the impact of place in the organization on perception.

Up to this point in Part One, we ask, "What are some of the influences on perceiving?" Next we reverse this question and ask, "What influence does accuracy of perceiving have on other behavior?" focusing particularly on its influence in producing effective interpersonal relations. Does it matter whether or not we perceive accurately?

Before going further, we might well caution the reader on one point. There is evidence here as elsewhere to support the cliche that a little learning can be a dangerous thing. A study by Crow, for example, found that a group of senior medical students were somewhat less accurate in their perceptions of others after training in physician-patient relationships than was an untrained control group. Not every training program that is designed to bring about change will do so. The danger is that a little learning may encourage the perceiver to respond with increased sensitivity to some kinds of individual differences. But he cannot gauge, without further observation, the significance of the differences he has seen, nor can he know that he is observing relevant kinds of differences. However, the reader need not lose heart, at this early stage. Although the Crow study offers a necessary caution, other studies have not been as discouraging (Stock and Thelen). Ultimately all sound practice must be based on knowledge. A little learning may be a dangerous thing, a thorough grounding in knowledge cannot be.

CHAPTER ONE

Nature
of the
Perceptual
Process

Some Basic Factors Influencing Perception, Including Need and Set

A good way to begin applying behavioral science research to administrative practice is to put aside the attitude of naive realism—the attitude that suggests that our perceptions simply register what is "out there." In fact, of course, they don't. We need ask: What are the major variables that form our perceptions and judgments of the outside world? Some of the variables identified in the literature up to the time of his review (1945) of research on object perception (where distortion may be less severe than with perception of people) led Johnson to suggest the following:

1. The perceiver may be influenced by considerations that he may not be able to identify; he responds to cues which are below the threshold, as it is called, of his awareness. That is, a judgment as to the dimensions of an object may be influenced by its color even though the perceiver may not be attending to the color.

2. When required to form difficult perceptual judgments, he may respond to irrelevant cues to arrive at a judgment. That is, in trying to assess honesty, it has been shown that the other person's smiling or not smiling is used as a cue to judge his honesty.

3. In making abstract or intellectual judgments, he may be influenced by emotional factors—what is right is actually perceived on the basis of what is liked.

4. He will weigh perceptual evidence coming from respected (or favored sources) more heavily than that coming from other sources.
5. A perceiver may not be able to identify all the factors on which his judgments are based. Even if he is aware of these factors he is unlikely to realize how much weight he gives them.

This does not mean that we respond *only* to the subtle or irrelevant cues or to emotional factors. We often perceive the obvious, obviously; but we are quite likely to respond as well to the less obvious and less objective.

Bruner, in the reading that follows, summarizes some more recent research than that on which Johnson's conclusions are based, and provides a systematically worked-out answer to the question: What considerations influence perception? He describes research, indicating the importance of our values and needs as perceptual determinants, and on the basis of this research suggests that the perceiver brings to the task a grid of categories into which events will be forced. He develops his concept of "perceptual readiness" as a basic consideration that influences the perceptual end-product.

READING 1-1

The "New Look" in Perception[1]

JEROME BRUNER

Perhaps the immediate impetus to contemporary concern with the role of perceptual processes in social behavior came from a series of experiments on determinants of perceptual organization—determinants that could be called "behavioral" which relate to such influences as need, social values, attitudes, stress, cultural background, etc., in contrast to "autochthonous" which refers to stimulus factors. These experiments, taken as a sequence, came, rather waggishly, to be called the "New Look" in perception. A sampling of some of the principal studies carried out will serve to highlight some of the critical problems that have faced the theorist concerned with formulating a model of the perceptual process that has some relevance to the understanding of social behavior. In the final section we shall return to the nature of such a theoretical model.[2]

The early studies were principally concerned with showing the nature of "distortion" in perception and the sources

[1] Abridged from "Social Psychology and Perception" in *Readings in Social Psychology* (3rd ed.), E. Maccoby, T. Newcomb, and E. Hartley, eds. Copyright © 1958 by Holt, Rinehart and Winston, Inc. By permission. This article was specially written for the Maccoby Readings book.

[2] Since there have appeared several hundred experimental investigations of motivational and social determinants of perception, it is indeed difficult and certainly arbitrary to select a few for special mention. The choice of the experiments is based partly upon the degree to which they illustrate basic theoretical issues, and partly on expository convenience—in about that order.

of perceptual inaccuracy and were, in the main, influenced by thinking imported from clinical psychiatry where such doctrines as "autistic thinking," "defense," "primary process" (hypothesized infantile wishful hallucination) had become dominant as a result of Freud's pioneering work. The studies of Gardner Murphy and his colleagues are a case in point. Levine, Chein, and Murphy[3] showed their subjects a set of food pictures behind a ground-glass screen that obscured them to the point of ambiguity. The subjects were then asked to give the first association that the obscured pictures brought to mind. They found that associations connected with food and eating increased as the hours of food deprivation of the subjects increased, reaching a maximum around ten to 12 hours of starvation. After this, the number of food associations declined. The authors attempted to explain the finding in terms of the pleasure principle operating under conditions of mild drive, being supplanted by the reality principle when hunger became severe. Like many pioneering experiments, there was much wrong with the design of this study—the kind of associational response employed, the fact that the subjects knew they would be fed after the requisite number of hours of being without food, etc. But it stimulated many follow-up studies. We now know that the results of Levine, Chein, and Murphy are a special case of a more general one whose nature is not yet clear.

McClelland and Atkinson,[4] for example, worked with subjects who were unaware of the relation between their hunger and the perceptual test they were being given. The subjects, sailors at a submarine base, were asked to "recognize" "barely perceptible" objects on a screen. Actually the screen was blank. The men showed an increase in instrumental food response—seeing eating utensils and the like—but no increase with hours of deprivation in the number of consummatory food objects seen.

Yet, in another study, under conditions of prolonged and chronic semistarvation, conscientious objectors show no increase at all in the number or quality of food associations or readiness to perceive food objects (see the wartime work of Brozek and his colleagues[5]). Here the question may well have been one of pride: these dedicated young men were doing their service by serving as subjects in an experiment. Giving in to hunger may have been something to avoid as almost a matter of honor. With respect to chronically food-deprived prisoners of war and concentration camp victims that I have interviewed shortly after release, one finds that there is repeated mention of two extreme types: those preoccupied with food and those who avoid the topic as much as possible. One can cite other studies that add further subtleties to the complex pattern that seems to emerge, but there is now enough evidence before us to suggest that not the *amount* of need but the *way* in which a person learns to *handle* his needs determines the manner in which motivation and cognitive selectivity will interact. Autism or wishful thinking are scarcely universal modes of coping with one's needs. It is conceivable that in a

[3] R. Levine, I. Chein, and G. Murphy, "The Relation of the Intensity of a Need to the Amount of Perceptual Distortion, a Preliminary Report," *J. Psychol.*, 1942, XIII, 283-293.

[4] D. C. McClelland and J. W. Atkinson, "The Projective Expression of Needs: I. The effect of different Intensities of the Hunger drive on Perception," *J. Psychol.*, 1948, XXV, 205-222.

[5] J. Brozek, H. Guetzkow, and M. G. Baldwin, "A Quantitative Study of Perception and Association in Experimental Semistarvation," *J. Pers.*, 1951, XIX, 245-264.

culture or in a family setting where emphasis is placed upon asceticism and denial of needs, autism would be the exception. On the whole, then, selectivity reflects the nature of the person's mode of striving for goals rather than the amount of need which he seems to be undergoing.

Closely related to this line of investigation are studies on the role of interest, value, and attitude, and this work brings up several additional subtleties. The experimental work of Postman, Bruner, and McGinnies[6] indicated that the speed and ease with which words were recognized when briefly presented in a fast-exposure apparatus (tachistoscope) was a function of the value areas these words represented and of the interest the subjects in the experiment evinced in these various value areas as measured by the Allport-Vernon Study of Values which tests for the relative dominance of religious, esthetic, political, social, theoretical, and economic interests. The general finding was that the greater the dominance of a value in the person, the more rapidly he would recognize words representing that area. The authors found that the hypotheses offered by subjects prior to correct recognition were particularly revealing, suggesting that in the presence of low-value words there was some form of defensive avoidance—the perceiving of blanks, scrambled letters, or even derogatory words which the authors called "contravaluant hypotheses." With high-value words, on the contrary, subjects tended in excess of chance to propose guesses that were in the value area of the stimulus word prior to correct recognition, in keeping with a subsequent finding of Bricker and

Chapanis[7] that subjects can obtain partial information from words when they are presented below threshold. Later studies by Bruner and Postman[8] on blocks in perceiving personally threatening words and by McGinnies[9] on the raising of identification thresholds for taboo words led to the development of the concept of "perceptual defense," a kind of blocking or recognition for classes of materials that were personally and/or culturally unacceptable to the perceiver, a "proscribed list" at the entry port so to speak.

It was argued by Solomon and Howes[10] that the finding on the effect of values could be accounted for by a factor of frequency—that the person interested in religion was more likely to have selective exposure to religious words and symbols. Howes[11] then went on to show that the amount of time required to recognize a word in the English language could be expressed rather precisely as a function of the logarithm of the frequency with which the word appeared in printed English as recorded in the useful Thorndike-Lorge frequency count.[12] But since economic

---

[6] L. Postman, J. S. Bruner, and E. McGinnies, "Personal Values as Selective Factors in Perception," *J. Abnorm. Soc. Psychol.*, 1948, XXCIII, 148-153.

[7] P. D. Bricker and A. Chapanis, "Do Incorrectly Perceived Tachistoscopic Stimuli Convey Some Information?," *Psychol. Rev.*, 1953, LX, 181-188.

[8] J. S. Bruner and L. Postman, "Emotional Selectivity in Perception and Reaction," *J. Pers.*, 1947, XVI, 69-77.

[9] E. McGinnies, "Emotionality and Perceptual Defense," *Psychol. Rev.*, 1949, LVI, 244-251.

[10] R. L. Solomon and D. W. Howes, "Word Frequency, Personal Values, and Visual Deviation Thresholds," *Psychol. Rev.*, 1951, LVIII, 256-270.

[11] D. Howes, "On the Interpretation of Word Frequency as a Variable Affecting Speed of Recognition," *J. Exp. Psychol.*, 1954, XLVIII, 106-122.

[12] E. L. Thorndike and I. Lorge, *The Teacher's Word Book of 30,000 Words* (New York: Teachers College, Columbia University, 1944).

words are likely to be more frequently encountered in printed English than theoretical words, the general frequency of words in English would not be sufficient grounds to explain why some individuals, high in theoretical interests, recognize theoretical words more quickly than economic words such as "money" or "price." We must invoke a notion of "idiosyncratic frequency," an individual's frequency of encounter without regard to frequency in English. Indeed, Postman and Schneider[13] showed that for very common words drawn from the six value-areas of the Allport-Vernon test, the relative position of the values for the subject made little difference. With rarer words it did, with the more valued ones being recognized more easily.

The upshot of this debate, it would appear, is twofold and of considerable significance. Perceptual readiness, the ease with which items are recognized under less than optimal viewing conditions, seems to reflect not only the needs and modes of striving of an organism but also to reflect the requirement that surprise be minimized—that perceptual readiness be predictive in the sense of being tuned to what is likely to be present in the environment as well as what is needed for the pursuit of our enterprises. The predictive nature of perceptual readiness, however, reflects more than the frequency with which things occur. Rather, it is best thought of as the matching of perceptual readiness to the probable *sequences* of events in the environments. We come to learn what goes with what. We *hear* the approaching whistle of a train and are readied to *see* the train. We learn, if you will, the probabilistic texture of the world, conserve this learning, use it as a guide to

tuning our perceptual readiness to what is most likely next. It is this that permits us to "go beyond the information given." That there is danger in using such a guide is illustrated in a study by Bruner and Postman on the perception of incongruity.[14] If playing cards with suit and color reversed—a red four of clubs, say—are presented to subjects for brief intervals of a few milliseconds, what occurs is perceptual completion according to high probability linkages we have already learned; the subject "sees" a red four of hearts or a black four of clubs. Thresholds of identification increase grossly: when subjects are presented with these incongruous stimuli, it takes them an inordinately long exposure time to "see" what is actually there. But human organisms unlearn and learn quickly: having seen the incongruity finally, later instances are much more rapidly identified correctly.

It is characteristic of perceptual identification of things that the larger the number of alternatives the person is expecting, the more difficult it is to recognize any single one of the alternatives that does occur. In an experiment by Bruner, Miller, and Zimmerman[15] it was found that it is much easier to recognize a word when it is one of four that may occur than when it is one of eight or 16 or 32 that may occur. This suggests that where speed is required in perception—as under stress conditions or under conditions of exigent motivation—that the likelihood of erroneous perception increases. That is to say, to gain speed, we limit the alternative hypotheses that we are willing to

13 L. Postman and B. Schneider, "Personal Values, Visual Recognition, and Recall," *Psychol. Rev.*, 1951, LVIII, 271-284.

14 J. S. Bruner and L. Postman, "On the Perception of Incongruity: A Paradigm," *J. Pers.*, 1949, XVIII, 206-223.

15 J. S. Bruner, G. A. Miller, and C. Zimmerman, "Discriminative Skill and Discriminative Matching in Perceptual Recognition," *J. Exp. Psychol.*, 1955, XLIX, 187-192.

entertain. In the event of ambiguous stimulation, as in social perception generally, such speed-producing monopolistic hypotheses are likely to be confirmed. We expect, for example, a hostile action from a disliked person; he does something equivocal; we "see" it as a hostile act and thus confirm our expectation. It is the case, moreover, that under conditions where alternative expectancies must be limited, we will be more likely to adopt socially conventional expectancies or ones that reflect our more basic needs. It is in this sense that stress and social pressure serve to reduce the subtlety of the registration process.

One final matter must be mentioned before turning briefly to theory. It has to do with the perception of magnitude, a subject which does not at first seem closely related to social psychology. An early study by Bruner and Goodman[16] opened the issue. The study was simply conceived—in both a good and a bad sense. Children, ages 10 to 11, divided into those from fairly prosperous homes and those from a slum settlement house, were given the task of adjusting a variable patch of light to the sizes of pennies, nickels, dimes, quarters, and half dollars. Half the subjects worked with coins in hand, half from memory. Control groups adjusted the light patch to cardboard discs of the same sizes. The findings, in general, were that the sizes of the more valuable coins were overestimated, of less valuable coins underestimated. The effects were greater for the memory condition than for the condition with coin present. No significant effect was found for paper discs. In general, the economically well-to-do children showed less of the value-distortion effect than the poor children.

The study has been repeated several times, and as McCurdy[17] and Tajfel[18] point out, the same effect found more often than not under a variety of conditions. One experiment by Carter and Schooler[19] found somewhat contrary results. The same trends were observed, but they fell short of statistical significance save for the condition where size was estimated from memory, where significant results were observed. A later study by Bruner and Rodrigues[20] pointed up one faulty assumption of the earlier studies mentioned. Overestimation and underestimation of size is always stated with respect to the measured sizes of the coins, the "physically accurate" size. This is a psychologically naïve way of describing what goes on in judgment of magnitude. Rather, one should ask about the *relative* subjective sizes of coins of different value. The study by Bruner and Rodrigues had as its principal object to show that there was a *greater separation* in subjective size between a nickel and a quarter than there was for comparable-sized white metal discs. Tajfel[21] has developed this point in an interesting theoretical paper, pointing out that it is one of the functions of perceptual judgment to accentuate the apparent difference in magnitudes between objects that differ in value, provided that the difference in magnitude is associated

---

[16] J. S. Bruner and C. C. Goodman, "Value and Need as Organizing Factors in Perception," *J. Abnorm. & Soc. Psychol.*, 1947, XLII, 33-44.

[17] H. G. McCurdy, "Coin Perception Studies and the Concept of Schemata," *Psychol. Rev.*, 1956, LXIII, 160-168.
[18] H. Tajfel, "Value and the Perceptual Judgment of Magnitude," *Psychol. Rev.*, 1957, LXIV, 192-204.
[19] L. F. Carter and K. Schooler, "Value, Need and Other Factors in Perception," *Psychol. Rev.*, 1949, LVI, 200-207.
[20] J. S. Bruner and J. S. Rodrigues, "Some Determinants of Apparent Size," *J. Abnorm. & Soc. Psychol.*, 1953, XLVIII, 17-24.
[21] Tajfel, *op. cit.*

with the difference in value—as if, so to speak, the two attributes, value and magnitude, are confounded in a way to point up and accentuate value difference. In short, even in the estimation of magnitude, judgmental processes reflect the social conventions that establish values for various elements of the environment.[22]

On Theoretical Models of Perception

. . .

The first, and perhaps most self-evident point upon reflection, is that perceiving or registering on an object or an event in the environment involves an act of categorization. We "place" things in categories. That is a "man" and he is "honest" and he is now "walking" in a manner that is "leisurely" with the "intention" of "getting some relaxation." Each of the words in quotation marks involves a sorting or placement of stimulus input on the basis of certain cues that we learn how to use. Now it is of great importance to bear in mind that most of the categories into which we sort for identification are learned on the basis of experience, by virtue of our membership in a culture and a linguistic community, and by the nature of the needs we must fulfill in order to exist beyond some degraded level. Not only are the categories learned, but we learn to estimate the likelihood that placement of an event into a category on the basis of a few cues will be "accurate"—by which we mean, *predictive* in the sense that a closer look will bear it out or that it will be consensually validated when other perceivers come on the scene or it

will be confirmed by technological inspection.

We may take it as self-evident that some categories we employ are more amenable to check by prediction. The cues we use for judging an object "distant" or a surface "impenetrable" are checked a thousand times a day in getting about: walking, driving, reaching. Others are less readily checked. Whether, on the basis of a few signs, we can judge whether a man is "honorable," given the difficulty of establishing a quick and adequate criterion, is questionable. The category, established by a culture in response to its social needs, resists validation. It is perhaps the case that modes of categorizing that are amenable to firm and immediate validation with respect to predictiveness are the ones that are more universal to the human race, more easily diffused and learned. The less readily a form of categorizing is able to be predictively validated, the more will it reflect the idiosyncrasies of a culture. It is not surprising that the famous Cambridge expedition to the Torres Straits[23] at the opening of this century found so few differences in the perception of distance, size, etc., in comparing primitive Pacific Islanders and English undergraduates.

It is also apparent that the categories of events with which we become accustomed to dealing are organized into systems or structures, bound together in various ways: by virtue of the fact that one class of events is likely to follow another or because classes of events are closely bound by some other principle than mere association as, for example, that several are required in order for certain objectives to be reached. Thus, displacement of a dot from one position

---

[22] So brief a summary of a field of research as complicated as magnitude estimation and the role of value factors in it is bound to be oversimplified. For a fuller account, the reader is referred to the excellent papers of Tajfel, *op. cit.*, and McCurdy, *op. cit.*

---

[23] W. H. R. Rivers, "Vision," *Reports of the Cambridge Anthropological Expedition to Torres Straits*, 1901, II, 1-132.

to another is categorized as "a dot moving" and not as "first a dot at position *A*, then another dot at position *B*." As we have noted before, recoding into systems serves to keep mental life from becoming burdened with a diversity of unrelated particulars. Highly practiced perception is a case in point. A practiced baseball spectator joins and meshes a highly complex set of categorized events into a structure called a "double play."

In addition to the problem of categories and category systems and how they are formed, there is also a question of the accessibility of such categories for use by a perceiver. It is often the case that we fail to identify an event properly although we are knowledgeable about the class of events which it exemplifies; fail to do so even though the cues are clear. And as the work cited earlier in this paper has shown, certain categories manifest their accessability by permitting rapid identification of relevant objects under conditions of very brief or very "fuzzy" exposure. What makes certain kinds of categorizing responses sometimes available and sometimes not? What can be said in general is that category accessibility reflects two sets of factors. Need and interest states, as we have implied, increase accessibility of those categories of objects that relate to their fulfillment or furthering—not necessarily in a wish-fulfilling or autistic way, as noted before, but in a manner consonant with achieving realistically a desired goal. The second set of factors governing category accessibility has to do with the predictive requirements of perception and the need to avoid disruptive mistakes. These requirements tune the readiness of the perceiver to match the likelihood of events in the environment. When we are hungry, we tend to be alerted to signs of restaurants, if we usually assuage hunger in restaurants. We notice ones we have never noticed before. Our "restaurant"

category has become highly "available." But we look for and expect restaurants at the street level and not in the sky or atop trees. It is this balancing of need-induced alertness and event-matching expectancy that makes it possible for perception to act in the service of needs and interests and, at the same time, with due regard for reality.

In conclusion, perceptual readiness reflects the dual requirements of coping with an environment—directedness with respect to goals—and efficiency with respect to the means by which the goals can be attained. It is no matter of idle interest that a religious man picks up perceptually things that are relevant to his interest more easily and more quickly than other things, and at the same time, this efficiency continues to reflect what is likely to occur in his surroundings. What it suggests is that once a society has patterned a man's interests and trained him to expect what is likely in that society, it has gained a great measure of control not only on his thought processes, but also on the very material on which thought works—the experienced data of perception. It is not surprising, then, that the social psychologist has shown a renewed interest in the process of perceiving. To understand the manner in which man responds to and copes with his social environment we must know what that environment is *to him*. The physicist provides a description of the nature of stimulation in such terms as wave lengths, radiant energy, chemical compounds. Nobody confuses these descriptions with what we experience—colors, brightness, tastes. The student of society, like the physicist, provides descriptions of the "external environment" in terms of stratification, totemic clans, moities. The question is how people perceive or register upon these features of the social environment. That is what is crucial in determining how we respond.

For our second reading, we have selected a paper originally presented by psychologist Hadley Cantril to a group of psychiatrists. He provides the reader with an opportunity to travel a little of the same territory as that previously traveled with Bruner but along a different path, and with a different perspective. The result, we believe, is a deeper awareness and a fuller conviction that every judgment about the outside can be viewed as a transaction between the perceiver and the perceived. The consequences of this negotiation process thus takes on coloring from both the perceiver and the object (or person) he is perceiving. We never completely lose ourselves; nor do we ever completely break through the outer shell of our own being. Cantril anticipates later chapters in identifying some characteristics of the perceiver that have significant impact on his judgments.

READING 1-2

Perception and Interpersonal Relations[1]

HADLEY CANTRIL

. . . the more one studies perception, the more one sees that what we label "perception" is essentially a process which man utilizes to make his purposive behavior more effective and satisfying, and that this behavior always stems from and is rooted in a personal behavioral center. Thus perception involves numerous aspects of behavior which we rather artificially and necessarily differentiate in order to get a toehold for understanding, but which, in the on-going process of living, orchestrate together in a most interdependent way.

This means, then, that the nature of perception can only be understood if somehow we manage to start off with what some of us call a "first person point of view" represented by the traditional psychological investigator. . . . A very

nice expression of [the] state of affairs was, incidentally, recently made by Aldous Huxley in his book *The Genius and the Goddess:*

> What a gulf between *im*pression and *ex*pression! That's our ironic fate—to have Shakespearian feelings and (unless by billion-to-one chance we happen to *be* Shakespeare) to talk about them like automobile salesmen or teen-agers or college professors. We practice alchemy in reverse—touch gold and it turns to lead; touch the pure lyrics of experience, and they turn into the verbal equivalents of tripe and hogwash.

Background

. . . [A] point of view . . . has developed rather recently in psychology and has been dubbed "transactional psychology." While I do not want to spend time here repeating what has been published in a variety of sources, I might at least very briefly note some of the major

[1] Read at the A. P. A. Regional Meeting in Montreal, Nov. 8-11, 1956. Abridged from *American Journal of Psychiatry, 114* (2) (1957), pp. 119-126.

emphases of transactional psychology before discussing certain aspects and some experimental results (1, 2, 3, 4). . . . Here, then, are some of the emphases of transactional psychology which may give us a take-off for discussion:

Our perception depends in large part on the assumptions we bring to any particular occasion. It is, as Dewey and Bentley long ago pointed out, not a "reaction to" stimuli in the environment but may be more accurately described as a "transaction with" an environment.

This implies that the meanings and significances we assign to things, to symbols, to people, and to events are the meanings and significances we have built up through our past experience, and are not inherent or intrinsic in the "stimulus" itself.

Since our experience is concerned with purposive behavior, our perceptions are learned in terms of our purposes and in terms of what is important and useful to us.

Since the situations we are in seldom repeat themselves exactly and since change seems to be the rule of nature and of life, our perception is largely a matter of weighing probabilities, of guessing, of making hunches concerning the probable significance or meaning of "what is out there" and of what our reaction should be toward it, in order to protect or preserve ourselves and our satisfactions, or to enhance our satisfactions. This process of weighing the innumerable cues involved in nearly any perception is, of course, a process that we are generally not aware of.

Creating Constancies

Since things in the world outside us— the physical world and more especially the social world—are by no means static, are not entirely determined and predictable, experience for most of us often carries at least some mild overtone of "concern" which we can label "curiosity," "doubt" or "anxiety" depending on the circumstances involved.

One of my favorite illustrations of this point is an incident described by Carl Sandburg in his autobiography, *Always the Young Strangers.*

> I have always enjoyed riding up front in a smoking car, in a seat back of the "deadheads," the railroaders going back to the home base. Their talk about each other runs free. . . . Once I saw a young fireman in overalls take a seat and slouch down easy and comfortable. After a while a brakeman in blue uniform came along and planted himself alongside the fireman. They didn't say anything. The train ran along. The two of them didn't even look at each other. Then the brakeman, looking straight ahead, was saying, "Well, what do you know today?" and kept looking straight ahead till suddenly he turned and stared the fireman in the face, adding, "For sure." I thought it was a keen and intelligent question. "What do you know today—for *sure?*" I remember the answer. It came slow and honest. The fireman made it plain what he knew that day for sure: "Not a damn thing!" . . .

Thus we seldom can count on complete 100% surety in terms of a perfect correspondence between our assumptions concerning the exact experience we may have if we do a certain thing and the experience we actually do have as the consequence of the action we undertake.

In an attempt to try to minimize our potential lack of surety concerning any single occasion and thereby maximize our sense of surety concerning the effectiveness of our action in achieving our intent, we build up "constancies" and begin to count on them. While a great deal of experimental work has been done on "constancies" in the psychological laboratory, we still have much more to learn. And above all, we have a great deal to learn about constancy as we extend this concept into the field of our interpersonal relations.

Parenthetically, one of the most important things we have to learn is that the "constancy" we create and that we describe usually by means of some word, symbol, or abstract concept *is* man's creation, the validity of which can only be tested and the meaning of which can only be experienced in terms of some behavior which has consequences to us and signals to us what the concept refers to.

We create these constancies by attributing certain *consistent* and *repeatable* characteristics to what they refer to, so that we can guess with a fair degree of accuracy what the significances and meanings are of the various sensory cues that impinge upon us. We do this so that we will not have to make fresh guesses at every turn.

These significances we build up about objects, people, symbols, and events, or about ideas all orchestrate together to give us what we might call our own unique *"reality world."* This "reality world" as we experience it includes, of course, our own fears and hopes, frustrations and aspirations, our own anxiety and our own faith. For these psychological characteristics of life . . . are just as real for us in determining our behavior as are chairs, stones or mountains or automobiles. It seems to me that anything that takes on significance for us in terms of our own personal behavioral center *is* "real" in the psychological sense.

Assigning Significances

Let me illustrate with reference to a few recent experiments the way in which

the significance we attach to others "out there" seems to be affected by what we bring to the situation. Incidentally but important: I do want to underscore that the experiments mentioned here are only exploratory; are only, I believe, opening up interesting vistas ahead. I am in no sense attempting to indicate what their full theoretical implications may be . . . [I . . .] mention them because of my deep conviction that psychology can be both humanistic and methodologically rigorous.

A whole series of most promising experiments now seems possible with the use of a modern adaptation of an old-fashioned piece of psychological equipment, the stereoscope. Dr. Edward Engel who devised the apparatus has already published a description of it and reported some of his first findings (5). As you know, the stereoscope in a psychological laboratory has been used to study binocular rivalry and fusion but the material viewed almost always consisted of dots and lines or geometrical patterns. Engel was curious to see what would happen if meaningful figures were used instead of the traditional material.

The results are really most exciting. In Engel's experiments he prepares what he calls "stereograms" consisting of photographs 2 x 2 inches, one of which is seen with the left eye, the other with the right. The photographs he used first were those of members of the Princeton football team just as they appeared in the football program. Although there were slight differences in the size and position of the heads and in the characteristics of light and shadow, still there was sufficient superimposition to get binocular fusion. And what happens? A person looks into the stereoscope and sees one face. He describes this face. And it almost invariably turns out that he is describing neither the face of the man seen with the left eye nor the face of the man seen with the right eye. He is describing a new and different face, a face that he has created out of the features of the two he is looking at. Generally the face seen in this particular case is made up of the dominant features of the two individuals. And generally the face created by the observer in this situation is more attractive and appealing than either of those seen separately. When the observer is shown the trick of the experiment by asking him to close first one eye and then the other and to compare the face he originally saw with the other two, he himself characterizes the face he created as more handsome, more pleasant, a fellow he'd like better, etc.

I hasten to add, however, that we should by no means jump to the conclusion that an individual picks out the "best" or "most attractive" features of figures presented to him in a situation of binocular fusion. For example, Professor Gordon Allport recently took one of Engel's stereoscopes with him to South Africa and initiated some experimental work there, using photographs of members of the different racial groups which make up that complex community.

While the experiments in South Africa have only just begun and no conclusion should be drawn, it is significant to note that in recent letters communicating the early results, Allport reported that when the stereograms consist of a European paired with an Indian, a colored person compared with an Indian, etc., the Zulus see an overwhelming preponderance of Indians. For the Zulu is most strongly prejudiced against the Indian who represents a real threat to him. Allport also reports that when Europeans in South Africa view the stereogram they tend to see more colored faces than white. It would seem, then, that a person sees what is "significant" with significance

defined in terms of his relationship to what he is looking at.

One pair of slides we use in demonstrating this piece of equipment consists of two stereograms, each a photograph of a statue in the Louvre. One of the statues is that of a Madonna with Child, the other a lovely young female nude. While I am unable so far to predict what any given individual will "see," no doubt such a prediction might be made after some good psychiatric interviewing. But let me describe what happened in a typical viewing of these stereograms. The viewers happened to be two distinguished psychologists who were visiting me one morning, one from Harvard, the other from Yale. The first looked into the stereoscope and reported that he saw a Madonna with Child. A few seconds later he exclaimed, "But my God, she is undressing." What had happened so far was that somehow she had lost the baby she was holding and her robe had slipped down from her shoulders and stopped just above the breast line. Then in a few more seconds she lost her robe completely and became the young nude. For this particular professor, the nude never did get dressed again. Then my second friend took his turn. For a few seconds he could see nothing but the nude and then he exclaimed, "But now a robe is wrapping itself around her." And very soon he ended up with the Madonna with Child and as far as I know still remains with that vision. Some people will never see the nude; others will never see the Madonna if they keep the intensity of light the same on both stereograms.

In the situation described above, we do not have conditions for genuine fusion, but rather a condition which introduces conflict and choice in the possible meaning of the content represented. In order to learn whether or not there might be differences in choice that would be culturally determined, a cross cultural comparison was made by Dr. James Bagby.[6] He constructed pairs of stereograms that would create binocular rivalry: in one stereogram of each pair he had a picture of some individual, object or symbol that would be of particular interest to Mexicans; in the other stereogram he had a picture that would be of particular significance to Americans. For example, one pair of slides consisted of a picture of a bull fighter matched with a stereogram picturing a baseball player. When these pairs were shown to a sample of Mexican school teachers, an overwhelming proportion of them "saw" the Mexican symbol; when the same slides were presented to a group of American school teachers, the overwhelming proportion "saw" the American symbol.

Incidentally, the Engel stereoscope is so constructed that one can get some idea of the relative "strength" of each of the stereograms by adjusting the intensity of the lighting on each. Hence, if the lighting is equivalent on two stereograms in a rivalry situation, one can reduce the amount of lighting on the one that originally predominates, increase the amount of light on the one that was not "seen" and find the point where the first one disappears and the second one "comes in."

A modification of the stereoscope has just been completed by Mr. Adlerstein in the Princeton laboratory. Our thought was that it might be extremely useful both in the clinical and social areas, if instead of having to use photographs of objects or people, a person could view the real thing—that is, the faces of real, live individuals or pairs of actual objects. So by means of prisms and mirrors, this device was constructed and I have only very recently had the opportunity of experiencing the resulting phenomena. I must say it is strange and wonderful. For example, when I viewed Mr. Adlerstein

and Mrs. Pauline Smith, Curator of our Demonstration Center, I seemed to be looking at a very effeminate Mr. Adlerstein who was wearing Mrs. Smith's glasses. Though weird, he was extremely "real." At one point while I was observing them Mrs. Smith began to talk yet it was Adlerstein's lips that were moving! Tingling with excitement and with a certain amount of anxiety, I drove home and asked my wife and daughter to come down to the laboratory so that I could take a look at them. I was, of course, fearful that I might see only one or the other. But fortunately, again I got an amazing fusion—a quite real and lovely head composed of a blending of my daughter's hair and chin and my wife's eyes and mouth—an harmonious composition that would do justice to any artist and which I created almost instantaneously and without any awareness of what was going on. These pieces of apparatus seem to me to have enormous potential usefulness for studying the way in which we create the world around us. I am hoping, for example, that before long someone in a position to do so may use this sort of equipment in a study of disturbed children. The child—having two eyes and two parents—might in some situations and in a very few seconds reveal a good bit about his inner life and his interpersonal family relations.

. . .

We could continue at some length reporting experiments which seem to show that what we "perceive" is, as already emphasized, in large part our own creation and depends on the assumptions we bring to the particular occasion. We seem to give meaning and order to sensory impingements in terms of our own needs and purposes and this process of selection is actively creative.

Social Constancies and Self-Constancy

It is clear that when we look for constancies in other people either as individuals or as members of a group a variety of complications is introduced. For when people are involved, as contrasted to inorganic objects or most forms of life, we are dealing with purposes, with motives, with intentions which we have to take into account in our perceptual process—the purposes, motives and intensions of other people often difficult to understand. The purposes and intentions of these other people will, of course, change as conditions change; and they will change as behavior progresses from one goal to another. Other people's purposes will be affected by our purposes, just as our purposes will be affected by theirs.

It is by no means a quick and easy process, then, to endow the people with whom we participate in our interpersonal relations with constancies and repeatabilities that we can always rely on. And yet we must, of course, continue the attempt to do so, so that our own purposeful action will have a greater chance of bringing about the satisfying consequences we intended. So we try to pigeonhole people according to some role, status, or position. We create constancies concerning people and social situations. These provide us with certain consistent characteristics that will ease our interpretation and make our actions more effective so long as there is some correspondence between the attribution we make and the consequence we experience from it in our own action.

The "social constancies" we learn obviously involve the relationships between ourselves and others. So if any social constancy is to be operational, there must also be a sense of "self-constancy." The two are interdependent. Since the human being necessarily derives so much of his value satisfaction from association with other human beings, his conception of his "self," his own "self-constancy" and "self-significance" is determined to a large extent by the significance he has to other people and the way they behave toward him. . . .

Perceptual Change

Laboratory experimentation as well as research in the field of opinion and attitude change seems to demonstrate beyond a shadow of a doubt that the major condition for a change in our perception, our attitudes or opinions is a frustration experienced in carrying out our purposes effectively because we are acting on the basis of assumptions that prove "wrong." For example, Dr. Kilpatrick has demonstrated that apparently the only way in which we can "learn" to see our distorted room distorted is to become frustrated with the assumption that the room is "square" in the process of trying to carry out some action in the room (8). It is clear that an "intellectual," "rational," or "logical" understanding of a situation is by no means sufficient to alter perception. The psychotherapist has taught us how successful reconditioning requires a therapy which simplifies goals so that their accomplishment can be assured through an individual's action as he experiences the successful consequences of his own behavior and thereby rebuilds his confidence in himself.

In this connection I recall a conversation I had in 1948 in Paris with an extremely intelligent woman who was at that time a staff member of the Soviet Embassy in Paris. We were at some social gathering and she began to ask me about American elections and the two-party system. She just couldn't understand it. She wasn't trying to be "smart" or supercilious. She was simply baffled. She couldn't "see" why we had to have 2 parties. For, obviously, one man was better than another and why wasn't he made President and kept as President as long as he proved to be the best man? It was a difficult argument for me to understand, just as my argument was impossible for her to understand. It was much more than a matter of opinion, stereotype or prejudice on either side. We were simply living in different reality worlds, actually experiencing entirely different significances in happenings which might appear to "an objective" "outside" observer to be the same for both of us.

Parenthetically, while one of the outstanding characteristics of man is often said to be his amazing capacity to learn, it seems to me that an equally outstanding characteristic is man's amazing capacity to "unlearn" which is, I think, not the exact opposite. Because man is not entirely a creature of habit, he has the fortunate ability to slough off what is no longer of use to him.

The Reality of Abstractions and the Commonness of Purposes

In order to ease our interpersonal relations and to increase the commonness of the significances we may attribute to the happenings around us, man has created abstractions in his attempt to bring order into disorder and to find more universal guides for living no matter what the unique and individual purposes and circumstances of an individual may be. Such abstractions are represented by our scientific formulations, our ethical, political, legal and religious systems. The abstractions can be recalled and repeated at will. They can be communicated. They are repeatable because they are static and have fixed characteristics.

The value of these abstractions for us in our interpersonal relations seems to be that when the tangibles of our personal reality world break down, we can turn to the intangible—to the abstractions we

have learned that have been created by others and have presumably proved useful to them. We can begin to check our own particular situation, possibly a frustrating one, against the abstraction and thereby, perhaps experience for ourselves what the abstraction is referring to. Only then will the abstraction become real for us. For when it does become functional for us in our own individual lives, it *is* real as a determinant of our experience and behavior.

I will close this discussion of perception and interpersonal relations with a story which seems to sum a good deal of what I have been talking about. The story concerns three baseball umpires who were discussing the problems of their profession. The first umpire said, "Some's balls and some's strikes and I calls 'em as they is." The second umpire said, "Some's balls and some's strikes and I calls 'em as I sees 'em." While the third umpire said, "Some's balls and some's strikes but they ain't nothin' till I calls 'em."

Bibliography

1. Cantril, Hadley. The "Why" of Man's Experience. New York: Macmillan, 1950.
2. Kilpatrick, F. P. (ed.). Human Behavior from the Transactional Point of View. Hanover, N.H.: Institute for Associated Research, 1952.
3. Kilpatrick, F. P. Recent Transactional Perceptual Research, a summary. Final Report, Navy Contract N6onr 27014, Princeton University, May, 1955.
4. Cantril, Hadley. ETC: A Review of General Semantics, 12: No. 4, 278, 1955.
5. Engel, Edward. Amer. J. Psychol., 69: No. I, 87, 1956.
6. Bagby, James. A Cross Cultural Study of Perceptual Predominance in Binocular Rivalry, 1956 (to be published).
7. Wittreich, Warren. J. Abnorm. Soc. Psychol. 47:705, 1952.
8. Kilpatrick, F. P. J. Exp. Psychol., 47: No. 362, 1954.

Bruner and Cantril emphasize the influence of needs and values in influencing the perceptual experience. Bruner's concept of perceptual readiness, and Cantril's transactional process also suggest the importance of set or expectation. Kelley and Strickland, in two separate researches that are summarized in Research Summaries 1-1 and 1-2, illustrate different ways in which expectations can distort our judgments of other people.

<table>
<tr>
<td>

RESEARCH

SUMMARY

1-1

</td>
<td>

The Warm-Cold Variable in First Impressions of Persons. Will what we are told about a person ahead of time really influence how we see him? Won't the person's actual behavior minimize the influence of our initial set? Kelley, in an experiment at M.I.T., was concerned with studying the effects of attaching a crucial personality label to a person to see if it transformed the entire impression of the person. Many studies of stereotyping have shown that indicating a person's group membership (for example, German, Negro) makes a difference in the impressions we have. The trait label that Kelley used was whether a person was "warm" or "cold." Various undergraduate classes were told that their regular instructor was out of town and that a substitute would take over. The experimenters indicated that as part of their own interest in the general problem of how various classes react to different instructors, the students would later be given some forms to fill out about him. (They were assured this wouldn't affect their own grades or the substitute's status). A short biographical note about the newcomer was given out; the notes were identical, except that one form described him as being, among other things, "very warm" and the other form called him "rather cold." The material was given without people knowing that there were two kinds of information being distributed. The "stimulus person" then appeared and led the class in a twenty minute discussion. A record was kept of how often each student participated in the discussion. Then, subjects wrote free descriptions of the instructor, and rated him on a set of fifteen rating scales.

The results showed clearly that the instructor was consistently rated more favorably by those told that he was "warm" than by those who had been told that he was "cold." Although they all "saw" the situation, those set to see the person as "warm" rated him as being more considerate of others, more informal, more sociable, more popular, more humorous, and more humane. (It obviously pays to have people think of you ahead of time as a "warm" person.)

Did their set affect their own behavior, or just the ratings? Apparently it affected behavior also, for a larger proportion of those who had been told that the instructor was "warm" participated in discussions than of those that were told he was "cold." This is in line with the principle that perception serves to guide and steer the person's behavior in his social environment, and that an unfavorable perception and set can lead to cutting down on our interactions with others.

</td>
</tr>
</table>

Surveillance and Trust. Are feelings of trust in another person always a function of the other's trustworthy behavior? Do we trust people because we have direct experience with their behavior to justify the feeling? Or, is trust of others sometimes a function of our own expectations or set?

Strickland, working with college students at the University of North Carolina, provided data indicating that a perceiver can trust one person and not another, even though each behaves in an equally trustworthy way. The study suggests that the perceiver's own behavior builds a set or expectation, leading to trust in one person and not another.

In the experimental situation, students (designated as supervisors) demanded from two workers, who could not be seen directly by the subject (and, as a matter of fact, were fictitious) a high level of work on a dull task. (Care was taken that subjects believed that workers were present through an arrangement of screens, tape-recorders, and so on.) The supervisor had the power to check performance of his "workers" and to punish them by firing them if they did not meet specified standards. In the experimental design, he had much greater monitoring power over worker A than over worker B in the initial series of ten work periods. He was, thus, set to watch A's results more closely. It was made apparent to the supervisor at the end of the work period that A and B had actually produced equal amounts, meeting or exceeding his standards, except for one period when both failed to meet the standard.

In other words, as far as the supervisor knew, two people worked at the same task for the same time and performed equally satisfactorily. The supervisor had, to his knowledge, watched more closely the work of one than the other. Thus, the only significant difference between the two workers was in amount of supervision received; and this was a characteristic of the supervisor's behavior, not the worker's.

What effect did his differential response to the two workers have on the supervisor's feelings about A and B? In the second part of the experiment, when offered a choice as to whom it was more necessary to supervise, the supervisor chose to watch A more than B. He expressed less trust in A, felt B to be more dependable, and apparently acted accordingly.

The conclusion must be drawn that the supervisor had formed a set that B had performed well of his own will, and A, only because he has been supervised. Trust, then, grew out of the perceiver's own unfounded set rather than the behavior of people he was judging. Strickland's results imply that the supervisor may attribute the employee's acceptable performance to the fact that he was supervised closely, whereas this was obviously not the cause. Once we are set to watch more closely, we can easily justify to ourselves why we don't dare relax our vigilance—if we did, performance would surely suffer.

An administrator might well question his judgments about loyalty, capacity to work without supervision, or trustworthiness, asking himself whether the basis for his judgments can be found in his own expectations rather than the behavior of those judged.

CHAPTER TWO

Forming
Impressions
of
Others

We are all confronted many times with the task of forming an impression of another person—a new employee at our desk, a visiting member of the home office, a staff member we have not personally met before. Our own values, needs, and expectations will play a part in the impression we form. Are there other factors that typically operate in this area of administrative life? One of the more obvious influences is physical appearance. Many of us agree (although without a sound basis) about what qualities of physical appearances are associated with different kinds of behavior or personality. Mason, in a study of this point, was able to demonstrate first, that people agree on what a leader should look like, and second, that there is no relation between the facial characteristics agreed upon and those possessed by actual leaders. Krech and Crutchfield (1948, p. 437) amplify the point, listing physical stature, strong face, and an air of self-confidence as physical traits that predispose people to form an impression that the other person has leadership ability. In effect, then, we have ideas about what leaders look like, and we can give examples, but we ignore the many exceptions that statistically cancel out the examples. Our agreed upon ideas just don't fit the facts.

There is evidence of still another influence that may distort our impression of the other person. In the sometimes casual, always transitory situations in which we have to form impressions of others, it is a most natural tendency to jump to conclusions, and form impressions without adequate evidence. In Research Summary 1-1 we saw the influence of set before contact with the person. In Research Summary 1-3 we see the impact of premature conclusions after brief contact on subsequent understanding of a person.

RESEARCH SUMMARY 1-3

The Influence of First Impression. Almost everyone believes that first impressions are lasting. Not so openly admitted is a widely held corollary—first impressions are accurate. Dailey, in a series of experiments on forming impressions of others, provides some data to test both statements.

In one of his experiments, his subjects were required to assess the personality of an unknown individual by reading some of the person's autobiographical material. The assessment was of a more specific type than is usually undertaken in most interpersonal situations, because Dailey's subjects were required to fill out a personality test as they believed the person himself would. Half of his subject group were asked to judge the person after a short segment of the autobiography was read (first impression) and then again after all of it was read. The remaining half were instructed not to try to form an impression until they had completed the autobiographical material. By comparing the actual test responses of the person to be judged with those attributed to him by both groups, the accuracy of the two maxims mentioned at the beginning of our summary could be tested. Dailey found that first impressions are lasting (at least under his experimental conditions): the early assessment showed a high correlation with the later assessment. He also discovered that first impressions tended to be inaccurate: subjects who had not formed first impressions were more accurate in predicting actual responses than were those who had allowed first impressions to color their final judgments.

In a second experiment, he showed that when first impressions are based on significant relevant material (as compared with unimportant or irrelevant material) they are not only lasting but can also be substantially accurate. The difficulty in the everyday world is that we can't always arrange to have our first impressions based on significant material. Thus, the only safeguard is to avoid forming impressions too early in the perceptual process.

First impressions are lasting because they influence the way in which we will "see" all subsequent data about the person. Unfortunately, they are more likely than not to be inaccurate. To the administrator facing the problems of knowing the other person, Dailey's work suggests that he postpone inferences and speculations about what kind of person he is observing until all the data are in—that is, until the end of the interview; until the complete application blank is read; or until a sufficient variety of contacts with the person has provided a comprehensive picture. Even then, an open approach to seeing new data is appropriate.

But our perceptual troubles are not yet all spelled out; there are other distorting influences on the process of forming impressions. Research over the years has brought into sharp focus some typical errors. The more important of these are: stereotyping, the halo effect, projection, and perceptual defenses. Their role in forming impressions is suggested in the readings and commentary that follow.

Stereotyping

Used by typographers to refer to a previously made-up block of type, the word "stereotyping" was first applied to bias in perceiving people by Walter Lippmann in 1922. He wrote of "pictures in peoples heads," called stereotypes, that guided (distorted) their perceptions of others. Allport has pointed out that a stereotype is not just a category but "a fixed idea" that accompanies the category (p. 191). The term *bias* has long been used to describe judgments made about people on the basis of their ethnic group membership; for example, some say Herman Schmidt (being German) is industrious. Stereotyping also predisposes judgments in many other areas of interpersonal relations. Stereotypes have developed about many types of groups, and they help to prejudice our perceptions of their members. Examples of stereotyped groups (in addition to those based on ethnic identification) come readily to mind: bankers, supervisors, union members, poor people, rich people, and administrators. A great variety of qualities are assigned to people principally because of such group memberships.

In the next reading, Haire gives us a research demonstration of the stereotyping of union and management representatives. Concerning this research, Stagner (p. 35) has pointed out, "It is plain that unionists perceiving company officials in a stereotyped way are less efficient than would be desirable. Similarly, company executives who see all labor unions as identical are not showing good judgment or discrimination." Haire's research follows.

READING 1-3

Role-Perception in Labor-Management Relations: An Experimental Approach*

MASON HAIRE

Almost everyone who concerns himself with problems of human relationships soon comes to see the problem of roles in relationships as a central one. It soon becomes clear that the roles

* Abridged from *Industrial and Labor Relations Review*, 8(2) (1955), pp. 204-216.

which are seen for one another by two people function as a kind of oversimplifying summary configuration of a complex mass of stimuli. Moreover, while the role is usually thought of as centering around a particular function or position, it is also clear that it goes beyond this in its influence on what will be seen and on the behavior of the participants (other than seeing). Essentially, seeing a person in a particular role defines him in the sense of limiting the alternative responses that are likely to be made to him. In addition, a similar restriction of behavior possibilities is forced on the person who perceives the role by virtue of the fact that a certain complementariness of roles tends to be demanded and by virtue of the limitation of response implied in the initial role-organization of the perception of the other. It also seems, in many cases, that this limitation of response possibilities, which initially appears to be associated with a particular function or position, extends widely beyond the specific area from which it arises.

These considerations lead us to look at and to worry about the problem of roles in relationships. However, it is usually very difficult to go much beyond this. Most theoretical statements of the nature of roles are not sufficiently clear or sufficiently independent to allow us to understand or predict behavior. We cannot say beforehand much about what the specific shape of the role will be, nor how it will broadly influence another's perception of the role-taker or his own perception of himself, nor how the role will influence his other behavior. We have very little evidence at the level of specifics and details.

Fortunately, there is a small body of empirical work on which we can build. Asch,[1] in an ingenious series of demonstration-experiments, has shown us the way in which the perception of a single personality variable influences the perception of other aspects of the personality. In Asch's experiments, two people were described as having identical per-

sonality attributes with one exception —in this case, one was described as "warm," the other as "cold." As a result of this single change, the subjects completely and consistently saw them as two distinct personalities. Haire and Grunes,[2] using a procedure similar to Asch's, have shown that the same kind of influences occur when the perception of a stereotypic role character is substituted for the personality characteristics Asch used. Here, the perception of a person in the role of a factory worker modified various other aspects of the observer's view of the person.

Both of these experiments were done with words rather than people. Kelley[3] extended the process [See Research Summary 1-1], again using essentially the same technique, and investigated the perception of people (as stimuli) when the observer was similarly influenced by single, simple characteristics. Again it was clear that the addition of a single personality characteristic changes the whole organization of the way in which a person is seen, and also changes other aspects of the observer's behavior with respect to the subject.

These experiments lead, step by step, to the matter at hand: (1) a single adjective reorganizes the whole view of the person described, its effect going far beyond the simple, logical relevancy of the word; (2) in addition, such a reorganization modifies other aspects of the observer's behavior toward the subject. One is led to wonder what effect the perception of a person as being a member of labor or a member of management will

[1] S. E. Asch, "Forming Impressions of Personalities," *Journal of Abnormal and Social Psychology*, Vol. 41, July 1946, pp. 258-290.

[2] Mason Haire and Willa Grunes, "Perceptual Defense Processes Protecting and Organizing Perception of Another Personality," *Human Relations*, Vol. 3, Spring 1950, pp. 403-412.

[3] H. H. Kelley, "The Warm-Cold Variable in First Impressions of Personality," *Journal of Abnormal and Social Psychology*, Vol. 18, April 1950, pp. 431-439.

have on other aspects of another's perception of other aspects of his personality, and in what way it will alter other aspects of the perceiver's behavior. These two problems—the problem of the way in which perceptual organization is shaped as a role (whether it is one's perception of himself or of another) and the problem of the changes in other kinds of behavior which flow from this perceptual organization—need investigation if we are to understand the workings of roles in relationships. If we are to understand the relationship between labor and management, we must develop more information about the meaning of these roles for each of the parties, and about the way in which these role-perceptions influence other aspects of their view of one another and other kinds of behavior which they display toward one another.

One further line of thinking needs to be introduced at this point. Much of our analysis of the behavior of formal groups has been limited and distorted by a tendency to deal with things which we know are there in some logical sense, and to disregard things which do not have this kind of existence. This has often led us to overlook important psychological variables and to introduce others which, though they have a logical and institutional existence, have no psychological meaning at all. For instance, in thinking about labor-management relations, we are quite apt to stress the importance of such things as a tight labor market on the behavior of the two parties, because we know that such a market exists and that it must influence the positions of each of the members of the relation. However, the mere existence of such a condition as a tight labor market is no guarantee that it exists psychologically—that is, that it is effective in shaping the behavior of the two parties. Psychological facts acting as

determinants of behavior do not necessarily have a one-to-one coexistence with logical facts. A tight labor market may eventually keep a man from getting a job, but it will not necessarily alter his behavior at the time of a negotiation. It may be one of the many facts which are logically and externally true, but have no efficacy as psychological causes. Similarly, though we may know, independently, that a tight labor market does not exist, it may in fact exist as a determinant of behavior regardless of its external and logical nonexistence. In order to understand the behavior of the parties, we must know the things that are psychologically present and not those which are merely logically in existence.

Further, we must avoid an error of overinstitutionalizing our thinking about such public relationships. Although we, as scholars, may know that a representative of labor springs from a group that typifies the rise of the trade union movement, this historical fact is not a cause of his behavior except insofar as its effects are present in the person's own psychological field. The industry spokesman may, in fact, typify the managerial revolution, but if he sees himself instead as a specialized worker in a team of workers this latter impression may well be the active cause of behavior.

We need to know what the relationship is like; we need to know how it looks to both parties and how they look to themselves and to one another. We need to know what factors are psychologically or phenomenally present, and to disencumber our thinking from considering a group of factors which we know to be logically or physically present. In essence, we need the kind of thing MacLeod[4] described in his "Phenomeno-

---

[4] R. B. MacLeod, "The Phenomenological Approach to Social Psychology," *Psychological Review*, Vol. 54, July 1947, pp. 193-211.

logical Approach to Social Psychology"; we need to know in more realistic detail *what* is there before we worry about why it is there or how it works.

The present report follows the kind of experimental approach indicated above in the work of Asch, Kelley, and Haire and Grunes, and the general theoretical approach indicated in MacLeod's article in attempting to deal with labor-management relationships and their role-perceptions of one another. It will present: (1) an empirical study of the way in which a labor and management group see one another, and (2) another empirical study of the way in which behaviors in a collective bargaining negotiation were influenced by these role-perceptions. [This study is omitted in our reading.]

Labor and Management's Perception of One Another

The experimental question that is asked is: "How will the perception of the personality (broadly considered) be influenced by the functional role in which he is perceived?" Knowing from the Asch and Kelley studies referred to above (1) that one's impression of a personality will be altered in many details by the inclusion of a single detail, and (2) that one's behavior with respect to a person tends to follow the phenomenal organization of the personality, it is particularly interesting to see how a person is seen when he appears, alternatively, as a representative of management or of labor.

The subjects in this experiment were 76 members of a Central Labor Council and 108 representatives of management —industrial relations or personnel men from plants or employers' organizations. All members of both groups lived and worked in the San Francisco Bay area. Many members of these two groups

(though not necessarily all) have bargained with one another.

The test materials consisted of two pictures and four descriptions. The pictures were chosen in an attempt to represent "ordinary people"; they were middle-aged, moderately dressed men, with no particular expression on their faces. The four descriptions were made up in the following manner: all four descriptions contained the information that (1) the person was almost 46, (2) was healthy, (3) had been married for a long time and had a family, (4) had held several jobs, all successfully, (5) had few hobbies or interests outside of family and work, and (6) read newspapers and fixed things around the house. In half the cases these items were arranged in different order so that it did not sound like the identical man, though in fact the same items were present. Further, in half the cases the man pictured was described as "local manager of a small plant which is a branch of a large manufacturing concern," and in the other half as "Secretary-Treasurer of his Union."

The two pictures, the two descriptions, and the two roles were all counterbalanced. Picture 1, description A, and Manager appeared together 12½ percent of the time, as did each of the other combinations. Each subject was given two pictures (one of each man), and one of them was described as a representative of management, one as a union man.

The subjects were told that this was part of a research project to see how well people could analyze personality on the basis of a few facts. They were given one minute to study the picture and description, then were told to turn the page where they found a list of 290 adjectives relating to personality. At the head were the following instructions,

Directions: A number of common adjectives are listed below. Please read them over quickly and check all those you would consider to apply to the man in the photograph. Don't worry about duplications, contradictions, etc. Work quickly and do not spend much time on any one adjective. Check your first impression of each adjective. You may check as many or as few as you like.

This procedure yielded a set of descriptions in the following form (Table I):

TABLE I

| | Management Sees | | | | Labor Sees | | | |
	Person A (N-54) as Management	(N-54) as Labor	Person B (N-54) as Management	(N-54) as Labor	Person A (N-38) as Management	(N-38) as Labor	Person B (N-38) as Management	(N-38) as Labor
Absent-minded	....	....	....	....	....	....	....	....
Active	....	....	....	....	....	....	....	....
Adaptable	....	....	....	....	....	....	....	....
Adventurous, etc.	....	....	....	....	....	....	....	....

With these data it is possible to give an approximate answer to the question: "How does management see labor and management, and how does labor see labor and management?"

General Results

The most striking result is as follows: when a member of either group (management or labor) describes a person, the description varies markedly depending on the role of the person described, although the facts and the pictures are identical. Table II shows the way in which members of management responded to the two pictures and roles.

TABLE II

Adjectives Most Frequently Used by Managers in Describing Managers

	Percent of All Managers Choosing Adjective	Percent of Use in Describing Same Man as Union	Significance of Difference ° ° = 1% ° = 5%
Mr. A.			
Honest	74	50	° °
Conscientious	74	58	° °
Adaptable	71	58	
Mature	71	34	° °
Practical	71	52	° °
Dependable	71	47	° °
Mr. B.			
Conscientious	71	63	
Conservative	74	21	° °
Dependable	71	40	° °
Industrious	66	53	
Sincere	66	53	

Column I lists the adjectives most frequently used by managers in describing managers. Thus, 74 percent of the subjects in the managerial group chose the word "honest" as descriptive of Mr. A, *when he was identified as manager.* The same managerial subjects, however, chose the word "honest" to describe Mr. A only 50 percent of the time when he was identified as a representative of the union. Table II-a shows the frequency with which the same group chose words descriptive of union men. The most frequently used words are listed here.

TABLE II-a

Adjectives Most Frequently Used by Managers in Describing Union Men

	Percent of All Managers Choosing Adjective	Percent of Use in Describing Same Man as Manager	Significance of Difference ° ° = 1% ° = 5%
Mr. A.			
Alert	76	68	
Aggressive	68	60	
Determined	63	53	
Energetic	76	68	
Masculine	66	66	
Mr. B.			
Active	74	53	° °
Aggressive	58	18	° °
Argumentative	60	8	° °
Opinionated	58	10	° °
Outspoken	58	5	° °
Persistent	58	30	° °

Thus, 76 percent of management describe the labor man as "alert," but use the word only 68 percent of the time to describe the same man when he is identified as a member of management. Similarly, Table III lists the words used most frequently by union men to describe managers (and, for comparison, the frequency with which these same words describe union men), and Table III-a lists the words most frequently used by labor to describe labor representatives.

TABLE III

Adjectives Most Frequently Used by Union Men in Describing Managers

	Percent of All Union Men Choosing Adjective	Percent of Use in Describing Same Man as Union	Significance of Difference ° ° = 1% ° = 5%
Mr. A.			
Active	72	80	
Alert	65	69	
Capable	67	66	
Dependable	67	47	° °
Efficient	67	62	
Mr. B.			
Active	48	78	° °
Affectionate	39	23	
Ambitious	46	48	
Capable	43	48	
Friendly	39	60	
Honest	43	56	

TABLE III-a

Adjectives Most Frequently Used by Union Men in Describing Union Men

	Percent of All Union Men Choosing Adjective	Percent of Use in Describing Same Man as Manager	Significance of Difference ° ° = 1% ° = 5%
Mr. A.			
Active	80	72	
Aggressive	69	61	
Alert	69	65	
Ambitious	71	59	
Capable	66	67	
Mr. B.			
Active	78	48	° °
Aggressive	50	28	°
Dependable	54	37	
Efficient	52	30	°
Honest	56	43	

One would hardly know that the same people were being described, unless one had seen that it was a single picture and a single set of facts. Two kinds of differences are apparent in the tables.

In the first place, in simple rank order terms, the labels "manager" and "labor" elicit very different adjectives in the most frequent usages; the top five adjectives (six where there are ties) are quite different from one another. No single adjective which is used most frequently by management to describe either role is also used most frequently to describe the other. In the second place, the percentage frequency of applying these adjectives to the oppositely labeled man shows a difference significant at the 1-percent level in 16 out of the 22 cases. It seems quite likely that other aspects of one's behavior in response to Mr. B union would be very different from one's behavior in response to Mr. B manager, and likewise with the two Mr. A's present.

Similar figures are given in Table III and III-a for the responses from the group of representatives of labor. The differences are not quite as great as they were in the case of management's responses, but they are still far from being descriptions of the same person that was in fact presented. In the two lists of eleven, there are only five cases in which the same adjective appears in the top five ranking. Similarly, the percentage of application of a frequent adjective to the other group shows a sprinkling of significant differences beyond that expected if the two groups were in fact identical. It will also be seen from Tables II and III that there is a difference between Mr. A. and Mr. B., whether he is seen as manager or labor, and that this difference interacts with the management-labor dimension. Presumably these interactions arose from the fact that the experimenter's attempt to secure neutral stimuli was not entirely successful, and they show further evidence of the generality of the organizing effects of role-characteristics of this sort. An exploration of the stimulus variation in this area would be a real addition to our understanding of the process of forming impressions of others.

It seems clear that a single person looks very different depending on whether he is seen as a manager or a union secretary. Moreover, the nature of this difference depends on whether he is thus seen *by* a manager or a union man. This difference in the impression follows Asch's experience with trait-names. It seems probable that the different perceptions lead to different overt behavior here, too, as they did in Kelley's experiment.

Specific Role-Perceptions and Dimensions

When we look at specific clusters of adjectives that might be expected to lead to different behavior, the effect of role-perception is equally clear. For instance, there is a group of adjectives centering around the idea that one can count on another's word, that he will do what he says. Some of them are positive (dependable, conscientious, honest, responsible, sincere) and some negative (changeable, undependable). If we add the use of these adjectives by each group in referring to self and other, subtracting the positive from the negative, we have the following table (high score means high dependability):

TABLE IV

Dependability

Management Sees		Labor Sees	
Management	Labor	Management	Labor
252	176	200	231

(Large number means high value)
Chi square = 11.68
P < .01

Each sees himself as more dependable than the other; neither places as much trust in the other's agreement as he does in his own.

There is another cluster of words that

center around one's being able to see things from the other's point of view, to get outside his own perspective. Again, some of these are positive (considerate, cooperative, fair-minded, and appreciative) and some are negative (self-centered, selfish, self-seeking). Scoring as before, we find:

TABLE V

Seeing Others Problem

Management Sees		Labor Sees	
Management	Labor	Management	Labor
123	47	93	137

(Large number means high value)
Chi square = 38.4
P < .01

Again, each sees himself, and especially himself, as able to see both sides of the question.

There are many more such adjective syndromes that can be extracted and tabulated. They are not presented here because the sample is not in any sense representative of the whole population of labor and management, and it is not necessary to describe in detail the anatomy of the perceptions of these two particular groups. The example given here serves to show that there is a difference in this case, and that it is a large one.

It is also possible, with this technique, to see something of the kinds of dimensions in terms of which labor and management see self and other. Not only can we compare value judgments, but by seeing which adjectives are most heavily used, we can get a first approximation to the question "which dimensions stand out in one's perception of the other?"

To do this it is necessary to make some corrections for imbalances in the responses. In the first place, labor used fewer adjectives in toto than management. One hundred eight representatives of management used only 8,873 adjectives in describing the two men while

76 members of labor used 7,831; on a per capita basis, labor used 103, while management used 82, contrary to what might be expected from the general difference in educational and socioeconomic backgrounds. Further, each side described itself in more detail than it did the other. Management devoted 52.7 percent of all its adjectives to describing management, while labor devoted 51.6 percent of its adjectives to describing labor.[5]

Making allowance for these differences in total number of adjectives, we can see how each group uses various kinds of adjectives. In general, the percentages are remarkably similar (Table VI).

TABLE VI

Type of Adjective	Percent of All Adjectives Used by:	
	Labor	Management
Adjectives having to do with thinking	10.6	10.4
Emotion	6.0	6.0
Interpersonal relations	12.2	10.7

Labor, however, used (significantly) more adjectives having to do with interpersonal relations, and we can perhaps assume that this dimension of people is more salient in labor's perception than in management's.

In all three of these dimensions, each group (management and labor) sees itself as superior. Subtracting the negative from positive, as before, we have:

TABLE VII

	Management Sees		Labor Sees	
	Management	Labor	Management	Labor
Thinking	369	263	344	430
Emotion	136	84	150	195
Interpersonal relations	248	103	172	314

(High number means high value)

In summary, from looking at these data, we can say:

---

[5] Though these differences are relatively small, both are significantly different (1 percent) from a 50-50 split.

(1) The general impression of a person is radically different when he is seen as a member of management than when he is seen as a representative of labor.

(2) Further, the change effected by membership is different when it is seen by members of management and labor. The kind of effect of such a characteristic or group membership is influenced by the group membership of the perceiver himself.

(3) Management and labor each sees the other as less dependable than himself. (Table IV)

(4) Management and labor each sees the other as less appreciative of the other's position than he himself is. (Table V)

(5) Management and labor each sees the other as deficient in thinking, emotional characteristics, and interpersonal relations in comparison with himself. (Table VII)

(6) The difference in perception of one another mentioned in (4) immediately above occurs in spite of the fact that the two groups assign nearly the same weight to the three dimensions of behavior (thinking, emotionality, and interpersonal relations) as indicated by the number of adjectives used. (Table VI)

On the basis of these data it seems clear that labor and management are not talking to the same people when they confer with one another. Labor sees itself and management so differently and management sees itself and labor so differently that, although they are only two people in the room, four people seem to be involved in the conversation. Consider, for example, the meaning of a statement like "we are anxious to work with you." Let us suppose it is made by Mr. B., a labor representative. He is seen by labor to be honest, dependable, and efficient. However, by management he is seen as persistent, opinionated, argumentative, and outspoken. He is seen by labor to have high thinking ability, to be dependable, and to see the other's side of the problem. He is seen by management to be a less clear thinker than management is, to be relatively undependable, and to fail to see management's side of the problem. Under these circumstances, it seems hardly possible that the statement can mean the same thing to both parties. Though only one man speaks, the masks through which the statement comes are so different that it is hardly the same thing any longer.

Two words of caution should be added to the interpretation of these data: in the first place, they are not specifically generalizable to all members of management and labor. These particular perceptual values do not necessarily represent the way in which all members of each group would see all members of the other group. Furthermore, the experimental material is drawn from three different kinds of populations: the population of subjects who provided the response, the population of personality characteristics (adjective) which they were allowed to check, and the population of labor and management representatives from whom the stimulus pictures were drawn. The experimental material samples these three populations to very different degrees. The samples of subjects who took part in the experiment are probably a reasonable representation of the population of labor and management representatives who bargain with one another *in this area,* but it obviously does not necessarily represent similar populations of labor and management bargaining groups in other geographical areas. The sample of personality characteristics provided for the judges is probably quite adequate. It is a very large proportion of commonly used adjectives, and gave every evidence of allowing the judges all the freedom they wanted in making their response. The most serious sampling problem, however, is the degree to which the stimulus pictures represent management and labor in general. On this count, there is no pretense that the sample is representative of the total population of labor and management people who might be or are seen by labor and management people. It is both theoretically and practically very difficult to provide representative stimulus material in this case, and the photographs used were not designed with this attempt in mind, but rather in an attempt to use neutral pictures which would allow a sample of the perceptions that might occur in labor and management's view of one another. The data presented here thus do not provide specific values for the misperceptions of labor and management, but rather illustrate the kind of distortion that can occur.

The second precautionary note in the interpretation of these data is this: this experiment illustrates gross distortion in labor and management's perception of one another. It does suggest that this distortion is sufficient to give rise to considerable misunderstanding between them of the subject matter of their conversations. It does not suggest that this is the sole source of difference of opinion between labor and management in negotiation. The kind of distortion demonstrated here should probably be viewed primarily as a barrier to communication which makes doubly difficult the problem of resolving differences of opinion or purpose. Where there is in fact substantive disagreement between labor and management, it would seem to be of particular importance to have a clear statement of the view and aim of each side. The kind of misperception illustrated here must certainly inhibit an unambiguous understanding of whatever differences exist.

. . .

One troublesome aspect of stereotypes is that they are so widespread. Finding the same stereotypes from one end of the country to another almost tempts one to accept their accuracy, except that the "kernel of truth" idea has effectively been shown not to be correct. For example, Allport (p. 190) reports on a local California stereotype of Armenians as "dishonest, lying, deceitful." An objective check showed that Merchants' Association records gave them credit ratings as good as other groups, and that Armenians applied less for charity and appeared less in legal cases. When we point to specific instances to "prove" our stereotypes we are overgeneralizing; that some businessmen have exploited the people working for them does not mean that businessmen as a group are exploiters.

Bruner and Perlmutter document the international nature of the stereotypes for "businessman" and "teacher." They also indicate that the more widespread one's experience with diverse members of a group, the less their group membership will affect the impression formed. We might add that even if a higher percentage than usual of people in a given group *were* to have a certain characteristic, it does not mean that all members of the group have this trait.

An additional illustration of stereotyping at work is provided by Luft, whose research is summarized in Research Summary 1-4.

<table>
<tr>
<td>

**RESEARCH
SUMMARY
1-4**

</td>
<td>

Personality Stereotypes of the Poor and the Well-Off. Luft suggests that perception of personality adjustment may be influenced by stereotypes that associate adjustment with high income and maladjustment with low income.

He asked one-hundred and eleven college students to fill out the California Test of Personality, as an hypothetical person to be described to them might fill it out. Descriptions of the hypothetical man were the same, except for his income level. Half were told that he earned $42.50 a week, the other half, $250 a week. To provide comparison data as actually given by a low income group, working men in the area filled out the same questionnaire. The Personality adjustment scores assigned to the low income group were significantly lower than scores actually earned by this group, and lower also than the scores assigned to the well-off group. Stereotypes suggest that the poor are maladjusted and unhappy, and the rich are healthy, happy, and well adjusted.

Luft's study also suggests that the strength of the stereotypes is related to the income level of the students themselves. Middle income groups assigned higher scores to the well-off hypothetical man than did the low income student groups.

Although the conclusions are based on a small and narrowly selected sample of the population, they are in accord with theoretical expectations. From a practical point of view they provide still another instance of distorting influence on the perceptual process.

</td>
</tr>
</table>

Halo Effect

The term *halo effect* was first used by Thorndike in 1920 to describe a process in which a general impression that is favorable or unfavorable is used by judges to evaluate several specific traits—the "halo" in such case serves as a screen, keeping the perceiver from actually seeing the trait he is judging. Over the years, it has received most attention because of its effect on rating employee performance. In the rating situation, a supervisor may single out one trait— either good or bad—and use this as the basis for his judgment of all other traits, for example, an excellent attendance record causes judgments of highest productivity, quality of work, and so on. One study in the Army showed that well liked officers were judged as being more intelligent than those who were disliked, even though they had the same scores on intelligence tests.

We examine halo effect here because of its general effect on forming impressions. It is likely to be most extreme when we are forming impressions of traits that provide minimal cues in the individual's behavior, when the traits have moral overtones, or when we are required to judge traits with which we have little experience (Bruner and Taguiri). A rather disturbing conclusion is suggested by Symonds: that halo effect is more marked the longer we know the person being judged. George Bernard Shaw had a point, as usual, when he said that "My tailor is the only person who really understands me; he takes my measurements every time we meet."

A somewhat different aspect of halo is suggested by the research of Grove and Kerr (Research Summary 1-5). Here, an extreme aspect of the employment situation produces a halo among a group of employees in judging the specific aspects of the situation. Knowledge that the company is in receivership causes them to de-value otherwise superior working conditions.

RESEARCH **SUMMARY** **1-5**	*Stereotyped Judgments in the Work Situation.* In a Chicago firm that had been in receivership for six months, ten employee morale variables were measured on eighteen female office workers. Salaries and working conditions (for example private offices) were actually superior to those of typical similar Chicago jobs. A control group of fifty-eight people in a financially sound firm was compared with the group in the "insecure" company. Those in the insecure group were understandably lower than the controls on feelings of job security; but, more important, this feeling of low satisfaction spread and pervaded other areas, many of which were irrelevant to job security. A form of halo effect operated, with the employees expressing discontent with their actually superior pay and working conditions, as well as with their work associates and immediate superiors. We can thus see that anxiety and insecurity about the job can color many of our other work attitudes. Just as our impressions of a person influence our perceptions of specific traits, so too, the organizational context or climate influences our job attitudes. When there's one important "rotten" attitude, it can spoil the "barrel" of attitudes.

Psychologists have noted a tendency in perceivers to package certain traits, assuming, for example, that when a person is aggressive he will also have high energy, when a person is "warm" he will also be generous and have a good sense of humor. This logical error is a special form of the halo effect; it has been best illustrated in the research of Asch. In his study, the addition of one trait to a list of traits, produced a major change in the impression formed. Knowing that a person was intelligent, skillful, industrious, determined, practical, cautious, and *warm* led a group to judge him to be also wise, humorous, popular, and imaginative. When warm was replaced by cold, a radically different impression (beyond the difference between warm and cold) was formed. Kelley's research, previously described, illustrates the same type of error. This tendency is not indiscriminate; with the words "polite–blunt," less change was found than with the more central traits of "warm–cold."

In evaluating the effect of halo on perceptual distortion, we may obtain some comfort from knowing that traits that correlate more highly with each other are more likely to lead to a halo effect than traits that are unrelated (Wishner).

Kipnis has reviewed both studies of industrial ratings and studies in the area of interpersonal perception. On the one hand he indicates the likelihood that a rating will be based upon considerably less than the total information available about the ratee's performance; and suggests that, on the other hand, factors external to that performance will influence the judgment. He identifies three such external factors: Propinquity between ratee and rater, amount of pressure under which the supervisor is working, and the extent to which the supervisor expresses criticism of subordinates (thus reducing his hostility by letting off steam).

Projection

A defense mechanism available to all of us is to relieve our feelings of guilt or failure by projecting blame onto someone else (See Part Three). In its original use, the term *projection* referred to the mechanism for defending ourselves from our unacceptable feelings. There has been a tendency for the term to be used more broadly—to ascribe or attribute any of one's own characteristics to other people. An early study by Murray illustrates one use of the term and demonstrates the effect on perception. After playing a dramatic game of "Murder," his subjects assigned much more maliciousness to people whose photographs were judged than did a control group that had not played the game. The current emotional state of the perceiver tended to influence his perceptions of others, that is, frightened perceivers judged people to be frightening. More recently, Feshback and Singer revealed further dynamics of the process. In their study, subjects who had been made fearful judged a stimulus person (presented in a moving picture) as being both more fearful and more aggressive than did nonfearful perceivers. These authors were able to demonstrate further that projection was reduced when their subjects were encouraged to admit and talk about their own fears.

Sears provides an illustration of a somewhat different type of projection and its effect on perceiving. Projection in his study is a matter of seeing in other people our own undesirable personality characteristics. Sears demonstrates that people high on such traits as stinginess, obstinacy, and disorderliness tend to rate others much higher on these traits than do people who show less of these undesirable characteristics. The tendency to project was particularly marked among subjects who had the least insight into their own personalities.

Research thus suggests that our perceptions may characteristically be distorted by emotions we are experiencing or traits that we possess. Placed in the administrative setting, the research would suggest, for example, that a manager, frightened by rumored organizational changes, might judge others to be more frightened than they are and assess various policy decisions as more frightening than they are. Or, for instance, a general foreman, lacking insight into his own incapacity to delegate, might be over-sensitive to this trait in his superiors.

Perceptual Defense

Do we put on blinders to defend ourselves from seeing events that might bother us? Although the existence of a specific process of perceptual defense, distinct from the other distorting influences we have thus far identified, is a matter of technical controversy, the Haire and Grunes research that uses the concept offers an excellent description of perceptual distortion at work. What happens when you are confronted with a fact inconsistent with a stereotype you already hold about a person? Haire and Grunes suggest an answer.

READING 1-4

Perceptual Defenses: Processes Protecting an Organized Perception of Another Personality*

MASON HAIRE
AND
WILLA FREEMAN GRUNES[1]

The question "how does an individual perceive another personality, and what factors will lead him to change that perception?" is involved in much current work in human relations. In the course of a study primarily aimed else-

* Abridged from *Human Relations*, 1950, 3, pp. 403-412.
[1] The work described here is done under the auspices and support of the Institute of Industrial Relations of the University of California at Berkeley.

where, the authors have come across some evidence that casts light in this area.

. . .

We modified the engaging technique used by Asch (1) in his study of the way in which one forms impressions of the personality. Asch was interested in the way items of a personality description are put together into an experienced whole. Our interest is somewhat the other side of the coin; assuming the already-organized-wholes, what differences are there with and without the inclusion of specific items—in this case, union membership? To investigate this, we constructed a list of the hypothetical personality characteristics of two factory workers (given below). They were identical except that one man was said to go to union meetings, while this point was not raised in the other. Respondents are then asked to describe the individual. With an instrument of this sort it is hoped that it may be possible to get some clues about the perception of union members by specified groups.

SAMPLE FORM

Test of Personality Assessment Ability   Do not sign your name

The object of the test is to determine the extent to which people are capable of sizing up a person from just a few facts about him. Below is a brief description of a certain working-man. Describe in a paragraph what sort of a person you think he is. Indicate wherever possible which items gave you your impressions of him.

FORM I	FORM II
works in a factory	*works in factory*
reads a newspaper	*reads a newspaper*
goes to movies	*goes to movies*
average height	*goes to union meetings*
cracks jokes	*average height*
intelligent	*cracks jokes*
strong	*intelligent*
active	*strong*
	active

Early pre-testing showed that the word "intelligent," which was contained in the list, occasioned considerable difficulty among the respondents. It apparently did not fit well into the picture of a factory worker, and consequently it took up what was for our interest an inordinately large amount of their time. Consequently, for further pre-test, two more lists were prepared, excluding the characterization "intelligent." The two descriptions (*Forms III and IV*) are the result, and these were again pre-tested.

All four forms were given to 179

SAMPLE FORMS

Test of Personality Assessment Ability   Do not sign your name

The object of the test is to determine the extent to which people are capable of sizing up a person from just a few facts about him. Below is a brief description of a certain working-man. Describe in a paragraph what sort of a person you think he is. Indicate wherever possible which items gave you your impressions of him.

FORM III	FORM IV
works in a factory	*works in factory*
reads a newspaper	*reads a newspaper*
goes to movies	*goes to movies*
average height	*goes to union meetings*
cracks jokes	*average height*
strong	*cracks jokes*
active	*strong*
	active

students in the Introductory Psychology class at the University of California. Copies of the four forms were interleaved and the pile handed out so that each student took one and passed the rest on, and no one was aware of the existence of the three alternatives being used by his neighbors. In this way, about 45 students responded to each form. The content of their descriptions was analyzed, making it possible for us to see the picture of the basic "raw" worker, and the changes introduced by the addition of intelligence to this picture on the one hand, or of union membership on the other, or of both. There is no particular thought that, in society, the perception of union membership by students limits the roles that a union man can play. The results as far as union membership is concerned will be most relevant when we have tested union men and members of management. This study will be reported later. The students were chosen, as usual, because of their availability for pre-test.

Their handling of the variable "intelligent" yields some interesting insights into the dynamics of change in cognitive structure. The descriptions of the factory worker who was not specified as either intelligent or a union member (*Form III*) were very uniform. Virtually every description would fit into the pattern of a " 'typical American joe,' likeable and well-liked, mildly sociable, healthy, happy, uncomplicated, and well-adjusted in a sort of earthy way, not very intelligent, but trying to keep abreast of current trends, interested in sports and finding his pleasures in simple, undistinguished activities." Not all the pictures fit into this mold, of course, or have all the items, but none of them would be greatly at variance. The descriptions were, by and large, a little patronizing and snobbish. It will be noticed that intelligence

is not an outstanding characteristic of this individual.

As we come to the group who described the factory worker who is also listed as "intelligent" (*Form I* above) the picture is somewhat different. Clearly, intelligence, in sufficient quantity to deserve mention, does not go with the basic perception. How can it be handled? It is not possible simply to add it on to the picture of the "raw" factory worker in the way that we might add on, say, red-headedness. It must be *integrated* into the whole, and not just added on, and its membership in the whole changes the whole, changes the nature of the item itself, and changes the meaning of other items in the totality. The descriptions of this man are not nearly so uniform as they were without intelligence, but they do follow a clear pattern. The basic problem that is posed for the respondents is to make some adjustment to the presence in the objective stimulus of the attribute "intelligent" and still maintain the good organization which his picture of a factory worker has. They do it in a number of ways. The main lines of approach which the respondents take are:

1. *Straightforward denial of the existence of the disturbing element.*
2. *A modification of the attribute that involves either wrapping it up in another context so that the characteristic that conflicts with the stereotype is rendered impotent, or reinterpreting the attribute so that it loses the conflict-producing characteristic.*
3. *Allowing the new element to make a real change. This is handled either by (a) changing a dimension of the personality irrelevant to the worker-intelligent conflict, (b) modifying the interpretation of the term "worker" so that the stereotype*

that is in conflict with "intelligent" is not evoked, or (c) as a last resort, actually changing the basic picture of the worker.

4. *An explicit recognition of the conflict and simultaneous maintenance of the unchanged stereotype and the un-integrated conflict-producing attribute.*

Denial

Comparatively few people were able actually to deny the existence of the attribute (5 out of 43).[3] Some managed it, however, by saying such things as "Intelligence not notable even though it is stated," "He is intelligent, but not too much so, since he works in a factory." After this the man could be fitted into the previous mold. We also obtained a more sophisticated rationalization, saying that it was not known in terms of what group he was intelligent, so that the factor could be disregarded. Although only real denials of the existence of the attribute are included here, many of the modifications and re-interpretations below partake of much of the same character.

Encapsulation and Distortion

One of the most frequent forms of response fell in this general category.[4] The basic pattern is to explain away the apparent conflict by joining the intelligence with some item which the respondent supplied. This may be done

[3] There is no thought that the empirical frequencies given here will predict the likelihood that a given mode of response will be used in solving other problems of inconsistencies in the phenomenal environment. The figures are illustrative.
[4] 14 out of 45 subjects, 16 out of 50 tabulations. The number of tabulations slightly exceeds the number of cases. In a few cases one individual fell into more than one category.

either by letting the respondent-supplied characteristics change the item "intelligent," or by using the additional material to isolate it and render it harmless. Thus, eight people postulated a lack of drive to account for the concatenation of intelligence and factory work; e.g., "he is intelligent, but doesn't possess initiative to rise above his group," "does only enough work to get by but doesn't exert himself (because he is intelligent and only a factory worker)," "he evidently lacks the incentive or drive to strike out upon his own and make better use of his capabilities." Another four cases use his (projected) lack of education similarly; e.g., "seems to be working in a factory more from lack of formal education than anything else," "Probably never had a college education, or he would do a bigger and better job than the work in a factory." Thus, the intelligence is there, but due to lack of schooling it is a "raw" native intelligence and hence not effective, or, the intelligence is there but due to lack of incentive is not used, and hence not effective. Lack of opportunity (from poor family background, poverty, etc.) is used in the same manner. Thus, again, the apparently disturbing juxtaposition of factory work and intelligence need not be disturbing, because the intelligent man is there only because he had no opportunity, for various reasons, to remove himself. These explanations seem to have in them either a change in the nature of the attribute which prevents it from conflicting with the stereotypical perception of the worker, or a technique of wrapping the attribute up in (projected) contextual details so that it no longer conflicts.

One other group of response falls into this class. Two people account for the existence of the conflicting element in terms of a (projected) force away from something else; e.g., "this man works in a factory because he doesn't like office work," "a man who, though intelligent, dislikes the work of a business man in a stuffy office." This device is perhaps akin to the fictional technique whereby the rich scion, bored with his life of luxury, takes up life in the slums, and comes to know the poor but beautiful girl; with the same dynamics the incongruity of the items is explained away by accounting for the presence of one term by a force away from something else.

Change in organization

Of the 43 people, 17 fall in a class where the added item actually changes their organization. Not all of these, however, actually integrate the new fact into their stereotype and allow it to modify their perception of the worker. Even here, devious ways are used to preserve the original picture. The most frequent change (14 cases out of 21 tabulations) is to alter the social character of the worker. In the original picture (without the disturbing element "intelligent") the worker was a rather dull clod, uncultured and insensitive, with a relatively undifferentiated view of the work, and his humour seemed likely to be of the thigh-slapping guffaw variety. He now changes to a man who is "witty," "a good conversationalist," because of a "lively interest in the world around him." "Because of his intelligence I think he is little more interesting than the average, and, therefore, more fun to be around." "His intelligence and fondness for keeping up with the world, combined with a pleasant sense of humour, probably make him well liked at the factory." There is a real change here, though it is sometimes difficult to pin down because it often depends on subtle differences in the choice of words (e.g., in the case of the worker who is not described as intelligent, the phrase "cracks jokes" becomes "plays jokes," suggesting a practical joker, while in the

intelligent man, it becomes "witty" and "a pleasant sense of humour." Again, the unintelligent man "tries to keep up with what's going on" with an air of never quite succeeding, while the intelligent man "has a lively interest in the world around him"). It should be noted, though, that the change which is made is in a dimension of the personality that is irrelevant to the basic conflict between the possession of intelligence and factory work. The intelligence is "used up" in making him more competent and attractive in non-work-relevant ways, chiefly interpersonal relations.

Another group (5 cases) resolved the conflict by denying, not that he was intelligent, but by denying that he was a factory worker in the sense that that produced conflict with intelligence. They promoted him to foreman.[5] When the two items conflict, it is perhaps surprising that his status in the work-hierarchy is not changed more often to resolve the difficulty. Probably the expression "working-man" and the phrase "works in a factory" do not communicate well with the picture of a supervisory position. In any case, only a few admitted the intelligence and changed the surroundings; e.g., "this person seems to have a supervisory or foreman's job in a factory (intelligent)," "this person is perhaps a foreman at the factory where he works, because for this position he would have to be intelligent."

Recognition of incongruity

Three people more or less explicitly recognized the disparity between their picture of the worker and the attribute "intelligent"; e.g., "the traits seem to be conflicting . . . most factory workers I have heard about aren't too intelligent,"

---

[5] Of the 48 people who described the man who was not specified as intelligent, no one felt it necessary to make him a foreman.

"his sense of humor, intelligence, and activity result in his being quite likeable. I hope he works in a factory through necessity and not choice, because there are other occupations that would give me a better impression of him." One subject tried to work "intelligent" into his rationale and crossed it out, apparently feeling that it did not belong. He is included here.[6]

> *From this categorization of the responses it seems clear that:*
> *(a) The students have a clear, well-organized picture of a working-man.*
> *(b) The attribute "intelligent" does not fit well into the organization.*
> *(c) In order to preserve the original organization of their picture of a worker in the face of the disturbing item they:*
>   *(i) deny the existence of the item, or*
>   *(ii) distort it or encapsulate it in a context that renders it impotent, or*
>   *(iii) maintain the original picture, recognizing the incongruity of the added item, or*
>   *(iv) finally, integrate the item, allowing it to change the stereotype. In doing this, the change is made as innocuous as possible, preserving the main dimensions of the original.*

The similarity between these processes in the organization of the cognitive structure and phenomena with which we are familiar should be pointed out. They are basically the same as the processes mentioned by Cartwright (4) in his discussion of the maintenance of existing cognitive

structures under the impact of the mass media. He points out (p. 258), "When a 'message' is inconsistent with a person's prevailing cognitive structure it will either (a) be rejected, (b) be distorted, or (c) produce changes in the cognitive structure." These rubrics describe very well the phenomena reported here. Our findings are detailed spelling-out of the way in which Cartwright's processes work.

Ichheiser (7) speaks of misunderstandings in human relations that arise from overestimation of the unity of the personality, and a refusal to accept and incorporate into the perception behavior or characteristics that are at variance with the previous picture of the person. He says (p. 28), "Once the image of another person, shaped by primary mechanisms of one kind or another, is fixed in our minds, we tend either to overlook all factors in the other person which do not fit in with our preconceived scheme; or else, we misinterpret all unexpectedly emerging factors in order to preserve our preformed misconceptions." Both of these processes are exemplified in the work reported here. The processes which Ichheiser describes and which we find here, are essentially processes which preserve the identity of the perceived organization and protect it from change. One immediately wonders if we are employing the same concept used in early Gestalt discussions of stroboscopic movement (10), and worked out in detail in such studies as that of Ternus (9). In Ternus' experiments it is clear that in order to understand what kind of movement will be seen we must take into account the organized figural character of the stimulus constellation. So, in our situation, to know the meaning which the item "intelligent" will assume, we must take into account the perceived organized personality to which it is related.

---

[6] Five people are not included in the sample. Their responses either did not say enough or were not intelligible in terms of the categorizations used here.

It is suggestive to wonder also whether the refusal to admit the disturbing element in this case and its distortion and encapsulation do not parallel the processes of selection (2) and distortion (3) demonstrated by Bruner and his coworkers, among others. They have shown, as have Levine, Chein, and Murphy (8) that there is a tendency to distort one's perception under the influence of a need. This has been interpreted in terms of a sort of "emotional economy" in which it is less expensive, under the influence of mild needs, to distort the perception of the environment and see what one would like to see. Most of the processes shown here seem to fit this picture, and the existing order is preserved by selectively eliminating, encapsulating, or distorting disruptive elements. Following the findings of these investigators, we might expect, under conditions of extreme need-tension, to find the process reversed, and a reality-orientation setting in.

Finally, we know from experiments such as Gelb and Granit's (6) that the limen for the perception of an item is higher when it is projected on an area that is seen as figure than one that is seen as ground. Is this resistance to the intrusion of a disturbing item shown by a well-organized figure another example under the same general heading as the resistance reported here? To complete the parallel, it seems quite likely that if the hypothetical man had not been described as a worker there would have been little difficulty in incorporating and integrating intelligence into his description. It is the fact that the original perception is well organized and the new item is at variance with the organization that causes the difficulty.

The descriptions given here emphasize again the importance of the relational character of an item in giving it meaning. Two things seem to be true: (*a*) the meaning of an item is partly a function of its relation to other items, and (*b*) the phenomenal characteristics of items in an organization determine their relational effects. Asch (1) demonstrated the first part, when he showed that the "helpful" of a man who was "helpful, quick, and skillful" was quite different from the "helpful" of a man who was "helpful, slow, and clumsy." Similarly here, the basic problem lies in the relational role of "intelligent." Moreover, other characteristics change as a function of the way in which "intelligent" is integrated. For instance, when intelligence is explained by lack of drive, the attribute "activity" is by and large used up by his being "interested in enjoying life," "active in sports," "healthy (strong and active, works at manual labor)," "likes a good time," and the like. When "intelligence" is allowed to change the basic picture so that he is seen as a better companion, the "activity" is used more in terms of an active interest in the world around him, or in terms of activity in relations with people. This effect of the organization in determining characteristics of items in the whole has been shown, in simple perceptual problems, by Fuchs (5) in his demonstration of the effect of membership in a phenomenal organization on perceived color, and by others. Fuchs, for example, employed an objectively grey dot which could be seen as a member either of a square of yellow dots or a square of blue dots. The dot appears blue or yellow, depending upon the figure of which it is seen as a part. Once more, it is stimulating to inquire whether the similarity between processes occurring in the complex organization of the cognitive structure and well-known principles in simpler perception is only a superficial kinship, or whether it indicates the action of a single set of factors.

References

1. Asch, S. E. "Forming Impressions of the Personality," *Journal of Abnormal and Social Psychology*, 1946, *41*, 258-290.
2. Bruner, J. S., and Postman, Leo. "Emotional Selectivity in Perception and Reaction," *Journal of Personality*, 1947, *16*, 69-81.
3. Bruner, J. S., and Goodman, Cecile C. "Value and Need as Organizing Factors in Perception," *Journal of Abnormal and Social Psychology*, 1947, *42*, 33-44.
4. Cartwright, D. "Some Principles of Mass Persuasion," *Human Relations*, 1949, *2*, 253-267.
5. Fuchs, Wilhelm. "Experimentelle Untersuchungen über die Aenderung von Farben unter dem Einfluss von Gestalten," *Zeitschr. f. Psychol.*, 1923, *92*, 249-325. Abstracted in Ellis, *Source Book of Gestalt Psychology*, Harcourt Brace, 1938.
6. Gelb, A., and Granit, R. "Die Bedeutung von 'Figur' und 'Grund' für die Farbenschwelle," *Zeitschr. f. Psychol.*, 1923, *93*, 83-118. Cited in Koffka, *Principles of Gestalt Psychology*. Harcourt Brace, 1935.
7. Ichheiser, Gustave. "Misunderstandings in Human Relations," *American Journal of Sociology*, Vol. LV, No. 2, Part 2, 1949.
8. Levine, R., Chein, I., and Murphy, G. "The Relation of Intensity of a Need to the Amount of Perceptual Distortion," *Journal of Psychology*, 1942, *13*, 283-293.
9. Ternus, J. "Experimentelle Untersuchungen über phänomenale Identität." *Psychol. Forsch.*, 1926, 7, 81-136. Abstracted in Ellis, see 5 above.
10. Wertheimer, Max. "Experimentelle Untersuchungen über das Sehen von Bewegung," *Zeitschr. f. Psychol.*, 1912, *6*, 161-265.

CHAPTER THREE

Some Other Interpersonal Factors in Perception

Characteristics of the Perceiver

Except for our discussion of projection, we have thus far been talking largely about influences on the perceptual process, without specific regard to who is doing the perceiving and what his own characteristics are. Much of the recent research has tried to identify some characteristics of the perceiver and their influence on the perception of other people.

A thread that would seem to tie many current findings together is the tendency of a person to use himself as the norm or standard by which he perceives or judges others. If we examine current research, certain conclusions are suggested:

1. *Knowing yourself makes it easier to see others accurately.* When we are aware of what our own personal characteristics are, we make fewer errors in perceiving others (Norman). People with insight are less likely to view things in "black and white" terms (Weingarten) and to give extreme judgments about others.

2. *Our own characteristics affect the characteristics we are more likely to see in others.* Secure people (compared to those that are insecure) tend to see others as warm rather than cold (Bossom and Maslow). The extent of one's own sociability influences the degree of importance that we give to the sociability of other people when we form impressions of them. (Benedetti and Hill). The person with "authoritarian" tendencies is more likely to view

45

others in terms of power and is less sensitive to the psychological or personality characteristics of other people than is a nonauthoritarian (Jones). The relatively few categories we use in describing other people tend to be those we use in describing ourselves (Hastorf). Thus, traits that are important to us in ourselves will be used more when we form impressions of others. We have certain "constant tendencies" with regard to using certain categories in judging others, and to the amount of weight given to these categories, or traits (Cronbach).

3. *The person who accepts himself is more likely to be able to see favorable aspects of other people* (Omwake). This relates in part to the accuracy of our perceptions. If we accept ourselves as we are, we widen our range of vision in seeing others; we can look at them and be less likely to be very negative or critical.

   In those areas in which we ourselves are more insecure, we see more problems in other people (Weingarten). We are more likely to like others who have traits we accept in ourselves, and reject those who have the traits that we do not like in ourselves (Lundy *et al.*).

4. *A corollary is the finding that for people we like, we tend to perceive more accurately the ways in which they are similar to us, and are less accurate in viewing the unlike ways.* However, for people we do not like, we tend to see them as different from ourselves; we perceive most accurately their traits that are unlike our own, and their similar traits least accurately (Vroom, 1959).

5. *Accuracy in perceiving others is not a single skill that some people have and others do not.* Our accuracy level will depend on how sensitive we are to the differences among the people we are judging; thus, we will be more accurate in judging some types of people than others. It will also depend on what norms for judgment (outside ourselves) are available in the situation; thus, we will be more accurate in judging in some situations than in others (Gage; Taguiri *et al.*; Bronfenbrenner *et al.*; Taft).

We can understand these results by relating them to our previous analysis of the process of perception. The administrator (or any other individual) who wishes to perceive someone else accurately must be looking at the other person, not at himself. The things that he looks at in someone else are influenced by his own traits. But if he knows his own traits, he can be aware that they provide a frame of reference for him. The question we could ask when viewing another is: Am I looking at him, and forming my impression of his behavior in the situation, or am I just comparing him to myself?

There is the added problem, too, of being set to see the personality traits in another that we don't accept in ourselves. At the same time, we may make undue allowances in others for those of our own deficiencies that don't bother us, but might concern others, for example not following prescribed procedures.

Characteristics of the Perceived in the Situation

We turn now to some characteristics of the person perceived that give us perceptual difficulties. For example, the status of the other person is a variable, influencing our judgments about his behavior. Thibaut and Riecken have shown that even though two people behave in identical fashion, status differences between them cause a perceiver to assign different motivations for the behavior. In this experiment, after a high status person and a low status person were introduced to the subject, they were asked by the subject to comply with a request. At the same point in the experiment, both did. The subject, nevertheless, did not perceive both as equally cooperative. He judged the high status person as *wanting* to cooperate; the low status person as *having* to cooperate and, in turn, he expressed more liking for the high status than for the low status person. Presumably, more credit is given when the boss says "good morning" to us than when a subordinate says the same thing.

Recalling Bruner's description of the categories we use to simplify our perceptual activities, we can recognize that there are certain categories into which we class the person being perceived. Status is one type of category, and role provides another. Thus, the remarks of Mr. Jones, in the sales department, are perceived differently from those of Smith, in the purchasing department, although both may say the same thing. Also, one who knows Jones' role in the organization, will perceive his behavior differently from one who does not know Jones' role. The process of categorizing on the basis of roles is similar to, if not identical, with the stereotyping process described earlier.

Visibility of the traits we are judging is also an important variable, influencing the accuracy of our perception. Visibility will depend, for example, on how free the other person feels to express the trait. It has been demonstrated that we are more accurate in judging people who like us than people who dislike us (Tagiuri, Bruner and Blake). The suggested explanation is that most people in our society feel constraint in showing their dislike, and thus the cues are less visible.

Another influence on making certain kinds of behavior visible to the perceiver is the relevance of the behavior to the situation in which it is being judged. Judgments about the administrative skill of an acquaintance, whom we know only through sharing a train trip together, are not likely to be very accurate. Unfortunately, but frequently, equally irrelevant situations are used to appraise behavior. For example, seeing that a person appears to mix well at a social gathering may tell us a little bit about how, as a salesman, he would get along with people; but it would not tell us how clearly he explains the product, or closes a sale.

Finally, some traits are not visible, simply because they provide few external cues for their presence. Loyalty, for example, as opposed to level of energy, provides few early signs for observation. Even honesty cannot be seen as such in the situations in which most impressions are formed. As obvious as these comments might be, in forming impressions, many of us nevertheless continue to judge the presence of traits that are not really visible. Frequently, we do so because the practical situation demands judgments, but we should recognize the frail reeds upon which we are leaning and be prepared to observe further and revise our judgments as time goes along.

Soskin describes four limitations on our ability to form accurate impressions of others. He suggests first, that our impression is likely to be disproportionately affected by the type of situation or surroundings in which the impression is made, and influenced too little by the person who is being perceived. (Maslow and Mintz found that "energy" and "well-being" were judged more favorably from faces when the judgments were made in esthetically pleasing, rather than displeasing conditions.) Thus, the plush luncheon club in which we first meet a man will dominate our impression of the man himself. Secondly, although our impressions are frequently based on a limited sample of the other person's behavior, the impressions we draw will be quite sweeping, for example, judging a man to be taciturn because he had nothing to say while you and an old friend reminisced about old times, or because he has heard, possibly erroneously, that you like to do the talking. A third limitation reported by Soskin is that the situation may not provide an opportunity for the other person to show behavior that is relevant to the traits about which impressions are formed. Casual conversation or questions for example, provide few opportunities to demonstate intelligence or work characteristics, yet we often draw conclusions about these from an interview. Soskin's final point ties in with what Bruner and Cantril have implied. The impression of the other may be distorted by some highly individualized reaction of the perceiver—a personal distaste for colorful ties, for example. With these limitations in mind, we must give even greater weight to Dailey's warning against forming impressions too early in an acquaintance.

The Situational Influences: Organization and Interpersonal Relationships

Likert has pointed out that "an individual's reaction to any situation is always a function, not of the absolute character of the interaction, but of his perception of it. It is how he sees things that counts, not objective reality. Consequently, an individual will always interpret an interaction between himself and the organization in terms of his background and culture, his experience and expectations." (1959, p. 191)

Interpersonal. Some recent research clearly points to the conclusion that the whole process of interpersonal perception is also a function of the group (or interpersonal) context in which the perception occurs. The research has important theoretical implications for a psychology of interpersonal relations; in addition, it contains some suggestions of applied value for administrators. It is possible to identify four characteristics of the interpersonal climate that have direct effect on perceptual accuracy. As will be noted, these are characteristics that can be known, and in some cases controlled, in administrative situations.

Bieri provides data, suggesting that when people are given an opportunity to interact in a friendly situation, each tends to see the others as more like himself. Applying his suggestion to the administrative situation, we can reason as follows: Some difficulties of administrative practice grow out of beliefs that different interest groups in the organization are made up of different types of people. Obviously, once we believe that people in other groups are different, we'll be set to see the differences. We can thus find, from Bieri's and from Rosenbaum's work, an administrative approach for attacking the problem. If we can produce an interacting situation that is cooperative rather than competitive, the likelihood of seeing others as more like ourselves is increased.

Exline's studies (1957; 1960) enable us to add some other characteristics of the social context that may influence perception. Paraphrasing his conclusions to adapt them to the administrative scene, we can suggest that when a committee is made up of congenial members who are willing to continue work in the same group, their perceptions of the goal-directed behavior of fellow committee members will be more accurate. On the other hand, observations of purely personal behavior (as distinguished from task-centered behavior) may be less accurate. The findings would seem to have application in selecting committee and work group members: at the very least avoid throwing together those with a past history of major personal clashes. If they must be on the same committee, each must be helped to see that the other is working toward the same goal.

An interesting variation in this area of research is the suggestion (from a study by Ex) that our perceptions will be more influenced by relatively unfamiliar people in our group than by those who are our intimates. The concept needs further research but it interestingly assumes that we may give credit to strangers for having greater knowledge (because we don't really know) than to our intimates (whose backgrounds and limitations we feel we do know).

Organization. The organization, and one's place in it, also provides part of the context in which perceptions take place. The Dearborn and Simon reading that follows illustrates this point. Their data support the hypothesis that the administrators' perceptions will often be limited to those aspects of a situation that relate specifically to their own departments, despite an attempt to influence them away from such selectivity.

READING 1-5

Selective Perception: A Note on the Departmental Identifications of Executives*

DE WITT C. DEARBORN
AND
HERBERT A. SIMON

An important proposition in organization theory asserts that each executive will perceive those aspects of the situa-

* Abridged from *Sociometry*, 21 (1958), pp. 140-144.

tion that relate specifically to the activities and goals of his department (2, Ch. 5, 10). The proposition is frequently supported by ancedotes of executives and observers in organizations, but little evidence of a systematic kind is available to test it. It is the purpose of this note to supply some such evidence.

The proposition we are considering is not peculiarly organizational. It is simply an application to organizational phenomena of a generalization that is central to any explanation of selective perception: Presented with a complex stimulus, the subject perceives in it what he is "ready" to perceive; the more complex or ambiguous the stimulus, the more the perception is determined by what is already "in" the subject and the less by what is in the stimulus (1, pp. 132-133).

Cognitive and motivational mechanisms mingle in the selective process, and it may be of some use to assess their relative contributions. We might suppose either: (1) selective attention to a part of a stimulus reflects a deliberate ignoring of the remainder as irrelevant to the subject's goals and motives, or (2) selective attention is a learned response stemming from some past history of reinforcement. In the latter case we might still be at some pains to determine the nature of the reinforcement, but by creating a situation from which any immediate motivation for selectivity is removed, we should be able to separate the second mechanism from the first. The situation in which we obtained our data meets this condition, and hence our data provide evidence for internalization of the selective processes.

Method of the Study

A group of 23 executives, all employed by a single large manufacturing concern and enrolled in a company sponsored executive training program, was asked to read a standard case that is widely used in instruction in business policy in business schools. The case, Castengo Steel Company, described the organization and activities of a company of moderate size specializing in the manufacture of seamless steel tubes, as of the end of World War II. The case, which is about 10,000 words in length, contains a wealth of descriptive material about the company and its industry and the recent history of both (up to 1945), but little evaluation. It is deliberately written to hold closely to concrete facts and to leave as much as possible of the burden of interpretation to the reader.

When the executives appeared at a class session to discuss the case, but before they had discussed it, they were asked by the instructor to write a brief statement of what they considered to be the most important problem facing the Castengo Steel Company—the problem a new company president should deal with first. Prior to this session, the group had discussed other cases, being reminded from time to time by the instructor that they were to assume the role of the top executive of the company in considering its problems.

The executives were a relatively homogeneous group in terms of status, being drawn from perhaps three levels of the company organization. They were in the range usually called "middle management," representing such positions as superintendent of a department in a large factory, product manager responsible for profitability of one of the ten product groups manufactured by the company, and works physician for a large factory. In terms of departmental affiliation, they fell in four groups:

Sales (6): Five product managers or assistant product managers, and one field sales supervisor.
Production (5): Three department superintendents, one assistant factory manager, and one construction engineer.
Accounting (4): An assistant chief accountant, and three accounting supervisors—for a budget division and two factory departments.
Miscellaneous (8): Two members of the legal department, two in research and development, and one

each from public relations, industrial relations, medical and purchasing.

The Data

. . .

We tested our hypothesis by determining whether there was a significant relation between the "most important problem" mentioned and the departmental affiliation of the mentioner. In the cases of executives who mentioned more than one problem, we counted all those they mentioned. We compared (1) the executives who mentioned "sales," "marketing," or "distribution" with those who did not; (2) the executives who mentioned "clarifying the organization" or some equivalent with those who did not; (3) the executives who mentioned "human relations," "employee relations" or "teamwork" with those who did not. The findings are summarized in the Table.

			Number Who Mentioned	
Department	Total Number of Executives	Sales	"Clarify Organization"	Human Relations
Sales	6	5	1	0
Production	5	1	4	0
Accounting	4	3	0	0
Miscellaneous	8	1	3	3
Totals	23	10	8	3

The difference between the percentages of sales executives (83%) and other executives (29%) who mentioned sales as the most important problem is significant at the 5 per cent level. Three of the five nonsales executives, moreover, who mentioned sales were in the accounting department, and all of these were in positions that involved analysis of product profitability. This accounting activity was, in fact, receiving considerable emphasis in the company at the time of the case discussion and the accounting executives had frequent and close contacts with the product managers in the sales department. If we combine sales and accounting executives, we find that 8 out of 10 of these mentioned sales as the most important problem; while only 2 of the remaining 13 executives did.

Organization problems (other than marketing organization) were mentioned by four out of five production executives, the two executives in research and development, and the factory physician, but by only one sales executive and no accounting executives. The difference between the percentage for production executives (80%) and other executives (22%) is also significant at the 5 per cent level. Examination of the Castengo case shows that the main issue discussed in the case that relates to manufacturing is the problem of poorly defined relations among the factory manager, the metallurgist, and the company president. The presence of the metallurgist in the situation may help to explain the sensitivity of the two research and development executives (both of whom were concerned with metallurgy) to this particular problem area. It is easy to conjecture why the public relations, industrial relations, and medical executives should all have mentioned some aspect of human relations, and why one of the two legal department executives should have mentioned the board of directors.

Conclusion

We have presented data on the selective perceptions of industrial executives exposed to case material that support the hypothesis that each executive will perceive those aspects of a situation that relate specifically to the activities and goals of his department. Since the situation is one in which the executives were motivated to look at the problem from a company-wide rather than a departmental viewpoint, the data indicate further that the criteria of selection have become internalized. Finally, the method for obtaining data that we have used holds considerable promise as a projective device for eliciting the attitudes and perceptions of executives.

References

1. Bruner, J. S., "On Perceptual Readiness," *Psychological Review*, 1957, 64, 123-152.
2. Simon, H. A., *Administrative Behavior*, New York: Macmillan, 1947.
   [Appendix omitted]

Perception of self, among populations at different levels in the hierarchy, also offers an opportunity for judging the influence of organizational context on perceptual activity. Porter's study of the self-descriptions of managers and line workers indicates that both groups see themselves in different terms, corresponding to their positions in the organization's hierarchy. He states that managers use leadership-type traits (for example, inventive) to describe themselves, whereas line workers use cooperative-follower terms (for example, cooperative). Which comes first: do managers see themselves this way because of their current position in the organization? Or, is this self-picture an expression of a more enduring personal characteristic that helped bring managers to their present positions? This study does not help to tell us if becoming a manager automatically brings with it an emphasis on certain traits; but it is consistent with other findings that relate changes in role with change in attitudes (see, for example, Reading 1-5).

Barrett has shown that if the superior and subordinate are in relative agreement in their perceptions of the importance of various aspects of the subordinate's job the superior expresses more satisfaction than when there is low agreement. And, in turn, when the subordinate's perception of how the job should be done is in line with his perception of the way the boss wants it done, then the subordinate is more satisfied with his job (than when agreement is low).

Perceptual Influences on Interpersonal Adjustment

Throughout Part One, we have examined a variety of influences on the perceptual process. In this discussion, we have implied that the operations of such influences on perception would in turn effect behavior that would follow. Common sense judgment suggests that being able to size up other people accurately facilitates smooth and effective interpersonal adjustments. Nevertheless, the relation between perception and consequent behavior itself needs direct analysis. Two aspects may be identified: (1) The effect of accuracy of perception on subsequent behavior, and (2) The effect of duration of the relation and the opportunity for receiving additional cues. We consider briefly research findings in each of these areas.

First then, we can ask a question that is crucial from the applied point of view—is there a relation between accuracy of social perception and adjustment to others? More specifically; does accurate social perception promote efficiency between people and, in group behavior, increased group effectiveness? Although both questions might suggest a quick affirmative answer, research findings are inconsistent about the relation between accuracy of social perception and interpersonal adjustment. Steiner has tried to resolve some of these inconsistencies by stating that accuracy does have an effect on interaction under the following conditions: (1) When the interacting persons are cooperatively motivated, (2) When the behavior that is accurately perceived is relevant to the activities of these persons, and (3) When members are free to alter their behavior on the basis of their perceptions.

As previously reported in Chapter Two, where interpersonal contact provides opportunity only to form an impression, a large number of subjective factors—set, stereotypes, and projections, operate to create an early impression that is frequently erroneous. In more enduring relationships, appraisal may become more balanced as increased interaction provides additional cues for judgment. Newcomb, in his study of the acquaintance process, points out that although early perception of favorable traits causes attraction to the person, over a four month period early cues for judging favorable traits of others become less influential. After time has passed, a much broader basis is used, including comparisons with others with whom one has established relationships. Such findings suggest that the warnings about perceptual inaccuracies implicit in the earlier chapters apply with even greater force to the short term process of impression forming than to relatively long term acquaintance building relationships. One would thus hope that rating an employee after a year of service would be a more objective performance than appraising him in a selection interview—a hope that will be achieved only when the rater has provided himself with opportunities for broadening the cues he uses to evaluate his first impressions.

Concluding Statement: Part One

We conclude our discussion of perception with a few straight-forward suggestions for raising the probability of more effective administrative action. One suggestion is that the administrator become aware of the intricacies of the perceptual process and thus be warned to avoid arbitrary and categorical judgments and to seek reliable evidence before judgments are made. A second suggestion grows out of the first—increased accuracy in one's self-perception can make possible the flexibility to go slowly, to seek evidence, and to shift positions as time provides additional evidence about others.

However, not every effort that is designed to improve perceptual accuracy will do so. The dangers of too complete reliance on formal training for perceptive accuracy are suggested by the study of Crow previously mentioned. The danger is that a little learning encourages the perceiver to respond with increased sensitivity to individual differences, without making it possible to gauge the real meaning of the differences he has seen.

Having offered this caveat, we conclude with a summary statement by Taft, made after his review of eighty-one studies in this field:

> The main attributes of the ability to judge others seem to lie in three areas: possessing appropriate judgmental norms, judging ability, and motivation. Where J [the judge] is similar in background to S [the subject] he has the advantage of being readily able to use appropriate *norms* for making his judgment. The relevant *judging ability* seems to be a combination of general intelligence and social intelligence, with the possibility of an additional specific factor for nonanalytic judgments ("intuition")—so far, only one study has distinguished such a factor. But probably the most important area of all is that of *motivation:* if the judge is motivated to make accurate judgments about his subject and if he feels himself free to be objective, then he has a good chance of achieving his aim, provided of course that he has the requisite ability and can use the appropriate judgmental norms. The act of judging one's fellows is a purposive piece of behavior that involves not only conscious motivation but also ingrained attitudes toward social relationships, including the relationships inherent in the act of judging itself.

PART TWO

Needs,
Motives,
and
Goals

Introduction

Everyone gives at least lip-service to the importance of motivation for administration. But acknowledging its importance, and even providing a catalogue of needs to be satisfied is quite different from being ready to perceive a person's specific needs in the work situation, and the individual way in which a particular person responds to his needs.

The complexity of motivation has fascinated mankind throughout recorded history. Novelists, playwrights, historians, detectives, and scientists, as well as all the rest of us are continually seeking the "why" of someone's behavior.

In Part Two we are going to try to summarize what has been learned in recent decades in scientific studies of motivation. We are *not* going to delve into specific case histories, nor will we focus on that part of the motivational picture that lies outside the administrator's scope. Thus, we do not include the physiological drives. Neither do we consider separately the intensive psychoanalytical theories of Freud and others, although many of our statements on motivation will show the influence of psychoanalytic concepts and research. The individual's reactions to frustration, anxiety, and conflict will be dealt with in Part Three.

Preview of Part Two

We examine motivation under three broad headings: basic human needs, some determinants of the individual's response to basic needs, and finally, incentives in the organization and their relation to job performance. Chapters Four and Five draw heavily on laboratory research; Chapter Six turns to research on employee groups in organizational settings. The theory and laboratory research provide a necessary backdrop for the work oriented organizational studies.

Over the past twenty years Maslow, a personality theorist and clinical psychologist, has been developing a theory of motivation that has more recently been widely adopted in management literature and practice as a useful framework within which to understand the motivation to work. He organizes motivation into a five-level hierarchy of needs: physiological, safety, membership, ego, and self-fulfillment. In Chapter Four, Maslow's theory is presented in a brief statement from his own writings and in an article by Clark, relating his theory to organizational behavior.

We next observe that although the same basic needs are almost universally felt by people in our culture, there is no universal pattern of response to them. Nor is there any simple way to predict behavior from a knowledge either of the need being experienced or the environmental source of satisfaction. The individual's life experiences have introduced a series of influences that intervene between the need and the source of satisfaction. His responses to his needs thus may be determined in a highly individual fashion. Behavioral science has not yet identified all these forces and their interactions, and so a complete understanding of the why of human behavior still eludes us. Recent theory and research has, however, identified some important influences. Among those discussed in Chapter Five are: Klein's concept of cognitive style; level of aspiration (presented in a reading by Lewin and several studies growing out of his original conceptions); expectancy; and the influences resulting from the individual's group memberships.

Chapter Six begins with a selection from Blauner's review of studies, describing the sources and qualities of satisfaction experienced by workers in the employment situation. Kahn's keen analysis of motivational factors related to worker productivity follows. We conclude with our summaries of several research studies that relate motivational factors to such aspects of job performance as turnover and quality of work.

CHAPTER FOUR

Basic
Human
Needs

Basic Human Needs

Psychology's earliest attempt to concern itself with the "why" of human behavior was to provide a catalogue of driving forces that, having been labelled instincts, were then said to "explain" behavior. More recently, the innate or constitutional nature of some of these forces has been questioned but the same cataloguing technique has been pursued—the motivational forces now being called drives or needs. Current motivational theory questions the usefulness of organizing our thinking around a mere listing of drives or needs.

Yet it is apparent that man's behavior is oriented around certain broad types of satisfactions. We can recognize this fact and set up a systematic list of the kinds of satisfactions that man requires; this can be a useful procedure if it is seen as a point of departure into the dynamics of motivation and not, as itself, the final answer. Maslow has constructed such an approach. His theory provides a list of needs as a foundation for a more penetrating and dynamic interpretation of the way in which man's behavior is motivated.

Our first very short reading is an abridgment of a series of propositions stated by Maslow to provide the broad outlines of his theory of motivation. These statements are followed by Clark's article that first provides a convenient description of pertinent details of Maslow's theory, and then relates the theoretical outline to organizational behavior, particularly productivity and employee turnover. We present this latter section as a separate reading in Chapter Six.

A Dynamic Theory of Human Motivation*

A. H. MASLOW

In a previous paper various propositions were presented which would have to be included in any theory of human motivation that could lay claim to being definitive. These conclusions may be briefly summarized as follows:

1. The integrated wholeness of the organism must be one of the foundation stones of motivation theory.

2. The hunger drive (or any other physiological drive) was rejected as a centering point or model for a definitive theory of motivation. Any drive that is somatically based and localizable was shown to be atypical rather than typical in human motivation.

3. Such a theory should stress and center itself upon ultimate or basic goals rather than partial or superficial ones, upon ends rather than means to these ends. Such a stress would imply a more central place for unconscious rather than conscious motivations.

4. There are usually available various cultural paths to the same goal. Therefore conscious, specific, local-cultural desires are not as fundamental in motivation theory as the more basic, unconscious goals.

5. Any motivated behavior, either preparatory or consummatory, must be understood to be a channel through which many basic needs may be simultaneously expressed or satisfied. Typically an act has *more* than one motivation.

6. Practically all organismic states are to be understood as motivated and as motivating.

7. Human needs arrange themselves in hierarchies of pre-potency. That is, the appearance of one need usually rests on the prior satisfaction of another, more prepotent need. Thus man is a perpetually wanting animal. . . .

8. *Lists* of drives will get us no place for various theoretical and practical reasons. Furthermore any classification of motivations must deal with the problem of levels of specificity or generalization of the motives to be classified.

9. Classifications of motivations must be based upon goals rather than upon instigating drives or motivated behavior.

10. Motivation theory should be human-centered rather than animal-centered.

11. The situation or the field in which the organism reacts must be taken into account but the field alone can rarely serve as an exclusive explanation for behavior. Furthermore the field itself must be interpreted in the organism's terms. . . .

12. Not only the integration of the organism must be taken into account, but also the possibility of isolated, specific, partial or segmented reactions.

It has since become necessary to add to these another affirmation.

13. Motivation theory is not synonymous with behavior theory. The motivations are only one class of determinants of behavior. While behavior is almost always motivated, it is also almost always biologically, culturally and situationally determined as well.

---

* Excerpted from *Psychological Review*, 50 (1943), pp. 370-373.

READING 2-2

Motivation in Work Groups:
A Tentative View*
(Part One)

JAMES V. CLARK

This paper represents an attempt to examine a number of different researches in the field of organizational behavior and to see if their similarities can be highlighted and tentatively explained by the use of Maslow's need-hierarchy concept.[1]

A recent research experience of mine (so far published only in case form)[2] suggested for me that this process might be a useful way of generating new hypotheses and methods of measurement. The present paper is presented in the hope that others can be stimulated in the same way.

More specifically, this paper makes no claim that the answers concerning employee motivation and its determinants are all in. Neither does it claim that the questions generated by the examination of several researches from the point of view of the need-hierarchy concept are all presently researchable in a strict operational sense. Rather, the paper puts up what, for me, appears to be a potentially operational scheme for analyzing motivation and its organizational determinants. With such a scheme, it appears possible to study a number of different organizations comparatively, an effort which the field of organizational behavior needs. . . .

The Need-Hierarchy Model

Let us start with McGregor's summary of Maslow's concepts, which is concise and simply put.

As most readers are probably aware, Maslow views an individual's motivations not in terms of a series of drives, but rather in terms of a hierarchy, certain "higher" needs becoming activated to the extent certain "lower" ones become satisfied. McGregor summarized these as follows:[4]

> *"Physiological Needs*
>
> Man is a wanting animal—as soon as one of his needs is satisfied, another appears in its place. This process is unending. It continues from birth to death.
>
> Man's needs are organized in a series of levels—a hierarchy of importance. At the lowest level, but preeminent in importance when they are thwarted, are his *physiological needs*. Man lives for bread alone, when there is no bread. Unless the circumstances are unusual, his needs for love, for status, for

---

* From *Human Organization,* 19 (1960-61), pp. 199-208. This reading is presented in two parts. The first, presented here, summarizes Maslow's theory of motivation; Part Two, examining industrial research to assess the relation between motivation and job performance is presented in Chapter Six as Reading 2-6.

[1] A. H. Maslow, *Motivation and Personality,* Harper and Bros., New York, 1954.

[2] "Century Co. (A)—(I)," Harvard Business School, EA-A 321-329.

---

[4] Douglas M. McGregor, 5th Anniversary Convocation, School of Industrial Management, Massachusetts Institute of Technology, Cambridge, Massachusetts.

recognition are inoperative when his stomach has been empty for awhile. But when he eats regularly and adequately, hunger ceases to be an important motivation. The same is true of the other physiological needs of man—for rest, exercise, shelter, protection from the elements.

A satisfied need is not a motivator of behavior! This is a fact of profound significance that is regularly ignored in the conventional approach to the management of ["normal"] people. Consider your own need for air; except as you are deprived of it, it has no appreciable motivating effect upon your behavior.

Safety Needs

When the physiological needs are reasonably satisfied, needs at the next higher level begin to dominate man's behavior, to motivate him. These are called *safety needs.* They are needs for protection against danger, threat, deprivation. Some people mistakenly refer to these as needs for security. However, unless man is in a dependent relationship where he fears arbitrary deprivation, he does not demand security. The need is for the "fairest possible break." When he is confident of this he is more willing to take risks. But when he feels threatened or dependent, his greatest need is for guarantees, for protection, for security.

The fact needs little emphasis that, since every industrial employee is in a dependent relationship, safety needs may assume considerable importance. Arbitrary management actions, behavior which arouses uncertainty with respect to continued employment or which reflects favoritism or discrimination, unpredictable administration of policy—these can be powerful motivators of the safety needs in the employment relationship at *every level,* from worker to vice president.

Social Needs

When man's physiological needs are satisfied and he is no longer fearful about his physical welfare, his *social needs* become important motivators of his behavior—needs for belonging, for association, for acceptance by his fellows, for giving and receiving friendship and love.

Management knows today of the existence of these needs, but it often assumes quite wrongly that they represent a threat to the organization. Many studies have demonstrated that the tightly knit, cohesive work group may, under proper conditions, be far more effective than an equal number of separate individuals in achieving organizational goals.

Yet management, fearing group hostility to its own objectives, often goes to considerable lengths to control and direct human efforts in ways that are inimical to the natural "groupiness" of human beings. When man's social needs—and perhaps his safety needs, too—are thus thwarted, he behaves in ways which tend to defeat organizational objectives. He becomes resistant, antagonistic, uncooperative. But this behavior is a consequence, not a cause.

Ego Needs

Above the social needs—in the sense that they do not become motivators until lower needs are reasonably satisfied—are the needs of greater significance to management and to man himself. They are the *egoistic* needs, and they are of two kinds:

1. Those needs that relate to one's self-esteem—needs for self-confidence, for independence, for achievement, for competence, for knowledge.

2. Those needs that relate to one's reputation—needs for status, for recognition, for appreciation, for the deserved respect of one's fellows.

Unlike the lower needs, these are rarely satisfied; man seeks indefinitely for more satisfaction of these needs once they·have become important to him. But they do not appear in any significant way until physiological, safety, and social needs are all reasonably satisfied.

The typical industrial organization offers few opportunities for the satisfaction of these egoistic needs to people at lower levels in the hierarchy. The conventional methods of organizing work, particularly in mass-production industries, give little heed to these aspects of human motivation. If the practices of scientific management were deliberately calculated to thwart these needs, they could hardly accomplish this purpose better than they do.

Self-Fulfillment Needs

Finally—a capstone, as it were, on the hierarchy of man's needs—there are what we may call the needs for *self-fulfillment*. These are the needs for realizing one's own potentialities, for continued self-development, for being creative in the broadest sense of that term.

It is clear that the conditions of modern life give only limited opportunity for these relatively weak needs to obtain expression. The deprivation most people experience with respect to other lower-level needs diverts their energies into the struggle to satisfy those needs, and the needs for self-fulfillment remain dormant."

For purposes of initial explanation and simplicity, McGregor spoke in terms of separate steps or levels. Actually, Maslow suggests that these levels are interdependent and overlapping, each higher-need level emerging before the lower needs have been satisfied completely. In our society, most people tend to be partially satisfied in each need area and partially unsatisfied. However, most individuals tend to have higher satisfaction at the lower-need level than at higher-need levels. Maslow helps to explain this by picturing the average citizen as (for illustrative purposes) 85 percent satisfied in his physiological needs, 70 percent satisfied in his safety needs, 50 percent in his belonging needs, 40 percent in his egoistic needs, and 10 percent in his self-fulfillment needs.

CHAPTER FIVE

Intervening
Influences
on
Responses
to
Needs

Differences are found among individuals when they are responding to the pattern of needs described by Maslow. Three principles implicit in his theory of motivation help us to understand these differences:

1. *The same need may lead to different responses.* Two individuals experiencing the same needs with equal intensity may use different ways to reach the same goal (for example, trying to get a raise). Among the possible "styles" are aggressive reaching out; passively being available and hopeful; open and frank approaches; or discreet, or even shrewd approaches. The administrator should know that there are more people who want, need, or expect a raise than those who ask for it. Hard workers are not the only people who have strong achievement needs, but they may be the ones who are more likely to get labelled as ambitious. We don't see people's needs directly. We tend to judge their needs by the behavior that they show. When their behavior seems self-effacing or diffident, we can too easily assume that this implies a lower need to get certain rewards, and fail to see that it may be their own individual way of responding to their needs.
2. *The same needs may be met by different satisfiers.* Hungry people, even in the same family, choose different foods. Achievement need may be satisfied

TABLE 2-1

Needs, Goals, and Intervening Influences

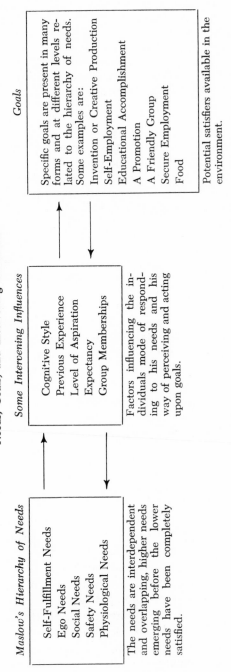

Maslow's Hierarchy of Needs

Self-Fulfillment Needs
Ego Needs
Social Needs
Safety Needs
Physiological Needs

The needs are interdependent and overlapping, higher needs emerging before the lower needs have been completely satisfied.

Some Intervening Influences

Cognitive Style
Previous Experience
Level of Aspiration
Expectancy
Group Memberships

Factors influencing the individuals mode of responding to his needs and his way of perceiving and acting upon goals.

Goals

Specific goals are present in many forms and at different levels related to the hierarchy of needs. Some examples are:

Invention or Creative Production
Self-Employment
Educational Accomplishment
A Promotion
A Friendly Group
Secure Employment
Food

Potential satisfiers available in the environment.

Needs, influences, and goals interact, creating new levels of equilibrium in the relationship.

by quantity or quality of performance. The need for status or for acceptance by others may be sought through a promotion within the formal organizational system, or through informal but important influence in the work group, or even outside the company organization in clubs or other groups.

3. *Similar behavior may be based on the operation of different needs.* Frequently, people are found in the same office who in one case turn out the work because they seek the admiration of others, and in the other case, because they must meet standards they have set for themselves. A promotion may be sought by one person because of the importance of more money and by another because of his need for increased power, or of greater status.

Even in choosing a job, people may choose the same job to satisfy quite different needs. Among the factors important in emphasizing one set of needs over another, Rim has suggested the relevance of cultural factors (there are, of course, many personal and familial factors operating as well). American and Israeli students were asked to indicate which of a series of job incentives would be most influential in their choice of jobs. The Americans (a group of Pittsburgh students) gave much more emphasis to job security; the Israeli students gave more emphasis to initiative. In commenting on his findings Rim notes: "[the difference] may reflect the Israeli reality of a very strong Labour Federation, which makes job security a matter of course. This may not be so in Pittsburgh, [it may also] reflect a different aspect of Israeli reality: Israel being a young and fast developing country puts a high premium on initiative."

Our readings and commentary in this Chapter attempt a more precise identification of factors that define how an individual will respond to the needs he is experiencing. (Refer to Table 2-1). In order to know how an individual will respond we have to know more than what need is active and what opportunities for its satisfaction are available. In the following sections we consider several influences that intervene between the individual's needs and his responses to satisfiers: cognitive style, his previous experience (success or failure), expectancy, level of aspiration and group membership.

Cognitive Style

One interpretation of the individual differences found in responding to existing needs and available satisfactions is offered in Klein's work on cognitive style. He suggests that each person works out his own individual way, or style, of handling his needs. The individual learns his style by receiving different rewards and punishments for different actions. The style involves some degree of cognitive (or rational) control, that directs his way of perceiving reality, thus influencing his responses to need and approaches to satisfiers.

At this point we can refer to a statement in the Bruner reading (Ch. One): ". . . there is now enough evidence to suggest that not the strength of need but the way in which a person learns to handle his needs determines the manner in which motivation and cognitive selectivity will interact." Bruner is talking about defense mechanisms, but Klein holds that cognitive style exists independently of the defense system of the individual. Both the patterns of using defense mechanisms and the cognitive style can account for individual and sometimes idiosyncratic motivational activities. The administrator cannot afford to think of motivation as a simple matter of matching needs and satisfiers. A complex series of factors intervene between these two elements of any motivational system, making the motivation of human behavior a challenging and frequently a frustrating puzzle.

Previous Experience, Level of Aspiration, Expectancy, and Achievement Need

Pursuing the same problem of relating the inner needs, the outer satisfiers, and the person's response to each of these, we next consider how past success or failure influences the future goals that an individual sets for himself. In 1931, Dembo and Hoppe, co-workers of Kurt Lewin, named this goal-setting behavior, level of aspiration. Since that time, much research activity has focused on the detailed way in which experiences of success or failure influence future behavior.

In this discussion we must distinguish at the start between goal-striving behavior and goal-setting behavior. The latter concerns the goal that the individual is willing to *set* for himself on the basis of *past* success or failure and consequent expectations of success. Goal striving is behavior directed toward reaching a goal that has already been set. Thus, a salesman may decide (with encouragement from his sales manager) to increase sales this year by ten per cent rather than five per cent, as in the year past (goal setting). The salesman now chooses actions that he believes will enable him to reach this ten per cent goal, for example, he plans his day's sales effort more carefully so that he can increase the number of visits made each day (goal striving). Goal setting and goal striving are, of course, related, in that experience (success or failure) in goal-striving behavior will significantly influence subsequent goals that are set.

Lewin's early article on the "Psychology of Success or Failure," which follows as our next reading, sets the stage for the subsequent summary of more recent research on level of aspiration.

READING 2-3

Psychology of Success and Failure*

KURT LEWIN

The great importance of success and failure is recognized by practically all psychological schools. Thorndike's law of effect,[1] as well as Adler's ideas, has close relation to this problem. Pedagogically, the importance of success is universally stressed.

---

* Abridged from *Occupations*, 14 (1936), pp. 926-930.
[1] Law of effect: One learns quickly those reactions which are accompanied or followed by a satisfying state of affairs; one does not learn quickly those which result in an annoying state of affairs or learns not to make such reactions.

Indeed, success and failure influence deeply the emotional status of the person, his goals, and his social relations. From the point of view of guidance, one can emphasize the fact that these problems are important throughout the whole age range and are as basic for the very young child as for the adult.

In spite of the common recognition of these factors, our knowledge about the psychology of success and failure is meager. The law of effect may, for instance, suggest that a person who has succeeded in a special activity will have a tendency to repeat that activity. Indeed, children of two or three years tend to repeat activities again and again. Yet, experiments show, at least for older persons, that a spontaneous repetition of a successful act is not very likely, and that in case it does occur, the activity is generally distinctly changed. As a matter of fact, the tendency to go back spontaneously to a special activity, is, as Ovsiankina has shown, about ninety times as high if the activity is not completed as if it is successfully completed. This shows, at least, that the whole problem is much more complicated than one might expect.

II

The first question one should be able to answer is: Under what conditions will a person experience success or failure? The experiments of Hoppe point to some fundamental facts which one could have learned from everyday experience; namely, it is not possible to correlate the objective achievement on the one side, with the feeling of success or failure on the other. The same achievement can result once in the feeling of great success, another time in the feeling of complete failure. This is true not only for different individuals, but even for the same individual. For instance, a person may throw a discus forty yards the first time. The second time he may reach fifty,

and feel very successful. After short practice, he may reach sixty-five. If he then throws fifty yards again, he will experience a definite failure in spite of the fact that he got a thrill out of the same achievement but a short time before. This means that the experience of success and failure does not depend upon the achievement as such, but rather upon the relation between the achievement and the person's expectation. One can speak, in this respect, about the person's "level of aspiration," and can say that the experience and the degree of success and failure depend upon whether the achievement is above or below the momentary level of aspiration.

One may ask whether a person always has a definite level of aspiration in respect to a certain task. The answer is no. If one, for instance, does something for the first time, one generally does not set himself a definite goal. It is interesting additional evidence of the relation between success and the level of aspiration that in such situations no strong failure is experienced. If one wishes to avoid or diminish the feeling of failure in the child, one often says to him: "Just try." In this way a definite level of aspiration is eliminated.

Not only is the level of aspiration fundamental for the experience of success and failure, but the level of aspiration itself is changed by success and failure. After success, a person generally sets himself a higher goal. After failure, his level of aspiration generally goes down. There are some exceptions to this general trend which one should notice. In the experiments of Hoppe, success led to a rise of the level of aspiration only in sixty-nine per cent; in seven per cent it remained the same; and in twenty-four per cent the person stopped the activity entirely. After failure, the level of aspiration was never raised, but it was lowered in only fifty per cent of the cases. In twenty-one per cent it remained the same, in two percent the person consoled himself by the realization of previous successes; and in twenty-seven per cent the person ceased the activity entirely. This varying behavior is due partly to the fact that there are cases which are neither clear successes nor clear failures. On the whole, the person is more ready to raise the level of aspiration after success than to lower it after failure.

It is important to note that a person instead of lowering his level of aspiration after failure, may stop entirely. There is a significant difference between individuals in this respect. Some persons are relatively easily influenced to lower their levels of aspiration, whereas others show a stiff backbone. The latter maintain their levels of aspiration in spite of failures, and may prefer to leave the field entirely rather than to lower it. Lack of persistence sometimes has to be attributed to such an unwillingness to yield. On the other hand, there are cases of apparent persistence, in which a person sticks to an activity only at the price of constantly lowering his level of aspiration . . . In problems of guidance involving unusually high or low persistency, the possible reasons behind such behavior should be carefully examined, because the advisable measures should be different in accordance with the underlying psychological facts.

Surprisingly enough a person may leave the field of activity not only after failure, but after success too. Such abandonment of the field after success occurs generally when this success follows a series of failures. One obviously does not like to quit a task after failure. One continues, eager to find a successful termination, and uses the first occasion to stop, out of fear that further repetitions may bring new failures.

III

One has to consider quite detailed facts in order to understand the forces which govern the level of aspiration.

The first point to mention is that any goal has a position within a set of goals. If a child is asked, "How much is three times four?" the answer, "twelve," determines a definite circumscribed goal he has to reach. The answer will be either right or wrong. But if the child has to write an English composition, or to translate a passage of French, or to build a wooden boat, there is no such absolutely determined goal, but, rather, a variety of possible achievements which may differ greatly in quality. Most tasks are of this nature. It is generally technically possible to order the different possible achievements of a task according to their degree of difficulty. This allows one to compare the achievement and the level of aspiration of different persons, and to determine in a given case, the effect of success and failure. The range of acceptable achievement has often a "natural maximum" and a "natural minimum." In Hoppe's experiment, for instance, the subject had to solve one of a group of puzzles, different in difficulty. A subject who was not able to solve any one of the puzzles, but who was able to return the stones to their proper places in the box would certainly not have reached the natural minimum of the task. On the other hand, it would be above the natural maximum to reach a solution of the most difficult puzzle within one second. Some tasks have no natural maximum. This holds, for instance, for many sport activities —there is always the possibility of jumping and running faster. The lack of this natural maximum within the goal structure of many sport activities has led to a biologically unsound race without end.

The individual usually is conscious of the variety of possible goals within the task. He conceives the single action in its significance for a larger field of actions. Besides the goals for the momentary act, he has some general goal in regard to this larger field. For instance, when a person in a competition throws a discus, his goal for a certain trial might be to throw at least fifty yards; his goal for the whole group of actions would be to win! There always exists besides the goal for the next act, or, as we may say, besides the immediate goal, an ideal goal. This ideal goal may be to become the best discus thrower of the college or even to become world champion.

Such a goal can possess any degree of reality or unreality. For the student who does well in the first weeks of his sporting activities, the ideal to become world champion may be only an occasional daydream without any significance. The ideal goal, to become the best player of the university, may have considerably more reality. In a vague way, a student entering college may dream about the possibility of becoming a leading surgeon, and without even confessing this goal to himself. If he progresses in college, and does well in medical school, this ideal goal may become somewhat more real. According to Hoppe, success narrows the gap between the immediate goal and the ideal goal, and brings the ideal goal from the level of unreality gradually down to the level of reality. Failure has the opposite effect: a previously real goal vanishes into the world of dreams. In case the ideal goal should be reached (a case more frequent in experiments than in life) generally a new ideal goal arises.

IV

If it is true that the degree of success and failure depends upon the amount of difference between the immediate goal and the achievement, it should be possible to create a very strong feeling of success by making the task so easy that the achievement will be much better than the task demands. On the other hand, it should be possible to create a very strong feeling of failure by assign-

ing a very difficult task. Experiments show that this is not true. If the task is above a certain degree of difficulty, no feeling of failure arises, and no feeling of success arises if the task is below a certain degree of difficulty. In other words, if one represents the possible degree of difficulty of a task on a scale, this scale is infinite in direction, both to greater ease and to greater difficulty. But an individual reacts with success and failure only to a small region within this scale. In fact, the tasks which an individual considers as "very easy," "easy," "medium," "difficult," and "very difficult," circumscribe only a small region in the scale. Above and below this region lie a great many tasks which the individual calls "too easy" or "too difficult." The "too difficult" tasks are considered as "objectively impossible," entirely out of the range of the individual's ability, and no feeling of failure is attached to such a task. Similarly, in the case of a "too easy" task, the achievement is taken so much for granted, that no feeling of success is aroused. Contrary to the scale of possible difficulties, the scale of possible achievements is not infinite, but has a definite upper limit for a given individual at a given time. Both success and failure occur only if the difficulty of the task lies close to the upper limit of achievement. In other words, the feeling of failure occurs only if there is a chance for success, and a feeling of success occurs only if there is a chance for failure. Behind success and failure, stands therefore always a conflict situation.

This conflict situation makes somewhat understandable the laws which govern the position and the change in the level of aspiration. These laws are probably among the most fundamental for all human behavior. They are quite complicated, and we are only beginning to understand them. If it were true that life is ruled by the tendency to get as much pleasure as possible, one might expect that everybody would keep his level of aspiration as low as possible, because in this case, his performance would be always above his level of aspiration, and he would feel successful. As a matter of fact, there is a marked tendency to keep the level of aspiration down out of fear of failure. On the other hand, there is at the same time, a strong tendency to raise the level of aspiration as high as possible. The experiments of J. D. Frank show that both tendencies are of different strength in different individuals, and that a third tendency may have to be distinguished, namely, the tendency to keep one's expectations about one's future performance as close as possible to reality. A cautious person usually starts with a relatively low level of aspiration, and after succeeding, he raises the level only by short steps. Other persons tend to maintain their levels of aspiration well above their achievements. The rigidity of the level of aspiration, i.e., the tendency to keep the level constant rather than to shift it, shows marked differences among individuals. Frank found that these differences are highly reliable and largely independent of the special nature of the task.

It is important to know whether success and failure change the level of aspiration only in the particular activity in question, or whether success and failure in one task influence the level of aspiration in another task too. This is important for problems of guidance, where the effects of achievement or failure in different fields of activity on each other are of great significance, as for instance, in the realm of school motivation and of delinquency. J. D. Frank found a marked relationship between success and failure in one task and the level of aspiration in another, if the tasks concerned had sufficient psychological relations. Mr. Jucknat's experiments verified this result but showed that this influence is weak or negligible if past experience has rigidly fixed the level of aspiration within a task.

V

These studies point to a relation between the level of aspiration for a specific task and something that one may call the self-esteem, which means the feeling of the person about his own status and general standards. All experiments indicate that this relation is very fundamental. There is, for instance, a marked tendency in the case of failure, to blame an inadequate tool or an accident for the lack of achievement. To experience success or failure the person has to attribute the result of an action to himself in a very specific way. In case of inadequate performance, the person often tries to get rid of the feeling of failure by cutting the tie of belongingness between him and the result, and by rejecting his responsibility for the outcome. Also the tendency to raise the level of aspiration as high as possible seems to be closely related to the self-esteem, particularly to the feeling of the person about his status in the social group. The level of aspiration is determined on the one side by the upper limit of the person's achievements; in other words, by his ability. A second fundamental factor is the level of achievement prevailing in the social group to which a person belongs; for instance, among his business friends, his comrades, his playmates. The social group can have a strong influence in keeping the level of aspiration either too high or too low for a person's ability. This is especially true for children. The expectation of his parents, or the standards of his group may keep the level of aspiration for the less able child too high, and lead to continuous failure and over-tension. Whereas the level of aspiration for the very able child may be kept too low. (This may be the reason for Wellman's finding that children with a relatively high IQ gain less in IQ in the nursery school than children with a relatively low IQ.)

Fajans has shown that success and failure influence greatly the degree of activeness among active and passive children. Chase found an increase in achievement following success. Fajans has fur-ther determined the degree to which praise has an effect similar to real success. The effects of being successful, and being socially recognized or being loved, resemble each other closely. This relation is important for adults, and even more so in the case of adolescents and children.

The effects of continued failure on level of aspiration.   The continuing current efforts to test hypotheses implicit in Lewin's statement are perhaps the best indicators of the strength of his original conceptions. In Research Summary 2-1, we examine a recent study that demonstrates experimentally the effect of stress, resulting from continued failure, on level of aspiration. The study is particularly interesting because it views level of aspiration and goal setting behavior in terms of a model frequently used for self-regulating physical and biological systems.

RESEARCH SUMMARY 2-1

The Effect of Continued Failure on Level of Aspiration. Some people assume that the way to motivate other people is to keep success always somewhat out of their grasp. They feel that the goal should always dangle, like a carrot for a donkey, ahead of the individual so that he does not reach it and then take it easy. Let us see how this view fits the work on level of aspiration.

Rao and Russell, in a study conducted at University College, London, on male high school students confirm earlier findings on the impact of failure on subsequent level of aspiration. In doing so, they have described the level of aspiration mechanism as similar to a feedback system or servo-mechanism. Thus, they provide a useful and currently popular model for analyzing their results. Briefly stated, the model is: feedback (knowledge of results) from the output (performance of a task) affects the individual in establishing or altering levels of aspiration, which in turn influence the future response (or output) of the system.

Their subjects were required to engage in a simple manual task comparable to a miniature shuffle board, and earned points based on the success of their performance. "Stress" trials were introduced for the experimental group of subjects, after a trial period of normal success. The game was fixed so that they failed to achieve their stated levels of aspiration. (For example, if the subject set twenty points for himself as a goal, he could only get fifteen.) Within the experimental group, sub-groups were exposed to ten, twenty, thirty, or forty of these "stress" trials. After the trial period of normal success, a control group continued on with forty normal or nonstress trials in which continued success was possible. All subjects then completed forty additional trials under normal conditions that allowed them to succeed. Thus, one group of subjects experienced only normal opportunities for success, and the other group experienced varying numbers of trials in which failure was assured. All participants were given their scores after each trial.

> In general, the authors found that the players were extremely sensitive in adjusting to the feedback provided. Under normal feedback conditions, the goals that subjects set for themselves (that is, their levels of aspiration) soon became stable at an adequately high level directly related to their performance. Under the stress conditions (of negative feedback), the level of aspiration first dropped sharply, and then tapered off to a relatively stable, but *low* level. There were indications that performance as well as aspirations also suffered from negative feedback (knowledge of failure). Nevertheless, both level of aspiration and performance quickly recovered to a high, stable level when the condition of imposed failure was eliminated, and the subjects could again experience success regularly.

The administrator who thinks that his subordinates will be challenged more by always giving them goals they are not quite able to reach might ponder these (and similar) findings. The view is sometimes held that letting the employee feel successful makes him go soft and coast on his laurels. But it is more likely that constant feelings of failure cause his sights to be lowered, and lead him to take it easy.

Expectancy. Another of the important outcomes of the research stimulated by Lewin's original discussion of success and failure was to bring into sharper focus the role of the person's expectations* as an influence on his subsequent behavior. Two studies, described below in Research Summaries 2 and 3, suggest quite different aspects of this role.

Evidence of the specific effect of past success or failure *and expectancy* on the future attractiveness of an activity is provided by Gebhard (Research Summary 2-2). She demonstrates that either a past experience of success or a reasonable expectation of future success increases the reported attractiveness of a task.

Although expectancy has some positive motivational implications, there are also negative possibilities. The hopeful individual is certainly going to be much more disappointed than the nonhopeful if success does not follow upon his effort or his goal seeking. Spector, whose research is summarized in Research Summary 2-3, makes this point in relation to expectations of a promotion.

RESEARCH SUMMARY 2-2	*Expectancy and the Attractiveness of a Future Task.* Gebhard arranged her experimental procedure so that some subjects experienced success, others failure; some were led to *expect* future success, others to *expect* failure on a task that they themselves had previously rated as being of neutral attractiveness. A second and later rating of the task showed an increase in its attractiveness for those who had experienced success or had been led to expect success on it.

---

* Let us note a distinction: level of aspiration refers to the performance level which the individual hopes to reach, that is, what he hopes to *do;* expectation refers to the incentive, reward or satisfaction which he feels will be provided for performing, that is, what he hopes to *get.*

RESEARCH
SUMMARY
2-3

Expectancy and the Effect of Success or Failure. Spector became interested in a paradoxical morale situation, previously reported in Stouffer's study of the American soldier. Stouffer had noted that the men who were most dissatisfied with the promotion system were in branches that had the highest rate of promotion (the Air Force). On the other hand, men most satisfied with the promotion system were in the Military Police, which had the lowest rate of promotions. Stouffer explained these results by suggesting that failure to be promoted was frustrating or not, depending on whether one's peer's expected one to be promoted. The Air Force did; the Military Police did not. It was not the fact of deprivation, but what Stouffer considered as relative deprivation.

The Army work suggested an experimental test of a similar question to Spector—what effect do one's own expectations have on satisfaction with a promotion, or dissatisfaction with failure to be promoted? Using college sophomores who were in his Psychology classes, Spector arranged for small groups of them to work on simulated military problems. They were all told that promotion from corporal to sergeant was possible and the status value of the promotion was emphasized. Some of the group were led to high expectations, others to low expectations of promotion. The experimental design was completed by arranging it so that some high expecters were promoted, others not, and some low expecters were promoted, others not. The level of satisfaction of each participant was measured on a six item morale scale.

The most satisfied members of the group were those who had least expectation of promotion and yet were promoted. The least happy members were those with high expectations who did not receive a promotion. Over-all, as one might expect, those who were promoted were happier than those who were not. But at the same time, regardless of promotion, those with low expectations were more satisfied than those with high expectations.

Spector's findings provide empirical support for a statement made many years ago by William James:

> With no attempt there can be no failure; with no failure no humiliation. So our self-feeling in this world depends entirely on what we *back* ourselves to be and do. It is determined by the ratio of our actualities to our supposed potentialities; a fraction of which, our pretensions, are the denominator and the numerator our success; thus:
>
> $$\text{Self-esteem} = \frac{\text{Success}}{\text{Pretensions.}}$$
>
> Such a fraction may be increased as well by diminishing the denominator as by increasing the numerator.

Expectancy may not only link to satisfaction, but to later job performance, as well. Weitz found that later job turnover was lower for a group of newly hired life insurance agents who had been given a clear detailed picture of what to expect on the job (through a descriptive booklet) than for a comparable group not provided with clear cut expectation of what the job entailed.

Differences in Aspiration and Motivational Strength for Achievement.
For the administrator attempting to motivate the individual employee, Atkinson

has added an additional significant dimension to a model of motivational analysis, that is, the willingness to assume risk. He suggests that there are two different motivational influences; (a) desire to achieve success, and (b) desire to avoid failure, and that people characteristically differ in the strength of these influences. He further suggests that people who are clearly failure-avoiders will choose only a goal that they are certain to achieve, whereas those clearly success-seekers will choose goals even though they cannot be sure of success.

Awareness of these differences between people in their desire for success and their fear of failure developed out of broader studies by McClelland (1953, 1955a, 1955b), Atkinson (1957, 1958, 1959) and others on the strength of motivation to achieve. Research Summary 2-4 presents an aspect of this work particularly relevant for business.

RESEARCH SUMMARY 2-4	*Need Achievement and Managerial Success.* In *The Achieving Society*, McClelland reports a fascinating and challenging study of n Achievement,° conducted over several years by a group of his associates and students. Two major hypotheses of interest to us are proposed.

1. The economic growth rate of a country is a function of the value its culture places on n Achievement—particularly the value placed on n Achievement during the early formative years of the men running its businesses. No brief summary can do justice to the sweep of the analysis McClelland makes in testing the hypothesis. We attempt merely to suggest the nature of their approach.

In a complex balancing of natural resources against actual national productivity, they identify some of the nations of the modern world (1950) as economic achievers, others as economic non-achievers. They measure n Achievement in these countries by analyzing for achievement themes the children's readers widely used in respective school systems at two time periods, 1925 and 1950, (Their procedure here is based upon widely accepted procedures for analyzing material produced in the projective testing of individuals.) Their findings suggest that countries high in n Achievement for the 1925 period tend to be among those showing strong economic achievement in 1950; those low in n Achievement in 1925, tend to show up as under-achievers economically in 1950. With respect to rates of growth after 1950, countries high in n Achievement as measured in 1950 (not always the same countries as were high in 1925) showed more rapid growth than countries low in n Achievement. Using the same basic approach for societies of the past, they report the same relationship between high value placed on n Achievement in the culture and subsequent economic growth.

Economists and others will not accept these findings without much question and further verification. The esoteric nature of the process for measuring n Achievement and the simplicity of the conclusion will keep many from ready acceptance. We can say, whether or not it is the only factor, or even the principal factor, n

---

° Need for Achievement.

Achievement seems to have been identified as an important value in a society for its subsequent economic growth.

How about its importance for the development of the individual as an entrepreneur and manager? Here more direct and precise measurement is possible. On this matter we state McClelland's second major hypothesis.

2. Men with high n Achievement more often become entrepreneurs and managers* than do those low in n Achievement, and, they are more successful in these roles.

In assessing n Achievement in individuals, rather than in society, it is possible to measure the strength of the drive directly. To do this, a series of pictures is offered to each individual and he is asked to make up a story based on the picture. The stories are then analyzed according to a highly detailed procedure to determine the presence and quality of achievement themes. All analyses, of course, must be done in a consistent fashion, established in advance, and without any knowledge of the individuals whose stories are being studied. Three findings will suggest the trend of Mc-Clelland's studies: (a) successful middle management executives showed higher n Achievement than did a random national sample of men of the same age and education but in other occupations; (b) in three out of four countries† managers showed higher n Achievement than did nonbusiness professionals of the same age, (c) most significant is the reported relation between n Achievement and success in business (in the role of manager and as measured by earnings [p. 269]). Although the relationship is a curvilinear one, the lowest money earners have the lowest measured n Achievement.

Here, as with McClelland's first hypothesis we need further study but the point remains that over many samples in different countries, a consistent relation is demonstrated to exist between entrepreneurial-managerial behavior and high n Achievement.

If under continued study, this relation holds up—as we would predict it will—a further analysis made by McClelland of the critical characteristics of the high n Achiever, will be of particular significance.

Many studies, most of them laboratory experiments, identify the following traits as characteristic of high n Achievers (and therefore, also, in view of the earlier findings, of the successful business man).

(a) Moderate risk-taking behavior when the outcome is dependent upon his skill, not chance. Where his skill can influence the result, the high n Achiever is willing to undertake a middle range of risk.

(b) Willingness to assume individual responsibility for making decisions. The high n Achiever finds both challenge and a possible source of reward in the responsibility of making decisions. For him it is an opportunity for achievement.

---

* Terms used by McClelland to identify men successful in business organizations as compared with such professionals as doctors, lawyers, educators, scientists, and theologians who may be successful in a nonentrepreneurial way.

† The fourth achievement country was Turkey and offsetting factors operate here to explain the discrepancy. For details cf. p. 263 of McClelland's book.

> (c) Need to operate under conditions in which there is feedback providing specific knowledge of results. The high n Achiever *tries* and he wants to know whether or not he has been successful. The value of money as a reward to some extent lies in its information value—a signal of successful performance.
>
> (d) A tendency to anticipate future possibilities. In McClelland's studies high n Achievers "think ahead" and more often tell stories about the remote future. Evidence also suggests they tend to take account of future exigencies and to take current action with such possibilities in mind. *

Even with our brief summary of McClelland's extensive study, several significant suggestions for administrators stand out. They are perhaps best phrased in questions the administrator might ask himself against the background of the McClelland study.

1. Are company recruitment and selection procedures likely to bring into the organization young people high in n Achievement?

2. Does company atmosphere provide opportunity for activities satisfying to high n Achievers: for example, knowledge of results and freedom to take moderate risks and assume individual responsibility?

3. Does the company "personality" place sufficient value on n Achievement so that young people in the company are strengthened in their achievement motivation for the day they will assume managerial responsibility?

4. Is there a relation between the degree to which the company culture values n Achievement and its over-all economic achievement, as is true between countries in McClelland's studies?

As we conclude this section, three suggestions of significance for the administrator emerge: (1) A man's prior history in an organization, particularly his successes and failures, narrows the choice of goals and performance levels he allows himself. Thus, among men twenty years in the company, the successful will have learned a different set of responses to their needs from the unsuccessful. (2) What a company, or a manager, or a colleague has caused a man to "expect" often is a more significant influence on his behavior and morale than the objective conditions; (3) Whether or not a man will take a risk—accept a promotion on trial, tackle a special job, venture a controversial opinion—can be a function of the relative strength of his personal needs for success or for avoidance of failure, respectively. This obviously cannot be gauged by simply asking the man himself, but techniques are emerging for the measurement of risk-taking propensity, and of achievement motivation.

---

* In addition, according to an extensive nationwide study (Morgan, *et al.*):

1. High n Achievers seem more likely to believe that success is related to hard work than to chance factors.

2. High n Achievers are also shown to have accumulated more capital income than low n Achievers, even when one controls for the influence of age and education.

Group Influences on Motivation

Although a description of the dynamics of group behavior is not presented here, it is relevant to say that group membership, characteristics of the group, and the individual's place in the group all influence the way in which he responds to his needs. We select only three types of influence to illustrate the process. Group norms (standards of behavior set by the group for its members), for example, can determine whether achievement need will be channeled into work productivity or elsewhere. Lack of clarity in an individual's role in the group (of his place on a committee, for example) may inhibit his willingness to respond to his own needs. Finally, whether a group's influence will be decisive or not for individual drives will depend on the degree to which group members can interact freely and on the extent to which members are interdependent on each other for goal achievement. (See Chapter Twenty-Three for a discussion of other group factors.)

CHAPTER SIX

Motivation
and
Incentive
on the
Job

This chapter begins with an overview of some significant sources of job satisfaction. It then examines the significance of money as an incentive and concludes with a discussion of motivational factors that influence productivity, turnover, and other aspects of job performance.

Job Satisfaction

Approaching his subject as a sociologist and reporting the worker's own answers to questions about satisfactions Blauner, in the reading that follows, establishes three principal points: (1) Contrary to much written opinion, most workers are not unhappy with their occupational lot in life; as a matter of fact, the vast majority of workers are moderately or highly satisfied (or at least so they say); (2) From one occupational level to another there are marked differences in work attitudes and expectations; (3) The principal source of job satisfaction is autonomy and independence on the job;* other factors are also

---

* In studies of job motivations and job satisfactions in first level and middle level managers, Porter reports that lower levels report less opportunity to satisfy their needs for security, esteem, and autonomy than do higher levels. Both groups feel that there is not sufficient opportunity on their jobs to satisfy needs for personal growth and worthwhile accomplishment.

identified. The reader should recognize that industrial (blue-collar) data out-weigh data on white collar occupations in the studies he reviews.

Extent of Satisfaction: A Review of General Research*

ROBERT BLAUNER

Before considering occupational differences and the factors that account for them, I shall briefly consider evidence on the general extent of job satisfaction by looking at the results of six representative sample studies. In Table 1

TABLE 1

Proportion of Dissatisfied Workers in Major Job Situation Studies

Researchers	Scope of Sample	Composition of Study	Date	Per Cent Dissatisfied
Morse and Weiss°	Random national	401 employed men	1955	20
Centers†	Representative national	811 men	1949	17
Palmer‡	Norristown, Pa.	517 labor force members	1957	10
Shister and Reynolds§	New England city	800 manual workers	1949	12 21°°
Hoppock‖	New Hope, Pa.	309 labor force members	1935	15
Kornhauser¶	Detroit area	324 employed persons	1952	11

° Nancy C. Morse and Robert S. Weiss, "The Function and Meaning of Work and the Job," *American Sociological Review*, 20 (1955), pp. 191-198.
† Richard Centers, *The Psychology of Social Classes* (Princeton: Princeton University Press, 1949), p. 172.
‡ Gladys L. Palmer, "Attitudes toward Work in an Industrial Community," *American Journal of Sociology*, 63 (1957), pp. 17-26.
§ Joseph Shister and L. G. Reynolds, *Job Horizons: A Study of Job Satisfaction and Labor Mobility* (New York: Harper, 1949), p. 33.
‖ Robert Hoppock, *Job Satisfaction* (New York: Harper, 1935), p. 246.
¶ Arthur Kornhauser, *Detroit as the People See It* (Detroit: Wayne University Press, 1952), p. 54.
°° Two separate samples.

the figure in the extreme right-hand column indicates the percentage of workers who gave the dissatisfied re-

---

* Abridged from "Work Satisfaction and Industrial Trends in Modern Society," in *Labor and Trade Unionism* edited by W. Galenson and S. M. Lipset (New York: John Wiley & Sons, Inc., 1960), pp. 340-354. An 89 item bibliography is provided in Blauner's complete article.

sponse to such a question as "Taking into consideration all the things about your job (work), how satisfied or dissatisfied are you with it?"

In the 1946 issue of the *Personnel and Guidance Journal*, Robert Hoppock began summarizing the results of all published studies of job satisfaction, most of which were non-representative samples of individual companies or occupations.

When, by 1958, 406 percentages of the persons dissatisfied with their jobs in these several hundred studies had been averaged out, they yielded a median percentage of 13 per cent dissatisfied. This figure is quite similar to the summary percentages of dissatisfaction resulting from more representative labor force samples.

Thus the most recent American research on satisfaction attitudes seems to support the generalization that: "Even under the existing conditions, which are far from satisfactory, most workers like their jobs. Every survey of workers' attitudes which has been carried out, no matter in what industry, indicates that this is so."

But a caveat should be inserted at this point. Many of these studies, which seek to determine the proportion of workers who are satisfied or dissatisfied with their jobs, fail to specify sufficiently an inherently vague concept and ignore the cultural pressures on workers to exaggerate the degree of actual satisfaction. Despite this, the evidence shows that in the numerous samples of the labor force which have been interviewed, more than 80 per cent indicate general job satisfaction. Even though the methodological limitations make it hard to accept the findings of any one of these studies by itself, it is much harder to reject the weight of their cumulative evidence.

Although it is difficult, therefore, not to accept the proposition that at least the majority (and possibly a very large majority) of American workers are moderately satisfied in their work, such a finding is neither particularly surprising nor sociologically interesting. Under "normal" conditions there is a natural tendency for people to identify with, or at least to be somewhat positively oriented toward, those social arrangements in which they are implicated. Attitude surveys show that the majority of employees like their company, that the majority of members are satisfied with their unions, and undoubtedly research would show a preponderance of positive over negative attitudes toward one's own marriage, family, religion, and nation-state. It is the presence of marked occupational *differences* in work attitudes to which I turn in the next section that is of more theoretical interest.

Occupational Differences in Work Satisfaction

Work satisfaction varies greatly by occupation. Highest percentages of satisfied workers are usually found among professionals and businessmen. In a given plant, the proportion satisfied is higher among clerical workers than among factory workers, just as in general labor force samples it is higher among middle-class than among manual working class occupations. Within the manual working class, job satisfaction is highest among skilled workers, lowest among unskilled laborers and workers on assembly lines.

When a scale of relative job satisfaction is formed, based on general occupational categories, the resulting rank order is almost identical with the most commonly used occupational status classification—the Edwards scale of the Bureau of the Census. For example, the mean indexes of satisfaction in Table 2 resulted from a survey of all New Hope, Pa., job-holders in 1935.

TABLE 2

Occupational Group	Mean Index	Number in Sample
Professional and managerial	560	23
Semiprofessional, business, and supervisory	548	32
Skilled manual and white collar	510	84
Semiskilled manual workers	483	74
Unskilled manual workers	401	55

A similar rank order resulted in a national survey when the proportions of workers in each occupational group who would continue the same kind of work in the event they inherited enough money to live comfortably were computed (Table 3).

TABLE 3

Occupational Group	Per cent Who Would Continue Same Kind of Work	Number in Sample
Professionals	68	28
Sales	59	22
Managers	55	22
Skilled manual	40	86
Service	33	18
Semiskilled operatives	32	80
Unskilled	16	27

The generally higher level of job satisfaction of white-collar over blue-collar workers is confirmed by a study of twelve different factories in 1934, in which the scores of clerical workers on job satisfaction were considerably higher than those of factory workers; by the Centers national sample, which found that only 14 per cent of workers in middle-class occupations were dissatisfied with their jobs, compared to 21 per cent of those in working class occupations; and by a 1947 *Fortune* poll, which revealed that the proportion of employees who said their jobs were interesting was 92 per cent among professionals and executives, 72 per cent among salaried employees and 54 per cent among factory workers. However, a study of the Detroit area population found that only among such upper white-collar employees as secretaries, draftsmen, and bookkeepers was the incidence of job satisfaction greater than among manual workers; such lower white-collar employees as clerks, typists, and retail salespeople were somewhat less satisfied than blue-collar workers.

Further evidence of the relation of job satisfaction to occupational status is provided by studies of retirement plans. Although there are a number of factors which affect the retirement decision, it is plausible to argue that the more satisfying a job is to the worker, the more likely he will choose not to retire. In a study of work and retirement in six occupations it was found that the proportion of men who wanted to continue working or had actually continued working after age sixty-five was more than 67 per cent for physicians, 65 per cent for department store salesmen, 49 per cent for skilled printers, 42 per cent for coal miners, and 32 per cent for unskilled and semiskilled steelworkers.

As has been shown in the preceding section of this paper, the majority of workers in all occupations respond positively when asked whether or not they are satisfied with their jobs. But that does not mean they would not prefer other kinds of work. The average worker in a lower-status occupation says that he would choose another line of work if he had the chance to start his working life anew. This question then, is perhaps a more sentitive indicator of latent dissatisfactions and frustrations; the occupational differences it points to, though forming the same pattern as the other, are considerably greater. For example, when a survey of 13,000 Maryland youths was made during the depression it was found that 91 per cent of professional-technical workers preferred their own occupation to any other, compared to 45 per cent of managerial personnel and farm owners, 41 per cent of skilled manual workers, 37 per cent of domestic workers, 36 per cent of office and sales personnel, 14 per cent of unskilled, and 11 per cent of semiskilled manual workers.

More detailed data for a number of professional and manual working class occupations strongly confirms these general findings. Note how for six different professions, the proportion of satisfied persons ranges from 82 per cent to 91 per cent, whereas for seven manual occupations it varies from 16 per cent for unskilled automobile workers to 52 per cent for skilled printers. (See Table 4.)

TABLE 4

Proportion in Various Occupations Who Would Choose Same Kind of Work if Beginning Career Again

Professional Occupations, %		Working Class Occupations, %	
Mathematicians°	91	Skilled printers	52
Physicists°	89	Paper workers	52
		Skilled automobile	
Biologists°	89	workers	41
Chemists°	86	Skilled steelworkers	41
Lawyers†	83	Textile workers	31
Journalists‡	82	Unskilled steelworkers	21
		Unskilled automobile	
		workers	16

Sources:
° "The Scientists: A Group Portrait," *Fortune*, October 1948, pp. 106-112.
† "The U.S. Bar," *Fortune*, May 1939, p. 176.
‡ Leo Rosten, *The Washington Correspondents* (New York: Harcourt, Brace and Company, 1938), p. 347.
   These are unpublished data which have been computed from the IBM cards of a survey of 3,000 factory workers in 16 industries, conducted by Elmo Roper for *Fortune* magazine in 1947. A secondary analysis of this survey is being carried out by the Fund for the Republic's Trade Union Project. The general findings of the original study appeared in "The Fortune Survey," *Fortune*, May 1947, pp. 5-12, and June 1947, pp. 5-10.

To some extent, these findings on occupational differences in job satisfaction reflect not only differences in the objective conditions of work for people in various jobs, *but also occupational differences in the norms with respect to work attitudes*. The professional is expected to be dedicated to his profession and have an intense intrinsic interest in his area of specialized competence; the white-collar employee is expected to be "company" oriented and like his work; but the loyalty of the manual worker is never taken for granted and, more than any other occupational type, cultural norms permit him the privilege of griping. In fact, it has been asserted that "the natural state of the industrial worker . . . is one of discontent." The same point has been clearly made in an analysis of the latent function of the time clock:

The office staff does not "clock-in"—ostensibly because they are not paid by the hour, but it seems likely that at least part of the reason for this is the supposition that, unlike labourers, they do not necessarily dislike work and can be placed on their honour to be punctual. The working classes, as we have seen, are supposed to dislike work and therefore need "discipline" to keep them in order. Since "clocking-in" has been abolished in many firms, it cannot be accepted as absolutely necessary.

Factors that Account for Occupational Differences in Satisfaction

The literature on work is filled with numerous attempts to list and often to estimate the relative importance of the various components, elements, or factors involved in job satisfaction. These lists do not correspond neatly with one another; they bear a large number of labels, but they all are likely to include, in one way or another, such variables as the income attached to a job, supervision, working conditions, social relations, and the variety and skill intrinsic in the work itself. The classification of these items is quite arbitrary and the number of factors considered relevant can be broken down almost indefinitely.

Whereas most studies attempt to explain variations in job satisfaction among individual employees in the same company or occupation, the interest of the present paper is to explain the gross differences in work attitudes that exist among those in *different* occupations and industries. Four factors that seem useful in accounting for these differences are discussed: occupational prestige, control, integrated work groups, and occupational communities.

Occupational Prestige. Occupational prestige is the one best explanatory factor in the sense that if all occupations (for which sufficient data are available)

were ranked in order of extent of typical job satisfaction, and these ranks were compared with the rank order in which they partake of public esteem, the rank-order correlations would be higher than those resulting from any other factor. This is because the prestige of any occupation depends on the level of skill the job entails, the degree of education or training necessary, the amount of control and responsibility involved in the performance of the work, the income which is typically received—to mention the most readily apparent factors. Since occupational prestige as a kind of composite index partly subsumes within itself a number of factors which contribute heavily to differences in satisfaction, it is not surprising that it should be itself the best individual measure of satisfaction.

In addition, jobs that have high prestige will tend to be valued for their status rewards even when "objective" aspects of the work are undesirable; similarly, low-status jobs will tend to be undervalued and disliked.

> . . . the lowliness or nastiness of a job are subjective estimates. . . . A doctor or a nurse, for example, or a sanitary inspector, have to do some things which would disgust the most unskilled casual laborer who did not see these actions in their social context. Yet the status and prestige of such people is generally high. . . . Above all, it is the prestige of his working group and his position in it which will influence the worker's attitude to such jobs.

That the actual findings on difference in job satisfactions correspond quite closely to the scale of occupational prestige has been shown in the previous section. Professionals and business executives have the highest prestige in our society; they also consistently report the highest degree of work satisfaction. According to the most thorough occupational prestige study, doctors are the most esteemed major occupational group in the United States. It is not surprising therefore that this public esteem is an important source of their satisfaction with their work:

> [For] physicians . . . work is a source of prestige. Some doctors stated that to be a physician meant that one belonged to an elite class. It meant that one associated with important people and was in a position of leadership in the community.

Among non-professional or managerial employees, white-collar workers are generally more satisfied with their jobs than manual workers. Again status considerations play an important role. Even when white-collar work does not out-rank manual jobs in income or skill, office workers are accorded higher social prestige than blue-collar personnel.

Although this is so, manual work seems to be viewed with greater respect in America, with its democratic frontier traditions, than in many other nations. The historic "social inferiority complex," the "sense of social subordination" of the European industrial worker, to use the words of Henri DeMan, has never been well developed in the United States. We might expect, therefore, that the level of work satisfaction among manual workers would be higher in this country than in Europe. With the rapidly increasing number of attitude surveys of European workers since the war, such a comparison would be of considerable interest.

Within the world of manual work, occupational differences in satisfaction are also related to the differences in prestige that exist among various working class jobs. The higher incidence of positive work attitudes consistently found among skilled workers is not only caused by the skill factor per se; the craftsman takes pride in the fact that he is looked on with more respect in the community than the factory operative or the unskilled laborer. Moreover, those manual workers in occupations which are particularly looked down on will find difficulty in deriving overall positive satisfactions in their work. Interviewers of coal miners have remarked on the great pride with which they are shown various home improvements made possible by the higher wages of a period of prosperity, and on the sensitivity with which some miners react to the public image of the occupation, which has been, in part, created by the hostility of the mass media to the militancy of the union.

> I don't like to strike, because people all get mad at the miners then. I wish the people would realize that the miner has to live too, and not hate him when he tries to better conditions for himself. It bothers me the way people say bad things about the miners, and makes me ashamed of my job.

An attempt has been made to illustrate the manner in which variations in work satisfaction among different occupations tend to follow variations in occupational prestige. Although this generalization is, to an impressive extent, supported by the evidence, it does not hold unfailingly. We can note occupations with relatively high prestige whose general level of satisfaction is lower than would be expected, whereas some low-status jobs seem to be highly satisfying. This suggests that in certain cases other factors play a role even more important than status. A good test of the approach applied here is to see whether the other factors which have been advanced as critical ones can indeed account for discrepancies in the generally marked association between occupational prestige and job satisfaction.

Control. In a perceptive passage, the Belgian socialist Henri DeMan remarks that "all work is felt to be coercive." The fact that work inherently involves a surrender of control, a "subordination of the worker to remoter aims," is probably what makes the relative degree of control in work so important an aspect of job attitudes. As Max Weber, the German sociologist, suggested long ago, "no man easily yields to another full control over the effort, and especially over the amount of physical effort he must daily exert."

There seem to be significant cultural as well as individual differences in the need for control and independence in work. In America, where individual initiative has long been a cultural ideal, we would expect strong pressures in this direction. And we do find that surprising proportions of manual workers in this country have attempted to succeed in small business, and that for many others the idea of running a gas station or a number of tourist cabins is a compelling dream.

Lack of control over the conditions of work is most pronounced for industrial workers.

> The very evidence of his daily work life brings home to the manual worker the degree to which he is directed in his behavior with only limited free choices available. From the moment of starting work by punching a time clock, through work routines that are established at fixed times, until the day ends at the same mechanical time recorder, there is impressed upon the industrial worker his narrow niche in a complex and ordered system of interdependency . . . a system over which he, as an individual, exercises little direct control.

The factory worker is at the bottom of the bureaucratic hierarchy; he is a person for whom action is constantly being originated, but who himself originates little activity for others.

At the same time, diverse factory jobs and working class occupations vary greatly in the degree of control they permit over the conditions of work: it is these variations, of which workers are keenly aware, that are most interesting for the purpose of accounting for differences in satisfaction.

The notion of control in work, as I am using it, is, of course, a vague, *sensitizing* concept which covers a wide range of phenomena rather than a concept which is precisely delimited and identifiable by precise indicators. Among its most important dimensions are control over the use of one's *time* and physical *movement*, which is fundamentally control over the *pace* of the work process, control over the *environment*, both technical and social, and control as the *freedom* from *hierarchal authority*. Naturally, these dimensions are highly interrelated; a business executive high on the occupational ladder will tend to be high in each, whereas an unskilled laborer will have little control from any of these viewpoints. *It is possible to generalize on the basis of the evidence that the greater the degree of control that a worker has (either in a single dimension or as a total composite) the greater his job satisfaction.*

CONTROL OVER TIME, PHYSICAL MOVEMENT AND PACE OF WORK. Assembly line work in the automobile industry is a good example of the almost complete absence of this aspect of control.

> Its coerced rhythms, the inability to pause at will for a moment's rest, and the need for undeviating attention to simple routines made it work to be avoided if possible and to escape from if necessary. So demanding is the line that one worker, echoing others, complained: "You get the feeling, everybody gets the feeling, whenever the line jerks everybody is wishing, 'break down, baby!' "

The consensus of the work literature is that assembly line work, especially in the automobile industry, is more disliked than any other major occupation, and the prime factor in dissatisfaction with the assembly line is the lack of control over the pace of production. Workers in assembly line plants have strong preferences for jobs off the line. A study of the job aspirations of 180 men on the line found that the "workers' motivations were not what might normally be expected. It was not promotion or transfer in order to improve one's economic status. Rather, it was primarily a desire 'to get away from the line.' " *Only 8 per cent* were satisfied, in the sense of not preferring to get an off-line job. The difference between line and off-line jobs has been clearly stated by the sociologist Ely Chinoy who worked in an automobile plant and studied automobile workers:

> Work at a machine may be just as repetitive, require as few motions and as little thought as line assembly, but men prefer it because it does not keep them tied as tightly to their tasks. "I can stop occasionally when I want to," said a machine-operator. "I couldn't do that when I was on the line." Production standards for a particular machine may be disliked and felt to be excessive, but the machine operator need only approximate his production quota each day. The line-tender must do all the work that the endless belt brings before him. . . .

The greater dissatisfaction with mass production assembly line jobs is confirmed by the findings in an automobile plant that "men with highly repetitive jobs, conveyor paced, and so forth, were far more likely to take time off from work than those whose jobs did not contain such job characteristics," and that quit rates were almost twice as high among men on the assembly line as among men off the line. In a study of Maryland youth during the depression, it was found that the occupation most disliked by female workers was that of operator on cannery conveyor belts. Every one of the fifty-three cannery operatives in the sample expressed a preference for different work! The control of these workers over the pace of production is at least as minimal as that of automobile workers, and in addition they lack even the protection of a strong union.

A machine operator may go all out in the morning to produce 100 pieces, take it easy in the afternoon, only putting out 50; at any rate it is his own decision. In similar fashion a few assembly line workers may be able to build up a "bank" of automobile seats which they assemble to the oncoming bodies; a few try to get ahead and gain time for rest by working up the line, but for the great majority it is hopeless. Assembly line workers are "alienated," according to the researchers who have studied them. In their work they "can secure little significant experience of themselves as productive human beings." As one automobile worker put it a little wistfully:

> You understand, if you get a job that you're interested in, when you work you don't pay attention to the time, you don't wait for the whistle to blow to go home, you're all wrapped up in it and don't pay attention to other things. *I don't know one single job like that.*

According to David Riesman, what these wage earners are deprived of is "any chance to extend themselves, to go all-out." A stark example is the worker on the packinghouse assembly line who goes home after his day's work in order to "try to accomplish something for that day." How do these workers stand it? Here is the deadly answer of a Hormel meat worker: "The time passes."

Most workers are so busily engaged in pushing the flow of work that they do not *consciously* suffer from the inherent monotony of their work. They are well adjusted, because they have reduced their level of aspirations to the rather low level of the job. They coast along, keeping busy, visiting, talking, making time go by, and getting the work done in order to get "out of there" in order to get home!

The great dissatisfaction with automobile assembly work is an example of a discrepancy between occupational status and job satisfaction. The status of the automobile worker is not lower than that of other semiskilled American factory workers; in fact, the level of wages would suggest that it is higher than manual workers in many other industrial occupations, especially those in non-durable goods manufacturing. But the control of the automobile assembly line worker over the work process is considerably less than in other major industrial occupations, and this is a big factor in accounting for the prevalence of job discontent.

It is interesting to contrast automobile manufacturing with mining, an occupation which, though considered lower in prestige, seems to provide marked work satisfaction. Alvin Gouldner, in his study of a gypsum plant, found that although the miners had considerably less status in the community than surface workers, they showed much greater work motivation. He attributed this high job satisfaction to the fact that miners

> were not "alienated" from their machines; that is, they had an unusually high degree of control over their machine's operation. The pace at which the machines worked, the corners into which they were poked, what happened to them when they broke down, was determined mainly by the miners themselves. On the surface, though,

the speed at which the machines worked and the procedures followed were prescribed by superiors.

Finally, the higher job satisfaction of skilled workers (documented in the preceding sections of this paper) is related to the fact that they have a large measure of control over the pace of their work. The fact that craftsmen themselves largely determine the speed at which they work gives them a marked advantage over most factory workers.

CONTROL OVER THE TECHNICAL AND SOCIAL ENVIRONMENT. In those occupations in which the physical environment or the technological work process is particularly challenging, control over it seems to be an important aspect of job satisfaction. Coalminers have "a very personal sense of being pitted against their environment" and express "feelings of accomplishment and pride at having conquered it." That steel production is found fascinating is suggested by a mill worker: "It's sort of interesting. Sometimes you have a battle on your hands. You have to use your imagination and ability to figure out what move to make." Similarly, it has been noted that railroad workers derive a sense of power in "the manipulation of many tons of railroad equipment." Engineers derive more pleasure in running large engines rather than small ones; switchmen and brakemen "give the signals that move fifty or so freight cars back and forth like so many toys."

A further source of the dissatisfaction with automobile assembly, then, is the fact that these jobs provide so little scope for control over the technical environment; there is little that is challenging in the actual work operation. As a man on the line puts it:

> There is nothing more discouraging than having a barrel beside you with 10,000 bolts in it and using them all up. Then you

get a barrel with another 10,000 bolts, and you know that every one of those 10,000 bolts has to be picked up and put in exactly the same place as the last 10,000 bolts.

Paralleling the control of industrial workers over the technical environment is the satisfaction derived by professional and white-collar employees from control over a social environment, namely, clients and customers. A study of salespeople concluded that "the completion of the sale, the conquering of the customer, represents the challenge or the 'meaningful life-experience' of selling." As one salesclerk, contemplating the import of his retirement, said: "I think to be perfectly truthful about it, the thing I miss most is being able to project myself into a sphere, conquer it, and retire with a pleased feeling because I have conquered it."

CONTROL AS THE FREEDOM FROM DIRECT SUPERVISION. On a slightly different level of analysis is this third dimension, which refers not to the aspects of the work process under control, but rather to the locus of control. One of the most consistent findings of work research is that industrial workers consider light, infrequent supervision, "foremen who aren't drivers," a crucial element in their high regard for particular jobs and companies.

The absence of close supervision in the mines has been considered an important determinant of the miners' high level of satisfaction. And truck drivers and railroad workers, in explaining their preference for their own trades, stress the independence they experience in these jobs where the contact between employees and supervisor is so much less frequent than in factory work. As two railroad engineers put it:

> I'd work anywhere except at a shop or in the factory. Just don't like a place where someone is

watching you do your work all the time. That's why I like my job on the railroad now.

I wouldn't last three days in a shop with a foreman breathing down my neck. Here I'm my own boss when I run the trains, nobody tells me what to do. . . .

Such impressionistic evidence is confirmed by the more systematic comparisons of Hoppock, who found that the mean job satisfaction index of railroad employees ranked only below professional men and artists; it was higher than managers, clerical workers, small business proprietors, salesmen, and store-clerks! Although railroading is a high-status industrial occupation-railroaders have historically been part of the labor aristocracy—its occupational prestige is below most white-collar occupations. On the other hand, truck driving is a lower-status manual occupation (truck drivers are classified as semi-skilled operatives by the census, and the popular stereotypes of this occupation are somewhat derogatory), and yet in the Hoppock survey the satisfaction of truck drivers outranked all industrial occupations except railroading and was approximately the same level as that of salesmen.

It is plausible that the marked discrepancy between job satisfaction and occupational status in these industries can be explained by the high degree of control, especially as reflected in freedom from supervision, which the workers enjoy.

If control in the work process is a crucial determinant of a worker's subjective feelings of well-being on the job, as I am trying to demonstrate, the question whether industrial trends are increasing or decreasing these areas of control becomes quite significant. It is interesting that Faunce's recent study of an *automated* engine plant shows that various dimensions of control may not change in the same direction. Compared to work in a non-automated, non-assembly line engine plant, automation greatly decreased the worker's direct control over his machine and pace of work, and this was felt to be a source of serious dissatisfaction. On the other hand, the increased responsibility and control over a complex technical environment of automated equipment was seen as a source of greater satisfaction and heightened status. Thus, while Faunce was able to locate the elements which made for satisfaction and those which made for dissatisfaction in these jobs (his analysis seems very congruent with the present discussion), it was rather difficult to assess the overall effect of the change on work satisfaction.

Integrated Work Groups. A third factor that is important in explaining occupational differences in work satisfaction is the nature of on-the-job social relations. The technological structure of certain industries such as steel production and mining requires that the work be carried out by *teams* of men working closely together, whereas in industries such as automobile assembly the formation of regular work groups is virtually prohibited by the organization of production. There is much evidence to support the proposition that the greater the extent to which workers are members of integrated work teams on the job, the higher the level of job satisfaction.

In a steel mill in which 85 per cent of sixty-two workers interviewed were satisfied with their jobs, Charles Walker found that "the source of satisfaction most often articulated or implied was that of being part of, or having membership in, the hot mill crew." . . .

While recognizing that close kinship ties and a small town atmosphere encouraged [a] cooperative spirit, Walker attributed the principal cause of the integrated work teams to the basic technological process of making steel, which requires small group operations. He compared this technology and its results with that of the automobile assembly plants in which the technological structure is such that the majority of workers perform their operations individually. There, the pattern of social interaction produced by the moving line is such that although workers will talk to the man in front of them, behind them, and across from them, no worker will interact with exactly the same group of men as any other worker will; therefore, no stable work groups are formed. Walker considered this a major element in the greater dissatisfaction he found among automobile workers compared to steel workers.

Mining is another occupation where technological conditions seem to favor the development of closely knit work groups. Since, as one miner expressed it, "the mines are kind of a family affair," where "the quality of the sentiment is of a depth and complexity produced only by long years of intimate association," it is not surprising that many miners feel that the loss of social contacts at work is a major disadvantage of retirement. The dangerous nature of the work is another factor that knits miners together:

> To be an old-timer in the mines means something more than merely knowing the technique of a particular job; it also means awareness and acceptance of the responsibility which each man has for his fellow-workers. The sense of interdependence in relation to common dangers is undoubtedly an important factor in the spirit of solidarity which has characterized miners in all countries for many generations.

Within the same factory, departments and jobs vary considerably in the extent to which the work is carried out by individuals working alone or by groups; the consequences of these differences have been a major interest of the "human relations in industry" movement. A recent study of one department in a factory manufacturing rotating equipment found that the employees who were integrated members of informal work groups were, by and large, satisfied with both the intrinsic characteristics of their jobs, and such "extended characteristics" as pay, working conditions, and benefits, whereas the non-group members tended to be dissatisfied. Sixty-five per cent of "regular" group members were satisfied, compared to 43 per cent of members of groups which were deviant in accepting less fully the values of the factory community, and compared to only 28 per cent of isolated workers.

The classic investigations of the functions of informal work groups in industry have been produced by the "human relations in industry" school, associated most directly with the Harvard Business School and the writings of Elton Mayo, and represented by the pioneering experiments at the Hawthorne plant of the Western Electric Company. These studies have demonstrated that informal work groups establish and enforce norms which guide the productive and other behavior of workers on the job, and that such management problems as absenteeism, turnover, and morale can often be dealt with through the manipulation of work groups and supervisorial behavior. But it is striking that the human relations school has concerned itself so little with the job itself, with the relation between the worker and his work, rather than the relation between the worker and his mates. A typical human relations discussion of the conditions of employee morale is likely to give all its emphasis to matters of communication, supervision, and the personality of workers and ignore almost completely intrinsic job tasks. In a recent study by the Harvard Business School entitled *Worker Satisfaction and Development,* the only sources of work satisfaction discussed are those which directly concern workers' integration in work groups and cliques. Although creativity is a major concern of the author, it is the creativity of the *work group* to adapt to new circumstances, rather than the creative expression of an individual in his work, that he is interested in.

In its emphasis on the importance of integrated work groups the human relations approach has made an important contribution. But "a way of seeing is a way of not seeing," and its neglect of the other factors imposes serious limitations on the usefulness of this approach, at least in providing an adequate theory of the conditions of work satisfaction.

Occupational Communities. The nature of the association among workers *off-the-job* is also a factor in work satisfaction. The evidence of the work literature supports the notion that levels of work satisfaction are higher in those industries and in those kinds of jobs in which workers make up an "occupational community." One such industry is mining. Not only is the actual work carried out by solidary work groups, but, in addition, miners live in a community made up largely of fellow workers. This kind of "inbreeding" produces a devotion to the occupation which is not characteristic of many other working class jobs:

> Somehow when you get into mining and you like the men you work with, you just get to the place after a while that you don't want to leave. *Once that fever gets hold of a man, he'll never be good for anything else.*

Such occupational communities are likely to develop in occupations that are isolated, either spatially or on the basis of peculiar hours of work. Coal mining and textile industries characteristically

have grown up in *isolated small communities;* sailors, cowboys, and long-distance truck drivers are also isolated from contact with persons in other jobs. Similarly, *off-hours shifts* favor the development of occupational communities; this is the case with printers, a large proportion of whom work nights, steel workers, who often rotate between day, swing, and graveyard shifts, firemen, and, of course, railroad men.

The essential feature of an occupational community is that workers in their off-hours socialize more with persons in their own line of work than with a cross section of occupational types. Printers generally go to bars, movies, and baseball games with other printers. In a small town steel mill, 87 per cent of the workers had spent "in the last week," at least some time off the job with other workers in their department; almost half said they had seen many or almost all of their fellow workers. However, in a large tractor plant of 20,000 people only 41 per cent of the employees said that they got together socially outside the plant with employees from their own work groups. *Occupational communities rarely exist among urban factory workers.*

A second characteristic of an occupational community is that its participants "talk shop" in their off-hours. That this is true of farmers, fishermen, miners, and railroaders has been described far more by novelists than by social scientists. The significance of talking about work off the job has been well expressed by Fred Blum, who notes that the assembly line workers in the meat packing plant he studied rarely do so.

> Whether they are with their family or their friends, rare are the occasions when workers feel like talking about their work. In response to the question: "Do you talk with your friends about the work you are doing?" only a very small number indicated that they

do talk with their friends—or their wife—about their work. Quite a few said that they "only" talk with their friends "if they ask me" or that they talk "sometimes" or "seldom." Some workers are outspoken in saying that they do not like to talk about their work. "If we get out of there, we are through with that to the next day." Another worker said, "When I leave down there, I am through down there. I like to talk about something else." *He adds to this with some astonishment: "Railroadmen always want to talk about their work."*

Third, occupational communities are little worlds in themselves. For its members the occupation itself is the reference group; its standards of behavior, its system of status and rank, guide conduct.

> Railroading is something more than an occupation. Like thieving and music, it is a world by itself, with its own literature and mythology, with an irrational system of status which is unintelligible to the outsider, and a complicated rule book for distributing responsibility and rewards.

We can suggest a number of mechanisms by means of which occupational communities increase job satisfaction. First, when workers know their co-workers off the job, they will derive deeper social satisfactions on the job. In the second place, an effect of the isolation of the occupation is that workers are able to develop and maintain a pride in and devotion to their line of work; at the same time, isolation insulates them from having to come to grips with the general public's image of their status, which is likely to be considerably lower than their own. Participation in an occupational community means not only the reinforcement of the group's sense of general prestige; in such worlds one's skill and expertise in doing the actual

work becomes an important basis of individual status and prestige. Finally, unlike the "alienated" assembly line worker, who is characterized by a separation of his work sphere from his non-work sphere—a separation of work from life as Mills and Blum put it—the work and leisure interests of those in occupational communities are highly integrated. If the integration of work and non-work is an important element in general psychic adjustment, as some assert, then these workers should exhibit higher job satisfaction, since satisfaction with life in general seems to be highly related to satisfaction in work.

Conclusions

When we read modern accounts of what work and workers were like before the industrial revolution, we continually find that the dominant image of the worker of that period is the craftsman. Viewed as an independent producer in his home or small shop with complete control over the pace and scheduling of his work, making the whole product rather than a part of it, and taking pride in the creativity of his skilled tasks, his traits are typically contrasted with those of the alienated factory worker—the allegedly characteristic producer of modern society.

It is remarkable what an enormous impact this *contrast* of the craftsman with the factory hand has had on intellectual discussions of work and workers in modern society, *notwithstanding its lack of correspondence to present and historical realities.* For, indeed, craftsmen, far from being typical workers of the past era, accounted for less than 10 per cent of the medieval labor force, and the peasant, who was actually the representative laborer, was, in the words of the Belgian socialist Henri DeMan, "practically nothing more than a working beast."

Furthermore, the real character of the craftsman's work has been romanticized by the prevalent tendency to idealize the past, whereas much evidence suggests that modern work does not fit the black portrait of meaningless alienation. In fact, it has been asserted that in modern society there is far greater scope for skill and craftsmanship than in any previous society, and that far more people are in a position to use such skills.

For intellectuals, it seems to be particularly difficult to grasp both the subjective and relative character of monotony and the capacity of workers to inject meaning into "objectively meaningless" work. Their strong tendency to view workers as dissatisfied suggests the idea that the alienation thesis, though a direct descendant of Marxist theory and related to a particular political posture, also reflects an intellectual perspective (in the sociology of knowledge sense) on manual work.

Surprisingly enough, business executives also tend to view manual workers as alienated. Perhaps this attitude reflects, in part, the growing influence of intellectual ideas, including neo-Marxist ones, on the more progressive business circles; perhaps, more importantly, this stems again, as in the case of the intellectual, from the middle-class businessman's separation and distance from the workaday world of his industrial employees. At any rate, such industrial spokesmen as Peter Drucker and Alexander Heron are likely to generalize much as does James Worthy of Sears Roebuck, who, in discussing "overfunctionalization," has written:

> The worker cannot see that total process, he sees only the small and uninteresting part to which he and his fellows are assigned. In a real sense, the job loses its meaning for the worker—the meaning,

that is, in all terms except the pay envelope.

Thus a very large number of employees in American industry today have been deprived of the sense of performing interesting, significant work. In consequence, they have little feeling of responsibility for the tasks to which they are assigned.

But, *work has significant positive meanings to persons who do not find overall satisfaction in their immediate job.* A still viable consequence of the Protestant ethic in our society is that its work ethic (the notion of work as a calling, an obligation to one's family, society, and self-respect, if no longer to God), retains a powerful hold. This is most dramatically seen in the reactions of the retired and unemployed. The idea is quite common to American workers at all occupational levels that soon after a worker retires, he is likely to either "drop dead" or "go crazy" from sheer inactivity. An English industrial psychiatrist states that this is actually a common calamity in British industry. Similarly, the studies made in the 1930's of unemployed people show that the disruption of the work relationship often leads to the disruption of normal family relations, to political apathy, and to lack of interest in social organizations and leisure-time activities.

The studies of job satisfaction reviewed in this paper further question the prevailing thesis that most workers in modern society are alienated and estranged. There is a remarkable consistency in the findings that the vast majority of workers, in virtually all occupations and industries, are moderately or highly satisfied, rather than dissatisfied with their jobs.

However, the marked occupational differences in work attitudes and the great significance which workers impute to being, at least to some extent, masters of their destiny in the work process, along with the fact that surrender of such control seems to be the most important condition of strong dissatisfaction are findings at least as important as the overall one of general satisfaction. Perhaps the need for autonomy and independence may be a more deep-seated human motive than is recognized by those who characterize our society in terms of crowdlike conformity and the decline of individualism.

These findings also have clear implications for industrial engineering. If industry and society have an interest in workers' experiencing satisfaction and pride in their work, a major effort must be made to increase the areas of control which employees have over the work process, especially in those industries and occupations where control is at a minimum. Charles Walker, who has written perceptively of the automobile worker's lack of control, has advocated two major solutions for humanizing repetitive assembly line work: job rotation and job enlargement. Where job rotation was introduced in one section of the automobile plant he studied, job satisfaction increased without loss of efficiency or production. The idea of recombining a number of jobs into one enlarged job seems especially to appeal to the line workers: as one man said, "I'd like to do a whole fender myself from the raw material to the finished product." But such radical job enlargement would be a negation of the assembly line method of production. Therefore, we must anticipate the day when the utopian solution of eliminating assembly line production entirely will be the practical alternative for a society which is affluent and concerned at the same time that its members work with pride and human dignity.

Finally, the findings of this paper indicate a need for considerable further research on industrial statistics and industrial trends. If the evidence shows that extreme dissatisfaction is concentrated among assembly line workers, it becomes terribly important, for a total assessment of the conditions of work in modern America, to know what proportion of the labor force works on assembly lines or in other job contexts involving little control over their work activities. It is startling, considering the importance of such data, that such figures do not exist. This situation helps maintain the conventional belief that the mechanized assembly line worker is today's typical industrial worker in contrast to the craftsman of the past.

An indication that the actual proportion of assembly line workers is quite small is suggested by figures of the automobile industry, the conveyor belt industry par excellence. If we consider total employment in the industrial groupings involved in the manufacture, sales, repair, and servicing of automobiles, we find that assembly line workers make up less than 5 per cent of all workers in this complex. There are approximately 120,000 automobile workers who are line assemblers, yet the number of skilled repair mechanics in all branches of the industry, a job which in many ways resembles the craft ideal, exceeds 500,000. In addition, the 120,000 assemblers are outnumbered by 400,000 managers who own or operate gas stations, garages, new and used car lots, and wrecking yards, and by 200,000 *skilled* workers in automobile plants. Recent developments, especially automation, have served further to decrease the proportion of assembly line operatives in the industry.

If the situation in the automobile industry is at all typical, research might well show that those kinds of job contexts which are associated with high work satisfaction and control over one's time and destiny, such as skilled repair work and self-employment, are more representative than is commonly believed, and are even increasing over the long run. Such a prospect should bring considerable satisfaction to all those in the diverse intellectual traditions who have been concerned with what happens to human beings in the course of their major life activity, their work. And yet, this would not necessarily mean that the problem of the lack of fulfillment in work had become less serious. For as one industrial sociologist has suggested, this problem *may become more acute,* not because work itself has become more tedious, fractionated, and meaningless, but because the ideal of pride in creative effort is shared by an increasingly large proportion of the labor force as a result of the rise of democratic education and its emphasis on individualism and occupational mobility.

Herzberg, Mausner, and Snyderman, in a study of accountants and engineers, provides independent confirmation of the general conclusions of Blauner's review, although the Herzberg study gives more emphasis to the achievement need than did Blauner. One of the principal points made by Herzberg, *et al.* is that being satisfied is not the opposite of being dissatisfied. Different incentive conditions influence satisfaction and dissatisfaction. A summary of the study is presented in Research Summary 2-5.

| RESEARCH SUMMARY 2-5 | *Satisfactions and Dissatisfactions in the Work Situation.* Being content involves more than just being *not* actively discontented. In their book, *The Motivation to Work,* Herzberg and his two associates, building on an extensive survey of job attitudes completed in 1953, present a challenging analysis of satisfactions and dissatisfactions in the work situation, and the factors relating to each.
| | Two hundred middle-management engineers and accountants from nine different industrial organizations were asked in interviews to describe an actual job experience in which "they felt exceptionally good or a time when they felt exceptionally bad about their job." They were pressed to describe two or three such experiences and were then asked to indicate on a rating scale how seriously their feelings (good or bad) about their jobs had been affected by what had happened.
| | Favorable experiences emphasized the actual job *content* (the task performed by the person), and the principal sources of satisfaction were achievement, recognition, the work itself, responsibility or advancement. Experiences during which they felt bad about their job involved mainly conditions in the job *context:* supervision, and company policy or administration.°
| | Verification of these findings from a different sort of research approach is found in a mental health survey of a national sample of employed men, conducted by Gurin, Veroff, and Feld. They report that such ego satisfying factors as the nature of the work and opportunities it provided for the use of skill, were mentioned much more often as positive characteristics of the job.† On the

---

° The Herzberg findings have been substantiated in a study in the utility industry by Schwartz, Jenusaitis, and Stack on a population of supervisors.

† The mental health aspect of work is discussed by Friedman, who emphasizes that

other hand, factors extrinsic to the work itself—money, job security, and working conditions, were more frequently noted as complaints than as sources of satisfaction.

From the findings of both studies one can speculate that from a motivational point of view, employees may be clustered around three points on a morale continuum: satisfied, neutral (neither pleased nor complaining), and dissatisfied. If conditions surrounding the job are not unpleasant, the job is tolerable without being really satisfying. Real satisfaction, apparently, comes only from a job that provides some opportunity for self-actualization, achievement, or recognition. The administrator can see that if he concerns himself only with maintaining good environmental conditions he may be helping to keep dissatisfactions down. But it is in the area of providing the positive satisfactions that real skill will be needed.

"There is a risk in inferring the actual causes of satisfaction and dissatisfaction from descriptions of events by individuals. It seems possible that the obtained differences between events may reflect defensive processes at work within the individual. Individuals may be more likely to perceive the causes of satisfaction within the self and hence describe experiences involving their own achievement, recognition, or advancement in their job. On the other hand, they may tend to attribute dissatisfaction not to personal inadequacies or deficiencies but to factors in the work enviornment, that is, obstacles presented by company policies and supervision. This type of explanation is invoked by Gurin, Veroff, and Feld, who, while noting the possibility of the Herzberg et al. interpretation, state that: '. . . this finding suggests that there is relatively little introspection in analyzing the sources of distress on the job—that complaints tend to be externalized rather than cast in personality terms' " (Vroom and Maier, p. 433).

Money and Motivation. The place of money in motivating performance is still very much misunderstood. Management theory has turned from earlier beliefs of man at work as solely motivated by economic considerations, but in moving away from the economic man theory, it is now in danger of ignoring the very real importance of money in the American culture.

In his *Money and Motivation,* Whyte states:

Man is not born loving money. He has to learn to love it. This learning takes place in varying degrees in various parts of the world. In economically underdeveloped countries we find that the possibility of making more money does not lead people to do more work. On the contrary, they usually prefer to work a shorter number of days or hours to make the amount of money they have customarily earned. American and Western European businessmen have often been troubled by this phenomenon. Apparently the workers in these situations have not learned to want the consumers' goods that mean a rising standard of

---

work is not a compulsory activity undertaken for purely practical ends but an activity that makes for equilibrium and development of the individual. In this regard he quotes Freud as follows: "Stressing the importance of work has a greater effect than any other technique of living in binding the individual more closely to reality; in his work he is at least securely attached to a part of reality, the human community."

living. They are content to remain at the customary level. Factory work being unfamiliar to them anyway, they are quite happy to be able to maintain this standard of living by working a shorter time.

In our society too, the response to money is a learned response; nor is it uniform. Americans in general, including factory workers, seem to have a stronger interest in making more money and in the things that money can buy than seems to be found in most other parts of the world. Even in the United States, however, among factory workers there are a great many variations in this response to money, as Dalton has so well demonstrated. We must recognize also that money is not the only reward nor lack of money the only punishment available in any given situation. We can expect almost any American who is offered more money without any compensating dissatisfaction to respond to the money. The problem is that other rewards and punishments always go along with it. Different individuals strike different balances between rewards and punishments, including money (p. 210).

The worker is rarely faced with a choice of more money, uncomplicated by other conflicting considerations such as possible antagonism from the group, change to a less secure job, or less pleasant work. The importance of money is frequently not considered in absolute terms but rather in comparative terms: Do I make as much as X, who is doing the same kind of work or has the same skills (Patchen)? Finally, of course, the whole concept of money is beclouded by its symbolic value as a measure of recognition for accomplishment, status, and place in society.

In line with his distinction between sources of satisfaction and dissatisfaction, Herzberg *et al.* reports that low salaries, or those considered unfair, are a source of job dissatisfaction. The amount of money paid in itself is not a source of job satisfaction, except as a change in the amount, as in a salary increase, is a welcome sign of recognition. In that situation, in so far as job satisfaction is concerned, it is the symbolic value of money that is motivating.

Money may have operated as an incentive for an individual to *take* a job; it may have an effect in keeping an individual from *leaving* the organization. But these influences have to be distinguished from the influence of money as an incentive to performance (either more work, better work, or maintenance of the same level), and, separately, as an influence on satisfaction. For example, a shift to a financial incentive tends to increase production and take home pay. Nevertheless, one cannot say that tieing money directly to production (as in a piece rate) will maximize production in the average organization; in fact, there is some evidence to the contrary (Adams and Rosenbaum). Nor can it be said that high salaries assure job satisfaction.

Rothe has examined the extent to which various types of financial incentives meet the psychological conditions required for increasing productivity. He indicates that most plans or approaches, for example, profit sharing plans or negotiated increases, cannot be expected to influence productivity. Costello and Zalkind have suggested that a system of short-range merit bonuses might come closer to maintaining an influence on behavior than the usual merit increase plan.

Likert has pointed out that economic motivation will be tapped more effectively if the plan of compensation is seen by the employee as enhancing his feeling of personal worth and importance. The degree of acceptance of the method or plan of pay may be more important than the details of the plan in getting positive motivation.

Motivation and Productivity. Since 1947, the Survey Research Center at the University of Michigan has studied the relationships between employee attitudes and behavior in the organization. In view of the widely held belief that job satisfaction leads to high productivity, they have been particularly concerned to study the relation between the two. Kahn's paper on "Productivity and Job Satisfaction" (our next reading) describes their efforts as well as the related work of others. The accumulated evidence reveals job satisfaction to be multi-dimensional, and the various dimensions to be differently related to productivity in the organization. It is no longer possible to take for granted that happy workers are productive workers. Production depends on whether workers are motivated to produce or are merely contented, and on the nature of the goals of the work groups in which workers find their satisfactions.

READING 2-5

Productivity and Job Satisfaction*

ROBERT L. KAHN

I did not select the topic of this paper, although I am glad to address myself to it. My interest in doing so stems partly from the fact that a great deal of research on the determinants of productivity and job satisfaction has been done at the Survey Research Center [of the University of Michigan]. I have, however, a more personal reason for being interested in the Productivity and Satisfaction title: I am impressed to the point of fascination with the durability of the myth that productivity and job satisfaction are inseparable. I would like to begin by asserting, without qualification, that productivity and job satisfaction do not necessarily go together. The persistence with

which managers and managerial consultants place them in juxtaposition is much more revealing of their own value structure, I believe, than it is indicative of anything in the empirical research data on organizations. If I am to back up this mildly iconoclastic assertion, I will have to ask you to rehearse with me some of the programmatic history of the Survey Research Center.

First Findings

The work of the Survey Research Center in studying organizations began in 1947 with a prospectus by Rensis Likert and Daniel Katz. The objectives of the program were described in some detail. For our present purposes, the following quotation is particularly appropriate: "Specifically, the objectives have to

* From *Psychology in Administration: A Symposium. Personnel Psychology,* 13 (1960), pp. 275-287.

do with the conditions making for a high level of group functioning, and a high level of individual satisfaction of the group members." There is here no assertion that efficient functioning can be achieved only through the achievement of high levels of satisfaction, but it is perhaps significant that the notions of satisfaction and productivity were linked together even at the beginning of the research. The earliest project in this research program was conducted in a life insurance company, and it consisted of a systematic comparison of work groups which had been demonstrated to differ significantly in productivity, as measured by the accounting procedures of the company. The analysis plan was to determine what supervisory practices were associated with high and low levels of satisfaction, and with high and low levels of productivity.

Although satisfaction and productivity were both defined as dependent variables, there was also a clear intention to use satisfaction as an intervening variable. As Katz stated, "A second direction has been a consideration of psychological, dependent variables from another frame of reference; namely, as intervening variables that affect performance. We have considered the satisfactions or morale dimensions, then, both as dependent variables to be predicted from other factors, and as a reflection of intervening variables which could help to predict productivity" (Katz).

In this early study, a number of systematic differences in leadership were found to be associated with differences in productivity. These are fully described in the monograph, *Productivity, Supervision, and Morale in an Office Situation,* by Katz, Maccoby, and Morse (Institute for Social Research, 1950). For example, high-producing supervisors were found to spend more time in actual supervisory activities, and less time in performing tasks similar to those done by their subordinates. They were supervised less closely and were themselves less closely supervised by their own managers. They were judged by coders who read their interviews to be more employee-centered in their attitudes. The employees of high-producing supervisors were more likely to feel that their supervisors would defend their interests rather than those of management, if such a choice had to be made.

The behavior of supervisors proved to be less important in explaining the satisfactions of employees than in explaining their productivity. In some respects, however, the determinants of satisfaction present a more complex problem. This is true in part because satisfaction itself is not a unitary concept. In recognition of this, three indexes of satisfaction were employed in the present study: one reflecting satisfaction with the company as a whole, one reflecting satisfaction with financial and job status, and one reflecting satisfaction with the job itself. A fourth index was, in fact, less a measure of satisfaction than a measure of the perceived performance of the work group.

Rather different patterns of factors were correlated with each of these indexes. For example, the major determinant of job satisfaction appears to be the type of work actually done by the employee. Among people doing high-level technical work, 58 per cent indicated a high degree of intrinsic job satisfaction. Among people doing repetitious clerical work, only 23 per cent recorded equally high satisfaction scores. The behavior of the supervisor, as measured by the attitudes and perceptions of his subordinates, was associated with all of the satisfaction indexes in some degree. The association was strongest with respect to financial and job status satisfactions, and to over-all satisfactions with the company. The behavior of the supervisor appeared to be less related to intrinsic job satisfaction, and to attitudes toward the work group. The most important finding, however, for our present line of argument is that no significant relationships were discovered between any of the indexes of satisfaction and the productivity of the work group. In other words, employees in highly productive work groups were no more likely than employees in low-producing groups to be satisfied with their jobs with the company, or with their financial and status rewards.

The completion of the research in the insurance company left us with a number of unresolved questions, questions which were obvious candidates for attention in subsequent projects. One of these questions was the central issue around which this paper has been written: "Is there a relationship between satisfaction and productivity?" Other major questions included: "What is the cause and effect relationship underlying the correlations between the supervisor's tendency to delegate and the productivity of employees?" More specifically: "Does the granting of increased responsibility and autonomy by the supervisor produce higher motivation on the part of the employee, with subsequent gains in productivity?" Or, alternately: "Does the employee who demonstrates high productivity receive, as a consequence of that productivity, a more general and less detailed kind of supervision from his immediate superior?"

Another question requiring solution was the nature and reality of the dimension which had been identified in the insurance company study as "employee-centered—production-centered." Was a supervisor who tended to be production-centered necessarily less sensitive and less oriented to employee needs? Might not a supervisor be both employee-centered and production-centered?

Finally, the study in the insurance company left us with the question of how to interpret the single area of satisfaction which seemed to relate to productivity—satisfaction with the work group. Was the prideful response of the high-producing work groups a measure of the spirit and motivation which caused their higher productivity, or were the members of these high-producing groups merely reporting their accurate perception? Their groups were in fact better than others when it came to getting the job done.

Riddles and Replication

The second study in this series of organizational researches on the determinants of productivity was done on a railroad, among maintenance-of-way workers. This study, which involved about 300 laborers and 72 foremen, was very similar in design to the study of clerical workers in the insurance company. It was similar, also, in research purpose: to investigate the relationships among supervisory behavior, employee satisfaction, and productivity. The major difference between the two studies lay in the drastic contrast in setting. Manual labor was studied in place of clerical work, middle-aged workers instead of young people just out of high school graduating classes, men instead of girls. In addition, the two studies differed in the availability of performance information to workers. In the insurance company, the employees had available management's records of their group performance. In the railroad situation, such data were not available to employees. In fact, it was necessary for us to obtain rankings from management in order to determine the relative efficiency of work groups. We were looking to this second study to serve as a partial validation of the earlier research findings, and to illuminate the area of satisfaction and productivity, which had been characterized by such unexpected results in the first study.

As a study in validation, the research on the railroad must be considered successful. As in the insurance company the effective foreman on the railroad was able to differentiate his role from the role of the nonsupervisory employee. Compared to less successful supervisors, he spent more time planning the work, more time performing highly skilled tasks, and more time in actual supervision. As in the insurance company, the high-producing railroad foreman showed greater sensitivity to the needs of his employees. He was more employee-centered in this sense. He was, for example, more interested in the men's off-the-job problems, more helpful in training them for better jobs, more constructive and less punishing when mistakes were made. With respect to the area of delegation, the railroad study was less definitive than the study in the insurance company. There was, however, some validation of the earlier findings, especially in the tendency of high-producing supervisors to report themselves as under less pressure from their own superiors.

In the matter of productivity and satisfaction, the results of the railroad study were identical with those of the work in the insurance company. There was no systematic relationship between productivity and such morale variables as intrinsic job satisfaction, financial and job status satisfaction, and satisfaction with the company. In the matter of attitudes toward the work group as potential predictors of productivity, the railroad study goes somewhat beyond its predecessor, in that the employees were questioned not only about their evaluation of their work groups' performance, but also about their liking for the other men in the section, about their feeling that the men stick together well, and about their

reactions to good or poor workers in their group. In none of these respects did the workers in high-producing groups differ from those in low-producing groups. The high-producing workers did differ, however, in their evaluation of their work groups' performance. Men in high-producing maintenance-of-way sections were more likely than men in low-producing sections to see their work group as superior to other groups. The question of causality in the relationship between productivity and attitudes toward the work group remains beyond the scope of this second study so far as a definitive answer is concerned. The fact, however, that the men in the high-producing groups did not evaluate their groups as superior in all respects, but only with respect to the accomplishment of work, certainly questions the earlier interpretation that some factor such as group pride is operating to increase the level of productivity. The more plausible interpretation seems to be that despite the absence of official information regarding productivity, the men were able to form accurate judgments with respect to the relative accomplishment of work groups, including their own.

There are perhaps two additional findings in the railroad study which should be mentioned as significant amplifications of the previous research. The first of these lies in the area of role differentiation. In the low-producing sections on the railroad, the men more often said that one man in the section tended to speak up in their behalf when they wanted something. A possible interpretation of this finding is that in situations where the formal leader does not fill the leadership role adequately, there is a tendency for an informal leader to arise. If the foreman does not differentiate his role sufficiently from that of his subordinates to provide leadership, the men will, in effect, "elect" a kind of substitute leader of their own.

The second finding in the railroad study, which goes somewhat beyond the previous research, lies in the content area of employee-centered supervision. The section hands on the railroad were asked what their foreman did when someone did a bad job. Answers to this question were coded as reflecting punitive or nonpunitive behavior on the part of foremen. Nonpunitive behavior was more characteristic of foremen of high-producing sections, than of low-producing sections. A concern with penalties rather than remedies, and with the assignment of personal blame rather than the discovery of causes for mistakes, appeared to characterize the low-producing units.

The End of an Hypothesis

With the completion of the second study in this series on the determinants of productivity, we found ourselves again with a failure of the expected relationship between morale or satisfaction and the productivity of work groups. We decided in the third study to make an all-out effort to eliminate as many as possible of the reasons for this failure. Accordingly, we wished to find a research situation in which the number of subjects would be very large so that it would be possible to hold constant a substantial number of other variables while looking at the relationship between morale and productivity. We wanted also to find a research situation in which the range of skills and kinds of work represented was very substantial. In addition, we hoped to find a situation in which objective measures of individual productivity were available. We thought that the group measures of productivity, which were all that we had to work with in the first two studies, might tend to obscure relationships between individually-held attitudes and individual consequences of those atti-

tudes. All these requirements for a third study on the determinants of productivity were well met in a large midwestern cluster of factories manufacturing agricultural equipment and tractors.

A study was conducted in these factories, in which all of the approximately 20,000 employees were included. Of this number, approximately 6,000 were on jobs for which productivity standards had been established by time study, and for which daily productivity data were available. In this study we introduced a number of changes with respect to research design and analysis. We decided to explore further the characterization of supervisors as employee-centered or production-centered, and to learn more about the characteristics of work groups. (Problems of causality, for example in the relationship between delegation and productivity, we saw as being resolved in a different study of experimental design.)

In general, the findings in the tractor company repeated the findings of the two earlier studies. There were, however, some significant differences. In the matter of employee-centered supervision, for example, the high-producing employees in the tractor company more often reported, as expected, that their supervisors took a personal interest in them, that they got along with him well, that he let them know how they were doing on the job, that it was easy to talk to him about most things, and so on through the list of behaviors which we had categorized as employee-centered. However, the high-producing workers were also more likely to say that high production was important to their foremen, and that one of the ways in which their foremen supervised them was by seeing that production was kept up. If we put these two sets of findings together, they lead us to a re-interpretation of the relationship between employee-centered and production-centered supervision. In the studies in the insurance company and on the railroad, we had treated employee-centered and production-centered supervision as if they were the two opposite ends of a single continuum. We had assumed, in other words, that as a supervisor became more production-oriented, he must of necessity become less employee-oriented. The research data from the tractor company suggested instead that the quality of being production-centered and the quality of being employee-centered should be regarded as theoretically independent dimensions of supervision. Thus we may, for convenience, think of a four-celled table, with each cell representing a kind of supervision which combines differently the attributes of employee orientation and production orientation. The most successful supervisors in this scheme are those who combine employee-centered and production-centered qualities, working out their own creative way of synthesizing these two concerns. We can also discover supervisors who are interested in the employees and sensitive to their needs, but neglectful or even disinterested in the production goals of the organization. Our impressions are that this is a style of supervision which sometimes generates a superficial popularity among the men, although we would predict that in time this would be replaced by feelings of aimlessness and lack of accomplishment. The supervisor who emphasizes production to the detriment of employee requirements is, according to the data from the tractor company, less successful both with respect to the productivity of his group and the attitudes of his men. Finally, we can imagine a supervisor who is seriously interested neither in productivity nor in the employees. We have yet to do research on supervisors in this category, but observation suggests that there are in many organizations men in supervisory positions whose own needs are so overpowering that there is little supervisory energy left for investment in meeting either the needs of the employees or the requirements of the organization.

A clue to the way in which successful supervisors synthesize their interest in productivity and in the needs of employees was provided by the responses of foremen in the tractor company. In answering the question as to how interested their own supervisors were in productivity, the general foremen, were in productivity, more foremen of high- than low-producing sections reported that their supervisors felt high production was *one* of the most important things on the job, but not *the* most important thing. The foremen of lower producing units, however, were more likely to report that their own supervisors either overemphasized the achievement of high production by acting as if it were *the* most important thing on the job, or underestimated the importance of high production by acting as if it were not among the more important things on the job.

Another of the areas which had been marked for further clarification in the tractor study was group influences on productivity. In the insurance study the interpretation had been offered that group pride was a factor in generating a high level of productivity, and that the statement of employees in high-producing groups that their work group excelled others was primarily a reflection of this pride. In the railroad study, it was pointed out that the apparently prideful evaluation of work group performance might be no more than an accurate perception of the group's accomplishment, and should not be interpreted as a definite casual factor. In the tractor company study, a number of questions were asked employees regarding the characteristics of their work groups, and their individual relationship to the group. The results were to replicate the findings of the earlier studies. The high-producing employees in the tractor company again told us that their work groups were better than others when it came to getting a job done. But high-producing employees were also more likely to say that they really felt a part of the groups in which they worked. Low-producing employees were more likely to report that they felt accepted in some respects, but not in others. In addition, high-producing employees were apparently more anchored to their work groups. They were more likely to say that they would resist transfer to another group or to another job, even if the job were the same in content and the same pay were being offered for it. Finally, the foremen of high-producing work groups reported that their sections were better than most others in the way in which the men helped each other out on the job. The effect of these several findings was to convince us that there were significant differences between high- and low-producing groups in their peer relationships. The statement, obtained in three studies from high-producing employees, that their groups excelled low-producing groups now seemed neither a dispassionate statement of group achievement nor in itself a cause of high productivity.

The nature of these group differences has been well analyzed by Stanley Seashore, who began by contrasting groups with respect to cohesiveness, or the attraction of the group for the individual. Seashore reasoned, following the experimental research of Leon Festinger and his associates, that the more cohesive group, being by definition the group with greater attraction for its members, would by virtue of that attraction have greater power over the individuals in it. Each person, since he valued more highly his membership in the group, would be more responsive to the group's demands on him. If this were true, we would expect that the major differences between high-cohesive and low-cohesive work groups would be visible in their relative uniformity of member behaviors; that is, the closeness to which members conformed to the norms of the group. Differences between high-cohesive and low-cohesive groups should be most apparent, not in the level of productivity, but rather in the variance of productivity. We could imagine a highly cohesive group which would predict that all group members would tend to conform closely to that high productivity norm. However, another group of equal cohesiveness might have a productivity norm which was markedly low. In this case, we would predict that the group members would be equally faithful in conforming to the low productivity norm. In both cases, the cohesiveness of the group would show in the variance of the productivity distribution, rather than in its level. The data bore out this approach very well, and Seashore was able to show in addition that the crucial considerations, in determining the level of the productivity norm in a highly cohesive group, involved the relation of the employees to management and union. Peer relationships in the industrial situation can be a force which either implements or frustrates the goals of the organization, depending upon the basic relationship which has been established between management, union, and employees.

With regard to the hypothesized relationship between productivity and satisfaction, an all-out effort was made in the tractor company study. A factor analysis was done to identify the components of satisfaction among the approximately 6,000 workers for whom individual productivity scores were available. Four identifiable factors resulted from this analysis and were labeled: intrinsic job satisfaction, satisfaction with the company, satisfaction with supervision, and satisfaction with rewards and mobility opportunities. None of these factors was significantly related to the actual productivity of employees in the tractor factories.

For purposes of our present discussion, the completion of the study in the tractor company represents the end of a cycle. We decided that the evidence from these three studies was sufficiently powerful so that we should abandon, in our future research, the use of satisfaction or morale indexes as variables intervening between supervisory and organizational characteristics on the one hand, and productivity on the other. This, perhaps, is the major conclusion so far as the topic of this paper is concerned. There are, however, a number of others worth mentioning, perhaps because of their continuing influence.

They are as follows:

We dropped from our empirical research and from our theoretical formulations the concept of morale as a sum of satisfactions realized in the work situation. This we did on the grounds that the factor analysis had shown, and the results of the previous study also suggested, that the several dimensions of satisfaction were quite independent, both with respect to their determinants and in their consequences.

We recognized the necessity of developing alternative theoretical schemes to show the determinants of each dimension of satisfaction and of productivity in the work situation. A discussion of several such alternatives is beyond the scope of this paper, but has been attempted elsewhere by Basil Georgopoulos, Rensis Likert, Robert Kahn, and others.

It is necessary to consider the relative stability over time of different levels of satisfaction and productivity. For example, Likert has proposed that the combination of high productivity with low satisfaction may be difficult or impossible to maintain over a long period of time, because of the fact that such a combination reflects the consumption and deterioration of the human assets of the organization.

Related to the above point is the need to develop more adequate criteria of organizational effectiveness. The measures of productivity used in the three studies cited in this paper should be supplemented by measures of the costs of recruitment, training, turnover, and the like. Georgopoulos and Arnold Tannenbaum have proposed the definition of organizational effectiveness as "the extent to which an organization as a social system, given certain resources and means, fulfills its objectives without incapacitating its means and resources, and without placing undue strain upon its members."

But these questions and hunches wait their turn in the continuing programs of organizational studies. What can we say in the meantime about the applied value of what has already been done? We are convinced that the growing literature of empirical research in organizations, of which the studies I have cited are a small part, is heavy with implications of responsibility and opportunity for psychologists who interact with the leaders of organization. There is a terrible gap between the complexities of organizational life and the patent-medicine remedies which are peddled unceasingly at management's doorstep. The psychologist, as staff member or as consultant, can help management avoid the dismal sequence of oversold devices, unrealistic expectations, and undiscriminating disillusionment. He can offer the assistance of what research has already learned, and the realistic comfort of knowing when decisions must still be based on managerial intuition.

The second part of Clark's article which follows as Reading 2-6 comes to grips with somewhat the same problem analyzed by Kahn: the relation between satisfaction and performance.

Clark cites additional industrial research and attempts an integration of these findings into Maslow's hierarchical need structure, thus casting the research findings into a different framework from that offered by Kahn. We present it as a second way of looking at the complex problem of motivation on the job.

READING 2-6

Motivation in Work Groups:
A Tentative View*
(Part II)

JAMES V. CLARK

Some Suggested Uniformities Among Different Researches

Exhibit 1 shows how the need-hierarchy concept (Maslow's theory presented in the first section of Clark's paper, Reading 2-2) might be utilized to relate and explain the findings of a number of different studies. In other words, it takes McGregor's generalization of Maslow's theory, attempts to relate it to some existing studies, and concludes that workers under this or that combination of environmental conditions behave *as if* they were motivated in such-and-such a fashion.

Before we turn to this exhibit, however, a word of caution is in order. This way of relating and thinking about different organizational behavior researches is by no means perfect. First of all, the propositions which follow from the need-hierarchy theory are extremely difficult to test in a research sense. Secondly, the variety of environmental and internal-system factors affecting work-group behavior cannot be categorized so as to make all known descriptions of work situations directly comparable from some

one point of view. Finally, almost all researchers leave out, or find uncontrollable, some variables that are necessary for complete comparability. Nevertheless, some available researches suggest uniformities consistent with the need-hierarchy concept.

Exhibit 1 shows how a number of different "givens" in a work-group's environment can prevent or frustrate an individual's opportunity for need satisfaction at different levels of the need hierarchy. The exhibit is based on the assumption that all individuals have a potential for activating all the needs on the need hierarchy. Likewise, the exhibit assumes that an individual does not necessarily suspend or forget his unrealized needs during his hours on the job. Actually, in industrial situations, there are few data to support the first assumption, many data to support the second. Therefore, the exhibit can usefully be regarded as a tentative explanation of how and why most people, or an "average worker," would most typically react under different conditions at work.

The extreme left-hand scale of the middle block of graphs in Exhibit 1 represents the various levels of the need hierarchy (exclusive of the physiological

---

* *Op. cit.* Reading 2-2.

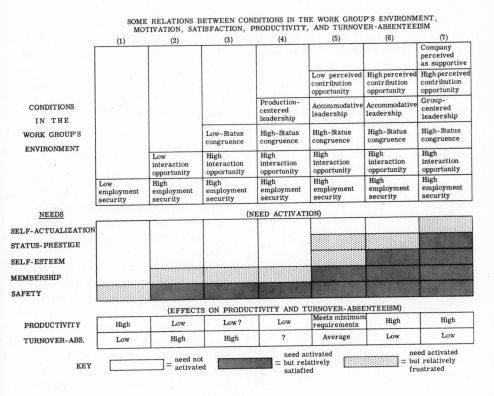

SOME RELATIONS BETWEEN CONDITIONS IN THE WORK GROUP'S ENVIRONMENT, MOTIVATION, SATISFACTION, PRODUCTIVITY, AND TURNOVER-ABSENTEEISM

Exhibit 1

needs). (In Maslow's description of his need hierarchy, the status-prestige need and the self-esteem need are placed side by side about the membership need. They are placed one on top of the other here for graphic simplicity.)

The remaining columns of the middle block depict the pattern of an individual's need activation and satisfaction under a number of different external conditions. These patterns will be discussed in this paper in relation to certain researches. (It is not possible to show all possible combinations of external conditions: researches have not been conducted under such a wide variety of conditions.)

Across the bottom of the exhibit are two rows which show "productivity" and "turnover and absenteeism" for each

column. These are by no means definitely established results but the researchers examined in this paper often suggested certain tendencies in regard to these variables which are shown. Consequently, by beginning with human needs, we can move to the relationship between the satisfaction of these needs, external conditions, and productivity and turnover-absenteeism.

Column 1 illustrates a situation in which employment security is extremely low. Such conditions might exist whenever alternative employment is unavailable (as in a depression) or is deemed by the workers to be not as desirable as present employment and where workers feel unprotected from a management which is perceived as arbitrary in its layoff and firing procedures.

Research by Goode and Fowler[5] in an automobile feeder plant illustrates this condition. In their study of a low morale, nonunion plant a small group of high service employees, for whom the job had become an absolute economic necessity, consistently produced according to management expectations. Turnover among other workers, for whom the job was less important, was high. They quit or were fired for not producing enough.

Interestingly enough, related situations were described some time ago, and were alluded to by Mitchell,[6] when he noted that the pace of work was slower in the flush times of 1900-1902 than it had been in the dull times of 1894-1896. He quoted a sample bit of testimony from the period. The superintendent of a company manufacturing electrical machinery said:

> . . . Five years ago men did not restrict their output, union or non-union men, because they wanted to hold their jobs, and a man would do anything and all he was told to do. Now a man knows that all he has to do is to walk across the street and get another job at the same rate of pay. . . .

Obviously, a group's productivity does not always increase in depression times: it fell off in the bank-wiring room[7] shortly before the final layoffs. The suggestion being made here is that under employment conditions which an individual perceives as economically threatening *and* arbitrary (and such conditions probably exist most often in a depression), his

higher needs cannot motivate. He is "stuck" on the safety level and his behavior can only work toward the immediate goal of economic survival. Under conditions of this kind, financial rewards tend to be the primary incentives which motivate workers toward higher productivity.

Frustrated Membership Needs

Columns 2 through 4 all show situations in which membership needs are active, but frustrated. They are shown separately, because apparently they occur under different environmental conditions.

Column 2 shows a situation where workers are less concerned with employment security, because they have it, but where the job technology imposes physical or spatial requirements where interaction is impossible or severely restricted. This condition reflects and is labelled "low interaction opportunity." Such conditions and their effects on satisfaction were described in two automobile assembly plant studies.

Walker and Guest[8] rated jobs according to their "mass production characteristics" (noise, repetitiveness, restricted opportunity for movement, etc.). Workers holding such jobs often reported social isolation to be an important reason for job dissatisfaction. Moreover, absenteeism and turnover (extremely high throughout the automotive industry) were nearly twice as high for persons whose jobs exhibited "extreme mass production characteristics."

Another study of automobile assembly workers by Jasinski[9] showed that the

[5] W. F. Goode and Irving Fowler, "Incentive Factors in a Low Morale Plant," *American Sociological Review,* XIV, No. 5 (1949).

[6] W. C. Mitchell, *Business Cycles and Their Causes,* University of California Press, Berkeley, Cal., 1941.

[7] F. J. Roethlisberger and W. J. Dickson, *Management and the Worker,* Harvard University Press, Cambridge, Mass., 1939.

[8] Charles R. Walker and Robert H. Guest, *The Man on the Assembly Line,* Harvard University Press, Cambridge, Mass., 1952.

[9] Frank J. Jasinski, "Technological Delimitation of Reciprocal Relationships: A Study of Interaction Patterns in Industry," *Human Organization,* XV, No. 2 (1956).

men resented not being able to follow conventional conversation patterns; looking at the listener, being able to pause for conversation, and to complete the "talk." A correlation was found between an individual's desire to talk on the job and his attitude towards his job: the higher the desire to talk, the less interesting the job.

It is possible that Van Zelst's study[10] of sociometrically restructured construction work groups may be illustrative of what happens when opportunities to interact are increased.

When men were allowed to work alongside others whom they themselves had chosen, turnover, labor cost and materials cost all dropped.

The inference can be drawn that these results occurred because membership level motivation was satisfied and higher needs became activated.

Another research, "The Case of the Changing Cage"[11] suggests what happens to a work group's productivity and satisfaction when interaction opportunities are suddenly lowered. (In this case, however, interaction opportunity was decreased by a combination of physical changes and another variable we will discuss later, leadership behavior.)

Workers in a voucher-check filing unit in an insurance company worked together well, kept up with the work load and expressed feelings of satisfaction. Their work area was inside a wire cage surrounded by filing cabinets and boxes through which the group's supervisors could not see. For efficiency purposes, the cage was moved to a new area in which the filing cabinets were arranged so that supervisors could see into the

cage and restrict worker interaction. The workers could no longer engage in social activities which had been important to them (games, chatting, eating, etc.). Their output declined drastically, the amount of time spent in nonwork activities increased substantially, and the workers expressed considerable dissatisfaction with the new setup.

In short, it appears that if there are any major physical or spatial technological factors which restrict opportunities for interaction (under conditions where safety-level needs are not primary), membership needs will be frustrated and, consequently, any higher-need levels will not be activated.

Column 3 illustrates a situation in which safety-level considerations are relatively unimportant because they are satisfied, interaction opportunities are high, but where workers are placed in low-status congruence work groups.

The need-hierarchy explanation of this situation would be as follows: safety needs are not active and membership needs are active but frustrated because social-status differences among persons in the work group are too large for the group to deal with effectively. Therefore no indications of higher-level needs are present. As a consequence, people would not see their work as something to which they could or should contribute. But why should low- or high-status congruence affect membership motivation?

In Zaleznik, Christensen, and Roethlisberger's recent study, a "theory of social certitude" was advanced to explain this on an individual level:

> In the condition of social certitude, the individual may be high, middle, or low in total status. But at whatever level, his status factors are well established. As a social entity, therefore, he can place himself and be placed readily in the structure of a group. People relate to him in terms of common ex-

10 R. J. Van Zelst, "Sociometrically Selected Work Teams Increase Productivity," *Personnel Psychology*, V, No. 3 (1953).
11 Cara B. Richards and Henry F. Dobyns, "Topography and Culture: The Case of the Changing Cage," *Human Organization*, XVI, No. 1 (1957).

pectations of behavior toward a person well established at his particular level of status. In turn, the individual knows what to expect from others. These expectations may or may not be functional for the group or the individual—there may be a more productive role for an individual than his status, well established as it is, allows him to play. Nevertheless, in a condition of social certitude the individual becomes "structured" into a group. Whether he is structured into the group at a high rank or low rank will depend on the level of the individual's total status.

The condition of ambiguity, where the individual's status factors are out of line, provides no readily apparent social position for him. As an ambiguous social entity, the group has no clear expectations regarding behavior from or toward such an individual. On the one hand, being high in one or more dimensions of status seems to require the form of behavior associated with a high status person. On the other hand, being simultaneously low in one or more dimensions of status seems to require behavior associated with a low status person. These mixed expectations create ambiguities and consequently anxiety in social relationships.[12]

This theory was advanced to explain why group members are attracted to or repelled by an *individual* whose status factors are out of line: some very high, some very low. Such an individual is ambiguous in relation to the group majority. The term "group-status congruence" refers to a collection of people

who share similar status factors, even if the factors themselves may be out of line with one another for a given individual. In this kind of a situation, an individual who exhibits status factors different from the majority tends to be avoided by the majority even if his status factors are in line with one another. He is likely to be described by others as "not our class" or "not our kind of person."[13] The four combinations between an individual and his group (high group-status congruence, high individual-status congruence; high group-status congruence, low individual-status congruence, etc.) have not been studied as such. At the present time, loosely stated, it appears that if, under most conditions, an individual has status factors to some extent different from the majority of people in the small-group social structure to which he belongs, he will tend to be regarded with anxiety.

Clark's supermarket research[14] was concerned with differences in group-status congruence between stores.

He found that groups with high group-status congruence (which he called "high status factors in common" groups) exhibited low turnover and low absenteeism, indications of membership-need level satisfaction. Moreover, he further found that stores which had high-status congruent groups in them also tended to have higher labor efficiency ratings. In addition, he found that members of these groups tended to speak of their work as more satisfying.

Adams' bomber crew study[15] was somewhat similar.

---

[12] A. Zaleznik, C. R. Christensen, and F. J. Roethlisberger, *The Motivation, Productivity and Satisfaction of Workers, A Prediction Study*, Harvard University Division of Research, Graduate School of Business Administration, Boston, Mass., 1958.

[13] James V. Clark, *Some Unconscious Assumptions Affecting Labor Efficiency in Eight Supermarkets* (unpublished D.B.A. thesis), Harvard Graduate School of Business Administration, 1958.
[14] *Ibid.*
[15] Stuart Adams, "Status Congruency as a Variable in Small Group Performance," *Social Forces*, XXXII, 16-22.

He showed that crews with high group-status congruence tended to report feelings of satisfaction with group membership. However, Adams also showed that while crews with high-status congruence showed high technical performance up to a point, beyond that point, as group-status congruence increased, technical performance decreased.

Therefore, while Clark's and Adams' studies showed similar results in the relation between group-status congruence and membership satisfaction, their findings on group-status congruence and performance were less clear.[16] It is difficult to explain with confidence why Adams' highest technical performance groups were low-status congruent. Comparable data on social structure, motivation, satisfaction, and formal leadership might have provided clearer explanations.

Not only the possible difference between these two studies, but the findings of other researchers in the general area of the status and how people react to it, all indicate that not enough is known yet about this subject to offer inclusive explanations for work-group behavior. For example, Zaleznik's machine shop workers[17] had developed a social structure which offered its members at least a minimal level of satisfaction. In comparison to other studies, his workers could be said to have exhibited low individual and group-status congruence, although

the congruence apparently was high enough for the group to form: it contained no Bolsheviks or Andaman Islanders. In short, the existing findings in this area suggest, but not conclusively, that under most industrial conditions, a group will be more cohesive to the extent to which its members exhibit individual and/or group-status congruence. (An important exception will be discussed under Column 7 of Exhibit 1).

The remaining columns, 4 through 7, show those situations where neither technological restrictions on interaction, nor the given sentiments of workers (e.g., notions of member attraction stemming from status factors in common) are such as to prevent the formation of a satisfying social structure. Rather the constrictions on group development portrayed here stem largely from the behavior of the formal leader of the work group.

Leadership Behavior

Since leadership is important here, it will be useful, before turning to the columns themselves, to describe roughly the leadership behavior under three different types.[18] The labels "accommodative," "production-centered," and "group-centered" will be briefly described, in that order.

The first, "accommodative," refers to situations where the leader's behavior neither challenges a group, nor seriously violates its norms of how a leader should behave. The group's determination of its own work procedures is left alone. As a result, the formal leader does not seriously threaten the group's survival as a group.

This condition is a common one and was described in the following reports:

---

[16] However, the two studies do not necessarily contradict each other on this point, since Clark studied no stores with status-congruence measures as high as some of the bomber crews studied by Adams. Also, the two studies used different status factors, and different ways to measure group-status congruence. Clark's research is continuing in an attempt to test for lower labor efficiency under conditions of higher group-status congruence.

[17] A. Zaleznik, *Worker Satisfaction and Development,* Harvard University Division of Research, Graduate School of Business Administration, Boston, Mass., 1956.

---

[18] It is beyond the scope of this article to evaluate these labels or to offer a different classification scheme.

In the Whirlwind Corporation[19] a group of workers developed an improved tool capable of increasing their productivity on a certain item fifty percent. Actually, they increased productivity ten percent and used the remaining time to improve quality on some products. A methods engineer was assigned to study the problem but the group withheld information about the tool from him. For some time, the foreman was aware of this but was "satisfied to let the men handle it their own way." He reasoned that at little expense he was able to get out production of high quality.

In Roy's research in a piecework machine shop[20] workers had an elaborate set of restriction-of-output activities. The foreman instructed new men in parts of this system. To one man he said:

> Say, when you punch off day work onto piecework, you ought to have your piecework already started. Run a few, then punch off day work, and you'll have a good start. You've got to chisel a little around here to make money.

In the Century Company,[21] workers in one area (B) reported that their foreman left them completely alone and had for several years. Prior to that time, he had supervised the men closely but they had taught him not to, by telling him that they would refuse to work if he didn't let them alone.

Although the three situations above point to different degrees of foreman involvement in the group, the uniformity among them is that the leader has ab-dicated any influence in the setting of work procedures. The group determines its procedures. A variety of labels other than "accommodative" have been devised to describe such a foreman: "laissez-faire," "abdicratic," etc.

Other researchers have pointed to the "production-centered" pattern of leadership behavior (and, moreover, suggested certain relations between such leadership and productivity).

In a study of productivity and leadership in an insurance company,[22] certain leaders were characterized as seeing their job primarily in terms of methods, procedures, and standards of production. Called production-centered leaders, by the researchers, it was noted that such leaders headed seven out of ten low-producing sections.

In the Century Company (I) case,[23] one foreman said this about his idea of a good worker:

> A good man is a man who is reasonable. . . . He does what the company tells him he should do. He does not try to do what he thinks he should do, but he does what he is told.

The people working for this foreman had these kinds of things to say about him:

> Whenever my foreman sees a man sitting down, he comes up to him and gives him something to do. . . . I don't think he'll be happy until he sees everybody running around all the time. [Our] foreman shouldn't yell at a man in front of everybody or nail him down. . . . This makes friction and breaks down the group.

Borrowing the phrase from the above-mentioned insurance company research,

---

[19] Paul Pigors and Charles H. Myers, *Personnel Administration, A Point of View and a Method*, McGraw-Hill Book Company, New York, 1956.
[20] Donald Roy, "Efficiency and the Fix: Informal Intergroup Relations in a Piecework Machine Shop," *American Journal of Sociology*, LX, No. 3 (1954).
[21] "Century Co. (A)–(I)," *op. cit.*

[22] Daniel Katz, N. Maccoby, and Nancy Morse, *Productivity, Supervision and Morale in an Office Situation*, Part I, Institute for Social Research, Ann Arbor, Mich., 1950.
[23] "Century Co. (A)–(I)," *op. cit.*

the Century Company researchers labelled this foreman "production-centered."

This kind of leader is the direct opposite of the accommodative type, in that he allows the employees little or no influence in the setting-up of work procedures. Influence is supposed to move downward only according to such a supervisor. Although we are calling such a leader production-centered, others have described him as "authoritarian," "autocratic," and "task-centered."

"Group-centered" leadership was indicated in the same two studies.

In the insurance company,[24] "employee-centered leadership" referred to supervisors who saw their job primarily in terms of the organization training, and motivation of subordinates. Such supervisors headed six of seven high-producing sections. The researchers said that:

> The supervisors of the high-producing sections . . . regard supervision as the most important part of their work. . . . Their method of supervision appears to be one of setting up certain general conditions for their employees and thus permitting their employees to work out the details of when and how the work will be handled.

In the Century Company case (I),[25] one foreman said this about his idea of a good worker:

> In my estimation, a good furnace worker is a man who has confidence in himself. . . . A foreman should show confidence in his men, and this should be real confidence. I'm always ready to show confidence in a man, even though at first sight I might think he doesn't deserve it. What I do is give some directions to a man and

then let him do his work without always being on his back. I want him to be free to do his work. . . . I realize that this requires a lot of talking on the part of the foreman. The men have to learn to trust their foreman. A foreman has to talk to his men to let himself be known by them. . . . Another thing, I like to tease the men, because it's one way for me to talk to them. It shows them I'm not dangerous.

The workers spoke about this foreman as follows:

> Last week when . . . . was our foreman we did not have any trouble. There were no complaints, no grievances, no beefs. It was hot and he understood that we were having more difficulty working at this temperature than at other times. After all a man needs encouragement.
>
> He knows how to run the men. I wish we could keep him for a long time. . . . We're not the only ones that have noticed he is good. Everywhere he has been in the company, people have been glad to work for him.

The researchers classified this foreman as "group-centered."

This kind of leader has been described as "democratic," "group-centered," "employee-centered," etc. In this paper, the group-centered label will be used. Regardless of the label, however, it can be seen that such a leader allows and encourages a *mutual* influence relationship with his men. Both the leader and his subordinates play a role in the setting-up of work procedures and the mutuality is made legitimate and encouraged by this kind of leader.

Returning to the Exhibit 1 diagram, *Column 4* shows the effects of the production-centered leadership condition in a situation where group formation potential is present. The behavior of a leader allowing low-influence oppor-

---

[24] Daniel Katz, N. Maccoby, and Nancy Morse, *op. cit.*
[25] "Century Co. (A)–(I)," *op. cit.*

tunity, as described above, would tend to prevent a group from forming a satisfying relationship with each other and to its environment. Because workers are more consciously forced to attend to their work, their membership needs are frustrated.

The Century Company[26] cases showed two groups of furnace workers, both with equal numbers of high and low individually status-congruent people. Workers in furnace area "A" had a production-centered foreman and exhibited less social development, while workers in furnace area "B" had an accommodative foreman and showed more social development. The researchers made an attempt to assess motivation, also, and there was considerably lower indication of membership need activation in area A than in area B. Moreover, of those judged active at this need level in area A, the majority appeared frustrated.

This study shows an instance in which membership needs were frustrated by a production-centered foreman: by holding workers rigidly to their required activities, he never permitted the social group to form, even though it was potentially capable of so forming. Incidentally, while accurate productivity data were not available for the two particular shift crews studied, area A as a whole (all four shift crews together) was producing much less than area B.

If production-centered leadership is introduced into a group that has already formed, however, there is some evidence to suggest that the group continues to function as a group: they unite around their hostility to management.

The "Case of the Changing Cage"[27] alluded to before illustrates this (although it contains no information about status congruence). The supervisor believed that

he could better control output by looking into this cage and thereby reducing nonwork behavior. In the old cage, he could not see in, but in the new cage he could. The result, however, was the nonwork activities actually increased (although they were less visible: the group went underground).

Whether or not such a situation is indicative of frustrated membership needs is difficult to say. Perhaps it can be said, though, that this group was simply elaborating its membership needs: under this condition, the nonwork behavior offered the only *possibility* for need satisfaction.

Columns 1 through 4 have all illustrated how environmental conditions can restrict the development of social structure in work groups. In addition, they also illustrated motivational consequences at lower-need levels only. The remaining columns show situations in which there is indication that higher-need levels can become activated. Since, in a formal organization, people activated at these higher-need levels show a tendency to contribute their judgment and productiveness to the organization's task, the term "contributive motivation" may sometimes be a useful shorthand for all the need levels above the membership level. We shall use it occasionally in the rest of this paper.

Column 5 shows two changes in comparison to Column 4. One, the satisfaction of membership needs, comes from the accommodative leader who, by not threatening the group too much, allows it to form and perpetuate itself. The second change is the frustration of the esteem needs, due to the introduction of a condition which might be labelled "low-perceived contribution opportunity." This refers to a worker's perception of a technological process as being predetermined for the most part. Here, except for the opportunity for an occasional

---

[26] *Ibid.*
[27] Cara Richards and Henry Dobyns, *op. cit.*

change in setup, technology, etc., a member of a social group at work sees no continuing opportunity to contribute anything, to make a difference, to initiate, along with other members of this group, something useful on his environment. The Column five situation has often been described in organizational behavior research at the worker level because it is undoubtedly the most common. The self-esteem and status-prestige needs are released, because membership needs are relatively satisfied, but, since the workers' jobs prevent any satisfying feelings of group competence or mastery to emerge, and because the accommodative foreman has no concept of getting his group involved in setting up any of its own procedures, the esteem needs are frustrated. Typical comments of workers in such situations are:

> A job is a job.
> You have to work so it might as well be here as anywhere.
> This job isn't bad: it's a nice bunch of guys but any moron could do the work [etc.].

It appears as if the "regulars" in the Zaleznik, Christensen, Roethlisberger prediction study[28] and the famous bank-wiring room workers[29] illustrate this column. Under such conditions, workers' productivity and satisfaction are determined mainly by their position in the social structure, since they are "stuck" on the membership level. Little, if any, opportunity for the satisfaction of contributive motivation exists.

Column 6 differs from Column 5 in that it shows the satisfied self-esteem need under conditions of a high perceived contribution opportunity, but a frustrated status-prestige need (frustrated by the lack of recognition on the part of an accommodative foreman) which the worker would feel was justified by his competence. The accommodative leader allows a group to develop simply by not being around or bothering to impede it. His *not* being around or *not* understanding the forces which motivate productiveness (i. e., self-esteem around job competence) make him less likely to reward the work with verbal or economic recognition of these perceived skills.

This motivational pattern and these environmental conditions were seen in the previously referred to Century Company case.[30] Workers in one furnace area (B) were glad their foreman was not around to interfere with their non-work activities and their exercising of skill and judgment in their work. However, they resented the fact that he did not *understand* the extent of their technical competence and hence could not reward them adequately when it came time for him to evaluate them.

Before leaving columns 1 through 6, which all illustrate one or another form of what Roethlisberger has called "frozen groups,"[31] another condition should be mentioned: "perception of company supportiveness." It has not been studied in enough situations to allow us to place it somewhere in columns 1 through 6; however two studies suggest its importance.

Seashore[32] found high cohesive groups tended to produce significantly higher than average when they reported a high perception of company supportiveness and to produce significantly lower than

28 A. Zaleznik, C. R. Christensen, and F. J. Roethlisberger, *op. cit.*
29 Where there is a suggestion (untested) that social structure was determined by individual status congruence. Cf. F. J. Roethlisberger and W. J. Dickson, *op. cit.*

30 "Century Co. (A)–(I)," *op. cit.*
31 A. Zaleznik, *op. cit.*
32 S. A. Seashore, *Group Cohesiveness in the Industrial Work Group,* Survey Research Center, University of Michigan, Ann Arbor, Mich., 1954.

average when they reported a low perception of company supportiveness.

In a piecework machine shop studied by Collins, *et al.*,[33] a work group had an elaborate system of output restriction. The accommodative foreman knew about and actively supported the system. The general superintendent, however, exerted much effort in an attempt to break it up. He told workers they should not accept group pressure to conform and that they were foolish and dishonest if they did. The men saw the over-all company as being hostile toward them and went to considerable lengths to restrict output: they often finished their day's work in three or four hours, they had jigs and fixtures which increased their hourly productivity but which were unknown to management, etc.

Column 7 shows a condition that has only recently been analytically studied on a continuing basis in industry. However, studies concerning group participation in the process of instituting technological change (e.g., the well-known relay assembly test room[34] and Coch and French[35] studies) might illustrate this situation for temporary periods where workers were involved in, and given recognition for, their ability to contribute to important organizational problems. Perhaps, too, the Lamson Company case[36] points to such a condition.

Skilled, experienced oil refinery workers were taken off their old job, given an extensive training course, and placed in a new tower. For several months they worked alongside the engineers who were installing and "de-bugging" the new and complicated equipment. Their suggestions were encouraged and accepted by the engineers and the men's behavior indicated they were highly satisfied with the experience.

Workers in such situations appear to be motivated at the higher need levels and to exist under maximal environmental conditions: they have a high opportunity to interact, a task to which they see a high opportunity to contribute and a leader who sets up a high opportunity for mutual influence between himself and his subordinates. Moreover, we can infer, too, that such workers would exist in an organizational environment which they saw as supportive. In addition, one study in an electronics factory (not yet published) suggests that the remaining environmental condition, high-status congruence, is a prerequisite for the motivation pattern seen in Column 7.

However, in a recently published research by Barnes[37] members of an engineering group exhibited low individual and group-status congruence, yet had high opportunity to interact, high opportunity for mutual influence and a high contribution opportunity. A few individuals, considered as a collection, had high group-status congruence, yet the social structure was not determined by this fact. Moreover, much of the group looked as if they might be exhibiting the need pattern seen in Column 7.

Barnes' research suggests, therefore, that, when all other conditions are met, a group's social behavior is not "frozen" by the status factors its members brought

---

[33] Orville Collins, Melville Dalton, and Donald Roy, "Restriction of Output and Social Cleavage in Industry," *Applied Anthropology*, V, No. 3 (1946).

[34] F. J. Roethlisberger and W. J. Dickson, *op. cit.*

[35] L. Coch and J. R. P. French, "Overcoming Resistance to Change," *Human Relations*, I, 512-532. [Presented as Reading in Part IV.]

[36] "Lamson Co.," Harvard Business School, HP 318.

[37] Louis B. Barnes, *Organizational Systems and Engineering Groups*, Harvard University Division of Research, Graduate School of Business Administration, Boston, Massachusetts, 1960.

with them. If one is interested in the growth and development of individuals in an organization, Barnes' study points to a helpful situation.

Summary and Conclusion

By carefully examining Exhibit 1 we have attempted to describe factors which both release and constrain different motivations in members of industrial work groups. In addition, we have shown how, according to Maslow's theory, relative satisfaction of certain needs may release other needs which alter the picture. Roughly, the following diagram illustrates this process and is nothing more than a simplified restatement of Exhibit 1.

Incidentally, the similarity between Exhibit 2 and the small group conceptual scheme of Homans'[38] is obvious. "Contribution opportunity" refers to the extent to which an individual's "required activities" are not so highly programmed that no room is left for the individual's contribution to them. "Interaction opportunity" refers to the extent to which an individual's "required interactions" do not limit him from getting together, on a social as well as task basis, with others. "Influence opportunity," a function of leadership behavior, has an effect on an individual's motivation because of the kinds of "given sentiments" most of us appear to have about leadership: when we are closely controlled or highly programmed, this violates our expectations of a satisfying superior-subordinate behavior. "Status congruence" refers to another large body of "given sentiments" most people seem to have: ideas about status and class which are widespread in our culture.

Any emergent small group behavior feeds back on the givens, however, as

Homans and others have observed. And Exhibit 2 is oversimplified insofar as this feedback is not shown. Nevertheless, its importance is obvious, particularly if one must understand and/or deal with a group through time. For example, a foreman of a work group which, for various reasons, was producing too little might change his leadership behavior from accommodative to production-centered, thus, perhaps, frustrating membership and self-esteem needs. Another example of such feedback might exist in a group under a group-centered leader who allowed mutual influence opportunities and whose members were active at the membership and contributive levels. Conceivably, these members would see continuous contribution opportunities in their jobs, thereby releasing further contributive motivation. Another example, and one which a number of my colleagues at the Harvard Business School and myself hope to test specifically in a current project, is the possibility that the structure of a group operating on higher need levels will be less determined by the status congruence of its members than it was at an earlier time, when it was operating more at the membership level.

In conclusion, the obvious fact remains to be emphasized that better techniques for the measurement of need activation in workers must be developed before this broad-stroke explanatory theory can be refined, altered, or rejected in the organizational behavior area. Only one of the studies cited—and that not yet published except in case form[39]—made an explicit attempt to assess motivation in Maslow's terms.

Research takes time, though, and those of us concerned directly with the immediate here-and-now problems of executives cannot always wait for our own

---

[38] George C. Homans, *The Human Group*, Harcourt, Brace & Co., New York, 1950.

[39] "Century Co. (A)–(I)," *op. cit.*

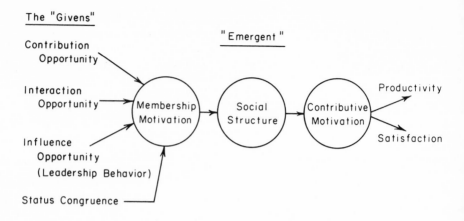

The "Givens"

Contribution
Opportunity

"Emergent"

Interaction
Opportunity

Membership
Motivation

Social
Structure

Contributive
Motivation

Productivity

Influence
Opportunity
(Leadership Behavior)

Satisfaction

Status Congruence

Exhibit 2

and others' patient and time-consuming testing of intriguing notions of potential utility to practicing administrators. And, it seems to me, an administrator *can* use this general way of thinking to predict, at least on a gross basis, that certain consequences are quite likely to follow from the "givens" in any situation. Such a prediction might be economically valuable to him. He might, for example, behave differently during a technological or organizational change than he would have if he were not aware of the suggested effects of low interaction opportunity and contribution potential on motivation, social structure and productivity, and satisfaction. Conversely, if he

were experiencing severe problems of dissatisfaction in his work force, he might seek to understand them in terms of this theory, and thereby highlight some "givens" which might be changed: interaction opportunity, for example. Such a change might cut down grievances, or even avert a strike.

Hopefully, this paper may serve to stimulate some better ways of testing the utility of Maslow's concepts for the study of organizational behavior. Certainly we are in need of integrative and operational concepts that both form the basis for replicable and comparative research and offer some utility to the practicing administrator.

Motivation and Employee Turnover. Because of its considerable contribution to labor costs, employee turnover has been the focus of much attention as Reading 2-6 has indicated. Two studies of turnover are of particular interest to us because of the additional light they shed on motivational factors in the work situation. Both emphasize the influence of psychological satisfactions, such as those described by Herzberg and Mausner on the rate of employee turnover. Summaries of the studies are presented in Research Summaries 2-6 and 2-7.

RESEARCH **SUMMARY** **2-6**	*Need Satisfaction and Employee Turnover.* In a study conducted at the Research Center for Group Dynamics of the University of Michigan, Ross and Zander obtained questionnaire data from 2,680 skilled female workers living in various large cities and em-

ployed in 48 sections of a large company. The study was designed to discover whether or not there was a demonstrable relation between the satisfaction of certain psychological needs in an employment situation and labor turnover. In testing this relation, the researchers sought data measuring the strength of five needs: affiliation, achievement, autonomy, recognition, and fair evaluation; and, in addition, the degree to which these needs were satisfied on the job. The questionnaire also provided data on the degree to which the job prevented gratification of needs in family and social life. Four months after the questionnaires were completed, 169 of the original group had resigned. For each of these individuals, two matched controls were selected from the same section, doing the same work, with comparable experiences, and in similar financial circumstances (so far as they could be determined). Job dissatisfaction scores were then computed for those who had resigned and for their controls by subtracting the degree of opportunity for satisfaction of each of the five needs on the job from the strength of this need expressed by the individual. The results indicate that where needs for recognition and autonomy, particularly, but also for achievement and fair evaluation were not being met, there was greater likelihood of turnover. In addition, where the job was seen as interfering with home and social life, there was greater turnover.

Ross and Zander here provide convincing evidence to support some aspects of current motivational theory and the findings of Blauner and Herzberg and the analysis presented by Clark. Their study is, of course, limited to an all-female group. The question must be asked whether these results can be generalized to male employees. Another limiting aspect of the study is that no evidence was available on the effect of increased salary as a substitute for deprivation of personal needs. Can you pay people enough so that they will stay on the job despite lack of opportunity for satisfying such important needs as those studied here? The next study by Wickert touches, as a side issue, on turnover and satisfaction with salary.

<table>
<tr><td>

RESEARCH

SUMMARY

2-7

</td><td>

Some Other Correlates of Employee Turnover. Trying to find the factors that determine turnover can lead down many paths. Wickert used a variety of empirical measures with almost 600 young women who were employees of the Michigan Bell Telephone Co. between 1945 and 1948. One path that he followed was to see if the "turnover-prone" employee could be predicted from the biographical data available at the time of employment; another path was to use employment test scores for the prediction. Neither of these sorts of data had any relation to turnover, nor did a score of "neurotic tendency" from 60 personality items show any relationship.

The path that led somewhere, in this study, had to do with the way the girls felt about their work. The point of striking difference between those who stayed with the company and those who left was the greater feeling of ego-involvement in the day-to-day operations of the company within those who stayed. This showed

</td></tr>
</table>

itself in two important ways: those who stayed with the company were much more likely to say that (1) they had a chance to make decisions on their jobs; and, (2) they felt they were making an important contribution to the success of the company. Although the difference between the groups in these attitudes was marked, for other attitude areas no relation to turnover was found. For instance, those girls who had left the company were not any more critical of company policies than those who stayed, and the former even felt better about their wages than those remaining. Thus, it is not, Wickert feels, a generalized attitude that was relevant to turnover, but the ego-involvement with the work. The administrator must be aware, in interpreting this study, that it is not whether *he* feels that the employees make decisions but whether *they* feel that they do that is important. He can also see that although women value such aspects of the working environment as congenial associates, attractive surroundings, and a pleasant supervisor, the interest of women in their work is more substantial than has often been thought. To tap the desire of employees—men or women—to feel that they are making a worthwhile contribution and participating in decisions is (as many other studies have shown) to tap an important source of high morale.

Concluding Statement: Needs, Job Satisfaction, and Job Performance

The impression should not be given that turnover, productivity, or any other organizational index will always correlate with satisfaction or morale. As Argyris has emphasized, there is no reason to assume that the needs of the individual and the needs of the organization should coincide. Sometimes turnover, absenteeism, or productivity figures have been related to attitudes and sometimes not, depending on conditions specific to the situation (Brayfield and Crockett). Katzell, Barrett, and Parker have found, for instance, that job satisfaction was associated neither with turnover, nor with quality of production, but was significantly related to quantity of production and to profitability. In their study, an important situational characteristic was that work settings showing a small town culture pattern were more likely to show high employee job satisfaction and productivity than situations with greater urbanization. Cureton and Katzell, in factor analyzing these data, found that the relation between degree of urbanization and job performance separated into two aspects: one, the small size of the plant and the community (low urbanization) was associated with relatively high productivity and profitability; but, two, low wages, absence of a union, and proportionately fewer male employees (regardless of degree of urbanization) were associated with high turnover. In other studies (as Readings 2-5 and 2-6 have shown), different specific situational factors may play a key role in determining the extent of the relation between satisfaction and performance.

It would be nice, then, but not accurate, to say that when an employee's

TABLE 2-2

Some Interacting Influences Affecting Feelings and Behavior on the Job

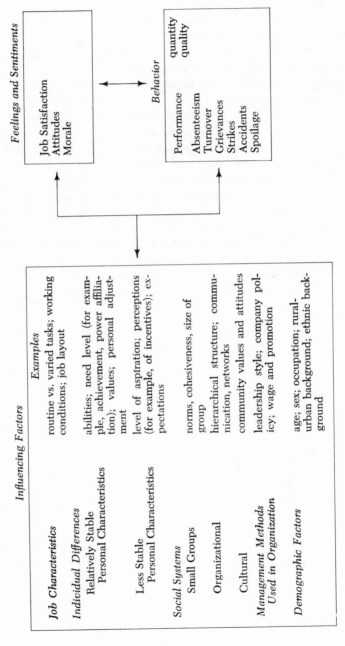

Feelings and Sentiments

Job Satisfaction
Attitudes
Morale

Behavior

Performance — quantity / quality
Absenteeism
Turnover
Grievances
Strikes
Accidents
Spoilage

Influencing Factors — *Examples*

Job Characteristics — routine vs. varied tasks; working conditions; job layout

Individual Differences
Relatively Stable Personal Characteristics — abilities; need level (for example, achievement, power affiliation); values; personal adjustment

Less Stable Personal Characteristics — level of aspiration; perceptions (for example, of incentives); expectations

Social Systems
Small Groups — norms, cohesiveness, size of group

Organizational — hierarchical structure; communication, networks

Cultural — community values and attitudes

Management Methods Used in Organization — leadership style; company policy; wage and promotion

Demographic Factors — age; sex; occupation; rural-urban background; ethnic background

needs are largely satisfied he always expresses this feeling of satisfaction in high level performance on the job.

The fact that satisfaction measures have not always related directly to performance does not remove the fact that they often do, and that the manager must recognize the possibility. For example, Kornhauser and Hagstrom describing a study of scientists in industry point out, "Where scientific standards and aspirations are weak (in the company or surrounding work groups) the quality of scientific performance (of the scientists) will not be high. Hence where industry dampens the motivation of scientists to participate in outside professional activities, industrial research suffers." The manager is in a position in which he can influence the degree to which people feel satisfied on the job and feel that their needs are being recognized and fulfilled. The extent to which the people are satisfied with their jobs may show directly, at times, in production, absenteeism, turnover, quality of work, or other performance indicators.

A variety of interacting influences make a simple and consistent relation between satisfaction and performance unlikely. Some idea of the complexity of the relationship is suggested in Table 2-2 which lists some of the major influences on: 1) feelings of satisfaction; 2) behavior on the job; and 3) the relation between the two. The hazards of sweeping generalizations can be seen in this sketch of the many specific and interacting influences that operate.

PART THREE

Reactions to Stress: Frustration, Anxiety, and Conflict

Introduction

Not all behavior that the administrator sees or must deal with in the organization results from someone's seeking satisfaction of such needs as we have discussed in Part Two. Some of the behavior he observes is the individual's reaction to a *failure* to satisfy his needs. In Part Two we described goal-oriented behavior; in the present part we discuss some of the things that happen when we do not reach our goals. Response to environmental stress that threatens or blocks need satisfaction is complex. Under some conditions, the resulting increase in internal tension may mobilize more energy for effective goal striving. Under other conditions, much of the activity may be directed toward reducing the unpleasant tensions indirectly through nongoal oriented defensive behavior.

Doob has labeled frustration, anxiety, and conflict—the principal feeling states that result from external stress—psychological adversities. They are normal adversities besetting anyone who must live in even the simplest society. The business organization, as a complex institution that plays a significant part in the life of its members, generates many such adversities for its managers and employees. Its competitive, hierarchical, and often authoritarian nature, as well as the necessary limits on available rewards, make feelings of frustration an inevitable, although preferably an occasional, experience. Both because it would be unwise (and impossible) to provide such absolute security as to eliminate all uncertainty and because people carry with them different predispositions to be anxious, anxiety develops as an important part of organizational life. Conditions associated with the individual's memberships in groups make conflict within people a frequent occurrence. Some of these conditions are the diversity of demands from formal and informal groups, explicit and implicit norms, uncertain role expectations and in general, a lack of sharply delineated, universally accepted values in the organization.

The administrator cannot hope to protect his people from psychological adversity, except extreme and unreasonable instances of it, but rather must try to understand behavior that results from such adversity, minimizing the negative influences for both the individual and the organization, and, where possible, turning these experiences to advantage. Although frustration, anxiety, and conflict are normal human experiences to be expected in an ordinary administrative day, in extreme form they can also provide the basis for unhealthy behavior. No one should expect the administrator to be a psychiatrist, but an understanding

FIGURE 3-1

A Schema Suggesting Some Relations Between Environmental Stress and Behavior

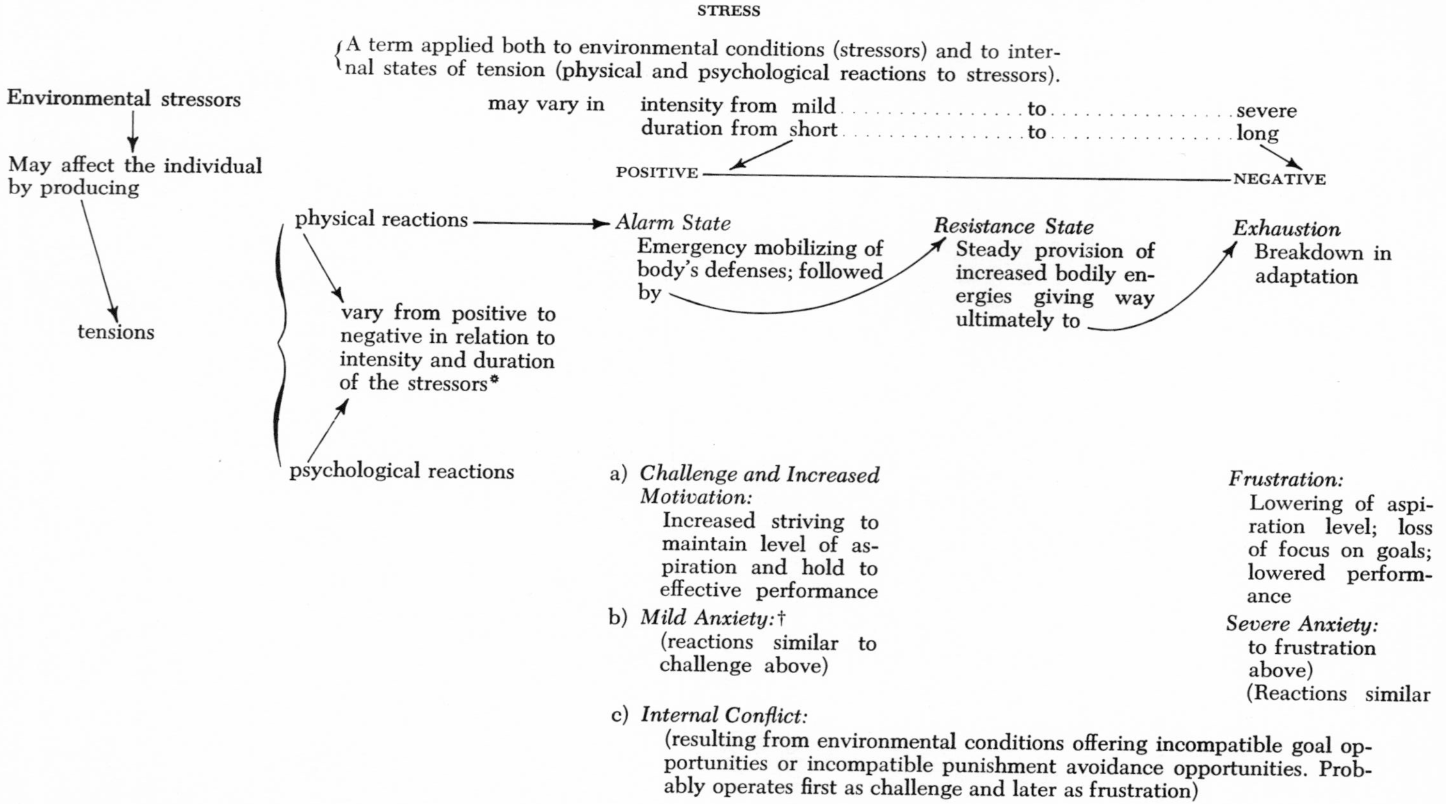

STRESS

{ A term applied both to environmental conditions (stressors) and to internal states of tension (physical and psychological reactions to stressors). }

may vary in   intensity from mild .... to .... severe

              duration from short .... to .... long

POSITIVE ———————————————— NEGATIVE

Alarm State
Emergency mobilizing of body's defenses; followed by

Resistance State
Steady provision of increased bodily energies giving way ultimately to

Exhaustion
Breakdown in adaptation

physical reactions ——→

vary from positive to negative in relation to intensity and duration of the stressors*

psychological reactions ——→

a) *Challenge and Increased Motivation:*
Increased striving to maintain level of aspiration and hold to effective performance

b) *Mild Anxiety:*†
(reactions similar to challenge above)

c) *Internal Conflict:*
(resulting from environmental conditions offering incompatible goal opportunities or incompatible punishment avoidance opportunities. Probably operates first as challenge and later as frustration)

Frustration:
Lowering of aspiration level; loss of focus on goals; lowered performance

Severe Anxiety:
to frustration above)
(Reactions similar

Environmental stressors

May affect the individual by producing

tensions

* The response shift from positive to negative is dependent not only on intensity and duration of stressors but also on characteristics of individuals, for example, strength of personal adjustment, prior exposure to stress.
† For anxiety-prone individuals mild stressors can raise already high levels of anxiety to cause negative reactions.

of the ways in which people in his organization respond to their tensions will aid him and his employees.

The problem in trying to provide that understanding is a two-fold one:

1. Authors writing in the field use similar terms with somewhat different meanings. For example, frustration is used to describe the process of interfering with an individual's direct progress toward a goal (see the Child and Waterhouse Reading (Ch. Seven); it is also used to describe a feeling or state *within* the individual (see Maier and McNeil Ch. Seven). Anxiety may be used in a psychiatric sense to suggest a disabling and unconsciously rooted dread of one's own impulses; it may also designate an appropriate response to some external threat to one's feelings of self-esteem. Conflict is used to describe behavior of groups that are pulling against each other, rivalries between individuals, and subjective uncertainty within the individual.

2. Each of the three terms overlap each other in many of their meanings. An individual experiencing conflict may be frustrated in his desire to achieve some goal. A threat to one's feelings of self-esteem resulting in anxiety may soon develop into real cause for experiencing a sense of deep frustration.

Despite confusion about terms, there are many well established facts in the area that administrators ought to know. In an effort to get at the facts and try to avoid the terminological confusion, we provide our own introductory schema. (See Figure 3-1.) With this schema, the reader can see the place of the subsequent readings and research summaries, so that the facts presented (about which there is agreement) can be brought into focus and the problem of terminology placed in the background.

Preview of Part Three

Immediately following this preview we cite the work of Torrance and of Selye (see Coleman), both of whom, from somewhat different points of view, analyze over-all response to stress. The chapters that follow provide a more detailed picture of response to particular types of stress: frustration, anxiety, and conflict.

Chapter Seven considers both the event that frustrates and the internal state of frustration. Child and Waterhouse describe aspects of such events that lead to a sense of challenge and motivation, and other aspects that lower performance level. Maier contrasts goal oriented behavior with frustrated, nongoal-oriented behavior. McNeil provides a comprehensive survey of research in the area and identifies some reactions to the internal state of frustration.

After starting with a reading by May that distinguishes normal from neurotic anxiety, Chapter Eight attempts to assess the effect of anxiety on performance. Three major problems are considered: the intensity of the anxiety, the anxiety proneness of the individual, and some forces that channelize behavior motivated by anxiety. The chapter provides a description of some specific effects of anxiety: for example, worry and psychosomatic ailment; and concludes with a discussion of some traits of the mature personality by Feinberg.

Chapter Nine considers internal conflict, psychologically described in a brief reading by McNeil. The remainder of the chapter considers two specialized aspects of conflict: cognitive dissonance and its motivating influence on behavior (Festinger), and the matter of post-decisional conflict (Janis). On the latter issue, Janis' study helps identify ways of minimizing conflict once a decision is made.

Reactions to Stress: General Statement

Because the word stress is used to refer both to an external event and to an internal state, our schema (Figure 3-1) uses the term "stressor" for the event, and "tension" for the internal experience. Stressor is thus defined as disturbance or strain in the environment. Under the heading of stressor we include such events as: obstacles in the paths of goals, unreasonable, exacting, or incompatible demands, and uncertain role prescriptions. Of a different sort, but also included under stressors are: noise, uncomfortable temperatures, food deprivation, and taxing work conditions.

Environmental stressors produce both physical and psychological tension states in the individual, and these may help or hinder him in his goal striving efforts. Figure 3-1 suggests some general relationships between stressors, internal tensions, and subsequent performance. The chapters that follow provide more specific detail and research on the matter.

Two things need to be said about stressors in this context:

1. The individual's response to a stressor will vary with its degree and duration, its nature, the quality of leadership available, the characteristics of the individual, and the group to which he belongs. (See the later summary of Torrance's research.)

2. The presence or absence of stressors in the organization environment, and their characteristics, are to some extent subject to control by the administrator. When he can, he will want to control (or use) them in relation to his knowledge of what effects particular stressors will have on the performance of organizational members.

Before proceeding to a more detailed description of the individual's response to particular stressors, we present two points of view that provide a more general picture of the effect of external stress on the individual. (See Research Summary 3-1 and Reading 3-1 following.)

RESEARCH **SUMMARY** **3-1**	*Some Conditions That Influence Response to Environmental Stressors.* For more than ten years, Torrance has been systematically studying the reactions of military groups to a wide variety of environmental stressors. He has conducted his studies under realistic field conditions but has, nevertheless, provided the necessary controls to assure careful observation and measurement. His 1961 summary of this research provides the basis for some generalizations about the effects of external stress. Torrance's work indicates that: 1. At least in their initial impact stressors increase the variability of behavior and reduce its consistency.

2. Moderate external stress tends to produce some performance improvements; severe stress results in disorganized performance.
3. The initial response to even moderate stressors is shock or resistance; this is followed by recovery and even overcompensation. If the stress is extreme or continues over a long period of time, lowered performance and, ultimately, collapse or breakdown occur.
4. Effective leadership and healthy interpersonal relations reduce the initial shock reaction and make possible a longer period of adaptation to unabated stress.*

Before an attempt is made to apply Torrance's conclusions to the administrative situation, several limiting characteristics of his studies must be allowed for: Torrance's subjects were all under military discipline and sensitive to the *esprit de corps* characteristic of well-trained military groups; all of his subjects were performing in a group setting with available support from closely associated peers and leaders; finally, his conclusions report averaged results, and the wide individual differences in response to stressors are not indicated in the conclusions we present. We will have opportunity to examine this latter problem in subsequent comment.

* Indik reports that for a group of 6,000 industrially employed individuals the amount of subjectively experienced tension, resulting from environmental stress is related to superior-subordinate relations. Where leadership is perceived as being supportive, stressors in the environment produce less tension.

READING 3-1

The General-Adaptation-Syndrome*

JAMES C. COLEMAN

. . .

A theoretical approach that helps to explain the effects of continued stress on the human system has been formulated by the prominent endocrinologist, Hans Selye. According to Selye's theory, the organism's reaction to severe, unresolved stress occurs in three major stages: the *alarm reaction,* the *stage of resistance,* and the *stage of exhaustion.*

1. *The alarm reaction.* The alarm reaction is a call-to-arms to the body's defense forces in the face of biological

or psychological stress. The alarm reaction consists of various biochemical changes mediated primarily by the autonomic nervous system which mobilize the organism's bodily defenses. The emergency mobilization already discussed is part of this process.

The initial physiological changes in response to stress tend to have much the same characteristics regardless of the nature of the stress. This accounts for the similarity of the general symptoms (such as fever, fatigue, and loss of appetite) of people suffering from different specific illnesses. Selye uses the term *general stress reaction* to refer to these changes.

* Excerpted from *Personality Dynamics and Effective Behavior,* copyright © 1960 by Scott, Foresman and Company, Chicago, pp. 170-172.

2. *The stage of resistance.* If the stressful situation continues, the alarm stage is typically followed by the stage of resistance in which the system evidently "learns" how to adapt to the particular stress, and the symptoms that occurred during the alarm stage disappear even though the stress continues. This resistance is achieved largely through increased activity of the anterior pituitary and the adrenal cortex, though more specific adaptations may also be made in blood chemistry, nutrition, or other processes. For example, continued exposure to lowered oxygen content in the air gradually results in an adaptation that permits subjects to perform work at high altitudes which would have been impossible at the beginning.

During the stage of resistance, most of the symptoms which occurred during the alarm reaction disappear, and physiological processes seem to resume normal functioning. If successful adaptation is achieved in this stage, the individual can cope with the stress over a considerable period of time. Sometimes, however, the hormonal defenses overshoot their mark and lead to bodily damage and pathology such as ulcers or other "diseases of adaptation."

3. *The stage of exhaustion.* If the stress continues too long or becomes too severe or if the organism is unable to make an effective adaptation during the stage of resistance, the bodily defenses eventually break down, leading to a stage of exhaustion. The anterior pituitary and the adrenal cortex are no longer able to continue secreting their hormones at the increased rate, so that there is a lowering in stress tolerance and a breakdown of whatever adaptation has been achieved. Now many of the symptoms which appeared during the alarm reaction begin to reappear, and the integration of the system is seriously impaired. Further exposure to the stress leads eventually to disintegration and death.

When the stress represents a threat to the self-structure rather than to the body, various psychological defenses are mustered in addition to the physiological ones described by Selye. Thus, the individual may be able to develop resistance to a psychological stress by learning new competencies or increasing his stress tolerance in other constructive ways. Or he may be able to erect defenses stable enough to protect him fairly well from the threat and allow him to maintain coordinated functioning. But any heavy, long-continued stress takes its toll, and eventually it may exceed his adjustive resources.

CHAPTER SEVEN

Frustrating
Events
and
Their
Effects

An Analysis of Factors Producing Positive and
Negative Reactions to Frustrating Stress

A particular kind of stress is the type that places obstacles in the direct path of the individual's movement toward a goal. We will call this frustrating stress. Although Child and Waterhouse, the authors of the reading that follows, use the term *frustration*, they clearly define it to mean an event, not an internal feeling state.

Torrance has indicated that mild to moderate stress improves performance; extreme stress lowers the performance level. Child and Waterhouse analyze in more detailed fashion the relationship between frustration (frustrating stress) and the quality of subsequent performance. They recognize that frustrating events may either improve or diminish the quality of performance.

Administrators, on the other hand, often uncritically think of the effects of frustrating stress upon employee performance from either of two extreme attitudinal positions: 1) frustrating stress will serve as a challenge to anyone, and, therefore, employees should not have things made too comfortable for them, or 2) trouble can be expected from an employee who has had to be frustrated, with resentment and a decline in work as the result. Neither attitude can be supported completely by the research evidence. The Child-Waterhouse analysis summarizes and interprets that evidence.

READING 3-2

Frustration and the Quality of Performance: II. A Theoretical Statement*

IRVIN L. CHILD AND
IAN K. WATERHOUSE

What is the effect of frustration on the quality of performance? There appears to be a dual tradition in the writings of psychologists and others who have given attention to this problem.

First, there is a tradition that frustration leads to improved quality of performance. Dewey's often cited account of why thinking occurs stresses the role of a problem or difficulty as the occasion for creative intellectual activity. Difficulty in such a situation often is an instance of frustration.[1] In more general accounts of the psychology of adjustment, unreduced tension is shown as giving rise to various forms of adjustment, of which some may be of high intellectual quality. On the level of

society as a whole there are notions such as Toynbee's—that the protracted existence of a challenge, often in the form of difficulty in meeting the needs of bare subsistence, is the condition for the joint constructive activity that produces a new civilization.

Second, there is also a tradition that frustration leads to lowered quality of performance. This is perhaps the more apparent part of the thesis of psychoanalysis and psychology of adjustment, since, on the whole, adjustments of poor quality to frustration have received the greater attention from therapists. This tradition is also evident in much of the discussion about the disorganizing effects of emotion (as reviewed, e.g., by Leeper), inasmuch as emotion is often produced by frustration. Barker, Dembo, and Lewin's study of frustration and regression is often cited in simple confirmation of this tradition, to the neglect of the rest of its content. Most recently this tradition is represented in Maier's systematization of the effects of frustration, as most of the effects he deals with would doubtless be considered to be of poor intellectual quality. [See Reading 3-3.]

There is, then, an apparent conflict of belief in this matter. Indeed, the conflict appears strikingly in some general textbooks in psychology. In a chapter on thinking and reasoning frustration

* Excerpted from Frustration and the Quality of Performance, *Psychological Review*, 60, # 2 (1953) pp. 138-39.
[1] We are using *frustration* in a broad sense to refer to prevention of a person's direct progress toward a goal, not wishing to prejudge by definition the importance of various distinctions that can be made among the variety of events that fit this definition. We heartily agree with Brown and Farber's emphasis on the need to distinguish sharply between this definition of frustration and its definition as referring to a state of the organism. But we feel it more useful to apply the term to the *event* of prevention of a person's progress toward his goal than to a *state* which may in some cases be inferred from the event.

is viewed as the condition for more organized behavior, and in a chapter on emotion it is viewed as the condition for less organized behavior. The failure to use a common term such as frustration in the two chapters apparently permits the contradiction to go unnoticed.

Is this apparent contradiction due merely to failure to appreciate the role of severity of frustration, minor frustra- tions leading in fact to an improvement in quality of performance and major frustrations to the opposite, as might be inferred from the settings in which these contrary effects are often discussed? Presumably not in any very uniform way, else why would anyone swear when he stubbed his toe, and how could any prisoner ever carry through successfully an ingenious plan for escape?

Child and Waterhouse continue by examining available relevant research on just how frustration does influence performance. From the research available, some conclusions are drawn by the authors; we summarize those that might appropriately be related to behavior in the organization.

The conclusions show the possibility of either positive or negative effects of frustration in three situations; some factors leading to either outcome are identified.

Frustration in Task A, and Its Effects on Task B

Negative Effects: In some individuals, under some circumstances, frustration* in one problem-solving area may lead to responses such as resentment, worry, or daydreaming that interfere with *other* problem-solving behavior, which the current situation may also demand. A concrete illustration may help to make the point. When a middle-management employee has been denied a request for a transfer to another branch of the company he may react with feelings of resentment and with tentative explorations to find another job. This response to frustration, of course, will interfere with his current work. Contrariwise, the absence of frustration might also interfere; if the transfer *were* arranged, it could divert attention from the important current assignment by introducing anticipatory thoughts of the new job, reduced motivation for the present tasks, and so on.

Positive Effects: For some individuals, under some circumstances, frustration of one activity may so increase the amount of drive or energy as to make more available for a second activity than would ordinarily be the case. This might be true where the second activity becomes more attractive to the individual because it is seen as the only available substitute. As Child and Waterhouse imply, an absolutely clear indication that the transfer is not coming through could clear the air in such fashion as to cause our hypothetical middle-management man to buckle down and concentrate on the work at hand. A manager, frustrated in his desire for a promotion, may accept appointment to a high status commitee as a substitute and work very hard at it. Available drive for other activities may also be increased where the frustration causes the in-

---

* Throughout our discussion of the Child and Waterhouse analysis, we use the word "frustration" in their sense of the word, a frustrating event, not a feeling state.

dividual to throw himself into other pursuits as a means of forgetting the original frustration. Needless to say, it is not easy to get frustrated people to do this.

Early Frustration in Task A, and Its Later Effects on Task A

What about the effect of *early* frustration in a problem-solving activity on the individual's continued efforts to solve the *same* problem? For example, suppose a staff member has begun early work on a special report and is rebuffed by his superior before he has proceeded very far. Are his subsequent efforts likely to be better or worse as a result of the frustration he experiences? We have discussed some effects on his level of aspiration (Part Two), but what of his performance?

In answering the question, Child and Waterhouse again suggest the danger of expecting the effect of such frustration to be either automatically positive or negative without taking account of the individual circumstances. The interacting effect of three influences would seem to be decisive: the degree to which the frustrated individual is involved in the problem-solving effort (in other words, how much does he care); the relevance and the adequacy of the early problem-solving effort; and finally, whether the frustrating situation or rebuff includes any cues for what would be considered more satisfactory behavior (that is, what can be done to improve). Two extreme illustrations may suggest how these factors influence the effect of frustration on behavior. Suppose that our staff member has fully committed himself to the task and has worked very hard, that his early efforts are the most adequate he can make for his ability and understanding of the problem, and furthermore that these efforts are simply rejected as unsuitable with no further comment. The resulting frustration will lead to even less satisfactory behavior, resentment will reduce his feelings of involvement, his next efforts will be at a lower level of competence, and his behavior will now lack goal direction. If any one of these factors had been different, the frustration might have raised the level of performance.

Stating the case in the opposite way, we can suggest conditions under which an *early* frustration can lead to improved performance. Suppose our individual has approached the task with only little interest, has worked at a level somewhat below his capacity, and the rejection included a description of what is really required to solve the problem. Under these conditions, and assuming an individual with normal security and self-confidence, the frustration should improve the level of his performance.

Major Frustration in Task A, and Its Effects on a Wide Range of Activity

The Child-Waterhouse analysis considers one other possibility. Where the frustration is pervasive and interferes with many of the individual's goal striving efforts, will its net effect on behavior be positive or negative? Once again, both possibilities must be considered. Which will actually prevail depends on the availability to the individual of skills, interests, and resources on which he might draw to overcome the negative influences of the frustration; the methods of responding (to frustration) that he has learned in his earlier life experiences,— for example, fight or flight or others—and the particular significance to the individual of the frustration.

Unfortunately, major adversity of the type described by Child and Water-house most often occurs when facilitating conditions are not present, and usually leads to progressive deterioration in the individual's adjustive efforts.

This, of course, is particularly true when the frustrating conditions continue over a long period of time or are widespread in the community. Rundquist and Sletto, in their study of the effects of the depression on personality, showed the demoralizing effects of not being able to find work, and the way in which despair and loss of self-confidence replaced drive for solving problems.

The Effect of Frustrating Stress as a Function of One's Expectations

Berkowitz, in reviewing other studies, and in several experiments of his own, gives further definition to the way in which frustrating stress affects behavior. His work and the evidence of two other studies presented in Research Summary 3-2 suggest the importance of what one expects in a situation in determining the effect of a frustrating event on behavior.

RESEARCH **SUMMARY** **3-2**	*Expectations and Frustrating Events.* In 1939, a classical analysis of the relation between frustration and aggressive reaction was presented by Dollard et al. These authors postulated that the strength of the aggressive reaction would depend on the strength of the response that was blocked by the frustrating event, the completeness with which the response was blocked, and the duration of the frustrating sequence. Berkowitz, in examining subsequent research on the last issue (the relation between duration and intensity of aggressive reaction) points to inconsistent findings. He cites two experiments. In one (Otis and McCandless) continuing frustrating stress produced increasing aggressive reaction. In the second (McClelland and Apicella) no relation was found between duration of the frustration and aggression. His analysis suggested that the explanation of the inconsistency might be found in the differing expectations held by subjects in the two experiments. In the first experiment, they simply did not expect to be continually blocked in their efforts: the aggressive responses, therefore, increased. In the second experiment, experimental conditions may have led the subjects to expect to be frustrated. What they expected, happened; consequently they showed less aggression to the continuing frustrating event. They nevertheless showed some aggressions.

With this possibility in mind, Berkowitz designed his own study to test the general hypothesis: the effect of a frustrating event on the victim's behavior (particularly the amount of aggression he shows) is in part a function of whether the frustrating event was expected or not.

In his experiment, subjects worked in pairs on a project that was named for their benefit "forming impressions." They were asked to make judgments of each other's personality on two separate occasions. The subjects were told that these judgments in each pair were being exchanged between the judge and the judged. Actually, statements prepared by the experimenter were substituted so that he could produce the following experimental conditions:

CONDITION I		CONDITION II	
First Judgment	*Second Judgment*	*First Judgment*	*Second Judgment*
Critical	Critical	Favorable	Critical

Under Condition II, with a frustrating critical evaluation not expected on the second judgment, the response to the frustrating event was much more hostile than under Condition I, in which the second critical judgment was expected.

Here then is evidence to identify another condition that influences the way in which an individual will respond to the stress of a frustrating event.

A study (Pepinsky et al.) of management strategy and team productivity conducted under laboratory conditions that simulated a bureaucratic organization's functioning, confirms Berkowitz' conclusion. It suggests, in addition, that when a group meets a frustrating event that is not expected, its organization and productivity suffer. Comparable teams of "employees" in "a toy manufacturing" operation worked under two different conditions. In one, "management" behaved according to previous commitment in approving or disapproving work procedures. In the second, "management" failed to back up its previous commitment to approve or disapprove in accordance with specified standards. Under the second condition, work teams met unexpected frustrating events. Groups working under condition two were disorganized and inefficient.

Spector's work on attitudes toward an expected or an unexpected promotion (previously cited in Chapter 5) supports the same point, negative outcomes of a frustrating event are most severe when the event is inconsistent with one's expectations.

From the evidence cited here, the administrator can draw two suggestions for his own practice: don't raise expectations that cannot be met; and, where possible, help people anticipate the possibility of meeting frustrations in their goal-striving behavior. In carrying out both suggestions, moderation and "common sense" are in order. Occasionally, plans have to be made with the concerned individual even before it is certain that an anticipated reward will occur. And in the other direction, too pessimistic an outlook on the part of the administrator can lower the individual's level of aspiration and also the intensity of his striving.

Reactions to Frustrating Stress: Summary Statement

As long as there are additional resources on which the individual can draw (additional energy, alternate paths to the goal) in the face of continuing frustrating stress, the individual will remain goal oriented and his performance may improve. He responds with a sense of challenge to the frustrating situation he faces.

At some point functionally related to both the resources and characteristics of the individual (for example, his expectations) *and* to the duration and intensity of the frustrating stress, the individual internalizes this sense of frustration. The focus is now on a frustrated individual, not the frustrating situation. He now begins to respond more to the unpleasantness of the feelings of frustration than he does to his previous goal.

A Comparison of Behavior Under Frustration and Under Motivation

Maier (1949), principally as an outcome of his own experimentation, has formulated a systematic approach to the problem of frustration as we are *now* defining it: a feeling state of the individual, not an external event. He makes a sharp distinction between frustrated behavior and motivated behavior. Once the distinction is made, the need to take different approaches in working with the two different types of behavior becomes apparent. We have selected a passage from Maier's book *Frustration: The Study of Behavior Without a Goal.* The author begins by listing the contrasting characteristics of frustrated and motivated behavior, and then suggests the different ways of dealing with each of the two types of behavior. Many of his suggestions can be readily carried over to the administrative situation with only slight modification.

READING 3-3

Behavior under Frustration and Motivation Contrasted[*]

NORMAN R. F. MAIER

When we assemble all the behavior properties associated with frustration and consider them to be descriptive of the frustration process, we find that they are quite different from those found in motivated problem solving and learning. At present a number of basic differences can be described.

1. A problem situation produces stereo- type behavior in the frustrated individual, whereas it produces variable behavior in the motivated individual.

2. Responses produced under frustration, in so far as they show fixation, are rigid and stereotyped to a degree that exceeds responses produced by rewarded learning. Thus the motivated individual is characterized by plasticity and the frustrated individual by rigidity.

3. Responses produced during frustration (such as abnormal fixations) are not responsive to alteration by punishment although reward-learned responses can be altered by punishment.

---

[*] Excerpted from *Frustration: The Study of Behavior Without a Goal,* N. R. F. Maier, McGraw-Hill Book Co., Inc., New York, 1949, pp. 159-161. Reprinted by University of Michigan Press: Ann Arbor Michigan, paperback series, 1961. Used by permission.

4. Punishment may serve as a frustrating agent and when this occurs a learned response may be replaced by a characteristic frustrated response.

5. Frustration-induced responses seem to be an end in themselves. They are not influenced by consequences except in so far as the consequences may alter the state of frustration, whereas motivated responses are a means to an end.

6. The method of guidance is highly effective for altering frustration-produced responses but it has no great value for replacing reward-learned responses.

7. Frustration-instigated responses are compulsive in nature whereas responses appearing in motivation situations are choice reactions.

8. The degree of frustration can be relieved by the expression of responses, regardless of whether or not the response is adaptive, whereas responses expressed by a motivated individual are satisfying only when the responses are adaptive.

9. Frustration-instigated responses are either nonconstructive or destructive in nature whereas motivated responses are constructive.

10. The response expressed during frustration is influenced to a great extent by its availability to the organism, whereas the response expressed in the state of motivation is influenced more by anticipated consequences than by availability.

11. Learning takes place under motivation and permits an increase in the number of differentiations the organism can make, whereas frustration leads to dedifferentiation (regression) and in some cases to convulsive . . . behavior.

12. The trait of resignation that may appear in frustration contrasts with the zest shown in states of motivation.

The number of contrasting features present in motivated and frustrated behavior offers great difficulty if one attempts to reduce them to the same basic principles. If the characteristics of each are assembled into two separate groups, however, consistency between the characteristics of each group can be obtained.

Reactions to Frustration

One of the most widely recognized possible reactions to frustration of the sort that Maier has described is aggression. Because frustration is so inevitable a part of social living, and thus of organizational life, aggression as a frequent consequence of frustration is an important human reaction. It is not *necessarily* maladaptive, although it may be; it is not always expressed in recognizable form; nor is the individual always aware that he is responding aggressively.

Levinson has suggested that one of the principal problems besetting today's large corporations is the absence of normal organizational channels for the discharge of aggression. The consequences frequently include covert and displaced aggressive behavior, the development of emotionally based physical symptoms, and feelings of alienation from work and company. Remedy of this situation will not come unless we see the normality of aggressive feeling, and better understand both the dynamic relationships between frustration and aggression, and some ways in which aggressive feeling can be ventilated in positive, helpful fashion.

McNeil's comprehensive survey of behavioral science research in the area provides perspective on the problem. We have selected those sections of it that seem most relevant to the administrative situation. This section of his report provides an over-all description of the nature of frustration, some ways in which aggression may result, and some defensive measures the individual is frequently forced to take.

READING 3-4

Psychology and Aggression*

ELTON B. MC NEIL

In man's attempt to apply the scientific method to human affairs, the study of aggression has commanded an inordinate amount of the energy of social scientists. Although recent events have expanded the scale on which human destructiveness can be expressed and have multiplied the urgency of the need for a solution to the riddle of hostility, the primary source of anxiety about aggressive behavior is still highly personal and quite mundane. The parent whose belligerent child is rejected by playmates, the schoolteacher whose ire is provoked by negativism, the policeman whose dignity is outraged by the defiance of a delinquent, and the average citizen whose rights have been trampled on—all experience an anguish that they cannot summon up when they consider the possibility that man may one day be the instrument of his own mass extinction.

Personal frustration is woven tightly into the fabric of the life of each of us, making aggressive feelings an inevitable human experience. The paradox which aggression presents is that, in all its abundance and despite the massive scrutiny it has endured since the beginning of time, it remains as enigmatic as if its presence had not yet been detected by man. An apt analogy might be to liken visible aggressive acts to a tree that is able to resist man's efforts to uproot it because he is only dimly aware of the meaning of the concept "roots." In many respects, the labors of the last forty years resemble such primitive efforts in our attempt to comprehend the notion of the roots of man's emotional life—roots which twist and turn in a seemingly incomprehensible fashion and plunge to depths to which man has seldom ventured. It is not surprising, then, that an account of this toil will inevitably contain murky observation, fanciful speculation, and valid as well as irrelevant and trivial fact. It is man's inability to distinguish between the momentous and the meaningless that constrains him from discarding what looks trivial but may, in fact be vital.

. . .

Frustration and Aggression

The bulk of human aggressiveness can be traced directly to frustration. The civilizing of the child cannot be accomplished without frustration of his needs, for the society insists that he must learn to satisfy his needs at specified times, in specified places, by specified techniques, and in relation only to specified objects. This systematic interference with the needs of its members seems to be a necessary condition of group living, for it makes the behavior of others a de-

* Abridged from *Journal of Conflict Resolution*, 3 (1959), pp. 200-206, 209-215. The complete article contains a bibliography of more than 400 items, not included here.

pendable and predictable event and allows planning for the common good. Although most well-socialized adults encounter many frustrations in the course of their daily lives, they use established patterns of reaction to overcome them to prevent their recurrence. The seeming ease with which adults remove, or adjust to, obstacles in their paths in a sharp contrast to the child's fumbling attempt to apply his limited skill and primitive understanding to the management of frustration. Not only do the child's needs seem to him to be overpowering, but the few alternative ways he knows of satisfying them offer little hope of an easy restoration of his emotional equilibrium. The child's methods of meeting his many frustrations tend to be quite simple and direct, and, until he learns a variety of ways to solve his problems, he is bound to feel like the helpless victim of the caprice of his environment. It is in this setting that some of the most fundamental personality characteristics of the individual are established, and his success or failure in mastering frustration has the utmost relevance to the aggressiveness with which he will manage his life.

Frustration involves interference with the gratification of a motive, need, or drive. The source of frustration may be perceived by the individual as internal or external, and it may take any of a number of forms. Frustration among children, for example, frequently appears as a physical obstruction, since they live in a world built to an adult scale. Frustration can be due to sheer satiation with a task from which there is no escape, or it can be caused by a discrepancy between an individual's desire to solve a problem and his ability to do so. Since so many of our working and social relationships are organized in terms of employers and employees and leaders and followers, frustration can issue directly

from unsatisfactory leadership which thwarts gratification of the needs of others. The interpretation of what constitutes frustration is a highly personal and individual matter and depends almost completely on the perception one has that gratification is being, or will be, withheld. To an intensely ambitious person, for example, life may be the continuous pursuit of gratification which, when achieved, is at once replaced by the demands of a new set of goals. As long as gratification is possible, it is a challenge rather than a frustration.

Rosenzweig pointed out that frustration can be delineated further as active or passive. The blocking of an individual's progress toward a goal, when the obstacle simply stands in the way of gratification, is passive frustration. Active frustration occurs when the interference with gratification is coupled with a threat of danger. Thus the passive frustration of a locked door may become an active frustration when the building is burning. The quality of frustration can also be distinguished by describing it in terms of privation, deprivation, or obstruction. The frustrations stemming from privations, for example, have a quite different meaning from those perceived as deprivations or obstructions. The privation of being born into poverty poses a series of frustrations for the individual, but his reaction to them differs considerably from his responses to being deprived of wealth, once he has possessed it. In much the same fashion, being born with a physical defect produces a psychological reaction distinct from that occurring when the defect is imposed by the carelessness of someone else.

The response to frustration is a complex affair, and its determinants include situational factors such as the setting in which it takes place, the intensity of the frustrating experience, its duration, the extent to which the victim sees a way to relieve his dilemma, and the individual's personal history of success or failure in dealing with states of tension. The fact that frustration regularly casts an aggressive shadow makes knowledge of its nature indispensable to an understanding of man's destructive impulses.

Attempts to explore the dimensions of frustration under controlled laboratory conditions have been the primary source of knowledge about its connection with aggression, but what laboratory studies gain in exactness they tend to lose in naturalness. Since experimentally induced frustration is an artificial sample of the normal annoyances of life, the conflict induced in a laboratory may not fit sensibly into the context of the subject's past experiences or affect needs which are important to his adjustment. Some of the confusing and contradictory findings that issue from "staged" frustration experiments can be traced to the use of techniques which do not duplicate, or even approximate, real-life situations. Most researchers offer too much safety to the subject or instigate such a low level of frustration that the subject has no reason to respond with socially unacceptable behavior. There can be unsuspected forces at work even in a controlled experiment. Some of the classic work on the psychology of frustration and aggression—work which became the prime mover of a decade of effort on the part of other researchers—required some reinterpretation when it became apparent that the arbitrariness of the frustration imposed by the experimenters, rather than the frustration itself, might have produced an aggressive response. Logically, the response to frustration resulting from personal inadequacy or from an inescapable fate would involve less overt expression of aggression than that resulting from the ego-deflation or deprivation imposed arbitrarily by someone else. A great deal of caution is needed in

tracking anger back to its origin, since there are many alluring but false trails. Zander recommended that laboratory frustration should be established by having the subject fail at a task at which he has previously succeeded. In this way the frustrated person will not channel his feelings at a target which has almost invited an attack.

The Response to Frustration. In what was probably the most important and stimulating theoretical presentation of frustration and aggression, Dollard and his associates at Yale stated that the existence of frustration inevitably leads to some form of aggression. The critics attacked this statement vigorously. Miller stated, two years later, that this might better be phrased to say that frustration produces instigation to different types of responses, one of which may be aggression. The enthusiasm with which the battle was joined pushed forward our understanding of frustration and aggression at a satisfying rate. The obverse of this statement—the contention that aggressive behavior always presupposes the existence of frustration—met with little resistance or criticism.

The strength of the aggressive motivation, according to the Dollard group, will vary with at least three factors: (1) the strength of the instigation to the frustrated response, (2) the degree of interference with the frustrated response, and (3) the number of frustrated response sequences that the individual endures. The term aggressive "motivation" rather than aggressive "behavior" is used because a factor such as the anticipation of punishment may influence the overtness of a hostile response. When aggressive behavior does appear, it is not always direct and overt; it may be deflected from its original goal, disguised, displaced, delayed, or otherwise altered. Individual differences in the capacity to tolerate frustration also help determine the point at which an aggressive response will occur. The research evidence bearing on each of these determinants of the strength of aggressive motivation can be considered in turn.

1. *The strength of instigation to the frustrated response.*—This factor is really twofold. It implies an estimate of the strength of the motive being frustrated, and it requires information about the strength of the individual's attachment to a particular object that will satisfy his need. If the motive is hunger, the stronger the hunger, the greater the likelihood of an aggressive response if he is deprived of food. If only certain kinds of foods or only food prepared in a certain way are acceptable need-satisfiers, then being offered an unacceptable substitute will produce frustration and instigate aggressive motivation. In an attempt to test this hypothesis, a number of researchers asked subjects to keep records of the incidents which provoked anger, the motives interfered with, and the nature of the frustration they felt. Although diaries and lists of things that annoy people are not the most reliable form of evidence, it seems clear that the stronger the drive being frustrated, the greater will be the instigation to an intense or aggressive response.

It is a familiar observation that, as one gets nearer to reaching a goal, the strength of the drive toward it tends to increase. This general rule is easily demonstrated in animals, in which close control can be maintained over their environment; it is somewhat more difficult to demonstrate in human beings, with whom such control is not always possible. A compromise can be effected by using children for experimental subjects, as did Haner and Brown. In their study they had children play a game which involved moving marbles toward a goal to win a reward. At various distances from the goal, the experimenters sounded a buzzer which ended the game

before the children could succeed. This buzzer continued to sound until the child pushed a plunger which would stop it. Assuming that the vigor with which the child slammed the plunger was an adequate indication of his aggressive feelings, Haner and Brown measured the pressure each child exerted on the plunger and compared it with how close he was to finishing the game. They found that the closer the child was to finishing the marble game when his task was interrupted, the greater the force with which he obliterated the offending buzzer. If we can accept this as an accurate measure of frustration, the evidence suggests a positive correlation between the strength of the drive being frustrated and the degree of aggressiveness of the response.

2. *The degree of interference with the frustrated response.*—Although introspective accounts are notoriously untrustworthy, people often report that their anger mounts apace with increased interference encountered in seeking a goal. When one interference follows on the heels of another, most people reach the limits of their tolerance. A more reliable measure of interference is the degree of anger or hostility apparent in the behavior of the victim of the interference. When an experimenter criticizes or insults a subject in order to frustrate him, the number of aggressive responses tends to increase as the tempo of insulting remarks is stepped up. As a check on this hypothesis, adolescent subjects were asked to indicate the most likely way a person would act when confronted with hostile situations ranging from being mildly disliked by another person to being struck by him. If we can accept the premise that a very hostile act directed toward a person will produce greater interference with his motives than a less hostile act, then the findings support the hypothesis that the strength of the aggressive response will vary with the degree of interference. Ex-

periments with groups of subjects interacting with one another have shown that those who were the victims of the greatest number of aggressive acts by others tended to be the ones who initiated the most aggression in return.* Even a good-natured ribbing will produce irritation if it exceeds the intensity that an individual can tolerate.

3. *The number of frustrated response sequences.*—This factor refers to a familiar situation in which there is an accumulation of aggressive motivations until the last straw is added to the load and the frustrated person can no longer carry the load. Thus, a series of minor frustrations of various sorts may culminate in an explosion that is out of proportion to the event which eventually triggers it. The longer the frustration continues without relief, the less attractive and satisfying are mature, non-aggressive responses and the greater the probability of an overt aggressive act. To demonstrate this phenomenon, Otis and McCandless arranged an eight-trial frustration task with which they could successfully continue frustrating a group of nursery-school children. From the first four to the last four of these trials, the children showed an increase in aggressive behavior and a decrease in non-aggressive behavior aimed at relieving the frustration. It is for this reason that parents tremble at the approach of the hour before supper. Hunger, when mixed with the day's accumulation of frustrations, can transform the family circle into a whining, shouting battleground. While television may not be very educational, it has certainly reduced family conflict in America between the hours of five and seven in the evening.

Further support for this hypothesis

was furnished by an intriguing experiment fashioned by Thibaut and Coules. In a group note-writing experiment with college students, the investigators, with the assistance of paid stooges pretending to be subjects in the experiment, angered the students by sending them insulting notes. A part of the group was permitted to reply in kind to the "student" who had angered them, while other members of the group were halted briefly in their note-writing activity. When the note-writing was resumed, a greater volume of aggression flowed from the students whose anger had been bottled up by the delay. As Berkowitz has since pointed out, it is a reasonable presumption that the irritation provided by the experimenters in interrupting the task at hand undoubtedly was added to that created by the faked notes. Nevertheless, this finding is congruent with Newcomb's insightful observation that when people get angry at one another, they tend to sever diplomatic relations, and communication between them ceases. Once this happens, it diminished the possibility of resolving the hostility they feel toward one another, and few constructive alternatives remain. Expressing resentment directly to one's tormenter will bring relief that cannot be matched by expressing anger toward substitute objects.

These general rules about the relationship of frustration to aggression have been powerful stimulants to the study of aggression, but they have also been the subject of healthy criticism and modification. The basic postulate that frustration leads to aggression has been qualified by some writers to apply only when certain kinds of frustration exist. Maslow, for example, maintained that sheer deprivation is likely to produce attempts to relieve the situation constructively, while aggression can be expected to occur only when the frustration is in the form of an attack or when it is

---

* Berkowitz' work, summarized in Research Summary 3-2 emphasizes the importance of expectation in this regard. The Berkowitz study is also relevant in considering McNeil's section 3.

threatening to the individual. Rosen-zweig's concept of active frustration would be a similar case in which aggressive responses would be a predictable outcome. McClelland added that the availability of a solution to the frustration would determine whether or not hostility would occur. Having an ace up one's sleeve, while dangerous in some social circles, would make the fall of the cards less frustrating and less an occasion for anger. In any case, the definition of what constitutes a threat and the perception of the availability of a solution remain highly individual issues and are not factors amenable to easy experimental verification. To an incurably optimistic person there may never be a situation without hope of resolution. Unfortunately, much of the research devoted to testing these hypotheses about the instigation to aggression employs a grossly circular logic. If, for example, the experimenter predicts that an increase in aggressive behavior will result from an increase in frustration, he cannot then use the aggressive behavior as proof that he has increased the frustration.

An additional difficulty is posed by the fact that most experimenters make the broad assumption that all forms of frustration are qualitatively the same, that they have the same meaning to each of the experimental subjects, and that the same needs and drives are being frustrated. Such assumptions are almost never tenable. Experimental work has yet to overcome these obstacles to a clear statement of the vital factors in the frustration-aggression hypothesis.

. . .

Defense Mechanisms, and Aggression

No attempt to understand the vicissitudes of human aggressive behavior is adequate without concepts similar to that of the defense mechanisms and the existence of an unconscious part of the self. The efforts, for centuries, to explain the motivation of human actions on a purely conscious and rational basis always produced embarrassing paradoxes or left a host of details unaccounted for. Emphasis on the intellectual rather than the emotional aspects of man's nature suggested that man, when faced with conflict, ought to be able to draw up a balance sheet of pros and cons and then, after examining the facts, make a rational decision. When psychoanalysis shifted the emphasis of psychiatric thinking to man's emotions, it became apparent that any attempt to add up the important facts could never strike a balance because essential facts were always missing. It was from these observations that a dynamic view of human functioning was formed and the notion of defense mechanisms evolved. . . .

Using hostility as the model of impulses to be dealt with, what are the ways in which it can be managed defensively? At a broad level, the choices of the individual are restricted to *changing the situation* through the process of conscious problem-solving and working out a new relationship with the person toward whom he is hostile; *escaping from the situation* by running away or retreating into a fantasy life, where the problems do not exist; or *changing his perception of the hostile situation* through defense mechanisms which render it innocuous.

Repression. Since all defense mechanisms are said to operate outside the sphere of conscious awareness of the individual, the removal from consciousness must be accomplished by the act of repression. Repression is a concept which describes the process by which impulses and thoughts are excluded from consciousness and made to remain inaccessible to it. As Sappenfield has pointed out, since repression is used to eliminate impulses which the conscious self finds repugnant, it might well be described as the process by which the "unthinkable" becomes truly *unthinkable*. Repression is a flight of the ego from danger by removing the danger and making it inaccessible to observation. Horney has indicated that we repress whatever we perceive as a threat to the success, recognition, and security of the personality and that it is especially necessary to keep internal destructive forces out of consciousness. Repression moves hostile impulses out of view, but it does not alter their strength or essential characteristics. This means that repression must operate continuously to keep these impulses from reasserting themselves or gaining access to consciousness. The most important aspect of repression is that, to the extent that it occurs, the individual will lose insight into some of his motivation. The loss of knowledge about what he really feels amounts to a surrender of part of the power of rational choice and a restriction on the reasonableness of future behavior. The seeming incomprehensibility of some forms of neurotic behavior can be accounted for in this way. If repression operates extensively, the individual is forced to behave in ways that he cannot explain and is powerless to change or control, since the hostile impulse has been withdrawn from the influence of the conscious part of the self. The repression of aggressive impulses is an often necessary, but always dangerous, method of solving emotional problems, since repression can fail and the impulses are reborn as a violent and destructive attack. . . .

Displacement. A quite commonplace method of dealing with hostile feelings which cannot be expressed toward the source of the frustration is through the mechanism of displacement. . . . Repression helps one to displace, for it allows the individual to "forget" the identity of the original object.

In learning to displace his feelings, the aggressive person selects a new target possessing certain characteristics. As nearly as he safely can, without having it apparent to himself or the original object, he chooses a new victim in terms of the similarity to the first object. This similarity is often more symbolic than real, so that a child may anger his teacher, instead of his mother, and yet gain the gratification of defying someone in authority. In general, the substitute target is one that is not capable of retaliation for the aggression meted out to it. A boss can displace his aggression against employees who are dependent on him, and a child can displace his anger against a smaller and weaker sibling or another innocent child. Displacement is made easier and more attractive when the new victim has done something to justify the punishment he is about to receive. Lacking any safe object, regardless of how distant it may be symbolically from the original, the angry person may be limited to a verbal abuse of high-level abstractions such as the state of the world, women drivers, minority groups, or baseball managers. Since the world offers a multitude of irritations and frustrations, the displacement of aggression to substitute objects can easily be accomplished. Displacement allows the person to maintain his relationship with the original object while venting his ire in safer surroundings—surroundings that are anxiety-free.

Projection. A more complex and sophisticated means of gaining relief from anxiety by getting rid of unacceptable thoughts, feelings, and impulses is through projection. A common meaning of projection is the reference of one's own thoughts and feelings to persons or objects in the outside world. It is a mechanism by which one is able to deny the reality that he cannot tolerate. Projection takes place in a series of steps. First, the intolerable feelings are removed from awareness by repression. The process of defense may stop here if repression is adequate to the task, but if the repressive forces fail to contain the hostility, then a further step must be taken. The dangerous thoughts are attributed to others. . . . Once he is convinced that others are against him and that he can expect only evil and mistreatment at their hands, his hostility toward them need not produce guilt or loss of self-esteem.

When someone projects his anger or resentment, he chooses objects for projection that offer some basis in reality for the feelings he ascribes to them. If you cut your finger, you become aware of that part of your hand in a thousand ways overlooked in daily life. The pain focuses attention on the finger, and it seems to be hurt at every turn. A normal person devoting a single day to searching for evidences of hostility in others would find it everywhere. Since no one is without hostility in one form or another, the person who projects can make a convincing case for his interpretation of the motives of others. Righteous indignation at the meanness of others coats the accuser with respectability, and in the act of hating hatred he is able to gratify the very impulse he denies so vehemently in himself. It is obvious that projection is the long way around to gratification, but such a circuitous route is demanded by an environment that makes onerous demands for conformity. A simple change in the environment (walking past a graveyard) can induce fear, which then becomes a fertile ground for seeing others as malicious and threatening.

Sublimation. Sublimation is regarded as one of the most adaptive of the defenses because it represents a form of substitution in which primitive impulses and behavior are replaced by behavior which is harmonious with the native impulse but more acceptable socially. Either the aim of the original impulse or its object may be the focus of substitution. . . . The aim is altered slightly, the object is rendered unrecognizable, and the source of the impulse and the impulse itself remain intact. With successful sublimation, an unacceptable impulse can be gratified in a second-best fashion, yet prove sufficient to strike a satisfactory emotional balance for life. Where repression of the impulse crushes it and forbids its expression, sublimation allows a slightly modified version to be expressed in an atmosphere that not only is free of guilt and anxiety but may produce the acclaim of one's fellow men.

Because they are socially rewarded, sublimations are seldom subjected to critical examination by the society. The motivation for deeds of service and self-sacrifice is not considered a polite or proper topic for speculation, since, according to the theory, this mechanism is at the base of the constructive parts of a culture. This concept has been resisted with great vigor by the lay public because it is considered degrading to man to have such magnificent edifices constructed of such elemental and shoddy materials. Theorists dedicated to the concept of sublimation have included, to the public's great dismay, most of man's proudest accomplishments under this rubric. Friendship is described as a sublimation of erotic and sexual attachments, and occupations, hobbies, art, literature, civic service, and religion are similarly described as polite forms of more reprehensible urges curbed in childhood. Since sex and aggression are so thoroughly regulated in this society, most sublimations are seen as stemming from one or the other of these impulses, and some theorists maintain that the anxiety connected with these urges is the factor that prevents the acceptance of the idea of sublimation. Photographic rather than actual "shots" of animals, the fighting spirit of sports, "killing" an audience with humor, and being a brilliant surgeon rather than Jack the Ripper are all ways in which socially positive behavior can issue, in slightly disguised form, from more primitive impulses. The amount of disguise necessary for hostile feelings will vary according to the particular demands of the environment and the resources of the individual and may range from highly competitive and destructive sports, such as boxing, to less obvious forms, such as chess. In some instances —the professional soldier, for example— little alteration of the aim is needed, and the impulse can be almost fully gratified.

It is certainly true that some event similar to sublimation must occur if aggressive urges are to be turned to socially acceptable ends. It is also true that many socially meaningful activities offer gratification for impulses that the society demands be denied expression on any other basis. The greatest public resistance is against assuming that *all* constructive activities draw their energy from forbidden urges that are remnants of the unsolved problems of childhood. There is undoubtedly more than one way to skin this psychological cat and more than one motivation for a person's way of life. The direct translation of primitive to civilized impulse does occur for some individuals, and, without the capacity to sublimate, more drastic measures might be needed to solve emotional conflicts. The simple alteration of the object of aggression provides a practical solution for aggressiveness, since aggressiveness has so many positive social uses.

This description of the way in which defense mechanisms can be used to solve the problem of managing hostility provides an accurate picture of the deviousness and complexity which sometimes characterize solutions to conflict over aggression. Defense mechanisms are necessary when all other attempts at solution have failed or are barred from use by the peculiarities of the individual's environment. They do not represent an "average" means of meeting the demands of civilized living. Defenses involve an unhealthy distortion of the world as it really is and exact an enormous toll on the integrity of the personality. Defenses cripple, but they do not destroy in the way that feelings of anxiety and worthlessness might if defenses were not available. If a neurotic personality results from the overuse of defenses in meeting the challenges of life, then it might rightfully be said that neurosis is the price we pay for civilization. The defensive maneuvers described are typical of those called upon to handle angry feelings, but this list of the twists and turns that may occur is far from complete or exhaustive. The human mind is most splendid in the evasions of which it is capable.

As drastic as defensive steps may seem, they may fail to be adequate, and a total destruction of the personality may occur in the form of psychosis. As the hastily erected defenses topple before the force of conflicts, last desperate attempts to stem the tide may appear. In a state of amnesia, the person may simply blot out the circumstances that surround him and become a different person, free to try a new approach to the same problems. In rare cases, nearly complete personalities are formed from the discards of emotional life and are hidden away in a closet of the mind where they lurk as invisible threats to the conscious personality. When defenses fail, as they do for an alarming proportion of our society, the personality may disintegrate and collapse into a psychosis in which the "unthinkable" finds its way to expression in shocking and easily recognizable forms. It is in psychosis that the intensity and destructiveness of the impulse life of humans appears in its least disguised form; it is a frightening apparition to behold.

While McNeil's discussion focusses chiefly around defense mechanisms operating in dealing with aggression or hostility, the mechanisms may also operate in connection with other drives, for example, sex, where the individual has learned through social pressures to control drive. And, equally important, they appear in connection not only with frustration, but in adjusting to feelings of conflict and to anxiety.

Defense mechanisms serve an important function for the individual. Everyone uses one or another or several of them at different times. Consequently, the administrator may find a knowledge of the defense mechanisms helpful in understanding the behavior of his people. Simply labeling behavior, however, is not enough; to be helpful, the label should suggest underlying dynamics that make the individual's behavior more meaningful and perhaps more tolerable. When used moderately, defense mechanisms suggest adjustive difficulties an emotionally healthy person is having; when they dominate behavior to the exclusion of more effective behavior, they can constitute a serious personality problem.

Table 3-1 presents a listing of the more common defense mechanisms, including several not in our selection from McNeil.

TABLE 3-1

Adjustive Reactions to Frustration, Conflict, and Anxiety

Adjustive Reactions	Psychological Process	Illustration
Compensation	Individual devotes himself to a pursuit with increased vigor to make up for some feeling of real or imagined inadequacy	Zealous, hard-working president of the Twenty-five Year Club who has never advanced very far in the company hierarchy
Conversion	Emotional conflicts are expressed in muscular, sensory, or bodily symptoms of disability, malfunctioning, or pain	A disabling headache keeping a staff member off the job, the day after a cherished project has been rejected
Displacement	Re-directing pent-up emotions toward persons, ideas, or objects other than the primary source of the emotion	Roughly rejecting a simple request from a subordinate after receiving a rebuff from the boss
Fantasy	Day-dreaming or other forms of imaginative activity provides an escape from reality and imagined satisfactions	An employee's day-dream of the day in the staff meeting when he corrects the boss' mistakes and is publicly acknowledged as the real leader of the industry
Identification	Individual enhances his self-esteem by patterning his own behavior after another's, frequently also internalizing the values and beliefs of the other; also vicariously sharing the glories or suffering in the reversals of other individuals or groups	The "assistant-to" who takes on the vocabulary, mannerisms, or even pomposity of his vice-presidential boss
Negativism	Active or passive resistance, operating unconsciously	The manager who, having been unsuccessful in getting out of a committee assignment, picks apart every suggestion that anyone makes in the meetings

Adjustive Reactions	*Psychological Process*	*Illustration*
Projection	Individual protects himself from awareness of his own undesirable traits or unacceptable feelings by attributing them to others	Unsuccessful person who, deep down, would like to block the rise of others in the organization and who continually feels that others are out to "get him"
Rationalization	Justifying inconsistent or undesirable behavior, beliefs, statements and motivations by providing acceptable explanations for them	Padding the expense account because "everybody does it"
Reaction-Formation	Urges not acceptable to consciousness are repressed and in their stead opposite attitudes or modes of behavior are expressed with considerable force	Employee who has not been promoted who overdoes the defense of his boss, vigorously upholding the company's policies
Regression	Individual returns to an earlier and less mature level of adjustment in the face of frustration	A manager having been blocked in some administrative pursuit busies himself with clerical duties or technical details, more appropriate for his subordinates
Repression	Completely excluding from consciousness impulses, experiences, and feelings which are psychologically disturbing because they arouse a sense of guilt or anxiety	A subordinate "forgetting" to tell his boss the circumstances of an embarrassing situation
Fixation	Maintaining a persistent nonadjustive reaction even though all the cues indicate the behavior will not cope with the problems	Persisting in carrying out an operational procedure long since declared by management to be uneconomical as a protest because the employee's opinion wasn't asked
Resignation, Apathy, and Boredom	Breaking psychological contact with the environment, withholding any sense of emotional or personal involvement	Employee who, receiving no reward, praise, or encouragement, no longer cares whether or not he does a good job
Flight or Withdrawal	Leaving the field in which frustration, anxiety, or conflict is experienced, either physically or psychologically	The salesman's big order falls through and he takes the rest of the day off; constant rebuff or rejection by superiors and colleagues, pushes an older worker toward being a loner and ignoring what friendly gestures are made

CHAPTER EIGHT

Anxiety

Introduction

Anxiety is a basic and almost universal human experience. It is often the central force of many psychiatric conditions but it also plays a part in the everyday experiences of normally functioning, healthy human beings. It manifests its presence in an array of symptoms, including the extreme of personality breakdown, purely physical symptoms, the defense mechanisms, and simple worry and fretting. It serves as a powerful motivating force, in some cases, forcing the most intense concentration on narrow and sometimes irrelevant aspects of the environment, thus leading to generalized maladjustment; in other cases, pressing the individual to venture forth, to intensify his efforts, and to accomplish more as a result of the anxiety.

Although a psychological experience related to frustration, anxiety must be distinguished from it. Frustration is a result of past or present painful feelings (need denial); anxiety is the apprehension concerning a possibly painful event. Frustration is response to an existing frustrating event; anxiety is response to the threat of such event.

In the readings and text that follows, we distinguish between neurotic anxiety and normal anxiety. In many ways, the effect of neurotic anxiety on behavior is similar to that of frustration (as Maier has described it), largely negative. On the other hand, normal anxiety is better considered in relation to our earlier discussion of level of aspiration (Ch. Five). Moderate anxiety tends to raise the sights of the individual (his level of aspiration) and help him mobilize increased energy to achieve the higher goals he has set. We have seen that an individual's level of aspiration is partially dependent on whether he tends toward high need achievement or failure avoidance. The effect of anxiety on behavior is also related to this characteristic of the individual's personality, as subsequently quoted research will indicate.

In considering the Readings and Research Summaries in this chapter, it will be helpful to keep in mind, as a useful if somewhat oversimplified guideline, that, in general, mild to moderate stress (of a type that generates mild to moderate anxiety), facilitates goal-oriented problem-solving behavior; extreme stress and the consequent extreme anxiety tend to result in defensive or maladjusted behavior. What constitutes moderate or extreme stress in a particular instance depends on the anxiety resistance of the individual.

So important and pervasive a human experience, of course, constitutes an important influence on work attitudes and job performance. It is from this point of view that we now consider a description of the various kinds of anxiety and an examination of the recent research that has identified the effects of normal anxiety on performance and attitudes. Our purpose is to help the administrator know the nature of anxiety as a normal human experience; to encourage him to recognize the possibilities for minimizing the negative effects of anxiety; and to consider the possibility that anxiety, under some conditions and for some people, can be used as a positive motivating force. The last point raises an interesting, and probably still controversial question: Can excellent performance ever be accomplished without a prior experience of motivating anxiety? More specifically asked, is some form of anxiety a *necessary* antecedent for all outstanding performance? Is this true for all people or only some? How do we distinguish the "clutch hitters" from those who fold under pressure? How do we use anxiety as an energizer rather than as a paralyzer?

The Nature of Anxiety

It is, of course, easier to raise questions than to provide the answers. May, in the excerpt from his book, *The Meaning of Anxiety*, that follows, describes some varieties of anxiety. His descriptions provide a basis for attempting some answers to the questions we have asked.

READING 3-5

The Nature of Anxiety*

ROLLO MAY

. . .

It is agreed by students of anxiety—Freud, Goldstein, Horney, to mention only three—that anxiety is a *diffuse* apprehension, and that the central difference between fear and anxiety is that

* Excerpted from *The Meaning of Anxiety* (New York: The Ronald Press, 1950), Ch. 6, pp. 190-191; 194-195; 226-229.

fear is a reaction to a specific danger while anxiety is unspecific, "vague," "objectless." The special characteristics of anxiety are the feelings of *uncertainty* and *helplessness* in the face of the danger. The nature of anxiety can be understood when we ask *what* is threatened in the experience which produces anxiety. The threat is to something in the "core or essence" of the personality. *Anxiety is* the apprehension cued off by a threat to some value which the individual holds essential to his existence as a personality. The threat may be to physical or psychological life (death, or loss of freedom), or it may be to some other value which the individual identifies with his existence (patriotism, the love of another person, "success," etc.). This identification of a value with one's existence as a personality is vividly illustrated in the remark of Tom[1] in his period of anxiety over whether he would be retained in his job or be forced to resort again to government relief: "If I couldn't support my family, I'd as soon jump off the end of the dock." This, put simply, is his way of saying that if he could not preserve the self-respecting position of being the responsible wage-earner, his whole life would have no meaning and he might as well not exist. The occasions of anxiety will vary with different people as widely as the values on which they depend vary, but what will always be true in anxiety is that the threat is to a value held by that particular individual to be essential to his existence and consequently to his security as a personality.

The terms "diffuse" and "vague" do not mean that anxiety is less intense in its painfulness than other affects. Indeed, other things being equal, anxiety is regularly more painful than fear. Nor do these terms refer merely to the generalized, "over-all" psychophysical quality of anxiety. Other emotions, like fear, anger, hostility, also permeate the whole organism. Rather, the diffuse and undifferentiated quality of anxiety refers to the *level* in the personality on which the threat is experienced. An individual experiences various fears on the basis of a security pattern he has developed; *but*

---

[1] [Major portions of Tom's gastric tract had been removed by surgery. He is more fully discussed in an earlier section of May's book, Ch. 3, p. 77.]

in anxiety it is this security pattern itself which is threatened.

. . .

Normal anxiety is, like any anxiety, a reaction to threats to values the individual holds essential to his existence as a personality; but normal anxiety is that reaction which (1) is not disproportionate to the objective threat, (2) does not involve repression or other mechanisms of intrapsychic conflict, and, as a corollary to the second point, (3) does not require neurotic defense mechanisms for its management, but can be confronted constructively on the level of conscious awareness *or* can be relieved if the objective situation is altered. . . .

Normal anxiety continues throughout life in the form of what Freud termed "objective anxiety." The existence of normal anxiety in adults is frequently overlooked because the intensity of the experience is often so much less than that of neurotic anxiety; and, since one characteristic or normal anxiety is that it can be managed constructively, it does not show itself in "panic" or in other dramatic forms. But the *quantity* of reaction should not be confused with its *quality*. The intensity of the reaction is important as a distinction between neurotic and normal anxiety only when we are considering the question of whether the reaction is proportionate to the objective threat. Every individual experiences greater or lesser threats to his existence and to values he identifies with his existence in the course of his normal development as a human being. But he normally confronts these experiences constructively, uses them as "learning experiences" (in the broad and profound meaning of that term), and moves on in his development.

. . .

Whereas the use of neurotic anxiety as a challenge for problem-solving has been agreed upon, it has often been overlooked that *normal* anxiety also indicates this possibility and may be used constructively. The tendency in our culture to regard fears and anxiety chiefly in a negative light, as results of unfortunate learning, is not only a oversimplification but tends by implication to remove the possibility of the constructive acceptance and use of the day-to-day anxiety experiences which cannot be called specifically neurotic. To be sure, neurotic anxiety is the result of unfortunate learning in the respect that the individual was forced to deal with threatening situations at a period—usually in early childhood—when he was incapable of coping directly or constructively with such experiences. In this respect, *neurotic anxiety is the result of the failure to cope with the previous anxiety situations in one's experiences.* But normal anxiety is not the result of unfortunate learning; it arises rather from a realistic appraisal of one's situation of danger. To the extent that a person can succeed in constructively meeting the normal day-to-day anxiety experiences as they arise, he avoids the repression and retrenchment which make for later neurotic anxiety.

In fine, the goal with regard to neurotic anxiety is the solving of the underlying problem and thus the overcoming of the anxiety. When we are thinking of neurotic anxiety, the oft-expressed criterion of mental health, "the ability to live without anxiety," is sound.[40] But

with regard to normal anxiety—the anxiety which arises from real threats, and which, as we have earlier pointed out, inheres in such aspects of human contingency as death, in the threat of isolation which accompanies the development of individuality, and so forth—the desideratum cannot be the complete absence of anxiety.

Our problem, therefore, is *how may normal anxiety-creating situations be used constructively?* Though this question has not generally been attacked in scientific writings, it was confronted directly by Kierkegaard[41] a century ago, and in our times has been attacked by Goldstein and, to a lesser extent, by Mowrer. [Goldstein has emphasized] that every human being encounters frequent anxiety shocks in the course of his normal development and that his capacities can be actualized only through an affirmative response to these threats to his existence. Goldstein's simple illustration is the healthy child's

---

40 The phrase, "living without anxiety," has its valuable ideal meaning, but when it is oversimplified, as it often is in general usage, to mean that the goal is a total absence of anxiety, the phrase becomes delusive and even dangerous. Needless to say, living totally without anxiety in a historical period like the present would imply an unrealistic and insensitive view of one's cultural situation and would betoken an irresponsible attitude toward one's duties as

a citizen. One could cite many demonstrations from the rise of fascism in Spain and Germany that the citizens who were unaware of the mortal danger became putty in the hands of the rising dictatorships. For another illustration, an officer who had no anxiety whatever for his men in time of battle would be irresponsible, and it would be dangerous to serve under him.

41 The constructive use of anxiety has been described at length by Kierkegaard. To him anxiety is a better "teacher" than reality, for while reality situations may be temporarily evaded, anxiety is an inner function which cannot be escaped short of constriction of the personality. Kierkegaard writes that only he who has been educated in the "school of anxiety"—i.e., has confronted and worked through previous anxiety experiences—is able to meet present and future anxiety experiences without being overwhelmed. In this connection, there is some evidence that soldiers in the last war who had experienced a fair degree of anxiety in their past lives and were in some cases relatively "high-strung" were better able to face anxiety experiences of combat than soldiers who had experienced relatively little anxiety before combat (Grinker and Spiegel).

learning to walk despite the fact that he falls and gets hurt many times in the process. When we try to understand the constructive use of normal anxiety from the *objective* side, we note that it is characterized by the individual's confronting the anxiety-creating situation directly, admitting his apprehensions but moving ahead despite the anxiety. In other words, it consists of moving *through* anxiety-creating experiences rather than moving *around* them or *retrenching* in the face of them. These ways of meeting anxiety were described countless times in studies of anxiety and fear among soldiers in combat during World War II. The most constructive attitude consisted of the soldier's frankly admitting his fear or anxiety about going into battle, but being subjectively prepared to act *despite*

his apprehension. As a corollary it has been frequently pointed out in these studies of soldiers that courage consisted not of the absence of fear and anxiety but of the capacity to move ahead even though one is afraid. This constructive confronting of normal anxiety in daily life and in crises which require moral rather than physical courage (such as the crises in self-development, often attended with profound anxiety, which occur during psychoanalysis), is sometimes accompanied by the effect of "adventure." At other times, however, when the anxiety-creating experience is more severe, confronting it may entail no pleasurable affect whatever but be accomplished only by the sheerest kind of dogged determination.

Laboratory Studies of Anxiety and Its Effects on Performance

The description of anxiety provided by May is drawn largely from clinical practice. His writing is a good illustration of the fact that often our knowledge of what is healthy can be increased by studying the sick. Such a procedure is only a good beginning; ultimately, to know the healthy we must observe them directly. In a series of researches beginning in the early 1950's, this has been done for the process of anxiety. Outside the clinics, among normally functioning people, the effect of anxiety on performance has been studied under laboratory conditions.

In describing this research on normal anxiety, we begin with two observations and some questions that follow from them: First, the administrator is confronted with people who vary in their characteristic level of anxiety, from highly anxious, almost continuously worried, individuals to those who show anxiety only under the most stressful conditions. This leads to a question, "What is the effect on performance of an already existing high level of anxiety?" Second, administrators, by virtue of their status and their control of significant sources of satisfaction for their people, can induce high levels of anxiety in others, either inadvertently or deliberately. We are then led to ask: "What is the effect on performance of anxiety induced by the administrator's demands?" The research results show that the answers to both questions are interwoven. In dealing with the second, we are led back to the first.

We begin by considering the growing evidence that identifies some people as success seekers and thus willing to set high levels of aspiration and others,

on the contrary, as failure-avoiders who set low levels of aspiration.* These
need tendencies are strongly influenced by early life experiences so that by
the time maturity is reached, reaction patterns to possible success or failure
have become relatively stable personality characteristics. The group for whom
the avoidance of failure is the more significant need may be considered anxiety
prone individuals in those achievement situations in which their performance
will be evaluated by others. The need-for-success group, on the other hand,
show little anxiety in such situations (Atkinson, 1961). It is not suggested here
that all persons can be dichotomized into one or the other group. Both traits
are probably normally distributed in any random population, so that there will
be many people who fall in the middle range of each characteristic. The significant points for the administrator are that there will be a substantial number
of people in his organization who differ significantly in achievement situations
by being oriented either principally toward the attainment of success or toward
the avoidance of failure, and that the latter group frequently show high anxiety.

Where it has been possible to identify high anxiety and low anxiety people
in achievement situations, differences in the quality of their performance have
been observed. High anxiety people do better than those with little anxiety
if they can be protected from feeling threatened. Thus, when the emphasis is
on the task rather than the person's ability to perform the task, anxiety seems to
aid performance. On the other hand, low anxiety people do better than high
anxiety people when the situation arouses a sense of threat (Sarason; Van
Buskirk).

We can understand these findings when we realize that anxiety can both
increase the drive to perform well (and so to please one's self and others) and
also tend to induce behavior that distracts the individual and interferes with his
achievement. Apparently, when the circumstances focus attention on the *task*,
the increased drive of the anxious individual helps him to superior performance; when the focus is on the *person* (and his possible failure) the anxiety
brings in a number of distracting responses (for example, worry or excuse-
making) that lower performance (Lowe). One study suggests the additional
possibility, under these circumstances, of a "vicious circle" reaction in which
knowledge that one is anxious increases the anxiety (Coppock, 1955).

Differences in the way in which high anxiety and low anxiety people respond to additional stress are sharply revealed in a study by Katchmar *et al.*
(1958). Although in the beginning of the experiment both groups performed
equally well on a complex problem, after both groups experienced failure,
performance of the low anxiety group improved, that of the high anxiety group
showed a decrement.

We may now return to the first question asked earlier in this section. What
is the effect on performance of an already existing high level of anxiety? The

---

* The position stated here is drawn principally from the work of Atkinson. A summary
statement of his position is presented in Atkinson (Annual Review, 1960). Other sources are
Atkinson, 1957, 1958; Atkinson and others 1960; Atkinson and Litwin 1960.

research findings clearly imply that whether the level of anxiety raises or lowers the level of performance is a function of the way the task is presented. Here is a condition that the administrator can control. For his high anxiety people, every situation is viewed by them as a test of themselves. The administrator will want to be supportive, assume some responsibility for the outcome himself, and focus attention on the task itself (and not on the employee and whether or not the latter can perform). He will avoid presenting the work as a challenge.

The evidence also should encourage the administrator to confront the *low* anxiety person with challenge and even a sense of stress to gain his maximum performance.°

The administrator has to use ordinary sensitivity to the reactions of others and to use his opportunities to observe performance in order to help him to know which of his people are success-seekers with a low potential for anxiety, and which are failure avoiders and thus frequently anxiety prone.

The answer to our second question, "What is the effect on performance of anxiety induced by the administrator's demands?" is a simple corollary of our answer to the first question. The administrator can improve performance by creating some anxiety for the low anxiety, high need achievement person, to keep his level of aspirations and subsequent performance high. He must minimize anxiety—producing demands for the high anxiety, failure avoiding person, to encourage him to work toward suitably high performance levels.

We thus return to our earlier generalization that moderate anxiety is facilitative, and severe anxiety is debilitative. A more precise statement of this generalization is presented in the summary Coleman (p. 171) has made which we quote in Research Summary 3-3.

RESEARCH SUMMARY 3-3	Effects of Anxiety°		
	Slight Anxiety	*Moderate Anxiety*	*Severe Anxiety*
	General alerting	Less spontaneity	Organization of behavior breaks down
	Increased sensitivity to outside events	Rigidity, reliance on "safe" habitual responses	Inability to distinguish between safe and harmful stimuli
	Physiological mobilization	Reduced ability to improvise	Stereotyped, unadaptive, random-appearing patterns
	Effective integration of behavior	More effort needed to maintain adequate behavior	Irritability, distractability
	Increase in ability for productive behavior	Narrowing and distortion of perception	Impaired learning, thinking

° These generalizations are drawn from many studies including Cannon, 1939; Liddell, 1944; Combs, 1952; Ausubel and others, 1954; Basowitz and others, 1955.

° We do not mean to imply that a person-centered approach should be used for low anxiety people and a production or task-centered approach for high anxiety people. Our point is that particularly when high anxiety people face achievement situations they be protected from the implied threat of an approach which emphasizes their personal stake in doing a good job.

Anxiety as a Motivating Influence

We have identified anxiety as one of life's psychological adversities, (a frequent and significant human experience), noted that there are differences among people in the amount of latent anxiety they bring into any situation, and, largely on the basis of laboratory studies, attempted to assess the effects of anxiety on performance. Anxiety, as has already been implied in earlier sections, is a compelling motivator (Farber), and anxiety-reduction, a universal goal.* Harry Stack Sullivan, founder of one of the principal psychoanalytic schools, expresses the thought this way: "I believe it fairly safe to say that anybody and everybody devotes much of his lifetime, and a great deal of his energy. . . . to avoiding more anxiety than he already has, and, if possible, to getting rid of some of this anxiety."

In Research Summaries 3-4 and 3-5 we present two quite different descriptions of organizational behavior; both, nevertheless, describe attempts to reduce anxiety.

RESEARCH SUMMARY 3-4	*Apprehension and the Fear of Failure: Anxiety in Successful Business Executives.* W. E. Henry studied the past job performance of more than a hundred business executives in a variety of middle-sized business organizations and established criteria enabling him to categorize each as successful or unsuccessful. All executives were given a battery of personality tests and a short undirected interview by a psychologist without knowledge of how the men had been categorized. The tests were then analyzed "blind," that is, without knowledge of whose tests were under study, and, independently of each other.

On the basis of the study, Henry was able to identify several personality characteristics that seemed to distinguish the successful from the unsuccessful executive. Among the traits that he found commonly characteristic of the successful executive (and absent in the personalities of the "failures") were: strong achievement drive (consistent with McClelland's study, Research Summary 2-4 . . .), a strong need for upward mobility, comfortable adjustment to authority and authority figures, high organizational abilities, decisiveness, a well-developed sense of self-identity, sensitivity to reality and its limitations, a high degree of activity and striving, a sense of identification and responsiveness to superiors, and strongly objective, detached ways of considering subordinates.

In addition, and of particular significance for our present discussion, the successful men exhibited a sense of dependency upon the policy and organizational framework of the company plus a pervasive sense of apprehension that they would not succeed in meeting organizational standards. This is, of course, the normal anxiety that May has described—an experiencing of threat to central values and one's sense of security.

---

* In *The Organizational Society* Presthus considers in detail the role of anxiety reduction in molding organizational behavior, conforming the individual's style to that of the organization (Ch. 4).

For these men, with strong achievement needs and an urge toward upward mobility, anxiety seems to motivate accomplishment. Their apprehensiveness presses them to work harder, invest more of themselves, and so, assure success. For them, movement toward success is the means of reducing anxiety.

The study reported in Research Summary 3-5 describes a quite different pattern of behavior, resulting presumably from the same need to reduce anxiety but found among individuals with different characteristics and in a different organizational setting.

RESEARCH
SUMMARY
3-5

Restricted Performance as a Defense Against Anxiety. When a job arouses strong feelings of anxiety and the social system surrounding the job does not provide a wholesome means of dealing with anxiety, individuals in the system will develop defenses that help them evade (rather than face) the anxiety; these defenses may be disruptive for the organization, interfering with the achievement of its goals. That is the picture drawn by Menzies in her study of a large British teaching hospital.

Brought in as a consultant to work out a more satisfactory allocation of staff and student time between patient service and training, Menzies soon saw the problem as a symptom, developed by the staff to help protect them from intense feelings of anxiety. The difficulty developed because the students allocated their time in ways more likely to minimize contact with anxiety arousing situations than to help patients or to train students.

Nursing in a hospital setting arouses strong feelings of anxiety in the individual. Death, pain, uncertainty, and strong emotional contacts, all surround the nurse. To deal with such strong anxiety, the individual requires support from the surrounding social system to help him confront the anxiety evoking experience and by so doing to develop capacities to tolerate and to deal more effectively with it. Menzies found that the hospital social system provided no such support. And, thus, the individuals (functioning through their profession and local group) developed some of the defenses stated below. These tend both to restrict the individual's own full development and accomplishment of the organization's goals.

Defense techniques identified by Menzies include:

splitting up the nurse-patient relationship so that several nurses were involved with each patient; each performing a somewhat different function (task specialization which reduced the intensity of patient-nurse contact);

depersonalizing the relationship by avoiding the use of patient names, referring to bed numbers, or patients by their illnesses;

performing tasks on a ritualistic basis to avoid the need for individual responsibility and to eliminate the need for decisions (Veblen's trained incapacity);

minimizing individual responsibility by building checks and counter checks into the system to protect everyone from feeling that he could make a fatal mistake;

a marked tendency to pass decisions up to superiors, student to nurse, to interne and so on.

Menzies, in her analysis of the situation, suggests that these defensive measures reduced the flexibility of operations, thus frequently producing a sense of administrative crisis, increased unnecessarily the shifting about of staff, created under-employment of student nurses, and deprived staff members of much real satisfaction in their jobs.

Here, then, we have another description of the possible effects of anxiety on behavior. In contrast to the executive group described in the Henry Study, who were prodded into superior performance by their anxiety, these hospital employees reduced anxiety by defenses that nevertheless narrowed their own satisfactions and their contributions to the organization goals.

Other studies: Worry, Psychosomatic Illness, and Emotional Disruption

We consider here research on several psychological and physical states which, if not anxiety are closely related to it. We have earlier stated that anxiety often expresses itself in worry and fretting. Neel, in a study that we have summarized in Research Summary 3-6 attempts to identify the specific worries of people who consider that the job makes them "nervous" or "jumpy." In Research Summary 3-7, still another possible expression of anxiety—psychosomatic ailment—is considered; in particular, the frequency with which certain kinds of psychosomatic ailment is found in executive and nonexecutive populations. In Reading 3-6, Schacter and his associates indicate the differential effect of emotional tension on routine nonchanging work assignments as compared with assignments undergoing methods changes. Summaries in these areas follow.

RESEARCH SUMMARY 3-6	*Some Typical Worries of Employee Groups.* Of some interest to administrators is the question of what specific things concern people who consider themselves jumpy or nervous on the job. Perhaps these are our anxiety-prone individuals. Neel has provided a tentative answer to the question for one group in the work force. After a group of 5,700 hourly rated workers of a manufacturing company had answered the question: "Does your work make you feel jumpy or nervous?", he correlated their *Yes-No* answers with answers to a series of specific worry questions. The highest correlations were found between general worries and worry about such specific matters as: health, failure to get ahead, accidents, or unhealthy job conditions, and temporary lay-offs. Moderately high correlations were found with: old age worries, lack of skill, and family problems. Lowest correlations on his list were money problems, feelings of being in a rut, and housing problems.

Neel's research is more interesting as an approach to an important problem than it is for any definitive answers it provides. His answers are suggestive but should *not* be substituted for an attempt to know the individual worrier and *his* particular concerns.

An earlier study of lifetime worries of a group of building trades employees suggests another important aspect of the problem. Van Zelst and Kerr found that lifetime worries fell into sequential clusters across the life span of their respondents. During the early adult years (up to 30) worries are largely personal—appearance, heterosexual adjustment, moral and religious concerns. During the early thirties, worries clustered around vocational success—meeting people, adjusting ambitions, and getting along with colleagues. Beginning in the late thirties and extending through the forties, there was a return to personal concerns, very similar to the concerns of the twenties. By the early fifties, this group began to show "declining years" types of worry: loss of work efficiency and loss of good health. The sequence here may be common for all work groups, however, the age breakdown probably differs for different occupational levels. And, of course, there will be individual variations.

RESEARCH SUMMARY 3-7	*Psychosomatic Illness in Executives.* Psychosomatic illness is a frequent response to stress. A widely held belief is that the demands made on executives are apparently more stressful than those faced by nonexecutives. This is supposed to cause a higher incidence of psychosomatic disorder in the executive population, with high blood pressure, heart attack, and gastric ulcers as the stereotyped "occupational" hazards. Lee and Schneider, in their study of a large population of executives and nonexecutives in the same age group and working in the same environment, report findings inconsistent with the stereotyped belief. Over a five-year period they compared the medical histories of 1,083 male executives with those of 293 nonexecutives. Both groups included only those over forty years of age and all participants in both groups worked for the same company in one building. They comment on their findings as follows:[*] The data . . . are surprising, for, in spite of the implied relationship between executive responsibilities and increased cardiovascular ailments, our data reveal no increase in incidence of either hypertensive or arteriosclerotic disease in the executive class. Hypertension generally appeared somewhat more frequently in subjects at lower levels of business duties. In considering arteriosclerotic disease as a whole, its occurrence among executives was significantly less than in persons in other work groups, of comparable age, and employed in the same office building. The incidence of certain diseases in employed personnel as determined by different observers may vary as much as twelvefold. For that reason, comparisons of the data obtained in the present study with those obtained by workers who were studying exclusively populations elsewhere must be made with this fact in mind. Nevertheless, in general terms, the incidence of hypertensive disease or arteriosclerotic disease in the executive and non-executive staffs studied herein compares favorably with, or is generally somewhat below that found in other studies. It is tempting to consider the possible reasons why even the

---

[*] R. E. Lee and R. F. Schneider, "Hypertension and Arterioclerosis in Executive and Nonexecutive Personnel," *Journal of the American Medical Association,* 167 (1958), pp. 1449-1450.

group of persons at the highest levels of executive responsibility showed no increase in incidence of the vascular states described and had notably fewer subjects with arteriosclerotic disease, as compared to less demanding positions from the business viewpoint. There is always the possibility that success in career attainment goes hand in hand with good health; in other words, the healthier go higher. A second possibility is that, with greater financial income, a person is able to afford a higher standard of living and perhaps more complete medical care from private physicians. This latter is not likely a major factor in the present study, because all of the subjects concerned have available to them and maintain the same medical followup program regardless of the level of duties within the organization. A third consideration should be to the matter of executive education and insight. The majority are college graduates, and several have postgraduate degrees. As a part of their training in the past, they have perhaps learned to realize the value of "escape valves" and the need for outside avenues of expression, such as hobbies. The benefit that may be derived from such endeavors has been emphasized repeatedly.

The lack of an increased incidence of hypertension among executives as a "stress" phenomenon further emphasized the importance of reaction by the individual to his environment, rather than the physical and intellectual demands of that environment per se. Stress is a relative and a subjective matter. When the inherent capacities of the individual to perform fail to measure up to the demands of his world, the harmonious balance between the subject and his environment is disrupted and a stress reaction takes place in the individual. This response occurs regardless of whether the factor in the external environment is a speedily approaching deadline for a frantic technical assistant or the threatened failure of a large business venture for the director in charge. From the medical viewpoint, one can therefore wonder whether at least a part of the recent emphasis on dangers of executive life to the vascular system may be based more in knowledge of the exceptions rather than of the rule.

Substantiation of the Lee and Schneider study is provided in a report from the DuPont Company (Fleming). In an early study, it was found that 700 top and junior executives showed no higher incidence of high blood pressure, coronary heart disease, and stomach ulcers than did a nonexecutive group of the same age. In a later study, 1,585 male salaried employees, 40 to 65 years of age were categorized into three management levels: top level executives, lower level executives, and nonexecutives. No significant differences were found among the groups in prevalence of high blood pressure, overweight, and hypercholesteremia. (Cholesterol level was lower among nonexecutives.) Smoking habits among the three groups were about the same, except that heavy smoking was more common among lower level executives than among top level executives.

READING 3-6

"Emotional Disruption and Productivity"*

S. SCHACTER, B. WILLERMAN,

L. FESTINGER, AND R. HYMAN

Though the introduction of new work procedures is a frequent event in many industries, the smoothness of the transition from one working procedure to another is usually unpredictable. Sometimes rebalancing an assembly line proceeds with no difficulty; at other times productivity drops precipitously after a change and it requires weeks for a work group to reach expected quality and production goals. Engineering, planning, supervision, and psychological factors are all involved in such a change, and it was the purpose of *this* study experimentally to examine the effects of emotional factors on the success of a planned change.

It is commonly assumed that emotional states such as anger and hostility are disruptive of performance. It is here hypothesized that such emotional states will be maximally disruptive of behavior that requires thought and concentration; but will have little effect on behaviors that are stereotyped, that is, behaviors such as walking or eating that are so

well mastered and habitual that they require neither attention nor thought. It is suggested that, once mastered, the typical assembly operation is of precisely this stereotyped character. The effect of introducing a change in working procedure is to convert the assembly operation from a completely stereotyped operation into one which requires, for a time, complete concentration. This analysis suggests the following hypotheses:

1. During regular factory operations, when no procedural changes are underway, the quality of production will be little affected by wide variations in emotional states disturbing the operators.
2. At times when changes in working procedures are being introduced, emotionally disturbed workers will have more difficulty making the transition than will relatively undisturbed operators.

To test these hypotheses, three independent field experiments were conducted on assembly groups working in General Electric factories. The results of all three studies support the hypotheses."

---

* Excerpted from *Journal of Applied Psychology*, 45, #4, pp. 212-213.

Some Characteristics of the Mature Personality

In assessing his own performance, as well as in understanding the behavior of others, the administrator needs some standards for judging what constitutes normal, healthy, and mature adjustment.

In the final reading of this chapter, Feinberg lists some characteristics of the mature personality. He attempts to synthesize current thinking and recently developed research on personality in a way that will be helpful to administrators. While he does not present research documentation for some statements, his paper does present, nevertheless, a good summary of present knowledge in a complex area.

Marks of Maturity *

MORTIMER R. FEINBERG

Psychologists and psychiatrists are all agreed on this: our ability to make the most of our lives depends on our emotional maturity, our constructive use of our inmost feelings.

The same emotional factors affect most of the other problems of our time—crime, delinquency, alcoholism, divorce, social conflict. In one way or another, each of these reflects a failure of personal maturity. The clue to personal success in growth, the progressive achievement of emotional maturity. To become more mature, we must first know what a mature person looks like—his make-up, the way he meets the challenge of his job and his family responsibilities, his outlook on the world.

The same problem of understanding maturity is important for an organization. Keyes[4] points out that, "Maturity—means the ability of an organization to respond to a variety of stimuli without resorting either to a fight or a flight from problems. When an organization is mature, it is able to deal with problems objectively. Its interests are broader and deeper than mere survival. It is able to operate with a degree of independence of its origins. It maintains a firm sense of reality. It is always flexible and adaptable, but it acts consistently in line with its purposes and its goals. It avoids ex-

pediency to gain short-range advantages for its corporate structure or for the administrative group which directs its destiny. It is able to produce more than it needs for survival; to give more than it gets."

The general principles are based on the thoughts of many psychologists. The insights are gleaned from both research and clinical observations. This paper will summarize and attempt to integrate some of the findings.[3, 5, 6, 10]

First some general questions about maturity.

A. *Is It a Matter of Intelligence?* A man may know the Encyclopedia Britannica by heart—and still be infantile in his emotions. All of us have seen how some of the most brilliant people are like children in controlling their feelings, in their overpowering need for affection from everybody they meet, in the way they handle themselves and others, or in their response to frustration.

But brilliance of intellect is no handicap to mature emotional development. Evidence suggests quite the contrary: bright people tend to effect superior emotional and social adjustments.[11]

B. *Is a Mature Person Always Happy?* Some people think that maturity means happiness. Freud once said that he considered himself successful if he changed a patient's neurosis into "common unhappiness." Emotional maturity does not guarantee freedom from worry and difficulty. Emotional maturity is demon-

---

* (Specially revised and adapted by the author from a report published by the Research Institute of America, 1956.)

strated by the way conflicts are solved, by the way pain is handled. People and organizations who have matured view their difficulties not as "disasters" but as "challenges."

C. *The Goal Is Unique for Each Individual.* A definition of maturity in Webster's Dictionary helps to clarify a point: "Mature—to advance towards perfection." The preposition is "towards," not "to." We can never advance to perfection but we can advance towards it, moving ever closer though we never reach it.

Further, the changes and growth of an individual as he advances towards maturity must be uniquely his own. Guidelines, such as the following, can be provided but each person must set up his own program. As the geneticist Dobzhansky[2] points out, "Evolution is not striving to achieve some foreordained goal; it is not the upholding of predetermined episodes and situations—evolutionary changes are *unique, non-recurrent,* and *creative.*"

Of the following six concepts of maturity, the first is the most important—and the hardest to achieve.

1. Acceptance of Self

Fundamental to mental health is the realization that the individual must accept himself as a human being. He is on the way to maturity if he can begin to appreciate himself without trying to be what he cannot possibly be. The mature person is able to appraise himself, and realizes that he has desirable traits as well as undesirable ones. He can direct his attention to the world outside because he is not busy fighting himself. To a great extent, this acceptance of self is a benefit of emotional health as well as a way to achieve it. Here are some guides:

a) A starting point is to know how you operate. Here the law of averages is on your side, for everybody has strengths, weaknesses, likes, dislikes.

b) Be fair to yourself. Acknowledge what you find. Recognize your own strengths and weaknesses without becoming over-proud or belittling yourself. If you can accept and enjoy your victories, you won't suffer unduly from defeats.

c) Keep a balanced attitude to avoid complacency. You have to accept what you can't change, but you must go about changing what you can. Constructive motivation, not fighting out losing battles, is the key to mental health.

The writer Somerset Maugham[8] in his autobiography, "The Summing Up," attributes his own success to his ability to confront his defects. He writes:

> I discovered my limitations and it seemed to me that the only sensible thing was to aim at what excellence I could within them. I knew that I had no lyrical quality. I had a small vocabulary, and no efforts that I could make to enlarge it much availed me. I had little gift of metaphor, the original and striking simile never occurred to me. Poetic flights and the great imaginative sweep were beyond my powers . . . I was tired of trying to do what did not come easily to me.
> On the other hand, I had an acute power of observation and it seemed to me that I could see a great many things that other people missed. I could put down in clear terms what I saw. I had a logical sense, and if no great feeling for the richness and strangeness of words, at all events a lively appreciation of their sound. I knew that I should never write as well as I could wish, *but I thought with pains I could arrive at writing as well as my natural defects allowed.*

The Hard Part: It's easy to admit our strengths—it's tough to tell ourselves just what our weaknesses are. But self-acceptance involves both. Each one of us has two sides to the scales, and we must be ready to weigh both.

If you're like most people, these are the realities you will find it hardest to accept about yourself: you have experienced failures because of your own deficiencies; there are some situations in your life that you handle awkwardly; you are not content with the place you now occupy in the world; you still have adolescent dreams that you have not yet given up.

To be mature, you must be willing to come to grips with your faults.

2. Accept Others

Only if a person can accept himself with all his faults, can he accept others in spite of their deficiencies. But notice that acceptance of others does not mean yielding to their follies. On the contrary, acceptance of others helps in recognizing and handling their faults. If you are tolerant of their faults, you will have no sense of guilt when you oppose their errors. You will be able to criticize them freely, knowing that you have no secret wish to injure them.

Besides, when you accept others with all their faults, you have the right to expect them to accept you with all of yours. You find that you don't have to give in to their whims in order to make them like you. The reason: a mature person doesn't constantly require the approval of others in order to respect himself.

3. Normal Dependency Needs

One of the advantages that flows from an acceptance of others is that fear at the idea of depending on others tends to disappear. In our complicated modern world, as in the 1600's, "no man is an island" sufficient unto himself. We must depend in part on the people we work for or who work with us; we cannot shoulder all the responsibility for every one of life's enterprises.

Once we admit to ourselves that we need others, we can accept them and depend on them without a feeling of anxiety. We can recognize our need for their affection, appreciation and approval without fear, shame or guilt.

But we have to avoid over-dependence. We must maintain a healthy level of dependency. Are there any standards for that? Here are some characteristics of mature dependency:

a) It is *occasional, not full time.* The mature person leans on others only in situations of real stress. But it is not his permanent way of life. Knowing himself, he consciously invites the aid of others to compensate for his weaknesses, but he remains independent in the area of his strengths.

b) It is *realistic.* A mature dependency is selective. It is directed only toward those who are able and willing to fulfill his needs. If those two tests are not met, he makes no further request for their assistance, and does not feel rejected or frustrated.

c) It is *reciprocal.* The traffic must move both ways. A mature person creates relationships in which he can not only be dependent but can also be depended upon.

Neither party in a relationship should always be giving while the other is always receiving. Indeed, taking and giving are two sides of the same emotional coin—one can't exist without the other. The mature person is capable of both.

4. Enjoy the Present

The mature person knows how to make the most of today. He doesn't live on an expectancy basis. He plans for the future, but he knows he must also live in the present. The mature person realizes that the best insurance for tomorrow is the effective use of today. Too much joy goes down life's drain because people fret about the past or worry about the future.

Immature people have a great fear of the future. Emotionally healthy individuals, however, do not allow the uncertainties of tomorrow to interfere with their enjoyment of present pleasures.

5. Patience with Problems

The mature person resists the temptation to seize upon the first answer to a problem. He is willing, at times, to wait out a problem until more facts are evaluated. The impulse to master all aspects of the environment may actually interfere with effective problem solving.

> Maslow[6] points out: . . . to the extent that we try to master the environment or be effective with it, to that extent do we cut off the possibility of full, objective, detached, non-interfering cognition. Only if we let it be, can we perceive fully. Again, to cite psychotherapeutic experience, the more eager we are to make a diagnosis and a plan of action, the *less* helpful do we become. The more eager we are to cure, the longer it takes. Every psychiatric researcher has to learn not to *try* to cure, *not* to be impatient. In this and in many other situations, to give in is to overcome, to be humble is to succeed. . . . But most important is my preliminary finding that this kind of cognition of the world is found more often in healthy people and may even turn out to be one of the defining characteristics of health.

6. Welcome Work

An emotionally healthy person knows how to enjoy the experience of work. He gets satisfaction from doing things well and may use work as a way of blowing off steam.

Here again, there is little difference among mature people, no matter what their walk of life. Appreciation of one's work is characteristic of the mature scholar and the mature bricklayer, the artist and the cook, the engineer and the lathe operator, the statistician and the stenographer. Each gets satisfaction out of life once he stops fighting his work and decides to enjoy it.

Just so, psychiatrist Abraham Meyerson[9] pointed out that even the simplest discovery comes from diligence. "A scholar," he wrote, "is like a pin, which as you know, must have a good sharp end as well as a good round end. The scholar's sharp end is to think with, his round end is to sit down to the job with. If he has only the sharp end, he becomes a dilletante flitting from job to job, accomplishing little. If he has only the round end, he is a pendant, unimaginative and uninspired."

No one matures overnight. No one matures completely. Growing is always a gradual, day-by-day process. It is a personal project with the full life span as the time table.

Bibliography

1. Darwin, F., *Life and Letters of Charles Darwin*, Vol. I. London: John Murray, 1887.
2. Dobzhansky, T., Evolution at Work. *Science*, May, 1958, 27.
3. Fiedler, F. E., The Concept of an Ideal Therapeutic Relationship. *Journal of Consulting Psychology*, 1950, 14, 239-245.
4. Keyes, E. J., *Maturity of an Organization*, paper presented at Eastern Psychological Association meeting, April, 1956.
5. Kornhauser, A., Toward an Assessment of the Mental Health of Factory Workers: A Detroit Study. *Human Organization*, 1962, 21, No. 1.

6. Maslow, A., *Motivation and Personality.* New York: Harper & Bros., 1954.

7. Maslow, A., *Health As a Transcendence of Environment,* paper presented at Eastern Psychological Association meeting, April, 1960, New York City.

8. Maugham, W. S., *The Summing Up.* New York: Doubleday & Co., 1946.

9. Meyerson, A., *Speaking of Man.* New York: Alfred A. Knopf, 1950.

10. Shaffer, L. and Shoben E., *The Psychology of Adjustment.* Boston and New York: Houghton Mifflin Co., 1956.

11. Terman, L. and Oden, M. H., *The Gifted Child Grows Up.* Stanford, Calif.: Stanford University Press, 1947.

CHAPTER NINE

Conflict

Introduction

We define conflict* as an internal state in which the individual is being pulled in opposite directions by forces within himself. Such forces may, of course, be stimulated by conditions in the environment (Cf. p. 124). Conflict is another one of the "psychological adversities" that influence behavior in the organization in complex ways. Here we focus largely on conflict as it is experienced by the individual, considering the many conflicting characteristics of the organization itself that may give rise to internalized conflict only indirectly.

The Nature of Conflict

A second excerpt from McNeil's article provides a good over-all description of the traditional psychological conception of conflict.

---

* We confine our discussion in this chapter to intra-psychic conflict. Conflict between individuals or groups is discussed briefly in relation to group problem solving in Ch. 23. A systematic presentation of inter-individual and inter-group conflict is presented in Anatol Rapoport's *Fights, Games and Debates*, and against a background of national and societal problems in Kenneth E. Boulding's *Conflict and Defense: A General Theory.*

READING 3-8

Conflict*

ELTON B. MC NEIL

It is not the more the merrier with drives. The simultaneous existence of one or more incompatible drives, urges,

---

* Excerpted from "Psychology and Aggression," *Journal of Conflict Resolution, 3,* (1959), pp. 200-201.

wishes, or needs heightens the risk of conflict—incompatible, in the sense that gratification of one would automatically eliminate the possibility of gratifying the other. The familiar conflicts of daily life are usually resolved simply by holding one need in abeyance while gratifying the other. Yet if the antagonistic needs are both intense or both vital to the emotional equilibrium of the individual, such conflict can be highly disruptive to the psychic economy. If conflict were a limited or self-contained process, it would play only a minor part in human adjustment; but, as Miller noted, conflict tends to spread to new situations and encompass an ever expanding share of the individual's emotional life.

Conflict may occur between incompatible needs, between incompatible modes of behavior aroused by the needs, or may exist in choosing a means of gratifying the needs. All conflicts are not of equal intensity; some involve merely choosing between simple alternatives, such as two television shows scheduled at the same time, which is easily resolved because the deprivation is not very great in either case. Successively more complicated are the conflicting attractions of two vital goals or two paths to the same goal. Although such conflicts can be crippling, the most extreme form of disruption is provided by catastrophic struggles in which no alternative is reasonable and all courses of action are equally threatening.

Another way of describing human conflict is in terms of whether the conflicting alternatives are viewed as positive or negative ones. If one has to choose between a Thunderbird and a Cadillac, both alternatives would appear to be positive. For convenience, these can be designated as plus-plus conflicts, to indicate the attractiveness of the alternatives. Conflicts of this sort are usually of minor significance and become severe only when they are rooted in other emotional problems. When need-satisfiers have both positive and negative aspects, such as the thorn that accompanies the rose, then vacillation, indecision, or worry is more likely to result. Minus-minus conflicts are highly threatening and evoke extreme forms of human behavior. "Out of the frying pan into the fire" is a minus-minus conflict. The complexity of human behavior allows an infinite variety of combinations of plus and minus characteristics and thus an infinite variety of conflicts.

An important aspect of the concept of conflict is the strength of the opposing forces. If the conflict is between an aggressive impulse and the prohibition of its expression and if both the impulse and the prohibition are intense, the person in whom the conflict rages can be reduced to helplessness by the battle of impulse versus restraint.

Cognitive Dissonance: A Form of Conflict

Festinger's recently developed concept of cognitive dissonance (1) establishes conflict resolution as a strong motivating force in human experience; (2) identifies particular tensions associated with conflict; and (3) suggests the dynamics frequently underlying conflict resolution. His position is presented in the reading that follows.

Cognitive Dissonance as a Motivating State[*]

LEON FESTINGER

. . . First of all, I should like to postulate the existence of *cognitive dissonance* as a motivating state in human beings. Since most of you probably never heard of cognitive dissonance, I assume that so far I have been no more informative than if I had said that I wish to postulate X as a motivating state. I will try, then, to provide a conceptual definition of cognitive dissonance. Let me start by trying to convey, in a loose way, what I have in mind. Afterward we can arrive at a more formal conceptual definition.

Definition of Dissonance

The word "dissonance" was not chosen arbitrarily to denote this motivating state. It was chosen because its ordinary meaning in the English language is close to the technical meaning I want to give it. The synonyms which the dictionary gives for the word "dissonant" are "harsh," "jarring," "grating," "unmelodious," "inharmonious," "inconsistent," "contradictory," "disagreeing," "incongruous," "discrepant." The word, in this ordinary meaning, specifies a relation between two things. In connection with musical tones, where it is usually used, the relation between the tones is such that they sound unpleasant together. In general, one might say that a dissonant relation

exists between two things which occur together, if, in some way, they do not belong together or fit together.

Cognitive dissonance refers to this kind of relation between cognitions which exist simultaneously for a person. If a person knows two things, for example, something about himself and something about the world in which he lives which somehow do not fit together, we will speak of this as cognitive dissonance. Thus, for example, a person might know that he is a very intelligent, highly capable person. At the same time, let us imagine, he knows that he meets repeated failure. These two cognitions would be dissonant —they do not fit together. In general, two cognitions are dissonant with each other if, considering these two cognitions alone, the obverse of one follows from the other. Thus, in the example we have given, it follows from the fact that a person is highly capable that he does not continually meet with failure.

The phrase "follows from" that was used in the previous two sentences needs some explaining. Without going into it in too great detail here, I should like to stress that we are concerned with psychological implication and not necessarily logical implication. The psychological implication which one cognition can have for another cognition can arise from a variety of circumstances. There can be psychological implication because of experience and what one has learned. Thus, if a person is out in the rain with no umbrella or raincoat, it follows from this that he will get wet. There can also be

[*] Abridged from "The Motivating Effect of Cognitive Dissonance," in *Assessment of Human Motives*, edited by Gardner Lindzey. Copyright © 1958 by Gardner Lindzey. Reprinted by permission of Holt, Rinehart and Winston, Inc., Publishers, pp. 65-86.

psychological implication because of cultural mores and definition. If one is at a highly formal dinner party, it follows from this that one does not pick up the food with one's fingers. . . .

How Cognitive Dissonance Resembles Other Need States. Thus far I have said nothing about the motivating aspects of cognitive dissonance. This is the next step. I wish to hypothesize that the existence of cognitive dissonance is comparable to any other need state. Just as hunger is motivating, cognitive dissonance is motivating. Cognitive dissonance will give rise to activity oriented toward or eliminating the dissonance. Successful reduction of dissonance is rewarding in the same sense that eating when one is hungry is rewarding.

In other words, if two cognitions are dissonant with each other there will be some tendency for the person to attempt to change one of them so that they do fit together, thus reducing or eliminating the dissonance. There are also other ways in which dissonance may be reduced but, not having the time to go into a complete discussion of this, I would rather confine myself to this one manifestation of the motivating character of cognitive dissonance.

Data Needed to Demonstrate the Motivating Character of Cognitive Dissonance. Before proceeding, let us consider for a moment the kinds of data one would like to have in order to document the contention that cognitive dissonance is a motivating state. One would like to have at least the following kinds of data:

1. Determination at Time 1 that a state of cognitive dissonance exists. This could be done either by measurement or by experimental manipulation.

2. Determination at Time 2 that the dissonance has been eliminated or reduced in magnitude.

3. Data concerning the behavioral process whereby the person has suc-

ceeded in changing some cognition, thus reducing the dissonance.

Actually, the above three items are minimal and would probably not be sufficient to demonstrate cogently the validity of the theory concerning cognitive dissonance.

. . .

. . . one has to demonstrate the effects of dissonance in circumstances where these effects are not easily explainable on the basis of other existing theories. Indeed, if one cannot do this, then one could well ask what the usefulness was of this new notion that explained nothing that was not already understood. Consequently, in order to persuade you of the validity of cognitive dissonance and its motivating characteristics I will give [an example of dissonance reduction].*

[An] intriguing example of the reduction of dissonance in a startling manner comes from a study I did together with Riecken and Schachter of a group of people who predicted that, on a given date, a catastrophic flood would overwhelm most of the world. This prediction of the catastrophic flood had been given to the people in direct communications from the gods and was an integral part of their religious beliefs. When the predicted date arrived and passed there was considerable dissonance established in these people. They continued to believe in their gods and in the validity of the communications from them, and at the same time they knew that the prediction of the flood had been wrong. We observed the movement as participants for approximately two months preceding and one month after this unequivocal disproof of part of their belief. The point of the study was, of course, to observe

---

* One of Festinger's examples is omitted here. See Prasad and also Sinha in bibliography at end of this reading.

how they would react to the dissonance. Let me give a few of the details of the disproof and how they reacted to it.

For some time it had been clear to the people in the group that those who were chosen were to be picked up by flying saucers before the cataclysm occurred. Some of the believers, these mainly college students, were advised to go home and wait individually for the flying saucer that would arrive for each of them. This was reasonable and plausible, since the date of the cataclysm happened to occur during an academic holiday. Most of the group, including the most central and most heavily committed members, gathered together in the home of the woman who received the messages from the gods to wait together for the arrival of the saucer. For these latter, disproof of the prediction, in the form of evidence that the messages were not valid, began to occur four days before the predicted event was to take place. A message informed them that a saucer would land in the back yard of the house at 4:00 P.M. to pick up the members of the group. With coat in hand they waited, but no saucer came. A later message told them there had been a delay—the saucer would arrive at midnight. Midst absolute secrecy (the neighbors and press must not know), they waited outdoors on a cold and snowy night for over an hour, but still no saucer came. Another message told them to continue waiting, but still no saucer came. At about 3:00 A.M. they gave up, interpreting the events of that night as a test, a drill, and a rehearsal for the real pickup which would still soon take place.

Tensely, they waited for the final orders to come through—for the messages which would tell them the time, place, and procedure for the actual pickup. Finally, on the day before the cataclysm was to strike, the messages came. At midnight a man would come to the door of the house and take them to the place where the flying saucer would be parked. More messages came that day, one after another, instructing them in the passwords that would be necessary in order to board the saucer, in preparatory procedures such as removal of metal from clothing, removal of personal identification, maintaining silence at certain times, and the like. The day was spent by the group in preparation and rehearsal of the necessary procedures and, when midnight came, the group sat waiting in readiness. But no knock came at the door, no one came to lead them to the flying saucer.

From midnight to five o'clock in the morning the group sat there struggling to understand what had happened, struggling to find some explanation that would enable them to recover somewhat from the shattering realization that they would not be picked up by a flying saucer and that consequently the flood itself would not occur as predicted. It is doubtful that anyone alone, without the support of the others, could have withstood the impact of this disproof of the prediction. Indeed, those members of the group who had gone to their homes to wait alone, alone in the sense that they did not have other believers with them, did not withstand it. Almost all of them became skeptics afterward. In other words, without easily obtainable social support to begin reducing the dissonance, the dissonance was sufficient to cause the belief to be discarded in spite of the commitment to it. But the members of the group that had gathered together in the home of the woman who received the messages could, and did, provide social support for one another. They kept reassuring one another of the validity of the messages and that some explanation would be found.

At fifteen minutes before five o'clock

that morning an explanation was found that was at least temporarily satisfactory. A message arrived from God which, in effect, said that He had saved the world and stayed the flood because of this group and the light and strength this group had spread throughout the world that night.

The behavior of these people from that moment onwards presented a revealing contrast to their previous behavior. These people who had been disinterested in publicity and even avoided it, became avid publicity seekers. For four successive days, finding a new reason each day, they invited the press into the house, gave lengthy interviews, and attempted to attract the public to their ideas. The first day they called all the newspapers and news services, informed them of the fact that the world had been saved and invited them to come and get interviews. The second day, a ban on having photographs taken was lifted, and the newspapers were once more called to inform them of the fact and to invite them to come to the house and take pictures. On the third day they once more called the press to inform them that on the next afternoon they would gather on their front lawn singing and that it was possible a space man would visit them at that time. What is more, the general public was specifically invited to come and watch. And on the fourth day, newspapermen and about two hundred people came to watch the group singing on their front lawn. There were almost no lengths to which these people would not go to attract publicity and potential believers in the validity of the messages. If, indeed, more and more converts could be found more and more people who believed in the messages and the things the messages said then the dissonance between their belief and the knowledge that the messages had not been correct could be reduced.

These examples, while they do illustrate attempts to reduce dissonance in rather surprising directions, still leave much to be desired. One would also like to be able to show that such dissonance-reduction phenomena do occur under controlled laboratory conditions and that the magnitude of the effect does depend upon the magnitude of the dissonance which exists. Consequently, I will describe for you a laboratory experiment which we have just completed at Stanford, one in which we investigated the reduction of dissonance following experimental manipulation of the magnitude of dissonance. The obtained results are, in my opinion, not easily interpreted in terms of other existing theories.

An Experimental Investigation. In this experiment, we created dissonance in the subjects by inducing them to say something which was at variance with their private opinion. It is clear that this kind of situation does produce dissonance between what the person believes and what he knows he has said. There are also cognitive consonances for the person. His cognitions concerning the things that induced him to make the public statement are consonant with his knowledge of having done it. The total magnitude of the dissonance between all other relevant cognitions taken together and the knowledge of what he has publicly said will, of course, be a function of the number and importance of the dissonances in relation to the number and importance of the consonances. One could, then, manipulate the total magnitude of dissonance experimentally by holding everything constant and varying the strength of the inducement for the person to state something publicly which was at variance with his private opinion. The *stronger* the inducement to do this, the *less* would be the over-all magnitude of dissonance created.

Let us imagine a concrete situation.

Suppose a number of people have had an experience to which they reacted negatively. Each of these persons, then, let us say, is offered a different amount of money to tell someone else that the experience was very pleasant and enjoyable. In each case, let us further imagine, the amount of money offered is at least large enough so that the person accepts the money and engages in the overt behavior required. Certainly, after telling someone that the experience was enjoyable, there is a dissonance between his cognition of what he has said and his own private opinion.

This dissonance could, clearly, be reduced if the person persuades himself that the experience was, indeed, fairly pleasant and enjoyable, that is, if he changes his private opinion so that it corresponds more closely with what he has said. The greater the dissonance, the more frequently should one observe such subsequent attitude change. We would expect then that, after the person had told someone else that the experience was pleasant and enjoyable, he would change his private opinions concerning the experience to some extent. We would further expect that the more money he was given to induce him to make the public statement, the smaller would be the subsequent opinion change, because less dissonance had been created initially.

Now for the details of the experiment. I will describe it as it proceeded for the subject, with occasional explanatory comments. Each subject had signed up for a two hour experiment on "measures of performance." The subjects were all students from the Introductory Psychology course at Stanford where they are required to serve a certain number of hours as subjects in experiments. When the student arrived he was met by the experimenter and, with a minimum of explanation, was given a repetitive motor task to work on. He packed a frame full of little spools, then emptied it, then packed it again, and so on for a half hour. He was then given another task to do in which he turned rows of pegs, each a quarter turn, then turned them all another quarter turn, and so on for another half hour. When he had finished, the experimenter informed him that the experiment was over, thanked him for his participation, and proceeded to explain to him what the experiment was about and what its purpose was.

From our point of view, the purpose of this initial part was to provide for each subject an experience which was rather dull, boring, and somewhat fatiguing. The student, however, believed this to be the whole experiment. The explanation of the experiment given to the student was that the experiment was concerned with the effect of preparatory set on performance. He was told that there were two conditions in the experiment, one of these being the condition he had experienced where the subject was told nothing ahead of time. The other condition, the experimenter explained, was one in which the subject, before working on the tasks, was led to expect that they were very enjoyable, very interesting, and lots of fun. The procedure for subjects in this other condition, the experimenter explained, proceeded in the following manner. A person working for us is introduced to the waiting subject as someone who has just finished the experiment and will tell the prospective subject a little about it. This person who works for us then tells the waiting subject that the experiment is very enjoyable, interesting, and lots of fun. In this way, the subjects in the other condition are given the set we want them to have. This concluded the false explanation of the experiment to the student and, in the control group, nothing more was done at this point.

In the experimental groups, however,

the experimenter continued by telling the subject that he had a rather unusual proposal to make. It seems that the next subject is scheduled to be in that condition where he is to be convinced in advance that the experiment is enjoyable and a lot of fun. The person who works for us and usually does this, however, although very reliable, could not do it today. We thought we would take a chance and ask him (the student) to do it for us. We would like, if agreeable to him, to hire him on the same basis that the other person was hired to work for us. We would like to put him on the payroll and pay him a lump sum of money to go tell the waiting subject that the experiment is enjoyable, interesting, and fun; and he was also to be on tap for us in case this kind of emergency arises again.

There were two experimental conditions which we actually conducted. The procedure was absolutely identical in both except for the amount of money that the subjects were paid as "the lump sum." In one condition they were paid one dollar for their immediate and possible future services. In the other condition they were paid twenty dollars. When the student agreed to do this, he was actually given the money and he signed a receipt for it. He was then taken into the room where the next subject was waiting and introduced to her by the experimenter, who said that the student has just been a subject in the experiment and would tell her a bit about it. The experimenter then went out, leaving student and the waiting subject together for two and a half minutes. The waiting subject was actually a girl in our employ. Her instructions were very simple. After the student had told her that the experiment was interesting, enjoyable and lots of fun, she was to say something like, "Oh, a friend of mine who took it yesterday told me it was dull and that if I could I

should get out of it." After that she was simply supposed to agree with whatever the student said. If, as almost always happened, the student reaffirmed that the experiment was fun, she was to say that she was glad to hear it.

· · ·

When the experimenter returned, after two and a half minutes, he sent the girl into the experimental room, telling her he would be there in a few minutes. He then obtained the student's phone number in order to continue the fiction that the student was to be available for future services of like nature. The experimenter then thanked the subject and made a brief speech in which he said that most subjects found the experimental tasks very interesting and enjoyed them, and that, when he thinks about it, he will probably agree. The purpose of this brief speech is to provide some cognitive material which the subject can use to reduce dissonance, assuming that such dissonance exists. The identical speech is, of course, made to the control subjects, too.

The only remaining problem in the experiment was to obtain a measure of what each subject honestly thought privately about the tasks on which he had worked for an hour. It seemed desirable, naturally, to obtain this measure in a situation where the subject would be inclined to be very frank in his statements. It also seemed desirable to obtain these measures quite independently of the actual experiment. This was done in the following manner. It had previously been announced by the instructor in the Introductory Psychology class that, since students were required to participate in experiments, the Psychology Department was going to do a study to assess the value of the experiences they had. The purpose of this, the instructor had explained, was to help improve the selection of experiments in the future. They were told that a sample of them, after serving in experiments, would be interviewed about them. It would be to their advantage, and to the advantage of future students in the course, for them to be very frank and honest in these interviews.

In our experiment, the student was told that someone from Introductory Psychology probably wanted to interview him. The experimenter confessed ignorance about what this impending interview was about but said he had been told that the subject would know about it. Usually at this point the subject nodded his head or otherwise indicated that he did, indeed, know what it was about. The experimenter then took him to an office where the interviewer was waiting, said good-bye to the subject, and left.

The interview itself was rather brief. Four questions were asked, namely, how interesting and enjoyable the experiment was, how much the subject learned from it, how important he thought it was scientifically, and how much he would like to participate in a similar experiment again. The important question, for us, is the first one concerning how interesting and enjoyable the experiment was, since this was the content area in which dissonance was established for the experimental subjects. The subject was encouraged to answer the question in some detail and then was asked to rate, on a scale running from -5 to $+5$, how he felt about it. The other questions were included to make the interview realistic and also to provide a comparison, since there seemed little reason to believe that there would or should be any difference among the three conditions on the questions concerning how much they learned and how important the experiment was. There might, of course, be differences on the question concerning their desire to

participate in a similar experiment, the answers to which would undoubtedly reflect, in part, how much they liked this one.

Needless to say, since it is standard practice, after the interview was concluded, the experimenter, the student, and the girl who posed as the waiting subject were brought together, and the truth about the whole experiment was explained in detail to the subject's satisfaction.

Some of you may wonder about the effectiveness of the experimental procedure. Were the subjects really taken in by all of it? Actually, if you have been wondering about this, let me assure you that it is a legitimate thing to wonder about. It took us several months of preliminary work to get the procedure in a form so that subjects did not become suspicious. In its present form, the procedure I have described works well. Of the forty subjects, twenty in each of the two experimental conditions (there were, of course, also twenty control subjects, but here there is no problem) only 5 gave evidence of suspecting that the experiment really dealt with having him talk to the waiting subject. These few subjects, of course, had to be omitted from the data.

Let us look, then, at what the results show. Figure 1 shows the average rating, for each of the three conditions, for the question concerning how interesting and enjoyable the experiment was. A rating of -5 meant extremely dull and boring, $+5$ meant extremely interesting and enjoyable, and 0 meant neutral. The subject could, of course, rate his reaction to the experiment anywhere between -5 and $+5$. The average rating for the control group is represented as a horizontal dotted line across the figure. It is done this way since the data from the control group actually provide a base line. This is how subjects reacted to the experiment

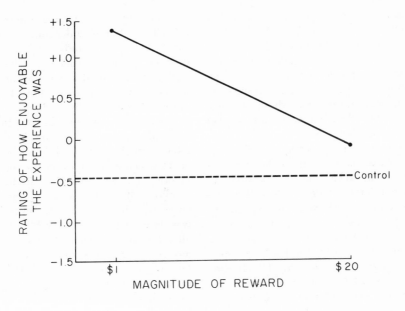

Figure 1

Relation Between Magnitude of Reward Used to Elicit Compliance and Subsequent
Rating of How Enjoyable the Experiment Was.

after having gone through it and having been told exactly the same things that the experimental subjects were told. They simply were never asked to, and never did, tell the waiting subject that the experiment was interesting, enjoyable, and lots of fun. It turns out that, on the average, the control group rates the experiment −.45 for how enjoyable it was, slightly below neutral. In the One Dollar experimental condition there is a definite increase over the control group. Here the average rating is +1.35, definitely on the positive side of the scale and significantly different from the control group at the 1 per cent level of confidence. In other words, in the One Dollar condition the dissonance between their private opinion of the experiment and their knowledge of what they had said to the waiting subject was reduced significantly by changing their private opinion somewhat, to bring it closer to what they had overtly said.

But now let us turn our attention to the Twenty Dollar condition. Here the magnitude of dissonance experimentally created was less than in the One Dollar condition because of the greater importance of the cognition that was consonant with what they knew they had done. It seems undeniable that twenty dollars is a good deal more important than one dollar. There should hence be less pressure to reduce the dissonance, and indeed, the average rating for the Twenty Dollar condition is −.05, only slightly above the Control condition and significantly different from the One Dollar condition at the 2 per cent level of confidence.

While I will not take the time to present the data on the other questions in detail, I will say that there were no significant differences on any of the other questions among the three conditions in the experiment. On the scale concerning how much they feel they learned from the experiment, the three means are virtually identical. On their desire to participate again in a similar experiment and on how scientifically important they think it is, the results are in the same direction as those we have shown, but the differences are smaller and not significant.

There is just one other point I would like to discuss about the data from this experiment. What are the possible alternative interpretations? Clearly, any interpretation which seeks to explain the opinion change in terms of reward or reinforcement is doomed to failure, since the smaller reward led to the larger opinion change. Janis and King (1954; King and Janis, 1956) have published two experiments in which they show that opinion change occurs after a person has made a speech favoring a particular point of view. They offer an explanation of their results mainly in terms of rehearsal of arguments, thinking up new arguments, and in this way convincing themselves. Could this be an explanation of the difference between the One and Twenty Dollar conditions? On the surface it appears implausible, since such an explanation would demand that the subjects in the One Dollar condition would have tried harder to be persuasive when talking to the waiting girl than the subjects in the Twenty Dollar condition. This would seem unlikely since, if anything, having received more money, they should be *more* motivated to do a good job in the Twenty Dollar condition. However, strange things sometimes happen; with this possibility in mind, we obtained recordings of the discussion between the subjects and the waiting girl. These have been rated for persuasiveness, number of different things the subject says, and other conceivably relevant variables. The ratings were, of course, done in ignorance of the experimental condition by two separate raters. The reliability of the independent ratings varies between .6 and .9. The ratings used in the actual analysis of the data were settled on by discussion of disagreements between the two raters. It turns out that there are no large differences between the two experimental conditions in what the subject said or how he said it. As one might expect, the small differences which do exist are in the direction favoring the $20 condition. In the $20 condition the subjects are a bit more emphatic about saying the experiment was interesting and enjoyable. Personally, I have not been able to think of any very satisfactory alternative explanation of the results. It is precisely this difficulty of devising alternative explanations that makes these results strongly supportive of the dissonance interpretation.

Summary and Conclusions

The evidence for the validity and usefulness of conceiving cognitive dissonance as motivating is as follows:

1. Evidence that the existence of cognitive dissonance sometimes leads to behavior that appears very strange indeed when viewed only from the standpoint of commonly accepted motives. Here I have had time only to give two examples illustrating this phenomenon.

2. Evidence that the amount of reduction of dissonance is a direct function of the magnitude of dissonance which exists. I illustrated this by describing a laboratory experiment where, under controlled conditions, the magnitude of dissonance was experimentally manipulated.

There is at least one further point that I would have liked to have made, and would have if I had supporting data. If cognitive dissonance is indeed a motivating state, one would like to be able to show, assuming that individual differences exist, which they almost certainly do, that those persons for whom it is more highly motivating react more strongly. In order to do this one would first have to have some way of measuring the degree to which cognitive dissonance is painful or uncomfortable for the individual. This I do not as yet have. It is, though, one of the clearly important goals of the future.

I stress this lack, not so much to emphasize that a measure of individual differences is missing, but rather to re-emphasize what I consider an important procedural point. I do not think it will be maximally fruitful in the long run to begin by developing tests to give measures of the strength of some hypothesized human need, and then to attempt to discover how this need operates. I believe strongly that it is better to proceed in the reverse order. After one has demonstrated the validity and usefulness of some hypothesized need is the time to start measuring individual variation. One then

knows much more clearly what one is trying to measure, why one is trying to measure it, and to what the individual measure should relate.

References

Festinger, Leon. *A theory of cognitive dissonance*. Evanston, Ill.: Row-Peterson, 1957.

————, Riecken, H. W., and Schachter, S. *When prophecy fails*. Minneapolis: University of Minnesota Press, 1956.

Janis, I. L., and King, B. T. The influence of role-playing on opinion change. *J. abnorm. soc. Psychol.*, 1954, *49*, 211-218.

King, B. T., and Janis, I. L. Comparison of the effectiveness of improvised versus non-improvised role-playing in producing opinion changes. *Human Relations*, 1956, *9*, 177-186.

Prasad, J. A comparative study of rumors and reports in earthquakes. *Brit. J. Psychol.*, 1950, *41*, 129-144.

Sinha, D. Behavior in a catastrophic situation: a psychological study of reports and rumors. *Brit. J. Psychol.*, 1952, *43*, 200-209.

Post-Decisional Conflict

We have thus far been talking about conflict prior to action—tensions leading to or resulting from an inability to make a decision. There is also the problem of looking back over one's shoulder after a decision has been made. Janis has carried out a series of researches on the process, which he calls post-decisional conflict. The point is, that conflict may either prevent a decision or block its implementation after the decision is made. Janis' research describes some conditions that cause people to worry, show blocking behavior, or other signs of conflict after a decision has been made.

Although Janis does not do so, his concept of post-decisional conflict can readily be cast into Festinger's theoretical development of cognitive dissonance: after a decision is made, a person finds himself committed to undertake an action that has some negative aspects to it.

Janis' work is represented first (Reading 3-10) by a summarizing general statement of his (excerpted from a longer discussion) that identifies important determinants of post-decisional conflict. Two studies of his are then presented in summarized form. The first (Reading 3-11) describes one way of adjusting to post-decisional conflict: Under conditions in which there are strong reasons for a person's wanting to carry out the decision, he will tend to deny the existence of reasons that should cause him not to carry out the decision. In the second (Reading 3-12) in a field experiment, Janis is able to identify preparatory actions that can be taken before the decision, to minimize conflict after the decision.

Motivational Factors in the Resolution of Decisional Conflicts*

I. L. JANIS

Determinants of the Mode of Resolution

The final *choice* of a mode of conflict-resolution probably depends upon many different predispositional and situational factors. By "choice" I do not, of course, mean to imply that the readjustive processes under discussion are carried out in a deliberate, fully conscious way; rather, I conceptualize the choice as often being the outcome of either preconsciousness or unconscious processes.

In a separate paper, I have presented a series of sample hypotheses and have illustrated some of the various determinants with historical examples from biographical studies bearing on the decisional conflicts of several American presidents and other national leaders who were responsible for important policy decisions affecting international war and peace. At this point I shall merely list six main types of determinants.

1. *Perceived status:* If a decision-maker perceives himself as having high status within the community and as having a high power position within the groups he belongs to, he will be much less re-

sponsive to signs that would ordinarily tend to evoke intense postdecisional conflict over potential loss of prestige, loss of social approval, or loss of self-esteem; as a consequence of the lower intensity of postdecisional conflict, such a person will tend to use less extreme modes of resolution (such as cognitive restructuring and compensatory actions) rather than more extreme modes (such as disaffiliation or self-condemnation) which tend to occur only when there is sustained postdecisional conflict at high level of intensity.

2. *Personality factors:* Chronic level of self-esteem and related personality factors probably determine the intensity of conflict engendered by information about failures and setbacks following major decisions. In recent years, systematic studies have been carried out on personality correlates of persuasibility, as measured by correlations between personality test scores and opinion change scores following exposure to persuasive communications. A number of these studies will soon be published in a forth-coming volume on *Personality and Persuasibility* by Hovland and myself, with the collaboration of R. P. Abelson, A. R. Cohen, and other coworkers in our Yale research project. Some of the main personality correlates isolated in these studies probably are applicable to those special classes of communications which a) arouse deci-

* In *Nebraska Symposium on Motivation*, M. R. Jones, Ed.; 1959. University of Nebraska Press, Lincoln, Nebraska, pp. 219-221. Bibliographic items omitted. Readings 3-10, 3-11, and 3-12 are all excerpted from this article by Janis.

sional conflicts, and b) urge the conflicted decision-maker to adopt a mode of resolution requiring relatively drastic changes in attitudes.

3. *Effortfulness of the mode of resolution:* A person's anticipation of the amount of time and energy required for a given compensatory activity will partially determine whether or not he will initially try it out. If the first, relatively noneffortful modes (such as cognitive restructuring) do not succeed in alleviating the emotional tension generated by a postdecisional crisis, more effortful modes will be resorted to. Certain modes (such as disaffiliating from a primary group, which may entail changing one's entire daily life patterns) would consume an enormous amount of one's available energy, and, partly for this reason, will be among the last ones to be tried out.

4. *Institutionalized patterns and traditions:* Policy-makers in an organizational or governmental hierarchy are likely to be encouraged to use certain modes of resolution and discouraged from using others on the basis of institutionalized practices or "operational codes" which foster compensatory behavior, persuasive efforts, overt self-condemnation, or some other form of action as the preferred mode of resolving acute postdecisional conflicts.

5. *Availability of postdecisional information:* When a person is in the throes of an acute postdecisional conflict, he will tend to seek for information that is relevant to his choice of a mode of resolution. Most pertinent of all is information as to which types of activity are most likely to be successful in warding off the threatened loss or disapproval. For example, certain bits of information available to an organizational leader may make him feel that although there is little chance of persuading fellow officers to support his policy, he can be quite optimistic about winning their esteem if he volunteers to take on certain additional administrative tasks, as a compensatory action.

6. *Advance warnings and predictions:* Another important type of information consists of advance warnings and predictions to which the decision maker is exposed *before* an acute postdecisional crisis arises. Appropriate preparatory communications can probably diminish the impact of subsequent setbacks and reduce the chances of thoughtless, impulsive attempts at resolving the postdecisional conflict. A great deal of my own theoretical thinking and empirical research has been centered on problems concerning long-run effects of preparatory communications.

Denial as a Means of Resolving Post-Decisional Conflict

Sometimes a decision to continue activity that is pleasant or rewarding in a special way is conflicted by the presentation of information suggesting negative or even harmful outcomes. One of Janis' experiments provides a description of one method used to resolve the post-decisional conflict that develops. The method would seem to be an unwholesome one: denial of the evidence that suggests the negative outcome.

Janis' subjects were habitual smokers who faced a dilemma when they were given impressive information about the harmful effects of the smoking habit. A group of nonsmokers served as controls.

READING 3-11

An Experimental Demonstration of Denial as a Means of Resolving Post-Decisional Conflict*

I. L. JANIS

The study was carried out by Janis and Terwilliger with a sample of 31 adults of ages 18 through 55, representing a broad range of occupations and educational levels. This group contained roughly equal numbers of smokers and nonsmokers.

Each subject was given a private interview, during which he was exposed to a communication which promoted the conclusion that heavy smoking causes cancer and which recommended that everyone should avoid or cut down on cigarette smoking. The basic communication consisted of 16 paragraphs and was made up mainly of authentic quotations from medical authorities. For half of the subjects, a *strong fear appeal* was inserted into the basic communication, which consisted of seven additional paragraphs containing vivid descriptions of the suffering and poor prognosis of cancer victims. For the other half of the subjects, a *mild fear appeal* was inserted, which used more objective language and did not elaborate on the most threatening aspects of the disease. Another communication variable (involving the massing versus spacing of reassuring statements that minimize the threat) was also experimentally manipulated and systematically investigated in this study.

The communication was presented to the subject one paragraph at a time. The instructions involved reading every paragraph of the communication out loud and then giving any and all of one's thoughts and feelings about the statements as he read them. The subject was seated in a booth so that the experimenter was out of sight during the actual running of the experiment. An experimental device was used which I have been developing and which could be called an auditory feedback suppressor. By the use of this apparatus, which delivers a white noise through earphones worn by the subject, the subject was able to speak aloud without hearing the sound of his own voice. This device was used because it was expected that the subject's verbalizations would more closely approximate his own silent thoughts than if he could hear himself talk. This expectation was based on the assumption that the sound of one's own voice is a socially reinforced cue such that one automatically sets himself to produce audible speech in a manner that takes account of the presence of listeners. Thus the absence of such social cues might lead to a better representation of the subject's private thoughts and feelings.

Tape recordings of the subject's verbalizations were transcribed and the associations were analyzed according to a systematic content analysis procedure. The findings for strong versus mild fear

---

* From *Nebraska Symposium on Motivation*, ibid., pp. 213-215.

appeals tended to confirm a hypothesis derived from an earlier experiment by Janis and Feshback on the effects of dental hygiene communications, which asserts that when a relatively high level of fear arousal is induced by a communication, the recipient will become motivated to develop psychological *resistance* to the to the communicator's message.

Of primary interest for our inquiry into the resolution of decisional conflicts are the findings which compare smokers with nonsmokers. For the nonsmokers, the fear-arousing material stimulated some degree of anxiety about cancer, but this anxiety did not involve a postdecisional conflict, inasmuch as the communication bolstered their current policy of abstaining from smoking. For the smok-ers, on the other hand, the anxiety about suffering from a horrible disease became a central component in a postdecisional conflict. Thus the communication introduced a powerful minus element, the fear of loss of health, which can be regarded as a personal utilitarian loss. The subject's spontaneous associations enabled us to descern that pitted against this minus component were some strong plus elements that motivated adherence to the smoking habit. For example, many subjects referred to the anticipated utilitarian gain of pleasure of relaxation and the anticipated social approval from friends with whom the habit is shared. Some of them spoke vaguely about a sense of maturity or sophistication as a smoker that seemed to involve the type of self-

TABLE 1

Type of Statement	Mean Number of Statements			
	Smokers (N = 14)	Nonsmokers (N = 17)	F	p-value
1. Worry about the threat	1.19	1.36	0.25	non-sig
2. Detachment from the threat	1.29	0.55	4.58	$< .05$
3. Explicit acceptance of pamphlet	4.52	6.71	5.33	$< .05$
4. Explicit rejection of pamphlet	14.58	10.15	1.98	non-sig

Content analysis of verbal associations given by smokers and nonsmokers during exposures to a fear-arousing pamphlet on the harmful effect of smoking (from an experiment by Janis and Terwilliger, 1959).

approval that comes from adhering to one's ego ideals.

On a common-sense basis, one might expect the smokers to show much more concern about the dangers of smoking, since the threat is much more ego-involving to them than to the nonsmokers. The content analysis results shown in Table 1, however, indicate that smokers tended to adopt a defensive reaction. The smokers made many *more* statements than the nonsmokers to the effect that they were *unconcerned* about the possibility of developing cancer or of suffering from the disease. In addition to making significantly more statements of detachment from the threat, the smokers also made significantly *fewer explicit accept-ance* statements than the nonsmokers. By "explicit acceptance" is meant any comment in which a subject asserts that he agrees with or accepts any of the main points made in the communication.

The subjects themselves were quite unaware of the resistance they were showing at the time of exposure to the communication. Follow-up interviews conducted from two to five weeks later indicated that some of the subjects subsequently became aware of their original defensive attitude toward the communication and experienced considerable anxiety when they thought about its content later on. Thus the pattern of resistance appears to be the *preconscious* level. The general picture that emerges from this experiment, then, is that denial constitutes one of the dominant types of preconscious affective mechanisms under conditions where a postdecisional conflict is stimulated by fear-arousing information about anticipated loss of an important utilitarian value (such as maintaining good health). Our subjects manifested denial of their personal vulnerability to the threat as well as denial of the impressiveness of the fear-arousing information. In terms of the balance sheet for analyzing decisional conflict, I am inclined to interpret the results as indicating that the denial responses on the part of the smokers allows the plus considerations (which motivate continuation of the smoking habit) to remain dominant by preventing a huge minus consideration from developing in the "utilitarian loss to self" category. In this way, these people manage to remain at least temporarily free from intense postdecisional conflict.

The experiment I have just described provides some preliminary evidence concerning the psychological mechanisms that are likely to come into play when postdecisional conflicts are aroused. The main purpose of reporting it here is to indicate a line of experimental research which, in my opinion, can eventually furnish rich and dependable evidence concerning factors which determine how people deal with and resolve their decisional conflicts.

Further experimental studies are obviously needed not only to investigate additional factors that influence reactions to fear-arousing communications of the type used in our experiments, but also to determine the alternative modes of resolution that come into play when communications arouse different types of postdecisional conflicts where the source of conflict involves other types of utilitarian losses, or external threats of social approval, or the moral dilemmas that entail anticipations of self-disapproval.

Anticipating Post-Decisional Conflict

Janis' second study (as will be seen in the reading that follows) provides suggestions similar to those drawn from the previously described work on the relation between one's expectations and the effect of frustrating stress. As he makes decisions himself, or helps others to make them, the administrator will find that anticipating the negative consequences of decisions that are made will help reduce later post-decisional conflict.

READING 3-12

Psychological Preparation for Postdecisional Crises*

I. L. JANIS

Awareness of the threat of potential failures and setbacks in advance, and

---

* In *Nebraska Symposium on Motivation, ibid.,* pp. 221-223.

especially before the decision has been made, can be expected to influence the choice of the mode of resolution in several different ways. In my own research, I have been especially concerned with finding out how advance warning facilitates psychological preparation and reduces the emotional impact of a stressful event when it subsequently occurs. Most of the hypotheses I have developed in this area have grown out of observations obtained in the series of studies of surgical patients, although some of my thinking has also been influenced by my clinical experience in conducting psychotherapy and counseling with persons who are facing serious marital problems and other crises. In the discussion which follows I shall summarize the main empirical findings of the surgery study and indicate how they are related to a central theoretical construct which I refer to as "the work of worrying." (A much more detailed presentation of the evidence and the theoretical inferences drawn from the surgery studies can be found in my book on *Psychological Stress*.)

For the purpose of understanding how preoperative emotional reactions are linked with postoperative adjustment, a combination of research techniques was used:

1. A small series of hospitalized patients was studied intensively before and after surgery, using data obtained from (a) intensive preoperative and postoperative interviews conducted by the author, and (b) daily behavioral records made by the hospital staff.

2. A questionnaire survey dealing with the emotional impact of surgical experiences was conducted among several hundred male adolescents who had undergone operations within the past few years.

The method of controlled comparisons was used in analyzing the observational data from the case study series as well as from the questionnaire survey. The following three hypotheses emerged from the intensive case study series and were supported by correlational data from the survey research:

1. Persons who were *extremely fearful* before the operation were *more* likely than others to be *anxiety ridden* again afterwards, and their excessive fears of body damage were linked with numerous clinical signs of chronic neurotic disturbance.

2. Persons who displayed a *moderate* degree of preoperative fear were significantly *less* likely than than others to display *any apparent form of emotional disturbance* during the stressful period of postoperative convalescence.

3. Persons who showed a relative *absence* of preoperative fear were *more* likely than others to display reactions of *anger and intense resentment* during postoperative convalescence.

Many additional observations contribute evidence in support of the following general theoretical proposition: The arousal of anticipatory fear prior to exposure to a stressful life situation is one of the necessary conditions for developing inner defenses that enable the person to cope effectively with the stress stimuli. There is considerable supplementary evidence, to be discussed shortly, which indicates that the nature of the inner defenses that are erected depends upon the degree to which one can overcome the powerful spontaneous tendency to *deny* the possibility of being personally affected by an impending source of danger. The evidence strongly suggests that if certain (nondenial) types of inner attitudes are formed before the danger materializes, the chances of developing traumatic or disorganized emotional symptoms are greatly reduced.

When we investigate those cases in whom anticipatory fear had been aroused before the operation, we find that they had fantasied or mentally rehearsed various unpleasant occurrences which they had thought would be in store for them.

Their anticipatory fears seem to have motivated them to seek out and to take account of realistic information about the painful and distressing experiences they would be likely to undergo after awakening from the anesthesia and during the period of convalescence. The conceptions these persons develop prior to the operation often turn out to be essentially correct, so that when unpleasant episodes occur, they not only are relatively unsurprised, but feel reassured that events during the recovery phase are proceeding in the expected fashion.

Some individuals (notably those who displayed excessively high anxiety before the operation) appeared to benefit relatively little from having mentally rehearsed the dangers in advance. Most of these cases, as already stated, were persons who chronically suffered from neurotic anxiety, and their postoperative emotional reactions can be regarded as a continuation of their neuroses. Both before and after the operation they seemed to be unable to develop any effective inner defenses to cope with the threat of body damage. Evidently their fears were grounded not so much in the external dangers of surgery as in long-standing unconscious conflicts that were ready to be touched off by any such environmental provocation. But the psychological situation appears to have been quite different among the patients in the "moderate anticipatory fear" group. These people appeared to be highly responsive to authoritative reassurances from the hospital staff and seemed to have developed a variety of ways and means of reassuring themselves at moments when their fears were strongly aroused. Such patients would frequently report instances of self-reassurance in their postoperative interviews; for example, "I

knew that there might be some bad pains and so when my side started to ache I told myself that this doesn't mean anything has gone wrong."

Such self-reassurances appeared to be rare among the patients who had been relatively free from anticipatory fears before the operation. These persons remained emotionally calm during the period when they were able to deny the possibility of danger and suffering, but they reacted quite differently as soon as they began to experience the pains and other harassments that accompany the usual recovery from a major surgical operation. They became extremely agitated and tended to assume that they should not have agreed to have the operation because it made them worse rather than better. They felt that the hospital authorities must be to blame for their suffering.

In a few such cases, it seemed quite probable that this way of reacting to external dangers was a manifestation of a characteristic personality tendency and might be quite unrelated to any specific occurrences either before or after the operation. In most of the other cases, however, it seemed extremely likely that the individual's lack of worry beforehand —and the consequent lack of inner preparation for coping with the stresses of surgery was a consequence of the *lack of adequate preparatory communications*. In several cases, the interview data and the hospital records indicated that, on the occasion of an earlier operation, their reactions had been of a markedly different character, so that neither the preoperative lack of fear nor the postoperative agitation and resentment could be regarded as typical for these personalities.

Concluding Statement: Some Administrative Implications

As each of the concepts of Part Three was presented, we have tried to indicate its place in furthering an understanding of organizational behavior. In concluding our chapter we want to state more explicitly some of the suggestions for administrative practices of the psychological material presented. In doing so, we also summarize the section.

The administrator must (1) recognize frustration, anxiety, or conflict where he finds it; (2) try to understand its underlying dynamics; (3) tolerate its presence, but (4) avoid being drawn into the "stewing" behavior that frequently accompanies it. His job, once he has taken these preliminary steps is to work to lead the individual away from distracting or defensive behavior and into situations where motivation can be organized around achievable goals. For example, when frustration leads to griping, and/or hostile or aggressive feeling, the expression of this feeling ought to be accepted. Research suggests that, up to a point, ventilation of feelings is desirable (Feshback). The administrator has to avoid intensifying the response either by too much sympathy or by arguing against it. His skill lies in timing his attempt to re-focus attention in another area where accomplishment may be possible.

A useful general principle is to recognize symptoms, allow a reasonable expression of them, and avoid confusing them with causes. Working with symptoms only is an unrewarding job. Stemming the flow of aggression or even of day dreaming may be necessary under some circumstances; sooner or later opportunity must be provided for alternative satisfactions if efficient adjustment is to result.

We have suggested the possibility of anxiety arousal as a means of intensifying motivation to do a better job. The matter is a complex one. On the one hand, the idea that others ought to be protected from anxiety at all costs frequently causes mediocre performance. On the other hand, it has been demonstrated that for anxiety prone individuals, the anxiety induced by the administrator can block rather than facilitate performance. The administrator must learn which of his people will give a poor performance when he puts the pressure on; he may even need to risk reducing the anxiety or sense of implicit threat in order to see if some of his people don't perform better.

In life generally, and in such an important aspect of it as our work adjustment, all of us prefer harmony and consistency in the facts before us. Dissonance is unpleasant and we are usually motivated to eliminate it, as Festinger has emphasized. But sometimes in organizational life, the facts coming from different sources or represented by the views of different people cannot easily be made consistent. The drive to reduce the dissonance should not tempt the administrator to ignore the inconsistent facts, to cut himself off from their source, or to surround himself only with people who can maintain the harmony or consonance of his thinking. The very nature of executive leadership requires that a manager live with dissonance, with inconsistent values, attitudes, and data brought out by the various parts of his organization. The psychologist might say of him that he should have high tolerance for ambiguity (and of disharmony, as well). Policy formulation must develop and decisions made; it is better that they grow out of a variety of views, frequently discordant, than that all preceding thought and discussion be harmoniously one-sided.

Janis' work clearly holds for administrators the suggestion that they recognize that the worry, backing, and filling that frequently follows a decision need not be a function of the decision-maker's personality. It is often a consequence of the way the decision-making situation was originally presented. Clear presentation, before the decision is made, of the possible negative consequences and the aspects of a decision to be feared will make for a more effective implementation of the decision once it is made. Hoodwinking a man (whether boss, subordinate, or colleague) into making a decision when only half-informed is certainly worse than having him make no decision, or even a contrary one. The hoodwinking process cannot be condoned even when tried by a hit-and-run salesman; it certainly is not sound practice for people who must live together in the organization.

We return again to a point made early in Part Three. The research clearly indicates that none of the psychological adversities we have described can be assumed always to have either a certain positive or negative influence on individual performance. Their impact is a complex function of the kind of individual, the way each condition is presented and the degree to which other conditions facilitate or hamper alternative behavior.

In Parts Two and Three, we have emphasized the importance of understanding motivational aspects of human behavior. It will be helpful here, in concluding this section, to place the matter of motivation in proper perspective, as one of several important factors that influence an individual's behavior. Ghiselli and Brown, in the following excerpt from their book, cite a study of Mackworth's that makes just this point.

> Even a cursory glance at current writings in the field of worker problems will reveal a consuming interest in motivation and allied matters. This stress undoubtedly is far too great. The implication is that such factors as ability, learning, equipment design, and conditions of work are of little or no importance. Essentially the point of view taken is that high motivation will compensate for all manner of unfavorable conditions whether they are within the individual, such as low ability, or environmental, such as noise.
>
> This position obviously is too extreme since the significance of other factors has been amply demonstrated. This is not to minimize the importance of motivation but rather to point out that motivation is only one of many factors that determine workers' behavior. The role played by motivation should be given its appropriate emphasis, no more, no less.
>
> The relative effects of motivation, conditions of work, and ability can be seen in an investigation conducted by Mackworth. This investigator had men perform heavy muscular work under various temperature conditions. In some cases the men worked under low conditions of motivation and in others under high conditions involving rewards, praise, competition, and individually set

goals. All men underwent all conditions of temperature and motivation and were divided into the upper half and lower half in terms of their ability to perform the work. The results . . . clearly show that *performance under high motivation is superior to that under low motivation.* It is also apparent from these results that *high motivation did not compensate for adverse atmospheric conditions.* With higher temperatures, performance decreased regardless of whether motivation was high or low. Furthermore, *at no point did high motivation overcome the effects of low ability.* The point being made is not that motivation is unimportant but rather that other factors may be equally important or even more important than motivation in determining workers' performance" (p. 415).

Effecting
Change
in
Human
Behavior:
The Learning Process

Introduction

The American Culture, in its short history, has had much opportunity to change and grow. Our economy continues to expand and requires change—organizations, for example, go from centralized to decentralized structure and sometimes, back again to recentralized. Our technologies grow on the new information developed in many of the physical sciences, soon requiring adaptive changes by those who will use them. Within the organization itself, younger people move in and press upward, recent arrivals from other fields bring different ideas, management development programs focus on changing people. There is a continuous need for change: in organizational relationships, in technologies, in knowledge, in interpersonal relations, and in specific skills.

Preview of Part Four

The change process may be considered at any one of three levels: recognition of, and responding to, the need for change; the decision to change (or innovate) in a particular way; and the implementation of the decision for change by producing change in the behavior of organizational members. The later chapters in Part Four consider in detail only the third of these—changing the behavior of people. It is thus, essentially, a discussion of the psychology of learning. But first in Chapter Ten, and before proceeding with a discussion of the learning process, we can view some aspects of the earlier phases of organizational change.

We move from a statement of the basic conditions for learning and effecting change in behavior to a more precise account of how skills can be acquired. In beginning Chapter Eleven we consider the essential conditions for effecting change of any type in human behavior. These conditions have been well-established in laboratory research, but they are not always applied in business and industry. McGehee, in our first brief reading, identifies some principles that can be used in the organization. A more fully developed discussion of the significance of reinforcement in effecting change, drawn from Skinner's book, follows. Among those managers and trainers who are looking toward psychology for a better understanding of administrative practice, Skinnerian theory today is probably the most influential of all learning theories.

Drawing upon a number of experimental studies, we next discuss some varieties of reinforcement and their effect on behavior. A final section in this chapter compares the effectiveness of different time schedules of reinforcement. In combination, the readings and research summaries make these points: some type of reinforcement (reward or knowledge of successful performance) is necessary to produce change; some types of rewards are more effective for use in the organization than are others; and lastly, the speed with which learning takes place and also how lasting its effects will be is determined by the timing of reinforcement.

Even when we provide desirable reinforcements at the proper time, there are other factors that must also be considered to make the most effective use of what we know about learning. Some of these factors are: the importance of letting a trainee know how he is doing; preparing him for learning; the impact of previously existing attitudes on learning; the cross-effects of one learning experience on another (transfer of training); the importance of thorough learning as compared to minimal learning; the importance of organization of and meaningfulness of material; and, the best conditions for practice in order to promote long lasting learning. Our approach in Chapter Twelve is to summarize laboratory research under each of the points mentioned in such a way as to point up their practical implications for the administrator.

The question of resistance to change is next considered (Chapter Thirteen) and a classical research on overcoming such resistance is described in the Coch and French selection. Part Four concludes with a summary statement emphasizing the fact that individual differences operate. We suggest that administrators keep these differences in mind when forming expectations about the outcome of their educational efforts and, where possible, choose methods suitable to the individual differences they find.

CHAPTER TEN

Some
Aspects
of
Change
Within
Organizations

Here we consider several characteristics of the change process in organizations: recognizing and responding to the need for change; aspects of the decision to change, and the importance in the change process of the executive's role as an educator.

Recognizing and Responding to the Need for Change. Despite the pressures on business organizations to change and to innovate, there are many forces within the organization that operate against a ready response to the need for change. For example, those in the organization high enough in the hierarchy to initiate change are the very ones who have benefitted most from the already existing order. Consequently, there can be a certain reluctance on their part to change what has worked out well for them.* They are also likely to be an older group with well-established ways of thinking and patterns of doing business and, thus, perhaps resistive to initiating change. Ginzberg (1962)

---

* Costello, Kubis, and Shaffer have shown, for example, that attitudes toward a planned merger were most favorable among the least successful group of managers in one of the merging organizations. The most successful managers held attitudes unfavorable to the merger.

suggests still another factor. The hazards of change are likely to appear early in the process, the positive outcomes much later, perhaps even after the men with decision-making authority are no longer around. For example, a decision to merge with another organization brings immediate organizational stress; the financial returns and ultimate strengthening of the firm might not be manifest until years later. Ginzberg suggests that under such circumstances a slowness to respond to the need for change will often be found.

There is the additional difficulty that those immediately below the men who must ultimately direct that a change be made, may oppose change. These are frequently the men responsible for providing the information to be used for any decision to change. If they strongly oppose change they can so distort the data as to delay change or even make it seem unnecessary or unwise. Illustrating the point, Festinger *et al.* report a field study in which community change was delayed by a hostile rumor started by people opposed to the change.

There are several reasons why organizational members just below top management levels might be opposed to change. For one thing, their identifications sometimes are more strongly with a functional area than with the organization as a whole (Cf. Reading 1-5 by Dearborn and Simon). The change, although good for the organization, might weaken or destroy their functional area.

A second reason is that change threatens to disturb carefully worked out role and status relationships among such a group. Third is the possibility that the change under consideration might eliminate systems or technologies that they have established. People rarely relish destruction of their own creations or those around which they have developed highly specialized skills (thus causing the fear of becoming out-moded).

It is understandable then, that despite the continued demand for change and innovation, a ready response to that demand may be found neither at the top of the organization nor in the lower ranks.

Behavioral scientists are beginning to study the conditions that facilitate the initiation of change* but relatively little data is available now to help in the process.

We summarize two studies of change in Research Summaries 4-1 and 4-2. In addition, two readings that appear in later sections also deal with the process of initiating change in a significant way: the Mann reading on Studying and Creating Change (Reading 5-7), and the Cyert, Simon, and Trow reading on Decision Theory and Business Decisions (Reading 6-6).

---

* See for example W. G. Bennis, K. D. Benne, and R. Chin, *The Planning of Change*, New York: Holt, Rinehart and Winston, 1961; R. H. Guest, *Organizational Change: The Effect of Successful Leadership*, Homewood, Ill.: The Dorsey Press, Inc. and Richard D. Irwin, Inc., 1962; E. Ginzberg and E. W. Reilley, *Effecting Change in Large Organizations*, New York: Columbia University Press, 1957. Also of interest in this area, is E. Roger's interdisciplinary analysis of innovation, *Diffusion of Innovations*, New York: The Free Press of Glencoe, 1962.

A Case Study of Innovation. Morison, in an insightful analysis of innovation in the American Navy during the 1890's, demonstrates that history has its uses for the forward looking business organization. He identifies some characteristics of the innovator, and situational characteristics that encourage the development of innovative ideas; and on the other side he draws a sharp description of resistive response to innovation, leading ultimately to the intervention of authority outside the naval organization.

The innovation Morison describes was a shift to continuous-aim firing from a system, previously used, that allowed the gunner to take his aim and fire at the target only at one point in the ship's roll. There were two serious disadvantages to the old system. Rate of firing was controlled by the rolling period of the ship and accuracy of firing was low. Sir Percy Scott, an admiral in the British Navy, had worked out some technical changes, inexpensively installed, that enabled men aboard his ship to keep their guns trained on the target continuously throughout the roll of the ship. Sims, a junior officer in the American Navy, worked with Scott and, impressed with Scott's invention, attempted to get the U.S. Navy to install the system on their vessels. Here he met resistance that could only be resolved when he drew in the President of the country, and obtained his support.

We follow Morison's analysis, first in identifying some traits of these two innovators: both Scott and Sims possessed a "savage indignation" at inflexibility, needless routine, and bureaucracy. And, because they were unwilling to keep their opinions to themselves, they were not very popular officers. Both had a strong sense of curiosity and a capacity to tinker. To develop their innovations, both had to be willing to accept ideas from others and build on them. The traits Morison reports are consistent with those more recent research has identified. (Cf. Chapter 22.)

There are also situational factors that help develop innovative ideas: time to be curious and follow out leads, and organizational freedom to experiment. Before pressing their idea, both men engaged in experimental trials on their own ships, apparently without the need to obtain official permission.

Resistance developed in the American Navy when Sims urged that the Navy adopt the system generally. Resistance first took the form of not responding at all to Sims' findings and suggestions. They were thought to be impossible and so were quickly filed away. Driven by Sims' importunate demands (13 documented reports in all) the next response was one of rationalizing official disagreement. Reasons were provided to suggest (all at the same time) "our equipment works better than anybody's," if it does not, "it is the fault of the Navy personnel who operate the equipment; they have not been trained properly," if there is something wrong with the equipment, "your idea is not the answer—it won't work."

Morison, in analyzing the source of the resistance, identifies these elements: "honest disbelief in the dramatic but substantiated claims of the new process; protection of the existing devices and instruments with which [the resistors] identified themselves; and maintenance of the existing society with which they were identified" (p. 602).

Only by writing to President Roosevelt himself, was Sims able to accomplish his goal. The President, identified with the super-ordinate goal of national defense, not in the social groupings in the Navy, and having no pride of authorship to protect, took the action to initiate effective change.

Generalizing from his case presentation, Morison suggests that resistance to change, in part at least, grows out of too narrow an identification—on the part of the resistor and the innovator both. He suggests a tendency to identify with a product, rather than a process. The resistor over-identifies with products already being used—and so is blind to improvement; the innovator identifies with his invention and ignores the feelings and ideas of those opposed. His suggestion is that if an organization is to be responsive to innovation it must first develop a strong sense of identification with the grand object (or process) of the enterprise—part of which must be a continuous adaptability to the new changes which are part of any organization's life. This over-all identification with the organization's process can then serve as "a unifying agent against the disruptive local allegiance of the inevitable smaller elements that compose any group" (p. 604).

RESEARCH
SUMMARY
4-2

Organizational Change: The Effect of Successful Leadership. During the early 1950's, Guest and his colleagues of the Technology Project of the Yale Institute of Human Relations were studying the impact of modern technological methods on work satisfaction and interpersonal relations among hourly rated employees and first-line supervisors in two large automobile plants. Their method of study utilized naturalistic field observation, depending heavily on direct observation of on-the-job performance over a long period of time, on interviews and on objective performance data.

One of the two plants became the focus of special study because its performance was far below that of the five other plants in the company. The study we report here considers the need for change in this plant and how the change was ultimately accomplished.

In 1953, on every measure of organizational performance, the plant was last, or next to last, among the company's other plants. It utilized 16% more direct-labor personnel than standards called for. It exceeded the maximum standards for defects and rejections. Indirect-labor costs were higher than for any other plant, as were its rates of absenteeism, accidents, and labor turnover. 1953 was typical of its performance for the several preceding years. There was obviously a need for change.

During this period, upper management tried a variety of pressures to improve plant performance. Telephone calls, letters, and memoranda flooded the plant manager. Plant visitations by upper management were frequent. Staff members from headquarters visited and worked with their counterparts in the plant, apparently to no avail. The plant manager and his subordinates knew that things were wrong and needed changing, but the actions they took only seemed to make things worse.

Finally, toward the end of 1953, after first considering closing the plant, management retired the plant manager and brought in as a replacement the production manager of one of the other plants. Because this took place only after a costly plant walkout, it illustrates the point, that too often, change is initiated only when things get even worse than they have been.

Guest, in his report, indicates that upper management made no changes other than replacing the old manager. Company management, formal structure in the plant, supervisory personnel, and product line remained the same. The striking improvement that resulted by 1956 seemed largely, if not exclusively, to have resulted from the actions taken by the new manager. And, following Guest's analysis of the situation we now examine briefly the steps taken by the new manager to accomplish the change. Before doing so it has to be pointed out, that once top management had made its own change decision (to replace the previous plant manager) its own behavior toward the plant changed—all the pressure was taken off. The influence of reducing the pressure is difficult to assess but it certainly must have been helpful. The question can be asked, would such a change (in upper management's behavior) have enabled the previous manager to have done what the new man did. Guest apparently believes not. The differences between the two men *and* their different histories, as well as the behavior of upper management accounted for the changes.

The new manager introduced no dramatic changes; as a matter of fact he took his time about introducing any changes. As Guest describes his behavior, he seemed at first to be primarily concerned about getting the men to know him in an informal way and, in turn, getting to know them; for example, very early in his regime he sent a letter to all foremen asking to be invited to visit the foreman's section. He arranged to meet with the union shop committee. His orientation period soon acquainted him with the emergency and crisis basis of operations in the plant and the need for planning. His response was the initiation, bit by bit, of an extensive set of group meetings, on a more planned basis, involving broader representation, and dealing with more significant activity than had ever been the case before. There were monthly meetings of all plant supervision, weekly meetings of the manager with his staff, cost meetings, specialized meetings focusing on quality control, materials control, and so on. The man below the manager soon followed his example, without needing any orders, and meetings became a frequent and scheduled way of getting the plant's work planned and coordinated. Although the new manager clearly avoided the invitation offered him by top management to "clean house," he soon did begin a rather extensive but carefully planned program of transferring supervisory level personnel throughout the plant. This approach apparently avoided creating either insecurity or resentment. Also there were changes introduced in the physical facilities—the first, improvements in the accommodations (washrooms, lockers, cafeteria) for the employees. Then, systematically, improvements in equipment and changes in systems were introduced. These were introduced gradually and in cooperation with the concerned personnel. Emphasis seemed to be placed on changes that would make it possible for the men to work together more smoothly and more efficiently.

By 1956, before the new plant manager was promoted out of the plant, interpersonal and intergroup relations had improved, and on most performance criteria the plant was leading the other plants in the company. Guest suggests in his overview of what had taken place that in this plant a "point" had been reached when it was not capable of changing itself internally. Some agent outside the organization—in this case the new manager—was required.

In generalizing from his study, Guest sets up the following "observations" about the change process as possible guide lines for further research on the process:

"(1) When an organization is a subordinate unit to a larger organization, and when the patterns of internal relationships within the subordinate organization are similar to those linking it to the larger, changes leading to more successful performance with the subordinate organization will take place after there has been a change in the pattern of relationships (interactions and sentiments linking the larger to the subordinate organization.") (p. 114-115).

"(2) The length of time required for an organization to improve its performance results is a function of:

    a. The size of the organization in terms of the number of individuals

    b. The number of levels in the hierarchy

    c. The number of specialized service, reporting, and control groups

    d. The complexity of technical operations

    e. The degree of intensity of personal insecurity and of interpersonal hostility at the outset of the change process" (p. 115-116).

"(3) For a complex organization to move from one pattern of behavior to another it is not necessary that its formal structure be altered" (p. 116).

"(4) The process of successful change in a hierarchical organization will start and continue to the extent that the members perceive the behavior of superiors, peers, and subordinates to be more in keeping with the norms of behavior in the larger culture" (p. 117).*

From the point of the organization wishing to draw on its own resources for initiating desirable change or innovation, both of these studies are essentially reports of failure. The proposal to change naval firing tactics was implemented only after intervention by a force outside the organization; the President gave obvious support and increased status to the man suggesting the innovation. In Guest's industrial study, plant operations were changed to a pattern of effectiveness only after higher management brought in a new plant manager, who then initiated the necessary changes. Neither study identifies the conditions that make it possible for forces within the organization itself to initiate the change.

The opinion has been expressed a number of times by organizational

---

* Excerpted from R. H. Guest, *Organizational Change: The Effect of Successful Leadership,* Homewood, Ill., The Dorsey Press, Inc. and Richard D. Irwin, 1962, pp. 114-117.

theorists that when organizational tensions and strains become severe enough they become "instrumental in leading to changes in the system" (Merton). Haire phrases the same thought somewhat differently by hypothesizing "that the organization will grow strongest when the forces tending to destroy it are strongest." Reasoning analogously, he bases his idea on the biological fact that a living organism mobilizes its strength to ward off infection or destructive attack (p. 11; pp. 272-306).

The thought that the business organization will initiate significant change only *after* it has begun to deteriorate although it may turn out to be factual, is a bleak one, as is the idea that an organism may not successfully resist infection. What we are emphasizing here is the need to anticipate or use the "symptoms" of organizational difficulties as cues to plan for changes that must be made.

Perhaps the time of responding to the need for change can be advanced somewhat if an organization will leave itself open to outside influence— whether that outside influence takes the form of information gathered in economic and market surveys, management consultants, or a superior management body. Leverage from outside the organization certainly seems helpful in breaking a fixed set—whether from a perceptual, a problem solving, or an initiating point of view.

Going beyond the research evidence to speculate, we might expect a readier response to the need for change within the organization itself:—if older management were eased into consultative roles and younger managers given increased responsibility for decision making; if creative and inventive staff were assigned the exclusive job of developing innovative plans to recommend to management; if high need achievement and thus willingness to take reasonable risks (Cf. Research Summary 2-4) were used as a basis for selecting those to be placed at the entrepreneurial edge of the organization.

Decision to Change: The Forms of Change. Whatever the mode is, through which the need for change is recognized and responded to, the form the change takes also needs to be considered. What about the organization should be changed; in which direction does the change move?

1. The decision to change can set new over-all organizational objectives. Examples are: diversify product output; reduce costs (advertising, labor, scrap, maintenance); increase percentage of total market.

2. The decision to change can also prescribe changes in the organization itself. These, presumably will be linked to some organization objective. A convenient way of grouping such changes is under the headings of: size, structure, and process.

(a) *Size.* The change decision can be one to *increase* the size of the organization, for example, through merger with another firm, or by acquisition of smaller companies, by additional capital investment in plant or equipment. Plans for a reduction in size may be made, for instance, through selling off unprofitable suboperations, or by deciding to buy certain items rather than make them. Over-all size may be kept constant, with a decision to change the size of different parts of the organization.

(b) *Structure.* By deciding to change the relationships between the various parts of the organization, the structure, as pictured, for example, in organizational charts may be affected. Examples of structural changes are: a decision to decentralize; a change in the chain of command, rearranging the reporting-to relations; an adjustment in the relations between certain line and staff activities, for instance, creating an independent research and development unit with its own vice-president.

(c) *Processes.* Here the changes might involve *social processes*, having to do principally with the frequency and quality of interactions between superiors and subordinates or with peer groups. An example is instituting regular staff conferences on the basis of horizontal groupings (for example department heads) or vertical groupings, (all management levels in the research and development department). Any other change in style of leadership would fall into this category of change.

A second type of process change would be one in *technology*, involving changes in systems and methods as well as mechanical or automated changes in production or data processing. The effect of this change on size, structure, or social process is frequently the basis for hostility to new technological systems.

3. The decision to change may take the form of changing significant personnel.° New leadership may be brought in from outside the company or from another division through significant promotions or internal transfers.

The Decision to Change: Interactive Effects. In attempting to understand the process of organizational change (even in the preliminary way to which we limit ourselves in this book) we might begin by considering the organization's "steady state" prior to change (Bennis, Benne and Chin, p. 205). A state of fluid balance among the parts of the organization has been achieved by a melding of formal and informal organization. The melding is a pattern of activities, interactions, and sentiments (to use Homan's terminology, p. 90) that has emerged out of the adjustive response of organizational members, with particular background and personal characteristics, to established organizational constraints. There is, of course, some "give" or elasticity to the balance that has been achieved so that movement and limited change (in minor personnel or procedures for example) does take place.

Significant change in the organization upsets this balance by throwing the steady relation between formal and informal structure out of alignment and by providing a new set of constraints around which new patterns of activities, interactions, and sentiments have to emerge. During the state of disequilibrium introduced by the change, it is almost certain that major symptoms of malfunction—increased turnover, absenteeism, lowered performance—will tempo-

---

° Decisions described under paragraphs 1, 2, and 3 above (change in objectives, changes in organization, and changes in personnel) are, of course, inter-related, for example—a new plant manager may be brought in (3) who will be expected to cut back the die-casting operation (2) in order to reduce costs (1).

rarily appear, continuing until a new balance has been achieved (or is in sight).

The inter-relationships in an organization are so complex that significant change along any one of the dimensions of size, structure, or process will almost inevitably bring change in each of the other dimensions. Several studies of organizational change provide evidence for the point. Guest, for example, in the study previously cited reports a detailed case study in which organizational change was initiated by changing plant managers. The new leadership soon initiated changes in superior-subordinates relations and in peer relations. New systems were soon installed. The point can be made here, of course, that new leadership was provided for the very purpose of initiating such changes.

But even where this is not the case, where the intention is to initiate only one type of change—a change in technology—changes in other directions seem inevitably to follow. Mann and Hoffman, in their study of automation in the electric power industry, show that an initial decision to change technological process also ultimately changed the size dimension—smaller work groups resulted and the social process dimension as well—relationships between superior and subordinates become much more open and permissive.

Haire has demonstrated the relation between a change in over-all size and the consequent changes in the size of various parts of the organization. Using a biological model that suggested that as the volume of an organism increases by a cubic function its surface will increase only by a square, he analyzed the growth patterns of four expanding industrial firms. Inside employees (production workers) increased by a cubic function, outside employees (purchasing and shipping staff) increased by a square. There were as well other structural realignments between staff and line, supervisors and subordinates, and white collar and blue collar employee groups.

Without research, we can surmise that increased size is likely to change social or technological process, for example, making more elaborate or highly specialized technologies possible. And certainly if organizational objectives are changed, ultimately, if they are to be accomplished, there must be consequent change in the organization and even in its manpower.

Summary Statement: Organizational Change.   In drawing our brief analysis of organizational change to its conclusion, we point up two considerations.

1. Change will not readily be initiated simply because it is needed. Sometimes things have to become very much worse before the pressures to make them better are created. Occasionally external forces will have to reach in to initiate the change. (And, of course, at times, essential changes will not be recognized, or initiated by those in authority.)

Even when the need for change is met, for whatever reason, there is the danger that a one-shot or merely accommodative solution will be attempted. Here, for example, the symptoms may be seen as the problem and a decision is made that merely eliminates (or appears to eliminate) the symptoms. An illustration is a company that in the face of a sharp decline in profits decides to change by cutting back the budget of its Research and Development department (a costly unit that has not recently "done anything"). Such one-shot or accommodative "solutions" result only in a short term gain (if any at all) and, frequently limit either the kinds of decisions that can be made in the future or the outcomes of such decisions. In the example used, a subsequent decision to diversify or substitute new materials in the product would be seriously hampered by the prior restrictions placed on the Research and Development department.

2. Change in any direction, once initiated, unleashes a variety of forces that interact with many other facets of the organization Two dangers may be present:

(a) So much attention may be directed toward the planned change that other changes that result are ignored and unplanned for, for example, attending to the technological side of a change toward automation may cause management to ignore the serious strain on interpersonal relations in the concerned department.

(b) In order for a change in one direction to work out successfully, changes along other dimensions may also be required. In this regard, Rice has described the impossibility of successfully installing modern machinery and work methods until changes in the social setting in which the work was done were also initiated. When employees were organized into small, self-sufficient work groups they accepted and successfully used equipment that they previously apparently couldn't handle.

Change in Behavior of Organizational Members: The Executive's Role as Educator.   Regardless of the direction of the proposed change, or the complexity of the change process, change in the organization resulting in improved organizational performance is obviously only possible if change takes place in the behavior of individuals. The administrator then has responsibility not only for recognizing the need to change, and deciding upon the direction of change, with an awareness of the interacting forces unleashed by any such decision; he also holds responsibility for creating organizational conditions under which change in the behavior of organizational members will take place in conformity with his decisions.

Such responsibility leads him to the point where he must be concerned with the process of learning (discussed in the following chapters), with attitudes and attitude change procedures (Part Five) and thinking and problem-solving (Part Six). It places an emphasis on his role of educator equal to that of the many other roles identified for him—decision maker, planner, coordinator, and group leader.

His role of educator goes beyond the problems of producing adjustment to a specific change decision here and now. There is need as well to teach the grand purposes of the enterprise (see Barnard, p. 233) and to engender an identification with this goal and a willingness to put aside merely local identifications. As Barnard (p. 87) has clearly indicated there is, in addition, the educational process of inculcating a belief in the real *existence* of a common purpose. Beyond these primary educational processes a continuing readiness for change itself must be taught, based on the point of view that change, adaptive to the goals of the enterprise (which, themselves, may change) is the only way in which organizations survive. There are as well, specific skills to be developed and information to be imparted.

From the psychological point of view, which this book takes, the process of education means the learning process. Education means that people learn to react differently, to change.* In Part Four, we consider in detail some important principles of learning. We take as our point of departure the statement: people who know something about learning can more effectively change the behavior of others (and thus effect change in the organization) than those who do not.†

Changing the behavior of others also frequently must concern itself with modifying attitudes resistive to change and building favorable attitudes. We discuss this area in Part Five. (See, particularly, attitude change procedures used in industry, Chapter Eighteen.) Maintaining a readiness for change and making wise decisions about change is a matter of thinking and problem solving and is discussed in Part Six.

---

* Cartwright, in his paper on "Achieving Change in People" cites some of the words that are used in preference to "change," a term that frequently arouses emotional response. He suggests that people would rather have someone educate them than change them, although, of course, education will produce change. Other terms he mentions are training, counselling, guidance, and orientation. We can mention, in addition, shaping or influencing. Each of these terms, of course, has a specific educational meaning; each is used in a particular context. All have the common goal of producing change in people. The discussion that follows in Chapters Eleven and Twelve does not deal separately with any of these change procedures. We believe the same basic principles of learning apply to all, although some learning procedures will be more useful for some than others.

† Maier, quoting a Bavelas study, makes the additional point that the training of trainers in techniques of establishing favorable social interrelations, in methods of increasing motivation, and in procedures for leading and guiding rather than pushing will increase the effectiveness of their training. By training the individual for the role of trainer, new attitudes toward the job of teaching and toward trainees are developed. The result in the Bavelas study was a clear increase in the speed with which trainees learned their jobs after trainers had learned something about training. It was not only knowing how the trainee should do the job, but knowing about the climate and factors of learning that made a difference.

CHAPTER ELEVEN

Some
Essential
Principles
of
Learning

People learn throughout their lives. Because each experience and response a person makes shapes all his subsequent behavior, it is accurate to say that people are continuously learning. They may not learn what we believe we are teaching them. They may even resist our efforts to change them, but this very resistance has been learned and the current act of resistance to change (if appropriately reinforced) may itself teach the person to continue his resistance.

Every aspect of human behavior is responsive to learning experiences. Knowledge, language, and skills, of course; but also attitudes, value systems, and personality characteristics. All the individual's activities in the organization—his loyalties, awareness of organizational goals, job performance, even his safety record—have been learned, in the largest sense of that term.

All this learning has not, of course, taken place in the organization. Much of it was well-set in early childhood, in school, or in prior job experiences. Some of it has taken place more recently, but off the job—in the family circle, in community life, at extension courses, in union headquarters. Some of it has taken place in the organization but not with management assistance (or even their knowledge)—in his informal work group, in his on-the-job experiences, in casual but unplanned exchanges with managers at all levels and in all functional areas. But much of it is subject to planned influence by management.

An administrator does not determine whether or not a man *will* learn. He can count on the fact that the man will learn. The administrator must be interested rather in *what* is learned. To develop his people so that they contribute to the organization's goals—and to make them responsive to the variety of changes that are part of organizational life, he must use learning principles and procedures that develop what he wants them to learn. Thus, his responsibility here is first, a matter of setting educational goals: the kinds of behavior required, necessary job skills, requisite information, and so on; and, secondly, a matter of creating organizational and work conditions under which effective principles of learning can operate to influence the individual toward the desired goal.

Psychologists now know some of the essential conditions that must be met if someone's behavior is to be changed. It must be quickly added that they do not know how to produce these conditions in every organization in which learning takes place. In the business organization, that should be the job of the administrator in his role as educator.

McGehee, in the short first reading of this chapter, briefly describes the learning process from the psychologist's point of view.

READING 4-1

"Are We Using What We Know about Training— Learning Theory and Training"*

WILLIAM MC GEHEE

The following generalizations concerning the learning process have evolved. They may be considered a statement of "what happens" when an individual learns. They can serve as guide posts for ordering experiences planned to modify behavior, i.e., train the individual. I shall leave it to you to judge how nearly they describe learning. Later I want to cite their implications for industrial training. These statements are:

The learner has a goal or goals, i.e., he wants something.
The learner makes a response, i.e.,

he does something to attain what he wants.
The responses, which he makes initially and continues to make in trying to attain what he wants, are limited by:
The sum total of his past responses and his abilities.
His interpretation of the goal situation.
The feed back from his responses, i.e., the consequences of his response.
The learner, having achieved his goal (or goal substitute), can make responses which prior to his goal seeking he could not make. He has learned.

* Excerpted from *Personnel Psychology*, 11, 1958, pp. 1-12.

Any current statement on the essential conditions for effecting change can be well-illustrated through the work of Skinner and his associates. Our second reading for this chapter is a selection from Skinner describing some basic principles for effecting change in behavior. Because the behavior of animals is simpler and more subject to control, much of the work referred to has been on pigeon and rat subjects, and he refers to this work in the reading. There is ample evidence to show that the principles described also apply to human learning.* As a matter of fact, one major approach in the new field of programmed teaching is based upon Skinner's principles of learning.†

---

* For example, see Keller and Schoenfeld; Greenspoon; Verplanck (1955, 1956); also from another point of view, Dollard and Miller.

† See Christian for a short review of the field and a comprehensive survey of the literature in the field; see Pressey for a word of caution about the value of programmed instruction.

READING 4-2

Operant Behavior*

B. F. SKINNER

One of the first serious attempts to study the changes brought about by the consequences of behavior was made by E. L. Thorndike in 1898. . . .

If a cat is placed in a box from which it can escape only by unlatching a door, it will exhibit many different kinds of behavior, some of which may be effective in opening the door. Thorndike found that when a cat was put into such a box again and again, the behavior which led to escape tended to occur sooner and sooner until eventually escape was as simple and quick as possible. The cat had solved its problem as well as if it were a "reasoning" human being, though perhaps not so speedily. Yet Thorndike observed no "thought-process" and argued that none was needed by way of explanation. He could describe his results simply by saying that a part of

---

* Excerpt reprinted with permission of the publisher from *Science and Human Behavior.* Copyright 1953 by The Macmillan Company, Ch. 5, pp. 59-72.

the cat's behavior was "stamped in" because it was followed by the opening of the door.

The fact that behavior is stamped in when followed by certain consequences, Thorndike called "The Law of Effect." What he had observed was that certain behavior occurred more and more readily in comparison with other behavior characteristic of the same situation. By noting the successive delays in getting out of the box and plotting them on a graph he constructed a "learning curve." This early attempt to show a quantitative process in behavior, similar to the processes of physics and biology, was heralded as an important advance. It revealed a process which took place over a considerable period of time and which was not obvious to casual inspection. Thorndike, in short, had made a discovery. Many similar curves have since been recorded and have become the substance of chapters on learning in psychology texts.

Learning curves do not, however, describe the basic process of stamping in. Thorndike's measure—the time taken to escape—involved the elimination of other behavior, and his curve depended upon the number of different things a cat might do in a particular box. It also depended upon the behavior which the experimenter or the apparatus happened to select as "successful" and upon whether this was common or rare in comparison with other behavior evoked in the box. A learning curve obtained in this way might be said to reflect the properties of the latch box rather than the behavior of the cat. . . .

Operant Conditioning

To get at the core of Thorndike's Law of Effect, we need to clarify the notion of "probability of response." This is an extremely important concept; unfortunately, it is also a difficult one. In discussing human behavior, we often refer to "tendencies" or "predispositions" to behave in particular ways. Almost every theory of behavior uses some such term as "excitatory potential," "habit strength," or "determining tendency." But how do we observe a tendency? And how can we measure one?

If a given sample of behavior existed in only two states, in one of which it always occurred and in the other never, we should be almost helpless in following a program of functional analysis. An all-or-none subject matter lends itself only to primitive forms of description. It is a great advantage to suppose instead that the *probability* that a response will occur ranges continuously between these all-or-none extremes. We can then deal with variables which, unlike the eliciting stimulus, do not "cause a given bit of behavior to occur" but simply make the occurrence more probable. We may then proceed to deal, for example, with the combined effect of more than one such variable.

The everyday expressions which carry the notion of probability, tendency, or predisposition describe the frequencies with which bits of behavior occur. We never observe a probability as such. We say that someone is "enthusiastic" about bridge when we observe that he plays bridge often and talks about it often. To be "greatly interested" in music is to play, listen to, and talk about music a good deal. The "inveterate" gambler is one who gambles frequently. The camera "fan" is to be found taking pictures, developing them, and looking at pictures made by himself and others. The "highly sexed" person frequently engages in sexual behavior. The "dipsomaniac" drinks frequently.

In characterizing a man's behavior in terms of frequency, we assume certain standard conditions: he must be able to execute and repeat a given act, and other behavior must not interfere appreciably. We cannot be sure of the extent of a man's interest in music, for example, if he is necessarily busy with other things. When we come to refine the notion of probability of response for scientific use, we find that here, too, our data are frequencies and that the conditions under which they are observed must be specified. The main technical problem in designing a controlled experiment is to provide for the observation and interpretation of frequencies. We eliminate, or at least hold constant, any condition which encourages behavior which competes with the behavior we are to study. An organism is placed in a quiet box where its behavior may be observed through a one-way screen or recorded mechanically. This is by no means an environmental vacuum, for the organism will react to the features of the box in many ways; but its behavior will eventually reach a fairly stable level, against which the frequency of a selected response may be investigated.

To study the process which Thorndike called stamping in, we must have a "consequence." Giving food to a hungry organism will do. We can feed our subject conveniently with a small food tray which is operated electrically. When the tray is first opened, the organism will probably react to it in ways which interfere with the process we plan to observe. Eventually, after being fed from the tray repeatedly, it eats readily, and we are then ready to make this consequence contingent upon behavior and to observe the result.

We select a relatively simple bit of behavior which may be freely and rapidly repeated, and which is easily observed and recorded. If our experimental subject is a pigeon, for example, the behavior of raising the head above a given height is convenient. This may be observed by sighting across the pigeon's head at a scale pinned on the far wall of the box. We first study the height at which the head is normally held and select some line on the scale which is reached only infrequently. Keeping our eye on the scale we then begin to open the food tray very quickly whenever the head rises above the line. If the experiment is conducted according to specifications, the result is invariable: we observe an immediate change in the frequency with which the head crosses the line. We also observe, and this is of some importance theoretically, that higher lines are now being crossed. We may advance almost immediately to a higher line in determining when food is to be presented. In a minute or two, the bird's posture has changed so that the top of the head seldom falls below the line which we first chose.

When we demonstrate the process of stamping in in this relatively simple way, we see that certain common interpretations of Thorndike's experiment are superfluous. The expression "trial-and-error learning," which is frequently associated with the Law of Effect, is clearly out of place here. We are reading something into our observations when we call any upward movement of the head a "trial," and there is no reason to call any movement which does not achieve a specified consequence an "error." Even the term "learning" is misleading. The statement that the bird "learns that it will get food by stretching its neck" is an inaccurate report of what has happened. To say that it has acquired the "habit" of stretching its neck is merely to resort to an explanatory fiction, since our only evidence of the habit is the acquired tendency to perform the act. The barest possible statement of the process is this: we make a given consequence contingent upon certain physical properties of behavior (the upward movement of the head), and the behavior is then observed to increase in frequency.

It is customary to refer to any movement of the organism as a "response." The word is borrowed from the field of reflex action and implies an act which, so to speak, answers a prior event—the stimulus. But we may make an event contingent upon behavior without identifying, or being able to identify, a prior stimulus. We did not alter the environment of the pigeon to *elicit* the upward movement of the head. It is probably impossible to show that any single stimulus invariably precedes this movement. Behavior of this sort may come under the control of stimuli, but the relation is not that of elicitation. The term "response" is therefore not wholly appropriate but is so well established that we shall use it in the following discussion.

A response which has already occurred cannot, of course, be predicted or controlled. We can only predict that *similar* responses will occur in the future. The unit of a predictive science is, therefore, not a response but a class of responses.

The word "operant" will be used to describe this class. The term emphasizes the fact that the behavior *operates* upon the environment to generate consequences. The consequences define the properties with respect to which responses are called similar. The term will be used both as an adjective (operant behavior) and as a noun to designate the behavior defined by a given consequence.

A single instance in which a pigeon raises its head is a *response*. It is a bit of history which may be reported in any frame of reference we wish to use. The behavior called "raising the head," regardless of when specific instances occur, is an *operant*. It can be described, not as an accomplished act, but rather as a set of acts defined by the property of the height to which the head is raised. In this sense an operant is defined by an effect which may be specified in physical terms; the "cutoff" at a certain height is a property of behavior.

The term "learning" may profitably be saved in its traditional sense to describe the reassortment of responses in a complex situation. Terms for the process of stamping in may be borrowed from Pavlov's analysis of the conditioned reflex. Pavlov himself called all events which strengthened behavior "reinforcement" and all the resulting changes "conditioning." In the Pavlovian experiment, however, a reinforcer is paired with a *stimulus;* whereas in operant behavior it is contingent upon a *response*. Operant reinforcement is therefore a separate process and requires a separate analysis. In both cases, the strengthening of behavior which results from reinforcement is appropriately called "conditioning." In operant conditioning we "strengthen" an operant in the sense of making a response more probable or in actual fact more frequent. In Pavlovian or "respondent" conditioning we simply increase the magnitude of the response elicited by the conditioned stimulus and shorten the time which elapses between stimulus and response. (We note, incidentally, that these two cases exhaust the possibilities: an organism is conditioned when a reinforcer [1] accompanies another stimulus or [2] follows upon the organism's own behavior. Any event which does neither has no effect in changing a probability of response.) In the pigeon experiment, then, food is the *reinforcer* and presenting food when a response is emitted is the *reinforcement*. The *operant* is defined by the property upon which reinforcement is contingent—the height to which the head must be raised. The change in frequency with which the head is lifted to this height is the process of *operant conditioning*.

While we are awake, we act upon the environment constantly, and many of the consequences of our actions are reinforcing. Through operant conditioning the environment builds the basic repertoire with which we keep our balance, walk, play games, handle instruments and tools, talk, write, sail a boat, drive a car, or fly a plane. A change in the environment—a new car, a new friend, a new field of interest, a new job, a new location—may find us unprepared, but our behavior usually adjusts quickly as we acquire new responses and discard old. [It is possible to show] that operant reinforcement does more than build a behavioral repertoire. It improves the efficiency of behavior and maintains behavior in strength long after acquisition or efficiency has ceased to be of interest.

Quantitative Properties

It is not easy to obtain a curve for operant conditioning. We cannot isolate an operant completely, nor can we eliminate all arbitrary details. In our example we might plot a curve showing how the frequency with which the pigeon's head is lifted to a given height changes with time or the number of reinforcements, but the total effect is clearly broader than this. There is a shift in a larger pattern of behavior, and to describe it fully we should have to follow all movements of the head. Even so, our account would not be complete. The height to which the head was to be lifted was chosen arbitrarily, and the effect of reinforcement depends upon this selection. If we reinforce a height which is seldom reached, the change in pattern will be far greater than if we had chosen a commoner height. For an adequate account we need a set of curves covering all the possibilities. Still another arbitrary element appears if we force the head to a higher and higher position, since we may follow different schedules in advancing the line selected for reinforcement. Each schedule will yield its own curve, and the picture would be complete only if it covered all possible schedules.

We cannot avoid these problems by selecting a response which is more sharply defined by features of the environment—for example, the behavior of operating a door latch. Some mechanical indicator of behavior is, of course, an advantage—for example, in helping us to reinforce consistently. We could record the height of a pigeon's head with a photocell arrangement, but it is simpler to select a response which makes a more easily recorded change in the environment. If the bird is conditioned to peck a small disk on the wall of the experimental box, we may use the movement of the disk to close an electric circuit—both to operate the food tray and to count or record responses. Such a response seems to be different from stretching the neck in that it has an all-or-none character. But we shall see in a moment that the mechanical features of striking a key do not define a "response" which is any less arbitrary than neck-stretching.

An experimental arrangement need not be perfect in order to provide important quantative data in operant conditioning. We are already in a position to evaluate many factors. The importance of feedback is clear. The organism must be stimulated by the consequences of its behavior if conditioning is to take place. In learning to wiggle one's ears, for example, it is necessary to know when the ears move if responses which produce movement are to be strengthened in comparison with responses which do not. In re-educating the patient in the use of a partially paralyzed limb, it may be of help to amplify the feed-back from slight movements, either with instruments or through the report of an instructor. The deaf-mute learns to talk only when he receives a feed-back from his own behavior which can be compared with the stimulation he receives from other speakers. One function of the educator is to supply arbitrary (sometimes spurious) consequences for the sake of feed-back. Conditioning depends also upon the kind, amount, and immediacy of reinforcement, as well as many other factors.

A single reinforcement may have a considerable effect. Under good conditions the frequency of a response shifts from a prevailing low value to a stable high value in a single abrupt step. More commonly we observe a substantial increase as the result of a single reinforcement, and additional increases from later reinforcements. The observation is not incompatible with the assumption of an instantaneous change to a maximal probability, since we have by no means isolated a single operant. The increased frequency must be interpreted with respect to other behavior characteristic of the situation. The fact that conditioning can be so rapid in an organism as "low" as the rat or pigeon has interesting implications. Differences in what is commonly called intelligence are attributed in part to differences in speed of learning. But there can be no faster learning than an instantaneous increase in probability of response. The superiority of human behavior is, therefore, of some other sort.

The Control of Operant Behavior

The experimental procedure in operant conditioning is straightforward. We arrange a contingency of reinforcement and expose an organism to it for a given period. We then explain the frequent emission of the response by pointing to this history. But what improvement has been made in the prediction and control of the behavior in the future? What variables enable us to predict whether or not the organism will respond? What variables must we now control in order to induce it to respond?

We have been experimenting with a *hungry* pigeon. . . . This means a pigeon which has been deprived of food for a certain length of time or until its usual body-weight has been slightly reduced. Contrary to what one might expect, experimental studies have shown that the magnitude of the reinforcing effect of food may not depend upon the degree of such deprivation. But the frequency of response which results from reinforcement depends upon the degree of deprivation at the time the response is observed. Even though we have conditioned a pigeon to stretch its neck, it does not do this if it is not hungry. We have, therefore, a new sort of control over its behavior: in order to get the pigeon to stretch its neck, we simply make it hungry. A selected operant has been added to all those things which a hungry pigeon will do. Our control over the response has been pooled with our control over food deprivation . . . an operant may also come under the control of an external stimulus, which is another vari-

able to be used in predicting and controlling the behavior. We should note, however, that both these variables are to be distinguished from operant reinforcement itself.

Operant Extinction

When reinforcement is no longer forthcoming, a response becomes less and less frequent in what is called "operant extinction." If food is withheld, the pigeon will eventually stop lifting its head. In general when we engage in behavior which no longer "pays off," we find ourselves less inclined to behave in that way again. If we lose a fountain pen, we reach less and less often into the pocket which formerly held it. If we get no answer to telephone calls, we eventually stop telephoning. If our piano goes out of tune, we gradually play it less and less. If our radio becomes noisy or if programs become worse, we stop listening.

Since operant extinction takes place much more slowly than operant conditioning, the process may be followed more easily. Under suitable conditions smooth curves are obtained in which the rate of response is seen to decline slowly, perhaps over a period of many hours. The curves reveal properties which could not possibly be observed through casual inspection. We may "get the impression" that an organism is responding less and less often, but the orderliness of the change can be seen only when the behavior is recorded. The curves suggest that there is a fairly uniform process which determines the output of behavior during extinction.

Under some circumstances the curve is disturbed by an emotional effect. The failure of a response to be reinforced leads not only to operant extinction but also to a reaction commonly spoken of as frustration or rage. A pigeon which has failed to receive reinforcement turns away from the key, cooing, flapping its wings, and engaging in other emotional behavior. . . . The human organism shows a similar double effect. The child whose tricycle no longer responds to pedaling not only stops pedaling but engages in a possibly violent emotional display. The adult who finds a desk drawer stuck may soon stop pulling, but he may also pound the desk, exclaim "Damn it!," or exhibit other signs of rage. Just as the child eventually goes back to the tricycle, and the adult to the drawer, so the pigeon will turn again to the key when the emotional response has subsided. As other responses go unreinforced, another emotional episode may ensue. Extinction curves under such circumstances show a cyclic oscillation as the emotional response builds up, disappears, and builds up again. If we eliminate the emotion by repeated exposure to extinction, or in other ways, the curve emerges in a simpler form.

Behavior during extinction is the result of the conditioning which has preceded it, and in this sense the extinction curve gives an additional measure of the effect of reinforcement. If only a few responses have been reinforced, extinction occurs quickly. A long history of reinforcement is followed by protracted responding. The resistance to extinction cannot be predicted from the probability of response observed at any given moment. We must know the history of reinforcement. For example, though we have been reinforced with an excellent meal in a new restaurant, a bad meal may reduce our patronage to zero; but if we have found excellent food in a restaurant for many years, several poor meals must be eaten there, other things being equal, before we lose the inclination to patronize it again.

There is no simple relation between the number of responses reinforced and the number which appear in extinction

. . . the resistance to extinction generated by *intermittent* reinforcement may be much greater than if the same number of reinforcements are given for consecutive responses. Thus if we only occasionally reinforce a child for good behavior, the behavior survives after we discontinue reinforcement much longer than if we had reinforced every instance up to the same total number of reinforcements. This is of practical importance where the available reinforcers are limited. Problems of this sort arise in education, industry, economics, and many other fields. Under some schedules of intermittent reinforcement as many as 10,000 responses may appear in the behavior of a pigeon before extinction is substantially complete.

Extinction is an effective way of removing an operant from the repertoire of an organism. It should not be confused with other procedures designed to have the same effect. The currently preferred technique is punishment, which . . . involves different processes and is of questionable effectiveness. Forgetting is frequently confused with extinction. In forgetting, the effect of conditioning is lost simply as time passes, whereas extinction requires that the response be emitted without reinforcement. Usually forgetting does not take place quickly; sizeable extinction curves have been obtained from pigeons as long as six years after the response had last been reinforced. Six years is about half the normal life span of the pigeon. During the interval the pigeons lived under circumstances in which the response could not possibly have been reinforced. In human behavior skilled responses generated by relatively precise contingencies frequently survive unused for as much as half a lifetime. The assertion that early experiences determine the personality of the mature organism assumes that the effect of operant reinforcement is long-lasting. Thus if, because of early childhood experiences, a man marries a woman who resembles his mother, the effect of certain reinforcements must have survived for a long time. Most cases of forgetting involve operant behavior under the control of specific stimuli.

. . .

The Nature of Reinforcement

As an agent of change, the administrator must see himself as a manager of reinforcement. How he manages the reinforcements available for use in the organization will be the most important determiner of whether or not change will take place and in what direction. Practice without reinforcement may provide only fatigue, or elimination of a response. Psychologists have not only demonstrated the essential nature of reinforcement for effecting a change in behavior, but they have also drawn some conclusions, based on research, about the effect of various types of reinforcement and the influence of different time sequences in reinforcement. We briefly examine some of these conclusions in three areas: extrinsic vs. intrinsic rewards; the effect of punishment; and variations in the reinforcement "schedules" or the timing.

*Extrinsic vs. Intrinsic Rewards.**   A reinforcement, in a sense, can be considered as an event that satisfies the individual; it may be the presentation of something he wants (for example, a salary increase) or the reduction or elimination of something unpleasant (for example, lowering of anxiety when a job is done well).† Part Two details the great variety of motives that make a variety of satisfiers appealing. Considering these potential satisfiers as reinforcements, we may conveniently and with practical advantage group them into two categories: extrinsic and intrinsic reinforcements. Extrinsic reinforcements are those that bear no inherent relationship to the behavior itself, but are selected artificially, and in some cases, arbitrarily, to reinforce the behavior in which change is sought. A suggestion system that awards money for acceptable suggestions is an example. The money unquestionably serves to reinforce the behavior of providing suggestions, but the award is not a natural consequence of the behavior. Intrinsic reinforcements are those that are a natural consequence of the behavior; from the individual's point of view they bear a psychologically expected relationship to the behavior itself. Knowledge of a job well done, the experience of knowing that you have worked up to capacity, or becoming qualified to do a different kind of work are illustrations.

Any management must consider whether it is placing too much emphasis on the desirability of using only extrinsic rewards—a salary increase, a bonus, a special prize, and so on. It has tended to ignore the possibility that other types

---

* Our presentation in this and the following section follows closely the position presented by F. H. Sanford in *Psychology*, San Francisco: Wadsworth Publishing Company, Inc., 1961, pp. 339-343.

† Where an individual wants to perform well, knowledge of results (of successful performance) serves as a reinforcement. Knowledge of results as a condition of learning is discussed more fully in Chapter 12.

of satisfactions are just as reinforcing. Although economic and other extrinsic rewards must continue to hold a place in the reinforcement system of an organization, exclusive dependence on such rewards has two definite disadvantages: Such reinforcers are available only in limited supply and can be used for only some of the people in the organization. A second more subtle disadvantage is that they focus attention on the external incentive, such as getting a raise, rather than on good and satisfying performance. Many people soon learn other techniques, less acceptable to management, for obtaining this kind of reinforcement, for example, putting pressure on for a salary increase. At times, the work may even be viewed as a source of frustration, a barrier to reward, rather than as a process providing a variety of intrinsic satisfactions (Stagner, p. 134-135).

Intrinsic reinforcements are more difficult to use than are extrinsic reinforcements. Nevertheless, in the long run, they must be used in the organization. They will not be used, though, unless the administrator keeps in mind the whole array of satisfactions that can be used to reinforce behavior and depends on extrinsic reinforcement only when it is appropriate. To think of extrinsic financial incentives as the only workable type of reinforcement is as damaging as to ignore them altogether. (See Chapter Six.)

The Effects of Punishment.   Common sense, as well as the traditions of our society, suggest that the opposite of reward is punishment. Sometimes psychological research confirms common sense, in this case it does not. Research indicates that, seen from the point of view of reinforcement theory, the effect of punishment is not simply the opposite of reward. Reward tends to increase the probability of a response's future occurrence; the effect of punishment cannot be said, unequivocally, to decrease its probability. In some cases, it may even increase the likelihood of the occurrence of a response by singling it out in an effective fashion, for example, a child who discovers the significance of a swear word in his vocabulary because he was drastically punished for using it may often use it more frequently in the future, although not in his parents' presence; it may even be used more with the parents' around, because the need involved may be to get attention and the parents' response reinforces this. Here, what was administered and perceived by the parent as punishment is experienced as reward by the recipient.

Many years ago, Thorndike demonstrated in a controlled experiment that a simple punishment (telling the subject he was wrong) did not weaken the strength of the punished response. Quite the contrary, in his research the punished responses tended to occur somewhat more frequently than nonpunished (but also, nonrewarded) responses.

The Thorndike research doesn't reveal the full picture. If we are seeking a way to find punishment to be the opposite of reward, perhaps, the answer can be found by saying the impact of reward on behavior is *simple* (it reinforces it); the impact of *punishment* on behavior is *complex*. There is research to suggest that punishment under differing circumstances may function in any of the following ways: (1) increase the occurrence of undesired behavior (Thorndike); (2) cause undesired behavior to last longer (Estes); (3) have a short-lived deterrent effect (Estes); (4) cause the individual to vary his behavior at the impact of punishment but not control the *direction* of the variability (Whiting and Mowrer); (5) tend to arouse negative feelings that often serve as the instigation for even less desired behavior; and, finally and, in a sense confusingly, (6) mild punishment may help improve behavior by at least providing negative feedback on performance, thus calling the individual's attention to incorrect behavior (Stevenson, Weir, and Zigler). Experience also suggests that severe punishment will deter specific behavior but usually with many negative side effects.

In the face of these variations in the effect of punishment on behavior, the reason can be seen for our suggesting to administrators: that reward will be more useful in trying to change behavior than punishment will. The results are more predictable when reward is used. The administrator has to make possible the positive reinforcement of *right* responses. Where incorrect or undesired behavior occurs, the suggestion is that it be ignored (in cases where desired or correct behavior is being reinforced). If the latter condition does not exist, punishment when used should be mild—a simple verbal statement, for example, "that is wrong," "that is not wanted," and punishment should be viewed as simply a signal to the individual to help him know right from wrong, good from bad behavior. Where punishment is tried it will be useless and occasionally harmful, unless help is provided to direct the person to the *right* response that must then be reinforced. There are often dozens of wrong ways for people to do things; the administrator can guide others to the right responses only by reinforcing them.

The Timing and the Schedules of Reinforcement. The effect of reinforcement on behavior is not only a matter of *what* the reinforcement is, but also *when* and on *what schedule* or pattern of presentation it is offered. Two questions are involved, timing and scheduling. The best timing for reinforcement is immediately after the desired response, each time it occurs. The least effective timing of reinforcement is one in which the reinforcement is provided on a fixed time basis, every hour, every week, at a yearly bonus time, and so on with no relationship to the behavior involved (Skinner, pp. 384-391).

There is also the question of the pattern of scheduling of reinforcement. At this point, we must draw on the distinction between *learning* a response, and establishing resistance to the *extinction* of a response. The learning process is one of *acquiring* responses to certain situations or stimuli and of becoming aware of those specific stimuli to which to respond; the extinction process is the elimination or dropping out of a response previously made to certain stimuli. In teaching an individual, we want to reinforce the correct responses and extinguish the incorrect. But we also want the correct response to continue beyond the initial learning period, to resist extinction. Concerning the schedules of reinforcement, immediate reinforcement may aid quick learning but other schedules of reinforcement are involved for the best resistance to extinction under later conditions of no reinforcement.

For the administrator, providing continuous reinforcement, except in the very beginning of any learning experience, seems too impractical when extrinsic rewards are used. This suggests an additional advantage for using intrinsic rewards. A most effective and practical approach in using either extrinsic or intrinsic rewards is some adaptation of a variable reinforcement schedule. For example, salary raises and appraisal interviews might be planned more in relation to what a man is doing than to the calendar. Two precautions must be taken—the raise, or interview must not be perceived as occurring on the basis of the administrator's whim of the moment and the interview must not be felt to be a threatening situation that occurs only if mistakes are made. The calendar should provide a framework to remind the administrator to be aware that the employee expects some periodic review with a report of how he is doing; it should not be the sole determinant of the timing of such a review. The important fact is that the reinforcement be seen as linked to desired performance.

CHAPTER TWELVE

Factors Facilitating Learning

In this chapter we summarize a number of specific conditions identified in psychological research as facilitating the learning process. Some of the statements apply generally to learning of all types; others vary in applicability with the type of learning involved, for example; skill acquisition, verbal learning, complex problem solving. In establishing an overview of the relationship between the essential principles described in the previous sections and those we describe below, we can say that the latter go beyond the question of reinforcement to spell out additional specific conditions that the administrator can strive to set up in his efforts to train his staff. The conditions described below apply more specifically to the problems of acquiring particular skills; the earlier principles can be equally well-applied to both the broader kinds of behavioral change and to specific skill acquisition.

Knowledge of Results

One of the safest generalizations one can draw about favorable conditions for learning is that learning is facilitated in direct proportion to the amount of feedback the learner is given about his performance. Ammons summarizes research in this area around several generalizations that we present below in adapted form.

1. Knowledge of the results of one's learning effort almost universally increases the speed of learning and the level of proficiency achieved. The as-

sumption that a person should be a "self-starter" and go on his own is not appropriate with a trainee who doesn't know what to do.

2. The more specific the knowledge of performance the more rapid is the improvement and the higher is the level of performance.

3. The longer the delay in giving knowledge of performance, the less effect the given information has. Letting the person "sink or swim" may seem easier for you (at the moment) and may be rationalized as "developing character" but it is not helping the person to learn.

4. Giving the learner knowledge of his results tends to increase his motivation to learn.

It may be noted here that programmed learning, which is now being developed for industrial as well as academic training, exemplifies the application of each of these generalizations.

Of considerable relevance to the administrator is Ammons' statement that where the educator (teacher, trainer) does not provide knowledge of results in relation to the educator's own criterion, the learner sets up some subjective criterion and evaluates his performance in relation to this irrelevant and perhaps undesirable criterion. He cites one study in which blind-folded subjects were asked to draw lines of a given length. They were given no information on their performance. After a time the subjects showed increasing self-consistency around incorrect lengths of line. In other words, they decided what was right and generated their own feedback on performance, but in relation to an unsatisfactory goal.

For anyone generally familiar with the work and learning habits of many industrial and clerical workers, and management level staff as well, no experiment is needed to make the same point. If a superior won't take the trouble to provide knowledge of results, the man will seek his own, but in relation to the employee's goals and his understanding of the job.

Intention to Learn

We have in our discussion of changing behavior thus far emphasized the effect of what takes place after an individual makes a response; also of importance are some things that take place *before* the learning (so to speak) begins.

Motivation. The learner will learn better if he is motivated to learn. The administrator can help to motivate learning sometimes simply by letting people know they are expected to learn or by identifying the reasons that make change (and learning) necessary.

Torrance describes a subtle interference with motivation to learn—a resistance to learning because the activity-to-be learned is experienced as inconsistent with the individual's concept of himself. When the learner is not aware of his resistance the problem is even more difficult. Torrance gives an example of his own difficulties in learning to march in military fashion at a time when he did not see himself as a soldier:

As an army private in basic training, I was strongly motivated to learn to march in step. I think I really wanted to learn to keep in step as much as I have wanted to learn anything. There was no lack of external nor internal motivation. There was no negativism; I tried every device anyone suggested and practiced during spare moments. Still I was always out of step. It was not until months later in a technical school with men of backgrounds of interests and experiences similar to my own that I "suddenly" learned to keep in step. Neither lack of motivation nor negativism would seem to describe what happened to me. Unconscious resistance due to the way I had learned to define myself would seem to be a more adequate way of describing the phenomenon. (p. 592)

Such resistance can also be found in the business organization. Miner describes a problem with scientist-supervisors, who were carrying out their supervisory roles ineffectively, largely because their self-images did not include this role. He found that a series of lectures utilizing some psychological concepts was helpful in broadening their self-concepts and thus making supervisory behavior more acceptable to them. (For a description of this research, see Reading 5-6.)

Set. Specific set as to what is to be learned, as well as more generalized motives for learning, will influence the learning process. Relevant to this matter of set is a research of Postman and Senders.

RESEARCH **SUMMARY** **4-3**	*The Effect of Pre-learning Set on What is Learned.* Suppose fifty college students are all asked to read a detailed selection from a short story not previously known to them. Will they all tend to remember the same type of information from the story? Of course, there will be differences in the *amount* remembered from one individual to another, depending on the general memory ability of each; an isolated individual or two may well find one or another aspect especially relevant to some well-remembered personal experience. But, in general, will most of the readers tend to remember the same type of material from the story?

Postman and Senders have conducted an experimental test of this question and their results indicate that the answer is yes *if* the subjects all have the same kind of intention to learn. When they subdivided the group into six subgroups, giving each a different intention to learn (through different instructions to each group) then, what was learned tended to vary from group to group as a function of the kind of instruction given. Each of the six groups was given one of the following types of instruction before reading the selection: (Group 1) "Read the selection so we can know how long it takes" (no instructions to learn); (Group 2) "Read for memory, you will be tested for your general comprehension." Instructions 3 to 6 were the same as 2 except that subjects were told they would be tested on (Group 3) sequence of events; (Group 4) details of content; (Group 5) details of wording; and, (Group 6) details of physical appearance.

Even when subjects were not given the assignment to learn |

(Group 1) they apparently brought to the task an implicit intention to learn. Under this condition, what they learned was mostly general comprehension of the material. When they were told to remember the passage and that they would be tested on general comprehension (Group 2) this increased sharply the amount of detail they remembered. On the other hand, when they were told to focus on some aspect of the details (Groups 3-6) while recall of this particular detail in most cases was improved, general comprehension was also improved. The results of these varied instructions on what was learned are a little bit surprising and certainly indicate the importance of carefully considering what impact instructions will have on learning.

The problem of the research is very much like the questions that might well occur to any administrator who is introducing another person to a learning situation—can I assume his intention to learn? Ought I direct his attention in one way or another? Will there be any impact on learning from what I say before he begins?

For the administrator we can say, how a learning assignment is introduced does make a difference. Merely counting on the learner's built-in intention to learn produces only an over-all familiarity; while focusing attention on an aspect significant for later usefulness increases recall of this aspect, as well as improving general comprehension.

The importance of how the administrator prepares the learner, what instructions he emphasizes, and what preliminary actions he asks the learner to take prior to the presentation of the material to be learned is suggested in two other laboratory studies of skill acquisition. Strahm demonstrates that even so simple an addition to the instructions as: "errors will be recorded" resulted in an over-all change in the way a task was learned, with greater learning taking place. The point here is not that the particular instruction is good or bad but that the administrator must realize that what he does to develop expectation, set, or intention in his instructions will alter the end product he will get. Ray carries the point a little further when he demonstrates that if learners are asked to tell ahead of time what their plan of learning is, they make fewer errors and require fewer trials to learn the task.

The intention and set to learn effectively can be developed through a process that has been called "learning to learn" (Duncan). Subjects who practiced on a series of similar tasks showed gradual improvement in later performance on other tasks beyond that anticipated in terms of the mere time invested. This positive transfer phenomenon can be useful in training situations involving the learning of a complex assignment that ordinarily might produce slow and discouraging learning. If the administrator will design a series of similar but simpler tasks and allow his people to practice learning these, he will find that they will learn to learn and ultimately do much better on the training task itself. It would seem of particular interest that slow learners benefit greatly from having a chance to learn how to learn.

Effect of Attitudes on Learning

In view of what we have said in our chapter on perceiving, it is no surprise to discover that attitude plays an important part in influencing what will be learned and how it will be learned. Although earlier studies made the same point, a study by Levine and Murphy most clearly describes the effect of attitudes on learning. They compared first, the speed of learning two types of prose material,—one consistent and the other inconsistent with the attitudes of the learners and then, after learning had taken place, compared the rates of forgetting for the same material. Their results provide experimental evidence for what we might expect in such a situation. It took longer to learn material inconsistent with one's attitude and, later on, this "unacceptable" material was more rapidly forgotten.

Jones and Kohler describe an additional interesting aspect of this process. They show that we *do* remember some of the arguments against our own position but we do so selectively, remembering principally the implausible arguments of the other side. At the same time, we remember the plausible arguments supporting our own attitudes.

Strong attitudes may make it necessary to exclude an individual from a certain type of training. For example, suppose a bank officer has built up attitudinal resistance to the idea of mutual funds. Can he be expected to learn the details of administering the mutual funds department of the bank rapidly enough to take over a new assignment? In another instance, we might question the idea of persuading a young college recruit to take a job with a large oil company after discovering that he is convinced that petroleum is not a growth industry. Later on, these negative attitudes may handicap him in his efforts to be developed as a manager. At the same time, it must be kept in mind that administrators can work to change attitudes, though this is complex and difficult. (Cf. Part Five.)

Transfer of Training

For the busy administrator it would be a pleasant experience to discover that the training job he did for one group of skills or for one aspect of management development could be readily transferred to other training his people needed, to situations other than those specifically presented in training. In this area, psychologists can provide some guidance. Training in one activity can be transferred to another activity that has to be learned under two conditions:

(a) Transfer of training in one activity will transfer to another one in which there are similar components, although the total activity may be somewhat different. The manager can facilitate this process, of course, by pointing out the transferability of skills now being learned to future skills that will have to be learned, or by indicating the similar components in an old job, previously learned, and the new job to be learned.

(b) Transfer of training is also facilitated to the extent that the learner discovers methods, techniques, principles, systems, or shortcuts in one learning activity that may be useful in others.* Here the manager can do much to insure that his early training emphasizes the broad transferable concepts as well as the skills immediately needed for job performance.

RESEARCH **SUMMARY** **4-4**	*How to Aid Transfer of Training.* An interesting illustration of a transfer effect that was facilitated by teaching transferable principles is the experiment of Hendrickson and Schroeder. The assigned task was to shoot at a submerged target. One group was first taught some basic principles of light refraction so that they understood their target would appear displaced from its original position. A control group received no such training. Both groups then practiced shooting at the submerged target until they had developed skill in the task (equal levels of skill for each group). The target depth was then changed. The control group had to practice all over again; in contrast, the group which had been specially trained readily learned to hit the new target.

Duncan's research, on learning to learn, which we have previously mentioned, is also an illustration of a helpful means of using transfer of training to facilitate the acquisition of a skill.

The principles underlying transfer of training have meaning for management development. For example, where case method is used as a basis of training, a statement of the principles involved ought to supplement the discussion. The case method can also help develop in the management trainee a set to learn; the case discussions can constitute the basis of his learning to learn. Specific on-the-job experience should be generalized through identifying the principles underlying a successful effort.

Repetition and Thorough Learning

Mere repetition of a response, without reinforcement, will not facilitate the performance's being learned to any observable degree. Nevertheless repetition provides an opportunity for the right response to be reinforced and associated interfering responses to be eliminated. Being able to do something right once is not enough to assure learning. It is generally necessary to repeat a situation until the individual learns appropriate stimuli or cues and produces a smooth, habitual performance. Practicing the response to assure "over-learning" or thorough learning, is necessary to give the learner a chance to eliminate some unnecessary or interfering responses that he has probably also learned while achieving the first right response.

Thus, for example, in training a supervisor to do an appraisal interview, a manager should not consider training complete with the first good performance.

---

* Woodworth and Schlosberg summarize the research on these and other aspects of the transfer process, Ch. 24. See also Osgood, pp. 520-540.

Repetition of other appraisal interviews under training conditions ought to be continued until the correct pattern has been effectively discriminated from all other patterns by thorough learning with appropriate reinforcement.

Some Efficient Conditions for Practice

Because some type of practice, followed by appropriate reinforcement is helpful, and frequently necessary, for all types of learning, we now consider the question of what form that practice or repetition should take.

Distribution of Practice. One of the most thoroughly investigated research questions in this area is whether practice should be massed in a concentrated time period or distributed over a longer period of time (Underwood). Should the practice be "piled on heavy" and all at one time, or should the same amount of time on the training be spread over a longer time with more breaks between sessions? A reasonably safe conclusion to draw is that some distribution over a period of time is essential to provide long-term retention of learned material. Different kinds of material to be learned require different patterns of distribution—for example, several very short periods distributed over two weeks; somewhat longer periods distributed over one week; one long session later followed by several short sessions, and so on. For the administrator to know which pattern is best for the training, he may have to experiment with different patterns. Research in the field suggests these guidelines:

1. Where the task requires the learner to develop insights or to discover things for himself, a long period of massed effort first, followed by shorter periods later on to strengthen the learning, seems most effective (Eriksen). The learning of complex materials that require the consideration of a variety of interrelations is also easier with a long period of practice in the beginning (Kidd; Riley). Learning to prepare a departmental budget, for example, may best be done in a week's concentrated effort, rather than in five one-day sessions distributed over five weeks.

2. On the other hand, work that is fatiguing or that demands rote memorizing of verbal materials (for example, the steps to follow in a detailed clerical transaction to be learned from a procedures manual) is best learned in short periods distributed over a week or two.

3. Where the material to be learned is meaningful, verbal in form, and is of high intrinsic interest to the learner, distributed practice tends to lose its advantage (McGeoch & Irion).

4. When the task is a problem-solving one, a wrong mental set may persist and thus massed practice may prevent a solution of the problem, whereas distributed practice would facilitate an interruption of the set and thus help the learner approach the task from a new point of view (Kendler, Greenberg, and Richman). Analyzing a system or a methods problem would fall into this category.

Whole vs. Part Learning. Although much research over the years has been directed to answering the question of whether or not it is better to learn the whole task or break it up into parts, only one relevant suggestion can be made to the administrator with regard to this aspect of practice. A flexible method, combining the advantages of whole and part learning seems best. Begin with an overview of the whole problem or material, discover the difficult parts and practice them, then integrate them into the whole process as a final step. Where the material can be rearranged, presenting it originally in a sequence that moves from the simple to the complex will frequently (although not always) be helpful (Fryer, Feinberg, and Zalkind, p. 97-98).

The administrator must keep in mind, though, that what *he* views as a small amount of easy material might contain much that is new or complicated to the person seeking to learn. Ryan and Smith (p. 450-452) have pointed out, for example, that a person starting on a new job often will have a great many new details or pieces of information to learn in the first day on the job.

Active Practice. The adage "we learn by doing" although widely recognized is frequently violated. The administrator who expects the trainee to learn simply by listening will be disappointed. Yet, often the attempt is made to teach interviewing, conference leadership, and even motor skills just by explaining them. Verbal orientation is helpful in the beginning to provide an overview, point up key suggestions, or produce the right set, but to learn, the learner must do the job himself. Active involvement is always to be preferred to passive listening or watching.

Organization and Meaningfulness

Learning, whether considered from the point of view of speed, subsequent recall, or transferability is a direct function of the meaningfulness of the material and the way in which it is organized. This is particularly so when the rote memory aspect of learning is an important part of the learning task. Much research establishes the relative ease of learning a list of words compared to a list of nonsense syllables. Learning poetry is easier than learning prose because the poetry is not only meaningful but is also more tightly organized (or grouped). Katona provides another example: Remembering twelve digits, arranged as follows, 581215192226, is difficult. Organizing them into groups of three's, 581, 215, 192, 226 makes it easier. We can make the task even easier by providing some meaning for the way the digits are arranged, in this case, by pointing out that if we begin with 5 and add alternately 3 and 4 to the last preceding number we can produce the list accurately.

Information theory (an interdisciplinary study dealing with the transmission of bits of information, messages, or signals) suggests that meaningful or well-organized material is learned more rapidly because it requires that we learn less. The pattern of the meaning or the organization is already known; we have only to fit into the pattern the new information or the context of what is to be learned. When the material is not organized for us, we have to learn both pattern (or organization) and content (Miller and Selfridge).

Pressey points out that most important matter to be learned has structure and that learning is integrative and judgmental. To learn effectively, a person must be able to see the structure (pattern or organization) and to explore it to know where the parts go and what the various relationships are (p. 1).

There are many ways in which an administrator can implement the principle we have described here. For example, he can take time to arrange the material to be learned into units that can then be assembled into meaningful patterns. The administrator, himself, may not be the one to do this, but he should insist that someone do it. Occasionally all that has to be done by an administrator to obtain the benefit of meaningfulness or organization is to begin a training session with such a statement as: "Our goal is to accomplish thus and so . . . and we believe we can do so if you do the following things."

Unless time is taken to provide reasons and meaning, learning will be slow and inefficient. In addition, even when learning does take place, there is the danger of developing what Veblen has called "trained incapacity": rules are learned well—through years of experience—but without an understanding of the meaning behind them. The rules are then applied but often without achieving the objective for which the rules were designed.

CHAPTER THIRTEEN

Resistance
to
Change

In one sense, everyone resists change.* To give up well-established and, therefore, easy habits, to spend time to acquire new knowledge, or to experience the possible threat of new conditions of work, all upset the even tenor of our adjustment. Unless there is more to be gained than lost and unless the gain is made apparent, we naturally resist having to change. Too often, changes required of people in the organization are presented only as a management demand. When this happens, and the individual fails to see any value in it for himself, there may be either a passive dragging of feet or a more active kind of resistance to the change. Fryer, Feinberg, and Zalkind (pp. 34-35) suggest two other factors that arouse resistance to change: training for change disrupts the regular work of the individual causing him to fall behind and to lose the satisfaction of getting done; and change is often seen as a further move to a more efficient, less personal, more highly specialized type of activity that will disturb the personal and social adjustment the individual has made. One can easily imagine a great variety of other fears that change might suggest to people at any level in the organization. It is not going too far to suggest that the administrator must expect that change will be met by resistance and that he initiate the change in such fashion as to prevent the development of re-

---

* Cf. earlier discussion of resistance to the initiation of change by upper management, in the Introduction to Part Four.

sistance or use approaches to overcome the resistance when it does develop.

Resistance to change that is rooted in well-established attitudes will be discussed in Part Five. Our next reading may well serve as both an introduction to Part Five and as a good description of resistance to change in industry and what was done to overcome this resistance. The excerpt from the Coch and French study that follows provides dramatic evidence of resistance to even small changes in the performance of relatively unskilled work. The resistance took the form of a sharp and long-lasting lowering of productivity, plus an increase in turnover. A program of explaining the reasons that made change necessary, followed by an opportunity for the employees to participate in implementing the change (not participation in the decision to change) had striking results in eliminating the symptoms of resistance to the change.

READING 4-3

Overcoming Resistance to Change*

LESTER COCH

AND

JOHN R. P. FRENCH, JR.

It has always been characteristic of American industry to change products and methods of doing jobs as often as competitive conditions or engineering progress dictates. This makes frequent changes in an individual's work necessary. In addition, the markedly greater turnover and absenteeism of recent years result in unbalanced production lines, which again makes for frequent shifting of individuals from one job to another. One of the most serious production problems faced at the Harwood Manufacturing Corporation has been the resistance of production workers to the necessary changes in methods and jobs. This resistance expressed itself in several ways, such as grievances about the piece rates that went with the new methods, high turnover, very low efficiency, restriction

of output, and marked aggression against management. Despite these undesirable effects, it was necessary that changes in methods and jobs continue.

Efforts were made to solve this serious problem by the use of a special monetary allowance for transfers, by trying to enlist the cooperation and aid of the union, by making necessary layoffs on the basis of efficiency, etc. In all cases, these actions did little or nothing to overcome the resistance to change. On the basis of these data, it was felt that the pressing problem of resistance to change demanded further research for its solution. From the point of view of factory management, there were two purposes to the research: (a) Why do people resist change so strongly? and (b) What can be done to overcome this resistance?

Starting with a series of observations about the behavior of changed groups, the first step in the program was to de-

* Abridged from *Human Relations*, 1948, *1*, 512-532.

vise a preliminary theory to account for the resistance to change. Then, on the basis of the theory, a real-life action experiment was devised and conducted within the context of the factory situation. Finally, the results of the experiment were interpreted in the light of the preliminary theory and the new data.

Background

The main plant of the Harwood Manufacturing Corporation, where the present research was done, is located in the small town of Marion, Virginia. The plant produces pajamas and, like most sewing plants, employs mostly women. The plant's population is about 500 women and 100 men. The workers are recruited from the rural, mountainous areas surrounding the town, and are usually employed without previous industrial experience. The average age of the workers is 23. The average education is eight years of grammar school.

The policies of the company in regard to labor relations are liberal and progressive. A high value has been placed on fair and open dealing with the employees and they are encouraged to take up any problems or grievances with the management at any time. Every effort is made to help foremen find effective solutions to their problems in human relations, using conferences and role-playing methods. Carefully planned orientation, designed to help overcome the discouragement and frustrations attending entrance upon the new and unfamiliar situation, is used. Plantwide votes are conducted where possible to resolve problems affecting the whole working population. The company has invested both time and money in employee services such as industrial music, health services, lunchroom, and recreation programs. In the same spirit, the management has been conscious of the importance of public relations in the local community; they have supported, both financially and otherwise, any activity which would build up good will for the company. As a result of these policies, the company has enjoyed good labor relations since the day it commenced operations.

Harwood employees work on an individual incentive system. Piece rates are set by time study and are expressed in terms of units. One unit is equal to one minute of standard work: 60 units per hour equal the standard efficiency rating. Thus, if on a particular operation the piece rate for one dozen is 10 units, the operator would have to produce six dozen per hour to achieve the standard efficiency rating of 60 units per hour. The skill required to reach 60 units per hour is great. On some jobs, an average trainee may take 34 weeks to reach the skill level necessary to perform at 60 units per hour. Her first few weeks of work may be on an efficiency level of 5 to 20 units per hour.

The amount of pay received is directly proportional to the weekly average efficiency rating achieved. Thus, an operator with an average efficiency rating of 75 units per hour (25% more than standard) would receive 25% more than base pay. However, there are two minimum wages below which no operator may fall. The first is the plant-wide minimum, the hiring-in wage; the second is a minimum wage based on six months' employment and is 22% higher than the plant-wide minimum wage. Both minima are smaller than the base pay for 60 units per hour efficiency rating.

The rating of every piece worker is computed every day, and the results are published in a daily record of production which is shown to every operator. This daily record of production for each production line carries the names of all the operators on that line arranged in rank order of efficiency rating, with the highest rating girl at the top of the list. The supervisors speak to each operator each day about her unit ratings. Because of the above procedures, many operators do not claim credit for all the work done in a given day. Instead, they save a few of the piece rate tickets as a "cushion" against a rainy day when they may not feel well or may have a great amount of machine trouble.

When it is necessary to change an operator from one type of work to another, a transfer bonus is given. This bonus is so designed that the changed operator who relearns at an average rate will suffer no loss in earnings after change. Despite this allowance, the general attitudes toward job changes in the factory are markedly negative. Such expressions as, "When you make your units [standard production], they change your job," are all too frequent. Many operators refuse to change, preferring to quit.

The Transfer Learning Curve

An analysis of the after-change relearning curves of several hundred experienced operators rating standard or better prior to change showed that 38% of the changed operators recovered to the standard unit rating of 60 units per hour. The other 62% either became chronically substandard operators or quit during the relearning period.

The average relearning curve for those who recover to standard production on the simplest type of job in the plant is eight weeks long, and, when smoothed, provides the basis for the transfer bonus. The bonus is the percentage difference between this expected efficiency rating and the standard of 60 units per hour.

The relearning period for an experienced operator is longer than the learning period for a new operator. This is true despite the fact that the majority of transfers—the failures who never recover to standard—are omitted from the curve.

However, changed operators rarely complain of "wanting to do it the old way" after the first week or two of change, and time and motion studies show few false moves after the first week of change. From this evidence it is deduced that proactive inhibition, or the interference of previous habits in learning the new skill, is either nonexistent or very slight after the first two weeks of change.

An analysis of the relearning curves for 41 experienced operators who were changed to very difficult jobs gives a comparison between the recovery rates for operators making standard or better prior to change, and those below standard prior to change. Both classes of operators dropped to a little below 30 units per hour and recovered at a very slow but similar rate. These curves show a general (though by no means universal) phenomenon: the efficiency rating prior to change does not indicate a faster or slower recovery rate after change.

A Preliminary Theory of Resistance to Change

The fact that relearning after transfer to a new job is so often slower than initial learning on first entering the factory would indicate, on the face of it, that the resistance to change and the slow relearning is primarily a motivational problem. The similar recovery rates of skilled and unskilled operators tend to confirm the hypothesis that skill is a minor factor and motivation is the major determinant of the rate of recovery. Earlier experiments at Harwood by Alex Bavelas demonstrated this point conclusively. He found that the use of group decision techniques on operators who had just been transferred resulted in very marked increases in the rate of relearning, even though no skill training was given and there were no other changes in working conditions (3).

Interviews with operators who have

been transferred to a new job reveal a common pattern of feelings and attitudes which are distinctly different from those of successful nontransfers. In addition to resentment against the management for transferring them, the employees typically show feelings of frustration, loss of hope of ever regaining their former level of production and status in the factory, feelings of failure, and a very low level of aspiration. In this respect, these transferred operators are similar to the chronically slow workers studied previously.

Earlier unpublished research at Harwood has shown that the nontransferred employees generally have an explicit goal of reaching and maintaining an efficiency rating of 60 units per hour. A questionnaire administered to several groups of operators indicated that a large majority of them accept as their goal the management's quota of 60 units per hour. This standard of production is the level of aspiration according to which the operators measure their own success or failure, and those who fall below standard lose status in the eyes of their fellow employees. Relatively few operators set a goal appreciably above 60 units per hour.

The actual production records confirm the effectiveness of this goal of standard production. The distribution of the total population of operators in accordance with their production levels is by no means a normal curve. Instead there is a large number of operators who rate 60 to 63 units per hour, and relatively few operators who rate just above or just below this range. Thus we may conclude that:

Proposition 1. There is a force acting on the operator in the direction of achieving a production level of 60 units per hour or more. It is assumed that the strength of this driving force (acting on an operator below standard) increases as

she gets nearer the goal—a typical goal gradient.

On the other hand, restraining forces operate to hinder or prevent her reaching this goal. These restraining forces consist, among other things, of the difficulty of the job in relation to the operator's level of skill. Other things being equal, the faster an operator is sewing the more difficult it is to increase her speed by a given amount. Thus we may conclude that:

Proposition 2. The strength of the restraining force hindering higher production increases with increasing level of production.

In line with previous studies, it is assumed that the conflict of these two opposing forces—the driving force corresponding to the goal of reaching 60 and the restraining force of the difficulty of the job—produces frustration. In such a conflict situation, the strength of frustration will depend on the strength of these forces. If the restraining force against increasing production is weak, then the frustration will be weak. But if the driving force toward higher production, i.e., the motivation is weak, then the frustration will also be weak. Probably both of the conflicting forces must be above a certain minimum strength before any frustration is produced, for all goal-directed activity involves some degree of conflict of this type; yet a person is not usually frustrated so long as he is making satisfactory progress toward his goal. Consequently we assume that:

Proposition 3. The strength of frustration is a function of the weaker of these two opposing forces, provided that the weaker force is stronger than a certain minimum necessary to produce frustration (3).

From Propositions 1, 2, and 3, we may derive that the strength of frustration (a) should be greater for operators who are below standard in production than for operators who have already achieved the goal of standard production; (b) should be greater for operators on difficult jobs than for operators on easy jobs; and (c) should increase with increasing efficiency rating below standard production. Previous research would suggest:

Proposition 4. One consequence of frustration is escape from the field (2).

An analysis of the effects of such frustration in the factory showed that it resulted, among other things, in high turnover and absenteeism. The rate of turnover for successful operators with efficiency ratings above standard was much lower than for unsuccessful operators. Likewise, operators on the more difficult jobs quit more frequently than those on the easier jobs. Presumably the effect of being transferred is a severe frustration which should result in similar attempts to escape from the field.

In line with this theory of frustration and the finding that job turnover is one resultant of frustration, an analysis was made of the turnover rate of transferred operators as compared with the rate among operators who had not been transferred recently. For the year September, 1946, to September, 1947, there were 198 operators who had not been transferred recently; that is, within the 34-week period allowed for relearning after transfer. There was a second group of 85 operators who had been transferred recently; that is, within the time allowed for relearning the new job. Each of these two groups was divided into seven classifications according to their unit rating at the time of quitting. For each classification the percentage turnover per month, based on the total number of employees in that classification, was computed.

The results are given in Figure 1. Both the levels of turnover and the form of the curves are strikingly different for the two groups. Among operators who have not been transferred recently the average turnover per month is about 4½%; among recent transfers the monthly turnover is nearly 12%. Consistent with the previous studies, both groups show a very marked drop in the turnover curve after an operator becomes a success by reaching 60 units per hour, or standard production. However, the form of the curves at lower unit ratings is markedly different for the two groups. The nontransferred operators show a gradually increasing rate of turnover up to a rating of 55 to 59 units per hour. The transferred operators, on the other hand, show a high peak at the lowest unit rating of 30 to 34 units per hour, decreasing sharply to a low point at 45 to 49 units per hour. Since most changed operators drop to a unit rating of around 30 units per hour when changed and then drop no further, it is obvious that the rate of turnover was highest for these operators just after they were changed and again much later just before they reached standard. Why?

It is assumed that the strength of frustration for an operator who has not been transferred gradually increases because both the driving force toward the goal of reaching 60 and the restraining force of the difficulty of the job increase with increasing unit rating. This is in line with Propositions 1, 2, and 3, above. For the transferred operator, on the other hand, the frustration is greatest immediately after transfer when the contrast of her present status with her former status is most evident. At this point, the strength of the restraining forces is at a maximum because the difficulty is unusually great due to proactive inhibition. Then, as she overcomes the interference effects between the two jobs and learns the new job, the difficulty and the frustration gradually decrease and the rate of turnover declines until the operator reaches 45-49 units per hour. Then at higher

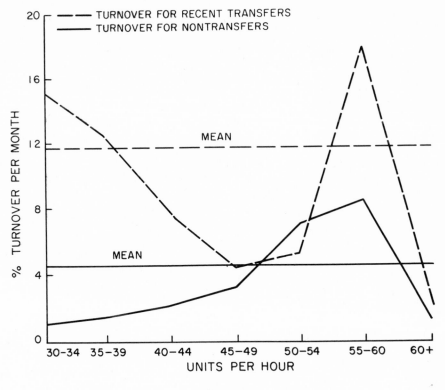

20 — — — TURNOVER FOR RECENT TRANSFERS
— TURNOVER FOR NONTRANSFERS

% TURNOVER PER MONTH

MEAN

MEAN

30-34 35-39   40-44   45-49   50-54   55-60   60+
UNITS PER HOUR

Figure 1

The Rate of Turnover at Various Levels of Production for Transfers as Compared With Nontransfers.

levels of production the difficulty starts to increase again and the transferred operator shows the same peak in frustration and turnover at 55-59 units per hour.

Though our theory of frustration explains the forms of the two turnover curves in Figure 1, it seems hardly adequate to account for the markedly higher level of turnover for transfers as compared to nontransfers. On the basis of the difficulty of the job, it is especially difficult to explain the higher rate of turnover at 55-59 units per hour for transfers. Evidently, additional forces are operating.

Another factor which seems to affect recovery rates of changed operators is the amount of cohesiveness. Observations seem to indicate that a strong psycho-logical subgroup with negative attitudes toward management will display the strongest resistance to change. On the other hand, changed groups with high cohesiveness and positive cooperative attitudes are the best relearners. Collections of individuals with little or no cohesiveness display some resistance to change, but not so strongly as the groups with high cohesiveness and negative attitudes toward management.

.   .   .

One common result in a cohesive subgroup is the setting of a group standard concerning production. Where the attitudes toward management are antagonistic, [the] group standard may take the form of a definite restriction of production to a given level. This phenomenon of restriction is particularly likely to happen in a group that has been transferred to a job where a new piece rate has been set, for they have some hope that, if production never approaches the standard, the management may change the piece rate in their favor.

. . .

The Experiments

On the basis of the preliminary theory that resistance to change is a combination of an individual reaction to frustration with strong group-induced forces, it seemed that the most appropriate methods for overcoming the resistance to change would be group methods. Consequently, an experiment was designed (Experiment I) employing three degrees of participation in handling groups to be transferred. The first variation, the control group, involved *no participation* by employees in planning the changes, though an explanation was given to them. The second variation involved *participation through representation* of the workers in designing the changes to be made in the jobs. The third variation consisted of *total participation* by all members of the group in designing the changes. Two experimental groups received the total participation treatment. The four experimental groups were roughly matched with respect to (*a*) the efficiency ratings of the groups before transfer; (*b*) the degree of change involved in the transfer; and (*c*) the amount of cohesiveness observed in the groups.

In no case was more than a minor change in the work routines and time allowances made. The no-participation group, 18 hand pressers, had formerly stacked their work in half-dozen lots on a flat piece of cardboard the size of the finished product. The new job called for stacking their work in half-dozen lots in a box the size of the finished product. The box was located in the same place the cardboard had been. An additional two minutes per dozen was allowed (by the time study) for this new part of the job. This represented a total change of 8.8%.

The group treated with participation through representation, 13 pajama folders, had formerly folded coats with prefolded pants. The new job called for the folding of coats with unfolded pants. An additional 1.8 minutes per dozen was allowed (by time study) for this new part of the job. This represented a total change of 9.4%.

The two total participation groups, consisting of eight and seven pajama examiners, respectively, had formerly clipped threads from the entire garment and examined every seam. The new job called for pulling only certain threads off and examining every seam. An average of 1.2 minutes per dozen was subtracted (by time study) from the total time on these two jobs. This represented a total job change of 8%.

The no-participation group of hand pressers went through the usual factory routine when they were changed. The production department modified the job, and the new piece rate was set. A group meeting was then held in which the group was told that the change was necessary because of competitive conditions, and that a new piece rate had been set. The new piece rate was thoroughly explained by the time-study man, questions were answered, and the meeting dismissed.

The group which participated through representatives was changed in a different manner. Before any changes took place, a group meeting was held with all the operators to be changed. The need for the change was presented as dramatically as possible, showing two identical garments produced in the factory;

one was produced in 1946 and had sold for 100% more than its fellow in 1947. The group was asked to identify the cheaper one and could not do it. This demonstration effectively shared with the group the entire problem of the necessity of cost reduction. A general agreement was reached that a savings could be effected by removing the "frills" and "fancy" work from the garment without affecting the folders' opportunity to achieve a high efficiency rating. Management then presented a plan to set the new job and piece rate:

1. Make a check study of the job as it was being done.
2. Eliminate all unnecessary work.
3. Train several operators in the correct methods.
4. Set the piece rate by time studies on these specially trained operators.
5. Explain the new job and rate to all the operators.
6. Train all operators in the new method so they can reach a high rate of production within a short time.

The group approved this plan (though no formal group decision was reached), and chose the operators to be specially trained. A submeeting with the "special" operators was held immediately following the meeting with the entire group. They displayed a cooperative and interested attitude and immediately presented many good suggestions. This attitude carried over into the working out of the details of the new job, and when the new job and piece rates were set the "special" operators referred to the resultants as "our job," "our rate," etc. The new job and piece rates were presented at a second group meeting to all the operators involved. The "special" operators served to train the other operators on the new job.

The total participation groups went through much the same kind of meetings.

The groups were smaller, and a more intimate atmosphere was established. The need for a change was once again made dramatically clear. The same general plan was presented by management. However, since the groups were small, all operators were chosen as "special" operators; that is, all operators were to participate directly in the designing of the new jobs, and all operators would be studied by the time-study man. It is interesting to observe that in the meetings with these two groups suggestions were immediately made in such quantity that the stenographer had great difficulty in recording them. The group approved of the plans, but again no formal group decision was reached.

Results

The results of the experiment are summarized in graphic form in Figure 2. The gaps in the production curves occur because these groups were paid on a time-work basis for a day or two. The no-participation group improved little beyond their early efficiency ratings. Resistance developed almost immediately after the change occurred. Marked expressions of aggression against management occurred, such as conflict with the methods engineer, expression of hostility against the supervisor, deliberate restriction of production, and lack of cooperation with the supervisor. There were 17% quits in the first 40 days. Grievances were filed about the piece rate, but when the rate was checked, it was found to be a little "loose."

The representation group showed an unusually good relearning curve. At the end of 14 days, the group averaged 61 units per hour. During the 14 days, the attitude was cooperative and permissive. They worked well with the methods engineer, the training staff, and the supervisor. (The supervisor was the same per-

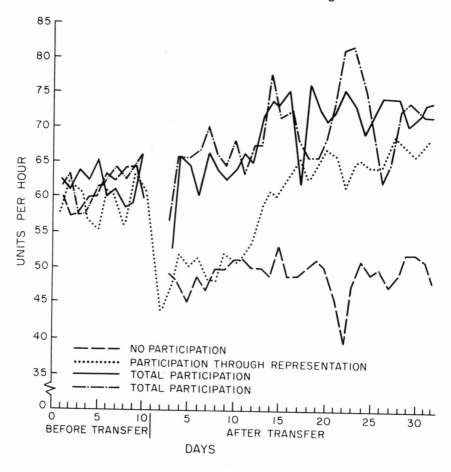

Figure 2

The Effects of Participation Through Representation and of Total Participation on Recovery After an Easy Transfer.

son in the cases of the first two groups.) There were no quits in this group in the first 40 days. This group might have presented a better learning record if work had not been scarce during the first seven days. There was one act of aggression against the supervisor recorded in the first 40 days. We should note that the three special representative operators recovered at about the same rate as the rest of their group.

The total participation groups recovered faster than the others. After a slight drop on the first day of change, the efficiency ratings returned to a prechange level and showed sustained progress thereafter to a level about 14% higher than the prechange level. No additional training was provided them after the second day. They worked well with their supervisors and no indications of aggression were observed from these groups. There were no quits in either of these groups in the first 40 days.

(A fifth experimental group, composed of only two sewing operators, was trans-

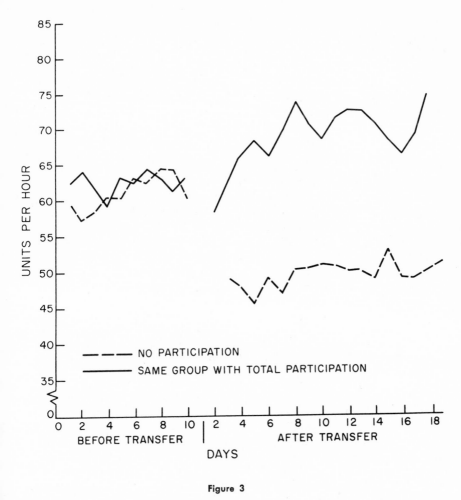

UNITS PER HOUR

DAYS

BEFORE TRANSFER | AFTER TRANSFER

- - - - NO PARTICIPATION
———— SAME GROUP WITH TOTAL PARTICIPATION

Figure 3

A Comparison of the Effect of No Participation With the Total Participation Procedure on the Same Group.

ferred by the total participation technique. Their new job was one of the most difficult jobs in the factory, in contrast to the easy jobs for the other four experimental groups. As expected, the total participation technique again resulted in an unusually fast recovery rate and a final level of production well above the level before transfer.)

In the first experiment, the no-participation group made no progress after transfer for a period of 32 days. At the end of this period the group was broken up, and the individuals were reassigned to new jobs scattered throughout the factory. Two and a half months after their dispersal, the 13 remaining members of the original no-participation group were again brought together as a group for a second experiment (Experiment II).

This second experiment consisted of transferring the group to a new job, using the total participation technique. The new job was a pressing job of comparable difficulty to the new job in the first experiment. On the average, it involved about the same degree of change. In the meetings, no reference was made to the previous behavior of the group on being transferred.

The results of the second experiment were in sharp contrast to the first (see Fig. 3). With the total participation technique, the same group now recovered rapidly to their previous efficiency rating and, like the other groups under this treatment, continued on beyond it to a new high level of production. There was no aggression or turnover in the group for 19 days after change, a marked modification of their previous behavior after transfer. Some anxiety concerning their seniority status was expressed, but this was resolved in a meeting of their elected delegate, the union business agent, and a management representative.

Interpretation

. . . The first experiment showed that the rate of recovery is directly proportional to the amount of participation, and that the rates of turnover and aggression are inversely proportional to the amount of participation. The second experiment demonstrated more conclusively that the results obtained depended on the experimental treatment rather than on personality factors like skill or aggressiveness, for identical individuals yielded markedly different results in the no-participation treatment as contrasted with the total-participation treatment.

Apparently total participation has the same type of effect as participation through representation, but the former has a stronger influence. In regard to recovery rates, this difference is not unequivocal because the experiment was unfortunately confounded. Right after transfer, the latter group had insufficient material to work on for a period of seven days. Hence, their slower recovery during this period is at least in part due to insufficient work. In succeeding days, however, there was an adequate supply of work and the differential recovery rate still persisted. Therefore, we are inclined to believe that participation through representation results in slower recovery than does total participation.

. . .

There are three main component forces influencing production in a downward direction: (a) the difficulty of the job; (b) a force corresponding to avoidance of strain; and (c) a force corresponding to a group standard to restrict production to a given level. The resultant force upward in the direction of greater production is composed of three additional component forces: (a) the force corresponding to the goal of standard production; (b) a force corresponding to pressures induced by the management through supervision; and (c) a force corresponding to a group standard of competition.

. . .

Management Pressure. On all operators below standard the management exerts a pressure for higher production. This pressure is no harsh and autocratic treatment involving threats; rather, it takes the form of persuasion and encouragement by the supervisors. They attempt to induce the low rating operator to improve her performance and to attain standard production.

Such an attempt to induce a psychological force on another person may have several results. In the first place the person may ignore the attempt of the inducing agent, in which case there is no induced force acting on the person. On the other hand, the attempt may succeed so that an induced force on the person exists. Other things being equal, whenever there is an induced force acting on a person, the person will locomote in the direction of the force. An induced force which depends on the power field of an inducing agent—some other individual or group—will cease to exist when the inducing power field is withdrawn. In this respect it is different from an "own" force which stems from a person's own needs and goals.

The reaction of a person to an effective induced force will vary depending, among other things, on the person's relation to the inducing agent. A force induced by a friend may be accepted in such a way that it acts more like an own force. An effective force induced by an enemy may be resisted and rejected so that the person complies unwillingly and shows signs of conflict and tension. Thus in addition to what might be called a "neutral" induced force, we also distinguish an *accepted* induced force and a *rejected* induced force. Naturally, the acceptance and the rejection of an induced force can vary in degree from zero (i.e., a neutral induced force) to very strong acceptance or rejection.

. . .

Group Standards. Probably the most important force affecting the recovery under the no-participation procedure was a group standard, set by the group, restricting the level of production to 50 units per hour. Evidently this explicit agreement to restrict production is related to the group's rejection of the change and of the new job as arbitrary and unreasonable. Perhaps they had faint hopes of demonstrating that standard production could not be attained and thereby obtain a more favorable piece rate. In any case there was a definite group phenomenon which affected all the members of the group. We have already noted the striking example of the presser whose production was restricted in the group situation to about half the level she attained as an individual. In the no-participation group, we would also expect the group to induce strong forces

on the members. The more a member deviates above the standard, the stronger would be the group-induced force to conform to the standard, for such deviations both negate any possibility of management's increasing the piece rate and at the same time expose the other members to increased pressure from management. Thus individual differences in levels of production should be sharply curtailed in this group after transfer.

An analysis was made, for all groups, of the individual differences within each group in levels of production. In Experiment I, the 40 days before change were compared with the 30 days after change; in Experiment II, the 10 days before change were compared to the 17 days after change. As a measure of variability, the standard deviation was calculated each day for each group. The average daily standard deviations before and after change were as follows:

Experiment I	*Before Change*	*After Change*
No participation	9.8	1.9
Participation through representation	9.7	3.8
Total participation	10.3	2.7
Total participation	9.9	2.4
Experiment II		
Total participation	12.7	2.9

There is, indeed, a marked decrease in individual differences within the no-participation group after their first transfer. In fact, the restriction of production resulted in a lower variability than in any other group. . . . It is also clear that the group standard to restrict production is a major reason for the lack of recovery in the no-participation group.

The table of variability also shows that the experimental treatments markedly reduced variability in the other four groups after transfer. In the group having participation by representation, this smallest reduction of variability was produced by a group standard of individual competition. Competition among members of the group was reported by the supervisor soon after transfer. This competition was a force toward higher production which resulted in good recovery to standard and continued progress beyond standard.

The total-participation groups showed a greater reduction in variability following transfer. These two groups were transferred on the same day. Group competition developed between the two groups, and this competition, which evidently resulted in stronger forces on the members than did the individual competition, was an effective group standard. The standard gradually moved to higher and higher levels of production, with the result that the groups not only reached but far exceeded their previous levels of production.

Probably a major determinant of the strength of these group standards is the cohesiveness of the group (1). Whether this power of the group over the members was used to increase or to decrease productivity seemed to depend upon the use of participation (4).

Turnover and Aggression

Returning now to our preliminary theory of frustration, we can see several revisions. The difficulty of the job and its relation to skill and strain avoidance has been clarified in Proposition 5. It is now clear that the driving force toward 60 is a complex affair: it is partly a negative driving force corresponding to the negative valence of low pay, low status, failure, and job insecurity. Turnover results not only from the frustration produced by the conflict of these two forces, but also from a direct attempt to escape from the region of these negative valences. For the members of the no-participation group, the group standard to restrict production prevented escape by increasing production, so that quitting their jobs was the only remaining escape. In the participation groups, on the contrary,

both the group standards and the additional own forces resulting from the acceptance of management induced forces combined to make increasing production the distinguished path of escape from this region of negative valence.

In considering turnover as a form of escape from the field, it is not enough to look only at the psychological present; one must also consider the psychological future. The employee's decision to quit the job is rarely made exclusively on the basis of a momentary frustration or an undesirable present situation. She usually quits when she also sees the future as equally hopeless. The operator transferred by the usual factory procedure (including the no-participation group) has, in fact, a realistic view of the probability of continued failure because, as we have already noted, 62% of transfers do fail to recover to standard production. Thus, the higher rate of quitting for transfers as compared to nontransfers results from a more pessimistic view of the future.

The no-participation procedure had the effect for the members of setting up management as a hostile power field. They rejected the forces induced by this hostile power field, and group standards to restrict production developed within the group in opposition to management. In this conflict between the power field of management and the power field of the group, the group attempted to reduce the strength of the hostile power field relative to the strength of their own power field. This change was accomplished in three ways: (*a*) The group increased its own power by developing a more cohesive and well-disciplined group. (*b*) They secured "allies" by getting the backing of the union in filing a formal grievance about the new piece rate. (*c*) They attacked the hostile power field directly in the form of aggression against the supervisor, the time-study engineer, and the higher management. Thus the aggression was derived not only from individual frustration, but also from the conflict between two groups. Furthermore, this situation of group conflict both helped to define management as the frustrating agent and gave the members strength to express any aggressive impulses produced by frustration.

Conclusions

It is possible for management to modify greatly or to remove completely group resistance to changes in methods of work and the ensuing piece rates. This change can be accomplished by the use of group meetings in which management effectively communicates the need for change and stimulates group participation in planning the changes.

For Harwood's management, and presumably for managements of other industries using an incentive system, this experiment has important implications in the field of labor relations. A majority of all grievances presented at Harwood have always stemmed from a change situation. By preventing or greatly modifying group resistance to change, this concomitant to change may well be greatly reduced. The reduction of such costly phenomena as turnover and slow relearning rates presents another distinct advantage.

Harwood's management has long felt that action research, such as the present experiment, is the only key to better labor-management relations. It is only by discovering the basic principles and applying them to the true causes of conflict that an intelligent, effective effort can be made to correct the undesirable effects of the conflict.

References

1. Festinger, L., Back, K., Schachter, S., Kelley, H., & Thibaut, J. *Theory and experiment in social communication.* Ann Arbor, Mich.: Institute for Social Research, 1950.
2. French, John R. P., Jr. The behavior of organized and unorganized groups under conditions of frustration and fear. *University of Iowa Studies in Child Welfare*, 1944, **20**, 229-308.
3. Lewin, Kurt. Frontiers in group dynamics. *Human Relations*, 1947, **1**, 5-41.
4. Schachter, S., Ellertson, N., McBride, Dorothy, & Gregory, Doris. An experimental study of cohesiveness and productivity. *Human Relations*, 1951, **4**, 229-238.

Concluding
Statement

Individual Differences in Learning

The specific conditions of learning will vary from one individual to another. What is necessary here is to spell out (1) what significant aspects of the learning process vary with individual differences, that is, the results of training and (2) what characteristics of the individual are particularly significant in the job of learning. Under our first heading, we can state three specific propositions:

The Results of Training

(a) Given the same training, the individuals in a group will learn to various levels of proficiency and at differing rates of speed. In the same training situation for example, Barbara will ultimately learn to type 80 words per minute whereas Joan will only learn 60 WPM no matter how much she practices. Ruth will learn to type 40 WPM after ten hours of practice. Anne will be able to type only 30 WPM after the same amount of practice.

(b) Given the same organizational setting and opportunities to learn, different people will learn different aspects best. For example, John will select for his learning a thorough knowledge of the characteristics of important customers, and Henry will become skillful in keeping the business machines operating.

(c) Training methods vary in their effectiveness for different types of employees. A study done by Edgerton for the Office of Naval Research provides a good illustration of this point.

He found that whether a *rote method of teaching* or a *method that provided explanations* worked best depended on the patterning of the trainees' abilities. The first method worked best with some trainees whereas the second method proved better with others. He also found evidence that morale level was higher for some trainees when the method of training matched the pattern of their abilities. One other significant finding in his study is that the relative effectiveness of two methods of training may depend on the characterstics and prior experience of the trainers themselves. Siegel and Siegel in research on college students, report comparable findings.

Significant Characteristics of the Individual

In a sense, practically every characteristic of the individual may be a significant determinant of how he learns. We single out those that we believe require special consideration by the administrator.

(a) The Edgerton study suggests that not only the sheer amount of ability but also the particular patterning of ability is significant in accounting for differences in training results.

(b) Miles reports that individuals differ in the previously established habits they bring to a learning task, and that these differences produce different training results. Some people habitually analyze a problem before attempting to solve it; others approach it on a trial and error basis. Training the two types of individuals with the same methods will produce different results.

(c) Recent research (some previously cited in Chapters Five and Nine) indicates the relevance of knowing what needs are present, and the level of anxiety, in understanding how an individual will respond to a learning situation.

(d) Differences in initial ability are, of course, relevant in any discussion of learning. Everyone knows that there are slow learners and rapid learners. Many administrators seem to believe that the slow learner, although he takes longer to learn something, somehow or other learns it better and will retain it longer. There is no research evidence to support such a conclusion. On the contrary, the faster learner maintains his advantage and retains material longer.

The question is sometimes asked, "Does training increase or decrease the differences between people of varying initial ability levels?"[*] The answer is that it may do either, depending on the complexity of the task to be learned. If the task is relatively simple, with a relatively low ceiling for accomplishment, continued practice cannot benefit the most able people. As a result, the less able will narrow the gap between themselves and the most able although the evidence indicates that they will not actually surpass those of superior ability. Where a task is complex, research indicates that variability in performance in-

---

[*] The research on which conclusions drawn in this section are based is summarized in Joseph Tiffin and Edward J. McCormick, *Industrial Psychology*, 4th Edition, Englewood Cliffs, New Jersey: Prentice-Hall, 1958.

creases with length of training or experience on the job: those of high initial ability outstrip the others in response to training. Training will also increase variability in performance on a task in which all beginners have no knowledge of the task or useful skill in its performance.

Can we extrapolate these research findings, based as they are entirely on skill training, to management development and supervisory training? Not easily, and certainly not without qualification. Unless our training groups have been selected to be extremely homogeneous, they will bring with them considerable variability in attitudes, personality characteristics, knowledge, and skill. Running them through a management or supervisory training program may move extreme characteristics, particularly extreme attitudes and ways of acting, closer to a middle, normative position. Under these conditions variability in the group, after training (if it is effective) is, of course, diminished. Consequently one might well consider as one of the dangers of some types of management and supervisory training a uniform molding process with a subsequent reduction in management's later capacity for versatile and flexible performance.

Summary

Administrators regularly face the problem of effecting change in the behavior of others; employees regularly face the problem of learning the expected changes. Over the years, a steadily accumulating body of research, much of it conducted in laboratories, has made possible the identification of those conditions that are *necessary* for learning to take place, for example, reinforcement of the desired response; and other conditions that *facilitate* the process, for example, providing specific knowledge of results.

In describing some of this research, Part Four emphasizes two principal points: (1) that one of the administrator's main functions is to serve as an agent of change and in this function his management of reinforcement (the reward system available for his use) is of utmost significance; and (2) that effecting change in others requires an understanding of the scientific principles that describe the process of learning.

PART FIVE

Attitudes and Attitude Change

Introduction

An administrator who is seeking to influence the behavior of others—whether these others are subordinates, superiors, or colleagues in his own organization, or those he deals with in other organizations—soon becomes aware of the importance of their attitudes. He may be surprised at some of the attitudes they have and wonder how they can hold some of the views they do (if these views differ from his own). He may be perplexed when others do not change their attitudes even after he has presented facts that "obviously" should cause them to change.

Scientists studying behavior have devoted much effort to the field of attitudes. They have gathered data on the functions that attitudes serve, the ways in which they develop, the conditions that lead to change in attitudes, and the resistance to change of attitudes. Our earlier discussions of perception, motivation, adjustment, conflict, and learning will serve as background for understanding more about attitudes.

Preview of Part Five

Our examination of attitudes is organized into five chapters. We start by considering the nature of attitudes. In our first reading, Katz is concerned with the functions that attitudes serve, and as a framework for his comprehensive discussion, provides four categories: adjustive, ego-defensive, ego-evaluative, and knowledge-serving. Following Katz's summary and discussion of much attitude research, our chapter goes on to consider how attitudes develop. In connection with the way in which an individual learns his attitudes, we describe various influences on attitude development: cultural, family, group membership, class and peer group, as well as previous work influences. We are thus dealing with the development of attitudes where apparently none existed before; the development process is to be distinguished from the changing of attitudes that are already held by the individual. This distinction provides the basis for separating Chapter Fourteen from the later chapters in Part Five.

In Chapter Fifteen, certain basic principles of attitude change are given with emphasis on arousing a need to change. Another excerpt from Katz's article relates the functional classification to various principles of attitude arousal and change. We then present a few links for relating these principles to administrative situations.

We next move, in Chapter Sixteen, to describing certain conditions for attitude change. The first of these involves the concept of role; an article by Lieberman describes the differential changes in attitudes that took place when, from the same basic group, some men were made foremen and some shop stewards. Next, we consider the part that group membership and interpersonal influence can play in changing attitudes, and touch for a moment on the question of conformity.

There has been much debate on the effectiveness of rules and regulations on changing attitudes. The research on the effects of enforced changes on behavior is discussed, using a contemporary distinction between compliance, identification, and internalization.

Much work in recent years has concerned the effects of information or communications on attitudes. Our discussion of information as a condition for attitude change is followed by the sections on situational influences, and on the effects of contact with other people. Finally, the role of participation is indicated, (cf, the article by Coch and French, Chapter Thirteen), but discussed at greater length in Chapter Eighteen.

The reader's hunch that attitude change is not easily obtained is underscored by Chapter Seventeen on Special Problems. In this, we attempt to use the concept of cognitive dissonance; the research it has provided, can serve as a way of tying together some of the complex problems of attitude change. An excerpt is given from Festinger's work on some of the reactions to feelings of dissonance.

Using dissonance as the thread, we attempt to tie together some of the research on the effects of inducements, commitment and choice, and seeking information. The ubiquitous question of individual differences is then considered; the chapter ends with an overview that seeks to provide an administrator with a guide to the complexities he faces on those occasions when, in good conscience, he has decided to modify the attitudes of other individuals.

Our final chapter covers some of the systematic attempts that industry has made to modify attitudes of its employees. Descriptions of these are provided in readings by Schein, Miner, Mann, Mann and Neff, and Levine and Butler.

CHAPTER FOURTEEN

The Nature
of Attitudes
and
Their Development

The Functions of Attitudes

Psychologists have taken various approaches in studying attitudes. In our first reading, Katz traces these approaches and presents a contemporary functional approach, one which seeks "to understand the reasons people hold the attitudes they do." He then goes on to a comprehensive discussion of four different functions that attitudes serve. The administrator must recognize that all attitudes are not the same if he is to understand how to change attitudes or overcome resistance to change of attitudes. Smith, Bruner, and White have asked "Of what use to a man are his opinions?" Katz organizes the uses for us. The framework Katz provides will be used later in this chapter along with subsequent excerpts from his article.

The Functional Approach to the Study of Attitudes*

DANIEL KATZ

. . .

Early Approaches to the Study of Attitude and Opinion

There have been two main streams of thinking with respect to the determination of man's attitudes. The one tradition assumes an irrational model of man: specifically it holds that men have very limited powers of reason and reflection, weak capacity to discriminate, only the most primitive self-insight, and very short memories. Whatever mental capacities people do possess are easily overwhelmed by emotional forces and appeals to self-interest and vanity. The early books on the psychology of advertising, with their emphasis on the doctrine of suggestion, exemplify this approach. One expression of this philosophy is in the propagandist's concern with tricks and traps to manipulate the public. A modern form of it appears in *The Hidden Persuaders,* or the use of subliminal and marginal suggestion, or the devices supposedly employed by "the Madison Avenue boys." Experiments to support this line of thinking started with laboratory demonstrations of the power of hypnotic suggestion and were soon extended to show that people would change their attitudes in an uncritical manner under the influence of the prestige of authority and numbers. For example, individuals would accept or reject the same idea depending upon

whether it came from a positive or a negative prestige source.[1]

The second approach is that of the ideologist who invokes a rational model of man. It assumes that the human being has a cerebral cortex, that he seeks understanding, that he consistently attempts to make sense of the world about him, that he possesses discriminating and reasoning powers which will assert themselves over time, and that he is capable of self-criticism and self-insight. It relies heavily upon getting adequate information to people. Our educational system is based upon this rational model. The present emphasis upon the improvement of communication, upon developing more adequate channels of two-way communication, of conferences and institutes, upon bringing people together to interchange ideas, are all indications of the belief in the importance of intelligence and comprehension in the formation and change of men's opinions.

Now either school of thought can point to evidence which supports its assumptions, and can make fairly damaging criticisms or its opponent. Solomon Asch and his colleagues, in attacking the irrational model, have called attention to the biased character of the old experiments on prestige suggestion which gave the subject little opportunity to demonstrate critical thinking.[2] And further exploration of sub-

* Excerpted from *Public Opinion Quarterly,* 1960, *24,* 163-176. A second part of this article appears as Reading 5-2.

[1] Muzafer Sherif, *The Psychology of Social Norms,* New York, Harper, 1936.
[2] Solomon E. Asch, *Social Pyschology,* Englewood Cliffs, N.J.: Prentice-Hall Inc., 1952.

jects in these stupid situations does indicate that they try to make sense of a nonsensical matter as far as possible. Though the same statement is presented by the experimenter to two groups, the first time as coming from a positive source and the second time as coming from a negative source, it is given a different meaning dependent upon the context in which it appears.[3] Thus the experimental subject does his best to give some rational meaning to the problem. On the other hand, a large body of experimental work indicates that there are many limitations in the rational approach in that people see their world in terms of their own needs, remember what they want to remember, and interpret information on the basis of wishful thinking. H. H. Hyman and P. Sheatsley have demonstrated that these experimental results have direct relevance to information campaigns directed at influencing public opinion.[4] These authors assembled facts about such campaigns and showed conclusively that increasing the flow of information to people does not necessarily increase the knowledge absorbed or produce the attitude changes desired.

The major difficulty with these conflicting approaches is their lack of specification of the conditions under which men do act as the theory would predict. For the facts are that people do act at

times as if they had been decorticated and at times with intelligence and comprehension. And people themselves do recognize that on occasion they have behaved blindly, impulsively, and thoughtlessly. A second major difficulty is that the rationality-irrationality dimension is not clearly defined. At the extremes it is easy to point to examples, as in the case of the acceptance of stupid suggestions under emotional stress on the one hand, or brilliant problem solving on the other; but this does not provide adequate guidance for the many cases in the middle of the scale where one attempts to discriminate between rationalization and reason.

Reconciliation of the Conflict in a Functional Approach

The conflict between the rationality and irrationality models was saved from becoming a worthless debate because of the experimentation and research suggested by these models. The findings of this research pointed toward the elements of truth in each approach and gave some indication of the conditions under which each model could make fairly accurate predictions. In general the irrational approach was at its best where the situation imposed heavy restrictions upon search behavior and response alternatives. Where individuals must give quick responses without adequate opportunities to explore the nature of the problem, where there are few response alternatives available to them, where their own deep emotional needs are aroused, they will in general react much as does the unthinking subject under hypnosis. On the other hand, where the individual can have more adequate commerce with the relevant environmental setting, where he has time to obtain more feedback from his reality testing, and where he has a number of realistic choices, his behavior

---

[3] *Ibid.*, pp. 426-427. The following statement was attributed to its rightful author, John Adams, for some subjects and to Karl Marx for others: "those who hold and those who are without property have ever formed distinct interests in society." When the statement was attributed to Marx, this type of comment appeared: "Marx is stressing the need for a redistribution of wealth." When it was attributed to Adams, this comment appeared: "This social division is innate in mankind."

[4] Herbert H. Hyman and Paul B. Sheatsley, "Some Reasons Why Information Campaigns Fail," *Public Opinion Quarterly*, Vol. 11, 1947, pp. 413-423.

will reflect the use of his rational faculties.[5] The child will often respond to the directive of the parent not by implicit obedience but by testing out whether or not the parent really meant what he said.

. . .

The theory of psychological consonance, or cognitive balance, assumes that man attempts to reduce discrepancies in his beliefs, attitudes, and behavior by appropriate changes in these processes. [See Festinger, Reading 3-9.] While the emphasis here is upon consistency or logicality, the theory deals with all dissonances, no matter how produced. Thus they could result from irrational factors of distorted perception and wishful thinking as well as from rational factors of realistic appraisal of a problem and an accurate estimate of its consequences. Moreover, the theory would predict only that the individual will move to reduce dissonance, whether such movement is a good adjustment to the world or leads to the delusional systems of the paranoiac. In a sense, then, this theory would avoid the conflict between the old approaches of the rational and the irrational man by not dealing with the specific antecedent causes of behavior or with the particular ways in which the individual solves his problems.

In addition to the present preoccupation with the development of formal models concerned with cognitive balance and consonance, there is a growing interest in a more comprehensive framework for dealing with the complex variables and for bringing order within the field. . . . [One] point of departure is represented by two groups of workers who have organized their theories around the functions which attitudes perform for the personality. Sarnoff, Katz, and McClintock, in taking this functional approach, have given primary attention to the motivational bases of attitudes and the processes of attitude change.[6] The basic assumption of this group is that both attitude formation and attitude change must be understood in terms of the needs they serve and that, as these motivational processes differ, so too will the conditions and techniques for attitude change. Smith, Bruner, and White have also analyzed the different functions which attitudes perform for the personality.[7] Both groups present essentially the same functions, but Smith, Bruner, and White give more attention to perceptual and cognitive processes and Sarnoff, Katz, and McClintock to the specific conditions of attitude change.

The importance of the functional approach is threefold. (1) Many previous studies of attitude change have dealt with factors which are not genuine psychological variables, for example, the effect on group prejudice of contact between two groups, or the exposure of a group of subjects to a communication in the mass media. Now contact serves different psychological functions for the individual and merely knowing that people have seen a movie or watched a television program tells us nothing about the personal values engaged or not engaged by such a presentation.

---

[5] William A. Scott points out that in the area of international relations the incompleteness and remoteness of the information and the lack of pressures on the individual to defend his views results in inconsistencies. Inconsistent elements with respect to a system of international beliefs may, however, be consistent with the larger system of the personality. "Rationality and Non-rationality of International Attitudes," *Journal of Conflict Resolution,* Vol. 2, 1958, pp. 9-16.

[6] Irving Sarnoff and Daniel Katz, "The Motivational Bases of Attitude Chance," *Journal of Abnormal and Social Psychology,* Vol. 49, 1954, pp. 115-124.

[7] M. Brewster Smith, Jerome S. Bruner, and Robert W. White, *Opinions and Personality,* New York, Wiley, 1956.

. . .

(2) By concerning ourselves with the different functions attitudes can perform we can avoid the great error of oversimplification—the error of attributing a single cause to given types of attitude. It was once popular to ascribe radicalism in economic and political matters to the psychopathology of the insecure and to attribute conservatism to the rigidity of the mentally aged. At the present time it is common practice to see in attitudes of group prejudice the repressed hostilities stemming from childhood frustrations, though Hyman and Sheatsley have pointed out that prejudiced attitudes can serve a normative function of gaining acceptance in one's own group as readily as releasing unconscious hatred.[8] In short, not only are there a number of motivational forces to take into account in considering attitudes and behavior, but the same attitude can have a different motivational basis in different people.

(3) Finally, recognition of the complex motivational sources of behavior can help to remedy the neglect in general theories which lack specification of conditions under which given types of attitude will change.

. . .

Before we attempt a detailed analysis of the four major functions which attitudes can serve, it is appropriate to consider the nature of attitudes, their dimensions, and their relations to other psychological structures and processes.

Nature of Attitudes: Their Dimensions

Attitude is the predisposition of the

individual to evaluate some symbol or object or aspect of his world in a favorable or unfavorable manner. Opinion is the verbal expression of an attitude, but attitudes can also be expressed in nonverbal behavior. Attitudes include both the affective, or feeling core of liking or disliking, and the cognitive, or belief, elements which describe the object of the attitude, its characteristics, and its relations to other objects. All attitudes thus include beliefs, but not all beliefs are attitudes. When specific attitudes are organized into a hierarchical structure, they comprise *value systems*. Thus a person may not only hold specific attitudes against deficit spending and unbalanced budgets but may also have a systematic organization of such beliefs and attitudes in the form of a value system of economic conservatism.

The dimensions of attitudes can be stated more precisely if the above distinctions between beliefs and feelings and attitudes and value systems are kept in mind. The *intensity* of an attitude refers to the strength of the *affective* component. In fact, rating scales and even Thurstone scales deal primarily with the intensity of feeling of the individual for or against some social object. The cognitive, or belief, component suggests two additional dimensions, the *specificity* or *generality* of the attitude and the *degree of differentiation* of the beliefs. Differentiation refers to the number of beliefs or cognitive items contained in the attitude, and the general assumption is that the simpler the attitude in cognitive structure the easier it is to change.[9] For simple structures there is no defense in depth, and once a single item of belief has been changed the attitude will change. A rather different dimension of

---

[8] Herbert H. Hyman and Paul B. Sheatsley, "The Authoritarian Personality: A Methodological Critique," in Richard Christie and Marie Jahoda, editors, *Studies in the Scope and Method of the Authoritarian Personality*, Glencoe, Ill., Free Press, 1954, pp. 50-122.

[9] David Krech and Richard S. Crutchfield, *Theory and Problems of Social Psychology*, New York, McGraw-Hill, 1948, pp. 160-163.

attitude is the *number and strength of its linkages to a related value system.* If an attitude favoring budget balancing by the Federal government is tied in strongly with a value system of economic conservatism, it will be more difficult to change than if it were a fairly isolated attitude of the person. Finally, the relation of the value system to the personality is a consideration of first importance. If an attitude is tied to a value system which is closely related to, or which consists of, the individual's conception of himself, then the appropriate change procedures become more complex. The *centrality* of an attitude refers to its role as part of a value system which is closely related to the individual's self-concept.

An additional aspect of attitudes is not clearly described in most theories, namely, their relation to action or overt behavior. Though behavior related to the attitude has other determinants than the attitude itself, it is also true that some attitudes in themselves have more of what Cartwright calls an action structure than do others.[10] Brewster Smith refers to this dimension as policy orientation[11] and Katz and Stotland speak of it as the action component.[12] For example, while many people have attitudes of approval toward one or the other of the two political parties, these attitudes will differ in their structure with respect to relevant action. One may be prepared to vote on election day and will know where and when he should vote and will go to the

polls no matter what the weather or how great the inconvenience. Another man will only vote if a party worker calls for him in a car. Himmelstrand's work is concerned with all aspects of the relationship between attitude and behavior, but he deals with the action structure of the attitude itself by distinguishing between attitudes where the affect is tied to verbal expression and attitudes where the affect is tied to behavior concerned with more objective referents of the attitude.[13] In the first case an individual derives satisfaction from talking about a problem; in the second case he derives satisfaction from taking some form of concrete action.

Attempts to change attitudes can be directed primarily at the belief component or at the feeling, or affective, component. Rosenberg theorizes that an effective change in one component will result in changes in the other component and presents experimental evidence to confirm this hypothesis.[14] For example, a political candidate will often attempt to win people by making them like him and dislike his opponent, and thus communicate affect rather than ideas. If he is successful, people will not only like him but entertain favorable beliefs about him. Another candidate may deal primarily with ideas and hope that, if he can change people's beliefs about an issue, their feelings will also change.

Four Functions Which Attitudes Perform for the Individual

The major functions which attitudes perform for the personality can be grouped according to their motivational basis as follows:

1. *The instrumental, adjustive, or utilitarian function* upon which Jeremy Bentham and the utilitarians constructed their model of man. A modern expression of

---

[10] Dorwin Cartwright, "Some Principles of Mass Persuasion," *Human Relations.* Vol. 2, 1949, pp. 253-267.

[11] M. Brewster Smith, "The Personal Setting of Public Opinions: A Study of Attitudes toward Russia," *Public Opinion Quarterly,* Vol. 11, 1947, pp. 507-523.

[12] Daniel Katz and Ezra Stotalnd, "A Preliminary Statement to a Theory of Attitude Structure and Change," in Sigmund Koch, editor, *Psychology: A Study of a Science,* Vol. 3, New York, McGraw-Hill, 1959, pp. 423-475.

[13] See pages 224-250 of [*Public Opinion Quarterly,* 1960, *24*].

[14] See pages 319-340 [*Ibid.*].

this approach can be found in behavioristic learning theory.

2. *The ego-defensive function* in which the person protects himself from acknowledging the basic truths about himself or the harsh realities in his external world. Freudian psychology and neo-Freudian thinking have been been preoccupied with this type of motivation and its outcomes.

3. *The value-expressive function* in which the individual derives satisfactions from expressing attitudes appropriate to his personal values and to his concept of himself. This function is central to doctrines of ego psychology which stress the importance of self-expression, self-development, and self-realization.

4. *The knowledge function* based upon the individual's need to give adequate structure to his universe. The search for meaning, the need to understand, the trend toward better organization of perceptions and beliefs to provide clarity and consistency for the individual, are other descriptions of this function. The development of principles about perceptual and cognitive structure have been the contribution of Gestalt psychology.

Stated simply, the functional approach is the attempt to understand the reasons people hold the attitudes they do. The reasons, however, are at the level of psychological motivations and not of the accidents of external events and circumstances. Unless we know the psychological need which is met by the holding of an attitude we are in a poor position to predict when and how it will change. Moreover, the same attitude expressed toward a political candidate may not perform the same function for all the people who express it. And while many attitudes are predominantly in the service of a single type of motivational process, as described above, other attitudes may

serve more than one purpose for the individual. A fuller discussion of how attitudes serve the above four functions is in order.

1. The adjustment function. Essentially this function is a recognition of the fact that people strive to maximize the rewards in their external environment and to minimize the penalties. The child develops favorable attitudes toward the objects in his world which are associated with the satisfactions of his needs and unfavorable attitudes toward objects which thwart him or punish him. Attitudes acquired in the service of the adjustment function are either the means for reaching the desired goal or avoiding the undesirable one, or are affective associations based upon experiences in attaining motive satisfactions.[15] The attitudes of the worker favoring a political party which will advance his economic lot are an example of the first type of utilitarian attitude. The pleasant image one has of one's favorite food is an example of the second type of utilitarian attitude.

In general, then, the dynamics of attitude formation with respect to the adjustment function are dependent upon present or past perceptions of the utility of the attitudinal object for the individual. The clarity, consistency, and nearness of rewards and punishments, as they relate to the individual's activities and goals, are important factors in the acquisition of such attitudes. Both attitudes and habits are formed toward specific objects, people, and symbols as they satisfy specific needs. The closer these objects are to actual need satisfaction and the more they are clearly perceived as relevant to need satisfaction, the greater are the probabilities of positive attitude formation. These principles of attitude formation are often observed in the breach rather than the compliance. In industry,

---

15 Katz and Stotland, *op. cit.*, pp. 434–449.

management frequently expects to create favorable attitudes toward job performance through programs for making the company more attractive to the worker, such as providing recreational facilities and fringe benefits. Such programs, however, are much more likely to produce favorable attitudes toward the company as a desirable place to work than toward performance on the job. The company benefits and advantages are applied across the board to all employees and are not specifically relevant to increased effort in task performance by the individual worker.

Consistency of reward and punishment also contributes to the clarity of the instrumental object for goal attainment. If a political party bestows recognition and favors on party workers in an unpredictable and inconsistent fashion, it will destroy the favorable evaluation of the importance of working hard for the party among those whose motivation is of the utilitarian sort. But, curiously, while consistency of reward needs to be observed, 100 per cent consistency is not as effective as a pattern which is usually consistent but in which there are some lapses. When animal or human subjects are invariably rewarded for a correct performance, they do not retain their learned responses as well as when the reward is sometimes skipped.[16]

2. The ego-defensive function. People not only seek to make the most of their external world and what it offers, but they also expend a great deal of their energy on living with themselves. The mechanisms by which the individual protects his ego from his own unacceptable impulses and from the knowledge of threatening forces from without, and the methods by which he reduces his anxieties created by such problems, are known as mechanisms of ego defense.[17] They include the devices by which the individual avoids facing either the inner reality of the kind of person he is, or the outer reality of the dangers the world holds for him. They stem basically from internal conflict with its resulting insecurities. In one sense the mechanisms of defense are adaptive in temporarily removing the sharp edges of conflict in saving the individual from complete disaster. In another sense they are not adaptive in that they handicap the individual in his social adjustments and in obtaining the maximum satisfactions available to him from the world in which he lives. The worker who persistently quarrels with his boss and with his fellow workers, because he is acting out some of his own internal conflicts, may in this manner relieve himself of some of the emotional tensions which beset him. He is not, however, solving his problem of adjusting to his work situation and thus may deprive himself of advancement or even of steady employment.

Defense mechanisms, Miller and Swanson point out, may be classified into two families on the basis of the more or less primitive nature of the devices employed.[18] The first family, more primitive in nature, are more socially handicapping and consist of denial and complete avoidance. The individual in such cases obliterates through withdrawal and denial the realities which confront him. The exaggerated case of such primitive mechanisms is the fantasy world of the paranoiac. The second type of defense is less handicapping and makes for distortion rather than denial. It includes ra-

---

[16] William O. Jenkins and Julian C. Stanley, "Partial Reinforcement: A Review and Critique," *Psychological Bulletin*, Vol. 47, 1950, pp. 193-234.

[17] See pp. 251-279.
[18] Daniel R. Miller and Guy E. Swanson, *Inner Conflict and Defense*, New York, Holt, 1960, pp. 194-288.

tionalization, projection, and displacement.

Many of our attitudes have the function of defending our self-image. When we cannot admit to ourselves that we have deep feelings of inferiority we may project those feelings onto some convenient minority group and bolster our egos by attitudes of superiority toward this underprivileged group. The formation of such defensive attitudes differs in essential ways from the formation of attitudes which serve the adjustment function. They proceed from within the person, and the objects and situation to which they are attached are merely convenient outlets for their expression. Not all targets are equally satisfactory for a given defense mechanism, but the point is that the attitude is not created by the target but by the individual's emotional conflicts. And when no convenient target exists the individual will create one. Utilitarian attitudes, on the other hand, are formed with specific reference to the nature of the attitudinal object. They are thus appropriate to the nature of the social world to which they are geared. The high school student who values high grades because he wants to be admitted to a good college has a utilitarian attitude appropriate to the situation to which it is related.

All people employ defense mechanisms, but they differ with respect to the extent that they use them and some of their attitudes may be more defensive in function than others. It follows that the techniques and conditions for attitude change will not be the same for ego-defensive as for utilitarian attitudes.

Moreover, though people are ordinarily unaware of their defense mechanisms, especially at the time of employing them, they differ with respect to the amount of insight they may show at some later time about their use of defenses. In some cases they recognize that they have been protecting their egos without knowing the reason why. In other cases they may not even be aware of the devices they have been using to delude themselves.

3. The value-expressive function. While many attitudes have the function of preventing the individual from revealing to himself and others his true nature, other attitudes have the function of giving positive expression to his central values and to the type of person he conceives himself to be. A man may consider himself to be an enlightened conservative or an internationalist or a liberal, and will hold attitudes which are the appropriate indication of his central values. Thus we need to take account of the fact that not all behavior has the negative function of reducing the tensions of biological drives or of internal conflicts. Satisfactions also accrue to the person from the expression of attitudes which reflect his cherished beliefs and his self-image. The reward to the person in these instances is not so much a matter of gaining social recognition or monetary rewards as of establishing his self-identity and confirming his notion of the sort of person he sees himself to be. The gratifications obtained from value expression may go beyond the confirmation of self-identity. Just as we find satisfaction in the exercise of our talents and abilities, so we find reward in the expression of any attributes associated with our egos.

Value-expressive attitudes not only give clarity to the self-image but also mold that self-image closer to the heart's desire. The teenager who by dress and speech establishes his identity as similar to his own peer group may appear to the outsider a weakling and a craven conformer. To himself he is asserting his independence of the adult world to which he has rendered childlike subservience and conformity all his life. Very early in the development of the personality the need for clarity of self-image is important—the need to know "who I am." Later it may be even more important to know that in some measure I am the type of person I want to be. Even as adults, however, the clarity and stability of the self-image is of primary significance. Just as the kind, considerate person will cover over his acts of selfishness, so too will the ruthless individualist become confused and embarrassed by his acts of sympathetic compassion. One reason it is difficult to change the character of the adult is that he is not comfortable with the new "me." Group support for such personality change is almost a necessity, as in Alcoholics Anonymous, so that the individual is aware of approval of his new self by people who are like him.

The socialization process during the formative years sets the basic outlines for the individual's self-concept. Parents constantly hold up before the child the model of the good character they want him to be. A good boy eats his spinach, does not hit girls, etc. The candy and the stick are less in evidence in training the child than the constant appeal to his notion of his own character. It is small wonder, then, that children reflect the acceptance of this model by inquiring about the characters of the actors in every drama, whether it be a television play, a political contest, or a war, wanting to know who are the "good guys" and who are the "bad guys." Even as adults we persist in labeling others in the terms of such character images. Joe McCarthy and his cause collapsed in fantastic fashion when the telecast of the Army hearings showed him in the role of the villain attacking the gentle, good man represented by Joseph Welch.

A related but somewhat different process from childhood socialization takes place when individuals enter a new group or organization. The individual will often take over and internalize the values of the group. What accounts, however, for the fact that sometimes this occurs and sometimes it does not? Four factors are probably operative, and some combination of them may be necessary for internalization. (1) The values of the new group may be highly consistent with existing values central to the personality. The girl who enters the nursing profession finds it congenial to consider herself a good nurse because of previous values of the importance of contributing to the welfare of others. (2) The new group may in its ideology have a clear model of what the good group member should be like and may persistently indoctrinate group members in these terms. One of the reasons for the code of conduct for members of the armed forces, devised after the revelations about the conduct of American prisoners in the Korean War, was to attempt to establish a model for what a good soldier does and does not do. (3) The activities of the group in moving toward its goal permit the individual genuine opportunity for participation. To become ego-involved so that he can internalize group values, the new member must find one of two conditions. The group activity open to him must tap his talents and abilities so that his chance to show what he is worth can be tied into the group effort. Or else the activities of the group must give him an active voice in group decisions. His particular talents and abilities may not be tapped but he does have the opportunity to enter into group decisions, and thus his need for self-determination is satisfied. He then identifies with the group in which such opportunities for ego-involvement are available. It is not necessary that opportunities for self-expression and self-determination be of great magnitude in an objective sense, so long as they are important for the psychological economy of the individuals themselves. (4) Finally, the individual may come to see himself as a group member if he can share in the rewards of group activity which includes his own efforts. The worker may not play much of a part in building a ship or make any decisions in the process of building it. Nevertheless, if he and his fellow workers are given a share in every boat they build and a return on the proceeds from the earnings of the ship, they may soon come to identify with the ship-building company and see themselves as builders of ships.

4. *The knowledge function.* Individuals not only acquire beliefs in the interest of satisfying various specific needs, they also seek knowledge to give meaning to what would otherwise be an unorganized chaotic universe. People need standards or frames of reference for understanding their world, and attitudes help to supply such standards. The problem of understanding, as John Dewey made clear years ago, is one "of introducing (1) *definiteness* and *distinctiveness* and (2) *consistency* and *stability* of meaning into what is otherwise vague and wavering."[19] The definiteness and stability are provided in good measure by the norms of our culture, which give the otherwise perplexed individual ready-made attitudes for comprehending his universe. Walter Lippmann's classical contribution to the study of opinions and attitudes was his description of stereotypes and the way they provided order and clarity for a bewildering set of complexities.[20] The most interesting finding in Herzog's familiar study of the gratifications obtained by housewives in listening to daytime serials was the unsuspected

role of information and advice.[21] The stories were liked "because they explained things to the inarticulate listener."

The need to know does not of course imply that people are driven by a thirst for universal knowledge. The American public's appalling lack of political information has been documented many times. In 1956, for example, only 13 per cent of the people in Detroit could correctly name the two United States Senators from the state of Michigan and only 18 per cent knew the name of their own Congressman.[22] People are not avid seekers after knowledge as judged by what the educator or social reformer would desire. But they do want to understand the events which impinge directly on their own life. Moreover, many of the attitudes they have already acquired give them sufficient basis for interpreting much of what they perceive to be important for them. Our already existing stereotypes, in Lippmann's language, "are an ordered, more or less consistent picture of the world, to which our habits, our tastes, our capacities, our comforts and our hopes have adjusted themselves. They may not be a complete picture of the world, but they are a picture of a possible world to which we are adapted."[23] It follows that new information will not modify old attitudes unless there is some inadequacy or incompleteness or inconsistency in the existing attitudinal structure as it relates to the perceptions of new situations.

---

[19] John Dewey, *How We Think,* New York, Macmillan, 1910.
[20] Walter Lippmann, *Public Opinion,* New York, Macmillan, 1922.

[21] Herta Herzog, "What Do We Really Know about Daytime Serial Listeners?" in Paul F. Lazarsfeld and Frank N. Stanton, editors, *Radio Research 1942-1943,* New York, Duell, Sloan & Pearce, 1944, pp. 3-33.
[22] From a study of the impact of party organization on political behavior in the Detroit area, by Daniel Katz and Samuel Eldersveld, in manuscript.
[23] Lippmann, *op. cit.,* p. 95.

THE DEVELOPMENT OF ATTITUDES

Attitudes are learned. Thus, the major determinants of all that the individual learns as he grows will also play a role in the formation of his attitudes. Morgan (p. 529) has indicated that the more important of these determinants are the culture (that is, society), the family, class and various peer groups.

Cultural Influences

The term culture is used to mean the customs, habits, and traditions that characterize a people or a social group (Morgan). This naturally includes the attitudes and beliefs that are prevalent in the society. Anthropologists have shown many areas of difference in attitudes between one society and another (for example, see the works of M. Mead or R. Benedict). Attitudes vary with respect to ways of responding to other people, raising children, private property, the use of authority, respect for the aged, and the proper ways to get social approval. Vast cultural differences have been shown with regard to competitiveness, acquisitiveness, the importance of the family, the relationships with other groups, the seeking of status, and the importance of individual achievement (Klineberg). We often tend to take it for granted that our attitudes toward many things are really "the ways things are supposed to be" and that they are determined by "human nature." Human nature simply allows us to learn any set of attitudes. Our society provides us with the material to be learned.

RESEARCH **SUMMARY** **5-1**	*A Cultural Influence on Attitudes.* One boundary line that frequently sets the framework within which some attitudes develop is the nation in which the person lives. A psychological study done in 1946 by McGranahan illustrates the point (cited in Morgan). Comparing youths (14-18 years of age) in a town in Germany with those from a comparable American town, McGranahan found, for example, that concerning the press, 43 per cent of the German youths, compared to 17 per cent of the Americans, felt newspapers should report only what they thought to be "for the good of the people" and not what the papers wished to. Concerning those who "unjustly criticized the government of a country" 36 per cent of the Germans and 21 per cent of the Americans felt they should be thrown in jail. Although this does not justify our jumping to the conclusion that all members of a national group hold the same attitudes, or that no shifts occur over the years, it does illustrate national influences.

Summaries of public opinion polls conducted in various countries at about the same times often reveal the extent to which major differences in feelings exist from country to country.* Cultural influences show themselves from the

---

* For example, see compilation of polls in *Public Opinion Quarterly*, 1961, 25 (#2) pp. 300-316.

most deep-set ways of behaving and thinking about the world and about people to the most minor matters.

Major Group Membership

Each individual in our complex society is influenced by the many groups of which he is a part. Geographic, religious, educational, and socio-economic class group memberships all provide a person with norms or standards as to what attitudes he "should" learn. Sometimes the different group attitudes to which he is exposed may be in conflict among themselves, for example the national may conflict with those of other groups which influence him, such as regional or economic groups.

Many attitudes growing out of the individual's group memberships are relevant to the work situations and industrial society. For instance, as the individual grows he forms attitudes toward management and labor. These are influenced by his own socio-economic class. Even within a given socio-economic class, rural or urban practices in child rearing, for instance, may be exerting influences on attitudes. Katzell, Barrett, and Parker have shown some indirect aspects of performance related to such a background difference. In one situation which they studied, it was found that a culture pattern closer to the small-town than to the urban was related both to greater employee satisfaction and to higher quantity of production. (Cf. Chapter Six.) Dalton, in another study showed that "rate-busters" in a work group were more likely to have come from rural than urban surroundings. Worthy reports that, within the same organization, morale tends to be higher in smaller, less complex communities, as compared to larger cities.

There is hardly an attitude survey or opinion poll that does not consider the effects of social class on attitudes. R. Centers, in 1945, showed the extent to which social class membership can permeate our thinking on political issues, whereas Converse, writing in 1958, provides evidence that the extent of the specific relationships found may vary over a period of time. Remmers and Radler show that attitudes of American adolescents toward the principles involved in the Bill of Rights may vary with region, income level, and urban or rural background. Even attitudes toward child-raising often vary with class (Bronfrenbrenner).

The Family

The chief direct influence on the development of the individual's attitudes is his family. This primary group is the usual filter through which the cultural, class, religious, and other sources will flow to the individual. Hyman has indicated, for instance, that many studies show a definite degree of similarity between the parents' political beliefs and those of their children. Certainly beyond the realm of politics, we see the individual generally acquiring his parents' religious beliefs, their national and regional outlooks, and so on.

In addition, many of their specific views on the ways to act and think become part of his attitudinal framework. As he grows the individual may think (in our society) that he rebels against the parental views. Although conscious of the areas of difference, he is less likely to be aware of the myriad of attitudes that he has absorbed from them but considers his own (Harsh and Schrickel); he may not recognize the basic similarity of his own and his family's attitudes (Morgan, p. 533).

The family provides many attitudes for the individual to learn and such attitudes are learned quite early in life. One classic research study, by Horowitz, showed the gradual and early development of attitudes toward other groups. Awareness of color differences and the learning of prejudiced attitudes (originally nonexistent in these children) toward Negroes was traced and shown to increase gradually during the formative years between 3 and 7. Exposure to a variety of group influences (particularly the family) led to the early learning of prejudice.

Peer Groups

One part of the learning process in our culture is, as we know, to learn to want approval. Linked to this is learning to rely on other members of a group for support of our own views. (Schein, 1958, emphasized the important role that the absence of group support of opinions played in "brain-washing" for some individuals in Korea.) The reliance on others' opinions shows itself as the individual moves out beyond the family into other groups, his own peer groups. Initially other children, playmates, acquaintances, and friends, later, perhaps students, then co-workers and others with whom he comes into contact, become influences on his attitudes. He may think they are right or he may simply not wish to risk disapproval, but his attitudes will in part be shaped by them. In an extensive study, Kornhauser, Mayer and Sheppard have shown the effect of various cross-currents of group membership and personal characteristics on the voting and the political attitudes of members of a major large labor union. However, not only their group membership outside the union, but also their personalities and feelings about life were related to their attitudes. Thus, for politicians to assume "bloc" voting has both convenience and hazards; although there may be such tendencies, there are also many influences—both group and personal—affecting the voter's choices.

Prior Work Experience

When he starts going out to work, the individual will carry with him the host of attitudes that have been acquired from the culture, (broadly the major group memberships including nationality, class, and religion) his family and peers, and those with whom he has previously worked. In addition, the various mass media have also been influencing him, although to a lesser degree than the personal influences of other people (Katz and Lazarsfeld).

By the time he goes to work in a specific organization (particularly if it is not his first job) he will hold many attitudes concerning such areas for example, as pay, working conditions, company policies, the way he should be supervised, and the ways of supervising others. He will have attitudes about the way work should be done, what constitutes a day's work, the way people should be treated, and the ways to sell a product. Such topics as the appropriate relationships with different units of the company as well as with customers, suppliers, and competitors will bring out views based on attitudes already formed. The approach toward manufacturing procedures, the role of research and development, the functions of executives, the nature of selection, and training procedures are all objects of varying attitudes.

The administrator will have to recognize the differing backgrounds of those with whom he works—that they come originally from different groups. Family, educational, social, geographic, occupational, economic, neighborhood, political, friendship, and other influences have operated. Prior organizational experiences (industrial and sometimes military) have influenced their attitudes. (The administrator cannot assume, however, that merely by knowing some of an individual's group memberships, he also knows his attitudes.) And underneath all are the personality functions of some of their attitudes. As Katz has indicated, the attitudes will come to serve a variety of functions for the individual. Regardless of their functions, they will have been learned.

Contemporary Influences

As important as historical factors may be in attitude formation, new attitudes may be formed in the contemporary situation. Staats and Staats have indicated a way in which they may be learned in the pattern of classical conditioning.

| RESEARCH SUMMARY 5-2 | *Learning an Attitude.* A name of a group or person (for example, Dutch; Jim) was presented to the subjects and was paired for some of them with a positively evaluative word (for example, gift; happy), and for others with a negatively evaluative word (for example, bitter; failure). Without the subjects being aware of it, the evaluative words conditioned an attitude response to the name used. When rating the names later, the favorableness ratings for the same names were different, depending on the direction in which the conditioning was set up, showing that attitudes were influenced (Cf. Kelley, Research Summary 1-1, for the comparable influence on behavior). |

CHAPTER FIFTEEN

The Modification
of Existing Attitudes:
Some Principles
of Attitude Change

We have traced the way in which attitudes develop and the functions that they serve. With attitudes developing along different paths and playing different parts in the person's life it should be apparent that the arousing and changing of attitudes will take different forms. In this chapter, we shall consider some principles underlying any approach to changing attitudes. Our next chapter will deal with specific conditions that can aid attitude change.

In the reading that follows, we return to Katz's article; the framework for the changing of attitudes is his categorization of attitudes into four functional types: the utilitarian or adjustment, the ego-defensive, the value-expressive, and the knowledge function.

READING 5-2

Determinants of Attitude Arousal and Attitude Change*

DANIEL KATZ

The problems of attitude arousal and of attitude change are separate problems. The first has to do with the fact that the individual has many predispositions to act and many influences playing upon him. Hence we need a more precise description of the appropriate conditions which will evoke a given attitude. The second problem is that of specifying the factors which will help to predict the modification of different types of attitude.

The most general statement that can be made concerning attitude arousal is that it is dependent upon the excitation of some need in the individual, or some relevant cue in the environment. When a man grows hungry, he talks of food. Even when not hungry he may express favorable attitudes toward a preferred food if an external stimulus cues him. The ego-defensive person who hates foreigners will express such attitudes under conditions of increased anxiety or threat or when a foreigner is perceived to be getting out of place.

The most general statement that can be made about the conditions conducive to attitude change is that the expression of the old attitude or its anticipated expression no longer gives satisfaction to its related need state. In other words, it no longer serves its function and the individual feels blocked or frustrated. Modifying an old attitude or replacing it with a new one is a process of learning, and

learning always starts with a problem, or being thwarted in coping with a situation. Being blocked is a necessary, but not a sufficient, condition for attitude change. Other factors must be operative and will vary in effectiveness depending upon the function involved.

Arousing and Changing Utilitarian Attitudes

Political† parties have both the problem of converting people with antagonistic attitudes (attitude change) and the problem of mobilizing the support of their own followers (attitude arousal). To accomplish the latter they attempt to revive the needs basic to old attitudes. For example, the Democrats still utilize the appeals of the New Deal and the Republicans still talk of the balanced budget. The assumption is that many people still hold attitudes acquired in earlier circumstances and that appropriate communication can reinstate the old needs. For most people, however, utilitarian needs are reinforced by experience and not by verbal appeals. Hence invoking the symbols of the New Deal will be relatively ineffective with respect to adjustive attitudes unless there are corresponding experiences with unemployment, decreased income, etc. Though the need state may not be under the control

---

* Abridged from *Public Opinion Quarterly*, 1960, *24*, 176-192.

† [Many of Katz examples are of political or social problems; the principles he illustrates are relevant wherever one must deal with attitudes, as is the case in the organization.]

of the propagandist, he can exaggerate or minimize its importance. In addition to playing upon states of need, the propagandist can make perceptible the old cues associated with the attitude he is trying to elicit. These cues may have associated with them favorable affect, or feeling, though the related needs are inactive. For example, the fighters for old causes can be paraded across the political platform in an attempt to arouse the attitudes of the past.

The two basic conditions, then, for the arousal of existing attitudes are the activation of their relevant need states and the perception of the appropriate cues associated with the content of the attitude.

To change attitudes which serve a utilitarian function, one of two conditions must prevail: (1) the attitude and the activities related to it no longer provide the satisfactions they once did, or (2) the individual's level of aspiration has been raised. The Chevrolet owner who had positive attitudes toward his old car may now want a more expensive car commensurate with his new status.

Attitudes toward political parties and voting behavior are often difficult to change if there is no widespread dissatisfaction with economic conditions and international relations. Currently, however, the polls show that even Republicans in the age group over sixty are worried about increased costs of medical care and the general inadequacy of retirement incomes. Thus many old people may change their political allegiance, if it becomes clear that the Democratic Party can furnish a program to take care of their needs.

Again the mass media play a role secondary to direct experience in changing attitudes directly related to economic matters. Once dissatisfaction exists, they can exert a potent influence in suggesting new ways of solving the problem. In the field of international affairs, mass media have a more primary role because in times of peace most people have no direct experience with other countries or their peoples. The threat of war comes from what they read, or see in the mass media.

The area of freedom for changing utilitarian attitudes is of course much greater in dealing with methods of satisfying needs than with needs themselves. Needs change more slowly than the means for gratifying them, even though one role of the advertiser is to create new needs. Change in attitudes occurs more readily when people perceive that they can accomplish their objectives through revising existing attitudes. Integration of white and Negro personnel in the armed forces came to pass partly because political leaders and military leaders perceived that such a move would strengthen our fighting forces. And one of the powerful arguments for changing our attitudes toward Negroes is that in the struggle for world democracy we need to put our own house in order to present a more convincing picture of our own society to other countries. Carlson has experimentally demonstrated that discriminatory attitudes toward minority groups can be altered by showing the relevance of more positive beliefs to such individual goals and values as American international prestige and democratic equalitarianism.[24]

Just as attitudes formed in the interests of adjustment can be negative evaluations of objects associated with avoidance of the harmful effects of the environment, so too can attitudes change because of unpleasant experiences or anticipation of harmful consequences. The more remote the cause of one's suffering the more likely he is to seize upon a readily iden-

---

[24] Earl R. Carlson, "Attitude Change through Modification of Attitude Structure," *Journal of Abnormal and Social Psychology*, Vol. 52, 1956, pp. 256-261.

tifiable target for his negative evaluation. Public officials, as highly visible objects, can easily be associated with states of dissatisfaction. Thus there is truth in the old observation that people vote more against the candidates they dislike than for the candidates they like. In the 1958 elections, in a period of mild recession, unemployment, and general uneasiness about atomic weapons, the incumbent governors (the more visible targets), whether Republican or Democratic, fared less well than the incumbent legislators.

The use of negative sanctions and of punishment to change utilitarian attitudes is more complex than the use of rewards. To be successful in changing attitudes and behavior, punishment should be used only when there is clearly available a course of action that will save the individual from the undesirable consequences. To arouse fear among the enemy in time of war does not necessarily result in desertion, surrender, or a disruption of the enemy war effort. Such channels of action may not be available to the people whose fears are aroused. The experiment of Janis and Feshback in using fear appeals to coerce children into good habits of dental hygiene had the interesting outcome of a negative relationship between the amount of fear and the degree of change. Lurid pictures of the gangrene jaws of old people who had not observed good dental habits were not effective.[25] Moreover, the group exposed to the strongest fear appeal was the most susceptible to counterpropaganda. One factor which helps to account for the results of this investigation was the lack of a clear-cut relation in the minds of the children between failure to brush their teeth in the prescribed manner and the pictures of the gangrene jaws of the aged.

The necessity of coupling fear appeals with clear channels of action is illustrated by a study of Nunnally and Bobren.[26] These investigators manipulated three variables in communications about mental health, namely, the relative amount of message anxiety, the degree to which messages gave apparent solutions, and the relative personal or impersonal phrasing of the message. The high-anxiety message described electric shock treatment of the psychotic in distressing detail. People showed the least willingness to receive communications that were high in anxiety, personalized, and offered no solutions. When solutions were offered in the communication, there was more willingness to accept the high-anxiety message.

The use of punishment and arousal of fear depend for their effectiveness upon the presence of well-defined paths for avoiding the punishment, i.e., negative sanctions are successful in redirecting rather than suppressing behavior. When there is no clearly perceptible relation between the punishment and the desired behavior, people may continue to behave as they did before, only now they have negative attitudes toward the persons and objects associated with the negative sanctions. There is, however, another possibility, if the punishment is severe or if the individual is unusually sensitive. He may develop a defensive avoidance of the whole situation. His behavior, then, is not directed at solving the problem but at escaping from the situation, even if such escape has to be negotiated by absorbing extra punishment. The attitudes under discussion are those based upon the adjustive or utilitarian function, but if the individual is traumatized by

[25] Irving L. Janis and Seymour Feshback, "Effect of Fear-arousing Communications," *Journal of Abnormal and Social Psychology,* Vol. 48, 1953, pp. 78-92.

[26] Jum C. Nunnally and Howard M. Bobren, "Variables Governing the Willingness to Receive Communications in Mental Health," *Journal of Personality,* Vol. 27, 1959, pp. 38-46.

a fearful experience he will shift from instrumental learning to defensive reactions.

Arousal and Change of Ego-defensive Attitudes

Attitudes which help to protect the individual from internally induced anxieties or from facing up to external dangers are readily elicited by any form of threat to the ego. The threat may be external, as in the case of a highly competitive situation, or a failure experience, or a derogatory remark. It is the stock in trade of demagogues to exaggerate the dangers confronting the people for instance, Joe McCarthy's tactics with respect to Communists in the State Department. Many people have existing attitudes of withdrawal or of aggression toward deviants or out-groups based upon their ego-defensive needs. When threatened, these attitudes come into play, and defensive people either avoid the unpleasant situation entirely, as is common in the desegregation controversy, or exhibit hostility.

Another condition for eliciting the ego-defensive attitude is the encouragement given to its expression by some form of social support. The agitator may appeal to repressed hatred by providing moral justification for its expression. A mob leader before an audience with emotionally held attitudes toward Negroes may call out these attitudes in the most violent form by invoking the good of the community or the honor of white womanhood.

A third condition for the arousal of ego-defensive attitudes is the appeal to authority. The insecurity of the defensive person makes him particularly susceptible to authoritarian suggestion. When this type of authoritarian command is in the direction already indicated by his attitudes of antipathy toward other people, he responds quickly and joyously. It is

no accident that movements of hate and aggression such as the Ku Klux Klan or the Nazi Party are authoritarian in their organized structure. Wagman, in an experimental investigation of the uses of authoritarian suggestion, found that students high in ego-defensiveness as measured by the F-scale were much more responsive to directives from military leaders than were less defensive students.[27] In fact, the subjects low in defensiveness were not affected at all by authoritarian suggestion when this influence ran counter to their own attitudes. The subjects high in F-scores could be moved in either direction, although they moved readily in the direction of their own beliefs.

A fourth condition for defensive arousal is the building up over time of inhibited drives in the individual, for example, repressed sex impulses. As the drive strength of forbidden impulses increases, anxiety mounts and release from tension is found in the expression of defensive attitudes. The deprivations of prison life, for example, build up tensions which can find expression in riots against the hated prison officials.

In other words, the drive strength for defensive reactions can be increased by situation frustration. Though the basic source is the long-standing internal conflict of the person, he can encounter additional frustration in immediate circumstances. Berkowitz has shown that anti-Semitic girls were more likely than less prejudiced girls to display aggression toward an innocent bystander when angered by a third person.[28] In a subse-

---

[27] Morton Wagman, "Attitude Change and the Authoritarian Personality," *Journal of Psychology*, Vol. 40, 1955, pp. 3-24. The F-scale is a measure of authoritarianism comprising items indicative of both defensiveness and ideology.

[28] Leonard Berkowitz, "Anti-Semitism and the Displacement of Aggression," *Journal of*

quent experiment, Berkowitz and Holmes created dislike by one group of subjects for their partners by giving them electric shocks which they thought were administered by their partners.[29] In a second session, subjects worked alone and were threatened by the experimenter. In a third session they were brought together with their partners for a cooperative task of problem solving. Aggression and hostility were displayed by subjects toward one another in the third session as a result of the frustration produced by the experimenter, and were directed more against the disliked partner than toward an innocuous partner.

Studies outside the laboratory have confirmed the principle that, where negative attitudes exist, frustration in areas unrelated to the attitude will increase the strength of the prejudice. Bettelheim and Janowitz found that war veterans who had suffered downward mobility were more anti-Semitic than other war veterans.[30] In a secondary analysis of the data from the Elmira study, Greenblum and Pearlin report that the socially mobile people, whether upward or downward mobile, were more prejudiced against Jews and Negroes than were stationary people, provided that the socially mobile were insecure about their new status.[31] Though it is clear in these studies that the situation frustration strengthens a negative attitude, it is not clear as to the origin of the negative attitude.

Abnormal and Social Psychology, Vol. 59, 1959, pp. 182-188.
[29] Leonard Berkowitz and Douglas S. Holmes, "The Generalization of Hostility to Disliked Objects," *Journal of Personality*, Vol. 27, 1959, pp. 565-577.
[30] Bruno Bettelheim and Morris Janowitz, *Dynamics of Prejudice*, New York, Harper, 1950.
[31] Joseph Greenblum and Leonard I. Pearlin, "Vertical Mobility and Prejudice," in Reinhard Bendix and Seymour M. Lipset, editors, *Class, Status and Power*, Glencoe, Ill., Free Press, 1953.

Most research on ego-defensive attitudes has been directed at beliefs concerning the undesirable character of minority groups or of deviants, with accompanying feelings of distrust, contempt, and hatred. Many ego-defensive attitudes, however, are not the projection of repressed aggression but are expressions of apathy or withdrawal. The individual protects himself from a difficult or demanding world and salvages his self-respect by retreating within his own shell. His attitudes toward political matters are anomic: "It does not make any difference to people like me which party is in power" or "There is no point in voting because I can't influence the outcome." Threat to people of this type takes the form of a complexity with which they cannot cope. Thus, they daydream when the lecturer talks about economic theories of inflation or the public official talks about disarmament proposals.

The usual procedures for changing attitudes and behavior have little positive effect upon attitudes geared into our ego defenses. In fact they may have a boomerang effect of making the individual cling more tenaciously to his emotionally held beliefs. In the category of usual procedures should be included increasing the flow of information, promising and bestowing rewards, and invoking penalties. As has already been indicated, punishment is threatening to the ego-defensive person and the increase of threat is the very condition which will feed ego-defensive behavior. The eneuretic youngster with emotional problems is rarely cured by punishment. Teachers and coaches know that there are some children who respond to censure and punishment by persevering in the forbidden behavior. But what is not as well recognized is that reward is also not effective in modifying the actions of the ego-defensive person. His attitudes are an expression of his inner conflicts and are not susceptible to external rewards. The shop-keeper who will not serve Negroes because they are a well-fixated target for his aggressions will risk the loss of income incurred by his discriminatory reaction.

Three basic factors, however, can help change ego-defensive attitudes. In the first place, the removal of threat is a necessary though not a sufficient condition. The permissive and even supportive atmosphere which the therapist attempts to create for his patients is a special instance of the removal of threat. Where the ego-defensive behavior of the delinquent is supported by his group, the social worker must gain a measure of group acceptance so as not to be perceived as a threat by the individual gang members. An objective, matter-of-fact approach can serve to remove threat, especially in situations where people are accustomed to emotional appeals. Humor can also be used to establish a non-threatening atmosphere, but it should not be directed against the audience or even against the problem. Cooper and Jahoda attempted to change prejudiced attitudes by ridicule, in the form of cartoons which made Mr. Biggott seem silly, especially when he rejected a blood transfusion which did not come from 100 per cent Americans.[32] Instead of changing their attitudes, the subjects in this experiment found ways of evading the meaning of the cartoons.

In the second place, catharsis or the ventilation of feelings can help to set the stage for attitude change. Mention has already been made of the building up of tension owing to the lack of discharge of inhibited impulses. When emotional tension is at a high level the individual will respond defensively and resist attempts

to change him. Hence, providing him with opportunities to blow off steam may often be necessary before attempting a serious discussion of new possibilities of behavior. Again, humor can serve this purpose.

There are many practical problems in the use of catharsis, however, because of its complex relationship to other variables. In his review of the experimental work on the expression of hostility Berkowitz reports more findings supporting than contradicting the catharsis hypothesis, but there is no clear agreement about the mechanisms involved.[33] Under certain circumstances permitting emotional outbursts can act as a reward. In a gripe session to allow individuals to express their complaints, group members can reinforce one another's negative attitudes. Unless there are positive forces in the situation which lead to a serious consideration of the problem, the gripe session may have boomerang effects. The technique often employed is to keep the group in session long enough for the malcontents to get talked out so that more sober voices can be heard. Catharsis may function at two levels. It can operate to release or drain off energy of the moment, as in the above description. It can also serve to bring to the surface something of the nature of the conflict affecting the individual. So long as his impulses are repressed and carefully disguised, the individual has little chance of gaining even rudimentary insight into himself.

In the third place, ego-defensive behavior can be altered as the individual acquires insight into his own mechanisms of defense. Information about the nature of the problem in the external world will not affect him. Information about his own functioning may have an in-

---

[32] Eunice Cooper and Marie Jahoda, "The Evasion of Propaganda: How Prejudiced People Respond to Anti-prejudice Propaganda," *Journal of Psychology*, Vol. 23, 1947, pp. 15-25.

[33] Leonard Berkowitz, "The Expression and Reduction of Hostility," *Psychological Bulletin*, Vol. 55, 1958, pp. 257-283.

fluence, if presented without threat, and if the defenses do not go too deep into the personality. In other words, only prolonged therapy can help the psychologically sick person. Many normal people, however, employ ego defenses about which they have some degree of awareness, though generally not at the time of the expression of such defenses. The frustrations of a tough day at work may result in an authoritarian father displacing his aggression that night on his family in yelling at his wife, or striking his youngsters. Afterward he may recognize the cause of his behavior. Not all defensive behavior, then, is so deep rooted in the personality as to be inaccessible to awareness and insight. Therefore, procedures for arousing self-insight can be utilized to change behavior, even in mass communications.

One technique is to show people the psychodynamics of attitudes, especially as they appear in the behavior of others. Allport's widely used pamphlet on the A B C's of Scapegoating is based upon the technique.[34] Katz, Sarnoff, and McClintock have conducted experimental investigations of the effects of insightful materials upon the reduction of prejudice.[35] In their procedure the psychodynamics of prejudice was presented in the case history of a subject sufficiently similar to the subjects as to appear as a sympathetic character. Two findings appeared in these investigations: (1) Subjects who were very high in defensiveness were not affected by the insight materials, but subjects of low or moderate defensiveness were significantly affected.

(2) The changes in attitude procedure by the arousal of self-insight persisted for a longer period of time than changes induced by information or conformity pressures. In a further experiment Stotland, Katz, and Patchen found that involving subjects in the task of understanding the dynamics of prejudice helped arouse self-insight and reduce prejudice.[36] McClintock compared an ethnocentric appeal, an information message, and self-insight materials, with similar results.[37] There was differential acceptance of these influences according to the personality pattern of the subject. McClintock also found a difference in F-scale items in predicting attitude change, with the projectivity items showing a different pattern from the conformity items.

. . .

Conditions for Arousing and Changing Value-Expressive Attitudes

Two conditions for the arousal of value-expressive attitudes can be specified. The first is the occurrence of the cue in the stimulus situation which has been associated with the attitude. The liberal Democrat, as a liberal Democrat, has always believed in principle that an income tax is more just than a sales tax. Now the issue has arisen in his state, and the group in which he happens to be at the moment are discussing an increase in sales tax. This will be sufficient to cue off his opposition to the proposal without consideration of the specific local aspects of the tax problem. The second condition for the arousal of this type of attitude is some degree of thwarting of the individual's expressive behavior in the immediate past. The housewife oc-

---

[34] Gordon W. Allport, *The Nature of Prejudice*, Cambridge, Mass., Addison-Wesley, 1954.
[35] Daniel Katz, Irving Sarnoff, and Charles McClintock, "Ego Defense and Attitude Change," *Human Relations*, Vol. 9, 1956, pp. 27-46. Also their "The Measurement of Ego Defense as Related to Attitude Change," *Journal of Personality*, Vol. 25, 1957, pp. 465-474.

[36] Ezra Stotland, Daniel Katz, and Martin Patchen, "The Reduction of Prejudice through the Arousal of Self-insight," *Journal of Personality*, Vol. 27, 1959, pp. 507-531.
[37] Charles McClintock, "Personality Syndromes and Attitude Change," *Journal of Personality*, Vol. 26, 1958, pp. 479-593.

cupied with the routine care of the home and the children during the day may seek opportunities to express her views to other women at the first social gathering she attends.

. . .

Again, two conditions are relevant in changing value-expressive attitudes:

1. Some degree of dissatisfaction with one's self-concept or its associated values is the opening wedge for fundamental change. The complacent person, smugly satisfied with all aspects of himself, is immune to attempts to change his values. Dissatisfaction with the self can result from failures or from the inadequacy of one's values in preserving a favorable image of oneself in a changing world. The man with pacifist values may have become dissatisfied with himself during a period of fascist expansion and terror. Once there is a crack in the individual's central belief systems, it can be exploited by appropriately directed influences. The techniques of brain washing employed by the Chinese Communists both on prisoners of war in Korea and in the thought reform of Chinese intellectuals were essentially procedures for changing value systems.

In the brain washing of Chinese intellectuals in the revolutionary college, the Communists took advantage of the confused identity of the student.[48] He had been both a faithful son and a rebellious reformer and perhaps even an uninvolved cynic. To make him an enthusiastic Communist the officials attempted to destroy his allegiance to his parents and to transfer his loyalty to Communist doctrines which could meet his values as a rebel. Group influences were mobilized to help bring about the change by intensifying guilt feelings and providing for atonement and redemption through the emotional catharsis of personal confession.

To convert American prisoners of war, the Communists made a careful study of the vulnerability of their victims. They found additional weaknesses through a system of informers and created new insecurities by giving the men no social support for their old values.[49] They manipulated group influences to support Communist values and exploited their ability to control behavior and all punishments and rewards in the situation. The direction of all their efforts, however, was to undermine old values and to supply new ones. The degree of their success has probably been exaggerated in the public prints, but from their point of view they did achieve some genuine gains. One estimate is that some 15 per cent of the returning prisoners of war were active collaborators, another 5 per cent resisters, and some 80 per cent "neutrals." Segal, in a study of a sample of 579 of these men, found that 12 per cent had to some degree accepted Communist ideology.[50]

2. Dissatisfaction with old attitudes as inappropriate to one's values can also lead to change. In fact, people are much less likely to find their values uncongenial than they are to find some of their attitudes inappropriate to their values. The discomfort with one's old attitudes may stem from new experiences or from the suggestions of other people. Senator Vandenburg, as an enlightened conservative changed his attitudes on foreign relations from an isolationist to an internationalist

---

[48] Robert J. Lifton, "Thought Reform of Chinese Intellectuals: A Psychiatric Evaluation," *Journal of Social Issues*, Vol. 13, No. 3, 1957, pp. 5-20.

[49] Edgar H. Schein, "Reaction Patterns to Severe, Chronic Stress in American Army Prisoners of War of the Chinese," *Journal of Social Issues*, Vol. 13, No. 3, 1957, pp. 21-30.
[50] Julius Segal, "Correlates of Collaboration and Resistance Behavior among U.S. Army POW's in Korea," *Journal of Social Issues*, Vol. 13, No. 3, 1957, pp. 31-40.

position when critical events in our history suggested change. The influences exerted upon people are often in the direction of showing the inappropriateness of their present ways of expressing their values. Union leaders attempt to show that good union men should not vote on the old personal basis of rewarding friends and punishing enemies but should instead demand party responsibility for a program. In an experiment by Stotland, Katz, and Patchen there was suggestive evidence of the readiness of subjects to change attitudes which they found inappropriate to their values.[51] Though an attempt was made to change the prejudices of the ego-defensive subjects, individuals who were not basically ego-defensive also changed. These subjects, who already approved of tolerance, apparently became aware of the inappropriateness of some of their negative evaluations of minority groups. This second factor in attitude change thus refers to the comparatively greater appropriateness of one set of means than another for confirming the individual's self-concept and realizing his central values.

We have already called attention to the role of values in the formation of attitudes in the early years of life. It is also true that attitude formation is a constant process and that influences are continually being brought to bear throughout life which suggest new attitudes as important in implementing existing values. An often-used method is to make salient some central value such as the thinking man, the man of distinction, or the virile man, and then depict a relatively new form of behavior consistent with this image. The role of motivational research in advertising is to discover the rudimentary image associated with a given

product, to use this as a basis for building up the image in more glorified terms, and then to cement the association of this image with the product.

Arousing and Changing Attitudes Which Serve the Knowledge Function

. . .

The factors which are productive of change of attitudes of this character are inadequacies of the existing attitudes to deal with new and changing situations. The person who has been taught that Orientals are treacherous may read extended accounts of the honesty of the Chinese or may have favorable interactions with Japanese. He finds his old attitudes in conflict with new information and new experience, and proceeds to modify his beliefs. In this instance we are dealing with fictitious stereotypes which never corresponded to reality. In other cases the beliefs may have been adequate to the situation but the world has changed. Thus, some British military men formerly in favor of armaments have changed their attitude toward disarmament because of the character of nuclear weapons. The theory of cognitive consistency . . . can draw its best examples from attitudes related to the knowledge function.

Any situation, then, which is ambiguous for the individual is likely to produce attitude change. His need for cognitive structure is such that he will either modify his beliefs to impose structure or accept some new formula presented by others. He seeks a meaningful picture of his universe, and when there is ambiguity he will reach for a ready solution. Rumors abound when information is unavailable. [In Table 5-1, Katz provides a summary of the principal points made in his preceding discussion.]

---

[51] Stotland, Katz, and Patchen, *op. cit.*

TABLE 5-1

Determinants of Attitude Formation, Arousal, and Change
in Relation to Type of Function

Function	Origin and Dynamics	Arousal Conditions	Change Conditions
Adjustment	Utility of attitudinal object in need satisfaction. Maximizing external rewards and minimizing punishments	1. Activation of needs 2. Salience of cues associated with need satisfaction	1. Need deprivation 2. Creation of new needs and new levels of aspiration 3. Shifting rewards and punishments 4. Emphasis on new and better paths for need satisfaction
Ego defense	Protecting against internal conflicts and external dangers	1. Posing of threats 2. Appeals to hatred and repressed impulses 3. Rise in frustrations 4. Use of authoritarian suggestion	1. Removal of threats 2. Catharsis 3. Development of self-insight
Value expression	Maintaining self identity; enhancing favorable self-image; self-expression and self-determination	1. Salience of cues associated with values 2. Appeals to individual to reassert self-image 3. Ambiguities which threaten self-concept	1. Some degree of dissatisfaction with self 2. Greater appropriateness of new attitude for the self 3. Control of all environmental supports to undermine old values.
Knowledge	Need for understanding, for meaningful cognitive organization, for consistency and clarity	1. Reinstatement of cues associated with old problem or of old problem itself	1. Ambiguity created by new information or change in environment 2. More meaningful information about problems

Some of the time, the type of attitude with which an administrator is dealing may be apparent to him. But often, he is faced with *not* knowing which sort of attitude is present. If he will observe the kinds of situation in which a person modifies his attitudes, and those in which he offers resistance, the administrator will develop clues as to the function of the attitude involved. Accordingly, he can gauge which principles of change might be more effectively used in present or future situations. By tentatively classifying the attitudes that are present, the administrator can select an approach more likely to work, try the approach, and check his predictions. This "classifying" can be a quick process, but even if it takes a bit of thought and time it still can lead to more productive results than the blithe assumption that an attitude should change because you have tried (one way) to change it.

Let us look back at Katz's statements and classifications and see what comments of relevance to administrators may be drawn from them. The basic premise for change must be emphasized: *For attitude change to occur, the need to change must be aroused.* With this as the underlying premise, a few comments can be made for each sort of attitude.

Adjustive or Utilitarian Attitudes

For changing adjustive or utilitarian attitudes the administrator must lead the subordinate into being dissatisfied with his (the latter's) own current attitude. One difficulty is to recognize that because *you* are dissatisfied with an individual's attitude is not a reason for *him* to want to change. His attitudes may be displeasing *to you* but satisfying to him. Suppose that the administrator is seeking to change attitudes that favor keeping an organization small. It might be shown that the individual's desires to have greater influence, prestige, or income are contingent upon an increase in the size of the organization. If, alternative attitudes can be seen by the person as getting him toward an objective that *he* accepts, then attitudes may begin to shift. Threat or punishment can force the person into avoiding the situation, or becoming ego-involved in not shifting.

Ego-Defensive Attitudes

Hostility or apathy may greet attempts at changing other's attitudes. When another person's attitudes seem to be serving the function of defending his ego, the problems of inducing change are more difficult than when dealing with other categories of attitude. Pouring in new information, or threatening may only stiffen resistance as Katz indicates. In a world of organizational and technological change, attitude changes can lag behind changes in events. When these external changes are seen as threatening—by the other person—then we are likely to find resistance. A change in work procedure or work hours, the installation of new equipment, or the encouragement of different sales techniques may all be seen by a subordinate as threatening. Of course, it is not only the subordinate who may feel this. A superior may be just as threatened by a procedural change. He may have grown up under the old system, or helped to institute it. It may be threatening to him merely to realize that systems and times change with the implied suggestion that people can be changed, or even let go. Not changing attitudes may merge with maintaining one's sense of identity.

For ego-defensive attitudes, the administrator must recognize the time-honored concept of "face-saving." Unless the individual can feel less threat in changing than in clinging to his old attitude, why should he change? It is of particular importance that he *not* feel that an attempt to change his attitude is an attack against him personally.

The idea, mentioned by Katz, of emotional "catharsis" or "letting off steam" provides the foundation for many sorts of helpful administrative approaches: a "permissive" group meeting; letting people air their objections to ideas; encouraging the person to see that *he* is not threatened as his views shift, allowing time for change, during which period frank discussion is encouraged.

One may well recognize, with Katz, that the psychologically sick individual, may have rigid attitudes and that only prolonged therapy may help him. Nevertheless, an administrator must be careful not to assume that a person is sick (or at best stubborn) because he won't change his views immediately.

Value-Expressive Attitudes

It may often be more important for the administrator to seek to arouse than to change value-expressive attitudes. For instance, in a current situation the norms on length of breaks or amount of work to be done may differ from some of the older attitudes that an individual may have once held, in which doing the best job possible expressed his values. A rearousal of older values might be of help in changing present attitudes.

Knowledge Serving Attitudes

For these, Katz has pointed out that in the ambiguous or unclear situation, the need to know may help to shift attitudes. It is here that providing information may be of value (under conditions to be described later). If the administrator can arouse a need to acquire more information attitudes may shift.* For instance, a salesman may have the attitude that certain geographic areas are not worth visiting because as a low income territory, he cannot make any sales there. If, through the prospects of increased sales, he can be brought to find (or provided with) information on the ways in which income is spent in that area, or the comparably priced items being bought, he may develop the attitude that a worthwhile market does exist.

---

* Consideration of the process of reducing inconsistencies is provided in Chapter Seventeen.

CHAPTER SIXTEEN

Conditions Facilitating Attitude Change

The principles of attitude change presented in our second selection from Katz can serve as a basis for understanding many specific conditions, approaches, or techniques useful to the administrator. A basic theme running through many of the principles suggests the following sequence: the individual becomes dissatisfied with his own attitudes (or is helped to do so) and sees that a shift is relevant to his self-image, his goals, or the satisfaction of his needs. The approach then encourages shifts of attitude to make them consistent with other values or goals, and avoids the arousal of ego-defense of the attitudes.

Whatever the function of the attitudes, attitude change follows the same laws as other learning. But because attitudes are often covert, the process is more complex. Each of the conditions discussed below can be considered as a situation allowing for reinforcement to operate. The individual learns new attitudes or shifts present ones as various reinforcements operate and relate to need satisfaction.

Anything that the administrator does to reward those needs leading to change, or to offer the anticipation of avoidance of punishments (consistent with the person's ego-needs and ego-defenses) should serve as a condition conducive to attitude change. We will consider first some of the most important of these conditions and then (Chapter Seventeen) some of the special problems that exist.

Role Changes

One means of changing another's attitudes is to give him a specific role, one that leads to adopting the attitudes sought. The role of an individual is often emphasized as basic to his behavior and his attitudes. (See Reading 1-5.) Lieberman, in a factory situation, has effectively shown the modification of attitudes that occur when some people get the new role of foremen and others become shop stewards. His article serves as our next reading.

READING 5-3

The Effects of Changes in Roles on the Attitudes of Role Occupants[1]

SEYMOUR LIEBERMAN

Problem

One of the fundamental postulates of role theory, as expounded by Newcomb (2), Parsons (3), and other role theorists, is that a person's attitudes will be influenced by the role that he occupies in a social system. Although this proposition appears to be a plausible one, surprisingly little evidence is available that bears directly on it. One source of evidence is found in common folk-lore. "Johnny is a changed boy since he was made a monitor in school." "She is a different woman since she got married." "You would never recognize him since he became foreman." As much as these expressions smack of the truth, they offer little in the way of systematic or scientific support for the proposition that a person's attitudes are influenced by his role.

Somewhat more scientific, but still not definitive, is the common finding, in many social-psychological studies, that relationships exist between attitudes and roles. In other words, different attitudes are held by people who occupy different roles. For example, Stouffer *et al.* (5) found that commissioned officers are more favorable toward the Army than are enlisted men. The problem here is that the mere existence of a relationship between attitudes and roles does not reveal the cause and effect nature of the relationship found. One interpretation of Stouffer's finding might be that being made a commissioned officer tends to result in a person's becoming pro-Army—i.e. the role a person occupies influences his attitudes. But an equally plausible interpretation might be that being pro-Army tends to result in a person's being made a commissioned officer—i.e. a person's attitudes influence the likelihood of his being selected for a given role. In the absence of longitudinal data, the relationship offers no clear evidence that roles were the "cause" and attitudes the "effect."

---

[1] Abridged from *Human Relations*, 1956, 9, 385-402. Our excerpt does not include the standard statistical analyses used by Lieberman or the discussion he provides of the relation between his findings and role theory. Readers are referred to the original article for these aspects of the study.

The present study was designed to examine the effects of roles on attitudes in a particular field situation. The study is based on longitudinal data obtained in a role-differentiated, hierarchical organization. By taking advantage of natural role changes among personnel in the organization, it was possible to examine people's attitudes both before and after they underwent changes in roles. Therefore, the extent to which changes in roles were followed by changes in attitudes could be determined, and the cause and effect nature of any relationships found would be clear.

Method: Phase I

The study was part of a larger project carried out in a medium-sized Midwestern company engaged in the production of home appliance equipment. Let us call the company the Rockwell Corporation. At the time that the study was done, Rockwell employed about 4,000 people. This total included about 2,500 factory workers and about 150 first-level foremen. The company was unionized and most of the factory workers belonged to the union local, which was an affiliate of the U.A.W., C.I.O. About 150 factory workers served as stewards in the union, or roughly one steward for every foreman.

The study consisted of a "natural field experiment." The experimental variable was a change in roles, and the experimental period was the period of exposure to the experimental variable. The experimental groups were those employees who underwent changes in roles during this period; the control groups were those employees who did not change roles during this period. The design may be described in terms of a three-step process: "before measurement," "experimental period," and "after measurement."

Before Measurement. In September and October 1951, attitude questionnaires were filled out by virtually all factory personnel at Rockwell—2,354 workers, 145 stewards, and 151 foremen. The questions dealt for the most part with employees' attitudes and perceptions about the company, the union, and various aspects of the job situation. The respondents were told that the questionnaire was part of an overall survey to determine how employees felt about working conditions at Rockwell.

Experimental Period. Between October 1951 and July 1952, twenty-three workers were made foremen and thirty-five workers became stewards. Most of the workers who became stewards during that period were elected during the annual steward elections held in May 1952. They replaced stewards who did not choose to run again or who were not re-elected by their constituents. In addition, a few workers replaced stewards who left the steward role for one reason or another throughout the year.

The workers who became foremen were not made foremen at any particular time. Promotions occurred as openings arose in supervisory positions. Some workers replaced foremen who retired or who left the company for other reasons; some replaced foremen who were shifted to other supervisory positions; and some filled newly created supervisory positions.

After Measurement. In December 1952, the same forms that had been filled out by the rank-and-file workers in 1951 were readministered to:

1. The workers who became foremen during the experimental period (N-23).
2. A control group of workers who did not become foremen during the experimental period (N-46).
3. The workers who became stewards during the experimental period (N-35).
4. A control group of workers who did not become stewards during the experimental period (N-35).

Each control group was matched with

its parallel experimental group on a number of demographic, attitudinal, and motivational variables. Therefore, any changes in attitudes that occurred in the experimental groups but did not occur in the control groups could not be attributed to initial differences between them.

The employees in these groups were told that the purpose of the follow-up questionnaire was to get up-to-date measures of their attitudes in 1952 and to compare how employees felt that year with the way that they felt the previous year. The groups were told that, instead of studying the entire universe of employees as was the case in 1951, only a sample was being studied this time. They were informed that the sample was chosen in such a way as to represent all kinds of employees at Rockwell—men and women, young and old, etc. The groups gave no indication that they understood the real bases on which they were chosen for the "after" measurement or that the effects of changes in roles were the critical factors being examined.[2]

· · ·

Results: Phase I

The major hypothesis tested in this study was that people who are placed in a role will tend to take on or develop attitudes that are congruent with the expectations associated with that role. Since the foreman role entails being a representative of management, it might be expected that workers who are chosen as foremen will tend to become more favorable toward management. Similarly, since the steward role entails being a representative of the union, it might be expected that workers who are elected as

---

[2] Some of the top officials of management and all of the top officers of the union at Rockwell knew about the nature of the follow-up study and the bases on which the experimental and control groups were selected.

stewards will tend to become more favorable toward the union. Moreover, in so far as the values of management and of the union are in conflict with each other, it might also be expected that workers who are made foremen will become less favorable toward the union and workers who are made stewards will become less favorable toward management.

Four attitudinal areas were examined: 1. attitudes toward management and officials of management; 2. attitudes toward the union and officials of the union; 3. attitudes toward the management-sponsored incentive system; and 4. attitudes toward the union-sponsored seniority system. The incentive system (whereby workers are paid according to the number of pieces they turn out) and the seniority system (whereby workers are promoted according to the seniority principle) are two areas in which conflicts between management and the union at Rockwell have been particularly intense. Furthermore, first-level foremen and stewards both play a part in the administration of these systems, and relevant groups hold expectations about foreman and steward behaviors with respect to these systems. Therefore, we examined the experimental and control groups' attitudes toward these two systems as well as their overall attitudes toward management and the union.

The data tend to support the hypothesis that being placed in the foreman and steward roles will have an impact on the attitudes of the role occupants. . . . both experimental groups undergo systematic changes in attitudes, in the predicted directions, from the "before" situation to the "after" situation. In the control groups, either no attitude changes occur, or less marked changes occur, from the "before" situation to the "after" situation.

Although a number of the differences are not statistically significant, those which are significant are all in the expected directions, and most of the non-significant differences are also in the expected directions. New foremen, among other things, come to see Rockwell as a better place to work compared with other companies, develop more positive perceptions of top management officers, and become more favorably disposed toward the principle and operation of the incentive system. New stewards come to look upon labor unions in general in a more favorable light, develop more positive perceptions of the top union officers at Rockwell, and come to prefer seniority to ability as a criterion of what should count in moving workers to better jobs. In general, the attitudes of workers who become foremen tend to gravitate in a pro-management direction and the attitudes of workers who become stewards tend to move in a pro-union direction.

A second kind of finding has to do with the relative *amount* of attitude change that takes place among new foremen in contrast to the amount that takes place among new stewards. On the whole, more pronounced and more widespread attitude changes occur among those who are made foremen than among those who are made stewards. . . .

The more pronounced and more widespread attitude changes that occur among new foremen than among new stewards can probably be accounted for in large measure by the kinds of differences that exist between the foreman and steward roles. For one thing, the foreman role represents a relatively permanent position, while many stewards take the steward role as a "one-shot" job and even if they want to run again their constituents may not re-elect them. Secondly, the foreman role is a full-time job, while most stewards spend just a few hours a week in the performance of their steward functions and spend the rest of the time carrying out their regular rank-and-file jobs. Thirdly, a worker who is made a foreman must give up his membership

in the union and become a surrogate of management, while a worker who is made a steward retains the union as a reference group and simply takes on new functions and responsibilities as a representative of it. All of these differences suggest that the change from worker to foreman is a more fundamental change in roles than the change from worker to steward. This, in turn, might account to a large extent for the finding that, although attitude changes accompany both changes in roles, they occur more sharply among new foremen than among new stewards.

A third finding has to do with the *kinds* of attitude changes which occur among workers who change roles. As expected, new foremen become more pro-management and new stewards become more pro-union. Somewhat less expected is the finding that new foremen become more anti-union but new stewards do not become more anti-management. Among workers who are made foremen, statistically significant shifts in an anti-union direction occur in four of the eight items dealing with the union and the union sponsored seniority system. Among workers who are made stewards, there are no statistically significant shifts in either direction on any of the eight items having to do with management and the management-sponsored incentive system.

The finding that new foremen become anti-union but that new stewards do not become anti-management may be related to the fact that workers who become stewards retain their status as employees of management. New foremen, subject to one main set of loyalties and called on to carry out a markedly new set of functions, tend to develop negative attitudes toward the union as well as positive attitudes toward management. New stewards, subject to overlapping group membership and still dependent on management for their livelihoods, tend to become more favorable toward the union but they do not turn against management, at least not within the relatively limited time period covered by the present research project. Over time, stewards might come to develop somewhat hostile attitudes toward management, but, under the conditions prevailing at Rockwell, there is apparently no tendency for such attitudes to be developed as soon as workers enter the steward role.

Method: Phase 2

One of the questions that may be raised about the results that have been presented up to this point concerns the extent to which the changed attitudes displayed by new foremen and new stewards are internalized by the role occupants. Are the changed attitudes expressed by new foremen and new stewards relatively stable, or are they ephemeral phenomena, to be held only as long as they occupy the foreman and steward roles? An unusual set of circumstances at Rockwell enabled the researchers to glean some data on this question.

A short time after the 1952 re-survey, the nation suffered an economic recession. In order to meet the lessening demand for its products, Rockwell, like many other firms, had to cut its work force. This resulted in many rank-and-file workers being laid off and a number of the foremen being returned to non-supervisory jobs. By June 1954, eight of the twenty-three workers who had been promoted to foreman had returned to the worker role and only twelve were still foremen. (The remaining three respondents had voluntarily left Rockwell by this time.)

Over the same period, a number of role changes had also been experienced by the thirty-five workers who had become stewards. Fourteen had returned to the worker role, either because they had

not sought re-election by their work groups or because they had failed to win re-election, and only six were still stewards. (The other fifteen respondents, who composed almost half of this group, had either voluntarily left Rockwell or had been laid off as part of the general reduction in force.)

Once again, in June 1954, the researchers returned to Rockwell to re-administer the questionnaires that the workers had filled out in 1951 and 1952. The instructions to the respondents were substantially the same as those given in 1952—i.e. a sample of employees had been chosen to get up-to-date measures of employees' attitudes toward working conditions at Rockwell and the same groups were selected this time as had been selected last time in order to lend greater stability to the results.

In this phase of the study, the number of cases with which we were dealing in the various groups were so small that the data could only be viewed as suggestive, and systematic statistical analysis of the data did not seem to be too meaningful. However, the unusual opportunity to throw some light on an important question suggests that a reporting of these results may be worthwhile.

Results: Phase 2

The principle question examined here was: on those items where a change in roles resulted in a change in attitudes between 1951 and 1952, how are these attitudes influenced by a reverse change in roles between 1952 and 1954?

The most consistent and widespread attitude changes noted between 1951 and 1952 were those that resulted when workers moved into the foreman role. What are the effects of moving out of the foreman role between 1952 and 1954? The data indicate that, in general, most of the "gains" that were observed when workers became foremen are "lost" when they become workers again. . . . On almost all of the items, the foremen who remain foremen either retain their favorable attitudes toward management or become even more favorable toward management between 1952 and 1954, while the demoted foremen show fairly consistent drops in the direction of re-adopting the attitudes they held when they had been in the worker role. On the whole, the attitudes held by demoted foremen in 1954, after they had left the foreman role, fall roughly to the same levels as they had been in 1951, before they had ever moved into the foreman role.

The results on the effects of moving out of the steward role are less clear-cut. . . . there is no marked tendency for ex-stewards to revert to earlier-held attitudes when they go from the steward role to the worker role. At the same time, it should be recalled that there had not been particularly marked changes in their attitudes when they initially changed from the worker role to the steward role. These findings, then, are consistent with the interpretation offered earlier that the change in roles between worker and steward is less significant than the change in roles between worker and foreman.

A question might be raised about what is represented in the reversal of attitudes found among ex-foremen. Does it represent a positive taking-on of attitudes appropriate for respondents who are re-entering the worker role, or does it constitute a negative, perhaps embittered reaction away from the attitudes they held before being demoted from the foreman role? A definitive answer to this question cannot be arrived at, but it might be suggested that if we were dealing with a situation where a reversion in roles did not constitute such a strong psychological blow to the role occupants (as was probably the case among demoted foremen), then such a marked reversion in attitudes might not have occurred.[4] . . .

The data indicate that changes in attitudes occurred soon after changes in roles took place. And inside a period of three years those who had remained in their new roles had developed almost diametrically opposed sets of attitudinal positions.

. . .

References

1. Jacobson, E., Charters, W. W., Jr., and Lieberman, S. "The use of the Role Concept in the Study of Complex Organizations." *J. Soc. Issues,* Vol. 7, No. 3, pp. 18-27, 1951.
2. Newcomb, T. M. *Social Psychology.* New York: The Dryden Press; London: Tavistock Publications, 1952.
3. Parsons, T. *The Social System.* Glencoe, Ill.: The Free Press; London: Tavistock Publications Ltd., 1951.
4. Riesman, D. *The Lonely Crowd.* New Haven: Yale Univ. Press, 1950.
5. Stouffer, S. A., Suchman, E. A., De-Vinney, L. C., Star, S. A. and Williams, R. M., Jr. *The American Soldier: Adjustment During Army Life* (Vol. 1). Princeton: Princeton University Press, 1949.
6. Walker, H. M., and Lev, J. *Statistical Inference.* New York: Henry Holt and Co., Inc., 1953.

---

[4] There were a number of reactions to demotion among the eight ex-foremen, as obtained from informal interviews with these respondents. Some reacted impunitively (i.e., they blamed uncontrollable situational determinants) and did not seem to be bothered by demotion. Others reacted extrapunitively (i.e., they blamed management) or intrapunitively (i.e., they blamed themselves) and appeared to be more disturbed by demotion. One way of testing the hypothesis that attitude reversion is a function of embitterment would be to see if sharper reversion occurs among extrapunitive and intrapunitive respondents. However, the small number of cases does not permit an analysis of this kind to be carried out in the present situation.

Some similar evidence from other nations may be of interest, to show that the role given to an individual is likely to influence his attitudes. Rim, in a unique study in Israel, has shown that whether a business is owned by private industry, labor unions, or the state, the attitudes of managers in each of the three situations resemble each other greatly. That presumably different financial ownership interests are being represented seems to have less influence on his attitudes than that of having the role of manager within the business. Granick, has postulated (though not with direct attitude survey data, but with other evidence) that managers of factories in Soviet Russia face many of the same problems and have some of the same attitudes—toward suppliers and workers—that exist in the United States or other countries where the enterprises are privately owned.

Failure to recognize the likelihood that attitudes change with changes in role can often lead to inaccurate predictions of the behavior of others, and to difficulties in dealing with them. When someone we've been friendly with at work, and whose attitudes we thought we knew, gets moved into a different job, we should not be surprised at changes, as Lieberman has shown. We may sometimes be inclined to forget that if an old associate in one department is shifted to a new role in another department his expectations about how *we* should behave toward him may change. As his new role effects changes in his attitudes toward many aspects of organizational life, our expectations about his behavior will also have to change. The attitudes appropriate for a member of a staff department may shift when he is placed in a line department. Before deciding that "the job has gone to his head," we must recognize that a new role brings some changed attitudes. As a matter of fact, if it doesn't, the individual may often not be able to hold the new position.

Even temporary role-playing has been shown to have attitudinal consequences (King and Janis). The changes in opinion have been shown to be greater when subjects were required to improvise their own speeches than when they played a role previously prepared for them (King and Janis). There are some people writing about attitude change who view the attitude changes resulting from role changes as evidence of the effects of the feeling of inconsistency, or of cognitive dissonance that is created. (We should not assume, however, that training by means of role-playing will necessarily bring long term attitude changes.)

Whatever the theoretical interpretation, there should be no doubt in the administrator's mind that providing a new role for an individual, *which he chooses to accept,* may effectively change attitudes. One caution is necessary here. To the administrator, it may seem that merely assigning an individual to a new role would automatically bring a shift in attitude. But the importance of choice or acceptance of the role by the individual should be pointed out (Cohen). A role, for example, a committee assignment, that is actively resented by the individual may produce a "freezing" rather than a shifting of attitudes.

Group and Interpersonal Influences

The entire pattern of the development of attitudes is, as we have seen, a question of learning the attitudes provided for us by the different groups to which we have been previously exposed. Thus, it is not surprising if we look to the influence of the group for means of changing attitudes. Although we are using the word group here chiefly to refer to face-to-face, or direct interpersonal influences,* we must not ignore the less direct effects of identification with so-called reference groups, that is, groups whose standards are used by the individual as a basis for his own.

The idea of using the pressure of the group leads right to the door of the much discussed problem of conformity, with all the feelings that this word arouses. To condemn something automatically because it smacks of "conformity" overlooks the fact that we are in a world of people inevitably influenced by social norms, whether in the procedures that seek to prevent chaos, such as traffic rules, or in the more complex societal procedures for developing such social values as honesty and decency.

On the other hand, to value something automatically because it brings about uniformity or conformity is to lose the vitality and value brought by diversity and the worth of personal individuality. In seeking to shift attitudes the administrator is seeking to increase the similarity of views; to heighten an aspect of "conformity." He must always be willing to ask himself if the consequences of the shift of attitudes are needed. He must also realize that he may gain from diverse attitudes, just as from diverse ideas (to be shown later in connection with research or production solving). Kelley and Shapiro have shown, for example, that conformity to group norms can be detrimental to group achievement. Not only the individual, but the group may suffer from the imposition of conformity (see also Blake and Mouton).

There are also, nevertheless, situations where an agreement in attitudes can make for effectiveness of group relations without injuring the individual's integrity. The administrator should not launch lightly into an attempt to shift attitudes until he has thought through why the attitudes should shift (for example, is it simply because he wants them to or is it because other goals will be accomplished?). From attempts to change attitudes and behavior, as with any process from fire to atomic energy, constructive or destructive results can occur.

If, to return to our theme, he has decided to seek to shift attitudes, what part can group pressures play?

The effects of group pressure are not just automatic. Defining conformity as "movement from one's own position toward a group norm or standard of

---

* The importance of personal influence in changing attitudes has been shown in studies of public opinion change (E. Katz and Lazarsfeld).

behavior," Walker and Heyns (p. 88) summarize their own research and present conclusions that fit the work of other experimenters (Asch; Sherif; Crutchfield) on the conditions for effective group pressure. Walker and Heyns indicate that: (1) "the stronger the need which can be served by conformity behavior, the greater will be the tendency to conform" (p. 92); (2) "the more familiar the subject is with the target of the attitude or behavior to be influenced by the norm, the less effective the pressure. . . . Susceptability to social pressure will vary with the degree of certainty the subject has in his own solution to the problem" (3) "the better the education, the more independent the behavior," and "the less the social pressure influence" (p. 94); (4) "the more ambiguous the situation, the more vague and numerous the alternate courses of action open, the more the conformity in response to social pressure" (p. 95).

The administrator can thus see that the time-honored approach of getting a person into a situation in which others can exert influence on him has experimental evidence as well as tradition to support it, if the individual sees conforming to pressure as achieving a desired acceptance by the group.

In this whole effort, it occasionally may be necessary to increase the persons actual awareness that he is a member of certain groups. This may be done by dramatizing the membership through rituals, ceremonies, or other informal reminders. The group thus becomes more salient for the individual and group norms become more influential in affecting his attitudes (Charters and Newcomb).

When an administrator's problem is to change the attitudes of an entire group (see Reading 5-7), he will find that attitudes "anchored" in a group are more resistant to change than those that are not (Kelley and Volkart; Gerard). Unfortunately, as Klapper (p. 27) has pointed out, our knowledge regarding the resistance of group-anchored attitudes is not sufficiently refined to permit wholly accurate predictions as to when changes will or will not occur.

One additional comment that can be made is that in cohesive groups uniform attitudes can be expected, and in less cohesive groups more varied attitudes are probable (Back). But, in our discussion of group pressures toward conformity, the importance of the expression of a minority viewpoint should not be overlooked. The administrator or any member of the group by being the first to speak up, may lead others with similar views to recognize that they are not unanimously opposed by the majority. The expression of a dissenting view may aid shifts within the group and may also help to prevent people from feeling "forced" to accede to a view contrary to their real feelings (Asch).

Enforced Changes in Behavior

The "importance of required behavior as a determinant of the individual's beliefs" has often been obscured (Katz and Stotland, p. 458); there is much evidence to suggest that behavior required of an individual can be a prelude to an attitude change. Of the four kinds of attitudes considered by Katz, the ego-defensive will be the one most likely to resist change through some imposed regulation or condition. The other three are more amenable to direct action and often they may be the more prevalent and more commonly held attitudes, but the administrator must remain sensitive to the possibility of defensiveness.

There is, for instance, much research demonstrating that the common view that "we cannot legislate attitudes" is both incomplete and incorrect. Evidence shows that a rule or a law *can* bring about changes in behavior, and then in turn, attitudes change. The law does not act directly on attitudes, but its indirect influences can be strong. Even in emotionally-charged areas, such as discrimination, a large amount of research (referred to by Katz) demonstrates this. Rules and laws that reduced discrimination, (for example, in housing, employment, and the military service) resulted in major reductions in feelings of prejudice despite relatively isolated instances of difficulties where group pressures and leadership have not been mobilized toward values of maintenance of law (Deutsch and Collins; Harding and Hogrefe; Star, *et al.*).

A rule or law often provides the basis for a socially-approved group norm. The other attitude change factors of increased equal status contact, the presence of new group norms, changes in role, and desires to reduce feelings of inconsistency all interrelate to allow enforced conditions to help change attitudes.

Assuming that the administrator is not aiming at shifting ego-defensive attitudes, there may be times that he can judiciously use the old "fait accompli" technique. However, he must be aware that behavioral and attitudinal changes may not be the same. The changes in behavior or attitude that may take place can be seen in the light of three processes of social influence described by Kelman. He distinguishes: (1) *compliance*—which can be said to occur "when an individual accepts influence from another person or from a group because he hopes to achieve a favorable reaction from the other;" (2) *identification*—when an individual adopts the behavior of another person or group because this behavior is associated with satisfactions tied in with the individual's self-image; and (3) *internalization*—when the content of the induced behavior is intrinsically rewarding and fits with the individual's value system.

We can see, then, that an enforced change may bring about compliance, but for this administrator this is the least satisfactory sort of change because it is directly dependent upon the rewarding and punishing power of the influencing agent. Continual surveillance is needed to see that the behavior changes are maintained, "if the cat's away. . . ." The overt behavior may change, but attitude changes will probably not follow, in the compliance situation. But, if the other person desires to keep a given relationship going smoothly, such as being on good terms with the boss or with people in other departments, then conditions facilitating the processes of identification or internalization may help attitude shifts to occur despite the actual content of the attitudes, even when there is not continual watching. In the identification situation, as in the internalization situation, more than compliance is obtained. Schein *et al.* (1961, p.

248) pointed out our lack of full knowledge about the interaction of these three processes; for the administrator, who seeks more than compliance, it is apparent that if he promulgates new rules or changes in procedure that are antagonistic to attitudes already held, then even though they be enforced changes, he should allow room for identification or internalization to take place. (See the discussion in Reading 5-5.)

The Effects of Information

From the extensive material concerning the effects of information or communication on attitude change, we should mention certain important factors.

Needs. There is ample demonstration that information relevant to an individual's needs will change attitudes more than information that is not (for example, Di Vesta and Merwin). Our earlier emphasis on sensitivity to the other person's needs and motives is relevant here. Giving information to an individual to change his attitudes will be disappointing in its effects if the receiver's needs are ignored. Of all the types of attitudes, ego-defensive attitudes will be least susceptible to change through providing information.

Credibility.[*] Credibility would seem to include two main components (whose interacting effects are not yet disentangled); trustworthiness and expertness. The administrator who hopes to have some influence on the attitudes of others (not necessarily just subordinates) should seek to maintain his standing as both trustworthy and knowledgeable in the information he conveys. Research reports and summaries show that a source considered to be highly credible will have more of an *immediate* effect on opinions than a source low in credibility.

If the information elicits some immediate action, lasting effects may take place. However, unless other influences are introduced to support the original information, the long range impact of credibility is less certain. Apparently over a longer time, the *content* of the information may be recalled independently of the recall of the source. With the passage of time, "the content of a statement is less likely to be spontaneously associated with the source; that is, people often remember what was said without thinking about who said it." Thus, we can see that in an organization, a rumor heard some weeks back may influence an employees' attitude to nearly the same degree as some of the boss's presumably accurate statements, once some time has passed. The boss should seek to maintain his credibility, but he must also seek to provide immediacy (possibly through repetition) of the information he is providing.

Personal characteristics. Although we are omitting most of the concern for differences in the characteristics of the persons being communicated *to,* (for example, intelligence, educational level) one point will be made. High status of the person providing information (compared to low status) may be more influential with people who tend to be more (measurably) dogmatic or

---

[*] Our discussion follows data presented in Hovland, Janis, and Kelley, pp. 35-41, and 259-270. Additional studies are reviewed by Abelson.

authoritarian, whereas low status information sources may carry greater weight with more "open-minded," less authoritarian people (Vidulich and Kaman). Thus, everyone should not be expected to respond in the same way to information conveyed to them. Their own "open-mindedness," their prior attitudes, the status and credibility of the communicator, the needs of the "receivers," and the relationship and ego-defensive attitudes to the information provided, are some of the factors involved in determining whether attitudes will shift with information. Willingness to expose oneself to the information provided has also been found to be important (Hovland, 1959).

We can see why it was stated (in the first Katz selection) that increasing the flow of information will not necessarily change attitudes, and why the administrator who feels it automatically will is in for a surprise when he "informs people" or "communicates," and then finds that nothing happens.

Situational Changes

Many of the influences that may be used to change attitudes overlap. Changing a person's role can be viewed as a situational change, as could enforcing a new rule. Despite some overlap, it may be of use to state that when situations change, attitudes may change. A change, for example, in economic conditions, or in the amount of profit the company has shown may lead to attitudinal changes. Frequently, however, the person may interpret the events to fit his attitude, rather than modify his attitudes (see Part One). Thus, his anticipation of the rewards or punishments to be expected in the changed situation will be important in the potential for attitude change. Relevant here is Kelman's distinction between compliance, identification, and internalization, any of which may result from a change in a situation and the perception of change.

In a study of bureaucratic organizations, Blau found Merton's concept of the latent functions and the unanticipated consequences of a change, useful in his study of bureaucratic organizations. Blau showed that introduction of the keeping of statistical records of performance had two effects: (1) by encouraging employees' attempts to improve work on their own initiative, supervisory criticism was cut down and more cordial attitudes developed between supervisor and subordinates; and (2) a competitive attitude toward each other was engendered among the employees that made it more difficult for them to complete their tasks. Thus, we see that a situational change, in the form of the sort of records kept, had unanticipated consequences and played a part in developing both favorable and less favorable attitudes. Situational factors will influence attitudes, but the administrator must be alert to some consequences that he may not have anticipated.

Effects of Personal Contact

For the administrator, there are a number of situations where he might be seeking to induce more favorable attitudes toward others; for instance, toward members of another department with whom there has been friction or toward the members of groups with different backgrounds or characteristics from those that predominate in the work group (handicapped workers; older workers; college graduates). Contact is often thought to change prejudiced attitudes toward other people. Krech and Crutchfield state, "though it is often true that the more information about people a person gains from contact with them the more favorable the attitudes are likely to be, this obviously is not always the case. The added information 'from contact' may make him see the people in a worse light than before" (p. 676). They point out that the question of the status of the individuals contacted is important, and cite Watson's study showing that equal status contact led to more favorable attitudes, whereas contact with minority group members of lower status than one's own led to less favorable attitudes toward them.

The administrator, thinking of using personal contact as an influence for favorable change, must remember that the contacts must not be of an "unequal status" sort. The changes that result in increased contact with other groups must be introduced as another aspect of the organizations goals—goals generally acceptable to all members of the organization. The administrator will have to guard against having the increased contacts perceived as an attack on the members of already established groups. As with providing information, so too with contact: the effects are neither automatic nor necessarily favorable.

The Effects of Participation

The principle of getting people to participate has formed the basis for various programs of attitude change. It is a useful principle in reducing ego-defensive attitudes as well as the other sorts. It can provide changes for equal status contact, group support, and identification; it also offers reinforcement for changing through satisfaction of ego-needs. It often operates to influence behavior as well as attitudes (see Reading 4-3). Emphasizing, at this point, that this is one of the most important principles, we will consider participation further on, in Chapter Eighteen, "Attitude Change Procedures Used in Industry."

CHAPTER SEVENTEEN

Special Problems
in Attitude Change
and
Some Guidelines

Throughout Part Five, we have stressed the idea that attitude change will not be easily accomplished. At this point, we would like to point out a special problem that runs throughout many of the ways of inducing attitude change. Paradoxically this factor—the reduction of inconsistency—is in one sense a complexity, (because it adds the difficulty of knowing what another person views as inconsistent) but in another sense it also provides a thread that helps to understand the operation of some of the previously suggested methods.

We have noted (in Part Three) that there seems to be a drive (or tendency) to try to reduce feelings of inconsistency or to reduce cognitive dissonance (to use Festinger's term). When some of the individuals attitudes, feelings, or beliefs are inconsistent (or dissonant) with other attitudes or behavior, he will seek to reduce the dissonance.*

Festinger, in our selection below, indicates what may occur.

---

* The concept has been identified under such other labels as: homeostasis (Maccoby and Maccoby); congruity (Osgood and Tannenbaum); balance (Heider); strain toward symmetry (Newcomb).

READING 5-4

The Reduction of Dissonance Stemming from Social Disagreement*

LEON FESTINGER

According to the theory, when there is dissonance there will be corresponding pressures to reduce the dissonance, the magnitude of these pressures depending upon the magnitude of the dissonance. . . . Three methods for reducing dissonance stemming from social disagreement readily suggest themselves.

1. The dissonance may be reduced, or perhaps even eliminated completely, by changing one's own opinion so that it corresponds more closely with one's knowledge of what others believe. Changing one's own opinion will effectively reduce dissonance only, of course, if there are not many persons who already agree with one's original opinion (who would then be disagreeing after the opinion change). This is completely analogous to changing existing cognition in other contexts.

2. Another way of reducing the dissonance would be to influence those persons who disagree to change their opinion so that it more closely corresponds to one's own. This is, of course, analogous to changing the environment and thereby changing the cognitive elements reflecting that environment. In the context of dissonance stemming from social disagreement, this is a major manifestation of pressure to reduce dissonance. These first two methods, taken together, represent the usual sort of influence process which

results in movement toward uniformity in groups in the presence of disagreement. Thus, recasting the theory of influence processes in terms of dissonance theory makes it quite easy to derive movement toward uniformity.

3. Another way of reducing dissonance between one's own opinion and the knowledge that someone else holds a different opinion is to make the other person, in some manner, not comparable to oneself. Such an allegation can take a number of forms. One can attribute different characteristics, experiences, or motives to the other person or one can even reject him and derogate him. Thus if some other person claims the grass is brown when I see it as green, the dissonance thus created can be effectively reduced if the characteristic of being color-blind can be attributed to the other person. There would be no dissonance between knowing the grass is green and knowing that a color-blind person asserted it was brown. Similarly, if one person believes that flying saucers are space ships from other planets and some other person voices the opinion that flying saucers, as such, do not even exist, the resulting dissonance in the cognition of the former may be reduced if he can believe that the latter is a stupid, ignorant, unfriendly, and bigoted individual.

Since all three of these processes, namely, changing one's own opinion, attempting to influence others, and attributing non-comparability to others, may potentially reduce dissonance, one would

---

* Reprinted from *A Theory of Cognitive Dissonance* by Leon Festinger, with the permission of the publishers, Stanford University Press. © 1957 by Leon Festinger.

expect to see all of them intensified in degree as the magnitude of the dissonance increased. Thus, as the magnitude of difference of opinion increased, as the relevance of the opinion to the group increased, as the attraction to the group increased, and as the number of other cognitive elements consonant with the opinion decreased, one would expect greater tendencies to change one's own opinion in response to disagreement, greater effort expended at influencing those who disagreed (especially those who disagreed most), and a greater tendency to make those who disagreed noncomparable. In short, returning once again to the basic theory, the pressure to reduce dissonance will be a function of the magnitude of the dissonance.

The Effect of Inducements

Much research has been taking place in recent years to follow up the implications of the dissonance theory. In one connection in particular, the theory has been of unique value in leading to predictions—verified by later research—that run counter to our everyday ideas of influencing attitudes—that is, the use of inducements.

Common sense might suggest that offering a person something might be one means of getting him to change an attitude he holds. Actually (although recognition of needs is vital) a specific inducement for a specific attitude change may not be effective and may even be resented if perceived as an attempt to "buy the individual off."

Trying to offer a reward or inducement of some sort to encourage attitude change poses some vexing problems. Some research (Smith) suggests that inducements offered to get someone to behave differently in the hope that he will also change his attitudes may help to bring about behavior changes, but may reduce any pressure within the individual to make his attitudes consistent with his changed behavior. In a common sense approach to this problem we might even believe that "a large inducement will be more useful in shifting attitudes than a small one;" but dissonance theory leads to predicting just the opposite. (See Reading 3-9.)

If the inducement is perceived as sufficiently large, there will be little feeling of dissonance within the person because he can justify his shift of behavior solely as a means of seeking the reward offered. Thus, compliance in overt behavior (despite an underlying attitude that would predispose an opposite kind of response) may occur, without a need for attitude change being induced. Research confirms this and shows that a specific large inducement may be less effective than a small one in shifting attitudes. If the administrator's goal is to change behavior without worrying about whether the attitude changes will also occur, to support the new behavior when the inducement is no longer present, then specific one-shot inducements may be of value. But greater value will come from the more complete process of changing attitudes by working to create a need for changing attitudes as well as for behavioral change.

An administrator might expect that beyond a certain level, the greater the added inducement the *less* the individual will shift his attitudes. The problem is that we cannot easily anticipate in advance the level or threshold for the other person above which an inducement is perceived as large, and thus produce behavioral, but not attitudinal shifts. It is the last mentioned difficulty that makes the use of inducements for attitude change a risky administrative procedure.

The Effects of Committment and of Choice

If the effects of offering inducements are complicated by dissonance, what about the relation of dissonance to getting a person to commit himself to something, or to make a choice? Schramm reviews the publication of some research on this (Rosenberg *et al.*).

> Dissonance, it has been demonstrated, arises from discrepancy between beliefs and behavior. Studies of role playing indicate that when a person devises and expresses argument contrary to his beliefs, he tends to modify his beliefs to some extent to accord with his role playing. Brehm wanted to find out whether it was necessary, in order to bring about his cognitive reorganization, actually to engage in discrepant behavior and be rewarded for it, or whether merely deciding to engage in discrepant behavior would be sufficient to bring about the change. With an experiment on eating unpopular foods he demonstrated quite clearly that it is not necessary to engage in the discrepant behavior, and that mere commitment to behavior inconsistent with one's beliefs will increase one's acceptance of a communication that supports the behavior and increase one's resistance to a communication that is nonsupporting.
>
> Brehm and Cohen then asked: How necessary is this act of *deciding* to engage in discrepant behavior? Suppose the individual has no choice; will an undesired event out of his control still lead to dissonance and consequently to attitude change in the direction of removing the dissonance? They found *that the act of "choice" is of major importance*. If the undesired event is thought to occur by "chance" there will still be some dissonance created, but the more the individual feels he could have avoided the event, the more he feels he had a choice, the more likely he is to reorganize his attitudes so as to support the event.

It would appear, then, that if an administrator gets a committment to some future action (or gives such a committment himself), the wheels are rolling toward a change in attitude. In addition, if the person feels that he had freedom to have chosen to behave differently, he is more amenable to change of attitude. The relation of this finding to the use (and our later discussion) of participation techniques is obvious.

The Effects on Seeking Information

One consequence of producing dissonance is that the seeking of information by the recipient may increase. It has been shown with some attitudes that people who are given information that produces feelings of dissonance will more likely seek additional information on the topic than those who received consonant information (Adams).

This can, of course, operate in two directions. For one, the person may look for more information to support his initial attitude. With ego-defensive attitudes, we might find this to be a likely possibility, with the individual discounting the new information. But, on the other hand, those whose attitudes *are* influenced by information communicated to them are likely at a later time to seek out conversations that reinforce their newly acquired beliefs. It was found (Maccoby, E. *et al.*) that these conversations helped to prevent "backsliding" to the original views. Relevant to this (and to the question of the importance of groups) is a study of Blau's (reported by Festinger, p. 208-9) showing that people who had more social contacts (and thus who can find more people to agree with the things they want to believe) changed opinions more than those with few social contacts.

The administrator might anticipate from these studies that providing access both to information (from respected sources) and to other people may help a person to reinforce newly acquired beliefs.

The Effect of Individual Differences

How does creating a feeling of dissonance affect people with extreme attitudes, as compared to those with moderate attitudes? Again, we could speculate in two directions: first, the extremes would hold out and be *less* likely to shift, or would shift only a small amount; or, second, that those who are most negative would feel more pressure to shift. As dissonance theory predicts, the latter hypothesis has been supported in several research studies (for example, Smith). Those who are extreme in attitude, shifted attitudes more than others (possibly because there was a greater distance available to move). Thus, creating dissonance may have more effect for those at the extremes than for those of moderate position.

A precaution to be aware of is that various stratagems for restoring feelings of consistency may be used by the individual. As Maccoby and Maccoby point out (p. 544) these alternatives include "(1) strengthening the original attitude by discounting the service of the disturbing communication; (2) refusal to attend to the message, or repressing it once it is received, and (3) compartmentalizing or fractionating the attitude so that inconsistencies are not so readily apparent." If such alternatives (similar in part to those mentioned above by Festinger) are blocked "the person might be expected to show a large amount of change" (Hovland and Rosenberg, p. 229).

In addition to the degree to which attitudes may be extreme or moderate, there is another important way in which individual differences may be displayed. Hovland and Rosenberg (p. 229) comment "there are certain settings in which, and certain persons in whom, motives favoring the *arousal and maintenance* of inconsistency are sometimes dominant." Some people may actually seek inconsistency; many people, who do not seek it, can still put up with such feelings better than others. Scientists, for example, while pressing to organize and reduce inconsistency may be less disturbed (or less surprised) than the laymen that things can't be neatly explained or understood. Many people have a higher tolerance than others for the ambiguous, the unclear, the inconsistent, and can live with these conditions more easily.

Many situations, too, may not permit complete explanation. Some readers of this book, for instance, may be perturbed that it is not possible to give direct, unqualified rules on how to deal with people, but the complexity of the research and the knowledge that there are not easy formulae, prevent this.

The administrator, pointing out inconsistencies in someone else's point of view may be upset by the fact that the other person does not seem bothered by these contradictions. He should be aware that what he feels to be inconsistent may not necessarily be perceived as such by another. A worker, for instance, may feel allegiance both to the company and to the union (Stagner; Purcell). Each of these organizations may be filling different needs for him, and he may have different roles in each. If the boss starts to oversimplify and imply "You're either for us or against us," he is not acting appropriately.

Some Guidelines

Our consideration of inconsistency or dissonance (and of inducements, choice, and so on) was introduced under the heading of Special Problems. Let us see what implications for administration emerge from this last section and tie them in to the major methods of attitude change previously discussed. In giving such an overview, the reader must recall the variety of hazards involved for each concept and not consider these as "rules" which can be used without concern for the previous, more extensive discussion. They interact and should not be viewed in isolation. Here, then, are some "guidelines."

The administrator should:

(a) Recognize that attitudes serve different functions. In order to change, the person must feel a need to change; a need stronger than the need to maintain the "old" attitude. One need that may at times be helpfully aroused is the need to reduce feelings of inconsistency or of dissonance.

(b) It is the need *to change* that must be aroused. Other needs that are satisfied by "outside" inducements may bring about compliance, but not bring a shift of attitudes that will serve as the basis for maintaining new behavior without the inducement. For example, a "reward" system for promptness may thus cut lateness when the reinforcements are sought by the individual, but may later decline in effectiveness, or may not work to change attitude toward lateness. The individuals may seek ways to "beat the system," or show up late if the rewards seem lost.

(c) Try to arouse values that are important to the other person, or encourage him to feel some dissatisfaction with his attitudes. Then, if he can see how a change in attitudes will be more consistent with other values he accepts, shifts may occur.

But . . .

(d) *Don't* arouse feelings of threat. If ego-defensiveness comes into play, the threats may boomerang, just as inducements may. The chance for the person to let off steam, and to express his ideas and feelings may allow him to see that a change is not a threat.

(e) Give the individual (or group) a special role, if possible, that leads to behavior that arouses feelings of dissonance and that leads to attitude changes. Or, use his present roles if he can be helped to see that a presently existing role is incompatible with certain attitudes.

(f) Use the group as a source of support for attitude shifts. A variety of needs are fulfilled in this way.

(g) Get an expression of commitment to changed behavior; if possible, to a kind of behavior that is linked to existing values or attitudes that may, in turn, act as magnets to attract other attitudes.

Getting the person to make some sort of effort (not "bribery") can lead to movement of attitudes. If that effort is based on values or attitudes consistent with the attitudes the administrator is trying to develop, it will be particularly effective.

(h) With all these suggestions, maximize the feeling of choice for the individual. Earlier attitudes will be viewed with less ego-defensiveness if the person feels he has chosen to behave in new ways and that these new ways lead to new attitudes.

(i) Recognize the useful limits of information. Seek to be (deservedly) credible as a source of information. Provide access to information, and if possible arouse needs that will lead the person to choose to use the valuable information. Provide a "low pressure" rationale (within a framework of the other guidelines).

(j) Notice individual differences—both in attitudes and in their "shiftability."

(k) Don't be surprised if—after trying all these ideas—attitudes still don't change (much).

Also, don't be surprised if, by ignoring all these ideas, you find that attitudes change even *less* than if you do heed these suggestions. The odds are more with you, if you understand some current knowledge on attitudes, even if the odds are not 100-1.

Finally, realize that attitude change can work in two directions. Others are seeking to change the administrator's attitudes too. And why (without being defensive) the administrator must ask himself, should *his* attitudes never change?

CHAPTER EIGHTEEN

Attitude Change
Procedures Used
in
Business and Industry

One can make a distinction between an organized program for changing attitudes and the individual efforts that an administrator must make in his interactions with others. The individual approach is the one with which we have been dealing so far. In this chapter, we focus on the attempts that have been made at an organizational level, in company programs. It must be remembered that the principles and conditions mentioned previously are also operative (or should be operative) in organized programs of attitude change.

We discuss three types of organized attitude change procedures used in industry: Management Development, Human Relations Programs, and Participation Methods. The categories overlap each other considerably. They were selected more for convenience of discussion than to represent totally different training activities. Participation methods are not formally considered training although they are frequently used to change attitudes and thus have a training function.

Both effective administration and good performance at lower levels spring from a foundation of appropriate, positive attitudes, as well as freedom from hampering negative attitudes. Therefore, the goal of all attitude change procedures must be a double one—the identification and change of undesired attitudes (a first step because the presence of negative attitudes frequently forestalls the growth of other attitudes) and the building of desired attitudes useful for effective performance in the organization.

Although the first three categories of attitude change procedures discussed in this chapter apply principally to managers and supervisors, we emphasize that some type of attitude change procedures must be available for all levels in the organization. Participation methods, as the Coch and French study demonstrates, are useful at the lower levels of the organization. Modified human relations training programs may also be used with lower level groups.

Management Development

Various approaches to management development are widely known. Schein considers them within the classical framework provided by Lewin for attitude change: unfreezing, movement, and refreezing. He provides as well a description of sensitivity training programs. Schein's paper appears as our next reading.

READING 5-5

Management Development as a Process of Influence*

EDGAR H. SCHEIN

The continuing rash of articles on the subject of developing better managers suggests, on the one hand, a continuing concern that existing methods are not providing the talent which is needed at the higher levels of industry and, on the other hand, that we continue to lack clear-cut formulations about the process by which such development occurs. We need more and better managers and we need more and better theories of how to get them.

In the present paper I would like to cast management development as the problem of how an organization can influence the beliefs, attitudes, and values (hereafter simply called attitudes) of an individual for the purpose of "develop-

* Abridged from *Industrial Management Review* of the School of Industrial Management, Massachusetts Institute of Technology, May 1961, 59-77.

ing" him, i.e. changing him in a direction which the organization regards to be in his own and the organization's best interests. Most of the existing conceptions of the development of human resources are built upon assumptions of how people learn and grow, and some of the more strikingly contrasting theories of management development derive from disagreements about such assumptions. I will attempt to build on a different base: instead of starting with assumptions about learning and growth, I will start with some assumptions from the social psychology of influence and attitude change.

Building on this base can be justified quite readily if we consider that adequate managerial performance at the higher levels is at least as much a matter of attitudes as it is a matter of knowledge and specific skills, and that the acquisition of such knowledge and skills is itself in part a function of attitudes. Yet we have given far more attention to the psychology which underlies change in the area of knowledge and abilities than we have to the psychology which underlies change in attitudes. We have surprisingly few studies of how a person develops loyalty to a company, commitment to a job, or a professional attitude toward the managerial role; how he comes to have the motives and attitudes which make possible the rendering of decisions concerning large quantities of money, materials, and human resources; how he develops attitudes toward himself, his co-workers, his employees, his customers, and society in general which give us confidence that he has a sense of responsibility and a set of ethics consistent with his responsible position, or at least which permit us to understand his behavior.

It is clear that management is becoming increasingly professionalized, as evidenced by increasing emphasis on undergraduate and graduate education in the field of management. But professionalization is not only a matter of teaching candidates increasing amounts about a set of relevant subjects and disciplines; it is equally a problem of preparing the candidate for a role which requires a certain set of attitudes. Studies of the medical profession (Merton, Reader, and Kendall, 1957), for example, have turned their attention increasingly to the unravelling of the difficult problem of how the medical student acquires those attitudes and values which enable him to make responsible decisions involving the lives of other people. Similar studies in other professions are sorely needed. When these are undertaken, it is likely to be discovered that much of the training of such attitudes is carried out implicitly and without a clearly formulated rationale. Law schools and medical schools provide various kinds of experiences which insure that the graduate is prepared to fulfill his professional role. Similarly, existing approaches to the development of managers probably provide ample opportunities for the manager to learn the attitudes he will need to fulfill high level jobs. But in this field, particularly, one gets the impression that such opportunities are more the result of intuition or chance than of clearly formulated policies. This is partly because the essential or pivotal aspects of the managerial role have not as yet been clearly delineated, leaving ambiguous both the area of knowledge to be mastered and the attitude to be acquired.

Existing practice in the field of management development involves activities such as: indoctrination and training programs conducted at various points in the manager's career; systematic job rotation involving changes both in the nature of the functions performed (e.g. moving from production into sales), in physical location, and in the individual's superiors; performance appraisal programs including various amounts of testing, general personality assessment, and counseling both within the organization and through the use of outside consultants; apprenticeships, systematic coaching, junior management boards, and special projects to facilitate practice by the young manager in functions he will have to perform later in his career; sponsorship and other comparable activities in which a select group of young managers is groomed systematically for high level jobs (i.e. made into "crown princes"); participation in special conferences and training programs, including professional association meetings, human relations workshops, advanced management programs conducted in business schools or by professional associations like the American Management Association, regular academic courses like the Sloan programs offered at Stanford and MIT, or liberal arts courses like those offered at the University of Pennsylvania, Dartmouth, Northwestern, etc. These and many other specific educational devices, along with elaborate schemes of selection, appraisal, and placement, form the basic paraphernalia of management development.

Most of the methods mentioned above stem from the basic conception that it is the responsibility of the business enterprise, as an institution, to define what kind of behavior and attitude change is to take place and to construct mechanisms by which such change is to occur. Decisions about the kind of activity which might be appropriate for a given manager are usually made by others above him or by specialists hired to make such decisions. Where he is to be rotated, how long he is to remain on a given assignment, or what kind of new training he should undertake, is masterminded by others whose concern is "career development." In a sense, the individual stands alone against the institution where his own career is concerned, because the basic assumption is that the institution knows better than the individual what kind of man it needs or wants in its higher levels of management. The kind of influence model which is relevant, then, is one which considers the whole range of resources available to an organization.

In . . . this paper I will attempt to spell out these general themes by first presenting a conceptual model for analyzing influence, then providing some illustrations from a variety of organizational influence situations,* and then testing its applicability to the management development situation.

A Model of Influence and Change

Most theories of influence or change accept the premise that change does not occur unless the individual is *motivated* and *ready* to change. This statement implies that the individual must perceive some need for change in himself, must be able to change, and must perceive the influencing agent as one who can facilitate such change in a direction acceptable to the individual. A model of the influence process, then, must account for the development of the motivation to change as well as the actual mechanisms by which the change occurs.

It is usually assumed that pointing out to a person some of his areas of deficiency, or some failure on his part in these areas, is sufficient to induce in him a readiness to change and to accept the influencing agent's guidance or recommendations. This assumption may be tenable if one is dealing with deficiencies in intellectual skills or technical knowledge. The young manager can see, with some help from his superiors, that he needs a greater knowledge of economics, or marketing, or production methods, and can accept the suggestion that spending a year in another department or six weeks at an advanced management course will give him the missing knowledge and/or skills.

However, when we are dealing with attitudes, the suggestion of deficiency or the need for change is much more likely to be perceived as a basic threat to the individual's sense of identity and to his status position vis-à-vis others in the organization. Attitudes are generally organized and integrated around the person's image of himself, and they result in stabilized, characteristic ways of dealing with others. The suggestion of the need for change not only implies some criticism of the person's image of himself, but also threatens the stability of his working relationships because change at this level implies that the expectations which others have about him will be upset, thus requiring the development of new rela-

---

* [This section of Schein's article is not included in the present excerpt.]

tionships. It is not at all uncommon for training programs in human relations to arouse resistance or to produce, at best, temporary change because the expectations of co-workers operate to keep the individual in his "normal" mold. Management development programs which ignore these psychological resistances to change are likely to be self-defeating, no matter how much attention is given to the actual presentation of the new desired attitudes.

Given these general assumptions about the integration of attitudes in the person, it is appropriate to consider influence as a process which occurs over time and which includes three phases:

(1) *Unfreezing:** an alteration of the forces acting on the individual, such that his stable equilibrium is disturbed sufficiently to motivate him and to make him ready to change; this can be accomplished either by increasing the pressure to change or by reducing some of the threats or resistances to change.

(2) *Changing:* the presentation of a direction of change and the actual process of learning new attitudes. This process occurs basically by one of two mechanisms: (a) *identification*†—the person learns new attitudes by identifying with and emulating some other person who holds those attitudes; or (b) *internalization*—the person learns new attitudes by being placed in a situation where new attitudes are demanded of him as a way of solving problems which confront him and which he cannot avoid: he discovers the new attitudes essentially for himself, though the situation may guide him or make it probable that he will discover only those attitudes which the influencing agent wishes him to discover.

———

* These phases of influence are a derivation of the change model developed by Lewin (1947).

† These mechanisms of attitude change are taken from Kelman (1958).

(3) *Refreezing:* the integration of the changed attitudes into the rest of the personality and/or into ongoing significant emotional relationships.

In proposing this kind of model of influence we are leaving out two important cases—the individual who changes because he is *forced* to change by the agent's direct manipulation of rewards and punishments (what Kelman calls "compliance") and the individual whose strong motivation to rise in the organizational hierarchy makes him eager to accept the attitudes and acquire the skills which he perceives to be necessary for advancement. I will ignore both of these cases for the same reason—they usually do not involve genuine, stable change, but merely involve the adoption of overt behaviors which imply to others that attitudes have changed, even if they have not. In the case of compliance, the individual drops the overt behavior as soon as surveillance by the influence agent is removed. Among the upwardly mobile individuals, there are those who are willing to be unfrozen and to undergo genuine attitude change (whose case fits the model to be presented below) and those whose overt behavior change is dictated by their changing perception of what the environment will reward, but whose underlying attitudes are never really changed or refrozen.

I do not wish to imply that a general reward-punishment model is incorrect or inappropriate for the analysis of attitude change. My purpose, rather, is to provide a more refined model in terms of which it becomes possible to specify the differential effects of various kinds of rewards and punishments, some of which have far more significance and impact than others. For example, as I will try to show, the rewarding effect of approval from an admired person is very different in its ultimate consequences from the rewarding effect of developing a personal solution to a difficult situation.

The processes of unfreezing, changing, and refreezing can be identified in a variety of different institutions in which they are manifested in varying degrees of intensity. The content of what may be taught in the influence process may vary widely from the values of Communism to the religious doctrines of a nun, and the process of influence may vary drastically in its intensity. . . . Because the value system of the business enterprise and its role conception of the manager are not as clear-cut as the values and role prescriptions in various other institutions, one may expect the processes of unfreezing, changing, and refreezing to occur with less intensity and to be less consciously rationalized in the business enterprise. But they are structurally the same as in other organizations.

. . .

The kind of model which has been discussed above might best be described by the term "coercive persuasion." "The influence of an organization on an individual is coercive in the sense that he is usually forced into situations which are likely to unfreeze him, in which there are many overt and covert pressures to recognize in himself a need for change, and in which the supports for his old attitudes are in varying degrees coercively removed. It is coercive also to the degree that the new attitudes to be learned are relatively rigidly prescribed. The individual either learns them or leaves the organization (if he can). At the same time, the actual process by which new attitudes are learned can best be described as persuasion. In effect, the individual is forced into a situation in which he is likely to be influenced. The organization can be highly coercive in unfreezing its potential influence targets, yet be quite open about the direction of attitude change it will tolerate. In those cases where the direction of change is itself coerced (as con-

trasted with letting it occur through identification or internalization), it is highly unlikely that anything is accomplished other than surface behavioral change in the target. And such surface change will be abandoned the moment the coercive force of the change agent is lessened. If behavioral changes are coerced at the same time as other unfreezing operations are undertaken, actual influence can be facilitated if the individual finds himself having to learn attitudes to justify the kinds of behavior he has been forced to exhibit. The salesman may not have an attitude of cynicism toward his customers initially. If, however, he is forced by his boss to behave as if he felt cynical, he might develop real cynicism as a way of justifying his actual behavior.

Management Development: Is It Coercive Persuasion?

Do the notions of coercive persuasion developed above fit the management development situation? Does the extent to which they do or do not fit such a model illuminate for us some of the implications of specific management development practices?

Unfreezing. It is reasonable to assume that the majority of managers who are being "developed" are not ready or able to change in the manner in which their organization might desire and therefore must be unfrozen before they can be influenced. They may be eager to change at a conscious motivation level, yet still be psychologically unprepared to give up certain attitudes and values in favor of untried, threatening new ones. I cannot support this assumption empirically, but the likelihood of its being valid is high because of a related fact which is empirically supportable. Most managers do not participate heavily in decisions which affect their careers, nor do they have a large voice in the kind of self-development in which they wish to participate. Rather, it is the man's superior or a staff specialist in career development who makes the key decisions concerning his career (Alfred, 1960). If the individual manager is not trained from the outset to take responsibility for his own career and given a heavy voice in diagnosing his own needs for a change, it is unlikely that he will readily be able to appreciate someone else's diagnosis. It may be unclear to him what basically is wanted of him or, worse, the ambiguity of the demands put upon him combined with his own inability to control his career development is likely to arouse anxiety and insecurity which would cause even greater resistance to genuine self-assessment and attitude change.* He becomes preoccupied with promotion in the abstract and attempts to acquire at a surface level the traits which he thinks are necessary for advancement.

If the decisions made by the organization do not seem valid to the manager, or if the unfreezing process turns out to be quite painful to him, to what extent can he leave the situation? His future career, his financial security, and his social status within the business community all stand to suffer if he resists the decisions made for him. Perhaps the most coercive feature is simply the psychological pressure that what he is being asked to do is "for his own ultimate welfare." Elementary loyalty to his organization and to his managerial role demands that he accept with good grace whatever happens to him in the name of his own career development. In this sense, then, I believe that the business organization has coercive forces at its disposal which are used by

it in a manner comparable to the uses made by other organizations.

Given the assumption that the manager who is to be developed needs to be unfrozen, and given that the organization has available coercive power to accomplish such unfreezing, what mechanisms does it actually use to unfreeze potential influence targets?

The essential elements to unfreezing are the removal of supports for the old attitudes, the saturation of the environment with the new attitudes to be acquired, a minimizing threat, and a maximizing of support for any change in the right direction. In terms of this model it becomes immediately apparent that training programs or other activities which are conducted in the organization at the place of work for a certain number of hours per day or week are far less likely to unfreeze and subsequently influence the participant than those programs which remove him for varying lengths of time from his regular work situation and normal social relationships.

Are appraisal interviews, used periodically to communicate to the manager his strengths, weaknesses and areas for improvement, likely to unfreeze him? Probably not, because as long as the individual is caught up in his regular routine and is responding, probably quite unconsciously, to a whole set of expectations which others have about his behavior and attitudes, it is virtually impossible for him to hear, at a psychological level, what his deficiencies or areas needing change are. Even if he can appreciate what is being communicated to him at an intellectual level, it is unlikely that he can emotionally accept the need for change, and even if he can accept it emotionally, it is unlikely that he can produce change in himself in an environment which supports all of his old ways of functioning. This statement does not mean that the man's co-workers

---

* An even greater hazard, of course, is that the organization communicates to the manager that he is not expected to take responsibility for his own career at the same time that it is trying to teach him how to be able to take responsibility for important decisions!

necessarily approve of the way he is operating or like the attitudes which he is exhibiting. They may want to see him change, but their very expectations concerning how he normally behaves operate as a constraint on him which makes attitude change difficult in that setting.

On the other hand, there are a variety of training activities which are used in management development which approximate more closely the conditions necessary for effective unfreezing. These would include programs offered at special training centers such as those maintained by IBM on Long Island and General Electric at Crotonville, N.Y.; university-sponsored courses in management, liberal arts, and/or the social sciences; and especially, workshops or laboratories in human relations such as those conducted at Arden House, N.Y., by the National Training Laboratories. Programs such as these remove the participant for some length of time from his normal routine, his regular job, and his social relationships (including his family in most cases), thus providing a kind of moratorium during which he can take stock of himself and determine where he is going and where he wants to go.

The almost total isolation from the pressures of daily life in the business world which a mountain chateau such as Arden House provides for a two-week period is supplemented by other unfreezing forces. The de-emphasis on the kind of job or title the participant holds in his company and the informal dress remove some of the symbolic or status supports upon which we all rely. Sharing a room and bath facilities with a roommate requires more than the accustomed exposure of private spheres of life to others. The total involvement of the participant in the laboratory program leaves little room for reflection about the back home situation. The climate of the laboratory communicates tremendous support for

any efforts at self-examination and attempts as much as possible to reduce the threats inherent in change by emphasizing the value of experimentation, the low cost and risk of trying a new response in the protected environment of the lab, and the high gains to be derived from finding new behavior patterns and attitudes which might improve back home performance. The content of the material presented in lectures and the kind of learning model which is used in the workshop facilitates self-examination, self-diagnosis based on usable feedback from other participants, and rational planning for change.*

The practice of rotating a manager from one kind of assignment to another over a period of years can have some of the same unfreezing effects and thus facilitate attitude change. Certainly his physical move from one setting to another removes many of the supports to his old attitudes, and in his new job the manager will have an opportunity to try new behaviors and become exposed to new attitudes. The practice of providing a moratorium in the form of a training program prior to assuming a new job would appear to maximize the gains from each approach, in that unfreezing would be maximally facilitated and change would most probably be lasting if the person did not go back to a situation in which his co-workers, superiors, and subordinates had stable expectations of how he should behave.

Another example of how unfreezing can be facilitated in the organizational context is the practice of temporarily reducing the formal rank and responsibilities of the manager by making him a trainee in a special program, or an apprentice on a special project, or an as-

---

* Although, as I will point out later, such effective unfreezing may lead to change which is not supported or considered desirable by the "back home" organization.

sistant to a high ranking member of the company. Such temporary lowering of formal rank can reduce the anxiety associated with changing and at the same time serves officially to destroy the old status and identity of the individual because he could not ordinarily return to his old position once he had accepted the path offered by the training program. He would have to move either up or out of the organization to maintain his sense of self-esteem. Of course, if such a training program is perceived by the trainee as an indication of his failing rather than a step toward a higher position, his anxiety about himself would be too high to facilitate effective change on his part. . . . If participants come to training programs believing they are being punished, they typically do not learn much.

The above discussion is intended to highlight the fact that some management development practices do facilitate the unfreezing of the influence target, but that such unfreezing is by no means automatic. Where programs fail, therefore, one of the first questions we must ask is whether they failed because they did not provide adequate conditions for unfreezing.

Changing. Turning now to the problem of the mechanisms by which changes actually occur, we must confront the question of whether the organization has relatively rigid prescribed goals concerning the direction of attitude change it expects of the young manager, or whether it is concerned with growth in the sense of providing increasing opportunities for the young manager to learn the attitudes appropriate to ever more challenging situations. It is undoubtedly true that most programs would claim growth as their goal, but the degree to which they accomplish it can only be assessed from an examination of their actual practice.

Basically the question is whether the organization influences attitudes primarily through the mechanism of identification or the mechanism of internalization. If the development programs stimulate psychological relationships between the influence target and a member of the organization who has the desired attitudes, they are thereby facilitating influence by identification but, at the same time, are limiting the alternatives available to the target and possibly the permanence of the change achieved. If they emphasize that the target must develop his own solutions to ever more demanding problems, they are risking that the attitudes learned will be incompatible with other parts of the organization's value system but are producing more permanent change because the solutions found are internalized. From the organization's point of view, therefore, it is crucial to know what kind of influence it is exerting and to assess the results of such influence in terms of the basic goals which the organization may have. If new approaches and new attitudes toward management problems are desired, for example, it is crucial that the conditions for internalization be created. If rapid learning of a given set of attitudes is desired, it is equally crucial that the conditions for identification with the right kind of models be created.

One obvious implication of this distinction is that programs conducted within the organization's orbit by its own influence agents are much more likely to facilitate identification and thereby the transmission of the "party line" or organization philosophy. On the other hand, programs like those conducted at universities or by the National Training Laboratories place much more emphasis on the finding of solutions by participants which fit their own particular needs and problems. The emphasis in the human relations courses is on "learning how to learn" from the participant's own interpersonal experiences and how to harness his emotional life and intellectual capacities to the accomplishment of his goals, rather than on specific principles of human relations. The nearest thing to an attitude which the laboratory staff, acting as influence agents, does care to communicate is an attitude of inquiry and experimentation, and to this end the learning of skills of observation, analysis, and diagnosis of interpersonal situations is given strong emphasis. The training group, which is the acknowledged core of the laboratory approach, provides its own unfreezing forces by being unstructured as to the content of discussion. But it is strongly committed to a method of learning by analysis of the member's own experiences in the group, which facilitates the discovery of the value of an attitude of inquiry and experimentation.

Mutual identification of the members of the group with each other and member identifications with the staff play some role in the acquisition of this attitude, but the basic power of the method is that the attitude of inquiry and experimentation *works* in the sense of providing for people valuable new insights about themselves, groups, and organizations. To the extent that it works and solves key problems for the participants, it is internalized and carried back into the home situation. To the extent that it is learned because participants wish to emulate a respected fellow member or staff member, it lasts only so long as the relationship with the model itself, or a surrogate of it, lasts (which may, of course, be a very long time).

The university program in management or liberal arts is more difficult to categorize in terms of an influence model, because within the program there are usually opportunities both for identification (e.g. with inspiring teachers) and internalization. It is a safe guess in either case, however, that the attitudes learned are likely to be in varying degrees out of phase with any given company's philosophy unless the company has learned from previous experience with a given course that the students are taught a point of view consistent with its own philosophy. Of course, universities, as much as laboratories, emphasize the value of a spirit of inquiry and, to the extent that they are successful in teaching this attitude, will be creating potential dissidents or innovators, depending on how the home company views the result.

Apprenticeships, special jobs in the role of "assistant to" somebody, job rotation, junior management boards, and so on stand in sharp contrast to the above methods in the degree to which they facilitate, indeed almost demand, that the young manager learn by watching those who are senior or more competent. It is probably not prescribed that in the process of acquiring knowledge and skills through the example of others he should also acquire their attitudes, but the probability that this will happen is very high if the trainee develops any degree of respect and liking for his teacher and/or supervisor. It makes little difference whether the teacher, coach, or supervisor intends to influence the attitudes of his trainee or not. If a good emotional relationship develops between them, it will facilitate the learning of knowledge and skills, and will, at the same time, result in some degree of attitude change. Consequently, such methods do not maximize the probability of new approaches being invented to management problems, nor do they really by themselves facilitate the growth of the manager in the sense of providing opportunities for him to develop solutions which fit his own needs best.

Job rotation, on the other hand, can facilitate growth and innovation provided it is managed in such a way as to insure the exposure of the trainee to a broad range of points of view as he moves from assignment to assignment. The practice of shifting the developing manager geographically as well as functionally both facilitates unfreezing and increases the likelihood of his being exposed to new attitudes. This same practice can, of course, be merely a convenient way of indoctrinating the individual by sending him on an assignment, for example, "in order to acquire the sales point of view from Jim down in New York," where higher management knows perfectly well what sort of view Jim will communicate to his subordinates.

Refreezing. Finally, a few words are in order about the problem of refreezing. Under what conditions will changed attitudes remain stable, and how do existing practices aid or hinder such stabilization? [There is evidence to suggest] the importance of social support for any attitudes which were learned through identification. Even the kind of training emphasized in the National Training Laboratories programs, which tends to be more internalized, does not produce stable attitude change unless others in the organization, especially superiors, peers, and subordinates, have undergone similar changes and give each other stimulation and support, because lack of support acts as a new unfreezing force producing new influence (possibly in the direction of the original attitudes).

If the young manager has been influenced primarily in the direction of what is already the company philosophy, he will, of course, obtain strong support and will have little difficulty maintaining his new attitudes. If, on the other hand, management development is supposed to lead to personal growth and organizational innovation, the organization must recognize the reality that new attitudes cannot be carried by isolated individuals. The lament that we no longer have strong individualists who are willing to try something new is a fallacy based on an incorrect diagnosis. Strong individuals have al-

ways gained a certain amount of their strength from the support of others, hence the organizational problem is how to create conditions which make possible the nurturing of new ideas, attitudes, and approaches. If organizations seem to lack innovators, it may be that the climate of the organization and its methods of management development do not foster innovation, not that its human resources are inadequate.

An organizational climate in which new attitudes which differ from company philosophy can nevertheless be maintained cannot be achieved merely by an intellectual or even emotional commitment on the part of higher-ranking managers to tolerance of new ideas and attitudes. Genuine support can come only from others who have themselves been influenced, which argues strongly that at least several members of a given department must be given the same training before such training can be expected to have effect. If the superior of the people involved can participate in it as well, this strengthens the group that much more, but it would not follow from my line of reasoning that this is a necessary condition. Only some support is needed, and this support can come as well from peers and subordinates.

From this point of view, the practice of sending more than one manager to any given program at a university or human relations workshop is very sound. The National Training Laboratories have emphasized from the beginning the desirability of having organizations send teams. Some organizations like Esso Standard have created their own laboratories for the training of the entire management complement of a given refinery, and all indications are that such a practice maximizes the possibility not only of the personal growth of the managers, but of the creative growth of the organization as a whole.

References

Alfred, T. M. Personal communication, 1960.

Hulme, K. *The nun's story.* Boston: Little, Brown, 1957.

Kelman, H. C. Compliance, identification, and internalization: three processes of attitude change. *Conflict Resolution,* 1958, *2,* 51-60.

Lewin, K. Frontiers in group dynamics: concept, method and reality in social science. *Hum. Relat.,* 1947, *I,* 5-42.

McGregor, D. *The human side of enterprise.* New York, McGraw-Hill, 1960.

Merton, R. K., Reader, G. G., and Kendall, Patricia L. *The student-physician.* Cambridge, Mass., Harvard University Press, 1957.

National Training Laboratory in Group Development: *Explorations in human relations training: an assessment of experience, 1947-1953.* Washington, D.C., National Education Association, 1953.

Schein, E. H. *Brainwashing.* Cambridge, Mass., Center for International Studies, M.I.T., 1961.

Schein, E. H. Interpersonal communication, group solidarity, and social influence. *Sociometry,* 1960, *23,* 148-161.

A beginning requirement for all participants in management development programs would seem to be a favorable attitude toward their administrative responsibilities. Miner, in the reading that follows, reports evidence that such an attitude is associated with effective performance in management. He goes on to describe a kind of management development course that changed the attitudes toward supervision and administration of a sizable number of the participants from unfavorable to favorable. Such unfavorable attitudes to administrative tasks are likely to be found in scientists and researchers who are brought into management, a frequent happening these days. The type of program he describes thus demands close attention.

READING 5-6

Management Development and Attitude Change*

JOHN B. MINER

Management development has in recent years become a major item in the industrial relations budget. In so far as this money has been spent on programs which impart specific knowledge, that can be directly put to work in managerial positions, there can be little question but what the investment has paid off. For various reasons, however, two other approaches have achieved considerable popularity and in many organizations have pushed the teaching of job-related knowledge into the back seat, if not completely out of the car. One of these, the program aimed at intellectual broadening through study of the humanities, emphasizes knowledge training, but learning is deliberately deflected into channels far removed from the managerial job. At least one research investigation has demonstrated the change-producing potential of such training.[1] There was a clear-cut

* From *Personnel Administration,* May-June, Vol. 24, No. 3. (1961), pp. 21-26.

[1] Morris S. Viteles, "Human Relations and the Humanities in the Education of Business Leaders: Evaluation of a Program of Humanistic Studies for Executives," *Personnel Psychology,* 1959, *12,* 1-28.

increase in knowledge of subject matter in the humanities and social sciences, a considerable development of interest in art, a decline in economic values, and a shift to less conservative and more liberal attitudes.

The third approach on the other hand, has achieved widespread popularity, and incidentally a sizable chunk of the management development budget, with only a very minimal amount of evidence available as to what it accomplishes. I have in mind the various programs designed to produce attitude change and personality development. There are, of course, a great diversity of such programs and one, at least, actually has been demonstrated to produce attitude change.[2] The various procedures designed to build confidence and those that have developed out of work in the areas of group dynamics and group psychotherapy remain, however, a completely unknown quantity in so far as their contribution to job effectiveness is concerned. It may be that management is investing wisely when it puts its money into such programs, but the evidence is surprisingly lacking.

The Research and Development Study: Procedure

For over three years now a research program intended to provide information on the relationship between management development and attitude change has been in progress. To date this work has been concentrated on the evaluation of a specific course designed toward the supervisory job. It has been our impression, and we have research evidence to support this,[3] that managers who like

supervisory activities tend to be considered better managers. Accordingly it seemed logical to assume that any procedure which created a more favorable attitude toward the supervisory job would also serve a valuable management development function. The first opportunity to investigate this conclusion came when I was asked to conduct a course for a group of 72 supervisors in the R & D Department of a large corporation. These men had clearly subordinated their supervisory activities to their scientific interests. Many had very negative attitudes toward the job of supervisor.

A course was devised which we hoped would produce a change in this attitude and in doing so bring about a shift to a more effective level of supervisory performance. There were 10 weekly sessions lasting approximately one and a half hours each. In order to permit discussion, the supervisors were split into 4 groups. However, the presentation was largely in lecture form and discussion was characteristically limited to clarification of specific points. The lecture content emphasized the diverse factors acting to bring about performance failure. Theoretical formulations and research findings drawn from the psychological literature made up a considerable part of the material. The men were put in the position of supervisors who had to figure out why one of their subordinates was performing ineffectively. Stress was placed on understanding the various strategic factors that might be involved in performance failure and on the techniques that might be used to correct it. The strategic factors discussed were those identified in the course of studies carried out by the staff of the Conservation of Human Resources Project at Columbia University. These studies utilized the personnel records of World War II soldiers and have been published in the three-volume

Ineffective Soldier series. The specific lecture topics were:[4]

1. Research evidence on the relationship between supervisor behavior and work group productivity.
2. The relationships between physical condition, motor dexterity, general intelligence, special abilities, and performance.
3. The nature of emotional disorder and its effect on performance.
4. Work motivation and work performance.
5. Family relationships and their effects on work.
6. The work group, its cohesiveness, morale and leadership as related to performance.
7. Organizational policy and individual performance.
8. Value conflict as a determinant of ineffective performance.
9. Situational factors, both real and imaginary, which produce and affect performance.
10. The fear-provoking aspects of the supervisory situation and their contribution to managerial ineffectiveness.

Throughout the presentation of these topics, the challenges and responsibilities of supervisory work were constantly emphasized.

In order to determine whether the course actually was changing attitudes as desired, a special measure of attitudes toward various aspects of supervisory work was developed and administered to 55 of the men just before they started training and again after the last session had been conducted. The questionnaire was of the sentence completion type and the items were so disguised as to keep from the supervisors any knowledge of what was actually being measured. Since the scoring procedure is rather complex, and in addition, has been described at length in another article,[5] no detailed explanation will be presented here. It is sufficient to note that the questionnaire has adequate reliability for group comparisons of this type and that it correlates significantly with management appraisal ratings of job performance and potential for advancement, as well as with managerial grade level.

Since it is important in studies like this to be sure that any changes detected are really a result of the training, a control group containing 30 supervisors in the R & D Department who did not take the course was also used. These men took the questionnaire as the course started and again as it ended. Any change in attitude found among those in training which was replicated in this control group, would obviously be a result of factors other than the management development effort proper.

The Research and Development Study: Results

A comparison of the pre-training questionnaire results with those obtained after the completion of the program indicated clearly that the desired results had been attained. Sixty-four per cent of the men had developed more favorable attitudes toward supervisory work during training, 14 per cent did not change, and 22 per cent became somewhat more negative in their attitudes. Obviously the positive effect was not universal, but when viewed in the context of what happened to the control group, it is rather striking. Only 20 per cent of those who did not take the

[4] See in particular the second volume—Eli Ginzberg, John B. Miner, James K. Anderson, Sol W. Ginsburg, and John L. Herma, *Breakdown and Recovery* (New York: Columbia University Press, 1959).

[5] John B. Miner, "The Effect of a Course in Psychology on the Attitudes of Research and Development Supervisors," *Journal of Applied Psychology*, 1960, *44*, 224-232.

course improved in attitude during the period, 20 per cent remained unchanged, and 60 per cent developed a more negative feeling about the supervisory job.

A more detailed analysis of the questionnaire responses indicated that the major change in the control group was a very marked increase in negative attitudes toward engaging in competitive activities. It is not exactly clear what caused this change, but there is some reason to believe it represented a response to the threat of departmental reorganization. Throughout the period during which the training program was in progress there were constant rumors that the R & D Department would be drastically reduced in size and changed in organizational structure. Apparently this threat had the general effect of forcing many supervisors to devalue their own individual ambitions and competitive wishes in order to present a united front against the forces external to the department which were pressing toward change. Those in the training program did not experience a similar attitude change even though the supervisors who participated in the course must have been subjected to exactly the same pressures as those who did not.

In addition to protecting the supervisors from external forces which otherwise would have produced negative attitudes toward competitive activities, the training also induced a considerable increase in positive attitudes toward imposing one's wishes on others, toward performing the routine administrative duties inherent in management positions, and toward the supervisory job generally. These changes were all reliable statistically. In view of our knowledge of the relationships between such attitudes and managerial performance, there seems to be little doubt but what this particular course did improve the caliber of supervision in the R & D Department.

How long this improvement may have lasted is unknown. The reorganization did occur and further study was impossible. However, because the questionnaires were filled out the second time over a six week period, with some men returning them immediately after training and some delaying for a considerable period of time, it was possible to get some check on permanency. A comparison of the attitude change existing immediately after training with that present two to six weeks later, produced no evidence of any difference. Clearly the improvement was maintained for well over a month.

The School of Business Study

More recently the effects of a similar course on the attitudes of undergraduate students in the School of Business at the University of Oregon have been investigated. In this instance the course content was expanded somewhat and presented in 25 one-hour lectures over an 11 week period. Since the class contained 59 students, there was practically no opportunity for discussion of the material. The cases in *Breakdown and Recovery* were used as supplementary reading and two examinations were given during the term. In general, however, the content of the training was practically identical with that employed in the R & D Department. The major changes were the shift to a straight lecture presentation and the utilization of students preparing for managerial work rather than practicing managers.

The results obtained from a comparison of attitude questionnaires administered at the beginning and end of the course were very similar to those of the previous study. Sixty-six per cent of the students developed a more positive attitude toward supervisory work, 10 per cent remained at the same level, and 24 per cent developed more negative attitudes. Although these percentages are almost identical with those found in the industrial setting, the extent of the positive shift in attitude among those who did improve was more pronounced among the students than among the supervisors. Thus, the over-all impact of training seems to have been somewhat greater for the student group.

Unfortunately, it was not possible to use a control group in connection with this preliminary study. However, the course was given again to a new group of students the following term and the attitude questionnaire was administered during the first meeting to a group of 71 students. These people had been in residence at the university and had been taking courses in the business school during the preceding term but had not taken the management development course. If the attitude change noted during the previous term was a direct result of training, then these new students should score at the same level on the questionnaire as the previous group had, before training started. Such a finding would provide at least presumptive evidence that factors external to the course had not induced the attitude change. Actually the average score for the new group was almost identical to that obtained when the first group started training. It looks very much as if the impact of the course on student attitudes is very similar to the effect on industrial managers. However, additional studies employing control groups are now in progress with a view to providing conclusive evidence on this point.

By way of addendum, I should note that our studies so far have given no indication that there is any relationship between the extent of attitude change and either the amount of learning (as determined by examinations based on course material) or intelligence. The same holds for initial attitude questionnaire score, job grade, performance ratings, and po-

tential for advancement ratings, when compared against the extent of attitude change.

Conclusions

Taken as a whole the research program to date has provided evidence for the following conclusions:

1. A favorable attitude toward supervisory work is an important factor in managerial performance. People who enjoy supervising others, who find pleasure in organizing and directing the work of subordinates, are more likely to be good managers than those who dislike such activities or find them emotionally disturbing.

2. Management development courses can modify attitudes, such as those toward supervisory work, which are directly related to the effectiveness of managerial performance. The change-producing potential of management development courses is not limited to the implanting of specific knowledge.

3. One very effective method of producing attitude change is a lecture course which places considerable emphasis on scientific theory and research findings relevant to supervisory practice; and which presents clearly the challenges, pleasures and responsibilities inherent in managerial work. This is not to say that other, very different approaches cannot achieve a similar result; only that the effectiveness of these other approaches has not yet been demonstrated.

4. Attitude change through management development is equally possible during the early stages of a man's career when he is preparing himself for a business position and at a later date when he has already assumed managerial responsibilities. The findings suggest that both the newly hired trainee and the more mature manager can benefit.

Human Relations Programs

Human relations training differs from management development in that it emphasizes, almost exclusively, the interpersonal aspects of the manager's role; and in focusing on relationships in his current job situation is less likely to be directly concerned with development for future promotion. The human relations emphasis in training originated as an outgrowth of the Hawthorne studies. It gained momentum in the period of World War II. During the decade 1950-1960 it was subject to considerable re-examination and some criticism, a process that has continued.

In 1957, Argyris (p. 139) described human relations as a "faddistic reaction" of management to the poor work habits of employees. He went on to decry the fact that such training was frequently offered as a panacea for most industrial ills. In the same year McNair while expressing his respect for human relations research in the social sciences and his awareness of the ethical canons demanding that we consider the dignity of the individual human being, nevertheless, severely criticized skill training in human relations. He listed, as some of its dangers, crude exploitation and manipulation, an undermining of personal responsibility, and its presumed tendency to reduce to unimportance in management the process of analysis, judgment, and decision making. Tannenbaum, in calmer tones, describes the several meanings of the term human relations as: an intra- and interpersonal phenomenon, a tool kit for practitioners, an ethical orientation, and a scientific discipline.

We avoid the lengthy controversial aspects of the topic. We identify human relations training (in all its varieties) as one means that business and industry has used to seek to change (or form) attitudes. We consider it as any program designed to focus on such qualities of supervision as employee-centeredness, considerateness behavior, or supportive leadership.*

A subcategory under human relations training is role-playing. Originally developed in the psychiatric field by Moreno, it has been widely described (Maier, *et al.*) as a helpful technique in attitude-change aspects of human relations training programs. In 1956 J. H. Mann summarized experimental studies of the effect of role-playing, suggesting that we have been expecting from it more than the evidence indicates it can deliver. Because of its dramatic and interest value, there is, nevertheless, every indication that it will continue to be used. In view of some positive results reported by Harvey and Beverly with a varied form of role-playing, its continued use may prove helpful.

The human relations effort in business and industry and its effectiveness in changing attitudes is described in the following excerpt of a paper by Mann. In view of the uncertain effects of human relations training programs, he and a number of his associates in the Human Relations Program of the University

---

* Terms used by Kahn, Shartle, and Likert at various points in the history of human relations training.

of Michigan Institute for Social Research have developed some techniques for effecting change in attitude and subsequent behavior. Their approach recognizes that effective change in attitude (leading to change in behavior) can be facilitated when the organizational setting itself is modified. To accomplish this, they suggest a system of information feedback at all levels of the organization. The basic elements of their feedback system involve: (1) the orderly collection of information about the functioning of the system; (2) the feeding of this information into the system; and (3) its use in making further adjustments.

READING 5-7

Studying and Creating Change: A Means to Understanding Social Organization*

F. C. MANN

. . .

Recurrent opportunities for social scientists to study a change process within an organizational setting are provided by human relations training programs for supervisors. As change procedures, these programs are formal, rational, purposeful efforts to alter institutional behavior. In contrast to the day-to-day attempts of management to bring about change, they are bounded in time and organizational space, and are thus easily studied intensively.

. . .

Management by the late forties began to be convinced that training might be useful for their supervisors, and there has since been a wholesale adoption of human relations training programs. While there was and still is a remarkable range in the content, methods, and settings of these programs, nearly all of them have

centered around improving supervisory skills in dealing with people—either as individuals or in face-to-face groups. They are frequently directed at teaching the supervisor how to work with an employee as an individual, occasionally at working with employees as members of a small group, but only rarely at understanding and working within the complex social system of the large corporation or factory. Another way of saying this is that the courses have drawn heavily from psychology, to a lesser extent from social psychology, and usually not at all from sociology.

There are no commonly agreed-upon ways by which these programs can be described. The following headings are, however, useful: objectives, content, methods, setting, training leader, and training unit. For example, the objectives of these programs are usually very general and quite ambitious: "to assist supervisors in developing the skills, knowledge, and attitudes needed to carry out their supervisory responsibilities," or "to improve morale, increase production, and

* From *Research in Industrial Human Relations,* edited by Conrad M. Arensberg, *et al.,* Copyright © 1957 by Harper & Row, Publishers, Incorporated. Reprinted with their permission.

reduce turnover." Their contents usually include human nature, personality, motivation, attitudes, and leadership, and other information about relevant psychological principles and research findings may also be included. More often than not the methods of training are some variant of the "lecture-discussion method." The settings are frequently in a classroom away from the job. The trainers are generally staff men whom the trainee did not know before the training; the trainees, first-line supervisors or foremen meeting with other supervisors from other parts of the organization.

Few systematic, quantitative studies have been made to investigate the effectiveness of these programs.[4] This is not to say that there has been no interest in evaluation. Any review of the literature will indicate many such attempts and many testimonials about the relative advantages of different procedures of training. Mahler and Monroe[5] reported a number of "evaluative studies" after reviewing the literature and conducting a survey of 150 companies known to have training programs. While these studies almost without fail acclaim the many benefits of such training, few of them meet more than a fraction of the requirements necessary for a rigorous test of the basic underlying assumptions.

What are these assumptions? In general, they are that training supervisors in human relations will result in changes in the supervisors' attitudes and philosophy, that these changes will be reflected in their behavior toward employees on the job, that this changed behavior will be seen by the employees, and that they will in turn become more satisfied with their work situation, then more highly motivated, and, ultimately, more productive workers.

While there is a good deal of evidence that human relations training programs do meet part of these assumptions—e.g., they do appear to change the verbal veneer of supervisors—there are few scientifically rigorous, quantitative studies which have demonstrated that these changes in what supervisors *know* affect their attitudes and behavior as seen or experienced by their subordinates. Few studies show that human relations training of supervisors is related to changes in the attitudes or productivity of employees under those supervisors.

It is not possible to make a complete review of these studies here. A review of the findings from several recent, major evaluative studies will, however, provide a good deal of evidence concerning the effectiveness of certain types of training programs. The findings will certainly emphasize the need for more systematic, quantitative research to assess the most effective combinations of content, methods, settings, training units, and trainers.

The Canter-Tyler Studies

In 1949, Canter[6] developed a human relations training course for first-line supervisors in the home offices of a large insurance company. The three objectives of the course were "(1) to establish facts and principles concerning psychological aspects of behavior and group functioning to enable supervisors to become more competent in their knowledge and under-

---

[4] A nonquantitative, but extraordinarily thorough and insightful study of foreman training was made by A. Zaleznik, *Foreman Training in a Growing Enterprise* (Boston: Graduate School of Business Administration, Harvard University, 1951).
[5] W. R. Mahler and W. H. Monroe, *How Industry Determines the Need for and Effectiveness of Training*, Personnel Research Section Report 929 (Washington: Department of the Army, 1952).

[6] R. R. Canter, "A Human Relations Training Program," *Journal of Applied Psychology*, XXXV (February 1951), pp. 38-45.

standing of human behavior; (2) to increase supervisors' capacities for observing human behavior; and (3) to present personality adjustment concepts to aid in integration of achievements made in the first two objectives." This training was designed to provide a foundation of information on which to build later through additional practice and "technique" training. Specific content was primarily psychological: human nature, personality, motivation, attitudes, leadership, and group structure. Method was lecture-discussion. The training occurred in the conference rooms of the company; Canter himself was the trainer. The trainees were eighteen supervisors whose superiors had participated in a preliminary run for executives. The course was presented in ten two-hour weekly sessions.

To determine the influence of this training, Canter employed a battery of paper-and-pencil questionnaires and tests which were given before and after training to two groups of supervisors: an experimental group of eighteen from one department who received the training, and a control group of eighteen from two other departments who did not receive training. The two groups were similar in type of work performed, age (about thirty), education (thirteen years), and proportion of men and women. While the control group had more years of service with the company (7.5 and 4.6, respectively) and higher mean scores on a mental alertness test, the statistical technique used in the final analysis did not require prematched individuals or groups.

Six tests, yielding a total of twelve separate scores, were used. (1) General Psychological Facts and Principles; (2) "How Supervise"; (3) General Logical Reasoning; (4) Social Judgment Test; (5) Supervisory Questionnaire; and (6) Test for Ability to Estimate Group Opinion. The major findings were that the trained supervisors obtained mean scores on all tests better than would have been predicted on the basis of the performance of the untrained group alone. For five out of the twelve measures, the differences were statistically significant at the 5 per cent level; for two other measures, differences were significant at the 10 per cent level. Other important conclusions were that trained supervisors became more similar in abilities measured by the tests and more accurate in estimating the opinions of employees in their departments, but not their sections. It was also found that those holding highest scores initially gained the most on all measures except the Test of Ability to Estimate Group Opinion, where the opposite result was obtained.

While Canter assumed in his design that cognitive training—i.e., an ability to understand human relations concepts and principles—would have to precede any behavioral training in supervisory skill, practices, and attitudes, Tyler[7] designed a companion study to measure any changes in employee morale which might be attributed to this training. Her morale surveys indicated improvement in employee morale scores for *both* the experimental and control departments. Morale improved by an average of 11 points per section (range 2-25 points) in five of seven sections in the experimental group, and decreased slightly in two others. "In the control groups, morale increased in eight of the nine sections by an average of 14 points (range 5-32 points). The decrease in the other section was seven points. The only category which showed a somewhat consistent change among sections was 'supervision' on which scores for over half of the sections decreased." After warning the reader of the possible effect of the before-test experience, she

---

[7] B. B. Tyler, "A Study of Factors Contributing to Employee Morale" (Master's thesis, Ohio State University, 1949).

notes: "Undoubtedly, the difference in change in morale between the control and the experimental groups is not large enough to be significant" (page 47). Canter, however, points out that in Tyler's study "morale was quite high initially, which might account for the lack of any improvement in the experimental department over the control."

The strength of the Canter-Tyler studies is that they used both *before* and *after* measures for experimental and control groups. Canter's use of multiple criteria against which to evaluate the various sub-goals of the training program is also noteworthy. The use of Tyler's perceptual and employee morale measures in conjunction with Canter's attitudinal and cognitive measures permits an evaluation of the course's effectiveness at two levels: the supervisor's intent, and his on-the-job performance. The findings from this combination of studies make it obvious that classroom learning does not guarantee the translation of such learning into job performance. It should be remembered, however, that Canter did not set out to change supervisors' skills and practices, but only their understanding of human relations concepts and ideas.

Fleishman-Harris Studies

Working with the education and training staff of a large company manufacturing trucks and farm machinery, Fleishman[8] developed a study design and a battery of research instruments for measuring the continuing effectiveness of leadership training. The general objectives of this training[9] were to change

[8] Edwin A. Fleishman, "Leadership Climate, Human Relations Training, and Supervisory Behavior," *Personnel Psychology*, VI (Summer 1953), pp. 205-222.
[9] Charles L. Walker, Jr., "Education and Training at International Harvester," *Harvard Business Review*, XXVII (September 1949), pp. 542-558.

understanding, attitudes, habits, and skill of foremen by giving them solid foundation in four basic areas of industrial knowledge. These areas were personal development, human relations, economics, and company operations. The method was primarily lecture-discussion. The training staff included full-time instructors, former supervisors, and part-time university faculty. The training was given to foremen who were taken from a wide variety of operations and plants and sent to a central school in Chicago for two weeks of eight-hours-a-day intensive development.

To determine the effects of this course on foremen from one motor-truck plant who had taken this training, Fleishman employed an *ex post facto* design with four groups of about thirty each. One group had not received the training; the other three had, 2-10, 11-19, and 20-29 months earlier. The groups were alike on a number of background characteristics: age (early forties), education (eleven years), length of service (sixteen years), supervisory experience (seven years), size of work group (about twenty-eight), and supervisory experience with present work group (six years). Seven paper-and-pencil questionnaires were used to obtain opinion, expectation, and perceptual data about leadership practices from the trainees, their superiors, and their subordinates. This battery gave Fleishman an opportunity to investigate the differences between supervisory beliefs as reported by the foreman himself and supervisory practices as reported by his employees, and to explore the interaction of training effects with the supervisor's "leadership climate." Each questionnaire contained two independent leadership dimensions which had been identified by factor analysis: "consideration"—the extent to which the supervisor was considerate of the feelings of employees; and "initiating structure"—the extent to which the supervisor defined or facilitated group interactions toward goal attainment.

The results obtained by giving attitude questionnaires to foremen on the first and last days of their training in Chicago provide evidence of how the topics stressed in this leadership training affected these two dimensions. The results obtained from these before and after measures showed a significant increase in "consideration" (.05 level) and an even more marked decrease in "initiating structure" (.01 level). The on-the-job effects of the training, however, appeared to be "minimal." "The training did not produce any kind of permanent change in either the attitudes or behavior of the trained foremen." The employees under the most recently trained foremen actually saw them as *less* considerate than the employees under the untrained foremen saw their superiors. This statistically significant finding was supported by other trends toward more structuring and less consideration by those foremen who had the training. Thus, while the human relations approach was stressed in the course and understood at least well enough to be registered as an opinion change on a paper-and-pencil questionnaire, it was not evident in what trained foremen said they did, or what their employees saw them doing in the actual work situation.

The most important variable found to affect leadership was the climate within which the foreman worked. In fact, the kind of superior under whom the foreman operated seemed "more related to the attitudes and behavior of the foremen in the plant than did the fact that they had or had not received the leadership training."

These results, showing that the training was not meeting its objective of making foremen more human-relations oriented in the plant, left two alternatives

open: redesign the course, or initiate an intensive criterion study relating supervisory behavior to group effectiveness. The latter alternative was chosen, and Harris[10] designed a study in the same plant to investigate (1) the relationship between these two dimensions of leadership behavior and various measures of work efficiency, and (2) the effects of a training course planned as a brief refresher for the central school training in Chicago. It is the findings from this second objective in which we are primarily interested here.

The course, lasting one week, was given at a small nearby college. The effects were evaluated by field experimental design with before and after measures for experimental and control groups. Two groups of thirty-one foremen were established through matching on a number of variables, including length of time since attending the central school (almost three years), scores on before measures (including leadership climate), and other personal factors. One group was given the training. Questionnaires, similar to Fleishman's, were used to obtain information from employees and foremen about the foremen's attitudes and behavior.

Harris used several different methods of analyzing his findings. His most rigorous method indicated there were no statistically significant differences in the foremen's own leadership attitudes or the workers' descriptions of their foremen's behavior—before and after this additional refresher course. The only significant difference he found was a decrease in the degree to which the foremen in the *control* group showed structuring in their leadership behavior as described by their

---

[10] E. F. Harris, "Measuring Industrial Leadership and Its Implications for Training Supervisors" (Doctoral thesis, Ohio State University, 1952).

employees. Building on Fleishman's gradual decreases in structuring and increases in consideration the longer the foreman is back on the job, Harris suggests this finding might be interpreted to mean that the refresher course may have "tended to retard a general decrease in structuring."

Harris and Fleishman[11] in analyzing the data from both of their studies in the same plant have uncovered one finding which tends to qualify the general, completely negative conclusion of their findings regarding the effectiveness of this training. This finding concerns the stability of leadership patterns of individual foremen who did not have the training in contrast to those foremen who had the training. They find there is *less* stability in the pre-post measures for the foremen who had the training than for those foremen who did not have training. This suggests that the courses had markedly different effects on different foremen, and that "large individual shifts in scores occur in both directions." They conclude that their research findings show no significant changes in *group* means among trained foremen and that future research should be directed toward investigating personal and situational variables which interact with the effects of training.

At best, these two studies suggest that this type of training has little or no general effect on the behavior of foremen in the plant. At worst, they suggest that the unanticipated consequences of separating foremen from their work groups and making them keenly aware of their role in management more than offset the anticipated consequences of making the foremen more considerate of

employees as human beings. Fleishman's finding that *leadership climate* appeared to be a better predictor than *training* of foremen's plant attitudes and behavior underscores the importance of considering the constellation of expectation patterns in which the trainee is embedded. Training which does not take the trainee's regular social environment into account will probably have little chance of modifying behavior. It may very well be that human relations training—as a procedure for initiating social change—is most successful when it is designed to *remold the whole system of role relationships of the supervisor.*[12]

The findings from these four studies suggest that trainers, researchers, and others interested in social change need to rethink what forces are necessary to create and sustain changes in the orientation and behaviors of people in complex systems of relationships. There is a good deal of evidence that management and trainees are enthusiastic about these training courses in general. Management's enthusiasm may be an index of whether the training will continue, but it does not indicate whether training is achieving changes in behavior. And while trainee satisfaction and acceptance may be important as an antecedent to learning, these factors do not indicate whether the training will produce attitudinal and, more significantly, on-the-job behavioral changes.

It should be stressed that the criterion which has been used here for measuring the effects of human relations training is not easily met. There is ample quantitative evidence in the preceding studies that supervisors' information about, and verbal understanding of, human relations

---

[11] E. F. Harris and E. A. Fleishman, "Human Relations Training and the Stability of Leadership Patterns," *Journal of Applied Psychology,* XXXIX (February 1955), pp. 20-25.

[12] For a full account of these two studies combined, see E. A. Fleishman, E. F. Harris, and H. E. Burtt, *Leadership and Supervision in Industry* (Columbus: Personnel Research Board, Ohio State University, 1955).

principles can be increased. There is much less evidence that these courses have an effect on the trainee's on-the-job behavior as seen by those working under him. And the hard fact remains that there are no quantitative studies which indicate that these courses in leadership affect workers' job satisfactions or motivations.

FEEDBACK: CHANGING PATTERNS
OF RELATIONSHIPS BETWEEN SUPERIORS
AND SUBORDINATES BY USING
SURVEY FINDINGS

Long-range interest in the actual varying of significant variables in organizations has necessitated that members of the Human Relations Program of the Institute for Social Research, University of Michigan, not only study existing programs for training and changing people in organizations, but that we *develop* new techniques for changing relationships, and that we learn how to *measure* the effects of such changes within organizations. As a result, we have invested a good deal of professional effort in exploring the effectiveness of different procedures for changing attitudes, perceptions, and relationships among individuals in complex hierarchies without changing the personnel of the units. The latter is an important qualification, for we have found that the changes in subordinates' perceptions and attitudes which follow a change in supervisory personnel are frequently of a much larger order than those generated by training or other procedures for changing the attitudes or behavior of incumbents.

Exploratory and Developmental Phase

One procedure which we developed and subsequently found to be effective in changing perceptions and relationships within organizations has been called "feedback." This change process evolved over a period of years as we[13] tried to learn how to report findings from human relations research into organizations so that they would be understood and used in day-to-day operations. Work began on this process in 1948 following a company-wide study of employee and management attitudes and opinions. Over a period of two years, three different sets of data were fed back: (1) information on the attitudes and perceptions of 8000 nonsupervisory employees toward their work, promotion opportunities, supervision, fellow employees, etc.; (2) first- and second-line supervisor's feelings about the various aspects of their jobs and supervisory beliefs; and (3) information from intermediate and top levels of management about their supervisory philosophies, roles in policy formation, problems of organizational integration, etc. We had several aims in this exploratory phase: (1) to develop through first-hand experience an understanding of the problems of producing change; (2) to improve relationships; (3) to identify factors which affected the extent of the change; and (4) to develop working hypotheses for later, more directed research.

The process which finally appeared to maximize the acceptance and utilization of survey and research findings can be described structurally as an interlocking chain of conferences. It began with a report of the major findings of the survey to the president and his senior officers, and progressed slowly down through the hierarchical levels along functional lines to where supervisors and their employees were discussing the data. These meetings

---

[13] A number of people contributed to the design of this feedback process during its developmental phase. They included Sylvester Leahy, Blair Swartz, Robert Schwab, and John Sparling from the Detroit Edison Company, and Rensis Likert, Daniel Katz, Everett Riemer, Frances Fielder, and Theodore Hariton from the Survey Research Center.

were structured in terms of organizational "families"[14] or units—each superior and his immediate subordinates considering the survey data together. The data presented to each group were those pertaining to their own group or for those subunits for which members of the organizational unit were responsible.

Members of each group were asked to help interpret the data and then decide what further analyses of the data should be made to aid them in formulating plans for constructive administrative actions. They also planned the introduction of the findings to the next level. The meetings were typically led by the line officer responsible for the coordination of the subunits at a particular level. Usually, a member of the Survey Research Center and the company's personnel staff assisted the line officer in preparing for these meetings, but attended the meetings only as resource people who could be called upon for information about the feasibility of additional analyses.

These meetings took place in the office of the line supervisor whose organizational unit was meeting, or in the department's own small conference room. All of the survey findings relative to each group were given to the leader and the members of his organizational unit; they decided what to consider first, how fast to work through each topic, and when they had gone as far as they could and needed to involve the next echelon in the process.

This feedback change procedure was developed in an organization where a great amount of effort had already been invested in the training of management and supervisors. During the war the company had participated in the various J-programs sponsored by the War Man-

power Commission, and more important, during the several years we were experimentally developing the feedback process, Dr. Norman R. F. Maier was working with all levels of management to improve their understanding of human relations and supervision.[15] The supervisors with whom we were working to increase their understanding of their own organizational units therefore had a great deal of training in the application of psychological principles to management.

Our observations of the feedback procedure as it developed suggested that it was a powerful process for creating and supporting changes within an organization.[16] However, there was no quantitative proof of this, for our work up to this point had been exploratory and developmental.

A Field Experiment in Accounting Departments

In 1950, when eight accounting departments in this same company asked for a second attitude and opinion survey of their seventy-eight supervisors and eight hundred employees, we[17] had an opportunity to initiate the steps necessary to measure the effects of this organizational change process. The questionnaires used in this resurvey were similar to those used in 1948 and provided the basis for a new cycle of feedback conferences. The general plan for the handling of these new resurvey data was to let everyone in the departments—employees

---

14 F. Mann and J. Dent, "The Supervisor: Member of Two Organizational Families," *Harvard Business Review*, XXXII (November-December 1954), pp. 103-112.

15 For a thorough description of this training, see N. R. F. Maier, *Principles of Human Relations* (New York: Wiley, 1952).

16 F. Mann and R. Likert, "The Need for Research on Communicating Research Results," *Human Organization*, XI (Winter 1952), pp. 15-19.

17 F. Mann and H. Baumgartel, *Survey Feedback Experiment: An Evaluation of a Program for the Utilization of Survey Findings*, monograph in preparation, Survey Research Center, University of Michigan.

and department heads—see the overall findings for eight accounting departments combined as soon as they were available, and then to work intensively on their use in *some* departments, but not in others until there had been a third survey.

While our objective was to test the effectiveness of the basic pattern of feedback developed during the preceding two years, we encouraged department heads and their supervisors to develop their own variations for reporting data to their units and maximizing their use in the solution of problems. After the all-department meetings had been concluded, the chief executive of the accounting departments held a meeting with each department head in the experimental group. At this meeting, the findings for the department head's unit were thoroughly reviewed. The findings included comparisons of (1) changes in employee attitudes from 1948 to 1950, (2) attitudes in that department with those in all other departments combined, and (3) employees' perceptions of supervisory behavior with supervisory statements about their behavior. Department heads were encouraged to go ahead with feedback meetings as soon as they felt ready, tentative next steps were discussed, and assistance from the researchers and the company personnel staffs was assured. Four departments launched feedback activities which were similar to each other in purpose but somewhat different in method. The programs varied in duration (13-33 weeks), in intensity (9-65 meetings), and in the extent to which nonsupervisory employees were involved in the process. During the eighteen months that these differences were unfolding, nothing was done in two of the remaining four departments after the first all-departments meetings. This was done so they might be available as "controls." Changes in key personnel eliminated the remaining two departments from any experimental design.

A third survey of attitudes was conducted in these departments in 1952 after the natural variations in the feedback programs had run their courses. In 1950 and 1952 surveys were then used as "before" and "after" measurements, the four departmental programs as "experimental variations," with the two inactive departments as "controls."

Our findings indicate that more significant positive changes occurred in employee attitudes and perceptions in the four experimental departments than in the two control departments. This was based on two measures of change: (1) a comparison of answers to sixty-one identical questions which were asked in 1950 and 1952, and (2) of a comparison of answers to seventeen "perceived change" questions in which employees had an opportunity to indicate what types of changes had occurred since the 1950 survey. In the experimental group, a fourth of the sixty-one items showed relative mean positive changes, significant at the .05 level or better; the change for another 57 per cent of the items was also positive in direction, but not statistically significant. Major positive changes occurred in the experimental groups in how employees felt about (1) the kind of work they do (job interest, importance, and level of responsibility); (2) their supervisor (his ability to handle people, give recognition, direct their work, and represent them in handling complaints); (3) their progress in the company; and (4) their group's ability to get the job done. The seventeen perceived-change items were designed specifically to measure changes in the areas where we expected the greatest shift in perceptions. Fifteen of these showed that a significantly higher proportion of employees in the experimental than in the control departments felt that change had occurred. More employees in the experimental departments saw changes in (1) how well the supervisors in their department got along together; (2) how often their supervisors held meetings; (3) how effective these meetings were; (4) how much their supervisor understood the way employees looked at and felt about things, etc. These indicate the extent to which the feedback's effectiveness lay in increasing understanding and communication as well as changing supervisory behavior.

Comparisons of the changes among the four experimental departments showed that the three departments which had the two feedback sessions with their employees all showed positive change relative to the control departments. The change which occurred in the fourth was directionally positive, but it was not significantly different from the control departments. In general, the greatest change occurred where the survey results were discussed in both the departmental organizational units *and* the first-line organizational units. The greater the involvement of all members of the organization through their organizational families—the department heads, the first-line supervisors, *and* the employees—the greater the change.

Implications of These Findings

The basic elements of this feedback process described above are not new. They involve (1) the orderly collection of information about the functioning of a system, and (2) the reporting of this information into the system for (3) its use in making further adjustments.

Work by Hall[18] and others who have had considerable practical experience with the use of information about a system for creating change show a similarity in both action steps and basic approach. This suggests there are certain psychological and sociological facts which must

---

[18] Milton Hall, "Supervising People—Closing the Gap Between What We Think and What We Do," *Advanced Management,* XII (September 1947), pp. 129-135.

be taken into consideration in attempting to change the attitudes and behavior of an *individual* or a *group of individuals* in an *organizational setting.*

1. Attitudes and behavior of an individual are functions of both basic personality and social role. *Change processes need to be concerned with altering both the forces within an individual and the forces in the organizational situation surrounding the individual.*

2. Organizations, as systems of hierarchically ordered, interlocking roles with rights and privileges, reciprocal expectations, and shared frames of reference, contain tremendous forces for stability or change in the behavior of individuals or subgroups. Change processes need to be designed to harness these forces for creating and supporting change. *As forces already in existence, they must first be made pliable, then altered or shifted, and finally made stable again to support the change.*

3. Essentially, unilateral power and authority structures underlie the hierarchical ordering of organizational roles. *Expectations of the superior are therefore more important forces for creating change in an individual than the expectations of his subordinates.* Also, those with a direct authority relationship—line superiors—have more influence than those without direct authority— staff trainers.

4. The attitudes, beliefs, and values of an individual are more firmly grounded in the groups which have continuing psychological meaning to him than in those where he has only temporary membership. The supervisor's role of interlocking the activities of two organizational units requires that he have continuing membership in two groups: (a) the organizational unit directed by his superior in which he is a subordinate along with his immediate peers; and (b)

the organizational unit for which he is responsible. *Change processes designed to work with individual supervisors off the job in temporarily created training groups contain less force for initiating and reinforcing change than those which work with an individual in situ.*

5. Information about the functioning of a system may introduce a need for change. This is especially true when the new data are seen as objective and at variance with common perceptions and expectations. Change processes organized around objective, new social facts about one's own organizational situation have more force for change than those organized around general principles about human behavior. *The more meaningful and relevant the material, the greater the likelihood of change.*

6. Involvement and participation in the planning, collection, analysis, and interpretation of information initiate powerful forces for change. Own facts are better understood, more emotionally acceptable, and more likely to be utilized than those of some "outside expert." *Participation in analysis and interpretation helps by-pass those resistances which arise from proceeding too rapidly or too slowly.*

7. Objective information on direction and magnitude of change —knowledge of results—facilitates further improvement. *Change processes which furnish adequate knowledge on process and specify criteria against which to measure improvement are apt to be more successful in creating and maintaining change than those which do not.*

Participation as a Method of Attitude Change

It seems accurate to state that providing personnel with a chance to participate in decisions concerning their own job performance is the most effective method of overcoming negative attitudes and building more useful ones. This is not to say that participation will always work, or even that it should always be tried. Furthermore, its effectiveness depends heavily on how it is done.

The following brief selection by Mann and Neff first identifies the salient values of a participative approach, and then cites research that suggests some limitations on the methods.

Involvement and Participation in Change[*]

F. C. MANN
AND
F. W. NEFF

. . .

Some current research findings have suggested that participation of individuals in decision-making regarding problems that concern them is an important source of positive motivation. Participation in such group decisions tends to give an individual:

. . . an opportunity to contribute his ideas

. . . an understanding of all the facets of the problem under decision

. . . a clearer definition of the objective

. . . a sense of responsibility for the success of the decision

. . . a feeling of satisfaction with the course of action agreed upon.

In a carefully designed field experiment, Coch and French[4] have shown that the extent to which individuals participate in decisions concerning how a change in production procedures is made directly relates to: (1) the rate of recovery of production rates and (2) the level of production attained following the change.

This experiment was replicated in a Norwegian factory in 1956.[5] It was found that participation helps to produce improved morale only to the extent that (1) the workers felt that they had the amount of influence on planning the changes that they thought they should legitimately have, and (2) there is no strong resistance to the methods of introducing change. This second experiment is important for it introduces the idea that the degree to which an individual feels it is legitimate for him to participate is a variable which affects the outcome of his participation. If people do not feel that it is right and proper for them to influence, and have a voice in a matter, sharing a problem with them will not result in the positive motivational effects attributed above to participation. More importantly, if they are given a voice, but less than they believe to be legitimate, then such participation may cause a negative reaction.

Other equally important factors have been found recently which alter the effects of participation on employee attitudes. They are the degree of authoritarianism and the strength of the need for independence of the participant. Both Tannenbaum[6] and Vroom[7] have shown that the outcome of psychological participation varied depending on the personality characteristics of the participant. The evidence suggests that authori-

[*] Excerpted from *Managing Major Change in Organizations* (Ann Arbor, Michigan: The Foundation for Research on Human Behavior, 1961), pp. 79-81.

[4] Coch, L. and French, J. R. P., Jr., "Overcoming Resistance to Change." Human Relations, 1948, 1, 512-532.

[5] French, J. R. P., Jr., Israel, J., and As, D. "An Experiment on Participation in a Norwegian Factory." *Human Relations*, 13, 1960, 3-19.

[6] Tannenbaum, A. The Relationship between Personality and Group Structure. Ph. D. thesis, Syracuse University, 1954.

[7] Vroom, V. H. *Some Personality Determinants of the Effects of Participation.* Prentice-Hall, Englewood Cliffs, N.J., 1960.

tarians and persons who do not have a strong need to be independent are not favorably affected by participation. Equalitarian-minded persons, and persons with strong needs for independence become more satisfied and perform better as a result of participation in decision-making. These findings contribute to our understanding of conditions under which the principle of participation is not effective, and point up the importance of analyzing carefully the personality needs and values of individuals who may be affected by a major change.

An equally important point is that the effect of participation on the individual is determined more by the extent of *psychological* participation than by the extent of *actual* participation. If he feels he has been personally involved, the amount of actual participation may not be important. Management would be well advised to try to obtain the benefits of encouraging employee participation through real, not apparent participation. People tend to see through such ruses, and react negatively quite rapidly. It does mean that management is most likely to effect change favorably through participation if it is made certain that people really do feel they are participating.

From findings showing that participation in departmental decision-making in general is not related to specific objec-tives like concern for cost, it can be inferred that participation, to be effective motivationally, must be directly related to the objective of the participation. Participation will be effective only to the extent that the problems that are shared deal with the specific change under consideration—not other less immediately consequential problems or topics. A general sharing of unrelated problems will not predispose individuals favorably toward accepting a specific change that will deeply affect them, and about which they have not been consulted.

In summary, we have suggested that involving people in problem-solving is important in bringing about motivation for change. We have indicated that the amount of participation an individual feels is related to his willingness to accept change, whether he expects to be involved, whether he feels he should have a voice, whether he prefers authoritarian or equalitarian relationships, and whether he has strong needs for independence will condition the effects of participation. These findings provide additional information for managers to use in determining the extent to which people in an organization should be encouraged, required, or permitted to participate in activities which are a part of the decisions concerning the change.

Our chapter concludes with a research demonstration in industry of a particular type of participation—the group decision process—first described by Lewin. The reader should note that group decision is directed toward behavior within the scope of the participant's job. It is not a program for making higher level management decisions.

READING 5-9

Lecture vs. Group Decision in Changing Behavior[*]

JACOB LEVINE

AND

JOHN BUTLER

· · ·

In this study, group decision is compared with formal lecture as a method of producing changes in socially undesirable behavior. Both methods are then compared with one in which no attempt is made to bring about any change. Thus, the experiment was designed to answer two questions: 1. Is the acquisition of knowledge enough to lead a group of individuals to change a socially undesirable behavior pattern? 2. Is group decision a more effective method of producing a change in behavior than is the formal lecture?

The Experiment

The subjects consisted of 29 supervisors of 395 workers in a large manufacturing plant. The workers were on an hourly rate. These factory workers represented a wide variety of jobs and skills, ranging from unskilled manual labor to the most highly skilled machinist and toolmakers. All of these jobs were classified into nine different grades on the basis of skill and training required.

Within each job grade three different hourly wage rates prevailed. The particular rate paid to any worker was determined in large part by the quality of his performance on the job. Performance was evaluated by one of the 29 foremen who supervised the work of these 395 men.

Every 6 months each worker was rated by his foreman on established rating scales for 5 factors: 1. Accuracy; 2. Effective use of working time; 3. Output; 4. Application of job knowledge; and 5. Cooperation. The sum of the scores on each of these five scales comprised a worker's total performance rating and determined what wage rate he would get.

. . . The foremen, in executing their ratings, tended to overrate those working in the higher job grades and to underrate those in the lower grades. This positive and negative "halo effect" resulted in the workers in the lower grades of jobs receiving the lowest of their respective wage rates while the more highly skilled workers consistently received the highest of their respective wage rates. Evidently the foremen were not rating performance of the individual worker but the grade of the job as well.

. . . Our objective was to help these supervisors see that their task in rating each worker was to consider only how well he did his job and not how difficult the job was. . . . The task of the present experiment was to determine which was the more effective method of achieving this change in behavior of the 29 rating supervisors, group decision or the formal lecture.

Experimental Procedure

The 29 supervisors were randomly divided into three groups of 9, 9, and 11.

[*] Abridged from *Journal of Applied Psychology*, 36, 1952, 29-33.

It may be pointed out that all supervisors were experienced raters and had been rating employees for a number of years. The first group, Group A, consisting of 9 supervisors of 120 workers, served as a control group, and received no special instructions prior to rating. The second group, Group B, consisted of 9 supervisors of 123 men and served as the discussion group. The third group, Group C, consisted of 11 supervisors of 152 men, and served as the lecture group.

Several days prior to rating, the members of Group B were gathered together around a table with the discussion leader. The leader did not sit at the head of the table nor did he lead the discussion. He introduced the problem by showing a graph of the previous ratings and raised the question why it was that the high skilled workers were consistently rated higher in performance than the low skilled. From that point on, the leader merely acted as moderator and avoided injecting himself into the discussion. All decisions and opinions were made solely by the group members. The discussion lasted one hour and a half. The group expressed a number of ideas and arrived at several conclusions. They finally reached one decision acceptable to the group: The way to avoid the inequalities in rating was to disregard the difficulty of the jobs and rate only the man doing the job. Consideration was to be given only to how well a worker was doing his job. All 9 members agreed on this decision.

Group C, the Lecture group gathered in a formal lecture room and all sat facing the leader. They were given a detailed lecture on the technique and theory of employee performance rating. Some background material on wage administration and job evaluation was also included. The lecture carefully pointed out the errors of their previous ratings and interpreted the reasons for their occur-

rence. He illustrated his lecture with graphs and figures. He finally explained what each rater was supposed to do: that he was to rate individual performance and not difficulty of the job. After the lecture, questions were encouraged and asked by the raters; complete answers were given. The total session lasted about one hour and a half.

Experimental Results

Table 1 presents the results of the supervisors' ratings according to labor grade. For comparison, the previous ratings by the same supervisors are included. In the pre-training rating we see the gradual decrease in mean rating as we go down in the labor grade. This "halo effect" characterizes each of the three experimental groups. In the post-training rating some changes are observable.

For the sake of simplification of the results, the nine labor grades were arbitrarily divided into two categories: Low Group and High Group: the first four labor grades were placed in the High and the last five in the Low. When we compare the mean ratings of the Low and the High labor groups prior to training we find that the difference is significant at the 1% level of confidence for two groups and at the 7% level for the third. In each case the size of the difference is at least one-third of a rating unit in a total of three units.

In the second rating, only Group B shows any significant change in difference in the mean ratings of Low and High Grades. For Group A, the control group, the mean difference remains almost the same, and is still significant to the 1% level of confidence. Group C, the lecture group, shows a small decrease in the difference, but it is still significant to the 1% level.

TABLE 1

**Mean Rating Differences Between Low and High Labor Groups
Before and After Training Sessions**

Labor Grade	Group A Control Mean Rating		Signif.* (P)	Group B Group Decision Mean Rating		Signif.* (P)	Group C Lecture Mean Rating		Signif.* (P)
	1st	2nd		1st	2nd		1st	2nd	
Low	1.7	1.7		1.7	1.7	.31	1.8	1.7	.23
High	2.0	2.0	.81	2.0	1.7	.01	2.4	2.2	.23
Mean Diff.	.35	.37		.33	.00		.63	.45	
Signif.* (P)	.01	.01		.07	.84		.01	.01	

* This is the probability that a difference this great or greater could have arisen simply through errors of random sampling.

We may conclude that performance ratings were significantly affected only after the raters had had a group discussion and had reached a group decision. Neither increased experience in rating nor the learning about their previous errors in rating had any significant influence. Our findings completely confirm those of Lewin in demonstrating the greater effectiveness of group decision over the lecture method of training.

. . .

References

1. Lewin, K. *Group decision and social change.* In Newcomb, T., and Hartley (editors), *Readings in social psychology.* New York: Holt, 1947.
2. Marrow, A., and French, J. R. P. Changing a stereotype in industry. *J. soc. Issues,* 1945, 1, 33-37.
3. Radke, M., and Klisurich, D. Experiments in changing food habits. *J. Amer. Dietetic Assn.,* 1947, 23, 403-409.
4. Samelson, B. Does education diminish prejudice? *J. soc. Issues,* 1945, 1, 11-13.

In considering Levine and Butler's findings, the work of Pelz is relevant as to what may be happening in the group. Her research suggests that the process of being required to come to a decision, even if this decision is not publicly stated by the individual, may be the important factor; while not denying the importance of group norms or pressures, Pelz's work would imply that a lecture (formal, or perhaps informal when the boss says "You shall change your ways") is less effective in bringing about the change than getting the person to commit himself to change, even if he does so silently.

Thinking:
Problem Solving
Decision Making
Creativity

Introduction

A good case can be made for the point that the essential functions of the administrator are problem solving and decision making, often with the additional requirement that his efforts also be original and creative. In emphasizing the importance of thinking as an executive activity, *Fortune* magazine quotes a DuPont executive as saying: "The number and cost of '$10,000 mistakes' made in our company as a result of faulty thinking are more staggering than anyone would wish to contemplate" (Stryker). The world-wide use by IBM of the admonition to Think is but another sign of industry's concern with problem solving and creativity.

In a larger sense, the organization itself can be viewed as a problem-solving, decision-making system. A major function of its executives, beyond their personal decision-making responsibilities is to improve the organization's problem solving and decision making. They can do this partly by improving individual performance, through training, for example, and partly by improving the system itself—the organization structure and the formalized decision procedures, for example. The goal of Part Six is to survey what is known about the psychology of thinking, to suggest applications for individual problem solving and decision making, and to suggest, as well, ways of looking at the organization to make it a more effective problem-solving system.

In this, the final section of our book, we describe first the psychological nature of the thinking processes and their inter-relationships; then examine the principal factors that facilitate or inhibit these processes.

Some Definitions

Although the cognitive processes were one of the first aspects of behavior studied by early experimental psychologists, the terms used to discuss different types of cognitive activity (thinking, problem solving, decision making, and creativity) have still not been clearly disentangled one from another. We present some definitions of the terms, not to attempt a resolution of the problem, but rather to identify the point of view we take in the following chapters.

We consider that an individual is thinking when, through the use of symbols or images, he internally represents or "constructs a model of"* the

---

* A concept used by Galenter and Gerstenhaber.

world or some aspect of it—whether that part of the world is immediately present or not. Thus, reverie, reminiscence, fantasy, dreaming, and remembering are all thinking activities; so are more directed efforts, such as re-integrating past experiences to solve a problem, or consciously weighing two courses of action to make a decision. (The question of whether an individual can think, in our definition of it, at a completely unconscious level would lead us into theoretical questions without any practical gain. However, there is no doubt that the individual frequently thinks without being able to verbalize his thought processes.)

Problem solving, as we will use the term, is thinking activity directed toward reaching some goal; it generally involves thoughtful effort to get around or overcome an obstacle. It is, of course, a different kind of response from those to frustration or emotional stress; these latter responses may also be elicited by obstacles in our path. (Cf. the Maier reading in Part Three.) For our purposes, problem solving will be distinguished as well from reactions in which the individual simply uses alternate but well habituated responses to overcome an immediate obstacle. Thus, trouble shooting in the programming of data processing illustrates problem solving in our use of the term; pressing a release lever when a calculator jams illustrates routine adjustive behavior.

The terms decision making and problem solving are often used interchangeably. We feel that it would be helpful for our purposes to distinguish between the two. Thus, as we have previously indicated, we use problem solving for the process of thoughtfully and deliberately striving to overcome obstacles in the path toward a goal. (The term reasoning is also often used in this way.) We confine the term decision making* to the choice process, choosing one from among several possibilities. The two processes are, of course, psychologically interwoven, and it will not always be possible to hold the line on the distinction we have made between them. (Some authors whom we will quote use both terms almost synonymously.)

The final forms of thinking we consider in this part of our book are originality and creativity. Thus, we can speak of thinking as varying from highly original to conventional. Original thinking would produce ideas or concepts infrequently thought of by others. When we speak of creative thinking we usually mean not only that it is original but also ingenious, clever, uniquely adaptive, or that it results in a new esthetically pleasing or innovative and valuable production.

People differ in the total amount of time they devote to various sorts of thinking, in the content areas in which they do most of their thinking, and in the level (efficiency, success, degree of abstraction) of their thinking. Individual differences in thinking may be a function of environment, personality, physical conditions, physiological functioning, language, intelligence, personal background factors, and group memberships.

---

* In Chapter Twenty-one, which more fully discusses decisions, further distinctions will be made involving the term decision making.

The beginning definitions we have offered introduce the subject; our further discussions and readings on the thinking processes will provide more detailed descriptions.

THINKING AS AN ACTIVITY OF THE TOTAL PERSONALITY

Psychologists consider thinking as having its place in the continuum of the learning processes, which have as one end, conditioned responses and well-established habits and on the other end, thinking. As with any learning process, thinking is subject to influence from perceptual, motivational, and attitudinal activities. Thus, thinking is integrally woven into the entire fabric of the behavior of the individual; and although it may be considered man's highest achievement, allowing him to soar to great intellectual heights, thinking is only one expression of the human personality, interacting with and affected by all other aspects of that personality.

A person may often be unable to describe accurately what is happening while he is thinking. He may be unaware of what many of the real influences are on his thinking. In addition to the factors immediately present in the situation, he will be influenced by his prior experience and early attitudes. The society and the groups in which he lives will influence his thinking—the process as well as the content. The structure of his language, for instance, will play a part in the kinds of problems he envisages and the ways he has for dealing with them.

Preview of Part Six

The very nature of thought—that it is some internal symbolic activity not always manifest in external observable behavior—gives us a clue to the difficulties encountered in thinking about thinking. Just as the description of someone throwing a baseball or walking fails to give us the full picture of the myriad of muscular, circulatory, and neural changes that are taking place, so the even less observable thought processes challenge total description.

Anyone who has attempted to catch his thoughts on the wing and recall or record in exact detail what they were (in a given situation) can sympathize with the difficulties of a researcher in the thinking area. The ephemeral, brief, short-cutting, and symbolic nature of the fast movement of thoughts would seem to defy description. In literature, writers have struggled to capture the "stream of consciousness," to deal with the fact that what takes a long time for them to describe may be happening in a brief moment. The scientist, then, who wishes not only to present, but also to analyze, and understand (and perhaps improve) the way in which thoughts occur, is faced with great hurdles.

That only the subject can introspectively report reliably on what he is thinking has naturally led to some attempts to describe the process by getting verbal reports after or during the event. (Our readings by Dewey and Duncker illustrate these attempts.) But other approaches have aimed at getting around the difficulties posed by the inadequacy and incompleteness of such reports. They seek to observe what changes in behavior or performance occur when changes in a problem or task situation are made by the experimenter (for example, Bruner and Maier). Thus, although someone studying electricity may not have an accurate detailed picture of any given instant in electrical activity, he might still discover what a change in certain physical conditions can do to the effective output of current.

In our selections on problem solving, we hope to show both the descriptive and the experimental approaches.

In Chapter Nineteen, the selection from Dewey suggests phases in the thinking process; Duncker's analysis, which follows, provides a more precise description by tracing the subject's thinking processes through his verbalizations of these processes. The Newell and Simon reading uses the same experimental strategy—having subjects think aloud; then by programming a computer to carry out the same processes, Newell and Simon demonstrate the value of computer simulation for a better understanding of human thinking. The selection by Katona compares problem solving behavior, and, habitual, associative behavior. Here too we consider the concept forming phase of the problem solving process.

Chapter Twenty summarizes research on problem solving under five principal headings—environmental factors influencing thinking; the principal cognitive barriers to effective thinking; some suggestions for surmounting the barriers; then, on the research thus far examined, a training program in problem solving is outlined. The chapter concludes with a consideration of individual differences in problem solving.

Decision theory, decision making and making business decisions comprise the subject matter of Chapter Twenty-one. Distinctions are drawn among these terms. The reading by Edwards is an example of the writing of the decision theorists, illustrating their emphasis and the type of contribution they make to theory and practice. The Cyert, Simon, and Trow reading compares the theory of decision making and the practical job of making decisions in the business setting. They present a case analysis of a company's decision to utilize electronic data processing. In the final reading, Mosel provides a practical illustration of the use of decision theory to pinpoint some problems in an industrial incentive program.

An active area of research is that of originality and creativity. In Chapter Twenty-two, in the only reading of the chapter, MacKinnon relates creativity to personality. Later in the chapter we also examine data relating creativity to age. Brief consideration is given to some of the measuring techniques developed to assess creative talent. In addition Maltzman's research in training for creativity is summarized.

Our final chapter considers some of the many variables that operate in group problem solving. No certain answer is provided for the question: is group problem solving better than individual problem solving. Rather, factors relevant to answering the question such as the nature of the problem and the cohesiveness of the group are identified. The Taylor, Block, and Berry reading demonstrates the superiority of individual brainstorming over group brainstorming. Other factors discussed in the chapter are leadership, communication, and semantics; all are considered in relation to group problem solving.

CHAPTER NINETEEN

Some Approaches
to
Problem Solving

Our chapter moves from an early, largely deductive description of problem solving through more recent experimental work. The terrain is crossed several times but in different company and from different directions. The hope is that the reading selections will shed light on both the nature of the problem solving process and the complexities of studying it.

AN EARLY DESCRIPTION OF THE PROBLEM-SOLVING PROCESS

One place to find a description of problem solving as it has been traditionally viewed is in John Dewey's *How We Think*. Dewey did not write as a psychologist but as a philosopher, and thus he offers here a logical, not necessarily a psychological, analysis of the problem-solving process.* And yet, keeping in mind the fact that the "perplexed" don't always take their steps in sequence, that they do not experience the various steps as discrete nor even always as recognizably separate, that they may occasionally respond with habit, stereotype, or emotion, instead of reflective thinking, we begin with Dewey's analysis as an influential, useful description of systematic problem solving. As a matter of fact, many of the modern approaches to problem solving are adaptations or psychological elaborations of the Dewey analysis and are acknowledged as such. Simon (1960, p. 3) for example, in presenting his contemporary analysis of decision making, notes the resemblance to Dewey's stages in problem solving.

---

* Dewey uses the terms "reflective thinking" and "problem solving" to refer to the same process.

READING 6-1

The Pattern of Reflective Thinking*

JOHN DEWEY

· · ·

The two limits of every unit of thinking are perplexed, troubled, or confused situation at the beginning and a cleared-up, unified, resolved situation at the close. The first of these situations may be called pre-reflective. It sets the problem to be solved; out of it grows the question that reflection has to answer. In the final situation the doubt has been dispelled; the situation is *post*-reflective; there results a direct experience of mastery, satisfaction, enjoyment. Here, then, are the limits within which reflection falls.

In between, as states of thinking, are (1) *suggestions*, in which the mind leaps forward to a possible solution; (2) an intellectualization of the difficulty or perplexity that has been *felt* (directly experienced) into a *problem* to be solved, a question for which the answer must be sought; (3) the use of one suggestion after another as a leading idea, or *hypothesis*, to initiate and guide observation and other operations in collection of factual material; (4) the mental elaboration of the idea or supposition as an idea or supposition (*reasoning*, in the sense in which reasoning is a part, not the whole, of inference); and (5) testing the hypothesis by overt or imaginative action.

The five phases, terminals, or functions of thought that we have noted do not follow one another in a set order. On the

contrary, each step in genuine thinking does something to perfect the information of a suggestion and promote its change into a leading idea or directive hypothesis. It does something to promote the location and definition of the problem. Each improvement in the idea leads to new observations that yield new facts or data and help the mind judge more accurately the relevancy of facts already at hand. The elaboration of the hypothesis does not wait until the problem has been defined and adequate hypothesis has been arrived at; it may come in at any intermediate time. And as we have just seen, any particular overt test need not be final; it may be introductory to new observations and new suggestions, according to what happens in consequence of it.

There is, however, an important difference between test by overt action in practical deliberations and in scientific investigations. In the former the practical commitment involved in overt action is much more serious than in the latter. An astronomer or a chemist performs overt actions, but they are for the sake of knowledge; they serve to test and develop his conceptions and theories. In practical matters, the main result desired lies outside of knowledge. One of the great values of thinking, accordingly, is that it defers the commitment to action that is irretrievable, that, once made, cannot be revoked. Even in moral and other practical matters, therefore, a thoughtful person treats his overt deeds as experimental so far as possible; that

---

* Excerpted from *How We Think*, Revised Edition (New York: D. C. Heath & Co., 1933), as reprinted in *Intelligence in the Modern World* (Ed. by J. Ratner), Modern Library, 1939, pp. 851-857.

is to say, while he cannot call them back and must stand their consequences, he gives alert attention to what they teach him about his conduct as well as to the non-intellectual consequences. He makes a problem out of consequences of conduct, looking into the causes from which they probably resulted, especially the causes that lie in his own habits and desires.

In complicated cases some of the five phases are so extensive that they include definite subphases within themselves. In this case it is arbitrary whether the minor functions are regarded as parts or are listed as distinct phases. There is nothing especially sacred about the number five.

In conclusion, we point out that the five phases of reflection that have been described represent only in outline the indispensable traits of reflective thinking. In practice, two of them may telescope, some of them may be passed over hurriedly, and the burden of reaching a conclusion may fall mainly on a single phase, which will then require a seemingly disproportionate development. No set rules can be laid down on such matters. The way they are managed depends upon the intellectual tact and sensitiveness of the individual. When things have come out wrong, it is, however, a wise practice to review the methods by which the unwise decision was reached, and see where the mis-step was made.

A SECOND DESCRIPTION OF THE PROBLEM-SOLVING PROCESS

Facing a problem of moderate complexity and of immediate principle importance, as Dewey has suggested, a person will call up out of memory items of relevant information, obtain other items from outside sources, and will consider these in relation to each other, imagining the consequences of taking various actions; he may then soon "see" a solution that he tries and verifies. A somewhat different version of the process has been described for problems that are more complex or demand highly creative solutions. Along these lines, Wallas has named "four stages of creative thought": preparation, incubation, illumination, and verification. Since his formulation, abundant evidence gathered from scientists, inventors, artists, and poets confirm the existence of comparable stages in problem solving and creative effort* (Woodworth and Schlosberg).

Within the loose framework suggested by these stages, many factors will determine widely different and individual approaches to the solution of a problem: the special nature of the task, personality and motivational factors, individual work habits, intelligence, or environmentally influenced opportunities. We describe the four stages then as a useful description of the broad phases that many successful problem solvers have experienced in their thinking. The description is useful not as a prescription for successful problem solving but as a framework within which any administrator can analyze and better understand his own problem-solving efforts and the hindrances to these efforts.

Preparation is a process of encountering, confronting, and coming to know

---

* Subsequent writers vary slightly in their labeling of the stages or emphasize a total of three, four, or five stages in covering essentially the same sequence. For example, one group of researchers adds the phase of "reapplication" (Merrifield, Guilford, *et al.*).

the problem. During this phase the problem solver saturates himself with knowledge about the problem: he will read about it, pick it up, study it, and search out its characteristics. He may literally as well as figuratively walk around the problem, looking at what he believes are all aspects of it. On the basis of information obtained, certain hypotheses may be formulated and discussed. Often, this phase blends with the phase of illumination as an hypothesis that is set up then seems to provide the answer.

Adequate preparation—within the time limits set by practical circumstances—must be considered an essential foundation for the administrator's own problem-solving efforts. When solutions are sought too early in the process, important facts in the case are overlooked, blind alleys are entered and the process is, in the long run, delayed.

At times, the process of preparation ends with no solution in view. Fatigued or blocked in his efforts, the scientist, inventor, artist, or business executive often puts the problem aside, occasionally even "dismissing it," at least for the time being. Much evidence, some of it only anecdotal but nevertheless persuasive, suggests that at a later time—during a period of relaxation, or as a by-product of another activity—an insight into the old problem seems suddenly to appear. The insight is frequently a preliminary one, pointing the way to a possible solution, rather than providing the completed solution itself. The period between preparation and illumination is thought of as a period of *incubation* and may last from a few minutes to months or, in some cases, years.

There are many psychologically acceptable explanations for the value of an incubation period in effective problem solving: freedom from fatigue, the elimination of a hampering set, the unconscious continuance of the problem-solving effort, and opportunity for the arousal of new and relevant associations.

The immediate point of interest to the administrator is: putting a problem aside after a period of thorough preparation, with no solution in sight, can be a helpful step. Needless to say, problems don't solve themselves merely through incubation—the preparatory work must be done, and frequently as much work has to be done after the period of *illumination* as in the period of preparation. One can say the new insight has to be engineered into a solution that can be put into production. The original "givens" of the problem have to be checked. New data must be sought. Preliminary tests of subhypotheses have to be worked through. Finally the "solution" must be verified.

Facets of the *verification* process have already been described in our Dewey reading. We might point up two items of particular concern to administrators: the question of an appropriate time for attempting verification, and the danger of unanticipated consequences. With respect to the time factor, it may be suggested that whether a solution is successful or not is sometimes a matter of when the question is asked: for example, after a week, or after six months. What is not working out now, may work, when given a little time; but it is also true that immediately successful solutions may falter with the additional complexities brought on as time goes by. The point is, of course, that both a short range and a long range point of view must be taken and necessary accommodations made.

In checking out a solution to a problem, the planned consequences are relatively easy to assess. The danger is that some unplanned and unanticipated consequences—perhaps indirect or even remote—may also be present. One of the real skills in administrative problem solving is ability to minimize the number of unanticipated consequences by careful study of the proposed solution, after it first comes to mind.

A FUNCTIONAL DESCRIPTION OF PROBLEM SOLVING

The descriptions by Dewey and Wallas emphasize the phases or stages through which the problem solver goes. Duncker has sought to get detailed verbal reports from subjects *while* they were dealing with a problem; he then analyzes this material in terms of the function being served by each approach the problem solver takes. In this manner, Duncker is able to describe a spiral-like approach to problem solving in which the problem solver goes at the problem at successively different and increasingly more specific functional levels. He identifies three such levels of attacking the problem: The problem solver first considers the "general range" of the problem, examining its requirements and seeking to identify some direction in which a solution might be sought; he next seeks a "functional solution" to the problem: what function has to be accomplished; what has to be done to solve the problem; and, finally, he seeks a "specific solution" in which the earlier functional solution is spelled out in relation to the exact requirements of the particular problem.

Duncker's study is classical in the field of problem-solving research. It provides a vivid picture of the advantages, as well as some of the difficulties, of experimental studies of the thinking processes.

READING 6-2

The Structure and Dynamics of Problem-Solving Processes*

K. DUNCKER

. . .

1. Introduction and Formulation of the Problem

A problem arises when a living creature has a goal but does not know how that goal is to be reached. Whenever one cannot go from the given situation to the desired situation simply by action, then there has to be recourse to thinking. (By action we here understand the performance of obvious operations.) Such thinking has the task of devising some action which may mediate between the existing and the desired situations. Thus the 'solution' of a practical problem must fulfill two demands: in the first place, its realization must bring about the goal situation, and in the second place one must be able to arrive at it from the given situation simply through action.

The practical problem whose solution was experimentally studied in greatest detail runs as follows: Given a human being with an inoperable stomach tumor, and rays which destroy organic tissue at sufficient intensity, by what procedure can one free him of the tumor by these rays and at the same time avoid destroying the healthy tissue which surrounds it?

. . .

In the present investigation the question is: *How does the solution arise from the problem situation? In what ways is the solution of a problem attained?*

* On Problem Solving, *Psychological Monographs*, 1945, 58, No. 270, excerpts from 1-14.

2. Experimental Procedure

The experiments proceeded as follows: The subjects (S_s), who were mostly students of universities or of colleges, were given various thinking problems, with the request that they think aloud. This instruction, *"Think aloud"*, is not identical with the instruction to introspect which has been common in experiments on thought-processes. While the introspecter makes himself as thinking the object of his attention, the subject who is thinking aloud remains immediately directed to the problem, so to speak allowing his activity to become verbal.

. . .

The subject (S) was emphatically warned not to leave unspoken even the most fleeting or foolish idea. He was told that where he did not feel completely informed, he might freely question the experimenter, but that no previous specialized knowledge was necessary to solve the problems.

3. A Protocol of the Radiation Problem

Let us begin with the radiation problem. Usually the schematic sketch shown in Fig. 1 was given with the problem. Thus, it was added, somebody had visualized the situation to begin with (cross-section through the body with the tumor in the middle and the radiation apparatus on the left); but obviously this would not do.

From my records I choose that sort of

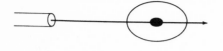

Figure 1

solution-process which was particularly rich in typical hunches and therefore also especially long and involved; the average process vacillated less and could be left to run its own course with considerably less guidance.

Protocol

1. Send rays through the esophagus.
2. Desensitize the healthy tissues by means of a chemical injection.
3. Expose the tumor by operating.
4. One ought to decrease the intensity of the rays on their way; for example—would this work?—turn the rays on at full strength only after the tumor has been reached. (Experimenter: False analogy; no injection is in question.)
5. One should swallow something inorganic (which would not allow passage of the rays) to protect the healthy stomach walls. (E: It is not merely the stomach walls which are to be protected.)
6. Either the rays must enter the body or the tumor must come out. Perhaps one could alter the location of the tumor but how? Through pressure? No.
7. Introduce a cannula. (E: What, in general, does one do when, with any agent one wishes to produce in a specific place an effect which he wishes to avoid on the way to that place?)
8. (Reply:) One neutralises the effect on the way. But that is what I have been attempting all the time.
9. Move the tumor toward the exterior. (Compare 6.) (The E repeats the problem and emphasizes, ". . . which destroy at sufficient intensity.")
10. The intensity ought to be variable. (Compare 4.)
11. Adaptation of the healthy tissues by previous weak application of the rays.

(E: How can it be brought about that the rays destroy only the region of the tumor?)

12. (Reply:) I see no more than two possibilities: either to protect the body or to make the rays harmless. (E: How could one decrease the intensity of the rays en route? [Compare 4.])
13. (Reply:) Somehow divert . . . diffuse rays . . . disperse . . . stop! Send a broad and weak bundle of rays through a lens in such a way that the tumor lies at the local point and thus receives intensive radiation.[4] (Total duration about half an hour.)

4. Impracticable "Solutions"

In the protocol given above, we can discern immediately that the whole process, from the original setting of the problem to the final solution, appears as a series of more or less concrete proposals. Of course, only the last one, or at least its principle, is practicable. All those preceding are in some respect inadequate to the problem, and therefore the process of solution cannot stop there. But however primitive they may be, this one thing is certain, that they cannot be discussed in terms of meaningless, blind, trial-and-error reactions. Let us take for an example the first proposal: "Send rays through the esophagus." Its clear meaning is that the rays should be guided into the stomach by some passage free from tissue. The basis of this proposal is, however, obviously an incorrect representation of the situation inasmuch as the rays are regarded as a sort of fluid, or the

---

[4] This solution is closely related to the "best" solution: *crossing of several weak bundles of rays at the tumor,* so that the intensity necessary for destruction is attained only here. Incidentally, it is quite true that the rays in question are not deflected by ordinary lenses; but this fact is of no consequence from the viewpoint of the psychology of thinking. See 4 below.

esophagus as offering a perfectly straight approach to the stomach, etc. Nevertheless, within the limits of this simplified concept of the situation, the proposal would actually fulfill the demands of the problem. It is therefore genuinely the solution of a problem, although not of the one which was actually presented. With the other proposals, the situation is about the same. The second presupposes that a means—for example, a chemical means—exists for making organic tissue insensitive to the rays. If such a means existed, then everything would be in order, and the solution-process would have already come to an end. The fourth proposal—that the rays be turned on at full strength only when the tumor has been reached—shows again very clearly its derivation from a false analogy, perhaps that of a syringe which is set in operation only when it has been introduced into the object. The sixth suggestion, finally, treats the body too much as analogous to a rubber ball, which can be deformed without injury. In short, it is evident that such proposals are anything but completely meaningless associations. Merely in the factual situation, they are wrecked on certain components of the situation not yet known or not yet considered by the subject.

Occasionally it is not so much the situation as the demand, whose distortion or simplification makes the proposal practically useless. In the case of the third suggestion, for example ("expose the tumor by operating"), the real reason why radiation was introduced seems to have escaped the subject. An operation is exactly what should be avoided. Similarly in the fifth proposal, the fact is forgotten that not only the healthy stomach-walls must be protected but also all parts of the healthy body which have to be penetrated by the rays.

A remark on principle may here be in order. The psychologist who is investigating, not a store of knowledge, but the genesis of a solution, is not interested primarily in whether a proposal is actually practicable, but only in whether it is formally practicable, that is, practicable in the framework of the subject's given premises. If in planning a project an engineer relies on incorrect formulae or on non-existent material, his project can nevertheless follow from the false premises as intelligently as another from correct premises. One can be "psychologically equivalent" to the other. In short, we are interested in knowing how a solution develops out of the system of its subjective premises, and how it is fitted to this system.

5. Classification of Proposals

If one compares the various tentative solutions in the protocol with one another, they fall naturally into certain groups. Proposals 1, 3, 5, 6, 7 and 9 have clearly in common the attempt to *avoid contact between the rays and the healthy tissue*. This goal is attained in quite different ways: in 1 by re-directing the rays over a path naturally free from tissue; in 3 by the removal of the healthy tissue from the original path of the rays by operation; in 5 by interposing a protective wall (which may already have been tacitly implied in 1 and 3); in 6 by translocating the tumor towards the exterior; and in 7, finally, by a combination of 3 and 5. In proposals 2 and 11, the problem is quite differently attacked: the accompanying destruction of healthy tissue is here to be avoided by the *desensitizing or immunizing of this tissue*. A third method is used in 4, perhaps in 8, in 10 and 13: *the reduction of radiation intensity on the way*. As one can see, the process of solution shifts noticeably back and forth between these three methods of approach.

· · · ·

6. Functional Value and Understanding

In this classification, the tentative solutions are grouped according to the manner in which they try to solve the problem, i.e., according to their "by-means-of-which," their "functional value." . . . The proposal to send rays through the esophagus. The S saw nothing at all about avoiding contact or about a free passage. Nevertheless, the solution-character of the esophagus in this context is due to no other characteristic than that of being a tissue-free path to the stomach. It functions as the embodiment solely of this property (not of the property of being a muscular pipe or of lying behind the windpipe, or the like). In short, in the context of this problem, the "by-means-of-which" the "functional value" of the esophagus is a free path to the stomach. The proposals "direct the rays by a natural approach," "expose by operation," "translocate the tumor toward the exterior," "protective wall," and "cannula" all embody the functional value: no contact between rays and healthy tissue. The functional value of the solution, "concentration of diffuse rays in the tumor," is the characteristic: "less intensity on the way, great intensity in the tumor." The functional value of the lens is the quality: "medium to concentrate rays," and so forth.

The functional value of a solution is indispensable for the understanding of its being a solution. It is exactly what is called the sense, the principle or the point of the solution. The subordinated more specialized characteristics and properties of a solution embody this principle, apply it to the particular circumstances of the situation. For example, the esophagus is in this way an application of the principle: "free passage to the stomach," to the particular circumstances of the human body. To understand the solution

as a solution is just the same as to comprehend the solution as embodying its functional value. When someone is asked, "Why is such-and-such a solution?," he necessarily has recourse to the functional value. In all my experiments, aside from two or three unmistakable exceptions, when the E asked about a proposal: "In what way is this a solution of the problem?," the S responded promptly with a statement of its functional value. (In spontaneous statements of the S's, the functional value was frequently left unmentioned as being too obvious.)

Incidentally, the realization of its functional value mediates understanding of a solution even where there is nothing but an "unintelligible" (though sufficiently general) relation between the functional value and the demand which it fulfills. Blowing on a weakly glimmering fire, for example, undoubtedly solves the problem of rekindling the fire because in this way fresh oxygen is supplied. In other words, the increase of the oxygen supply is the immediate functional value of blowing on the fire. But why combination with oxygen produces warmth and flame is ultimately not intelligible. Even if the whole of chemistry should be successfully and without a gap derived from the principles of atomic physics, these principles are not in themselves altogether intelligible, i.e., ultimately they must be "accepted as mere facts."

. . .

Thus, intelligibility frequently means no more than participation in, or derivability from, sufficiently elementary and universal causal relationships. But even if these general laws are not in themselves intelligible, reducibility to such general laws actually mediates a certain type of understanding.

To the same degree to which a solution is understood, it can be transposed, which means that under altered conditions it may be changed correspondingly in such a way as to preserve its functional value. For, one can transpose a solution only when one has grasped its functional value, its general principle, i.e., the invariants from which, by introduction of changed conditions, the corresponding variations of the solution follow each time.

An example: When, seen from the standpoint of a spectator, someone makes a detour around some obstacle, and yet acts from his own point of view in terms of nothing but, say, "now three yards to the left, then two yards straight ahead, then to the right . . ."—these properties of the solution would certainly satisfy the concrete circumstances of the special situation here and now. But so long as the person in question has not grasped the functional value, the general structure: "detour around an obstacle," he must necessarily fail when meeting a new obstacle which is differently located and of different shape. For to different obstacles correspond different final forms of the solution; but the structure, "detour around an obstacle," remains always the same. Whoever has grasped this structure is able to transpose a detour properly. . . . A solution conceived without functional understanding often betrays itself through nonsensical errors.

. . .

"Good" and "stupid" errors in Köhler's sense can be clearly distinguished as follows: In the case of good, intelligent errors, at least the general functional value of the situation is correctly outlined, only the specific manner of its realization is not adequate. For example, an ape stands a box on its corner under the goal object, which hangs high above, because in this way the box comes closer—to be sure, at the price of its stability. In the case of stupid errors, on the other hand, the outward form of an earlier, or an

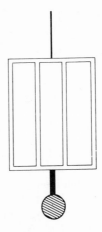

Figure 4

imitated solution is blindly reproduced without functional understanding. For example, an ape jumps into the air from a box—but the goal object is hanging at quite a different spot.

8. The Process of Solution as Development of the Problem

. . .

The final form of an individual solution is, in general, not reached by a single step from the original setting of the problem; on the contrary, the principle, the functional value of the solution, typically arises first, and the final form of the solution in question develops only as this principle becomes successively more and more concrete. In other words, the general or "essential" properties of a solution genetically precede the specific properties; the latter are developed out of the former.

. . .

The finding of a general property of a solution means each time a *reformulation of the original problem*. Consider for example the fourth proposal in the protocol above. Here it is clearly evident that at

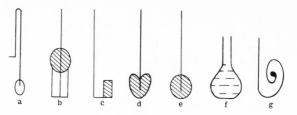

Figure 5, a-g

first there exists only the very general functional value of the solution: "one must decrease the intensity of the radiation on the way." But the decisive re-formulation of the original problem is thereby accomplished. No longer, as at the beginning, does the S seek simply a "means to apply rays to the tumor without also destroying healthy tissue," but already—over and above this—a means to decrease the intensity of the radiation on the way. The formulation of the problem has thus been made sharper, more specific—and the proposal not to turn the rays on at full strength until the tumor has been reached, although certainly wrong, arises only as a solution of this new, re-formulated problem. From this same reformulation of the problem there arises, at the end of the whole process, the practicable solution, "concentration of diffuse rays in the tumor." With the other proposals in the protocol, the case is similar, the solution-properties found at first, the functional values, *always serve as productive reformulations of the original problem.*

We can accordingly describe a process of solution either as development of the solution or as development of the problem. Every solution-principle found in the process, which is itself not yet ripe for concrete realization, and which therefore fulfills only the first of the two demands given on page 1, functions from then on as reformulation, as sharpening of the original setting of the problem. *It is therefore meaningful to say that what is really done in any solution of problems consists in formulating the problem more productively.*

To sum up: *The final form of a solution is typically attained by way of mediating phases of the process, of which each one, in retrospect, possesses the character of a solution, and, in prospect, that of a problem.*

. . .

9. Implicit Solution-Phases

Not all phases of the various solution-processes are given in a family tree of the kind graphically represented on page 5: rather, only the more prominent and relatively independent among them are given. Aside from these, there exist phases which are not explicit enough and, above all, too, banal ever to appear in a protocol. In the case of the radiation problem, for instance, it is clear to all Ss from the start that, in any case, to find a solution, something must be done with the actual circumstances concerned, with the rays and the body. As modern Europeans, they do not think of looking for suitable magic formulae; nor would they anticipate that some change in another place would lead to a solution. Similarly in the case of the prime numbers problem, from the beginning there is no doubt that the solution is to be sought in the province of numbers, and not, for example, in the province of physical processes. In short, from the very first, the deliberating and searching is always confined to a province which is relatively narrow as to space and context. Thus preparation is made for the mere discrete phases of a solution by certain *approximate regional demarcations*, i.e., by phases in which necessary but not yet sufficient properties of the solution are demanded. Such implicit phases of a solution do not quite fulfill even the first prerequisite of a solution mentioned [previously].

This is valid not only for thinking, but also for attempts at solution by action (trial and error). When a layman wishes to adjust the spacing between lines on a typewriter, this much at least of the solution is known to him: "I must screw or press somewhere on the machine." He will not knock on the wall, for instance, nor does he anticipate that any change of the given colors would do. In general, one seeks to achieve mechanical effects by mechanical alterations in the critical object.

. . .

10. Insufficiency of a Protocol

The reader has probably received the impression that the discussions of the preceding paragraphs left the data of the protocol a long way behind. In the case of the very first proposal, for instance, that of the esophagus, there was no mention at all of "redirecting over a tissue-free path," or even of "avoiding contact." That some such thing appeared in other protocols in an analogous place naturally proves nothing about the psychological origin of just this individual proposal.

This is the place in which to say something essential about protocols. One could formulate it thus: A protocol is relatively reliable only for what it positively contains, but not for that which it omits. For even the best-intentioned protocol is only a very scanty record of what actually happens. The reasons for this insufficiency of protocols which are based on spoken thoughts must interest us also as characteristic of a solution-process as

such. Mediating phases which lead at once to their concrete final realization, and thus are not separated from the solution by clear phase-boundaries, will often not be explicitly mentioned. They blend too thoroughly with their final solutions. On the other hand, mediating phases which must persist as temporary tasks until they find their final "application" to the situation have a better chance of being explicitly formulated. Furthermore, many super-ordinate phases do not appear in the protocol, because the situation does not appear to the S promising enough for them. Therefore, they are at once suppressed. In other words, they are too fleeting, too provisional, too tentative, occasionally also too "foolish," to cross the threshold of the spoken word.

In very many cases, the mediating phases are not mentioned because the S simply does not realize that he has already modified the original demand of the problem. The thing seems to him so self-evident that he does not have at all the feeling of having already taken a step forward. This can go so far that the S deprives himself of freedom of movement to a dangerous degree. By substituting unawares a much narrower problem for the original he will therefore remain in the framework of this narrower problem, just because he confuses it with the original.

. . .

12. Learning from Mistakes (Corrective Phases)

As yet we have dealt only with the progress from the superordinate to the subordinate phases (or vice versa), in other words, with progress along a given genealogical line. That this is not the only kind of phase succession is, one should think, sufficiently indicated by the protocol given above. Here the line itself is continually changed, and one way of approach gives way to another. Such a *transition to phases in another line* takes place typically when some tentative solution does not satisfy, or when one makes no further progress in a given direction. *Another* solution, more or less clearly defined, is then looked for. For instance, the first proposal (esophagus) having been recognized as unsatisfactory, quite a radical change in direction takes place. The attempt to avoid contact is completely given up and a means to desensitize tissues is sought in its place. In the third proposal, however, the S has already returned to old tactics, although with a new variation. And such shifting back and forth occurs frequently.

It will be realized that, in the transition to phases in another line, the thought-process may range more or less widely. Every such transition involves a return to an earlier phase of the problem; an earlier task is set anew; a new branching off from an old point in the family tree occurs. Sometimes a S returns to the original setting of the problem, sometimes just to the immediately preceding phase. An example for the latter case: From the ingenious proposal, to apply the rays in adequate amounts by rotation of the body around the tumor as a center, a S made a prompt transition to the neighboring proposal: "One could also have the radiation apparatus rotate around the body." Another example: The S who has just realized that the proposal of the esophagus is unsatisfactory may look for another natural approach to the stomach. This would be the most "direct" transition, that is, the transition which retrogresses least. Or, renouncing the natural approach to the stomach, he looks for

another method of avoiding contact. Or, again, he looks for an altogether different way to avoid the destruction of healthy tissue. Therewith, everything which can be given up at all would have been given up; a "completely different" solution would have to be sought.

In such retrogression thinking would naturally not be taken back to precisely the point where it had been before. For the failure of a certain solution has at least the result that now one tries *"in another way."* While remaining in the framework of the old *Problemstellung*, one looks for another starting point. Or again, the original setting may itself be altered *in a definite direction*, because there is the newly added demand: From now on, that property of the unsatisfactory solution must be avoided which makes it incompatible with the given conditions.

.   .   .

Such learning from errors plays as great a rôle in the solution-process as in everyday life.[13] While the simple realization, *that* something does not work, can lead only to some variation of the old method, the realization of *why* it does not work, the recognition of the *ground of the conflict*, results in a correspondingly definite *variation* which corrects the recognized defect.

---

[13] Life is of course, among other things, a sum total of solution-processes which refer to innumerable problems, great and small. It goes without saying that of these only a small fraction emerge into consciousness. Character, so far as it is shaped by living, is of the type of a resultant solution.

A COMPARISON OF PROBLEM SOLVING AND HABIT FORMATION

Having considered the phases of problem solving and their functions we now compare problem solving with the more routinized type of adjustive behavior: associative learning and habit formation.

We have chosen a brief excerpt from an article by Katona, in which he describes the values of using psychological principles, particularly learning theory principles, to clarify some basic questions in economic theory. The reading extends our earlier descriptions of the problem-solving process.

READING 6-3

Habitual Behavior and Genuine Decision Making*

G. KATONA

. . .

. . . In trying to give noneconomic examples of "rational calculus," economic theorists have often referred to gambling. From some textbooks one might conclude that the most rational place in the world is the Casino in Monte Carlo where odds and probabilities can be calculated exactly. In contrast, some mathematicians and psychologists have considered scientific discovery and the thought processes of scientists as the best examples of rational or intelligent behavior.[4] An inquiry about the possible contributions of psychology to the analysis of rationality may then begin with a formulation of the differences between (a) associative learning and habit formation and (b) problem solving and thinking.

The basic principle of the first form of behavior is repetition. Here the argument of Guthrie holds: "The most certain and dependable information concerning what a man will do in any situation is information concerning what he did in that

situation on its last occurrence" (4, p. 228). This form of behavior depends upon the frequency of repetition as well as on its recency and on the success of past performances. The origins of habit formation have been demonstrated by experiments about learning nonsense syllables, lists of words, mazes, and conditioned responses. Habits thus formed are to some extent automatic and inflexible.

In contrast, problem-solving behavior has been characterized by the arousal of a problem or question, by deliberation that involves reorganization and "direction," by understanding of the requirements of the situation, by weighing of alternatives and taking their consequences into consideration and, finally, by choosing among alternative courses of action.[5] Scientific discovery is not the only example of such procedures; they have been demonstrated in the psychological laboratory as well as in a variety of real-life situations. Problem solving results in action which is new rather than repetitive; the actor may have never behaved in the same way before and may not have

---

* Excerpted from Rational Behavior and Economic Behavior, *Psychological Review*, 1953, *60*, 309-311.

[4]Reference should be made first of all to Max Wertheimer who in his book *Productive Thinking* (17) uses the terms "sensible" and "intelligent" rather than "rational." Since we are mainly interested here in deriving conclusions from the psychology of thinking, the discussion of psychological principles will be kept extremely brief.

[5] Cf. the following statement by a leading psychoanalyst: "Rational behavior is behavior that is effectively guided by an understanding of the situation to which one is reacting" . . . French adds two steps that follow the choice between alternative goals, namely, commitment to a goal and commitment to a plan to reach a goal.

learned of any others having behaved in the same way.

Some of the above terms, defined and analyzed by psychologists, are also being used by economists in their discussion of rational behavior. In discussing, for example, a manufacturer's choice between erecting or not erecting a new factory, or raising or not raising his prices or output, reference is usually made to deliberation and to taking the consequences of alternative choices into consideration. Nevertheless, it is not justified to identify problem-solving behavior with rational behavior. From the point of view of an outside observer, habitual behavior may prove to be fully rational or the most appropriate way of action under certain circumstances. All that is claimed here is that the analysis of two forms of behavior—habitual versus genuine decision making—may serve to clarify problems of rationality. We shall proceed therefore by deriving six propositions from the psychological principles. To some extent, or in certain fields of behavior, these are findings or empirical generalizations; to some extent, or in other fields of behavior, they are hypotheses.

1. Problem-solving behavior is a relatively rare occurrence. It would be incorrect to assume that everyday behavior consistently manifests such features as arousal of a problem, deliberation, or taking consequences of the action into consideration. Behavior which does not manifest these characteristics predominates in everyday life and in economic activities as well.

2. The main alternative to problem-solving behavior is not whimsical or impulsive behavior (which was considered the major example of "irrational" behavior by nineteenth century philosophers). When genuine decision making does not take place, habitual behavior is the most usual occurrence: people act as they have acted before under similar circumstances, without deliberating and choosing.

3. Problem-solving behavior is recognized most commonly as a deviation from habitual behavior. Observance of the established routine is abandoned when in driving home from my office, for example, I learn that there is a parade in town and choose a different route, instead of automatically taking the usual one. Or, to mention an example of economic behavior: many businessmen have rules of thumb concerning the timing for reorders of merchandise; yet sometimes they decide to place new orders even though their inventories have not reached the usual level of depletion (for instance, because they anticipate price increases), or not to order merchandise even though that level has been reached (because they expect a slump in sales).

4. Strong motivational forces—stronger than those which elicit habitual behavior —must be present to call forth problem-solving behavior. Being in a "crossroad situation," facing "choice points," or perceiving that something new has occurred are typical instances in which we are motivated to deliberate and choose. Pearl Harbor and the Korean aggression are extreme examples of "new" events; economic behavior of the problem-solving type was found to have prevailed widely after these events.

5. Group belonging and group reinforcement play a substantial role in changes of behavior due to problem solving. Many people become aware of the same events at the same time; our mass media provide the same information and often the same interpretation of events to groups of people (to businessmen, trade union members, sometimes to all Americans). Changes in behavior resulting from new events may therefore occur among very many people at the same time. Some economists (for instance, Lord Keynes) argued that consumer optimism

and pessimism are unimportant because usually they will cancel out; in the light of sociopsychological principles, however, it is probable, and has been confirmed by recent surveys, that a change from optimistic to pessimistic attitudes, or vice versa, sometimes occurs among millions of people at the same time.

6. Changes in behavior due to genuine decision making will tend to be substantial and abrupt, rather than small and gradual. Typical examples of action that results from genuine decisions are cessation of purchases or buying waves, the shutting down of plants or the building of new plants, rather than an increase or decrease of production by 5 or 10 per cent.[6]

---

[6] Some empirical evidence supporting these six propositions in the area of economic behavior has been assembled by the Survey Research Center of the University of Michigan.

CONCEPT FORMATION

An aspect of the thinking and problem-solving process that we have not yet mentioned is concept formation. The formation of a concept is often a necessary early step in problem solving; it may *be* the problem at times. Early work in psychology sought to describe the process of forming a concept; and some of the recent research continues the effort. We consider some examples of this research for the light they can shed on the problem-solving process itself. We will recognize the unsettled and controversial points in current psychological theory on concept formation, without—we hope—becoming entangled in them.

Concept formation is acquiring or utilizing a common response to dissimilar stimuli.* It requires what is often called the "abstracting" of a common property from several different objects, events, or situations. Two examples will help identify the process. Hull, in one of the early experimental demonstrations of concept formation, taught his subjects to associate a particular nonsense syllable with a variety of Chinese symbols—all different except for one common element in each symbol. Later on, the subjects used this nonsense syllable to identify Chinese symbols, not previously seen, containing the same common element. They had formed a concept. Comparably, in the business setting, a new executive may learn to identify a group of dissimilar people— accountants, bookkeepers, clerks, and secretaries—as members of the auditing department. He has formed a concept that causes him to respond, in some sense, to dissimilar people in the same way. Because the development of such concepts constitutes an important part of the problem-solving effort, we are interested in knowing what takes place when concept formation is attempted and what influences facilitate or hamper the process. In Research Summaries 6-1 and 6-2, we consider some theories of concept formation and postpone our discussion of influencing factors until Chapter Twenty.

Two different theoretical orientations toward concept formation hold the

---

* This definition and the discussion which follows are based on: T. S. Kendler, "Concept Formation," in *Annual Review of Psychology*, 1961, p. 447.

field. In one, forming a concept is considered a matter of *discriminating* a feature that several different stimuli have in common. This position theorizes that a concept is formed directly through a stimulus-response connection, without the intervention of any internal (cognitive) mediating process taking place between the stimulus and response. The second, and perhaps more widely held orientation, is that concept formation is a process that goes on *between* the presentation of the stimulus (or the problem) and the making of the response (the solution). The evidence supporting one or the other position is not yet all in, so we cannot simplify our presentation by describing *the* one process of forming concepts. As a matter of fact, a useful knowledge of how people form concepts can be developed by following the reasoning and research of both schools of thought.

RESEARCH **SUMMARY** **6-1**	*Discrimination Theories of Concept Formation.* Skinner, whose work we have previously considered in Chapter Eleven, drawing on his extensive studies of the learning process, outlines a pattern of concept formation based on differential reinforcement. Any aspect of a stimulus, he suggests, that is present when a response is reinforced, gains a degree of control over the response; the control, or, increased likelihood for the response to occur when that aspect of the stimulus is present, continues even when it is present in combination with other stimuli not previously experienced.

Other theorists also emphasize the discrimination process in concept formations. For example, Bourne and Restle suggest the existence of two discrimination processes in "concept identification": conditioning to the relevant and rewarded cue, and adaptation to the irrelevant, unrewarded cue. The rate of learning to identify (or form) concepts accurately is considered a function of the ratio of relevant to irrelevant cues. Additional research suggests a linear relationship between the number of bits of irrelevant information and the difficulty in forming concepts (Bourne). The more we have to sort through and distinguish the irrelevant, the more difficulty we have. The introduction of only two instances of irrelevance can interfere with an individual's identification of regularly occurring similarities; this is a difficulty because he does not know which instances are the irrelevant ones (Bruner, Wallach, and Galenter).

In connection with concept formation, brief mention must also be made of Harlow's discussion of learning set, which he considers basic to concept formation. He describes learning set as a discrimination process in which inappropriate responses and response tendencies are inhibited, thus creating a set to make only the appropriate responses. For Harlow, concepts are formed in the same fashion as learning sets.

Before going on to a discussion of the other theory in the field, it will be well for us to find use for the theory we have already discussed by examining any implications it might have for the administrator.

The suggestion can be drawn that in a problem-solving effort, when concepts are to be drawn from direct observation of a number of events, care must be taken to eliminate, where possible, any irrelevant or unnecessary bits of data. In a sense, the problem must be stripped down to its essential characteristics. The interfering effect of irrelevant information is similar to the phenomenon of "mental dazzle"—too much useless information—that we describe later (Chapter Twenty).

In many administrative situations, it will be possible to form concepts from direct observation of a variety of events, without resort to any extended mediating cognitive process between observation and concept. For example, a problem may be posed that suggests differential handling of the various departments in a company. Direct examination of the organization chart and the manning tables may immediately suggest grouping them into large and small departments. Or, a quick survey of the functions performed by the departments may suggest a grouping based on whether they are entirely internal departments, or are departments having contact with the public—sales, purchasing, reception, and the like.

On the other hand, care must be taken lest such a quick conceptual grouping be considered the only legitimate one to use. It is possible, for example, to group departments together quickly on the basis of functions performed, whereas for effective problem solving a more useful conceptual grouping might be departments with high social interaction and those with low interaction. The latter concept may not be the one first developed, but may require further thinking and analysis.

Mediating Theories of Concept Formation

We now turn to the second principal interpretation of how concepts are formed, that which suggests the existence of a mediating cognitive process between problem (in this case, the occurrence of a series of events) and solution (in this case, the development of a concept uniting such events). To represent the orientation toward concept formation requiring such a mediating process, we choose the work of Bruner and his associates.

RESEARCH SUMMARY 6-2

Strategies in Forming Concepts. The experimental analysis of concept formation reported by Bruner, Goodnow, and Austin serves as a good illustration of the type of research now being done on the thinking process. Their experimental design enabled them to "externalize" the thought processes of the subject. The nature of the experimental task made it possible for the experimenters to infer what processes the subjects were using to achieve a solution. In addition, through logical analysis of the problem situation the experimenters were able to describe certain ideal processes (or strategies as they were called)—ideal in relation to criteria identified by the experimenters. They then compared the ideal strategies with those actually taken by the problem-solving subjects. They also sought to identify the factors that influenced their subjects to use one or another strategy.

The concept forming strategies are intervening cognitive activities; and it is his emphasis on these that distinguishes Bruner's approach from the discrimination theorists, whose work we have previously described.

A more specific description of the experimental procedure itself will help explain some possible strategies that can be taken to achieve a concept and to evaluate them in terms of the criteria identified by Bruner, *et al.*

They prepared 81 cards; each card was printed in one of three colors (red, green, or black), had on it one, two, or three similar figures (a cross, circle, or square). In addition, each card had a single, double, or triple border. Figure 6-1 pictures some of the designs that are possible. In Bruner's experiment, there were 255 possible ways of grouping the 81 cards, for example, all cards using circles (designs 1, 3, 5, 7 and 9); all cards containing two figures in a double border (designs 8, 9, 10); or all cards containing one figure, in a triple border and printed in black (design 5, 6, 11).

It will not be possible for us to follow completely the procedures used by Bruner; we select, for illustration, one possible experimental presentation of the material and two possible strategies used by

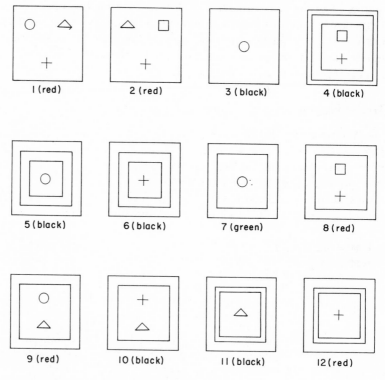

Figure 6-1

Illustrative Designs Useful in Studying Concept Formation. (Based on experiments of Bruner, Goodnow, and Austin.)

some of his subjects. In one experimental procedure, the cards were presented one at a time. For each run of the cards, one way of categorizing the cards was chosen by the experimenter as the right way, for example, all red cards using circles. The task for the subject was to discover this category system and thus form a concept. To make learning possible after each card was presented, the subject was told whether or not the card fell into the category. After each correctly selected card, he was asked to state his hypothesis as to what the category was and what characteristics on the card defined it; in this way his thinking processes could be better "seen."

In forming a concept under these conditions, one strategy a subject can use is to keep all the characteristics of the first correct card as the basis of his strategy—redness, two figures, which were circles, contained in a double border; then, test each subsequent positive instance to see which characteristic, if any, is not included. Another, riskier strategy is to select one or two characteristics as the basis of the category and test these on subsequent positive instances. Here, the subject might say "I'll bet its cards containing two figures in a double border."

Any strategy used can be evaluated by considering it in the light of three questions:

1. Does it make maximum use of all the information that is available?
2. Does it minimize the "cognitive strain" of holding in memory, all at once, a large number of bits of information?
3. Does it control the risk or probability of making decisions that are wrong?

The first strategy mentioned above makes maximum use of the information and is relatively safe, but it keeps the level of cognitive strain high. The second method is less strainful but is risky and uses information in a careless fashion.

Experiments such as Bruner's cannot, of course, describe all possible strategies that either the exigencies of the situation or the personal habits of thinking might dictate. The research does identify some ways in which any strategy can be evaluated.

Strategies similar to those identified by Bruner are used frequently by business men before making business decisions. Instances, cases, or items of information are presented to them. These must be categorized and related to other instances. When this process of concept formation is finished a decision is made. When it is verified the problem is solved.

For example, three complaints about delayed orders that come to the desk of the Sales Manager on the same day activate him to do something about the situation. He obtains from his file other recent complaints and sends them along to the Production Manager, whose problem it now becomes. The essence of his problem is, of course, to find the cause of the delay. From another point of view the problem might be solved were he to find common characteristics of each situation. In this effort he would, or at least, could, use Bruner's strategies. In doing so, he might be able to sort all instances into two common groupings: Group 1—all went through an understaffed department; Group 2—all required meeting unusual specifications. Further tracing of these findings would lead to action that could solve his problem. With knowledge of the advantages and disadvantages of the various strategies he might use, the businessman can perhaps plan his problem-solving efforts in a more informed fashion, choosing strategies in relation to the criteria that are most important in his situation.

Going Beyond the Information Given

There is still another way of describing concept formation and thinking that will be helpful for us to mention. We refer to Bruner's (1957) discussion of thinking as a process of "going beyond the information given,"—"a speck on the horizon surmounted by a plume of smoke is identified as a ship, so too a towering transatlantic liner at its dock," or, as another example, seeing that A is bigger than B on one occasion, and that B is larger than C on another, the observer goes beyond the immediate sensory information given to "know" that B is bigger than C. The ability to go beyond the information given is, Bruner states, a matter of the coding system (concept system), or ways of grouping and relating information that we have previously learned. Bruner points out the need to learn coding systems that have applicability beyond the situation in which they were first learned. How to do this touches on a problem of basic importance in any problem-solving effort and we shall want to consider some of the possibilities for accomplishing this in our next chapter.

Problem Solving: A Restatement

Thus far in this Chapter, we have attempted an examination of the psychological processes the individual employs to solve problems, as described by some of the early workers such as Dewey and Duncker, and as further analyzed through recent research. Gagne, in the introduction to his 1959 review of research in the area, provides a summary of the problem-solving process, incorporating both the old and the new. His description includes an indication of the phases in problem solving and concept formation (which we have discussed here) and decision making, which we will discuss in our next chapter:

> Problem solving begins with a stimulus situation, and instructions which establish sets and define the goal. The behavior is exhibited in a number of phases, which may be conceived as follows. Phase one is the reception of the stimulus situation. Sometimes, the situation is entirely apparent to the subject from the beginning; or, it may be presented in a sequential manner; or again, the subject's responses may change the situation as he proceeds. Concept formation or concept invention, is a second phase, which probably has its basis in transfer of training. This behavior is greatly influenced by strategies, that is, by rules that subjects adopt (whether or not they can state them clearly) to determine which parts of the stimulus situation to react to. Some kinds of problems (like trouble

shooting, solving mathematical problems) appear not to require concept invention.

Determining courses of action is a third and central phase in problem solving. The courses of action available to the subject may be few to very many. This phase is also influenced by strategies, which may be relatively "conservative" or relatively "risky," and which interact with the concepts of outcome probabilities the subject has. Decision making may be distinguished as a fourth phase of problem solving. It is a process of choice or judgment that occurs when two or more courses of action are known to the individual, each of which provides an "adequate" solution. Verification is the final stage.

COMPUTER SIMULATION OF THINKING

New insights into the problem-solving and thinking processes beyond those possible with traditional experimental methods, are being sought through computer simulation of human thinking. The interest here is not in attaining objectives beyond the scope of human capabilities through the use of the computer's high speed or its extensive storage capacities ("memories"). The computer's resources are used rather, to simulate, as closely as possible, the way in which a human being would think and solve problems. Information, identical with that which a person might have about a problem is stored in the computer. The machine is then programmed to process this information in a fashion similar to the sequence of steps that would be taken by the person solving the problem.

In 1956, Newell, Shaw, and Simon, in a pioneering study, evolved a theory of problem solving based on their analysis of a computer simulation of human problem solving in the field of symbolic logic.

An example of their work, using computer simulation as a means of describing human thinking is presented in the reading by Newell and Simon that follows. A theory of human problem solving and an illustration of how computer simulation is being used to study the thinking process are given.*

* For a comprehensive survey of other similar work being done readers are referred to Hovland or to Minsky's extensive bibliography.

READING 6-4

Computer Simulation of Human Thinking*

ALLEN NEWELL

AND HERBERT A. SIMON

The path of scientific investigation in any field of knowledge records a re-

* From *Science*, copyright 1961 (December 22) by the American Association for the Advancement of Science, *134*, 2011-2017.

sponse to two opposing pulls. On the one side, a powerful attraction is exerted by "good problems"—questions whose answers would represent fundamental advances in theory or would provide the basis for important applications. On the other side, strong pulls are exerted by "good techniques"—tools of observation and analysis that have proved to be incisive and reliable. The fortunate periods in a science are those in which these two pulls do not paralyze inquiry by their opposition but cooperate to draw research into fruitful channels.

When this happy condition is not substantially satisfied, science is threatened by schism. Some investigators will insist on working on important problems with methods that are insufficiently powerful and that lack rigor; others will insist on tackling problems that are easily handled with the available tools, however unimportant those problems may be.

Stress arising from the mismatch of ends and means is seldom completely absent from any science; examples could be provided from contemporary biology, meteorology, or mathematics. But it has been blatantly apparent in the science of psychology. This is true even if we leave out of account the tremendously important practical problems that are posed for the field by its potential applications in the clinic, in education, and in many areas of social policy. In basic research the disparity has been strikingly visible. We can fairly classify most psychological research, and even most research psychologists, by their orientation on this issue. "Gestaltism" is one of the labels applied to question-oriented psychology; "behaviorism" is the label most commonly applied to method-oriented psychology. It is no accident that research on human thinking, problem solving, personality, verbal behavior, and social phenomena has tended to attract psychologists closest to the "Gestalt" end of the continuum, while research on animal behavior, physiological psychology, rote memory, and simple motor skills has been primarily the domain of behaviorists.

It is commonly agreed that the dividing lines between the two points of view have become less clear since World War

II. Several reasons might be given for this trend, but a full explanation would include the impact of new ideas drawn from cybernetics and the rapidly developing communications sciences. Complex electronic devices using feedback mechanisms to secure adaptive behavior have clarified concepts such as "goal seeking" and "learning" and have showed how these concepts could be made operational. This clarification has encouraged problem-oriented psychologists to give more precise operational meaning to terms that had been vague, and has encouraged technique-oriented psychologists to tackle problems that earlier appeared too complex for their tools.

The developments now taking place in psychology involve much more, however, than just a borrowing of new terms and new metaphors from other sciences. They involve the use of the digital computer as a tool both for constructing theories and for testing them. Enough has already been learned about this tool and its potentialities to indicate that many of the "good problems" of psychology are now within reach of the "good techniques."

We should like to discuss here one of several important applications of the computer to psychological research—its use as a device for simulating the processes of human thinking. We shall not attempt a review of computer-based research in this one sphere of application but shall present instead a specific example drawn from our own work.

The Behavioral Phenomena

Let us begin with a sample of the phenomena we wish to explain. We seat a subject in the laboratory (a college sophomore, member of a ubiquitous species in psychological research). We present him with a problem, which we tell him is a problem in "recoding" symbolic expressions. We present a certain expression:

$$R.(\sim P \supset Q) \qquad (1)$$

and ask him to obtain from it a second expression:

$$(Q \vee P).R \qquad (2)$$

by applying to the first expression a succession of rules of transformation drawn from a list which we also put before him.

Readers familiar with symbolic logic will recognize the expressions and the rules, but the subjects were unacquainted with formal logic. The subjects read the first expression, for example as, "(r) dot (tilde-p horseshoe q)." They made no use of the meanings of the expressions in their usual interpretation but simply manipulated them as organized collections of symbols. If the reader wishes to follow the analysis in detail, he should adopt the same point of view.

We asked the subject to announce aloud each rule that he wished to apply and the expression that would result from its application. The experimenter then wrote the new expression on a blackboard. We also asked the subject to talk aloud about what he was doing—"what he was thinking about." We recorded the entire session on tape.

Here is the protocol of a subject working on the problem stated above (subject No. 9, problem α 1).

Subject: "I'm looking at the idea of reversing these two things now."

Experimenter: "Thinking about reversing what?"

Subject: "The R's . . . then I'd have a similar group at the beginning, but that seems to be . . . I could easily leave something like that 'til the end, except then I'll. . . ."

Experimenter: "Applying what rule?"

Subject: "Applying, . . . for instance, 2. That would require a sign change."

Experimenter: "Try to keep talking, if you can."

Subject: "Well . . . then I look down at rule 3 and that doesn't look any too practical. Now 4 looks interesting. It's

got three parts similar to that . . . and there are dots, so the connective . . . seems to work easily enough, but there's no switching of order. I need that P and Q changed, so . . . I've got a horseshoe there. That doesn't seem practical any place through here. I'm looking for a way, now, to get rid of that horseshoe. Ah . . . here it is, rule 6. So I'd apply rule 6 to the second part of what we have up there."

Experimenter: "Want to do that?"

Subject: "Yeah."

Experimenter: "OK, to line 1 you apply rule 6. Line 2 is $R.(P \vee Q)$."

Subject: "And now I'd use rule 1."

Experimenter: "Rule 1 on what part? You can use it with the entire expression or with the right part."

Subject: "I'd use it both places."

Experimenter: "Well, we'll do them one at a time . . . which do you want first?"

Subject: "Well, do it with P and Q."

Experimenter: "$R.(Q \vee P)$. Now the entire expression?"

Subject: "Yeah."

Experimenter: "On line 3, rule 1 . . . you'd get $(Q \vee P).R$."

Subject: "And . . . that's it."

Experimenter: "That's it all right; OK . . . that wasn't too hard."

The research problem, then, is to construct a theory of the processes causing the subject's behavior as he works on the problem, and to test the theory's explanation by comparing the behavior it predicts with the actual behavior of the subject. How can a computer help us to solve this problem?

Nonnumerical Computer Program as a Theory

An electronic digital computer is a device for adding, subtracting, multiplying, and dividing very rapidly. But it is now known to be much more than this. Speed in executing arithmetical operations is achieved by providing the computer with a program (usually stored in the computer memory) to govern the sequence of its operations, but designed to make that sequence conditional on the results of previous operations.

The instructions that make up the computer program, like the data on which it operates, are symbolic expressions. But while the data are normally interpreted as numbers, the instructions are interpreted as sequences of words— as sentences in the imperative mode. When the computer interprets the instruction "add *A* to *B*," it produces the same result that a person would produce if he were asked in English to "add the number labeled *A* to the number labeled *B*."

We see that a computer is not merely a number-manipulating device; it is a symbol-manipulating device, and the symbols it manipulates may represent numbers, letters, words, or even non-numerical, nonverbal patterns. The computer has quite general capacities for reading symbols or patterns presented by appropriate input devices, storing symbols in memory, copying symbols from one memory location to another, erasing symbols, comparing symbols for identity, detecting specific differences between their patterns, and behaving in a manner conditional on the results of its processes.

Let us return now to our human subject in the laboratory. His behavior, which we wish to explain, consists of a sequence of symbol emissions. This statement does not depend on the "thinking aloud" technique used in these experiments. It would be equally true if the subject had responded to the task in writing, or by pushing buttons. In all cases, his behavior can be interpreted as a sequence of symbol productions—in the last case cited, a sequence of *L*'s and *R*'s, where *L* stands for "left button" and *R* stands for "right button."

We can postulate that the processes going on inside the subject's skin—involving sensory organs, neural tissue, and muscular movements controlled by the neural signals—are also symbol-manipulating processes; that is, patterns in various encodings can be detected, recorded, transmitted, stored, copied, and so on, by the mechanisms of this system. We shall not defend the postulate in detail —its true defense lies in its power to explain the behavior. Nor shall we speculate in detail about the precise neurophysiological mechanisms and processes that correspond to terms such as *symbol transmission, stored symbol, copying,* and the like.

Instead we shall adopt the tactic, highly successful in other sciences, of allowing explanation at several distinct levels, without for a moment denying that the mechanisms producing the behavior are ultimately reducible to physiological mechanisms and that these, in turn, are reducible to chemical and physical mechanisms. Just as we explain what goes on in the test tube by chemical equations and subsequently explain the chemical equations by means of the mechanisms of quantum physics, so we will attempt to explain what goes on in the course of thinking and problem solving by organization of symbol-manipulation processes, putting to one side the task of explaining these processes in neurophysiological terms.

This approach to building a theory of complex behavior is depicted in Fig. 1. We are concerned with the top half of the figure—with reducing the overt behavior to information processes. If this reduction can be carried out, then a second body of theory will be needed to explain information processes on the basis of neurological mechanisms. Tunneling through our mountain of ignorance from both sides will prove simpler, we hope, than trying to penetrate the entire distance from one side only.

Using Fig. 1, we begin to see how a

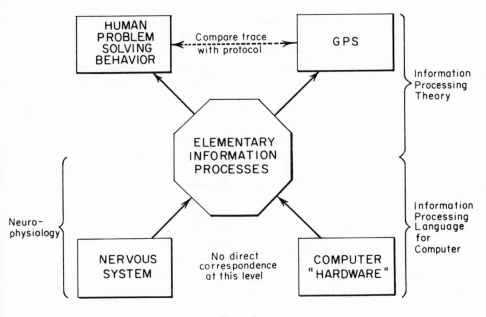

Figure 1

Levels in an Information Processing Theory of Human Thinking

computer can help with the half of the tunneling operation that concerns us here. We postulate that the subject's behavior is governed by a program organized from a set of elementary information processes. We encode a set of subprograms (subroutines) for a digital computer, each of which executes a process corresponding to one of these postulated information processes. Then we undertake to write a program, compounded from these subroutines, that will cause the computer to behave in the same way that the subject behaves—to emit substantially the same stream of symbols—when both are given the same problem. If we succeed in devising a program that simulates the subject's behavior rather closely over a significant range of problem-solving situations, then we can regard the program as a theory of the behavior. How highly we will prize the theory depends, as with all theories, on its generality and its parsimony—on how wide a range of phenomena it ex-

plains and on how economical of expression it is.

It can be seen that this approach does not assume that the "hardware" of computers and brains are similar, beyond assuming that both are general-purpose symbol-manipulating devices and that the computer can be programmed to execute elementary information processes that are functionally quite like those executed by the brain. When we begin to theorize about the reduction of information processes to hardware, the brain and the computer (at least the computer used in this particular way) part company (see Fig. 1). The former calls for a physiologist, the latter for an electrical engineer or physicist.

From a formal standpoint, a computer program used as a theory has the same epistemological status as a set of differential equations or difference equations used as a theory:

1) Given a set of initial and boundary conditions, the differential equations pre-

dict the successive states of the system at subsequent points in time.

2) Given a set of initial and subsequent environment inputs, the computer program predicts the successive states of the system (the subject's symbol emissions and the state of his memory) at subsequent points in time.

With this use of the computer we construct "equations" for nonnumerical symbol-manipulation phenomena without ever translating the phenomena into numerical form.

General Problem Solver

Our attempt to explain the problem-solving protocol, excerpted above, and others like it takes the form of a computer program that we call the General Problem Solver (GPS).

The program has means for representing internally (that is, in its memory) symbolic structures corresponding to the logic expressions, the rules for transforming expressions, and new expressions generated by applying the rules. The problem cited above is represented internally in the form of an expression that means "transform 1 into 2." We call the symbolic structures corresponding to the logic expressions *objects;* the structures corresponding to the problem statement and similar statements, *goals.* The program attains goals by applying *operators* to objects, thus transforming them into new objects.

The program has processes for applying operators to objects. It also has processes for comparing pairs of objects; these processes produce (internally) symbols that designate the differences between the objects compared. It has processes for generating new goals from given objects, operators, and differences.

The processes of GPS are organized around three types of goals and a small number of methods for attaining goals of these types (see Fig. 2).

1) *Transformation goals.* These are of the form already illustrated: Transform object *a* into object *b.*

Method 1. Compare *a* with *b* to find a difference, *d,* between them; if there is no difference, the problem is solved. Construct the goal of reducing difference *d* between *a* and *b.* If successful, the result will be a transformation of *a* into a new object, *c.* Now construct the new goal of transforming *c* into *b.* Attaining this goal will solve the original problem.

Method 1'. There is another method, the planning method, for attaining transformation goals. We do not have space to describe it in detail here. Briefly, it involves replacing the objects with corresponding abstracted objects, say, *a''* and *b'',* then transforming *a''* into *b''* by means of the other methods and using the resulting sequence of operations as a *plan* for transforming *a* into *b.*

2) *Operator application goals.* These are of the form: Apply operator *q* to object *a.*

Method 2. Determine whether *a* meets the conditions for application of *q.* If so, apply *q;* if not, determine a difference between *a* and an object to which *q* is applicable. Construct the goal of reducing this difference. If successful, a new object *a'* will be produced, which is a modification of *a.* Now try to apply *q* to *a'.*

3) *Difference reduction goals.* As we have just seen, these are of the form: Reduce difference *d* between objects *a* and *b.*

Method 3. Find an operator, *q,* that is *relevant* to the difference in question (the meaning of relevance will be explained in a moment). Construct the goal of applying *q* to *a.* If successful, the result will be a transformation of *a* into a new object, *c,* which will not differ as much from *b.*

Thus, the General Problem Solver is

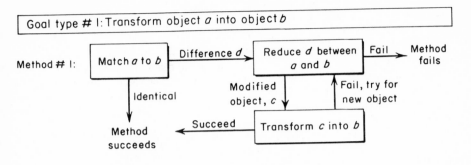

Goal type # 1: Transform object a into object b

Method # 1:

Match a to b — Difference d → Reduce d between a and b — Fail → Method fails

Identical ↓

Modified object, c ↓   Fail, try for new object ↑

Method succeeds ← Succeed — Transform c into b

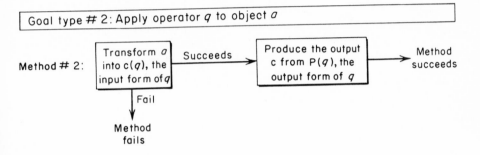

Goal type # 2: Apply operator q to object a

Method # 2:

Transform a into $c(q)$, the input form of q — Succeeds → Produce the output c from $P(q)$, the output form of q → Method succeeds

Fail ↓

Method fails

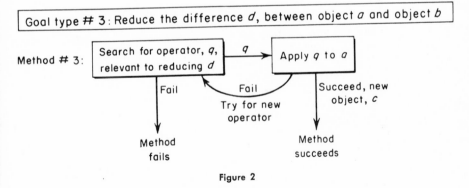

Goal type # 3: Reduce the difference d, between object a and object b

Method # 3:

Search for operator, q, relevant to reducing d — q → Apply q to a

Fail ↓   Fail, Try for new operator ↖   Succeed, new object, c ↓

Method fails   Method succeeds

Figure 2

Methods For Means-Ends Analysis

a computer program comprised of rather general processes for reasoning about ends (goals) and means (operators). It is general in the sense that the program itself makes no reference to the precise nature of the objects, differences, and operators with which it is dealing. Hence, its problem-solving capacities can be transferred from one kind of task to another if it is provided with information about the kinds of objects, differences, and operators that characterize and describe the particular task environment it is to handle. Thus, to solve logic problems, it must be provided with a format for representing logic expressions, tests for the differences that must be recognized between pairs of expressions, and a list of the allowable operators. The rules of the game it is to play must be described to it.

At present, the General Problem Solver is also provided with a "table of connections" that lists the operators that are potentially useful (relevant) for reducing each of the recognizable types of differences. We have indicated in another place how this program could use its own problem-solving processes to construct the table of differences, and how it might even evolve a suitable set of differences if these were not provided to it in a new task environment (1).

Testing the Theory

How adequate the program is as an information-processing theory of human problem solving can be asked at several levels of specificity. At the grossest level, we may ask whether the program does, in fact, solve problems of some of the sorts that humans solve. This it demonstrably does. Hence we may say that its program constitutes a system of mechanisms, constructed from elementary information processes, that is sufficient for solving some problems. It provides an unequivocal demonstration that a mechanism can solve problems by functional reasoning.

The general kinds of means-end analysis that the General Problem Solver uses are also the methods that turn up in the subjects' protocols. We have examined in fair detail some 20 protocols of subjects solving logic problems (2). Virtually all the behavior in these protocols falls within the general framework of means-end analysis. The three goal types we have described account for about three-fourths of the subjects' goals, and the additional goal types that appear in the protocols are closely related to those we have described. The three methods we have

outlined represent the vast majority of the methods applied to these problems by the subjects. In addition, the planning method, mentioned above, appears in several different forms in the protocols.

Protocols of human problem-solving behavior in a range of tasks—playing chess, solving puzzles, writing computer programs—contain many sequences of behavior that are also quite similar to the means-end analysis of the General Problem Solver. We may cite, for example, the following excerpt from the thinking-aloud protocol of a chess player: "Again I notice that one of his pieces is not defended, the rook, and there must be ways of taking advantage of this. Suppose now, if I push the pawn up at bishop 4, if the bishop retreats I have a queen check and I can pick up the rook. If the bishop takes the pawn, then I can win a piece by simply again bringing either the queen down with check, or knight takes bishop."

We cannot, of course, on the basis of this kind of evidence, conclude that GPS provides an adequate explanation for all these kinds of problem-solving behavior. Many other mechanisms may be involved besides those that are incorporated in it. Only when a program simulates the entire sequence of behavior—for example, makes the same chess analysis as the human player—do we have any assurance that we have postulated a set of processes that is sufficient to produce the behavior in question.

These tests are still very general and do not take into account differences among the programs of different subjects. Obviously, not all subjects solve the problems in exactly the same way. The evidence presented thus far suggests that programs of most subjects share the general qualitative features of GPS, but there are variations in detail. We can subject the theory to further tests by seeing what modifications in GPS, if any, will enable us to predict, in detail, the symbolic behavior of a particular subject during some interval of his problem-solving activity.

In Fig. 3 we compare, in parallel columns, the protocol segment introduced earlier with the output of a particular version of GPS set to the task of solving the same problem. The right-hand half of Fig. 3 is the human subject's protocol; the left-hand half is the trace of the program. The language of the subject is much less stylized than the language of the computer. To fit the theory, we must, for example, interpret a sentence such as, "I'm looking at the idea of reversing these two things now," as equivalent to "Construct the difference-reduction goal of eliminating the difference in position of corresponding subparts in objects L1 and L2." To make such a translation is, in practice, not too difficult, and having made it, we can determine in great detail the similarities and differences between the programs of the subject and the computer, respectively.

Let us consider some of the differences visible in the example at hand—differences that represent inadequacies of GPS in its present form as an accurate theory of the subject's behavior. Observe that the subject solves the entire problem in his head and then asks the experimenter to write the actual transformations on the blackboard. The GPS program, in the version shown here, makes no provision for such a distinction between the internal and external worlds; hence, the trace corresponds only to the subject's covert (but verbalized) problem solving. For example, GPS and the subject both discover in the same sequence the correct rules for transforming the problem expression, but the subject "publicly" applied these rules in the reverse order.

Another difference, characteristic of these data, and of such data in general, is that a number of things appear in the trace that have no correspondents in the human protocol—most prominently, the references here in the trace to rules 5, 7, and 8. We cannot tell whether these omissions indicate an error in the theory, or whether the subject noticed the rules in question but failed to mention them aloud.

In contrast to these differences, there is some striking correspondence in detail between the computer trace and the subject's protocol. First, in noticing differences between pairs of expressions, both GPS and the subject pay most attention to differences in the positions of symbols, next most attention to the presence or absence of "~" signs, and least attention to differences in connectives. This shows up, for example, in the refusal of both to apply rule 2, after mentioning it, to reorder the expression, because applying the rule involves changing a sign. Second, of the several possible paths to solution of the problem, both program and subject chose an application of rule 6 and two applications of rule 1.

These samples of success and failure will give the reader some indication of the kind of detailed comparison that can be made between theoretical predictions of computer models of this kind and actual human behavior. Much remains to be learned about how to make such comparisons and how to test their "goodness of fit." The fragmentary evidence we have obtained to date encourages us to think that GPS provides a rather good approximation to an information-processing theory of certain kinds of thinking and problem-solving behavior. The processes of thinking can no longer be regarded as completely mysterious.

Computer Trace

L0 (QvP).R
L1 R.(~P⊃Q)

GOAL 1 TRANSFORM *L1* INTO *L0*
   GOAL 2 CHANGE POSITION IN *L1*
      GOAL 3 APPLY *R1* TO *L1* [*A.B→ B.A*]
      PRODUCES *L2 (~P⊃Q).R*

   GOAL 4 TRANSFORM *L2* INTO *L0*
      GOAL 5 CHANGE POSITION IN LEFT *L2*
         GOAL 6 APPLY *R2* TO LEFT *L2* [*A⊃B → ~B⊃ ~A*]
         PRODUCES *L3 (~Q⊃P).R*

      GOAL 7 TRANSFORM *L3* INTO *L0*
         GOAL 8 CHANGE SIGN LEFT *L3*
         NONE FOUND

      GOAL 5
         GOAL 9 APPLY *R3* TO *L2* [*A.A → A*]
         REJECT, NOT DESIRABLE
         GOAL 10 APPLY *R4* TO *L2* [*(A.B).C → A.(B.C)*]
         REJECT, NOT DESIRABLE
         GOAL 11 APPLY *R5* TO *L2* [*A.B → ~(~Av~B)*]
         REJECT, NOT DESIRABLE
         GOAL 12 APPLY *R7* TO *L2* [*A.(BvC) → (A.B)vA.C)*]
         REJECT, NOT DESIRABLE
         GOAL 13 APPLY *R8* TO *L2* [*A.B → A*]
         REJECT, NOT DESIRABLE

      GOAL 5
         GOAL 14 APPLY *R1* TO *L2* [*AvB → BvA*]
         GOAL 15 CHANGE CONNECTIVE TO *V* IN LEFT *L2*
            GOAL 16 APPLY *R6* TO LEFT *L2* [*A⊃B → ~AvB*]
            PRODUCES *L4 (PvQ).R*

         GOAL 17 APPLY *R1* TO LEFT *L4* [*AvB → BvA*]
         PRODUCES *L5 (QvP).R*

      GOAL 18 TRANSFORM *L5* INTO *L0*
      IDENTICAL

Figure 3

Comparison of Computer Trace [p. 368] with Protocol of a Subject
[p. 369]. The rules are shown in square brackets in the computer trace.
In the protocol, the experimenter's words are [italicized].

Protocol of Subject

(*L0* is expression to be obtained)
(*L1* is expression given at start)
(Goal 1 is set by the experimenter)

I'm looking at the idea of reversing these two things now. *Thinking about reversing what?* The *R*'s . . . then I'd have a similar group at the beginning but that seems to be . . . I could easily leave something like that 'til the end, except then I'll. . . .
Applying what rule?
Applying, . . . for instance, 2.

That would require a sign change.

Try to keep talking, if you can.
Well . . . then I look down at rule 3 and that doesn't look any too practical.
Now 4 looks interesting. It's got three parts similar to that . . . and there are dots, so the connective . . . seems to work easily enough, but there's no switching of order.

I need that *P* and a *Q* changed, so . . .
I've got a horseshoe there. That doesn't seem practical any place through here. I'm looking for a way, now, to get rid of that horseshoe. Ah . . . here it is, rule 6.

So I'd apply rule 6 to the second part of what we have up there. *Want to do that?* Yeah. *OK, to line 1 you apply rule 6.* Line 2 is R.(PvQ). And now I'd use rule 1. *Rule 1 on what part?* You can use it with the entire expression or with the right part. I'd use it both places. *Well, we'll do them one at a time . . . which do you want first?* Well, do it with *P* and *Q*. R.(QvP). *Now the entire expression?* Yeah. *On line 3, rule 1 . . . you'd get* (QvP).R. And . . that's it. *That's it all right, OK . . . that wasn't too hard.*

Conclusion

A digital computer is a general-purpose symbol-manipulating device. If appropriate programs are written for it, it can be made to produce symbolic output that can be compared with the stream of verbalizations of a human being who is thinking aloud while solving problems. The General Problem Solver is a computer program that is capable of simulating, in first approximation, human behavior in a narrow but significant problem domain.

The General Problem Solver is not the only existing program of this type. There is a program, the predecessor of GPS, that also discovers proofs for theorems, but only in symbolic logic (3). There are programs for proving theorems in geometry (4), for designing electric motors, generators, and transformers (5), for writing music (6), and for playing chess (7). There are programs that "learn"—that is, that modify themselves in various respects on the basis of experience (8). We omit from the list those programs that make primary use of the computer's arithmetic capabilities and that are not particularly like human processes, even in their general organization. All of the programs listed, other than GPS, are limited to a single task environment, and none of them seeks to simulate the corresponding human processes in detail. Nevertheless, their underlying structures are all extremely similar, involving selective search for possible solutions based on rules of thumb, or heuristics. This communality provides further evidence of the basic correctness of the approach illustrated by the General Problem Solver in the construction of a theory of human thinking.

In our discussion we have limited ourselves to problem-solving programs. Several recent investigations undertake to simulate other kinds of human cognitive activity that have been studied in the psychological laboratory. Feldman (9) has written a simulation program for partial reinforcement experiments; Feigenbaum (10) and Feigenbaum and Simon have written a program that simulates subjects' behavior in rote memory experiments; Hunt and Hovland (11) and Laughery and Gregg have written programs that simulate concept-forming behavior. In addition, there are a substantial number of programs for pattern-recognition tasks. There are now a score or more of research psychologists who are constructing and testing information-processing theories of cognitive processes, formulating their theories as computer programs, and testing them by comparing the computer simulations with the protocols of human subjects.

Psychology has discovered an important new tool whose power appears to be commensurate with the complexity of the phenomena the science seeks to explain. As our skills in using this new tool develop, we may expect that the paralyzing conflict between the good problem in psychology and the good techniques will be greatly lessened (12).

References and Notes

1. A. Newell, J. C. Shaw, H. A. Simon, in *Self-Organizing Systems*, M. C. Yovits and S. Cameron, Eds. (Pergamon, New York, 1960), pp. 153-189.
2. For discussion of the comparison of the trace of slightly different versions of GPS with protocols, see A. Newell and H. A. Simon, in *Current Trends in Psychological Theory* (Univ. of Pittsburgh Press, Pittsburgh, 1961), pp. 152-179, and ———, *Proc. Conference on Learning Automata, Karlsruhe, Apr. 1961* (Oldenbourg, Munich, 1961).
3. A. Newell and H. A. Simon, *IRE Trans. on Inform. Theory* IT-2, No. 3, 61 (1956).
4. H. Gelernter, J. R. Hansen. D. W. Loveland, *Proc. Western Joint*

Computer Conf. 1960 (1960), pp. 143-150.

5. G. L. Goodwin, *Power* **102** (Apr. 1958).

6. L. A. Hiller and L. M. Isaacson, *Experimental Music* (McGraw-Hill, New York, 1959).

7. A. Newell, J. C. Shaw, H. A. Simon, *IBM J. Research and Develop.* **2**, 320 (1958).

8. A. L. Samuel, *ibid.* **3**, 210 (1959); A. Newell, J. C. Shaw, H. A. Simon, *Proc. Western Joint Computer Conf. 1957* (1957), pp. 218-230.

9. J. Feldman, *Proc. Western Joint Computer Conf. 1961* (1961), pp. 133-144.

10. E. A. Feigenbaum, *Proc. Western Joint Computer Conf. 1961* (1961), pp. 121-132.

11. C. I. Hovland and E. B. Hunt, *ibid.* (1961).

12. We acknowledge our debt to J. C. Shaw, our co-worker in the research described here.

CHAPTER TWENTY

Factors
in
Effective
Problem Solving

It is one thing to describe the process of problem solving but quite another, more difficult, matter to suggest means of improving the process. It is this latter question that we now face: what suggestions are there to make administrative problem-solving efforts more effective.* Within limits, the psychological research on the problem-solving process makes it possible to provide some—perhaps tentative—answers to the question. Suggestions can be helpful, of course, only to the extent that the individual problem solver has both sufficient basic intelligence and an adequate background of relevant knowledge. Our attempt here is to suggest some conditions under which a problem solver can make the best use of, or can be trained to make the best use of, whatever problem-solving equipment he already has.

The Environmental Background

The environment in which the problem-solving effort takes place, of course, will be a major influence on its success, even affecting the likelihood that the effort will be made at all. Some aspects of the environment relevant to successful problem solving are: access to necessary information, time free from

---

* Reflecting the emphasis in psychological research, this chapter considers suggestions principally for problem solving. Frequently, of course, these will also apply to creativity or originality and to making decisions.

the pressures of routine, a system of rewards or sanctions that motivate problem-solving efforts, stimulation obtained from interaction with other professions or technical specialties, and an atmosphere free from rigidity or threat. Fortunately, the administrator can influence these environmental features, and must do so if he wants to encourage effective and creative problem solving (Randall). For his own problem-solving efforts, he will have to seek from his superiors the same suitable environmental opportunity.

A relevant "law" that needs citing at this point is March and Simon's formulation of a "Gresham's law" of planning: when a person can choose between routine tasks and problem-solving effort, he will tend to give his time to the routine. On this basis, they suggest that if inventiveness is to be built into an organization, special departments must be set up in which the members are prohibited from performing routine tasks and rewarded only for problem-solving and inventive activities. Presumably, some adaptation of this is also possible within each department, and for qualified persons on an individual basis, through an allocation of some part of his week's work (for example, a day or half a day) exclusively to problem-solving activity.

Some Cognitive Difficulties in Effective Problem Solving

It will be helpful to us in considering an array of suggestions for improving problem-solving effectiveness if we first set down what seem to be the principal blocks in the way of such effectiveness.* The specific suggestions might then be examined from the point of view of their usefulness in breaking through the obstacles. Some of these barriers are:

Wrong Set. The problem solver often brings a set (attitude, approach, expectation) to the problem that is inappropriate and from which it is difficult to free himself. He may develop such a set while working on the problem. Persistence in the set keeps him from varying his approaches, testing other hypotheses, or drawing upon different kinds of information for the solution. Some problems are problems only because the problem solver has a wrong set; with a change in set the solution would be very easy to see.

Unavailability of Information. Information may have been acquired in such a specific way and tied so tightly to the original, concrete experience that even if it is known to the individual, the information is not available for application to new and somewhat different situations (Bruner, 1957, p. 9). Any conditions that interfere with search behavior, particularly at an early stage of the problem will also, of course, keep information unavailable; these conditions might be limiting the search of one's memory (for example, because of intense motivation or the stress of the situation) or limiting the search of outside sources because of time pressure, limited contacts, or negative attitudes as to appropriate sources to use.

---

* Experimental studies providing the basis for the statements that follow are described in: Woodworth and Schlosberg; Johnson; Thompson.

Ineffective Use of Information.   Even where all the necessary information is available, failure in problem solving may occur because the information was not applied to the problem or because the separate items of information were not seen in proper relation to each other. Bloom and Broder, for example, note that good and poor problem solvers differ not so much in learning relevant information but in applying it to a problem. Ineffective use of information may, of course, result from the wrong set toward the problem or toward the information.

Faulty Analysis of the Problem.   Every problem presents certain "givens" —the conditions that prevail now—financial, mechanical, human, and so on—and certain consequences or requirements to be met by the action proposed in any solution to the problem. Frequently, the problem solver fails to bridge the gap between the two, and in concern for what is given, overlooks some of the requirements, or in considering what is required, he forgets exactly what is given (Woodworth & Schlosberg, p. 821). Our earlier reading from Duncker provides examples of this weakness in problem solving.

Handicapping Characteristics of the Problem Solver.   Failure to solve a problem or inability, in general, to solve certain kinds of problems may simply reflect some handicapping characteristic of the problem solver himself: inadequate intelligence, faulty memory, such personality traits as rigidity or overwhelming anxiety, or lack of achievement need. As with all human behavior, so with problem solving, individual differences count, and notice must be taken of them—a fact that our readers by now have seen emphasized in every section of the book.

A characteristic that must be given special emphasis is the problem solver's level of motivation. The classical, early studies of animal problem-solving behavior (Osgood) as well as more recent human research (Cf. earlier discussion of stress, Part Three) indicate that where extreme motivation or unusual stress exist, problem-solving efficiency falls off and the problem had best be put aside or given to someone less emotionally involved. On the other extreme, if there is too little motivation, the persistent effort required for good problem solving will not be made. A moderate level of motivation is required. The problem solver must feel the need to solve the problem but not so urgently as to direct all his attention to the need and none to the means of solution.

EFFECTIVE PROBLEM-SOLVING PROCEDURES

We consider suggestions for effective problem solving under two principal headings: set and utilization of information. In addition, we provide a listing of other suggestions not classifiable under either heading.

Set

Our survey of the research on problem solving indicates that the question of set has received more attention than any other aspect of the problem-solving process. Whether this suggests that a wrong set is the principal problem in problem solving, or simply reflects the relative ease of studying the question, the fact of much research remains, and thereby makes it possible for us to provide hints for attacking the difficulty of set in problem-solving behavior.

Sources of Set

Structure of the Problem.   We begin by examining the sources of set. For one thing the problem situation itself may be so structured as to cause one aspect of it (not necessarily the most helpful for problem-solving purposes) to be more salient or obvious than others, thus causing us to consider this aspect while ignoring the others. An experiment by Judson and Cofer illustrates this point. Subjects were asked to exclude the one of four words that was different from the others. When the words were presented as: "skyscraper," "prayer," "temple," and "cathedral," 40 per cent of the subjects exclude "skyscraper;" when the words are presented as: "prayer," "skyscraper," "temple," and "cathedral," 70 per cent exclude "skyscraper." The set used to approach the problem—architectural or religious—seems in a significant way to grow out of the structure of the problem situation itself. Problems seem to have a figure-ground organization in that some elements of a problem stand out much more than others. Some elements furnish starting points much more than others and thus induce a set. (See also the discussion of set in perception, Chapter One.)

Sometimes the set may be brought on by the way the problem is introduced or the instructions that are given. A problem assigned in an offhand manner, for example, can suggest that a solution is easy to find thus keeping the problem solver from making the effort for a much more complex approach that may be necessary for the solution. Any problem solver will, therefore, have to work to restructure the problem in order to minimize problem-induced sets that promote fruitless problem-solving efforts (Bloom and Broder).

Characteristics of the Person.   The set also may grow out of characteristics of the individual himself. For example, in the Judson and Cofer study mentioned above, subjects with strong religious interests were much more likely to exclude skyscraper and include prayer as being like the other two words.

Prior Experience.   The immediately preceding problem-solving experiences, or a long history of using one or a few types of approaches, may set the individual toward a particular type of solution and keep him from seeking others when his first efforts fail (Krech and Crutchfield, pp. 383-384).

Shifting Set

Regardless of the sources of the set, the problem solver has to vary his behavior to shift from one approach to another, and occasionally to restructure the problem. In this way, he can minimize the carry-over effect of any wrong set that does exist. The following specific means of accomplishing this shift are suggested by the psychological research that has been done on problem solving.

Maier (1933) makes the preliminary suggestion that the least we ought to do is instruct the problem solver (or ourselves) to guard against habitual activities and persistent sets, so that he can clear the ground for new and different solutions to appear. Such instructions are no guarantee for the administrator hopeful of an easy means of eliminating harmful sets. Nevertheless, Maier's results on student groups indicate that this approach can be helpful.

Hints and suggestions of many types often significantly affect the problem solver's efforts (Duncan). Where an administrator can offer constructive hints to someone else or can seek out such hints from others for his own problem solving, he should do so. The value of being given the right "direction" in which to seek a solution has been demonstrated by Maier (1930). But the administrator will have to be equally concerned about carelessly or unwittingly giving suggestions or hints that build unrewarding sets.

Osgood (p. 637), in concluding his survey of the research in problem solving, suggests that *the problem solver vary his position in the field,* deliberately walk around the problem and look at it from different vantage points. For the administrator-problem solver this might mean that literally he move out of his office and walk through the situation where the problem exists, even taking a trip into the field to do so. In some types of problem, the suggestion might be to "walk" around the problem mentally, picking up (so to speak) each aspect of the problem for inspection and asking questions about it: for instance—can this have something to do with it, what part does that play. . . .

Several experimenters suggest the wisdom of *rearranging the problem—* either spatially or temporally. We can, for example, work a problem either backwards from the goal—asking how and what things would be different, if we achieved the goal—or forward, by beginning with an analysis of what needs changing in the present situation. We could begin by focusing on the "givens" of the problem or the "requirements." We could take all the relevant information and present it in varying time sequences or place it in different spatial relationships (Detambel and Stolurow). One of the key points in this suggestion is, of course, developing ingenious ways of varying the original structuring of the problem—practice in doing so on a variety of problems might very well be helpful. Even increasing the time interval between solving the various steps of a complex problem can be helpful in reducing the carry-over effect of hampering sets from one part of a problem to the next (Kendler, *et al.* 1952).

Backing away from a problem after working on it for some time can also be helpful. In a sense, the incubation phase of problem solving, described earlier (Ch. 19) accomplishes this. In one experiment, it was demonstrated that if time was allowed to lapse between the acquisition of a wrong set and actual work on the problem, more effective problem solving resulted (Adamson and Taylor). The administrator or his problem solver will not always know when he has a wrong set; but, when his problem-solving efforts seem of no avail, one possible cause is wrong set, and one way to reduce the force of this set is to turn to something else for some time and then return to the problem later.

Avoiding functional fixedness. One kind of set that we all bring to our problem-solving efforts is what Duncker has called functional fixedness: seeing common objects only in terms of their most common functions, for example, a pair of scissors is for cutting. Frequently, the set keeps us from seeing the other uses of the object necessary to a solution of the problem, for example, a scissors as a paperweight. Maier (1933) has also studied this problem and points out that even where the problem solver has prior experience relevant to his using the objects of the problem in a different way, functional fixedness may still operate. "Knowing" the right response is not enough if the set is wrong.

If an effort is made early in the problem-solving process to consider all the possible uses for any objects in the problem, even those not obviously relevant, there is evidence to indicate that the set (functional fixedness) will be reduced (Saugstad). In administrative situations, this suggests a preliminary conference or discussion about the problem situation and the various facets of it. It should encourage a preliminary listing of all the attributes of various objects in the problem situation, for example, a scissors is sharp, heavy, metallic, has a hand-grip, and so on. It could be used, therefore, to cut, as a weight, as a conductor, and to tie a string to. The goal is to make available in advance an awareness of a variety of uses, characteristics, and relationships before functional fixedness forces a set that hinders the problem-solving effort.

Seeking alternates. Some of the earliest work on problem solving was done on mechanical puzzles by Ruger. He found it helpful in combating wrong sets to ask a subject to state the assumption underlying his attempts to solve the problem, and then pressed him to consider what alternative assumptions were possible. The suggestion seems a likely one whether we are helping somone else or minimizing the harmful effect of set in our own problem-solving efforts.

Maier and Hoffman report a modification of Ruger's suggestion, applicable to group efforts at problem solving. Groups of four discussants were asked to work out a solution to a problem involving a work change. Each group was given 20 minutes to role-play the parts of a foreman and three workers and then to agree on a solution. When they had finished they were asked to find a second solution. When first and second solutions were compared, the second were found to be better. The possibility therefore exists that being forced to find a second solution helped some groups overcome early sets that narrowed the scope of their solution efforts.

Try another problem. If we assume that a particular set has grown from a narrow problem-solving horizon, existing at a particular time, then Polya's suggestion to try another problem: an analogous, auxiliary, or related problem, makes sense. The new problem may change our set by allowing a greater range of stimuli to come before us. The administrative problem solver might say, for example, "How would I solve this problem in a military setting, how would I solve it for a voluntary community group?" Or, "How would I solve it if all my people were experts, or, if all my people were new trainees?" Hopefully, solving a different problem will bring a different set that nevertheless may be appropriate to the original problem; at the very least, it will help eliminate a persisting, nonhelpful set originally developed.

Polya (pp. 121-122) summarizes the advantage of trying another problem as follows:

> when passing from one problem to another, we may often observe that the new, more ambitious problem is easier to handle than the original problem. More questions may be easier to answer than just one question. . . . The more ambitious plan may have more chances of success provided it is not based on mere pretension but on some vision of the things beyond those immediately present.

Spectator role. Become a "spectator at the problem" by watching it and asking what would happen if "this" or "that" were done. To the business leader beset by the urgency of finding a solution to today's problem right away, it may be easier for us to say this than for him to do it. Nevertheless, the watching attitude reduces the amount of self-involvement, and thus may minimize set and encourage openness to other possibilities (Heidbreder). An almost playful, trial and error approach (as if trying a game or puzzle) can also help reduce the binding effect of either rigid or narrow approaches to problem solving.

A "problem-solving set"—as an advantage. Following the pattern of psychological research, we have emphasized the negative effect of a wrong set and the need to follow procedures that encourage shifting and variability of response. We have now to recognize that there is also advantage in set, at least a certain kind of set. It seems possible to identify a "problem-solving set," perhaps comparable to what Harlow has called learning set or "learning to learn." This set is really not a set *within* the confines of the problem, but a set to *approach* the problem in certain ways. Such a set, or predisposition, must include at least the readiness to search before making decisions: to search for facts, opinions, and varied approaches to our problems. The "set to solve problems" is a question asking one: what are all the givens, what requirements must be met, what are all the things x can do, what are all its characteristics.

A good question to ask, of quite another kind, is, "Can such sets be built in those around us who must solve problems?" The answer is that we have to try to do so, through the example of our own problem-solving behavior, by precept, and by providing problem-solving experience on many different kinds of problems.

Problem Solving and Information

Information, relevant and available, is the very life blood of the problem-solving process. Every problem requires us to draw upon a store of information, from memory or acquired through external search. We fail to solve the problem when we don't have the information at all or when we don't have it available for use, such as, when we do not remember it or when we remember it in a non-useful way or form. We fail to solve the problem if we don't use the remembered information properly; for example, if we don't see appropriate relationships between separate bits of information.

And yet, at times, the presence of too much information dazzles us and keeps us from finding a proper use for the relevant information. Katz provides a simple example of "mental dazzle" from too much information, some of which is irrelevant to the problem solution.

Different groups of children were asked to add the same set of digits, presented in three different ways:

a) 10.50 plus 13.52 plus 6.89, and so on
b) $10.50 plus $13.52 plus $6.89, and so on
c) Kr 10.50 plus Kr 13.52 plus Kr 6.89

The addition of the irrelevant although familiar dollar sign made *b* more difficult than *a;* the addition of the irrelevant and unfamiliar foreign designation made *c* the most difficult of all. Even adults took longer to add *c* than *b* and *a;* and longer to add *b* than *a.* Excess information, when it is either irrelevant or unnecessary and particularly when it is unfamiliar interferes with problem solving.

We have already referred to Bourne and Restle's study (p. 354) in which they demonstrated the interfering aspects of irrelevant information in concept formation. The administrator must not be led to assume from this that all originally "foreign" or difficult information is, therefore, irrelevant. The value of information for problem solving provides us with a challenging paradox (Krech and Crutchfield, p. 325). It is true that the more information an individual has acquired in the past the more likely is it that he will be able to solve a particular problem. But it is also true that the less knowledge he has, the freer he will be of binding restrictions, the more flexible and open to new and unusual solutions, and the less distracted by irrelevant, unnecessary information. This is not the same as saying "Don't bother with the facts"; it does suggest a sifting of facts, while staying open to various solutions. For the administrator, the paradox can be reduced by seeking solutions to problems from both the well experienced person and the inexperienced, and, on some occasions, combining the solutions offered by both.

Specific suggestions fall into two areas: those that help increase the amount of information available and those that help us use most effectively the information we have.

Making More Information Available

Frequently making more information available is a matter of increasing the flow of associations stimulated by the problem. Associations will occur more readily if we separate the process of *producing* associations from the process of *evaluating* them. Jotting down all associations, thoughts, or ideas as they come without, at this point, considering their value, is likely to net more helpful ideas, than a process of sifting, judging, and sorting as the associations appear. Osborn (p. 84) has noted this point in the procedures he has established for "brain-storming" a program for group problem solving. Others have confirmed its value in individual problem solving (Parnes and Meadow, 1959, 1969). (We shall consider its value for groups in Chapter 23.) The suggestion has also been made (Johnson, p. 258) that an enthusiastic rather than a resigned or depressed approach to a problem facilitates the flow of associations. Fatigue, frustration, anxiety, and alcohol are all likely to diminish the flow of associations.

The suggestion to try another problem, previously quoted from Polya, in our discussion of set is relevant here too. Considering a different (simple or more complex) version of a problem increases the range of stimuli operating in the problem solver, and often not only breaks set but provides additional items of information available for use on the original problem.

Material that can't be retained in immediate memory is not readily available for use in solving a problem. Consequently, the severe limitation our span of immediate memory places on the amount of information we are able to receive, to process and to remember, serves as a major barrier to problem solving. One useful procedure in overcoming this information bottleneck is to organize informational input along several dimensions, and then to subdivide each dimension into parts. By forming assorted items of information into some sort of logical outline we "stretch" the span of memory and make more of the information available for ready application (Miller). Organized information is retained more easily than disorganized information.

Making Effective Use of the Information We Have

We have previously seen that unfamiliar bits of information—even when not needed for a solution to the problem of which they are a part—can interfere with our problem-solving efforts. Any preliminary work we do to reduce the unfamiliarity of the information in the problem before attempting to work on a solution will be helpful. Many inventors and scientists who have written about their problem-solving experiences, emphasize this matter "of getting things down pat" first before a solution was attempted. One of them phrases it this way, "It was always necessary first of all that I should have turned my problem over on all sides to such an extent that I had all its angles and complexities in my head and could run through them without writing. . . ." (Helmholtz, quoted in Sanford).

Recent experimentation verifies the point. Subjects who first took time to become more familiar with information later to be used in making a decision, made simpler, more accurate decisions than did those who had not made such advance preparation (Fitts and Switzer).

The arrangement of the information that we propose to use will often influence the way in which it is used. Just as the structure of the problem itself was shown to provide a set, so does the arrangement of the information being used to solve the problem. Re-arranging material or arranging it systematically can thus be a helpful step, following thorough search for the information. In this regard, we can draw a practical suggestion from the models of the decision theorists by arranging decision alternatives in terms of their utility under various conditions, with the probability of occurrence of each condition. The pay-off matrix to be described in Chapter Twenty-one illustrates the point.

Even a simple sorting of the information into categories, for example, arranging the plus-features and then the minus-features together, or grouping the information under such headings as financial, equipment, human factors, and the like, can be helpful in making the information more useful. But, simply listing the pros and cons does not take into account the relative weights or importance of the various features (Bristow and Gabard, p. 70).

Related to arranging the information is the possibility of transforming it. Some of us find it easier to deal with pictorial or graphic representations than we do with verbal summaries, or with words rather than abstract symbols. Frequently, the information itself is easier to understand in a form other than the one in which it originally appears. Consequently, the question of recasting the available information into a different form ought always be considered in a problem-solving effort. An interesting example of the effect of the form in which information appears, or the conclusion drawn is the following:

When the information is stated as: all A are B, then many people draw the conclusion, all B are A.

Yet, when the statement is made, all men are mammals, no one draws the conclusion that all mammals are men (Bruner 1957, pp. 43-44).

Additional Suggestions

Our attention thus far in this section has been focused on overcoming two of the chief obstacles to good problem solving—wrong set and inadequately available or improperly used information. We now bring together an assortment of additional suggestions that psychological research indicates can also be helpful in problem solving.

There is abundant evidence that being able to put a problem in words and talking it out facilitates the problem-solving process (Sanford, p. 363). This suggests, in the first place, the need to build a relevant vocabulary in the problem-solving area and then to become thoroughly familiar with it; and, in the second place, the helpfulness of discussion of the problem in informal groups before there is commitment to a particular solution. The results of two studies may emphasize these points: in one, problem solvers who were required to state their plans in advance were superior to those who did not (Ray); in the other, the simple process of talking out the steps taken in problem-solving practice helped problem solvers discover useful general principles and apply them in subsequent problem solving (Gagne and Smith).

As the complexity of a problem itself increases, the difficulties of solving it increases at a much faster rate. We can minimize the complexity of the problem by subdividing it into parts and solving each part, or by reintegrating some of the complexities into a simpler over-all pattern. We thus reduce the amount of information that has to be held in memory at one time and also cut back the multitudinous comparisons that must be made when the problem remains in complex form (Cook).

It is well to recognize that the revision stage of problem solving, when ideas are refined and more precise formulations attempted, ought to be seen as a process independent both of the search for information and the setting up of possible hypotheses. It is best placed in the last phases of the total problem solving effort, where it will not block the earlier search activities that at first require freedom and scope, not critical evaluation.

One final suggestion in this group, implicit in much that we have said in the chapter thus far, is the need to actively manipulate the problem. Where there aren't parts to be picked up and placed in different relation to each other, diagramming the relations among ideas, or even the activity of jotting down thoughts on a scratch pad may keep the activity level high. The need for actively doing something is important in all learning; it will consequently also be helpful in problem solving.

Training for Problem Solving

We begin by describing a training task in a business organization—a hypothetical task but one that will nevertheless allow us to make some realistic suggestions for training in problem solving.

A new methods department has been set up in the large long-established headquarters of a national insurance company. The department has been staffed with young, bright employees selected from various departments in the company on the recommendation of the personnel department. They will be required to analyze workflow problems in departments throughout the company. Some of their work will be initiated by a request from a department head, some of it will result from a continuing survey of methods and systems that will be set up by the new methods department itself. To be successful, they will be required to have sufficient human relations skill to minimize resistance to the changes they recommend; they will also need problem-solving skill to identify the better methods and systems they will ultimately recommend. Presumably, a basic grounding in the kind of knowledge about human behavior that we have described in our earlier chapters would help in developing human relations skills. But, in this chapter, we are specifically interested in training them for effective problem solving. What kind of training program for effective problem solving can the department head set up?

We see four interacting training approaches, the first two acting as foundations for the others: (1) increasing the trainee's technical competence by increasing the amount of information he has about the operations on which he will work; (2) providing orientation in the processes and difficulties of problem solving; (3) providing practice in solving problems, and (4) maintaining a training attitude toward their subsequent experiences.

1. Working from the broad to the detailed, and using as much in-company talent as is available, the department head will have to provide his staff with a description of the work done in the various departments, the objectives that the company has for their own department, and the tools, for example, methods or systems, the analyst might use. Problem solving requires a thorough familiarity with the information that ultimately must be used in finding a solution. The need for each man to prepare himself thoroughly in the specific work of each department in which he works, must also be emphasized as the first step in attacking a problem.

2. Providing a description of the phases of problem solving (for example, as cited in Chapter Nineteen), a listing of some usual barriers to effective problem solving, and some suggestions for overcoming these barriers (as listed in this chapter) will provide a meaningful preliminary experience to actual practice on problems. Although all learning takes place through active practice, transfer to other problem situations is most likely when the practice is founded on an understanding of meaningful principles (Duncan). Thus, a department head should look upon the orientation session in problem solving as a program of identifying transferable principles, useful in later work. To be most effective such principles will have to be reexamined in connection with practice on actual problems.

In 1950, R. L. Thorndike described some goals that ought to be emphasized in problem-solving behavior. He was writing for teachers and indicating what the schools might do to develop problem-solving attitudes and skills. Nevertheless, his suggestions also outline some useful goals for this orientation phase of the department heads' training programs. He might thus follow Thorndike in emphasizing to his staff (a) that perseverance and flexibility are required; (b) that the source of information must be evaluated critically; (c) that problem solvers must be willing to withhold judgment until all the evidence is in; and finally, (d) that conclusions, no matter how logical, must be viewed empirically.

3. The next step must be to provide practice in actual problems. Here we look to research to try to identify the type of practice problem that will provide the most transfer value in later problem solving on the job. One of the advantages of any practice period in problem solving might well be the building of an expectancy in the trainee that his job is to solve problems. In some ways such an expectancy is a learning set, previously described.

Two suggestions, which at first may appear somewhat inconsistent, emerge from several studies: (Kendler, p. 454) it is helpful to the trainee to practice on a diversity of problems because it develops a set to shift his approaches; but transfer to new problems (and even ability to know when another problem is of a different type) depends on thorough mastery of the first problem. Apparently, a blending of thoroughness and variety of experience is in order. Many different problems ought to be selected for the practice experience, but each one should be introduced only after adequate mastery of the earlier problem has been accomplished. Skipping from one problem to another may let the problem solver know there are many types of problems without teaching him how to solve any one of them.

After the trainees have worked through several practice problems, it will prove helpful for the group to get together and critique each other's problem-solving performance, (Selz) although care must be exercised that they do not criticize each other, but focus on the problems. Following this, they might even be asked to rework their own problems, seeking alternative solutions to the ones they first found (Maier and Hoffman).

The goal of a problem-solving practice period such as we have just described must be to increase understanding of the ways in which a problem is solved, not to learn the solution to the particular problems. This goal will be accomplished only if continuous emphasis is placed on problem-solving processes and principles that can be generalized to any later problem-solving effort.

4. As the trainees gradually begin their real problem-solving efforts on the job, both the problem solver and the department head or administrator must maintain a willingness to be evaluative of both solution and problem-solving method. Occasional review bearing on problem-solving principles and obstacles, round-table critiques, and continued focus on the best methods for solving problems will all pay dividends in more effective problem solving. Giving each trainee a checklist of desirable problem-solving practices will serve as a continuing reminder of principles discussed in his earlier training (Bloom and Broder).

Before leaving our discussion of training for problem solving, one final and important point must be made: there is no one method of problem solving that is best for all individuals and all problems. There is room for, perhaps we might better say, need for, a variety of problem-solving approaches (Buswell). As previously stated, the goal of a training program is neither to teach a particular solution nor to teach a particular method of problem solving but rather to develop facility in using a variety of approaches based on sound principles. The individual must be helped to avoid seeking to fit the problem to a method that he finds comfortable, and encouraged to seek out whatever method or approach will help to reach a solution.

Individual Differences in Problem Solving

Some people are better problem solvers than others; not only because of specialized abilities and background of knowledge, but also because of personality characteristics and habits of thinking and working that favor effective problem solving. Carrying along our training example of the previous section, we now identify some characteristics that the personnel department might have considered in recommending employees for the job requiring high problem-solving ability. However, because our aim is more to alert the administrator to the presence of individual differences than to provide a set of selection criteria, we mention these characteristics only briefly.

The following personality and motivational characteristics have been identified as favoring effective problem solving: high achievement need; a tolerance of ambiguity and uncertainty; flexibility; habits of searching and exploration; and freedom from conventionalized attitudes in the area of the problem.*

In addition to personality differences, there is evidence also that well habituated differences in cognitive methods of approaching problems exist and influence problem-solving effectiveness. Bruner and Tajfel, for example, speak of broad categorizers and narrow categorizers, finding that the former group can maintain a certain distance from the immediate stimulus situation whereas the latter group would seem to be over-responsive to small changes in the situation. Although their research only suggests it, one could predict that broad categorizers would be better problem solvers. Along somewhat the same line, John reports in a study of training in the natural sciences as compared with training in other disciplines, that past training and experience bring about habituation to particular conceptual and organizational processes, which, of course, affect current problem-solving ability.

We are still far from the day when we will be able to discriminate accurately (let alone quickly) between the good and the poor problem solver. However, we have reached the point of being able to warn the administrator that he will not be able to train all his people to be effective problem solvers. When he has a choice among several people for assignment to a problem-solving job, keeping in mind the individual differences mentioned, he should seek out evidence of past or present problem-solving effectiveness before making his choice. Our department head in the earlier illustration might well find that one value of his training program is to help him discover employees who won't learn to solve problems effectively, even though they may function well in other tasks.

---

* From data presented respectively by French and Thomas; Krech and Crutchfield, p. 387; Johnson, pp. 261 and 285; Weaver and Madden.

CHAPTER TWENTY-ONE

Decision Theory
and
Making Decisions

Decision making, which has been identified thus far in our presentation as a phase of the process of problem solving, has itself become the focal point of, and the term applied by many to a major interdisciplinary effort of theorizing, model building, mathematical formulation, and empirical study since the late 1940's* with the term decision theory used by many as the name for this area of effort.

The importance of decision making in the administrative process has been most forcefully expressed by Simon in the opening statement of his fundamental text in the field.

> Although any practical activity involves both "deciding" and "doing" it has not commonly been recognized that a theory of administration should be concerned with the processes of decision as well as with the processes of action. This neglect perhaps stems from the notion that decision making is confined to the formulation of over-all policy. On the contrary, the process of decision does not come to an end when the general purpose of an organization has been determined. The task of deciding pervades the entire admininstrative organization quite as much as does the task of doing—indeed, it is integrally tied up with the latter. A general theory of administration must include principles of organization that will insure correct decision making, just as it must include principles that will insure effective action.

---

* Edwards (1961) provides a review of the work done since 1954; his earlier review (1954) goes back to 1930, however, the bulk of the work was done after World War II, although with strong roots in economic theory long before that.

There is good reason then for us to examine in some detail the work being done by psychologists and others on the decision-making process.

Beginning in economics, with theoretical explanations of man's economic behavior as he made decisions to maximize utility, the work in this area has drawn on the several behavioral sciences and has been extended to much of man's decision-making and choice behavior. Today, theory and research on decision making are at the center of a variegated array of problems and applications, of significance alike to the behavioral science theorist and the business practitioner: from learning theory on the one hand to computer applications on the other, from a micro-analytic approach of problem solving to broad descriptions of administrative behavior. The field has developed useful constructs for analyzing human behavior and potentially useful theories for the ultimate prediction of human behavior. Although it has not yet become possible to provide specific prescriptions for more effective decision making, what has been accomplished is to bring into sharp focus, for both practitioner and scientist, the need for a better understanding of the process of making a decision.

It is necessary to distinguish between decision making, as it is described in decision theory, and making a decision in a real life situation as, for example, decisions made by administrators to hire a particular man, to bring in a consultant on a technical problem, or to go into production on a new product. Decision theory largely considers decision as the process of making a single choice among courses of action at a particular point in time. Because a person actually making a decision almost always includes any choice in a sequence of other choices, descriptions of a single choice can only approximate the complex process of making a decision. We do gain, nevertheless, the advantage of clarity and simplicity in studying the process when we confine our descriptions to a single choice.

Another point of difference between *decision making* (a term we will use from now on only when referring to decision theory) and *making a decision* is the emphasis placed by decision theorists on the rational aspects of the process. Recent models of decision making, particularly those developed by psychologists, are beginning to include psychological influences, with decision making models being integrated with other psychological processes (for example, level of aspiration and personality processes [see later Edwards reading]); nevertheless, the fact remains that decision theory has not yet been able to describe fully the complex circumstances and problems that must be faced by the person when he makes a decision. Nonetheless, as decision theorists continue to exert more influence on those thinking and writing about organizations, the administrator ought to be aware of their ideas.

There is one further introductory comment that has to be made. The terms, decision making and problem solving, are often used interchangeably. They are related through one of the major concepts of decision theory, which represents possible future behavior as a "tree" with a number of branches radiating from each choice point. The individual selects at each such point the appropriate branch to follow. (Also see comment in Simon, xxvii.) A problem becomes a process of making a series of decisions in an effort to move toward a specified goal. Thus, the problem of handling a break-down in inventory control might be attacked by deciding, in the first place, to consider automatic data processing as a possible solution, then deciding between one company's system and another's, and so on.

We first present in this chapter some material on decision theory, and follow this with two readings that consider the actual making of a decision in the business setting.

DECISION THEORY

An Economist's Matrix for Analyzing a Decision

The economists have been long at work analyzing the rational process of making a choice. Although psychologists point out that choices are not always made on a rational basis,* it will, nevertheless, be helpful if we begin with a simple rational analysis of a business decision as it might be made by an economist, in one of the simplest of decision theory models.†

A New York City bank must decide whether to open a branch office at a particular location in an adjoining suburb. The officers of Bank X do not know whether or not a competing institution (Bank Y) will follow their example and open a branch on an available location across the street. The decision of Bank X may be analyzed more precisely by considering the following table:

TABLE 6-1

Illustrative Payoff Matrix

| | Behavior of Bank X | |
	I *Opens a Branch*	II *Does not Open a Branch*
Behavior of Competing Bank Y: a. follows example of Bank X	sustains losses from uneconomic situation	lack of growth
b. does not follow example of Bank X	gain new business; make profit	lack of growth

The table is a typical pay-off matrix, suggesting the outcomes from the possible actions that might be taken. We can read it as follows: The behavior of Bank X may be either (I) to open a branch or (II) not to open a branch. If

---

* For a discussion of rational and irrational elements in administrative decision making see Simon, pp. XXII-XXIX and chapters 4 and 5.
† The model that follows is loosely adapted from Marschak.

it does I, and the competing institution follows its example (a), it will suffer a loss; if it does I, and the competing bank does not follow its example (b) it will gain new business. If Bank X does not open a branch (II), it experiences a lack of growth.*

From the bank's point of view, we may assume that gains are preferable to a lack of growth, and a lack of growth is preferable to losses. These are the utilities to be considered. In addition to considerations of utility, the probability of either type of behavior on the part of the competing institution must also be estimated. Supposing the probability of competing Bank Y's *not* following the first bank's example is 100%. Then policy I produces a result (gains) preferable to the result (lack of growth) of policy II. The bank officers, therefore, "should" choose policy I. If the probability of *b* were zero (thus, the likelihood of *a* would be 100%) he "should" choose policy II.

Of course, rarely are probabilities certain in this way. Usually the probability of an event's occurrence in such a situation falls at a point intermediate between zero and 100%. And we frequently are required to choose when an event is "almost certain," "more likely than not," and so on.

The interacting forces in making a choice are: the utilities or subjective values resulting from each course of action (that is, what is it worth to us) and the subjective probabilities—our estimate of how likely it is that an event will occur. The objective, or "real" probability cannot be known, as a rule. Presumably, the higher the utility of the outcome of a particular action, the greater risk we will be willing to take concerning the probability of that outcome. To put it more specifically, we can say that if utility is very high, we will make the decision even though the probability of occurrence is below 50%. In our example, a new bank, very much in need of growth, might choose to open a branch even though there is a 50-50 chance that a competing institution will follow its example. A large, well-established bank, not placing so much value on growth, might not open a branch unless the likelihood of finding undesirable competition was less than 25%.

The analysis illustrates the use of a pay-off matrix and of the two principal elements in a rational choice; utility and probability. Using such an analysis as a point of departure, economists have gone on to structure more complex mathematical models around the ingredients identified. In doing so, they have been able to state the variables more precisely and to consider the whole process of decision making at a higher level of abstraction—one leading to important theoretical development.

We cannot examine in any detail the theory in the field, nor consider the knotty problems growing out of attempts to measure utility and subjective probability. Our concern is to provide the administrator with an overview of some approaches taken by decision theorists with the thought that some of these approaches may be useful in the decisions he makes.

---

* Our example ignores the possibility that Bank Y may open a branch even if Bank X does not.

The SEU Model

Although the economists have had a running start in the field of decision theory, psychologists are now following close behind. Among psychologists, one of the most widely considered models for analyzing decision making is the subjectively expected utility maximization model (SEU model), named by Ward Edwards.

Taking the four possible considerations that might determine a decision: objective values, subjective value (utility), objective probability and subjective probability, Edwards has examined the four models and the equations that might be developed from the several pairings of the four listed considerations.

In commenting on the SEU model from an administrator's point of view, one point should be underscored: the distinction between objective and subjective probability. Too often, we forget that when we indicate the probability of some event occurring, we are talking of our estimate or guess as to its probability. We proceed to act as if this estimate *is* the objective probability (which may not be determinable) and thus may fail to think through what different decision might be made if some other probability estimate were considered.

Our first reading in this chapter describes the SEU model more fully and relates it to other decision theory models. The reader will see in the article how experiments involving gambling and games can readily be set up to study the influence of psychological variables, such as level of aspiration, personality characteristics, or amount of reinforcement on decision making.

READING 6-5

Utility, Subjective Probability, Their Interaction, and Variance Preferences[*]

WARD EDWARDS

The Subjectively Expected Utility Maximization Model

In 1738 Daniel Bernoulli, puzzled about why people buy insurance even though insurance companies must take in more money as premiums than they pay out in benefits, proposed a theory of decision-making which asserts that people choose among risky courses of action in such a way as to maximize their expected utility (Bernoulli, 1738; Sommer, 1954). The word utility is a name for the concept of subjective value, which may be quite different from objective or dollar value. This theory was put into modern and sophisticated mathematical form in 1944 by von Neumann and Morgenstern in their famous book, *Theory of Games and Economic Behavior* (von Neumann and Morgenstern, 1957). During the remainder of the '40s and the early '50s it attracted an increasing amount of theoretical attention and a small amount of experimental attention as well. Unfortunately, the theory did not hold up very well under experimental analysis. The difficulty seemed to be that people made decisions in risky situations on the basis of the probabilities as they perceived them, rather than the objective probabilities. This experimental finding, combined with the difficulties which arise for an expected utility maximization model when objective probabili-

ties cannot be meaningfully defined, led several theorists to propose a new theory, which asserts that people choose among risky courses of action in such a way as to maximize what has come to be called subjectively expected utility. The subjectively expected utility of a course of action is defined as follows:

$$SEU = \psi_1 u_1 + \psi_2 u_2 + \ldots + \psi_n u_n,$$

where there are n possible outcomes of the course of action, the first outcome has utility u_1 and subjective probability ψ_1, and so on. Although a number of psychologists have expressed some severe reservations about the merits of this model in the face of the data, it remains the dominant model for static decision-making to this day—although nowadays it is usually complicated by a stochastic formulation which causes it to predict a probability that one course of action will be preferred to another, rather than a choice. For reviews of this literature, see (Edwards, 1954d, 1961).

Non-independence of Values and Probabilities

One important feature of the subjectively expected utility maximization model is that the utilities are ordinarily assumed to be functions only of the possible outcomes of the course of action, while the subjective probabilities are ordinarily assumed to be functions only of the objective probabilities of those outcomes. Neither of these assumptions is

[*] From *Journal of Conflict Resolution*, 1962, 6, 42-51.

necessary to the mathematical content of the model itself, but it is very difficult to see how the model could be applied to real decisions unless some such assumptions were made. Nevertheless, a number of people have proposed that utility is determined both by objective probability and by objective value, and that subjective probability is also determined both by objective probability and by objective value.

Specifically, two propositions of this sort have been defended. One asserts that an outcome which has a low probability will, by virtue of that low probability, have a higher value or utility than the same outcome would have if it had a high probability. The assertion that the grass is greener on the other side of the fence embodies the essence of this proposition. Since this hypothesis was originally brought to prominence in psychology by Kurt Lewin and his students, I will call it the Lewin utility theory. The other common proposition concerns the determiners of subjective probability; it says that people will overestimate the likeliness of desirable events and underestimate the likeliness of undesirable ones. A number of psychologists have proposed this second hypothesis in one form or another. Since Francis W. Irwin is an early and effective proponent of this view, I shall call it the Irwin subjective probability theory (Irwin, 1953). It is important to note that although both of these theories are inconsistent with the simple version of the SEU maximization model, they are nevertheless two completely independent theories; either one could be correct while the other was wrong.

Before evaluating the validity of the Lewin utility theory and the Irwin subjective probability theory, we must first decide what the simpler hypothesis is with which both of these theories disagree. This is not as easy as it sounds.

Unfortunately, neither subjective probability nor utility is usually conceived of as directly observable, or even as easily inferred from observations. We usually suppose that choices among risky courses of action are determined by both utilities and subjective probabilities, and we then attempt to infer appropriate values of these quantities to account for observed sets of choices. Since we permit considerable arbitrariness in determining utility and subjective probability values, it takes some substantial set of observations, very carefully chosen, to obtain a contradiction of the SEU model. Without discussing the evidence in detail, I would like to assert that I know of no experiment in the psychological literature, including Irwin's recent one (personal communication), which cannot be explained in terms of appropriate utility and subjective probability functions. Consequently I am compelled to argue that no evidence against the SEU model and in favor of either the Lewin utility theory or the Irwin subjective probability theory exists.

I do not consider this fact to be in favor of the SEU model, however. What it means is that the SEU model, in the form in which it has usually been defended, is so vague that it is almost impossible to find a reasonable pattern of behavior which is inconsistent with it.[2] The SEU model can be made sufficiently specific so that it really means something only by specifying the forms of the utility and subjective probability functions which enter into it, or (what amounts to the same thing) by specifying

---

[2] Since this paper was written, I have reported (Edwards, 1962) a deduction from the SEU model so specific that it would be very easy to find data which violate it, which assumes nothing but continuity and monotonicity of utility and subjective probability functions. This implies that the SEU model is more vulnerable than I realized in 1960.

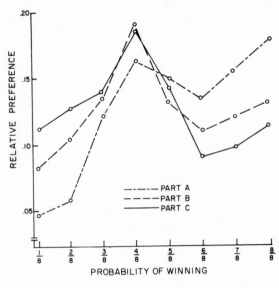

Figure 1

Preference as a Function of Probability for Positive Expected Value Bets. (Reproduced by permission from Edwards, 1953, p. 355.)

some operations by which utilities and subjective probabilities can be measured independently of the decisions they are supposed to predict. Just such a development is now in progress. Direct psychophysical methods are being applied to the measurement both of utility and of subjective probability. So far the results of using such directly obtained utility and subjective probability functions to predict decisions among bets have not been very favorable to SEU models. Unfortunately, they are not very favorable to the Lewin or Irwin theories either. Such experiments seem to show that the utility of money is more or less linear with its dollar value (for small amounts of money, at any rate), and that the estimated probability associated with a suitable probability display is very close to linear with the objective probability being displayed. In short, the data indicate that people perceive both values and probabilities correctly. Never-

theless, they do not make decisions which maximize objective expected value, so it must be concluded that although they perceive values and probabilities correctly, they use them incorrectly. In other words, on this interpretation it is the mathematical form of the SEU model, rather than the links between it and the real world of choices, which is at fault. (This argument is spelled out in detail in [Edwards, 1962]). I will discuss a specific hypothesis about how the mathematical form of the SEU model is at fault and how to correct it later in this paper.

**Evidence Concerning
Non-independence**

So far I have been treating the Lewin utility theory and the Irwin subjective probability theory as though they were alternatives to the SEU maximization model, to be adopted only if the SEU maximization model turns out not to work. But they can equally well be considered as models in their own right, to be used independently of the SEU model. When they are thought of in that way, a substantial amount of evidence bearing on them is available.

First, consider the evidence for the Irwin subjective probability theory. The results of several experiments show that people consider an event more likely to occur if its consequences are favorable than if its consequences are unfavorable (Crandall, Solomon, and Kellaway, 1955; Irwin, 1953; Marks, 1951). Some of the data from my probability preference experiments indicate more or less the same thing (Edwards, 1953, 1954a, 1954b). In those experiments subjects

were asked to make choices from pairs of bets. Both members of each pair had the same expected value, so there was never any objective reason for preferring one bet to the other. Figure 1 shows the results for positive expected value bets. The y-axis is a measure of the extent to which various bets are preferred, and the x-axis is the probability of winning of the bets. It is evident that people particularly like the 50-50 bet and particularly do not like the 6/8 bet; these findings are highly reproducible. Figure 2 shows the same information for negative expected value bets. Here the outstanding finding is that people prefer relatively low probabilities of losing (and relatively high amounts of loss) and avoid relatively high probabilities of losing, and relatively small amounts of loss.

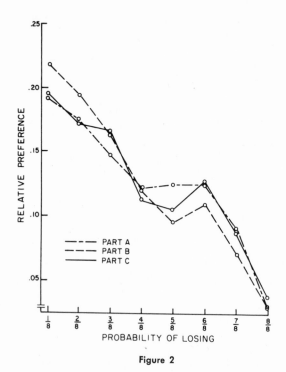

Figure 2

Preference as a Function of Probability for Negative Expected Value Bets. (Reproduced by permission from Edwards, 1953, p. 355.)

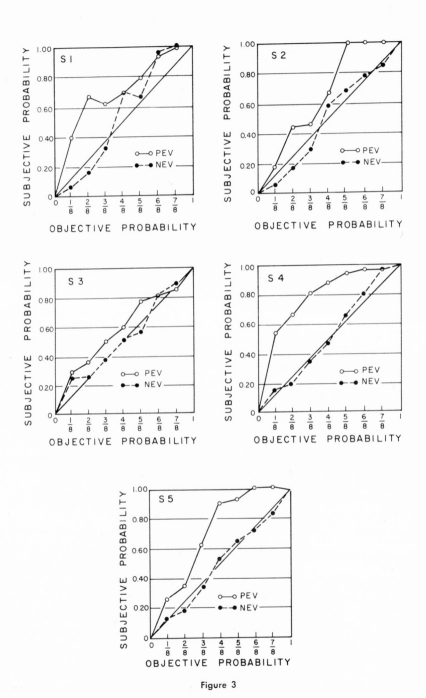

Figure 3

Subjective Probability as a Function of Objective Probability and Sign of Expected Value. (Reproduced by permission from Edwards, 1955, p. 208.)

These findings would be consistent with the hypothesis that people considered an event with a negative expected value to be less likely than the same event with a positive expected value, although of course they do not prove that hypothesis.

Another form of evidence comes from an experiment in which I actually obtained utility and subjective probability functions (Edwards, 1955). Again subjects made choices among bets, and these functions were inferred from their choices. The method used depended on a rather doubtful assumption, but the data obtained in the experiment provided internal consistency checks on the assumption which worked pretty well, so I have some confidence in the data even though I do not like the assumption used to obtain them. The data relevant to the Irwin subjective probability theory are presented in Figure 3. Ten subjective probability functions, two for each of five subjects, are shown. For each subject, one curve is his subjective probability function inferred from postitive expected value bets and the other is his subjective probability function inferred from negative expected value bets. It is apparent that most subjects remained pretty objective when choosing among negative expected value bets, but were over-optimistic when choosing among positive expected value bets.

A Conclusion about the Irwin Subjective Probability Theory

All of these findings strongly indicate that there is at least an interaction between the *sign* of the utility of a bet and the subjective probability associated with the event (note that the utility must be measured on a ratio scale for this statement to be meanirgful, and zero utility must be where you now are). Furthermore, the direction of the effects is in general the direction predicted by the Irwin subjective probability theory. None of the evidence, however, indicates an interaction between value and subjective probability provided that the signs of the utilities involved do not change. This is fortunate for the SEU model. It is not too difficult to think of an SEU model which requires up to five different functions relating subjective to objective probability, depending on the signs of the utilities involved. One such function might apply when all utilities were positive, another when the lowest utility was zero, a third when both positive and negative utilities were present, a fourth when the highest utility was zero, and a fifth when all utilities were negative. Some of the data on zero expected value bets suggests that there may be little or no difference between the first two or three of these cases. But I do not see how to formulate a model which would permit the dependence of subjective probability on amounts, as well as signs, of utilities. And I know of no evidence which requires anything more than interaction with sign. So, for the time being, perhaps we can afford to assume that the Irwin subjective probability theory is right, but that the dependence of subjective probability is on signs of utilities rather than on their values.

Atkinson's Form of the Lewin Utility Theory

Now consider the Lewin utility theory. I don't propose to examine it in Lewin's form; instead, I will take the model which Atkinson has proposed as my point of departure (Atkinson, 1957; Atkinson, Bastian, Earl, and Litwin, 1960). Atkinson believes that in situations in which a person perceives the outcome of a risky act as contingent on his skill, the variables which will control his decision are the motive to achieve success (M_s), the motive to avoid failure (M_f), the subjective probabilities of achieving success and avoiding failure $(P_s$ and $P_f)$ and the incentive values of achieving success and avoiding failure $(I_s$ and $I_f)$. He combines these six determiners of decisions into a single resultant motivation by simple multiplication; his equation for resultant motivation is:

$$(M_s \cdot P_s \cdot I_s) + (M_f \cdot P_f \cdot I_f)$$

Now Atkinson's crucial assumption is that the attractiveness of success is a positive linear function of task difficulty, and similarly that the attractiveness of failure, always a minus quantity, becomes increasingly negative for easier tasks. In symbols:

$$P_f = 1-P_s; \qquad I_s = 1-P_s; \qquad I_f = -P_s$$

It follows that Atkinson's equation for resultant motivation can be rewritten as follows:

$$P_s (1-P_s) (M_s-M_f)$$

You may already have noticed an interesting similarity between this equation for resultant motivation and a familiar statistical quantity: the variance of a two-outcome bet. If you can win $A with probability p and win $B with probability $1-p$, then the variance of the bet is

$$p (1-p) (A-B)^2$$

The only structual difference between the equation for variance and Atkinson's equation for resultant motivation is that in Atkinson's equation the difference between the two motives is not squared. This means that Atkinson's resultant motivation can be negative, while of course a variance cannot be less than zero.

Variance Preferences

This structural similarity suggests that Atkinson's model, though not couched in that language, is in fact a suggestion that people may in choosing among bets base their preferences not only on the first moment of the distribution of outcomes (the mean, or expected value, or SEU), but also on higher moments of the distribution. That suggestion has been made before; in fact, it has been perhaps the most persistent criticism of the school of thought about utility maximization which was started by von Neumann and Morgenstern (Allais, 1953). In 1954 I published an experiment addressed to the question, which concluded that variance preferences do indeed exist, but are minor in importance compared with utility and subjective probability as determiners of choices among bets (Edwards, 1954c). More recently, Coombs and Pruitt have performed an experiment in which they asked subjects to make choices from pairs of imaginary bets of fixed expected value which varied in variance and in skewness (Coombs and Pruitt, 1960). Data were rejected if they failed to satisfy weak stochastic transitivity, which is a fairly lenient kind of assumption that if A is preferred to B and B is preferred to C, then A ought to be preferred to C at least 50 percent of the time. The remaining data were analyzed according to Coombs' unfolding technique. The major findings were that most subjects chose consistently and transitively and that most subjects exhibited single-peaked variance preferences and (except for an undue preference for 50-50 bets) single-peaked skewness or probability preferences. The consistency found by Coombs and Pruitt was extraordinarily high; perhaps it is because their subjects made their choices among these imaginary bets at rates ranging from 3.4 to 22.4 choices per minute, and so cannot have taken much time for reflection. The two rules "Always choose the bet with the highest payoff for winning" and "Always choose the bet with the lowest cost for losing" together account for about 68 per cent of all the rank orderings Coombs and Pruitt obtained; these rules, of course, could be applied simply and mechanically to min-imize thought. It has been shown (Slovic, Lichtenstein, and Edwards, forthcoming) that more complex preference patterns, less easily interpreted as variance prefer-ences, occur when subjects make more careful choices, but of course this finding is not evidence against variance prefer-ences; in fact, the evidence suggests that they do exist, but not in the single-peaked form hypothesized by Coombs and Pruitt.

Unfortunately, for any bet which has only two outcomes, skewness is com-pletely confounded with probability of winning and variance is completely con-founded with utility. Consequently any experiment designed to examine variance preferences unequivocally must use bets with more than two possible outcomes. So neither my earlier experiment nor the Coombs-Pruitt experiment nor the Slovic-Lichtenstein-Edwards experiment has anything definitive to say about the existence or relative size of variance preferences. Nevertheless, it seems intui-tively plausible that such preferences exist, and Atkinson's theory can be rein-terpreted very simply to be an assertion that people with high need for achieve-ment and low need to avoid failure should prefer high-variance bets, while people with low need for achievement and high need to avoid failure should prefer low-variance bets—a hypothesis which is supported by a substantial amount of data.

A Conclusion Concerning the Lewin Theory

If variance preferences exist, then the SEU model is not very useful in predict-ing choices. But the notions of utility and subjective probability are necessary aside from their use in SEU models. People do make judgments about the values of things, and they do make judg-ments about the likeliness of events. These judgments can conveniently be called utilities and subjective probabili-ties, regardless of the usefulness or lack of usefulness of the SEU maximization model. But the Lewin utility theory says more than that variance preferences exist. It asserts that objects which are harder to obtain are more valuable than those which are easier to obtain. This hypothe-sis has meaning independent of choices among risky courses of action. But I am unclear, and have been unable to find out from the literature, which of two pos-sible interpretations of this statement is intended by those who make it. One in-terpretation simply asserts that our world is so constructed that the more desirable objects are harder to get. I feel confident that this is so, but I see no reason why this fact should be interpreted as a theory of behavior. It is instead a theory about the environment in which behavior takes place. The other possible interpretation is that exactly the same object is more valuable when it is hard to obtain than when it is easy to obtain. This hypothesis is intuitively plausible, but I know of no very convincing evidence that it is cor-rect.

Early in this paper, I said that the Lewin utility theory is summarized by the proverb "The grass is greener on the other side of the fence." I am now saying that there are two possible interpretations of this proverb. One is that the grass is really the same on both sides, but looks greener over there. The other, which seems to me more plausible, is that the grass is in fact greener over there—and indeed they put up the fence in the first place just to keep it that way. Until evidence against the second of these two interpretations accumulates, I find it more persuasive than the first.

Summary

The subjectively expected utility maxi-mization model, currently the dominant static model about how men make risky decisions, rests on the concepts of utility or subjective value, assumed to be a function only of amount and nature of the valued object, and subjective probability, assumed to be a function only of amount and display or means of realization of objective probability. But evidence, anecdotal and experimental, suggests that human judgments of value are affected by probability of obtaining the valued object, and human judgments of probability are affected by value of the possible payoffs of the risky course of action. Two specific theories of this sort are considered. The Irwin subjective probability theory asserts that people will over-estimate the likeliness of desirable events and underestimate the likeliness of undesirable events. Review of relevant data indicates that such an interaction indeed occurs, but that it is only with the signs, not with the amounts, of the possible payoffs. The Lewin utility theory asserts that an outcome with a low probability will have a higher value than the same outcome would have if it had a high probability. A specific version of this point of view proposed by Atkinson is reviewed and found to resemble closely the hypothesis that choices among risky courses of action depend on the variance as well as the expected value of each course. Evidence for such variance preferences is reviewed. It is concluded that the favorable evidence concerning variance preferences casts serious doubts on the validity of the subjectively expected utility maximization model. But judgments of value can occur independently of decisions, and so the Lewin utility theory is important even if the subjectively expected utility maximization model is wrong. The question is raised whether the attractiveness of improbable achievements is not a characteristic of the environment rather than of judgments of value. Doesn't the grass seem greener on the other side of the fence because it *is* greener, and wasn't the fence erected to keep it that way?

References

Allais, M. "Le comportement de l'homme rationnel devant le risque: critique des postulats et axiomes de l'école américaine," *Econometrica*, 21 (1953), 269-90.

———. "La psychologie de l'homme rationnel devant le risque: la théorie et l'expérience," *Journal de la Société de Statistique de Paris*, 94 (1953), 47-73.

Atkinson, J. W. "Motivational Determinants of Risk-taking Behavior," *Psychological Review*, 64 (1957), 359-72.

Atkinson, J. W., Bastian, J. R., Earl, R. W., and Litwin, G. H. "The Achievement Motive, Goal Setting, and Probability Preferences," *Journal of Abnormal and Social Psychology*, 60 (1960), 27-36.

Bernoulli, D. "Speciment theoriae novae de mensura sortis," *Comentarii Academiae Scientiarum Imperiales Petropolitanae* (1738), 175-92. Translation by L. Sommer in *Econometrica*, 22 (1954), 23-36.

Coombs, C. H. and Pruitt, D. G. "Components of Risk in Decision-making: Probability and Variance Preferences," *Journal of Experimental Psychology*, 60 (1960), 265-77.

Crandall, V. J., Solomon, D., and Kellaway, R. "Expectancy Statements and Decision Times as Functions of Objective Probabilities and Reinforcement Values," *Journal of Personality*, 24 (1955), 192-203.

Edwards, W. "Probability Preferences in Gambling," *American Journal of Psychology*, 66 (1953), 349-64.

———. "Probability Preferences among Bets with Differing Expected Values," *American Journal of Psychology*, 67 (1954a), 56-7.

———. "The Reliability of Probability Preferences," *ibid.* (1954b), 68-95.

———. "Variance Preferences in Gambling," *ibid.* (1954c), 441-52.

———. "The Theory of Decision-making," *Psychological Bulletin*, 51 (1954d), 380-417.

———. "The Prediction of Decisions among Bets," *Journal of Experimental Psychology*, 51 (1955), 201-14.

———. "Behavioral Decision Theory," *Annual Review of Psychology*, 12 (1961), 473-98.

————. "Subjective Probabilities Inferred from Decisions," *Psychological Review*, 69 (1962). (In press.)

Irwin, F. W. "Stated Expectations as Functions of Probability and Desirability of Outcomes," *Journal of Personality*, 21 (1953), 329-35.

Marks, R. W. "The Effect of Probability, Desirability, and 'Privilege' on the Stated Expectations of Children, *Journal of Personality*, 19 (1951), 332-51.

Phares, E. J. "Expectancy Shifts in Skills and Chance Situation," *Journal of Abnormal and Social Psychology*, 54 (1957), 339-42.

Slovic, P., Lichtenstein, S. C., and Edwards, W. "Boredom: A Vitiating Variable in Decision Experiments." (Forthcoming.)

von Neumann, J., and Morgenstern, O. *Theory of Games and Economic Behavior*. 2nd ed. Princeton, N.J.: Princeton University Press, 1957.

Decision Theory and Business Decisions

Throughout our presentation, we have emphasized that decision theory initially describes choices a *rational* man *should* make. The administrator is neither totally rational (that is, using strict logic and probability information) in his decisions nor does he find all the conditions requisite for rational choice present when he must make his decisions. There is then a considerable gap between choice as described in decision theory and the choices made in the business organization. It is important to recognize the limitations of mathematically modeled rational decisions when these models are applied to actual decisions; there is nevertheless the possibility of using them as a basis for a better understanding of what does take place when the administrator decides.

One way to accomplish such a goal is to study actual business decisions within the framework of decision theory. Cyert, Simon, and Trow have done this with regard to one company's decisions about the feasibility of using electronic data-processing equipment. Their work, which is presented in the next reading, suggests additions that must be made to a theory of decision making if it is to describe real business decisions.

READING 6-6

Observation of a Business Decision[*]

RICHARD M. CYERT,
HERBERT A. SIMON,
AND DONALD B. TROW

. . . [It] is extremely doubtful whether the only considerable body of decision-making theory that has been available in the past—that provided by economics—

————
[*] Reprinted from *The Journal of Business*, XXIX, 237-248, by permission of The University of Chicago Press. Copyright 1956 by the University of Chicago.

does in fact provide a realistic account of decision-making in large organizations operating in a complex world.

In economics and statistics the rational choice process is described somewhat as follows:

1. An individual is confronted with a number of different, specified alternative courses of action.

2. To each of these alternatives is attached a set of consequences that will ensue if that alternative is chosen.

3. The individual has a system of preferences or "utilities" that permit him to rank all sets of consequences according to preference and to chose that alternative that has the preferred consequences. In the case of business decisions the criterion for ranking is generally assumed to be profit.

If we try to use this framework to describe how real human beings go about making choices in a real world, we soon recognize that he need to incorporate in our description of the choice process several elements that are missing from the economic model:

1. The alternatives are not usually "given" but must be sought, and hence it is necessary to include the search for alternatives as an important part of the process.

2. The information as to what consequences are attached to which alternatives is seldom a "given," but, instead, the search for consequences is another important segment of the decision-making task.

3. The comparisons among alternatives are not usually made in terms of a simple, single criterion like profit. One reason is that there are often important consequences that are so intangible as to make an evaluation in terms of profit difficult or impossible. In place of searching for the "best" alternative, the decision-maker is usually concerned with finding a *satisfactory* alternative—one that will attain a specified goal and at the same time satisfy a number of auxiliary conditions.

4. Often, in the real world, the problem itself is not a "given," but, instead, searching for significant problems to which organizational attention should be turned becomes an important organizational task.

Decisions in organizations vary widely with respect to the extent to which the decision-making process is *programmed*. At one extreme we have repetitive, well-defined problems (e.g., quality control or production lot-size problems) involving tangible considerations, to which the economic models that call for finding the best among a set of pre-established alternatives can be applied rather literally. In contrast to these highly programmed and usually rather detailed decisions are problems of a non-repetitive sort, often involving basic long-range questions about the whole strategy of the firm or some part of it, arising initially in a highly unstructured form and requiring a great deal of the kinds of search processes listed above. In this whole continuum, from great specificity and repetition to extreme vagueness and uniqueness, we will call decisions that lie toward the former extreme *programmed*, and those lying toward the latter end *non-programmed*. This simple dichotomy is just a shorthand for the range of possibilities we have indicated.

It is our aim in the present paper to illustrate the distinctions we have introduced between the traditional theory of decision, which appears applicable only to highly programmed decision problems, and a revised theory, which will have to take account of the search processes and other information processes that are so prominent in and characteristic of non-programmed decision-making. We shall do this by recounting the stages through which an actual problem proceeded in an actual company and then commenting upon the significance of various items in this narrative for future decision-making theory.

The decision was captured and recorded by securing the company's permission to have a member of the research team present as an observer in the company's offices on substantially a full-time basis during the most active phases of the decision process. The observer spent most of his time with the executive who had been assigned the principal responsibility for handling this particular problem. In addition, he had full access to the files for information about events that preceded his period of observation and also interviewed all the participants who were involved to a major degree in the decision.

The Electronic Data-processing Decision

(1) The decision process to be described here concerns the feasibility of using electronic data-processing equipment in a medium size corporation that engages both in manufacturing and in selling through its own widely scattered outlets. In July, 1952, the company's controller assigned to Ronald Middleton, an assistant who was handling several special studies in the accounting department, the task of keeping abreast of electronic developments. The controller, and other accounting executives, thought that some of the current developments in electronic equipment might have application to the company's accounting processes. He gave Middleton the task of investigation, because the latter had a good background for understanding the technical aspects of computers.

(2) Middleton used three procedures to obtain information: letters to persons in established computer firms, discussions with computer salesmen, and discussions with persons in other companies that were experimenting with the use of electronic equipment in accounting. He also read the current journal literature about computer developments. He informed the controller about these matters principally through memorandums that described the current status of equipment and some of the procedures that would be necessary for an applications study in the company. Memorandums were written in November, 1952, October, 1953, and January, 1954. In them, in addition to

summarizing developments, he recommended that two computer companies be asked to propose possible installations in the company and that the company begin to adapt its accounting procedures to future electronic processing.

(3) In the spring of 1954 a computer company representative took the initiative to propose and make a brief equipment application study. In August he submitted a report to the company recommending an installation, but this was not acted upon—doubt as to the adequacy of the computer company's experience and knowledge in application being a major factor in the decision. A similar approach was made by another computer company in September, 1954, but terminated at an early stage without positive action. These experiences convinced Middleton and other executives, including the controller, that outside help was needed to develop and evaluate possible applications of electronic equipment.

(4) Middleton drew up a list of potential consultants and, by checking outside sources and using his own information, selected Alpha as the most suitable. After preliminary meetings in October and November, 1954, between representatives of Alpha and the company accounting executives, Alpha was asked to develop a plan for a study of the application of electronic data-processing to sales accounting. Additional meetings between Alpha and company personnel were held in February, 1955, and the proposal for the study was submitted to the controller in March.

(5) Although the proposal seemed competent and the price reasonable, it was felt that proposals should be obtained from another consulting firm as a double check. The controller agreed to this and himself selected Beta from Middleton's list. Subsequently representatives of Beta met with Middleton and other department executives. Middleton, in a memo-

randum to the controller, listed criteria for choosing between the two consultants. On the assumption that the written report from Beta was similar to the oral proposal made, the comparison indicated several advantages for Beta over Alpha.

(6) After the written report was received, on May 2, the company's management committee authorized a consulting agreement with Beta, and work began in July, 1955. The controller established a committee, headed by Middleton, to work on the project. Middleton was to devote full time to the assignment; the other two committee members, one from sales accounting and one from auditing, were to devote one-third time.

(7) The consulting firm assigned two staff members, Drs. Able and Baker, to the study. Their initial meetings with Middleton served the purpose of outlining a general approach to the problem and planning the first few steps. Twenty-three information-gathering studies were defined, which Middleton agreed to carry out, and it was also decided that the consultants would spend some time in field observation of the actual activities that the computer might replace.*

. . .

On February 15 (1956) the controller, in conference with the assistant controller and Middleton, dictated a letter to the company's president summarizing the conclusions and recommendations of the study [a complex study that went much beyond the one planned initially] and requesting that the accounting department be authorized to proceed with the electronics program.

On the following day the controller read the letter to the management committee. The letter reviewed briefly the

* [The authors' narrative continues with a detailed report of activities and decisions leading to the final action taken by the company.]

history of the project and summarized the conclusions contained in the consultants' report: that there was ample justification for an electronic-data-processing installation; that the installation would warrant use of the largest computers; and that it would produce savings, many intangible benefits, and excess computer capacity for other applications. The letter quoted the consultants' estimate of the cost of the installation and their recommendation that the company proceed at once to make such a conversion and to acquire the necessary equipment. It then cited the various cross-checks that had been made of the consultants' report and concluded with a repetition of the conclusions of the report—but estimating more conservatively the operating and installation costs—and a request for favorable management committee action. Supplementary information presented included a comparison of consultant and equipment company cost estimates and a list of present and proposed computer installations in other companies. After a few questions and brief discussion, the management committee voted favorably on the recommendation, and the controller informed Middleton of the decision when the meeting ended.

The Anatomy of the Decision

From this narrative, or more specifically from the actual data on which the narrative is based, one can list chronologically the various activities of which the decision process is composed. If we wish to describe a program for making a decision of this kind, each of these activities might be taken as one of the steps of the program. If the rules that determined when action would switch from one program step to another were specified, and if the program steps were described in enough detail, it would be possible to replicate the decision process.

The program steps taken together define in retrospect, then, a program for an originally unprogrammed decision. The program would be an inefficient one because it would contain all the false starts and blind alleys of the original process, and some of these could presumably be avoided if the process were repeated. However, describing the process that took place in terms of such a program is a useful way or organizing the data for purposes of analysis.

In order to make very specific what is meant here by a "program," Chart I has been prepared to show the broad outlines of the actual program for the first stages of the decision process (through the first seven paragraphs of the narrative).

CHART I

Program Steps from Inception of the Problem to Selection of a Consultant

Keeping-up program (paragraphs 1 and 2 of narrative):
  Search for and correspond with experts;
  Discuss with salesmen and with equipment users;
  Search for and read journals;
Procurement program (paragraph 3):
  Discuss applications study with salesmen who propose it;
  Choice: accept or reject proposed study;
  (If accepted) transfer control to salesmen;
  Choice: accept or reject application proposal;
  (If rejected) switch to consultant program;
Consultant program (paragraphs 4 through 7):
  Search for consultants;
  Choice: best consultant of several;
  Transfer control to chosen consultant;
  Choice: accept or reject proposal;
  (If accepted): begin double-check routine;
  Request expenditure of funds;
  (If authorized) transfer control to consultants;
  And so on.
Subprograms.   The various program steps of the decision process fall into

several subprograms, some of which have been indicated in Chart I. These subprograms are ways of organizing the activities *post factum,* and in Chart I the organizing principle is the method of approach taken by the company to the total problem. It remains a question as to whether this organizing principle will be useful in all cases. As in the present example, these subprograms may sometimes be false starts, but these must be regarded as parts of the total program, for they may contribute information for later use, and their outcomes determine the switching of activity to new subprograms.

In this particular case the reasons for switching from one subprogram to another were either the proved inadequacy of the first one or a redefinition of the problem. Other reasons for switching can be imagined, and a complete theory of the decision process will have to specify the conditions under which the switch from one line of attack to another will occur.

Common Processes.   In the whole decision-making program there are certain steps or "routines" that recur within several of the subprograms; they represent the basic activities of which the whole decision process is composed. For purposes of discussion we have classified these common processes in two categories: the first comprises processes relating to the communication requirements of the organization; the second comprises processes relating directly to the solution of the decisional problem.

Communication Processes.   Organizational decision-making requires a variety of communication activities that are absent when a decision is made in a single human head. If we had written out the program steps in greater detail, many more instances of contacts among different members of the organization would be recorded than are now explicit in the narrative. The contacts may be oral or written. Oral contacts are used for such purposes as giving orders, transmitting information, obtaining approval or criticism of proposed action; written communications generally take the form of memorandums having the purpose of transmitting information or proposing action.

The information-transmitting function is crucial to organizational decision-making, for it almost always involves acts of selection or "filtering" by the information source. In the present instance, which is rather typical in this respect, the consultants and subordinate executives are principal information sources; and the controller and other top executives must depend upon them for most of their technical information. Hence, the subordinate acts as an information filter and in this way secures a large influence over the decisions the superior can and does reach.

The influence of the information source over communications is partly controlled by checking processes—for example, retaining an independent expert to check consultants—which give the recipient an independent information source. This reduces, but by no means eliminates, filtering. The great differences in the amounts and kinds of information available to the various participants of the decision process described here emphasize the significance of filtering. It will be important to determine the relationship of the characteristics of the information to the resultant information change and to explore the effects of personal relations between people on the filtering process and hence upon the transmission of information.

Problem-solving Processes. Alongside the organizational communication processes, we find in the narrative a number of important processes directed toward the decision problem itself. One of the most prominent of these is the search for alternative courses of action. The first activities recounted in the narrative—writing letters, reading journals, and so on—were attempts to discover possible action alternatives. At subsequent points in the process searches were conducted to obtain lists of qualified consultants and experts. In addition to these, there were numerous searches—most of them only implicit in the condensed narrative—to find action alternatives that would overcome specific difficulties that emerged as detail was added to the broader alternatives.

The data support strongly the assertion made in the introduction that searches for alternative courses of action constitute a significant part of non-programmed decision-making—a part that is neglected by the classical theory of rational choice. In the present case the only alternatives that became available to the company without the expenditure of time and effort were the systems proposals made early in the process by representatives of two equipment companies, and these were both rejected. An important reason for the prominent role of search in the decision process is that the "problem" to be solved was in fact a whole series of "nested" problems, each alternative solution to a problem at one level leading to a new set of problems at the next level. In addition, the process of solving the substantive problems created many procedural problems for the organization: allocating time and work, planning agendas and report presentations, and so on.

Examination of the narrative shows that there is a rich variety of search processes. Many questions remain to be answered as to what determines the particular character of the search at a particular stage in the decision process: the possible differences between searches for procedural alternatives, on the one hand, and for substantive alternatives, on the other; the factors that determine how many alternatives will be sought before a choice is made; the conditions under which an alternative that has tentatively been chosen will be subjected to further check; the general types of search strategies.

The neglect of the search for alternatives in the classical theory of decision would be inconsequential if the search were so extensive that most of the alternatives available "in principle" were generally discovered and considered. In that case the search process would have no influence upon the alternative finally selected for action. The narrative suggests that this is very far from the truth —that, in fact, the search for alternatives terminates when a satisfactory solution has been discovered even though the field of possibilities has not been exhausted. Hence, we have reason to suppose that changes in the search process or its outcome will actually have major effects on the final decision.

A second class of common processes encompasses information-gathering and similar activity aimed at determining the consequences of each of several alternatives. In many decisions, certainly in the one we observed, these activities account for the largest share of man-hours, and it is through them that subproblems are discovered. The narrative suggests that there is an inverse relation between the cost or difficulty of this investigational task and the number of alternative courses of action that are examined carefully. Further work will be needed to determine if this relation holds up in a broader range of situations. The record also raises numerous questions about the *kinds* of consequences that are examined most closely or at all and about the conditions under which selection of criteria for choice is prior to, or subsequent to, the examination of consequences.

Another set of common processes are those concerned with the choices among alternatives. Such processes appear at many points in the narrative: the selection of a particular consulting firm from a list, the choice between centralized and decentralized electronic-data-processing systems, as well as numerous more detailed choices. These are the processes most closely allied to the classical theory of choice, but even here it is notable that traditional kinds of "maximizing" procedures appear only rarely.

In some situations the choice is between competing alternatives, but in many others it is one of acceptance or rejection of a single course of action— really a choice between doing *something* at this time and doing nothing. The first such occasion was the decision by the controller to assign Middleton to the task of watching developments in electronics, a decision that initiated the whole sequence of later choices. In decisions of this type the consequences of the single alternative are judged against some kind of explicit or implicit "level of aspiration" —perhaps expressed in terms of an amount of improvement over the existing situation —while in the multiple-alternative situations, the consequences of the several alternatives are compared with each other. This observation raises a host of new questions relating to the circumstances under which the decision will be formulated in terms of the one or the other of these frameworks and the personal and organizational factors that determine the aspiration levels that will be applied in the one-alternative case.

Another observation derivable from our data—though it is not obvious from the condensed narrative given here—is that comparability and non-comparability of the criteria of choice affects the decision processes in significant ways. For one thing, the criteria are not the same from one choice to another: one choice may be made on the basis of relative costs and savings, while the next may be based entirely on non-monetary criteria. Further, few, if any, of the choices were based on a single criterion. Middleton and the others recognized and struggled with this problem of comparing consequences that were sometimes measured in different, and incomparable, units, and even more often involved completely intangible considerations. The narrative raises, but does not answer, the question of how choices are made in the face of these incommensurabilities and the degree to which tangible considerations are overemphasized or underemphasized as compared with intangibles as a result.

Conclusion

We do not wish to try to transform one swallow into a summer by generalizing too far from a single example of a decision process. We have tried to illustrate, however, using a large relatively non-programmed decision in a business firm, some of the processes that are involved in business decision-making and to indicate the sort of theory of the choice mechanism that is needed to accommodate these processes. Our illustration suggests that search processes and information-gathering processes constitute significant parts of decision-making and must be incorporated in a theory of decision if it is to be adequate. While the framework employed here—and particularly the analysis of a decision in terms of a hierarchical structure of *programs*—is far from a complete or finished theory, it appears to provide a useful technique of analysis for researchers interested in the theory of decision as well as for business executives who may wish to review the decision-making procedures of their own companies.

Our final reading in this chapter provides an example of how some concepts derived from decision theory can be applied to a better understanding of incentive influences on employee behavior.

READING 6-7

Incentives, Supervision and Probability*

JAMES N. MOSEL

All managements rely upon the use of incentives to motivate employees to perform those actions required by the organization's mission and goals. These incentives generally fall into two classes: (a) *positive* incentives such as promotions and cash awards (i.e., outcomes people want), and (b) *negative* incentives or deterrents such as dismissal and repri-

mands (i.e., outcomes people want to avoid). Managers have traditionally assumed that the motivating power of such incentives is a function of their attractiveness to the employee (or repulsiveness, in the case of deterrents). Consequently, there has been a tendency to search for bigger and juicier carrots, and a bigger, more threatening club. However, recent developments in the field of behavioral decision theory have shown that there is much more to the story than

* From *Personnel Administration* (Jan.-Feb.) 1962, 25, 9-14.

this. Research on decision behavior has demonstrated that the effectiveness of an incentive is not determined by its attractiveness alone: it is also determined to a very significant degree by the *subjective probability* that the reward (or punishment) will follow the behavior to be motivated.[1] By subjective probability we mean the employee's *perceived* probability or *expectancy* (conscious or unconscious) that the reward will be forthcoming if he performs the action which the reward is intended to motivate; or, in the case of deterrents, the perceived likelihood that the punishment will occur if he commits the act which the punishment is intended to deter.

This relationship may be stated in the form of the following equation: $I = A \times P$, where I is the motivating power of the incentive, A the incentive's attractiveness ("utility" in decision theory) to the employee, and P the employee's subjective probability. (For deterrents we would substitute R for A to stand for the "repulsiveness" of the deterrent.)[2]

For example, this equation means that the incentive power of a cash award for a suggestion submitted in a suggestion plan is determined not only by the monetary value of the cash award, but also by the employee's belief about the likelihood that submitting a suggestion will lead to adoption and the award. It is

also apparent that this equation states in formal and precise terms what has traditionally been explained in terms of the consistency of discipline and the dependability of rewards.

This equation yields a very important conclusion: incentives frequently fail, not because they lack attractiveness to the employee, but because the employee has a very pessimistic attitude (i.e. low subjective probability) about his actions leading to the proffered reward. In view of this, it would seem that management gives too much emphasis to dangling rewards and punishments before the worker, but not enough to creating the conditions that will establish high subjective probabilities. Evidence [of] this defect in employee incentive systems will be presented shortly. We shall also see what effect the supervisor has upon the employee's subjective probabilities.

Measuring Subjective Probabilities in a Military Establishment

These principles have been used in this article to analyze and evaluate the incentives available to 900 civilian employees in a large branch of the military establishment. The employees studied were both men and women, with salaries ranging from $3,000 to $8,000 and over. The subjective probabilities of these employees were obtained for five events:

1. Promotion to a higher grade within the next 18 months if the employee was the most outstanding producer in his section.
2. Dismissal from employment within the next 18 months if he were the worst producer in his section.
3. Receipt of a cash award for sustained superior performance in the next 18 months.
4. Having a submitted suggestion adopted in the Suggestion Awards Program.
5. Supervisor writing a recommen-

---

[1] For a review of recent research on decision behavior see Ward Edwards, "Behavioral Decision Theory," in P. R. Farnsworth *et al.* (eds.), *Annual Review of Psychology*, Palo Alto, Annual Reviews, Inc., 1961. For applications to individual behavior, see Julian Rotter, *Social Learning and Clinical Psychology* (Prentice-Hall, 1954), Chap. 5. For applications to organizations, see James March and Herbert Simon, *Organizations* (Wiley, 1958).

[2] In decision theory there is a third independent variable which is omitted here as irrelevant to the present study, namely, "cost" (effort required, task difficulty, risk, etc.).

dation for cash award for sustained superior performance if such were warranted.

Subjective probabilities were estimated by having employees rate on a six-point scale the likelihood that the above five events would occur under the conditions specified. Thus there were 6 degrees of probability: 100% certain, very probable, fairly probable, uncertain (not sure), fairly improbable, and very improbable. "Uncertain" represents the point of equiprobability, i.e. the point where the chances are fifty-fifty.

TABLE 1

Employee Subjective Probabilities for Five Events

Per Cent of Employees with a Given Subjective Probability[1]

Event	100% Certain	Very Probable	Fairly Probable	Uncertain	Fairly Improbable	Very Improbable	Total
Promotion in next 18 months if most outstanding producer in section	4%	8%	17%	38%	13%	20%	100%
Dismissal in next 18 months if worst producer in section	11	12	22	37	12	6	100
Receipt of cash award for sustained superior performance if warranted	3	4	17	39	15	22	100
Having suggestion adopted in Suggestion Awards Program	3	4	19	54	13	7	100
Supervisor writing recommendation for cash award for sustained superior performance if warranted	24	14	24	17	11	10	100

[1] The total number of employees (100%) is 900.

Results on Subjective Probabilities of Incentives

Table 1 shows the distribution of subjective probabilities for each of the four incentive events and for supervisory support in getting a cash award.

These results reveal several very interesting findings. First we note that for all incentives there is a wide spread of probabilities with an appreciable number of employees with very low probabilities ("very improbable"). For instance, 20 per cent perceive promotion within the next 18 months (if the most outstanding employee) as very unlikely, while 22 per cent perceive the receipt of a cash award for sustained superior performance as very unlikely.

With the exception of "supervisory recommendation for warranted cash award," all incentives have the modal (most frequent) probability at "uncertain." In each of these cases, then, there is a plurality at the equiprobability point; for these employees the chances are fifty-fifty that the incentive event will occur. We notice that uncertainty is greatest (54%) for getting a suggestion accepted, followed in close order by earning a cash award for sustained superior performance (39%), being promoted if most outstanding (38%), and being dismissed if the worst producer (37%), with getting a supervisory recommendation for a cash award having the least uncertainty (17%) of all.

Supervisory support in getting a recommendation for a warranted cash award is notable in that its modal probability is higher than that for any of the other events; the plurality is at the "fairly probable" category. *Thus the supervisor's behavior in providing award recommendations is more certain and predictable than the organization's behavior in providing rewards.*

We also note that for two incentives—promotion and cash award for sustained superior performance—the distribution is *bimodal*, that is, there are two peaks in the distribution of subjective probabilities. In both cases the second mode or peak is at "very improbable." This suggests that for these two incentives employees tend to fall into two rather distinct groups: those who tend to be uncertain, and those who tend to be very sure they would *not* obtain the reward when warranted.

Furthermore, the distribution of probabilities for each incentive is *skewed*, i.e., lopsided, instead of being normal or bell-shaped. If we define "optimism" as all those probabilities to the left (i.e., "probable") side of "uncertain," and "pessimism" as all those probabilities to the right ("improbable") of "uncertain," then we can interpret skewness in terms of optimism and pessimism. We observe that employees tend to be "optimistic" as to supervisory support for cash awards (62% perceive this as "probable"), being dismissed if a worst producer (45% perceive this as "probable"), and getting a suggestion accepted (but only 26% perceive this as "probable"). ("Optimism" is perhaps not a good word in the case of dismissal since it implies that the employee is certain he will be dismissed if

he were the worst producer in his section.)

On the other hand, employees tend to be pessimistic with regard to promotion for outstanding work (33% see this as "improbable") and earning a cash award (37% see this as "improbable").

These results, in summary, indicate that employees' subjective probabilities cluster *below* the fifty-fifty point for the two main incentives which are commonly used to spur performance promotion for outstanding work and cash awards for sustained superior performance. In view of this we can conclude that these incentives have little motivating power, no matter how attractive they may be. On the other hand, the subjective probabilities cluster *above* the fifty-fifty point for getting an award recommendation from the supervisor and for being dismissed if a poor producer. It is clear that *being dismissed for poor work is somewhat more probable than being promoted for good work.*

Effect of Supervisor Upon Subjective Probabilities

Further analysis shows that the above distributions of subjective probabilities are not significantly related to the employee's age, sex, salary, marital status, or education. The above findings, then, hold regardless of these personal variables. This suggests the very significant conclusion that since the determinants of employees' subjective probabilities do not lie within the individual, they must lie somewhere *within the organization.*

What, then, determined the employee's expectations toward receiving these rewards? The data show quite clearly that the supervisor is a prime determinant. More specifically, we find that *the probability of the supervisor's writing a recommendation for a cash award has an effect upon the probabilities of the four incentive events.* This expectation toward the supervisor appears to be an important manifestation of what Rensis Likert and his researchers at the University of Michigan call the supervisor's "employee supportiveness."[3]

The nature of the supervisor's effect can be seen in Table 2 which shows how employees' probabilities for each of the four incentives differ according to whether they perceive the supervisor's support in getting a recommendation as "probable" (i.e. optimistic) or "improbable" (i.e. pessimistic). We observe that, with the exception of dismissal, there is a very high relationship between

TABLE 2

Effect of Supervisor Supportiveness on Subjective Probabilities of Four Incentives

Incentive	Probability	Supervisory Supportiveness[1]	
		High	Low
Promotion in next 18 months if most outstanding producer in section	Probable[2]	61	25
	Improbable[3]	39	75
		100%	100%
Dismissal in next 18 months if worst producer in section	Probable	73	55
	Improbable	27	45
		100%	100%
Receipt of cash award for sustained superior performance if warranted	Probable	59	11
	Improbable	41	89
		100%	100%
Having suggestion adopted in Suggestion Awards Program	Probable	68	22
	Improbable	32	78
		100%	100%

[1] "Supervisory supportiveness" is the subjective probability that the supervisor would write a recommendation for a cash award in the case of a warranted sustained superior performance. "High" means that this event is either "absolutely certain," "very probable," or "fairly probable." "Low" means this event is "fairly improbable" or "very improbable."
[2] "Probable" represents the combination of the "optimistic" subjective probabilities, i.e. "100% certain," "very probable," and "fairly probable."
[3] "Improbable" represents the combination of the "pessimistic" subjective probabilities, i.e. "fairly improbable" and "very improbable."

the perceived likelihood of getting the supervisor's recommendation and the probability of being promoted, earning a cash award, and having a suggestion accepted.

For instance, in the case of promotion for outstanding performance, we see that

among those who show some degree of probability that their supervisor would give them a recommendation when warranted, the majority (61%) believe that there is at least a fair probability that they would be promoted in the next 18 months if they were the most outstanding producer. Among those who are low in their confidence in the supervisor, the majority (75%) believe that such a promotion is improbable. For all incentives (except dismissal) the relationship is posi-

[3] See Rensis Likert, *Developing Patterns in Management,* General Management Series, No. 182, American Management Association, 1956.

tive, that is, the greater the confidence in the supervisor the more likely the rewards are seen to follow the actions in point.

Inspection of Table 2 shows that the relationship is highest (as one might expect) for cash awards, followed by adoption of suggestions, and being promoted. The supervisor's supportiveness, then, has its greatest effect on the incentive of a cash award, followed by the incentives of suggestion adoption and promotion, in that order. It is evident that *certain incentives are more sensitive to the supervisor's supportiveness than others.*

The one exception to this relationship is the negative incentive of dismissal. It is perhaps significant that this is also the only deterrent or negative incentive studied. We note that high confidence in the supervisor tends to be associated with the expectation that dismissal will follow poor work; however, the opposite is not true, for low confidence also tends to be associated with the same expectation, although the tendency is much weaker. The tendency is so weak, in fact, that for practical purposes low confidence in the supervisor makes very little difference in the subjective probability of dismissal.

This means that high confidence in the supervisor strengthens the deterrent effect of dismissal, but low confidence tends to strengthen the deterrence very slightly or not at all. In any case, low confidence does not weaken the deterrent of dismissal. Employees expect to be dismissed even when supervisory supportiveness is low, but they expect it much more when supportiveness is high.

The general conclusion from these findings is that the supervisor—via the effect of his supportiveness on employee subjective probabilities—has a considerable influence over the motivating power of management's formal incentives. Employees' confidence in him appears to have a "generalizing effect" which spreads out and conditions the subjective probabilities associated with the organization's official rewards. This spread of effect is differential in that it affects the subjective probabilities of certain incentives more than others. The implication is that the failure of incentives, especially positive incentives to motivate employees may in part be due to inadequate supervision and that the power of incentives can be boosted by increasing the supervisor's employee supportiveness.

Summary Statement

Decision theory today must be seen as the hub of a wheel in which spokes reach out to many areas of concern to the business man. It cannot be the only wheel on administration's wagon but it is a necessary one—the making of a decision is a central administrative process.

From our examination of some work in the area of making of decisions, we can see that the relationship between decision theory and real-life decisions is an outstanding example of the relationship that must always exist between science and practice. Science must first describe precisely, raise the level of thinking to the highest level of abstraction, and then explain a given set of phenomena in the most parsimonious fashion. Decision theory is now attempting to do this for business decisions. It has emphasized the basic concepts with which a business man can analyze his own decisions—utility and probability. It has indicated some relationships between these two factors. It is coming to grips with the means of quantifying both of them. Research is identifying other influences that operate on them. Finally, as application takes place, models are being developed that include additional elements that must be accounted for in the real life organizational setting—accidental features that, nevertheless, are critical.

For the administrator, it must certainly be apparent that as he and his organizational colleagues make decisions, recognition must be given to the different utilities that will be assigned to various outcomes and, as well to the different probabilities that will be assigned to these outcomes. All that makes each individual what he is—motivational pattern (for example, his current level of aspiration), learning experiences (for example, what prior decisions have been enforced and in what fashion), perceptual influences (for example, the existence of particular stereotypes) will cause him to assign utilities and to expect particular probabilities different from anyone else. An administrator may not be able to wait for unanimity before deciding, nor will he always be able to placate each individual in on the decision; he will, nevertheless, have to take some account of the differences that operate among individuals sharing an organization decision.

CHAPTER TWENTY-TWO

Originality
and
Creativity

Originality and creativity are attributes of some, but not all, processes of problem solving in the organization. Consequently, and in line with the growing trend in psychological research, we separate the topic of original and creative thinking from our general discussion of problem solving.

Problem solving and making decisions are major and continuing activities of the administrator; a high degree of originality and creativity, although essential for the organization's growth, are found only in the rare member of the organization. One is tempted to say that high originality and creativity *are tolerated* only in the exceptional member of the organization* and such individuals are often placed in some isolated department or in a staff capacity. It may very well be, that real originality and creativity can thrive only in such specially set up sections of the company (Cf. Simon's comment, p. 373).

Lyndall F. Urwick, an outstanding British authority on management, puts it this way:

First of all, the leader must administer his business. If he does not keep the organization running smoothly he will make less than he should today and

---

* In this connection, Hollander has developed the concept of "idiosyncrasy credit." The idea is that the organization informally keeps a kind of accounting system in which the individual accumulates credits by conforming to norms, demonstrating competence in group activities, and having high status inside or outside of the group. These credits may then be spent in occasional bouts of idiosyncratic behavior, such as innovation and deviation from expectations.

sell less than he could tomorrow. To run his business successfully he must encourage his administrators, the men who keep things tidy for him.

At the same time, if his business is to remain alive, he must have something new to make or to sell after tomorrow. To achieve this, he must help and encourage his lunatic fringe—his crazy people, the group who are irregular, who don't fit in—because it is out of this group that he is most likely to get new ideas which are of some value.

In particular he must protect this group from the wrath and just indignation of his administrators.

To expect originality and creativity only from a "lunatic fringe" is certainly an unnecessarily extremist view. But as a later reading will indicate, and as the reader's personal experience may already have taught him, the original and creative person often does not fit comfortably in an organization. Some of the very traits that make possible the originality and inventiveness of his thinking are those frequently resented in the typical organization.

Before going further into our chapter, it will be helpful to recall a distinction we previously drew between originality and creativity. *The measure of originality in a response is the uncommonness or rarity of its occurrence; the measure of creativeness is the value society places on it.* Creative responses are thus original responses but the reverse is not always true (Maltzman).

Research in the area has grown rapidly since 1950.* For our purposes, four major areas can be identified: attributes of creative persons, measurement of creative potential, training for originality and creativity, and the relation between age and productivity. In our chapter, we can only sample work done in each of these areas.

Creativity and Personality

In the pàst, two quite different speculations have been made of the relationship between personality and creativity. In one of these, a close association has often been said to exist between genius and insanity (and various vivid examples in the arts are cited). The research evidence provides no support for such a relationship (Cf. Stein and Heinze). It does suggest a different personality picture for the creative as compared with the noncreative, but not one based on pathology. For example, in the creative person there is a complexity and richness of personality, a general lack of defensiveness, an openness to experience, and especially to experience of one's inner life (MacKinnon, 1962a).

In the other speculation about creativity, made some time ago by psychologists as well as by others, and more implied than fully stated, is the suggestion that creativity is a matter of intelligence, not of personality.†

More systematic research provides support for neither position—creativity

---

* An annotated bibliography of contemporary work as well as earlier work in the area is provided by Stein and Heinze.

† See discussion of this point in Anastasi.

does not border on madness but neither is it just a function of high level intelligence in an otherwise average personality.

MacKinnon's summary of the extensive California study of creativity, presented as our next reading, indicates the particular personality traits of emotionally healthy and bright people that often appear with creativity.

READING 6-8

What Makes a Person Creative?*

DONALD W. MacKINNON

Six years ago, a group of psychologists began a nationwide study of human creativity. They wanted the scientific answers to the mystery of human personality, biology, intelligence, and intuition that makes some persons more creative than others.

Working under a grant by the Carnegie Corporation of New York, the researchers were faced with the usual stereotypes that picture the highly creative person as a genius with an I.Q. far above average, an eccentric not only in thinking but in appearance, dress, and behavior, a Bohemian, an egghead, a longhair. According to these unproved stereotypes, he was not only introverted but a true neurotic, withdrawn from society, inept in his relations with others, totally unable to carry on a conversation with others less gifted than himself. Still others held that the creative person might be profound but that his intelligence was highly onesided, in a rather narrow channel, and that he was emotionally unstable. Indeed, one of the most commonly held of these images was that he lived just this side of madness.

The psychological researchers who sought a more precise picture of the creative person conducted their investi-

gations on the Berkeley campus of the University of California in the Institute of Personality Assessment and Research. At the Institute, the persons to be studied have been brought together, usually ten at a time, for several days, most often a three-day weekend. There they have been examined by a variety of means— by the broad problem posed by the assessment situation itself, by problem-solving experiments, by tests designed to discover what a person does not know or is unable to reveal about himself, by tests and questionnaires that permit a person to manifest various aspects of his personality and to express his attitudes, interests, and values, by searching interviews.

The professional groups whose creative members were chosen for study were writers, architects, research workers in the physical sciences and engineering, and mathematicians. In no instance did the psychological assessors decide which highly creative persons should be studied. Rather, they were nominated by experts in their own fields; and to insure that the traits found to characterize the highly creative were related to their creativity rather than indigenous to all members of the profession a wider, more representative sample of persons in each of the professional groups was also chosen, though for somewhat less intensive study.

* From the *Saturday Review,* February 10, 1962, pp. 15-69.

All told, some 600 persons participated.

As the study has progressed it has become abundantly clear that creative persons seldom represent fully any of the common stereotypes, and yet in some respects and to some degree there are likenesses. It is not that such images of the creative person are fantastic but that they are caricatures rather than characterizations, heightening and sharpening traits and dispositions so as to yield a picture recognizable, yet still out of accord with reality. There are, of course, some stereotypes that reflect only error, but more often the distortion of the reality would seem to be less complete.

As for intellectual capacity, it will come as no surprise that highly creative persons have been found to be, in the main, well above average. But the relation between intelligence and creativity is not as clear-cut as this would suggest, if for no other reason than that intelligence is a many-faceted thing. There is no single psychological process to which the term "intelligence" applies; rather, there are many types of intellective functioning. There is verbal intelligence, and on a well-known test of this factor creative writers on the average score higher than any of the other groups. But there is also spatial intelligence—the capacity to perceive and to deal with spatial arrangements—and on a test of this aspect of intelligence creative writers as a group earn the lowest average score, while creative architects as a group are the star performers. There are, of course, many elements of intelligence in addition to these two.

If for the moment we ignore those patterns of intellective functioning which clearly and most interestingly differentiate one creative group from another, there are some more general observations that may be noted. It is quite apparent that creative persons have an unusual capacity to record and retain and have readily available the experiences of their life history. They are discerning, which is to say that they are observant in a differentiated fashion; they are alert, capable of concentrating attention readily and shifting it appropriately; they are fluent in scanning thoughts and producing those that serve to solve the problems they undertake; and, characteristically, they have a wide range of information at their command. As in the case of any intelligent person, the items of information which creative persons possess may readily enter into combinations, and the number of possible combinations is increased for such persons because of both a greater range of information and a greater fluency of combination. Since true creativity is defined by the adaptiveness of a response as well as its unusualness, it is apparent that intelligence alone will tend to produce creativity. The more combinations that are found, the more likely it is on purely statistical grounds that some of them will be creative.

Yet intelligence alone does not guarantee creativity. On a difficult, high-level test of the more general aspects of intelligence, creative persons score well above average, but their individual scores range widely, and in several of the creative groups the correlation of intelligence as measured by this test and creativity as rated by the experts is essentially zero.

Certainly this does not mean that over the whole range of creative endeavor there is no relation between general intelligence and creativity. No feeble-minded persons appeared in any of the creative groups. Clearly a certain degree of intelligence, and in general a rather high degree, is required for creativity, but above that point the degree of intelligence does not seem to determine the level of one's creativeness. In some fields of endeavor, mathematics and theoretical physics for example, the requisite intelligence for highly creative achievement is obviously high. But it does not follow that the theoretical physicist of very superior I.Q. will necessarily be creative, and in many fields of significant creative endeavor it is not necessary that a person be outstanding in intelligence to be recognized as highly creative, at least as intelligence is measured by intelligence tests.

Regardless of the level of his measured intelligence, what seems to characterize the creative person—and this is especially so for the artistically creative—is a relative absence of repression and supression as mechanisms for the control of impulse and imagery. Repression operates against creativity, regardless of how intelligent a person may be, because it makes unavailable to the individual large aspects of his own experience, particularly the life of impulse and experience which gets assimilated to the symbols of aggression and sexuality. Dissociated items of experience cannot combine with one another; there are barriers to communication among different systems of experience. The creative person, given to expression rather than suppression or repression, thus has fuller access to his own experience, both conscious and unconscious. Furthermore, because the unconscious operates more by symbols than by logic, the creative person is more open to the perception of complex equivalences in experience, facility in metaphor being one specific consequence of the creative person's greater openness to his own depths.

This openness to experience is one of the most striking characteristics of the highly creative person, and it reveals itself in many forms. It may be observed, for example, in the realm of sexual identifications and interests, where creative males give more expression to the feminine side of their nature than do less creative men. On a number of tests of masculinity-femininity, creative men score relatively high on femininity, and this despite the fact that, as a group, they do not present an effeminate appearance or give evidence of increased homosexual interests or experiences. Their elevated scores on femininity indicate rather an openness to their feelings and emotions, a sensitive intellect and understanding self-awareness, and wide-ranging interests including many which in the American culture are thought of as more feminine, and these traits are observed and confirmed by other techniques of assessment. If one were to use the language of the Swiss psychiatrist C. G. Jung, it might be said that creative persons are not so completely identified with their masculine *persona* roles as to blind themselves to or deny expression to the more feminine traits of the *anima*. For some, of course, the balance between masculine and feminine traits, interests, and identifications is a precarious one, and for several it would appear that their presently achieved reconciliation of these opposites of their nature has been barely achieved and only after considerable psychic stress and turmoil.

It is the creative person's openness to experience and his relative lack of self-defensiveness that make it possible for him to speak frankly and critically about his childhood and family, and equally openly about himself and his problems as an adult.

One gets the impression that by and large those persons who as adults are widely recognized for their creative achievements have had rather favorable early life circumstances, and yet they often recall their childhood as not having been especially happy.

In studying adult creative persons, one is dependent upon their own reports for the picture they give of their early years. Although they may often describe their early family life as less harmonious and happy than that of their peers, one cannot know for certain what the true state of affairs was. In reality the situation in their homes may not have been appreciably different from that of their peers. The differences may reside mainly in their perceptions and memories of childhood experiences, and it seems the more likely since one of the most striking things to be noted about creative persons is their unwillingness to deny or to repress things that are unpleasant or troubling.

The theme of remembered unhappiness in childhood is so recurrent that one is led to speculate about its role in fostering creative potential. In the absence of a sensitive awareness of one's own experience and of the world around one, without considerable development of and attention to one's own inner life, and lacking an interest in ideational, imaginal, and symbolic processes, highly creative responses can hardly be expected to occur. Something less than complete satisfaction with oneself and one's situation in childhood, if not a prerequisite for the development of a rich inner life and a concern for things of the mind and spirit, may nevertheless play an important contributory role.

There is no doubt, too, that some of the highly creative persons had, as children, endured rather cruel treatment at the hands of their fathers. These, to be sure, constitute the minority, but they appear today to be no less creative than those who could more easily identify with their fathers. There is some evidence, however, that those who were harshly treated in childhood have not been so effective or so successful in the financial and business (masculine) aspects of their profession as the others. There is in these persons more than a hint that they have had some difficulty in assuming an aggressive professional role because, through fear of their fathers, their masculine identifications were inhibited.

Both in psychiatric interviews that survey the individual's history and present psychological status, and in clinical tests of personality, creative persons tend to reveal a considerable amount of psychic turbulence. By and large they freely admit the existence of psychological problems and they speak frankly about their symptoms and complaints. But the manner in which they describe their problems is less suggestive of disabling psychopathology than of good intellect, richness and complexity of personality, and a general candor in self-description. They reveal clearly what clinical psychologists have long contended: that personal soundness is not an absence of problems but a way of reacting to them.

We may resort again to Jung's theory of the psychological functions and types of personality as an aid in depicting the psychology of the creative person. According to this view it might be said that whenever a person uses his mind for any purpose he either perceives (becomes aware of something) or he judges (comes to a conclusion about something). Everyone perceives and judges, but the creative person tends to prefer perceiving to judging. Where a judging person emphasizes the control and regulation of experience, the perceptive creative person is inclined to be more interested and curious, more open and receptive, seeking to experience life to the full. Indeed, the more perceptive a person is, the more creative he tends to be.

In his perceptions, both of the outer world and of inner experience, one may focus upon what is presented to his senses, upon the facts as they are, or he may seek to see, through intuition, their deeper meanings and possibilities. One would not expect creative persons in their perceptions to be bound to the presented stimulus or object but rather to be intuitively alert to that which is capable of occurring, to that which is not yet realized; this capacity is, in fact, especially characteristic of the creative person.

One judges or evaluates with thought or with feeling, thinking being a logical process aimed at an impersonal analysis of the facts, feeling, on the other hand, being a process of appreciation and evaluation of things which gives them a personal and subjective value. The creative person's preference for thinking or for feeling in his making of judgments is less related to his creativeness as such than it is to the type of material or concepts with which he deals. Artists, in general, show a preference for feeling, scientists and engineers a preference for thinking, while architects are more divided in their preference for one or the other of these two functions.

Everyone, of course, perceives and judges, senses and intuits, thinks and feels. It is not a matter of using one of the opposed functions to the exclusion of the other. It is rather a question of which of them is preferred, which gets emphasized, and which is most often used. So also is it with introversion and extroversion of interest, but two-thirds or more of each of the creative groups which have participated in the study have shown a rather clear tendency toward introversion. Yet, interestingly enough, extroverts, though they are in the minority in our samples, are rated as high on creativity as the introverts.

Whether introvert or extrovert, the creative individual is an impressive person, and he is so because he has to such a large degree realized his potentialities. He has become in great measure the person he was capable of becoming. Since he is not preoccupied with the impression he makes on others, and is not overconcerned with their opinion of him, he is freer than most to be himself. To

say that he is relatively free from conventional restraints and inhibitions might seem to suggest that he is to some degree socially irresponsible. He may seem to be, and in some instances he doubtless is if judged by the conventional standards of society, since his behavior is dictated more by his own set of values and by ethical standards that may not be precisely those of others around him.

The highly creative are not conformists in their ideas, but on the other hand they are not deliberate nonconformists, either. Instead, they are genuinely independent. They are often, in fact, quite conventional in matters and in actions that are not central to their areas of creative endeavor. It is in their creative striving that their independence of thought and autonomy of action are revealed. Indeed, it is characteristic of the highly creative person that he is strongly motivated to achieve in situations in which independence in thought and action are called for, but much less inclined to strive for achievement in situations where conforming behavior is expected or required. Flexibility with respect to means and goals is a striking characteristic of the groups we have studied.

On a test that measures the similarity of a person's expressed interests with the known interests of individuals successful in a variety of occupations and professions, creative persons reveal themselves as having interests similar to those of psychologists, architects, artists, writers, physicists, and musicians, and quite unlike those of purchasing agents, office men, bankers, farmers, carpenters, policemen, and morticians. These similarities and dissimilarities of interest are in themselves less significant than the abstractions and inferences that may be drawn from them. They suggest strongly that creative persons are relatively less interested in small details, in facts as such, and more concerned with their meanings and implications, possessed of considerable cognitive flexibility, verbally skillful, eager to communicate with others with nicety and precision, open to experience, and relatively uninterested in policing either their own impulses and images or those of others.

With respect to philosophical values —the theoretical, economic, esthetic, social, political, and religious as measured on one of our tests—there are two values most emphasized by all the creative groups. They are the theoretical and esthetic. One might think that there is some incompatibility and conflict between a cognitive and rational concern with truth and an emotional concern with form and beauty. If this is so, it would appear that the creative person has the capacity to tolerate the tension created in him by opposing strong values, and in his life and work he effects some reconciliation of them. Perhaps a less dramatic and more cautious interpretation of the simultaneous high valuing of the theoretical and the esthetic would be that for the truly creative person the solution of a problem is not sufficient; there is the further demand that it be elegant. The esthetic viewpoint permeates all of a creative person's work. He seeks not only truth but also beauty. Closely allied to his strong theoretical

and esthetic values is another pervasive trait of the creative, his preference for complexity, his delight in the challenging and unfinished, which evoke in him an urge, indeed a need, to discover unifying principles for ordering and integrating multiplicity.

In so brief a report, emphasis has had to be placed upon the generality of research findings. What needs to be equally emphasized is that there are many paths along which persons travel toward the full development and expression of their creative potential, and that there is no single mold into which all who are creative will fit. The full and complete picturing of the creative person will require many images. But if, despite this caution, one still insists on asking what most generally characterizes the creative individual as he has revealed himself in the Berkeley studies, it is his high level of effective intelligence, his openness to experience, his freedom from crippling restraints and impoverishing inhibitions, his esthetic sensitivity, his cognitive flexibility, his independence in thought and action, his high level of creative energy, his unquestioning commitment to creative endeavor, and his unceasing striving for solutions to the ever more difficult problems that he constantly sets for himself.

The Measurement of Creative Potential

Several possibilities exist for measurement of creative potential, none of them yet developed to the point of thoroughly reliable use in selecting individuals.

There are psychological tests designed to measure both creative intellectual endowment and creative temperament. Guilford and his co-workers have worked out tentative test items to measure some intellectual abilities they believe to be associated with creativity.* These latter are: ability to see problems, fluency of thinking, flexibility of thinking, originality, redefinition, and elaboration. He has also begun work on measuring what he calls the nonaptitude or temperamental characteristics for creativity.

---

* Also see R. L. Thorndike.

Indicating a similar approach to the problem, MacKinnon describes the ways in which a variety of already existing psychological tests have been used to assess traits that identify the creative person (as seen in our preceding reading).

Another likely possibility for meeting the problem of identifying the creative individual is to evaluate characteristics in his early history. There is now accumulating a wealth of data to suggest that the childhood and educational behavior of truly creative people falls into a different pattern from that of the noncreative person. On the basis of such data it may soon be possible to improve the chances of identifying the creative individual with the help of a careful biographical inventory that explores childhood and school interests and activities (Stein and Heinze).

Although even now industry is beginning to use both tests and biographical inventories to select creative individuals,* it is accurate to state that for business use the best (and until further research is done, the only) means of assessing creativity is past performance that was creative in comparable circumstances.

Training for Originality

Original and creative thinking is one form of learning activity. Consequently, any attempt to encourage this type of thinking must depend upon implementation of the basic laws of learning (Cf. Part Four).

In this section, we review some experimental attempts to apply learning theory concepts to eliciting more original thinking in the belief that there are some implications for administrators who may be interested in training for originality.

Prior to an examination of the training studies, it will be well to emphasize two points. The climate in the work situation must be such as to make original and creative thinking possible.† In addition, the individuals to be trained must have the intellectual capacity and the temperament for originality and creativity (Cf. the MacKinnon reading). Thus, training for originality and creativity begins with a selection program that brings into the organization appropriately talented people. Otherwise, the program will have only minimal effect, raising slightly the originality level of people whose capacity for creativity is slight.

Given a stimulating work climate and potentially talented employees, we can hope to raise their level of originality (and thus in talented people, their creativity) through formal training. Maltzman has conducted a series of researches that suggest some procedures usable in a business setting.

---

* See, for example, Smith *et al.* reporting on work done in the American Oil Company and the AC Test of Creative Ability (AC Spark Plug).

† Two studies of Van Zelst and Kerr, for example, indicate that the more productive (creative?) persons among a group of scientists and technicians expressed strong dislike for regimentation in choice of problem, working hours, deadlines, and other aspects of the work situation.

On the Training of Originality. A cardinal principle in shaping new behavior is that any occurrence of the desired behavior, or in the early phases of training, an approximation of the desired behavior, must be reinforced—paid for, recognized, praised, and be seen as worthwhile. The problem in *training for originality is that by its very nature* the original response occurs rarely; it may be dampened further by old habits of thinking and earlier organizational pressures. There is thus little or nothing to reinforce.

The problem then is how to increase the likelihood of its occurrence. Here, Maltzman's experimental techniques may be helpful. A description of his first experiment will provide a basis for understanding the conclusions he draws after a series of comparable experiments. Control and experimental groups were randomly assembled to equate for initial levels of creativity. The control group gave free associations to a list of 25 words (the training condition). They later gave free associations to a new list of 25 words (the test condition). The experimental group followed the same procedure except on the training condition. Here, the initial list of 25 words was presented to them five additional times with the instructions that they give a different response each time. When originality was measured by the uncommonness of responses on the second association list, the experimental group showed superior originality. Other research demonstrated that this originality also carried over to a different type of task—the Guilford Unusual Uses Test, a test of original thinking in which the subject is required to give as many uncommon uses as he can think of for common objects.

Maltzman has varied his training approaches in a series of researches. From his studies we draw the following conclusions:

1. Originality in responding to common objects can be increased by training. Training in one type of original response carries over to different tasks and seems to persist over a time period. Experimental findings are available only for relatively short time periods and for a narrow range of activities. With extended training sessions, a stable increase in originality of response over a wide area of activity might be hoped for.
2. The most effective training activity seems to be a free association activity in which the subjects (trainees) are pressed to give different responses to the same stimulus words from trial to trial. In addition, Maltzman did find that even the process of giving single responses to each of a variety of stimulus words can be helpful.
3. It is possible to train subjects to reduce their originality as well as to increase it. Some experimental procedures seemed to decrease originality of subsequent response. For example, when a control group was required to repeat the same response to a given stimulus word over five repetitions of a list, subsequent responses suffered a lowering of originality.

Fom the administrator's point of view, there are two important outcomes of Maltzman's work. First, the question: "Are there now any organizational activities which as one of their unanticipated consequences train to *reduce* originality?" Repetitively offered and accepted responses to any situation would tend to do so.

Second, Maltzman provides a demonstration that it is possible to increase originality of response. It is not too far-fetched to suggest that some adaptation of Maltzman's experimental procedure be built into the activities of any employee whose job requires problem solving, particularly original or inventive new solutions to problems. In some ways, Maltzman is suggesting a brainstorming operation for the individual. In this regard, the least we can require of our efforts to develop originality in the organization is that each problem solver first cite as many different solutions as he can before recommending any one solution.

Such a procedure has the advantage of possibly improving the solution to the specific problem being worked on; in addition, from Maltzman's work, it might be judged, that it would also increase the originality of approaches to subsequent problems.

Age and Productivity

Primarily as a result of the early work of Lehman, considerable attention has been given to the relationship between age and creativity. Lehman's work led him to conclude that the curve of creativity in the individual rises rapidly in early maturity and then declines slowly after attaining an early maximum. Dennis, in re-analyzing the Lehman data and in presenting other data of his own, has attempted to temper Lehman's conclusions by suggesting that for historical and biographical reasons a man's early productions are likely to be disproportionately emphasized. In addition, he points out that productivity, especially for creative persons, continues right on to ages beyond 60 even if it is conceded that creative production may be more abundant or of somewhat higher quality in early years.

Without taking sides in favor of Lehman or Dennis, Research Summary 6-4 summarizes Lehman's work to illustrate one other research approach to the study of creativity.

RESEARCH **SUMMARY** **6-4**	*Age and Achievement.* Lehman identified outstanding leaders in such fields as chemistry, mathematics, philosophy, literature, art, education, and public life. Since all his subjects were deceased, the productivity of their entire lives was available for analysis. Although his methods for the different fields varied, he sought some criterion to gauge the productivity and to evaluate it. He then plotted these measures against the age of the individual. The productivity peak of both quantity and quality was reached in practically all fields prior to the age of 45; in most fields, some time during the thirties. In public life, leadership was usually assumed most often after age 50 (N. B. Lehman's work was done before the Kennedy era). An exception among Lehman's subjects were those on annual salary, including business leaders. Among this group highest salary

was earned late in life, by which time salary obviously reflects many factors beyond creativity.

Lehman notes the difference between fields requiring new learning and those requiring an accumulation of past knowledge. Among the latter, presumably age would be an advantage. He concludes with the statement: "The conditions essential for creativity and originality . . . come earlier than those social skills which contribute to leadership and eminence and which inevitably must wait, not upon the insight of the leader himself, but upon the insight of society about him."

Keeping in mind the points of view both of Lehman and Dennis, the administrator for his purposes can safely conclude that outstanding creative contributions can be sought from talented people at an early age. But he must also keep in mind that the really creative people in his organization are likely to remain more creative than others for their entire career.

Summary

Although our chapter was designed more to illustrate the research on originality and creativity than to survey it all, we can draw certain conclusions. Highly creative people have superior intellectual endowment and in addition, personality traits that distinguish them from noncreative people. The identification of creative potential prior to actual creative performance is still not reliably possible although attempts are now being made to construct tests and biographical inventories to do so. There is the beginning of a body of experimental evidence to suggest the possibility of training people to be more original in their responses to problem situations. Creative productivity begins at an early age in many fields, particularly the sciences; but among talented individuals it continues to be present at a slowly diminishing rate until the seventies or later. Finally, an organizational climate that encourages and rewards creativity can be of great value in attracting, holding, and encouraging those with high creativity.

CHAPTER TWENTY-THREE

Group
Problem
Solving

Groups as well as individuals attempt to solve problems. And in the business organization the occasions for group problem solving are frequent. Committees, *ad hoc* groups, or staff teams are asked to recommend courses of action, that, first, require a collaborative, or at least a joint problem-solving effort before a specific recommendation can be made.

We do not raise the question of group problem solving because of any belief that groups necessarily will achieve superior technical solutions to problems than will individuals working alone, although this will occasionally be the case for some problems under circumstances that we will describe later on. The question is raised because sometimes group *acceptance* of a solution is more important than arriving at the technically most perfect solution, in which case, of course, group problem solving is more helpful than individual efforts even when the latter are made by the most competent individual available. Morale considerations or special organizational circumstances also occasionally demand group rather than individual effort. Whether it is because groups do better, or because it is made necessary for other reasons, attempts to solve problems will often be a group effort in the business organization.

Research on small groups, such as those that function in business organizations, is considerable. Much of it has been done in laboratory settings, although increasingly behavioral scientists are finding it possible to study groups in their natural setting (for example, Sayles or Whyte). Except for the special attention we pay to problem solving by groups, we will not be able to examine in detail the other research on small group processes. It will, nevertheless, be possible to identify some of the principal conclusions drawn about the general characteristics of small groups* before considering their problem-solving behavior.

THE SMALL GROUP

Group Goals and Individual Needs

The behavior of individuals in groups is a resultant of influences stemming from group goals (for example, to set up a methods program or to raise a sum of money) and individual needs and aspirations (such as the need for congenial company, or the status associated with group membership). In the first place, joining a group or maintaining membership in the group may be motivated by identification with the group's goals and activities or by personal satisfactions obtainable by group membership (for example, companionship, prestige). Most frequently, it will be an amalgam of both group and individual influences. Group goal satisfactions and personal satisfactions interact so that one feeds the other. A group of individuals finding social pleasures in membership may be expected frequently, but not always, also to contribute to the attainment of the group's goals. And, in the other direction, when a group successfully carries out its group functions, members will usually find it easier to satisfy personal needs through the group.

Hare gives a somewhat different emphasis to the dynamic forces within the group:

> . . . all groups have problems to solve in four areas. Two of these areas (are) achieving the group's purpose and arranging a satisfying social structure for the members. . . . The other two areas (are) achieving individual task goals and individual social-emotional goals. . . . Problems in the first two areas, the group task area and the group social-emotional area, are related to each other in a state of "dynamic balance" so that too much activity in the task area will leave unsolved problems in the social-emotional area. In its attempts to solve the social-emotional problems the group (or the individual) often swings too far in that direction and the task is left undone. The group then swings back and forth in its activity, tending toward a state of equilibrium (p. 341).

A full discussion of the process of working toward this "state of equilibrium" would have to show that the individual-group, need-goal interaction is affected by: the needs, aspirations, and expectations brought by the individual into the group; the effectiveness of the group situation in meeting these; the individual's identification with the goal; the goal and paths to it as instruments of need satisfaction; the degree of cooperation or competition in the

---

* The reader interested in this area might see Cartwright and Zander, *Group Dynamics* (2nd Ed.); Olmsted, *The Small Group;* or Hare, *Handbook of Small Group Research.*

group; the clarity of the goal; and the over-all organizational or social environment.

Group Norms or Standards

Groups tend to influence their members toward uniform or similar behavior and attitudes. This phenomenon sometimes identified as the conformity effect, may be stated more precisely as follows: a tendency on the part of individual group members to move toward the group norm or standard in their behavior and attitudes. The effectiveness of group norms and pressures will, of course, vary with the nature of the behavior being influenced and its significance to the individual, the relationship of the individual to the group, and the presence of extra-group or other group influences.

The following conditions tend to increase the likelihood of a conformity effect: high cohesiveness in the group,* the possession by the group of a significant set of sanctions and rewards, isolation from the influence of other groups, a judgmental setting and task that is ambiguous and uncertain for the individual, and the possibility of taking gradual steps toward the group standard (Walker and Heyns).

We are describing the conformity effect, neither encouraging nor condemning its use. Pressure toward conformity is an established group phenomenon. It may lead to desired or undesired behavior. The point is that an administrator should know about its existence and mode of functioning, then decide what to do about it.

In view of the conformity effect, it is understandable that a considerable body of research has demonstrated the power of group influence or interaction in changing well-set habits and attitudes (Lewin). The use of group interaction in this way was demonstrated in the Levine and Butler research on changing supervisor's rating practices (cf. page 328).

Leadership in the Group

Leadership behavior† available to the group is an important determinant of how it behaves.** Yet, there is no one pattern of leadership behavior that is best for all groups.†† As a matter of fact some groups function best under two different, co-existing patterns—one centered on task accomplishment, the other on social adjustment (Bales, 1958). One important function that leadership can serve is to make it possible for minority opinion that is correct to sway group opinion, and thus, at the same time, to change the usual direction of the conformity effect (Maier and Solem).

---

* Cohesiveness is considered more fully later in the chapter.

† Extensive and analytical surveys of experimental studies of leadership behavior are provided by Bass and by Stogdill.

** The point is made for different types of groups in different settings by Lippitt and White; Argyris (1952, 1957); Guest.

†† Katzell; Tannenbaum and Schmidt; Foa; Likert (1958); Wilensky; Vroom and Mann.

Informal Groups

Before going on to discuss more specifically the problem-solving behavior of groups, we need to point up the general significance to the business organization of informal groups. Management thinking is agreed that the existence of informal groups alongside the formal organization is essential for its healthy existence, as well as being inevitable. Barnard (p. 122) points out, for example, its function in extending vital communication channels. Others have demonstrated the potentially positive effect on job satisfaction, absenteeism, job turn-over, safety, and productivity of regular membership in a satisfying informal work group.*

At the same time, as the Western Electric studies (Roethlisberger and Dickson), and later others, including Zaleznik, have shown, the existence of informal groups can present management with problems. It is necessary to encourage the development of cohesive work groups, but unless they identify with management's goals, their very cohesiveness can encourage restriction of production and the isolation of nongroup members, to management's disadvantage.

GROUP VERSUS INDIVIDUAL PROBLEM SOLVING

We now return to our original concern with groups—their problem-solving efforts.

A question that can stimulate lively discussion among managers and others interested in the field is: do groups solve problems better than individuals working alone?†

Experimental studies, perhaps inevitably, provide no simple answers. In fact, the data suggest two other questions, "what kinds of problems" and "what kinds of groups."

In the section that follows, we indicate some of the factors to be considered. Before doing so, several general statements are in order.

1. Group performance is frequently better than that of the average individual; it is seldom better than the best individual (Lorge *et al.*). In fact, the group's superior performance may well result from the efforts of one superior problem solver (Taylor and McNemar).

2. The measure of a group's efficiency should be the total number of man-hours spent in solving the problem, not just the lapsed time spent by a group as compared with an individual.

3. Group problem solving may be preferred to individual problem solving, even though its superior efficiency cannot be demonstrated, when ac-

---

* For a summary statement of research see Likert, *New Patterns of Management*, 1961, Ch. 3.

† For two quite differently oriented discussions of the question see W. H. Whyte, Jr. (1956) and Tillman.

ceptance of the solution is important or when morale is a relevant consideration (Maier, 1960).

Social Factors

The one obvious way in which group problem solving is different from
the problem-solving efforts of an individual working alone, is, of course, that
there are immediate social factors at work in the former situation. The effect
of social factors on the problem-solving process is not easy to estimate. There
are several possibilities: the social factors may distract the group from its task
efforts, for example, the simple effort of keeping all in the group adjusted to
each other may leave little time for problem solving. The group norms may
serve to restrict the full efforts of some individuals in the group. Particularly
crucial may be the possibility that the group may inhibit the expression of
certain types of information, for example, personal or extreme (but perhaps
useful) points of view (Asch). Social interaction may spark emotion, possibly
negative expressions of emotion or tension, that may in turn reduce the
individual's problem-solving abilities, either because strong emotion generally interferes with intellectual performance, or because the constraints developed to control emotional expression may also limit participation and dis-
courage touching on delicate but crucial questions. Attempts (for example
brainstorming discussed below) to get around the barriers imposed by the
group have been varied but not a major benefit.

On the other hand, one can speculate on the existence of positive effects
(a kind of social facilitation) growing out of the simultaneous presence of
several people working on the same problem: intensity of effort can be
heightened, an *esprit de corps* can develop, the satisfaction of pleasant social
interactions can increase dedication to the task.

The studies conducted by Western Electric in their Hawthorne plant between 1927 and 1932, although not directly concerned with problem solving,
illustrate both the facilitating and inhibiting effect of the social factor on a
group's efforts. In one of their experiments, a group of women employees, who
had been assembled through mutual choice showed increased productivity,
partially as a result of the sense of team spirit that developed* (Roethlisberger
et al.). On the other hand, in another group, productivity was restricted to conform to performance norms established by the group and enforced through
various social pressures.

RESEARCH **SUMMARY** **6-5**	*Cooperation, Competition, and Conflict.* The social aspect of group problem solving, also, of course, introduces the possibility of either competitive or cooperative relationships. A cooperative or a com- petitive relationship among members of a group may be developed either through the type of external rewards offered for effective performance or through the kinds of motivations experienced by the individual members themselves. We cite a study showing the effects of each type of influence:

* Also see Van Zelst for a discussion of work teams formed by sociometric choice.

External Influence. A study by Deutsch, although taking place under laboratory conditions with college students, nevertheless provided these subjects with a realistic external reward system. In one case, the rewards encouraged students to work cooperatively and in the other competitively. At each of five sessions over a five week period subjects worked on two types of puzzle and in a later part of the session, discussed a human relations problem. Because they were participating in the experiment in place of their regular psychology course, the experimenter had the privilege of awarding each subject with a grade. To produce a cooperative atmosphere, subjects were told all members of a group would be given the same grade, to be determined by the group's position among other groups in the experiment; under competitive conditions, each student was told that his grade would be determined by comparing his performance with other members in the same group.

On many counts, the cooperative groups were superior to the competitive groups, particularly in types of behavior related to effective problem solving. Cooperative groups solved puzzles faster and offered better solutions to the human relations problems. They showed stronger individual motivation and better attitudes toward other group members. Coordination, interaction among members, and division of labor among members were superior to that in the competitive situation. They lisened to each other more and were more influenced by each other's ideas.

Internal Influence of Motivation. Occasionally, members of a group on their own account bring only self-oriented (rather than group oriented) needs into the group and behave largely in a self-serving way, thus building up a somewhat competitive atmosphere. In one study of this matter, conducted in an industrial setting, seventy-two decision-making conferences were observed, with a record kept by experimental observers without awareness of the participants. In a carefully worked out procedure, they recorded and tallied the kinds of interactions, comments, and behavior of the group members, for example, the amount of self-oriented behavior shown in each comment. (An example of self-serving behavior would be that in which an individual insisted that his department be included in a new procedure, despite the fact that nothing substantive would be contributed by doing so.) Under competitive conditions, that is where there was a high incidence of self-serving behavior by members, there was less satisfaction with the decision reached, with the meeting and with the chairman's behavior. Competitive groups also completed fewer items on their agenda than did cooperative groups (Marquis *et al.*).

The combined findings of both studies strongly support a suggestion made previously that when problem-solving groups are set up, any reward system be based on group, not individual performance. The second study, in addition, suggests that self-oriented behavior in problem-solving groups be sharply limited either by excluding those who are most likely to be so motivated or by suppressing such behavior through effective group conference leadership.

However much weight is given to the importance of cooperation, the impression should not be drawn that the best problem-solving groups are those free of disagreement or conflict. Two important studies suggest that conflict and disagreement, when properly controlled, can contribute to effective problem solving. In controlled observations of many discussion groups, Bales (1954) has observed that the best groups—presumably groups arriving at the best solution—were those in which some disagreement and even negative emotions were expressed. The absence of disagreement suggests either lack of commitment on the part of members or fear, causing them to inhibit disagreeing statements. After controlled research, another study concludes that the presence of conflict in a group could increase the frequency of high quality solutions to a problem. In particular, these authors found that when prior to the conference, they led subjects to have strong feelings about one important aspect of a task, it was possible to generate increased resistance among members of a group to a solution offered by a member in an authority position; the group delayed accepting an obvious, but not entirely satisfactory solution, when it did not take into account the important but neglected aspect (Hoffman *et al.*, 1962).

In their search for alternatives, they often found a solution that was better. Early agreement would have prevented this, and either fear or lack of personal commitment would have made such agreement easy.

The point is, of course, that where conflict or disagreement exists it must center about different methods for best solving the group's problems; it can not simply be a matter of gaining advantage for one's self, in a competitive sense.

Illustrative of one way in which social factors can inhibit spontaneously offered solutions to a problem is a study on "brain-storming." Although the brain-storming technique has widely been taken up by business as a useful means of group problem solving, the Taylor, Berry, and Block study presented as our next reading, indicates that individual brain-storming can be more effective than group brain-storming.

READING 6-9

Does Group Participation When Using Brainstorming Facilitate or Inhibit Creative Thinking?*

DONALD W. TAYLOR,

PAUL C. BERRY,

AND CLIFFORD H. BLOCK[1]

Brainstorming was originated and first used by Alex F. Osborn in 1939 in the advertising agency Batten, Barton, Durstine & Osborn, which he then headed.[2] Within recent years its use has grown rapidly. A large number of major companies, units of the Army, Navy, and Air Force, and various federal, state, and local civilian agencies have employed the technique, and instruction has been given in a number of colleges and universities in its use.[3] Although an occasional critical voice has been raised,[4] brainstorming may be said to have achieved wide acceptance as a means of facilitating creative thinking.

The purpose of brainstorming is to free individuals from inhibition, self-criticism, and criticism by others in order that in response to a specific problem they may produce as many different ideas as possible. The assumption is that the larger the number of ideas produced, the greater the probability of achieving an effective solution. Brainstorming is characterized by four basic rules:

(1) *Criticism is ruled out.* Adverse judgment of ideas must be withheld until later.

(2) *"Free-wheeling" is welcomed.* The wilder the idea, the better; it is easier to tame down than to think up.

(3) *Quantity is wanted.* The greater the number of ideas, the more the likelihood of winners.

(4) *Combination and improvement are sought.* In addition to contributing ideas of their own, participants should suggest how ideas of others can be turned into *better* ideas; or how two or more ideas can be joined into still another idea.[5]

Brainstorming ordinarily involves not only following the four basic rules but also group collaboration in attacking the problem. Osborn emphasizes the value of group interaction in facilitating the flow of ideas.[6] It was this characteristic of

* Abridged from *Administrative Science Quarterly*, 1958, 3, pp. 23-47. Reprinted by permission.
[1] [A] technical report previously issued under the [ONR] contract: Donald W. Taylor, Paul C. Berry, and Clifford H. Block, *Does Group Participation When Using Brainstorming Facilitate or Inhibit Creative Thinking?* (New Haven: Departments of Industrial Administration and Psychology, Yale University, 1957). Copies of this technical report are available in major university libraries. Permission is granted for reproduction, translation, publication, use, and disposal of the present article in whole or in part by or for the United States Government.
[2] Alex F. Osborn, *Applied Imagination,* rev. ed. (New York, 1957).
[3] *Ibid.* See also Brainstorming—New Ways to Find New Ideas, *Time,* 69 (Feb. 18, 1957), 90.
[4] Bernard S. Benson, Let's Toss This Idea Up . . . *Fortune,* 56 (Oct. 1957), 145-146.

[5] Osborn, *Applied Imagination,* p. 84.
[6] *Ibid.,* pp. 82-83.

brainstorming which was of primary interest in the present study. . . .

The present experiment employed a design previously developed by Taylor for use in studies of group problem solving where the problems involved have logically correct solutions.[8] Earlier studies of such group problem solving were concerned with a comparison of the achievement of groups of various sizes with that of individuals. However, the performance of a group should be superior to that of an individual, simply because in the group more individuals are working on the problem. On the assumption of the appropriate null hypothesis, namely, that working in a group has no effect either positive or negative upon individual performance, Taylor[9] and Lorge and Solomon[10] independently have presented a simple mathematical model for predicting the performance of a group of a given size from a knowledge of individual performance. By comparing actual group achievement with that predicted from the model, one can determine whether group participation facilitates or inhibits problem solving.

Taylor has also developed an experimental design which provides an alternative method of testing the same null hypothesis as that represented by the model.[11] Individuals are randomly assigned to work either alone or in groups of a given size on a series of problems.

The number of individuals working alone should be about equal to that working in groups. After the experiment is completed, those who actually worked alone are divided at random into nominal groups of the same size as the real groups. The performance of the nominal groups is then scored as though the members of the group had worked together. The achievement of the nominal groups thus provides a measure of the performance to be expected under the null hypothesis. If the performance of the real groups is superior to that of the nominal groups, group participation facilitates performance; if it is inferior, group participation inhibits it.

This design, with appropriate modification in the scoring of responses for nominal groups, was employed in the present experiment to provide an answer to the question: Does group participation when using brainstorming facilitate or inhibit creative thinking?

The Experiment

Subjects. The ninety-six Yale juniors and seniors who served as subjects in this experiment were all at the time enrolled in a course in Psychology of Personnel Administration taught by the first author. Each week, in addition to two lectures to the entire class, the course included an analysis of a case carried out in small discussion groups;[12] each group had its own student leader, this task being rotated among the members of the group. As a result of such case discussion and of the way in which subjects were assigned, each real group in the present experiment was not, as often must be

---

[8] Donald W. Taylor, "Problem Solving by Groups," in *Proceedings of the Fourteenth International Congress of Psychology, Montreal, June 1954* (Amsterdam, 1955), pp. 218-219. See also Donald W. Taylor and Olga W. McNemar, "Problem Solving and Thinking," in Calvin P. Stone, ed., *Annual Review of Psychology* (Stanford, Calif., 1955), VI, 455-482.

[9] Taylor, *op. cit.*

[10] Irving Lorge and Herbert Solomon, Two Models of Group Behavior in the Solution of Eureka-Type Problems, *Psychometrika*, 20 (1955), 139-148.

[11] Taylor, *op. cit.*

---

[12] Each period was devoted to discussion of a case selected from John D. Glover and Ralph M. Hower, *The Administrator* (Homewood, Ill., 1957). By the beginning of the present experiment, each group had completed a total of six cases.

the case in studies of group problem solving, an *ad hoc* group of individuals meeting for the first time; instead, each real group included men who not only knew each other but who also had worked together effectively in a small-group discussion over a considerable period of time. At the same time, the procedure used in assigning subjects was such that those assigned to work in groups and those assigned to work alone could legitimately be regarded as random samples from the same population. . . .

From each of the ten discussion groups in the class, four men were picked at random to form an experimental group, thus providing ten experimental groups; and from two of the ten discussion groups, an additional four men were picked at random to provide two more groups, for a total of twelve experimental groups. The remaining men in the ten discussion groups, forty-eight in all, served as individual subjects. Two points perhaps should be added here. The original registration of members of the class in the five sections was dependent primarily upon class schedules and had no known relation to ability. The division of these sections into two discussion groups was also unrelated to ability.

Problems . . . On the basis of this pretesting, three problems were selected which seemed to be of interest to Yale students, productive of many and varied responses, and appropriate for use with brainstorming. The three problems were as follows:

1. Each year a great many American tourists go to visit Europe. But now suppose that our country wished to get many more European tourists to come to visit America during their vacations. What steps can you suggest that would get more European tourists to come to this country?

2. We don't think this is very likely to happen, but imagine for a moment what would happen if everyone born after 1960 had an extra thumb on each hand. This extra thumb will be built just as the present one is, but located on the other side of the hand. It faces inward, so that it can press against the fingers, just as the regular thumb does now. Here is a picture to help you see how it will be. (A line drawing of a hand with two thumbs was shown by the experimenter at this point in the reading of the problem and then left in full view on the table during the entire period of work on the problem.[14]) Now the question is: What practical benefits or difficulties will arise when people start having this extra thumb?

3. Because of the rapidly increasing birth rate beginning in the 1940's, it is now clear that by 1970 public school enrollment will be very much greater than it is today. In fact, it has been estimated that if the student-teacher ratio were to be maintained at what it is today, 50 per cent of all individuals graduating from college would have to be induced to enter teaching. What different steps might be taken to insure that schools will continue to provide instruction at least equal in effectiveness to that now provided?

For brevity's sake, the three problems were referred to as the "Tourists Problem," the "Thumbs Problem," and the "Teachers Problem."[15]

·   ·   ·

Results

The first step following the completion of the experimental sessions was the division of the forty-eight individual

---

14 For a copy of the line drawing, see Taylor, Berry, and Block, *op. cit.*, p. 6.

15 Although the third problem would be more accurately described as the education problem, it was called the "Teachers Problem" for the sake of symmetry.

subjects into twelve nominal groups of four each. This was done in order to permit comparison of real group performance not only with that of individuals but also with that to be expected on the basis of the hypothesis that working in the group has no effect either positive or negative upon the performance of its members. A table of random numbers was employed to divide the twenty-four individual subjects who had worked with the first experimenter into six nominal groups of four; the same procedure was used to divide the twenty-four who had worked with the second experimenter into an additional six nominal groups. This particular procedure was necessary if a test were to be made of any possible difference between the two sets of six nominal groups resulting from

differences between the experimenters. Inspection of the data later obtained, however, revealed no possible significant difference between experimenters in the results. . . .

Table 1 presents the mean number of responses by individuals and real groups to each of the three problems. On each of the three problems, the mean number of ideas presented by real groups is much larger than that presented by individuals. The appropriate analysis of variance briefly summarized in Table 1 shows that this difference between real groups and individuals with an F of 71.2 is significant at well beyond the .0001 level. The analysis also shows that the differences among the three problems in mean number of responses is significant at the .001 level and that the interaction

TABLE 1
Mean Total Number of Responses to Each Problem by Individuals and Real Groups

	Tourists	Thumbs	Teachers	Mean of means
Individuals	20.7	19.9	18.2	19.6
Real groups	38.4	41.3	32.6	37.5
Mean of means	29.6	30.6	25.4	

Analysis of variance	d.f.	F	p
Individuals *vs.* real groups	1, 58	71.2	.0001
Among problems	2, 116	8.5	.001
Interaction	2, 116	4.96	.01

between the two primary variables is also significant.[21]

Table 2 shows that the mean number of responses produced by nominal groups was considerably larger than that produced by real groups on each of the three problems. The analysis of variance indicates that this superiority of nominal

---

[21] Interaction refers to the variation in the effect of one independent variable upon the dependent variable as a function of a second independent variable (see McNemar, *op. cit.*, pp. 283, 301-303).

to real groups is significant at far beyond the .0001 level. The difference among the three problems in number of responses is again significant, but in this case the interaction does not even approach significance.

It seemed important to compare the performance of real and nominal groups not only in terms of the number of ideas produced but also in terms of the originality and quality of these ideas. For this purpose, additional analyses were undertaken.

TABLE 2

Mean Total Number of Responses to Each Problem by Real Groups and Nominal Groups

	Tourists	Thumbs	Teachers	Mean of means
Real groups	38.4	41.3	32.6	37.5
Nominal groups	68.3	72.6	63.5	68.1
Mean of means	53.4	57.0	48.0	

Analysis of variance	d.f.	F	p
Real vs. nominal groups	1, 22	96.3	.0001
Among problems	2, 44	7.8	.005
Interaction	2, 44	.09	——

A large proportion of the responses to any one of the problems was, of course, produced by more than one of the nominal or real groups, a small number of the ideas on each of the problems being suggested by nearly all of the twenty-four groups. On each problem, however, an appreciable number of suggestions was made by only one of the twenty-four groups; these may be described as unique responses. The number of such unique ideas provides one satisfactory measure of the originality of the performance of a particular group.

In Table 3 are given the mean number of unique responses produced by real and nominal groups on each of the three problems. The superiority of the nominal to the real groups on this measure is significant at the .005 level. The difference among the three problems in mean number of unique responses is also significant, but the interaction is not. . . .

Detailed examination of the 483 dif-

TABLE 3

Mean Numbers of Unique Responses to Each Problem

	Tourists	Thumbs	Teachers	Mean of means
Real groups	7.5	17.7	7.3	10.8
Nominal groups	13.7	28.1	17.5	19.8
Mean of means	10.6	22.9	12.4	

Analysis of variance	d.f.	F	p
Real vs. nominal groups	1, 22	11.4	.005
Among problems	2, 44	42.1	.0001
Interaction	2, 44	1.29	——

ferent suggestions for solution of the Tourists Problem and of the 513 different suggestions for solution of the Teachers Problem indicated that these suggestions differed in quality with respect to at least three dimensions: feasibility, ef-

fectiveness, and generality. Accordingly, five-step rating scales were constructed for use in measuring these three. . . .

The 791 different responses made to the Thumbs Problem differed from those made to the other two problems in that they represented anticipated consequences instead of suggested steps for solution. For this reason only one of the three rating scales constructed for rating responses to the other two problems, namely, generality, appeared equally applicable in the case of the Thumbs Problem. For this problem, however, analogous to feasibility and effectiveness on the other problems were the dimensions of probability and significance, respectively. Accordingly, two additional rating scales were constructed by the same method to measure these latter variables.[25] . . . The responses to each problem were rated on three different scales by three different raters, presumably increasing the independence of the ratings of the three characteristics. Each rater employed a different scale for each of the three problems, thus presumably minimizing the possibility that a single idiosyncratic interpretation of any of the scales would occur for all three problems. . . .

One additional point concerning the procedure used in rating deserves emphasis. All ratings were made of the responses as they appeared on the master list for the given problem and without any knowledge of whether the response had been made by real or nominal groups. This was done, of course, to eliminate any possible tendency of any rater to bias his ratings to favor either real or nominal groups. . . . The score for each group for a given problem and a given dimension was simply the sum of the ratings on that dimension of the responses given by the group to that problem.

A comparison of the mean scores of real and nominal groups on each of the three rated dimensions [shows that] . . .

on each of the three dimensions for each of the three problems, the mean for the nominal groups is much larger than that for the real groups. The analyses of variance show that this superiority of the nominal to the real groups is significant well beyond the .0001 level for each of the three problems.*

. . .

Discussion

The first important finding was that on each of the three problems the mean total number of ideas produced by the twelve groups was considerably larger than the mean number produced by the forty-eight individuals, the difference being highly significant (Table 1). It is true that the interaction is significant, indicating that the difference between real group and individual performance does vary among the three problems. But on all three problems group performance is clearly superior to individual performance. Such group superiority may very well account for the widespread impression that group participation does facilitate production of ideas. The individual who compares his own performance working alone with that of a group in which he participates at another time may understandably conclude that group interaction stimulates creative thinking, whether or not this is in fact the case. Many of those participating in the groups in the present experiment made comments indicating that they believed such participation had been stimulating.

The comparison of group performance with individual performance does not, however, provide an adequate answer to the question: Does group participation when using brainstorming facilitate or inhibit creative thinking? To answer this question, the performance of the twelve real groups was compared with that of

---

[25] For a copy of each of the five rating scales, see Taylor, Berry, and Block, *op. cit.,* pp. 40-42. Inspection of these scales provides the best available definition of each of the variables.

---

* Tables 5, 6, and 7 are omitted.

the twelve nominal groups on each of the three problems with respect to (a) mean total number of ideas produced, (b) mean number of unique ideas produced, and (c) the three measures which involved the weighting of the ideas with respect to quality. The results of these several analyses were both clear-cut and consistent.

The performance of the twelve real groups is markedly inferior to that of the twelve nominal groups both in terms of number of ideas produced (Table 2) and in terms of number of unique ideas produced (Table 3). Since in neither case was the interaction significant, these findings apply equally to all three problems. The mean scores of the real groups on the three weighted measures were also markedly inferior to those of the nominal groups for the Tourists, Thumbs, and Teachers Problem. . . . In brief, the performance of the real groups is inferior to that of the nominal groups on all three problems with respect to each and all of the measures of performance employed.

To the extent that the results of the present experiment can be generalized, it must be concluded that group participa-

tion when using brainstorming *inhibits* creative thinking. What accounts for such inhibition? Although data are not available to provide an adequate answer, two suggestions may be made. In brainstorming strong emphasis is placed upon avoiding criticism both of one's own ideas and of the ideas of others. Nevertheless, it appears probable that the individual working in a group feels less free of possible criticism by others even when such criticism is not expressed at the time than does the individual working alone. To the extent that this is true, group participation is inhibiting. A second reason is that group participation may reduce the number of different ideas produced. A given number of individuals working in a group appear more likely to pursue the same train of thought—to have the same set or the same approach to the problem—than do the same number of individuals working alone. The greater the variety of set, train of thought, or approach, the greater would be the expected number of different ideas produced. To the extent that group participation reduces such variety, it inhibits production of ideas.

Before acting on the findings of the Taylor *et al.* study* an administrator might well consider an aspect of the problem not raised in the laboratory study. In the organization, when members are brought together to brainstorm, all are required to devote the specified time to the task, and the social pressures that are present cause most members to give the problem their attention and creative effort. If these same members were asked to do the same thing individually at their desks would they in reality allow the same amount of time for the task? Or would it get squeezed out by other activities with a net loss in worthwhile ideas as compared with the group effort? Apparently, only if we can be sure that individuals will work for as long a period of time as does the group, can we count on getting more and better ideas by assemblying the production of individuals who have been working alone. The administrator may speculate on his role in helping provide the idea-producing time for his subordinates.

---

* The Taylor study has been replicated with research scientists and advertising personnel by Dunnette, Campbell and Jaastad. They report similar findings with the additional suggestion that the superiority of individual brainstorming over group brainstorming was relatively greater when the former was preceded by group participation.

Social Effects: Summary Statement

There seems little doubt that under differing circumstances any of a number of social interactions can take place in problem solving groups. The research findings in the area* are neither consistently enough in one direction nor specific enough for an administrator to use in predicting with certainty the direction of influence of the social factor introduced by a group problem solving effort in the organizational setting. Two conclusions, nevertheless, can be drawn: (1) the social factor introduced by having people work together to solve a problem produces no magical effects (contrary to the expectations of some enthusiasts) and may be handicapping; and (2) the effect of leadership and planning can be decisive in determining the effect of social factors on problem-solving behavior. We examine the latter conclusion in more detail in a later section of this chapter.

Cognitive Factors

Social influences certainly differ between individual and group problem solving. Are there, as well, differences in some cognitive aspects of problem solving in comparing the two situations? Research does indicate some types of problems for which the cognitive resources available to the group seem more helpful than those available to the individual.

A problem of this type is one that requires the problem solver (or a group) to reason the way through a series of steps with the possibility of making an error at each of the several steps. With a number of people attending to each step and rationally checking it out, there is less possibility of error than when only one person can do this (Shaw). Even the best problem solver in the group can slip and make an error that would be identified by some other person in the group, thus making it possible for the group to be more efficient than any one of its members. It is likely also that where a clear cut division of labor is possible in the problem-solving effort, then "more hands" available in the group will expedite the problem-solving effort. If, for example, the problem requires the computation of several sets of independent figures, or the arrangement of different kinds of data, before a solution can be reached, the group will do it sooner in total lapsed time, although obviously there will be no saving in total man-hours of effort.

Perhaps the most significant advantage of groups over individuals is found in the type of problem that requires an extensive background of varied information for its solution. Here, different individuals coming with a variety of job experiences and a spread of specialized knowledge can contribute more to the solution than can the single individual, even though he himself might have a good fund of information. This type of problem frequently confronts the administrator requiring, for example, information about purchasing, current

---

* Social influences on productive effort have been the focus of studies going back to 1898. The work is summarized in Hare.

sales, personnel resources, and so on. Although the different kinds of information brought by members of the named departments may also be accompanied by different points of view that could lead to dissension, this may be a necessary price to pay for the required information. It might even be said that under good leadership the disagreement and conflict, provided all the relevant information is considered, would be helpful in hammering out a better solution to the problem (Hoffman *et al.*). Finally, there are some problems in which judgments have to be made about ambiguous situations, for example, the likelihood that Congress will pass a particular bill, or the probable number of employees who will choose to join a pension program (when it is not possible to ask them). Here the evidence suggests that the pool of opinion available in a group can lead to a more accurate judgment than could be made by the individual working alone. This is true even when the judgments of individual members are obtained without discussion and then statistically averaged.* In a business problem-solving group where discussion takes place, due to the conformity effect mentioned earlier, the ultimate group opinion is likely to be a modified average, weighted in favor of estimates made by high status members or those considered expert, but under good leadership it is usually not exclusively determined by such members. Even such a weighted average might well be better than individual opinion alone. Of course, we are talking here of judgments the group would be entitled to make through their general familiarity with the situation. If the group is not familiar with the situation to be judged, expert individual opinion is best sought (Wispe). An example of research demonstrating the value of group opinion and pooled opinions in judging the probability of certain social and technological events is given in Research Summary 6-6.

RESEARCH **SUMMARY** **6-6**	*Group and Individual Opinion in Predicting Events.* Kaplan, Skogstad, and Girshick asked their subjects—most of them college graduates, employed as mathematicians, statisticians, and engineers —to predict the outcome of various political, economic, and scientific events that would occur within the following 5 months. Some of the subjects worked alone and made their predictions without discussing them with other members (Condition 1); some were formed into small groups, discussed the event, and then formed their own opinion (Condition 2); still others, in small groups, discussed the event, and arrived at a collective decision (Condition 3). Decisions arrived at under Conditions 2 and 3 above were more accurate, that is they predicted the actual outcome more often, than those made by subjects under Condition 1. Group decisions were more accurate than individual decisions. When individual decisions were statistically pooled and a mean prediction computed, the mean prediction was almost as accurate as those that had benefitted from group discussion.

---

* See discussion by Kelley and Thibaut in the *Handbook of Social Psychology;* also Klugman.

Are there other kinds of problems that, in contrast to those we have been discussing, favor the solution seeking efforts of the individual working alone? Our earlier reading (6-9) provides evidence that when the criterion of a successful solution is novelty, uniqueness, or creativity the individual alone, free of a possible inhibiting effect from the presence of others, may do better than groups. There is also the belief that when a problem requires a single over-all insight an individual may often do better than the group (Krech and Crutchfield p. 687). Among the group factors that would interfere with the achievement of broad encompassing insights are (1) social influences that are distracting and (2) difficulties in managing the relevant information in relation to all the members, so that a single insight could be achieved. In any case, there would seem to be no basis for expecting a group to show superior performance in such problems.

RESEARCH SUMMARY 6-7

Individual and Group Risk Taking Behavior. An interesting possible difference between group and individual problem solving is the amount of risk that individual's working alone are willing to take in their decisions as compared with risk taken by the same individuals in a group setting.

Much work done in the field, as already indicated, suggests that when individuals come into a group, the group process tends to reduce the spread of extreme views previously expressed by them. In an apparent process of compromise and concession, an averaging effect is achieved in which deviant views are brought into close harmony with the central tendency of the group. Whyte has argued, more on a logical than an empirical basis, that committees and conferences in business tend to minimize boldness and risk taking.

Despite the inference suggested by this earlier work that group decisions will be less risky (since less extreme) than individual decisions, or at least no more risky than the average of the individual decisions, Wallach, *et al.* present compelling evidence to the contrary. In a direct test of the issue, they demonstrate that decisions taken on a unanimous group basis are consistently more risky than the average of decisions originally made by the same individuals on their own.

Twelve "life dilemma" situations were designed, in which a decision had to be made between two courses of action, one more risky, but also potentially more rewarding than the other. One of their decision situations will illustrate the pattern: "The president of an American corporation which is about to expand may build a new plant in the United States where returns on the investment would be moderate, or may decide to build in a foreign country with an unstable political history where, however, returns on the investment would be very high." Other decision situations varied widely, including career choices, health problems, game decisions, and additional business questions.

Subjects were college students paid for their efforts. Each subject had to indicate the lowest probability of success he would accept before deciding for the more satisfying (but risky) alternative.

Probabilities offered for selection were 1, 3, 5, 7, and 9 chances out of 10 and a final category—refusal to recommend the risky choice no matter what the probability of its success. After entering their individual choices, they were assembled into groups of six, and asked to discuss each question, until the group reached a unanimous decision. Then they were again separated and asked to enter their personal choices, once again, on an individual basis.

The results with striking consistency support two major conclusions:

1. Unanimous group decisions are riskier than decisions made by the same individuals working alone prior to group discussion.

2. Individual decisions made after the group decision are riskier than individual decisions made prior to the decision. This effect lasted for at least 2 to 6 weeks after the original experience.

Furthermore, in another aspect of the study, Wallach *et al.* were able to demonstrate that the individual seen by the group as most influential in the group discussion tended to be one whose original individual decision was on the risky side. Such influence was not a function of his popularity, nor of superior initial status (since there were no obvious status differences among the members).

The findings are clear and indirectly supported by other observations (for example, the daring behavior of crowds); nevertheless additional, more systematic testing of the phenomenon has to be done and, no doubt, will follow.

What implications are present for problem solving in the business setting? If the findings are supported, and if the evidence indicates they can be generalized, for example, to real life business situations, there are several. Innovative but risky ventures, more adventurous policy decisions, somewhat risky capital investment, even methods changes of some types are more likely to be recommended after group decision than by individual's forwarding their recommendations on an individual basis. Top management may want to test their own individual decisions against decisions reached in group session by lower level specialists. This effect of group discussion certainly must be allowed for before a pending decision is committed to group discussion and recommendation. A final word of caution: the research does not indicate that group decisions are better than individual decisions—only riskier—at least under the circumstances of the experiment. If the problem is to overcome individually expressed conservative views, then group discussion might result in "better" decisions.

CHARACTERISTICS OF EFFECTIVE PROBLEM-SOLVING GROUPS

There are, as we have just indicated, types of problems that may best be solved through group effort, and types on which the individual had best work on his own. Often the group setting, rather than an individual problem-solving approach, is used to raise morale or gain increased acceptance of any solution achieved. Regardless of the reason, in business organizations and elsewhere, groups do attempt to solve problems by assignment or on their own initiative. There is then the question of what kinds of groups best solve problems, or, more specifically stated, what characteristics of groups facilitate effective problem solving? In general those groups are effective: (1) whose practices and procedures enable them to carry out systematically the steps in problem solving and whose members have skills appropriate to the nature of the problems faced; (2) that have received training in problem-solving strategies and whose efforts are appropriately motivated; (3) that have a stable, status system, familiar to all its members; (4) whose size is large enough to accomplish the task but not so large as to introduce distracting organizational problems; (5) that are cohesive, interacting cooperatively with members possessing compatible personality characteristics, and (6) that are operating under mild to moderate, but not extreme stress. In addition to the factors mentioned, patterns of communication and leadership available to the group will also significantly affect their performance.

Group Cohesiveness

A feeling of cohesiveness among members of a group is unquestionably the most influential determinant of the group's behavior *as a group*. Although definitions of cohesiveness by researchers vary somewhat in their point of emphasis, there is agreement that cohesive groups experience a high degree of attraction to the group, feel good about their membership in the group, and tend to want to "stick together."

The Effects of Cohesiveness. Group cohesiveness has been extensively studied.* We list below some of the principal effects of cohesiveness in the group on performance selecting particularly those effects that seem relevant to the group's problem-solving behavior.

1. Highly cohesive groups work harder than those with low cohesiveness. Of particular significance is the fact that they are likely to do so regardless of outside supervision (Berkowitz, 1954).

2. On the other hand, what the members of a cohesive group work harder at is, of course, a question of their degree of enthusiasm for the group's goals.† It would be unwise for an administrator to assume that group members who like each other and get along well as a group will, solely because of such relationships, work efficiently on the assigned problem. In addition to feeling a sense of cohesiveness, the members must also be identified with, or feel enthusiastic about the *goals* of the group, that is the problem to be solved. A highly cohesive group is well-launched on a successful problem-solving venture if the members feel enthusiastic about the assigned problem—provided the solution is at all within reach of the group's capabilities.

3. In 1960, Cartwright and Zander (pg. 89) summarized prior research on the behavior of group members who felt highly attracted to their groups. In their summary, which follows, we can identify much behavior that would help a group be more efficient in its problem-solving efforts:

---

* See Newcomb; Cartwright and Zander; Krech, Crutchfield and Balachey.

† For a research oriented discussion of the problem see Kelley and Thibaut, pp. 752-758.

Responsible Activity. Those who are highly attracted to a group more often take on responsibilities for the organization, participate more readily in meetings, persist longer in working toward difficult goals, attend meetings more faithfully, and remain members longer.

Interpersonal Influence. Attracted members more readily try to influence others, are more willing to listen to others, are more accepting of others' opinions, and more often change their minds to take the views of fellow members.

Similarity of Values. Members who are strongly attracted to a group place greater value on the group goals, adhere more closely to the group's standards, and are more eager to protect the group's standards by exerting pressures upon or rejecting persons who transgress them.

Developing Cohesiveness

Because membership in cohesive groups increases the likelihood of member responses helpful in problem solving, the administrator ought to pay attention to the conditions that increase feelings of cohesiveness in groups. The research findings suggest that cohesiveness will increase under the following conditions: (1) When members feel that they are highly valued by the group; (2) When the members are in a cooperative rather than competitive relationship with each other; (3) When they have full opportunity for social interaction; and (4) When the group is a small one.

Group cohesiveness is reduced: (1) When false expectations are raised about the group; (2) When a few members dominate things; and (3) When disagreement or failure is too often experienced (Cartwright and Zander, p. 93).

The administrator, reading that list, may feel overwhelmed by the many things to keep in mind when forming a problem-solving group. Yet each factor, considered by itself, can readily be controlled by relatively simple efforts on the part of the group leader, or the administrator who is responsible for the group.

On the question of selecting members for the group, the question of personality compatibility has been raised by some psychological research. The findings in one study, although tentative, indicate that when it is possible to assess individual personality traits and to assemble groups whose members have compatible personalities* such groups are more productive than incompatible groups. It may be possible for administrators to keep this finding in mind generally but the assessment of personality is so complex a process as to raise questions about the feasibility of selecting compatible group members in any precise fashion in the organization setting.

Procedures Employed by Successful Groups

In a series of studies of airplane crews that had to solve the problem of surviving after bailing out over enemy territory, Torrance identifies three principal procedures followed by successful crews. They were able: (a) to

---

* Schutz has provided an instrument for attempting to measure compatibility.

make sense of an initially unstructured, unclear situation (a necessary first step in many problem situations); (b) to resume communication among members; and (c) to establish a goal to work toward (Torrance, 1954, 1955, 1962). The problems of business groups are rarely so critical, or presented in such challenging settings, yet the procedures for solving problems, presumably, should be the same. The simple step of making the procedures (described above) explicit for the group should help them. If, in addition, the group's leader holds them to these procedures, improved problem solving should result. This does not mean limiting the alternative solutions available to them, but specifying the procedure available to reach a solution. Hare suggests that in a particular problem, one or another of the phases of problem solving (which he designates as observation or fact gathering, hypothesizing and proposing action) may be especially important. If so, it will be necessary to have in the group members who have the required capacities: if, for example, the observational phase is critical then the groups should have one or several members who have skills in the kinds of observation needed to solve the problem. If the problem particularly depended upon setting up possible hypotheses, then we would need members who were analytical or creative in their approaches.

The point is obvious but, nevertheless, frequently not considered: for a group to solve problems its members must have the set and skills to use procedures required by the nature of the problem. A group successful in working out problems in a well-structured context, for example, allocating portions of an over-all budget, may not be successful with a loosely structured problem, for example, improving communications among departments. The requirements of the problem constitute one important item to be considered in deciding which members will make up the group.

RESEARCH **SUMMARY** **6-8**	*Phases in Problem Solving.* In Chapter 19, the various phases or steps in individual problem solving were discussed. Bales and Strodtbeck have pointed out that "most of the theories about steps or stages in group problem solving seem to be more or less direct extrapolations of steps or stages assumed to exist 'in individual mental processes.' " They set about seeing whether the interactions which occur in group problem solving can be categorized objectively into phases. A phase they consider to be a qualitatively different sub-period in some continuous period of interaction. Following such previous research of Bales and others, they used a system of categories into which each comment or act of the member of a group can be placed by an observer (or data analyst working with a tape recording). These categories* are stated on p. 447. Analyzing twenty-two group situations (both laboratory and regular operating groups in organizations), they found that a series of comparable changes take place in group interaction, even though the nature of the problems being dealt with by the groups differed. In the first phase (a third of the total period of the meeting) *Orien-*

---

* Robert F. Bales, *Interaction Process Analysis*, 1950, p. 9 [as reproduced in Olmsted, M.S. The Small Group, p. 123.]

Bales' System of Observational Categories

Social- Emotional Area: Positive	A	1. *Shows solidarity,* raises other's status, gives help, reward. ◄─────┐
		2. *Shows tension release,* jokes, laughs, shows satisfaction. ◄
		3. *Agrees,* shows passive acceptance, understands, concurs, complies. ◄
Task Area: Neutral	B	4. *Gives suggestion,* direction, implying autonomy for other. ◄
		5. *Gives opinion,* evaluation, analysis, expresses feeling, wish. ◄
		6. *Gives orientation,* information, repeats, clarifies, confirms. ◄
		a b c d e f
	C	7. *Asks for orientation,* information, repetition, confirmation. ◄
		8. *Asks for opinion,* evaluation, analysis, expression of feeling. ◄
		9. *Asks for suggestion,* direction, possible ways of action. ◄
Social- Emotional Area: Negative	D	10. *Disagrees,* shows passive rejection, formality, withholds help. ◄
		11. *Shows tension,* asks for help, withdraws out of the field. ◄
		12. *Shows antagonism,* deflates other's status, defends or asserts self. ◄

Key

a = Problems of Communication   d = Problems of Decision
b = Problems of Evaluation   e = Problems of Tension Reduction
c = Problems of Control   f = Problems of Reintegration

A = Positive Reactions   C = Questions
B = Attempted Answers   D = Negative Reactions

tation (Categories 6 and 7) seems to occur more than it does later; although individuals possess facts relevant to a decision, they also have a degree of ignorance and uncertainty about other relevant facts (perhaps possessed by others in the group). In the second phase, *Evaluation* is proportionally more in evidence (Categories 5 and 8). Assuming the solution not to be "open and shut," the different values and interests of the members are more apparent, both directly and as the criteria for making a decision. The *Control* phase follows, with the group shifting to more concern over reaching a group decision, and expecting further joint action.

For the administrator, it is worth noting that he should not be surprised if a group does not go directly to the final phase of Control, as he might hope. He and others may wish that the group "get down to business" right away, but part of that business involves the people getting oriented, seeing the gaps that exist in information, sorting out the values and viewpoints held, and then moving toward consensus.* It might be noted, too, that these phases seem to occur where there are no marked status differences in the group which would deny people the feeling that they can participate and influence the group planning or decision. Perhaps, too, the administrator, if he is conducting the meeting, might even set sub-goals for the group, for example, getting most of the facts listed first, then the advantages and disadvantages of different approaches, before moving to the "What do we do?" part of the meeting.

---

* See also Guetzkow and Gyr.

Training

Earlier in this section, we descibed a possible program for training employees in individual creative thinking; the desirabilty of training *groups* for group problem solving must also be considered. We know that it is possible to improve skills in discussion leadership for more effective problem solving, but little work has been' done on training the group itself in the procedures of problem solving (Maier, 1953). (The training program described in Chapter Twenty might easily be adapted for group purposes.)

Motivation and Incentives in Group Problem Solving

Too often, the principal need operating in members of a problem-solving group is that of finishing the job and "getting back to our own work." Occasionally there is the motivation for individuals to exploit a group problem situation for private and departmental ends, frequently at the expense of a really good solution to the group's problem. It is unusual to find an organization providing incentives directed at efficient *group* functioning. And yet we know that groups, as well as individuals, respond to increased motivation or specific incentives for successful group performance.*

It may require imagination to find means in the average organization to reward effective group performance. It has been done and as long as problem solving is attempted in group settings it must be done to raise the level of the group's efforts.† Among some methods that might be tried are: relating salary recommendations to cooperative group performance, giving high prestige to group assignments (but controlling those who will seek only the prestige), giving feedback on group performance from a high level source in the organization, including group problem solving as one of the standards of performance set for the individual. Unless the group incentive is present, one of two undesirable consequences tend to result: mediocre performance is accepted to "get the job done" or competitive individual performance is stimulated to the ultimate disadvantage of the group and the over-all organization. If we are going to depend on individual performance, it may be better to do so outside the group setting.

Structural Characteristics of Successful
Problem-Solving Groups

There are indications that when a group has been newly formed of members who are not familiar with each other, or of members whose status levels have not been clearly established, the problem-solving effort may suffer. A lack of familiarity may tend to inhibit the information giving or opinion expressing of some members (Nash and Wolfe). Where status among members is uncer-

---

* For example, see Mayo; Berkowitz (1957); or Leavitt (1962).
† One approach is that taken by Scanlon. See Lesieur.

tain, the task functioning of the group may be shunted aside in a power struggle to establish status through domineering performance (Sayles). It may also happen that members are being judged along two different status dimensions, for example, age and education. The status level for one dimension may be inconsistent with the level in the other dimension (for example, a very young, highly educated member and an older member with little education).* This will produce a socially ambiguous situation. The consequent attempt to clarify status may distract the group from its problem solving goal. Newly formed groups that have two or more members contesting for superiority were found less effective in a highly interdependent task than groups where the outstandingly superior member was uncontested (Ghiselli and Lodahl). In setting up a problem-solving group, an attempt should be made to control these difficulties. For example, organizational members who do not know each other may be given opportunity to become familiar with each other by working first on less critical problems. To throw them together for the first time to solve a challenging problem or one in a highly sensitive area can only result in half-hearted effort and mediocre solutions. Or, to choose an example in the area of status, it may be better to wait until a new young man has worked out his status relationships in the organization before assigning him to a problem-solving group. Management can even hasten the process and strengthen his hand by giving him job experiences that increase his perceived usefulness prior to assigning him to group tasks.

It may not always be possible to form groups to avoid the difficulties introduced by unfamiliarity or status uncertainty. Where this is the case, awareness of the possible difficulties should make it possible for the group leader to use the early part of the session to resolve the social uncertainties, postponing decisions about the problem itself until later. Doing this, he may be able to keep the social struggle disentangled from the struggle with the problem itself. The problem then may be solved on its own merits rather than on the basis of irrelevant social factors.

The question of group size also has to be mentioned. In determining how large a problem-solving group should be, it is well to use Thelen's "principle of the least group size." A group should be only large enough to have present all the relevant information and skills for solving the problem. The larger a group becomes the more social matters such as control, limited opportunity for each member to speak, and lack of familiarity, reduce the efficiency of the real problem-solving effort.

Group Problem Solving Under Stress

A conclusion drawn about individual problem solving applies also to the group: Group performance is better under mild stress than under severe stress or no stress at all. One study suggests some reasons why.

---

* Homan's concept of status congruence is discussed in this connection by Zaleznik, *et al.*, pp. 56-65. A research suggesting the complexity of the problem is reported by Adams.

When a group is placed under stress the members tend to view the group as a source of security in the face of the external threat that is creating the stress. Consequently more behavior acceptable to the group develops: cooperation, friendliness, group discussion, and coordinated behavior. Behavior that would be rejected by the group is minimized: aggression, self-serving behavior, and competition (Lanzetta).

Although the study reported is a laboratory experiment, lacking in fully realistic circumstances, the type of stress used was one known to the administrator: setting a time limit. It seems safe enough to draw the implication that when an administrator can raise the stress level slightly by imposing a time limit or requiring the group to work under mildly uncomfortable (rather than soporifically comfortable) conditions, he can hope to raise the level of a group's performance. The point is made because often administrators behave as if they were reasoning in the very opposite way—giving them plenty of time to work under pleasant conditions will bring out the best in them. A small dilemma develops when the comfortable place to work is provided as a means of raising the group's prestige. It may then be better to count on the time limit to add the note of mild stress.

LEADERSHIP AND GROUP PROBLEM SOLVING

To devote a short section to the matter of leadership in the last chapter of our book would be the grossest type of under-emphasis in a discussion of administrative behavior, unless we can believe that we have been talking about leadership throughout the book—or at least the kind of knowledge about human behavior on which leadership can build effective action. In addition, up to now our discussion of the characteristics of effective problem-solving groups has largely sought to point up what leaders can do to help form effective groups.

Here we hope merely to identify a few further suggestions, highly specific to the group problem-solving situation, and confined to leadership of the group itself, rather than the broader type of administrative leadership we have described throughout the book. For example, a group leader may have to realize that he can gain group productivity on the problem only by restricting the social and emotional satisfactions of the members (Hare, p. 374). Consequently he will have to learn to survive without being the most popular member of the group and even be able to tolerate the development of a second leader of the group who is free to cater to the nontask needs of its members (Bales, 1953). At the same time, his problem-solving leadership will be effective to the extent that he typifies the group's idea of a leader for the task he has assumed (Greer). In other words, the group will expect him to "lead" them toward a solution of the problem in a skillful, acceptable way but may not reward him by increasing his popularity for doing so. Differently stated, popularity and group leadership (at least for problem-solving groups) are not the same. (This view would fit with much other research showing leadership not to be an across-the-board trait, but relevant to the situation.)

Still another component that must be integrated into the delicate balance required for successful leadership is the matter of an authoritarian or a democratic approach. An authoritarian approach is reported to increase the productivity of groups, particularly when members show a strong tendency to express self-oriented needs. Such would be the case in groups of low cohesiveness. The quality of product, however, may be higher in democratically led groups.

The inference is strong, although the actual data have not yet been fully developed, that the most effective style of leadership for problem-solving groups will vary with many characteristics of the group itself. Some of these are: the group's past history of success or failure, its task or social orientation, the level of cohesiveness, the personality characteristics of members, the size of the group and its problem-solving resources, and the characteristics of the leader himself, particularly, for example, the problem relevant information and skill that he possesses, and his status and perceived influence in the organization. One can surmise that in a highly cohesive group with a strong problem orientation, a permissive style of leadership might get problems solved better than a more authoritarian approach; on the other hand, if the group was either not so cohesive or not problem oriented, we could not so safely draw the same conclusion. A leader who is seen to have expert knowledge or highly useful problem skills may be quite authoritarian in his leadership practices without necessarily arousing negative emotional reactions; or he may be quite permissive without being seen as weak. Compared to a skilled leader, a leader who has neither useful skill nor knowledge will have to work much harder, be more careful about the style of his leadership, and in one way or another, find a role in which he can help the group achieve its goal of solving the problem. Otherwise he will either find someone else taking his place or the problem staying unsolved.

In studying the relation between styles of managerial practice and problem-solving behavior, Levy states: "Supporting and helping styles of managing employed by superiors do not only affect the degree of satisfaction or morale of their people, but also clearly affect the degree to which individuals and groups can operate productively and solve problems effectively within the organization."

We are not completely without more specific guidance about effective leadership for problem-solving groups. Maier's research in the area provides several guidelines for us.

RESEARCH **SUMMARY** **6-9**	*Some Guidelines for Group Problem Solving.* Since 1930, Maier has been interested in the psychological phases of problem-solving behavior. During the past decade or so, he and his associates at the University of Michigan have been studying group problem solving. In 1963, Maier summarized much of this research in a book on problem-solving discussions and conferences. We draw on his conclusions to suggest some guidelines for leaders of problem solving groups. The leader contributes to group problem solving when he:

1. Presents the problem in situational goal-oriented terms rather than personal terms. Talking about people or the behavior of groups tends to arouse defensiveness rather than problem-solving behavior.

2. Presents the problem free of any implied solution that he himself prefers. Solutions openly offered or implied by the leader are likely either to be too quickly accepted or rejected. Rarely are they openly and objectively discussed on their merits.

3. Encourages all members to participate in the discussion, offering full opportunity for minority opinion to be heard.

4. Creates an atmosphere free enough to encourage expressions of disagreement and conflict; but one that focusses the disagreement on the ideas and proposals, not on the people expressing them.

5. Periodically summarizes the discussion, both keeping the group on the problem and giving them a sense of movement and accomplishment.

The group works effectively when:

1. It uses the facts available even though it may feel the facts are not fully adequate. When abundant facts are not present, there is a temptation to fall back on old solutions that worked for other problems. The facts available should be examined, at least to determine the relevance of such old solutions or the need for different approaches.

2. Members direct their attention to the surmountable aspects of the problem, rather than endlessly attempting a solution to an insoluble aspect of the problem. Frequently, handling the most simple parts of a problem open up new paths for approaching the more difficult parts.

3. It is willing to separate the idea getting process (which should come first) from the idea evaluation process in problem solving. Evaluating ideas at the time they are expressed distracts the group from the process of producing ideas and tends to inhibit some members from expressing deviant but nevertheless useful ideas. In addition Maier suggests that a group ought first to be problem-minded and only much later solution-minded.

For effective problem solving:

1. The problem should be converted into a variety of alternatives. Unless this is done, the problem is often approached in terms of a single solution, perhaps implied in the way the problem was suggested.

2. Where a choice situation—either-or—is presented, it ought to be converted into a problem—what goal do we seek? After the goal is identified, often a two alternative choice gives way to a listing of many possibilities.*

COMMUNICATION IN PROBLEM-SOLVING GROUPS

The amount and quality of communication that can, and does, take place is, of course, an important influence on any relationship among people. We examine the communication process here in specific reference to its impact on

---

* For a full discussion of these and many other suggestions for group problem solving the reader is referred to Maier's book, *Problem-solving Discussions and Conferences.*

problem-solving efficiency in groups. One aspect of this is the content of the communication, particularly language factors; another, and probably more important aspect is the communication channels or networks available and used. Chapter Sixteen on Attitude Change has touched on characteristics of the communicator, for example, credibility, that may affect the receipt of information.

Communication Content (Language or Semantic Elements) and Group Problem Solving

When individuals come together to work on a problem, they are dependent upon language as a principal, if not exclusive, means of exchanging information, opinion, and suggestions. The semanticists, particularly Korzybski, warn us about some of the weaknesses and distorting influences in the words we use. Osgood has provided a means of quantifying the different meanings the same word holds for different people. This is not the place to describe the philosophical and logical orientation out of which Korzybski's work has developed. We choose, instead to identify some difficulties in the use of words and the practical suggestions offered by Korzybski to limit the resulting communication distortions.

The most basic difficulty in the use of words is the inevitable temptation to act as if the words were really the things they represent. Korzybski would have us recognize that words can only be a map of the actual territory, not the territory itself. The word, then, only approximates the thing. Different people may use different maps to represent the same things, or using the same maps, they may have a different scale of representation. A map will never be able to represent all aspects of the world; words cannot cover all they represent. It will be helpful to pin down the concepts to specific examples:

1. budget—as it might have meaning for different users of the term: a sum of money to be spent; an upper limit, not to be exceeded under any circumstances; not to be exceeded if departmental needs can be satisfied without doing so.
2. reasonable production (see Figure 6-2).
3. organization chart—may foolishly be assumed to be a description of the way in which people relate to each other in the organization. Frequently a reorganization is assumed to be accomplished when a new organization chart is published and distributed.

So, in group problem solving it is helpful to explore the map systems used by different participants and to understand that words used are tentative, inexact, incomplete representations of what it is the problem solver is talking about. It is necessary to accept the possibility that some words will stand in the way of seeing a solution or of gaining acceptance of a solution from other participants.

A particular difficulty, pointed out by Korzybski, is the use of the same word to refer to objects existing at different time periods. Here the map remains the same while the territory changes. As a corrective he suggests that

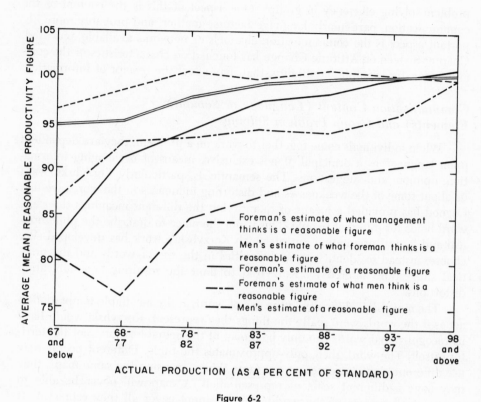

Figure 6-2

Actual Productivity and Average Perceived Reasonable Productivity Figure.

we add subscripts (or parenthetical notation) to some of our words to indicate the time period we have in mind, for example, "this company $_{1950}$," "our plans (January 15th)."

To help keep in a communicator's mind that he is never able to say all there is to say about a topic, the semanticists suggest adding *etc.* after any statement that presumes to do so. Our tendency to use *and* to place two objects or processes together suggests that they will remain the same after they have been associated with each other. To point up the fact that association may set up an interactive process changing both objects or processes, they suggest a hyphen joining the two words be substituted for *and*, for example, "Smith serves as controller-personnel director" rather than "Smith serves as controller and personnel director."

Members of problem-solving groups are not likely to use these suggestions in any literal sense. They can keep them in mind as warnings of some misunderstandings that creep into the communication process and block efficient problem solving.

Communication Networks

Whether we talk about problem-solving efforts in the organization itself or in a small face to face problem-solving group, it soon becomes apparent that although many channels for communication seem available, for various reasons only certain channels are used. Much research has been done demonstrating that both level of performance (here problem-solving efficiency) and level of satisfaction are dependent upon the communication networks or channels used.

Groups that solve problems in business organizations may be small *ad hoc* groups set up by one administrator who has drawn the group members only from his department; they may also be—may, as a matter of fact more frequently be—individuals from various parts of the organization or even outside the organization, in different roles, and even at different status levels, who are required to collaborate to solve a problem. It is for the latter type of group that a discussion of networks holds the most significance. Nevertheless, it is true that communication networks will develop in any social setting.

In 1948 Alex Bavelas while at M.I.T., designed a laboratory study to simulate some networks that might develop in an organization or group setting. His work stimulated an extensive analysis of the problem by many others. At this point, we refer to the Bavelas study only to picture some possible networks. We return later to examine some of the findings.

Placing each of five subjects in an individual cubicle, he assigned the group of five the task of discovering which of six symbols appeared on the cards given to each member. Each card had printed on it five different symbols, only one of which was printed on all the cards. Communication among the members was limited to a network decided upon in advance by Bavelas. Figure 6-3 illustrates some of the networks he studied. Each line indicates a two-way linkage between the two subjects named.

These networks were not designed to be literal imitations of organizational channels; nevertheless they do come very close to describing channels that as

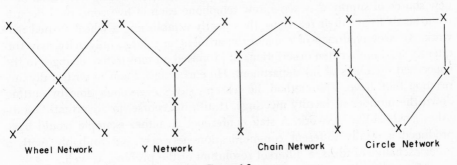

Figure 6-3

Illustrative Communication Networks.
Each line represents a two-way channel of communication between two members of the group.
After Bavelas.

a matter of fact, are used in business organizations. The wheel network describes a department head and four subordinates who report individually to him (even though the usual organization chart shows the relationship differently). The Y describes a hierarchical arrangement in which communication from subordinates proceeds up the line through higher echelons to the top man. The circle might very well represent communication among peers at the same level in the organization, whose most frequent communication contacts are limited to the colleagues on each side of them. These and other network patterns do develop in organizations, and even, in a less obvious way, in small face to face problem-solving groups.

We consider, first, some factors that determine communication networks, then some characteristics of these networks and their effects on performance and satisfaction.

Factors That Determine Communication Networks

Networks actually used in business organizations are determined by (a) the formal organization, (b) informal organization, and (c) the media used in communication. Some examples follow:

(a) *Formal Organization.* The vice president in charge of research and development, in the interest of conserving some of his own time, may designate an assistant vice president to be in contact with all project leaders. If the assistant does so on an individual basis he has produced a Y shaped network.

(b) *Informal Organization Through Unofficial Distortion of the Formal Organization.* In the same department under the same conditions, project leaders who have neither opportunity for group discussion nor direct access to their chief, may set up their own network, for example, a chain network ultimately centering on one senior or more expert project leader. Thus, A may interact with B who is in an adjoining section of the building. And E may interact with D on the same basis, with both D and B going separately to C who is considered by all to be somewhat more influential with top management.

(c) *Media of Communication.* A purchasing agent facing a decision on a new source of supply may separately telephone each of five concerned department heads to get their reactions, thus neatly establishing a wheel shaped network. An area chairman of a major department in a large university may frequently send out written descriptions of proposed administrative changes to the concerned members of his department. He encourages them to write fully any reaction they have. The method, he reasons, saves everyone's time by cutting down the number of faculty meetings. It also, of course, in advertently establishes a wheel-like network. A staff conference in either example would have produced a totally different communication network, and probably, with a fuller exchange of ideas, a different resolution of the problem as well.

Many other less explicit influences will also determine the communication channels chosen by members in an organization. Some of these are: status considerations other than those formally established in the organization, for example, age or educational levels; common background or professional training; known similarities in points of view; and simple personal friendships.

Characteristics of Networks and Their Effect

Now to return to the research stimulated by Bavelas' early study to examine the effects of different communication networks. The differently structured networks we have described vary in the number of communication channels they provide individual members in the network and in the amount of information they make available to each member. For example, in the circle, each member has two channels of communication; in the wheel, four members have one channel, one member has four channels. In the wheel, one member will have all the information; other members will have only some of the information. Research has demonstrated that both these factors, number of communication channels and amount of information, significantly affect both the performance and the attitudes of those in the network. These effects may be summarized* as follows:

Highly Centralized Networks (those in which one member has more channels and more information than others).	*Networks Low in Centralization* (those in which all members share an equal number of channels and have access to the same amount of information).
(1) facilitate efficient performance of routine problem solving, involving principally the assembling of information.	(1) Produce higher levels of satisfaction.
(2) strengthen the leadership position of the member most central in the network (having the largest number of channels and the most information).	(2) facilitate the handling of ambiguous and unpredictable situations.
(3) result in a quickly stabilized set of interactions among members.	(3) are likely to be more responsive to innovative and creative solutions.

The research does not identify one type of network as clearly more desirable than any other. It strongly suggests that the communication network is still another factor to be taken into account in the organization's problem-solving efforts. Members of problem-solving groups will communicate with each other through some network of channels, whether formally or informally established, explicitly stated or not. The structure of the network will influence the outcome of any problem-solving effort taking place within the confines of the network.

It is an administrative responsibility to be aware of the network used and to assess its appropriateness for particular problem-solving goals, both in terms of the sought after performance and satisfaction of the group members.

In concerning himself with the relationship between group problem solving and communication network, the administrator might also consider implications in two other lines of research: comparisons of two-way versus one-way

---

* For summaries of the research on communication networks see Hare, Chapter Ten; Glanzer and Glaser.

communication, and studies of the effect of status differences on flow of communication.

When communication is encouraged or allowed to take place in only one direction, with no opportunity for feedback from the communicatee in the form of acknowledgements, questions, or negative reactions then accuracy in communication is poor and both communicator and communicatee show low confidence in each other. (By accuracy of communication is meant a correspondence between what the person intends to say and what he is perceived as having said.) But when a period of free feedback is provided, even though it is limited to the early phases of the communication effort, considerable improvement takes place in both accuracy of communication and confidence between the two participants (Leavitt and Mueller). In addition, administrators will find that when they have to communicate criticism (or any form of hostility) subsequent relations with the criticized person will be friendlier if they allow opportunity for retort in the first place (Thibaut and Coules).

Two way communication seems unquestionably more effective than one way communication, even though it may seem to take more time and may occasionally produce some unpleasant "back talk." This is preferable to the continuation of negative feelings (unexpressed) and possible interference with future interaction.

Differences in status among members of a problem-solving group will affect the flow of communication, which, in turn, may affect the efficiency of problem solving. For example, one study indicates that lower status members of a three man problem-solving group emphasize material likely to make them "look good" in the eyes of the higher status people (thus perhaps not making their full contribution to the solution of the problem). Higher status members of the group tend to feel that members of lesser status are doing more talking than as a matter of fact they are, a feeling that may result in a show of impatience that could block the contribution of others. Perhaps the status problem can be illustrated if we imagine a problem-solving team made up of a general, a major, and a private. Let us also assume that all three are professionally trained. We can predict that if the order of problem-solving communication moves from the general to the major to the private, communication will be less full, with a less adequate solution than if the order were the reverse.* But under some conditions, a reversal of the order would also make for difficulties— for example, if after the private and the major made their contributions, the general totally ignored the contributions of both; or if neither the private nor major were informed enough about the problem to make any worthwhile contributions.

Obviously, no simple formula exists for eliminating the impact of status differences on the flow of communication. In some cases, the solution may be to assign only peers to problem-solving committees. At other times, it may be necessary to count on leadership in the problem-solving group to minimize the effect of status.

---

* For research on this point see Maier and Hoffman, 1960, 1961; also Torrance, pp. 482-492.

Concluding
Statement

The Organization as a Problem-Solving System

In the business setting, individual and group problem-solving efforts contribute to the goals of the organization as a whole. The organization itself also can be viewed as a problem-solving system; its design (the arrangement of its parts) and its functioning (the activities of its members) must be evaluated against the criteria of its effectiveness and its efficiency in problem solving.

In addition to the suggestions made previously, what do we know about thinking that can be applied to the organization's system of problem solving? We begin by considering some barriers frequently present in any problem-solving effort. Looking back at the chapters in Part Six, we see examples of such barriers as: wrong set, inadequate communication networks, and lack of information. The administrator must ask whether or not the organizational structure is one that will help to bypass these barriers. Let us examine first, the barrier of wrong set. Subgroups in the organization—marketing, purchasing, production—are narrowed in their thinking by working on problems only in their own field, communicating most often and freely with members of their own groups and not often being able to see the full contributions made by other subgroups to the over-all task. They tend, as a result, to develop sets or expectations that are too restrictive and that reduce their capacities for co-operative problem solving with other groups. Sales people take a marketing approach, production people often emphasize only technical aspects, and so on. There are certainly advantages to functional specialization but in order to overcome the rigid sets produced, some opportunity must be provided to break away from functional subgroups. Perhaps prior to permanent job placement, a planned rotation through the functional areas would help prevent a fixing of attitudes too early. After "permanent" placement, every major problem solver in the organization ought to be given opportunity for working with a different functional group on problems cutting across functional lines. Two examples are: production, purchasing, sales, and research people working on a project to build community good will or, marketing and public relations joining personnel and production groups in developing a safety program.

There are also barriers created by lack of information or by its unavailability for use in problem solving. From an organizational point of view, two sources of difficulty can be identified. The absence of communication channels between problem-solving groups dependent on each other for exchange of information is one. Consider, for example, two independent but parallel subgroups working on different subunits for assembly into a complex whole. Once original assignments have been outlined, little communication may be available to the groups.

The absence of opportunities for communication blocks flexibility and eliminates the exchange of learning experiences that might make possible, for example, new solutions, synthesizing the problem-solving efforts of all sub-groups. Absence of effective communications sometimes occurs because of lack of structuring for communication—information is traded but not in such a systematic or structured way as to assure its being delivered to the right spot on time for use in problem-solving decisions. Informal, unstructured communication exchange has its value more for the social aspect of the organization than for its problem-solving activities. To solve problems effectively an organization must provide formal (but not stuffy) channels of communication between subgroups whose problem-solving efforts may be interdependent, whether the channels flow vertically or horizontally in the organization.

The second major threat to adequate information for problem-solving is the presence of filters in the available communication networks. When information must move from one subgroup to another, through only one individual, his biases and inadequacies filter the information, often preventing vital aspects of it from reaching its appropriate destination. Reading 6-6 describes one means of overcoming this problem—increasing the number of filters operating independently of each other, through which the information will flow: asking two different individuals separately to prepare a report, for example, on the feasibility of a projected improvement.

A more basic and readily available means of both reducing the filter effect and of providing a formal communication exchange is systematically planned conferences—across vertical and horizontal organizational lines. As our discussion in Chapter Twenty-three indicates, skilled leadership is required. When carefully planned and well led, such conferences provide (a) an organizationally structured means of bringing a variety of information to bear on complex problems; (b) an effective means of eliminating the filtering effect, and (c) a way of broadening narrow sets growing out of functional specialization.

Our discussion of concept formation has implications for over-all management practice. Management frequently uses a conceptual system based solely on the formal functional areas of the organization. Problems are conceptualized as marketing or production problems, when, as a matter of fact, different conceptual schema might be more helpful. For example, problems might be sorted into such categories as time problems, human relations problems, or intergroup problems; the resources of several subgroups might then be sought in their solution. Or, a simple grouping into growth problems and maintenance problems might help in breaking out of nonhelpful sets that hamper organizational problem solving.

The vertical structure of the organization also forces the use of other categories or concept systems—for example, all purchase orders over $10,000 must be approved by headquarters. Here a classification system is being used to sort problems into large and small matters and to relate these to appropriate levels of the organization for resolution. Such a classification system provides an ordered set of concepts, helping to delineate areas of responsibility in specific terms. A danger is that the boundaries of the classification system outlive their usefulness. An upper limit of $10,000 is appropriate when such amounts occur only occasionally. The limit causes unnecessary delays when such amounts occur *often,* as they might with company growth or a change in purchasing practices.

Here, too, we can question whether the classification system frequently used by management—one based on amount of money to be spent, of equipment to be ordered, and so forth—is the most useful one. Are there other criteria that better indicate how important a choice is? For relating problems to hierarchical levels in the organization, the complexity of the problem (rather than the simple cost) might better be the basis of classification. Such questions as the following might be considered in formulating other conceptual schemas for sorting problems: Can the problem be solved only by going beyond stated policy? are other departments involved in decisions that will be made? will the problem solving commit the company to a course of action for a short or a long time span? The answer to any of these questions may provide a more useful basis for classifying problems than considering only the amount involved in the transaction.

From the chapter on decision making, certain additional implications appear. The organization can upgrade its problem solving by introducing thinking tools, for example, normative decision rules derived from decision theory, or any of a variety of other techniques: accounting procedures, psychological measuring instruments, or the mathematical procedures of operations research. Often, the problem is not to introduce the tools but to spread their use throughout the organization. Some seem naturally to have grown out of the work of particular functional areas. Though their usefulness as problem-solving aids goes beyond the original department, no one thinks to make them available throughout the organization. The identification of accounting techniques with the controller's department is an example. Some of the procedures in operations research seem to be suffering the same fate—confinement to one or two functional areas. At the same time, unfortunately, in these areas the procedures are often treated as ends in themselves rather than as useful means to the solving of organization problems.

Finally, we return to the organizational structure and the kind of problem-solving system it tends to create. The point of view espoused in our book would certainly emphasize the value of increasing face to face contact among members of an organization who must collaborate (or work jointly) to solve organizational problems. In these comments devoted to organizational problem solving, we consider all subgroups in the organization as falling into this category. Nevertheless, the success of interdependent problem-solving groups does not depend only on the amount of face to face communication available to them, but depends, as well, on the system of problem solving imposed on the groups by the organization.

Leavitt has pointed out that an organization's current structure is "probably in large part an outcome of (its) problem-solving (history). Given different task histories (for example, different products, different economic environments, and so on) at different stages of their growth, we would expect different present operating organization structures (for example, different distributions of line and staff roles, different proportions of jobs at different levels in the hierarchy, and so on," 1960, p. 235). The point for us to consider is that an organization's problem-solving system is more likely to be geared for past problems than for current or future ones. The challenge is to examine and modify conceptual schema, types of information available, and assignments made in the light of current and future conditions in order to minimize any dysfunctional carry-over from the organization's past. In the early phases of an organization's history, the most important problem-solving contributions might come from its technical staff—providing more efficient means of product manufacture; later on, the need might be for effective problem solving from its market organization, discovering additional uses for products or product improvements. The system will have to be changed to match the shift in type of problem.

In addition to the historical effect, there are other questions to be raised about the organization's system for problem solving: In what sequence does the organization present problems? We don't know a best sequence, but we do know that certain sequences influence the effectiveness of problem solving. For example, Leavitt (1960) has demonstrated, in a laboratory situation, that for one type of problem, moving from easy to difficult problems is more efficient than moving from difficult to easy problems.

Are solution systems encouraged or only accommodative, single shot solutions? A problem can be solved by accommodating to the particular obstacles and constraints present here and now, or it can be solved by developing a system that will provide a solution for all (or most) other problems of the same type. The latter is, of course, the more efficient procedure. Which one occurs is, no doubt, influenced by many factors. Zand and Costello have shown that one factor might be the requirement to work on a problem until its successful completion before going on to another form of the same type of problem. A large number of versions of the problem seemed to encourage development of a solution system; a relatively small number of versions encouraged only accommodative solutions.

Is the structure provided by the organization one that encourages original and creative problem solving? In our discussion of the network experiments (Ch. Twenty- three), we cited studies indicating that communication structure can affect the likelihood of innovative or novel solutions to problems. In addition to open networks for communicating, there is the question of providing units in the structure whose sole purpose is the generation of original proposals for problem solving.

In summarizing this final section on organizational problem solving, we can draw two major conclusions: (1) the organizational structure imposes a method of problem solving on its members. That method has to be studied to be sure that the most efficient problem-solving system is evolved. (2) Providing frequent formal (as well as informal) opportunities for face to face communication across functional areas and hierarchical lines increases the efficiency of the organization's problem-solving system.

Concluding Note

Any author who has attempted to write about human behavior in a systematic and comprehensive fashion must often have been tried by the impossibility of describing simultaneously all the facets of even the simplest human act. The piecemeal approach that we so often take in meeting the problem, leads us to describe first one aspect, then another, with the possibility of leaving the suggestion that each aspect is independent of the others.

A person is a unity and he perceives, as he is motivated, as he thinks, in the framework of his attitudes, while he is learning. Learning is an aspect of all human behavior, as is perception, thinking, motivation and so on. Each phase of behavior that we have written about must be seen as part of every other phase, growing out of it, interacting with it, and, in turn, giving rise to other behavior.

To our administrator readers, we can only suggest that as they well know—they cannot plan without organizing and controlling and directing—so they will find it unwise to focus on any one aspect of human behavior without considering its simultaneous interaction with all other facets of the human being's potential for response.

Bibliography

Part One: Perceiving People and Situations

Allport, G., *Nature of Predjudice*. Reading, Mass.: Addison-Wesley Publishing Co. 1954.

Asch, S., Forming Impressions of Personality. *Journal of Abnormal and Social Psychology*, 1946, *41*, 258-290.

Barrett, R. S., The Agreement Scale: A Preliminary Report. *Personnel Psychology*, 1961, *14*, 151-165.

Benedetti, D. T. and Hill, J. G., A Determiner of the Centrality of a Trait in Impression Formation. *Journal of Abnormal and Social Psychology*, 1960, *60*, 278-279.

Bieri, J., Change in Interpersonal Perception Following Interaction. *Journal of Abnormal and Social Psychology*, 1953, 48, 61-66.

Bossom, J. and Maslow, A. H., Security of Judges as a Factor in Impressions of Warmth in Others. *Journal of Abnormal and Social Psychology*, 1957, 55, 147-148.

Bronfenbrenner, U., Harding, J., and Gallwey, M., The Measurement of Skill in Social Perception. In McClelland, D. C., Baldwin, A. L., Bronfenbrenner, U., and Strodtbeck, F. L. (eds.), *Talent and Society*. Princeton, N.J.: D. Van Nostrand Co., Inc., 1958, pp. 29-111.

Bruner, J. S., Social Psychology and Perception. In Maccoby, E., Newcomb T., and Hartley, E. (eds.), *Readings in Social Psychology* (3rd ed.). New York: Holt Rinehart & Winston, Inc., 1958, 85-94.

————, and Perlmutter, H. V., Compatriot and Foreigner: A Study of Impression Formation in Three Countries. *Journal of Abnormal and Social Psychology*, 1957, 55, 253-260.

————, and Taguiri, R., *The Perception of People*. In G. Lindzey (ed.), *Handbook of Social Psychology*. Vol. II, Reading, Mass.: Addison-Wesley Publishing Co., 1954, Ch. 17.

Cantril, H., Perception and Interpersonal Relations. *American Journal of Psychiatry*, 1957, *114* (#2), 119-126.

Cronbach, L. J., Processes Affecting Scores on "Understanding of Others" and "Assumed Similarity." *Psychological Bulletin*, 1955, 52, 177-193.

Crow, W. J., Effect of Training on Interpersonal Perception. *Journal of Abnormal and Social Psychology*, 1957, 55, 355-359.

Dailey, C. A., The Effects of Premature Conclusion upon the Acquisition of Understanding of a Person. *Journal of Psychology*, 1952, 33, 133-152.

Dearborn, D. C. and Simon, H. A., Selective Perception: A Note on the Departmental Identifications of Executives. *Sociometry*, 1958, *21*, 140-144.

NOTE: This Bibliography includes only those items referred to in the text material. References used in the Readings in most cases are contained in each Reading.

Ex, J., The Nature of the Relation Between Two Persons and the Degree of Their Influence on Each Other. *Acta Psychologica*, 1960, *17*, 39-54.

Exline, R. V., Group Climate as a Factor in the Relevance and Accuracy of Social Perception. *Journal of Abnormal and Social Psychology*, 1957, *55*, 382-388.

————, Interrelations Among Two Dimensions of Sociometric Status, Group Congeniality and Accuracy of Social Perception. *Sociometry*, 1960, *23*, 85-101.

Feshback, S. and Singer, R. D., The Effects of Fear Arousal upon Social Perception. *Journal of Abnormal and Social Psychology*, 1957, *55*, 283-288.

Gage, N. L., Accuracy of Social Perception and Effectiveness in Interpersonal Relationships. *Journal of Personality*, 1953, *22*, 128-141.

Grove, B. A. and Kerr, W. A., Specific Evidence on Origin of Halo Effect in Measurement of Morals. *Journal of Social Psychology*, 1951, *34*, 165-170.

Haire, M., Role-Perceptions in Labor Management Relations: An Experimental Approach. *Industrial and Labor Relations Review*, 1955, *8*, 204-216.

———— and Grunes, W. F., Perceptual Defenses: Processes Protecting an Original Perception of Another Personality. *Human Relations*, 1950, *3*, 403-412.

Hastorf, A. H., Richardson, S. A., and Dornbusch, S. M., The Problem of Relevance in the Study of Person Perception. In Taguiri, R. and Petrullo, L. (eds.), *Person Perception and Interpersonal Behavior*. Stanford, California: Stanford University Press, 1958, pp. 54-62.

Johnson, D. M., A Systematic Treatment of Judgment. *Psychological Bulletin*, 1945, *41*, 193-224.

Jones, E. E., Authoritarianism as a Determinant of First Impressions Formation. *Journal of Personality*, 1954, *23*, 107-127.

Kelley, H. H., The Warm-Cold Variable in First Impressions of Persons. *Journal of Personality*, 1950, *18*, 431-439.

Kipnis, D., Some Determinants of Supervisory Esteem. *Personnel Psychology*, 1960, *13*, 377-391.

Krech, D. and Crutchfield, R. S., *Elements of Psychology*. New York: Alfred A. Knopf, Inc., 1958.

————, *Theory and Problems of Social Psychology*. New York: McGraw-Hill Book Company, Inc., 1948.

Likert, R., Motivational Approach to a Modified Theory of Organization and Management. In Haire, M. (ed.), *Modern Organization Theory*. New York: John Wiley & Sons, Inc., 1959.

————, *New Patterns of Management*. New York: McGraw-Hill Book Company, Inc., 1961.

Lippmann, W., *Public Opinion*. New York: The Macmillan Company, 1922.

Luft, J., Monetary Value and the Perception of Persons. *Journal of Social Psychology*, 1957, *46*, 245-251.

Lundy, R. M., Katkovsky, W., Cromwell, R. L., and Shoemaker, D. J., Self Acceptability and Descriptions of Sociometric Choices. *Journal of Abnormal and Social Psychology*, 1955, *51*, 260-262.

Maslow, A. H. and Mintz, N. L., Effects of Esthetic Surroundings: I. Initial Effects of Three Esthetic Conditions upon Perceiving "Energy" and "Well Being" in Faces. *Journal of Psychology*, 1956, *41*, 247-254.

Mason, D. J., Judgments of Leadership Based upon Physiognomic Cues. *Journal of Abnormal and Social Psychology*, 1957, *54*, 273-274.

Murray, H. A., The Effect of Fear upon Estimates of the Maliciousness of Other Personalities. *Journal of Social Psychology*, 1933, *4*, 310-329.

Newcomb, T. M., The Perception of Interpersonal Attraction. *American Psychologist*, 1956, *11*, 575-586; *The Aquaintance Process*, New York: Holt, Rinehart & Winston, Inc., 1961.

Norman, R. D., The Interrelationships Among Acceptance-Rejection, Self-Other Identity, Insight into Self, and Realistic Perception of Others. *Journal of Social Psychology*, 1953, 37, 205-235.

Omwake, K. T., The Relation Between Acceptance of Self and Acceptance of Others Shown by Three Personality Inventories. *Journal of Consulting Psychology*, 1954, *18*, 443-446.

Porter, L. W., Differential Self-Perceptions of Management Personnel and Line Workers. *Journal of Applied Psychology*, 1958, *42*, 105-109.

Rosenbaum, M. E., Social Perception and the Motivational Structure of Interpersonal Relations. *Journal of Abnormal and Social Psychology*, 1959, *59*, 130-133.

Sears, R. R., Experimental Studies of Projection, I. Attribution of Traits. *Journal of Social Psychology*, 1936, 7, 151-163.

Soskin, W. E., Influence of Information on Bias in Social Perception. *Journal of Personality*, 1953, 22, 118-127.

Stagner, R., *Psychology of Industrial Conflict*. New York: John Wiley & Sons, Inc., 1956.

Steiner, I., Interpersonal Behavior as Influenced by Accuracy of Social Perception. *Psychological Review*, 1955, *62*, 268-275.

Stock, D. and Thelen, H. A., *Emotional Dynamics and Group Culture*. New York: New York University, 1958.

Strickland, L. H., Surveillance and Trust. *Journal of Personality*, 1958, *26*, 200-215.

Symonds, P. M., Notes on Rating. *Journal of Applied Psychology*, 1925, 7, 188-195. Cited by Bruner and Taguiri; *op. cit.* in Lindzey, Vol. II. p. 641.

Taft, R., The Ability to Judge People. *Psychological Bulletin*, 1955, *52*, 1-21.

Taguiri, R., Bruner, J. S. and Blake, R., On the Relation Between Feelings and Perceptions of Feelings Among Members of Small Groups. In Maccoby, E. E. et al. (eds.), *Readings in Social Psychology* (3rd ed.). New York: Holt, Rinehart & Winston, Inc., 1958, 110-116.

Thibaut, J. W. and Riecken, H. W., Some Determinants and Consequences of the Perception of Social Casuality. *Journal of Personality*, 1955, *24*, 113-133.

Vroom, V. H., Projection, Negation and the Self Concept. *Human Relations*, 1959, *12*, 335-344.

Weingarten, E., A Study of Selective Perception in Clinical Judgment. *Journal of Personality*, 1949, *17*, 369-400.

Wishner, J., Reanalysis of "Impression of Personality." *Psychological Review*, 1960, *67*, 96-112.

Part Two: Needs, Motives, and Goals

Adams, J. S. and Rosenbaum, W., The Relationship of Worker Productivity to Cognitive Dissonance About Wage Inequities. *Journal of Applied Psychology*, 1962, *46*, 161-164.

Argyris, C., *Personality and Organization*. New York: Harper & Row, Publishers, 1957.

Atkinson, J. W., Motivational Determinants of Risk-taking Behavior. *Psychological Review*, 1957, *64*, 359-372.

————— (ed.), *Motives in Fantasy, Action, and Society*. Princeton, N.J.: D. Van Nostrand Co., Inc., 1958.

—————, Personality Dynamics. In Farnsworth, P. R. and McNemar, Q. (eds.), *Annual Review of Psychology*, Vol. II, Palo Alto, California: Annual Reviews, Inc., 1960, 255-290.

Blauner, R., Work Satisfaction and Industrial Trends in Modern Society. In Galenson, W. and Lipset, S. M. (eds.), *Labor and Trade Unionism*. New York: John Wiley & Sons, Inc., 1960, 340-354.

Brayfield, A. H. and Crockett, W. H., Employee Attitudes and Employee Performance. *Psychological Bulletin*, 1955, *52*, 396-424.

Bruner, J. S., Social Psychology and Perception. In Maccoby, E., *et al.* (eds.), *Readings in Social Psychology* (3rd ed.), New York: Holt, Rinehart & Winston, Inc., 1958, p. 89.

Clark, J. V., Motivation in Work Groups: A Tentative View. *Human Organization*, 1960-1961, *19* (#4), 199-208.

Costello, T. W. and Zalkind, S. S., Merit Raise or Merit Bonus: A Psychological Approach. *Personnel Administration*, 1962, *25* (#6), 10-17.

Cureton, E. E. and Katzell, R. A., A Further Analysis of the Relations Among Job Performance and Situational Variables. *Journal of Applied Psychology*, 1962, *46* (#3), 230.

Dembo, T., as cited in Lewin, K., Dembo, T., Festinger, L., and Sears, P., Level of Aspiration. In J. McV. Hunt (ed.), *Handbook of Personality and the Behavior Disorders*. New York: The Ronald Press Company, 1944, 333-378.

Friedmann, G., *The Anatomy of Work*. New York: The Free Press of Glencoe, Inc., 1961.

Gebhard, M. E., Effect of Success and Failure upon the Attractiveness of Activities as a Function of Experience, Expectation and Need. *Journal of Experimental Psychology*, 1948, *38*, 371-388.

Gurin, G., Veroff, J., and Feld, S., *Americans View Their Mental Health*. New York: Basic Books, Inc., 1960, 143-174.

Herzberg, F., Mausner, B., Peterson, R., and Capwell, D., *Job Attitudes: Review of Research and Opinion*. Pittsburgh, Pa.: Psychological Services, 1957.

—————, —————, and Snyderman, B. B., *The Motivation to Work* (2nd ed.), New York: John Wiley & Sons, Inc., 1959.

Hoppe, F., as cited by Lewin, K., Behavior and Development as a Function of the Total Situation. In L. Carmichael (ed.), *Manual of Child Psychology*. New York: John Wiley & Sons, Inc., 1954, p. 957.

James, W., *Principles of Psychology*. New York: Holt, Rinehart & Winston, Inc., 1918, Vol. 1, 210-311.

Kahn, R. L., Psychology in Administration: A Symposium. III. Productivity and Job Satisfaction. *Personnel Psychology*, 1960, *13*, 275-287.

Katzell, R. A., Barrett, R. S., and Parker, T. C., Job Satisfaction, Job Performance, and Situational Characteristics. *Journal of Applied Psychology*, 1961, *45*, 65-72.

Klein, G. S., Cognitive Control and Motivation. In Lindzey, G. (ed.), *Assessment of Human Motives*. New York: Holt, Rinehart & Winston, Inc., 1958, 88-89.

Kornhauser, W. and Hagstrom, W. O., *Scientists in Industry—Conflict and Accom-*

modation. Berkeley, California: University of California Press, 1962, 155.

Lewin, K., Psychology of Success and Failure. *Occupations*, 1936, *14*, 926-930.

Likert, R., An Emerging Theory of Organization, Leadership, and Management. In Petrullo, L. and Bass, B. M. (eds.), *Leadership and Interpersonal Behavior*. New York: Holt, Rinehart & Winston, Inc., 1961, 296-297.

Maslow, A. H., Dynamic Theory of Human Motivation. *Psychological Review*, 1943, *50*, 370-396.

McClelland, D. C., Atkinson, J. W., Clark, R. A., and Lowell, E. L., *The Achievement Motive*. New York: Appleton-Century-Crofts, Inc., 1953.

————— (ed.), *Studies in Motivation*. New York: Appleton-Century-Crofts, Inc., 1955 (a).

—————, Some Social Consequences of Achievement Motivation. In Jones, M. R. (ed.), *Nebraska Symposium on Motivation*. Lincoln, Nebraska: University of Nebraska Press, 1955 (b).

—————, *The Achieving Society*. Princeton, N.J.: D. Van Nostrand Co., Inc., 1961.

Morgan, James, David, M., Cohen, W., and Brazer, H., *Income and Welfare In the United States*. New York: McGraw Hill Book Company, Inc., 1962.

Patchen, M., *The Choice of Wage Comparisons*. Englewood Cliffs, N.J.: Prentice-Hall, Inc., 1961.

Porter, L. W., Job Attitudes in Management: I. Perceived Deficiencies in Need Fulfillment as a Function of Job Level. *Journal of Applied Psychology*, 1962, *46* (#6), 375-384.

—————, A Study of Perceived Need Satisfactions in Bottom and Middle Management Jobs. *Journal of Applied Psychology*, 1961, *45* (#1), 1-10.

Rao, K. V. and Russell, R. W., Effects of Stress on Goal Setting Behavior. *Journal of Abnormal and Social Psychology*, 1960, *61* (#3), 380-388.

Rim, Y., Dimensions of Job Incentives and Personality. *Acta Psychologica*, 1961, *18*, 332-336.

Ross, I. and Zander, A., Need Satisfactions and Employee Turnover. *Personnel Psychology*, 1957, *10*, 327-338.

Rothe, H. F., Does Higher Pay Bring Higher Productivity? *Personnel*, 1960, 37, 20-38.

Schwartz, M. M., Jenusaitis, E., and Stack, H., Motivational Factors Among Supervisors in the Utility Industry. *Personnel Psychology*, 1963, *16*, 45-53.

Spector, A. J., Expectations, Fulfillment, and Morale. *Journal of Abnormal and Social Psychology*, 1956, 52, 51-56.

Stouffer, S., Suchman, E. A., DeVinney, L. C., Star, S. A., and Williams, R. M., Jr., Who Were the Most Critical of the Army's Promotion Opportunities? In *The American Soldier, Adjustment During Army Life*. Vol. I, Princeton, N.J.: Princeton University Press, 1949, 250-258.

Vroom, V. and Maier, N. R. F., Industrial Social Psychology. In Farnsworth, P., *et al.* (eds.), *Annual Review of Psychology*. Vol. 12, Palo Alto, California: Annual Reviews, Inc., 1961, pp. 413-446.

Weitz, J., Job Expectancy and Survival. *Journal of Applied Psychology*, 1956, *40*, 245-247.

Whyte, W. F., Dalton, M., Roy, D., Sayles, L., Collins, O., Miller, F., Strauss, G., Fuerstenberg, F., and Bavelas, A., *Money and Motivation*. New York: Harper & Row, Publishers, 1955, 210.

Wickert, F. R., Turnover and Employees' Feelings of Ego-Involvement in the Day-to-Day Operation of a Company. *Personnel Psychology*, 1951, *4*, 185-197.

Part Three: Reactions to Stress: Frustration, Anxiety, and Conflict

Atkinson, J. W., Motivational Determinants of Risk-Taking Behavior. *Psychological Review*, 1957, *64*, 359-372.

—————— (ed.), *Motives in Fantasy, Action, and Society*. Princeton, N.J.: D. Van Nostrand Co., Inc., 1958.

——————, Personality Dynamics. In Farnsworth, P. R. and McNemar, Q. (eds.), *Annual Review of Psychology*, Vol. 12, Palo Alto, Calif.: Annual Reviews, Inc., 1960, pp. 255-290.

——————, Bastion, J. R., Earl, R. W., and Litwin, G. H., The Achievement Motive, Goal Setting, and Probability Preferences. *Journal of Abnormal and Social Psychology*, 1960, *60*, 27-36.

—————— and Litwin, G. H., Achievement Motive and Test Anxiety Conceived as Motive to Approach Success and Motive to Avoid Failure. *Journal of Abnormal and Social Psychology*. 1960, *60*, 52-63.

Berkowitz, L., Repeated Frustrations and Expectations in Hostility Arousal. *Journal of Abnormal and Social Psychology*, 1960, *60*, 422-429.

Boulding, K., *Conflict and Defense: A General Theory*. New York: Harper & Row, Publishers, 1962.

Child, I. L. and Waterhouse, I. K., Frustration and the Quality of Performance. *Psychological Review*, 1953, *60* (#2), 127-139.

Coleman, J. C., *Personality Dynamics and Effective Behavior*. Chicago, Ill.: Scott, Foresman & Company, 1960.

Coppock, H. W., Responses of Subjects to Their Own Galvanic Skin Responses. *Journal of Abnormal and Social Psychology*, 1955, *50*, 25-28.

Dollard, J., Doob, L., Miller, N., Mowrer, O., and Sears, R., *Frustration and Aggression*. New Haven, Conn.: Yale University Press, 1939.

Doob, L., *Social Psychology*. New York: Holt, Rinehart & Winston, Inc., 1952 (Ch. 4).

Farber, I. E., Anxiety as a Drive State. In M. R. Jones (ed.), *Nebraska Symposium on Motivation*. Lincoln, Nebraska: University of Nebraska Press, 1954, 1-46.

Feinberg, M. R., *Marks of Maturity*. Specially adapted by the author from a report published by the Research Institute of America, 1956.

Feshbach, S., The Drive-Reducing Function of Fantasy Behavior. *Journal of Abnormal and Social Psychology*, 1955, *50*, 3-11.

Festinger, L., The Motivating Effect of Cognitive Dissonance. In Lindzey, G. (ed.), *Assessment of Human Motives*. New York: Holt, Rinehart & Winston, Inc., 1958, pp. 65-86.

Fleming, A. J., Executive Stress . . . Excessive or Not? Advanced Management-Office Executive, 1962, *1*, No. 5, 11-12.

Ghiselli, E. E. and Brown, C. W., *Personnel and Industrial Psychology* (2nd ed.). New York: McGraw-Hill Book Company, Inc., 1955.

Henry, W. E., The Business Executive: The Psychodynamics of a Social Role. *American Journal of Sociology*, 1949, *54*, 286-291.

Indik, B. P., Some Individual and Environmental Factors that Tend to Lessen the Effects of High Job Related Stress. Reported at the Eastern Psychological Association Meetings, April, 1963, New York, N.Y.

Janis, J. L., Motivational Factors in the Resolution of Decisional Conflicts. In Jones, M. R. (ed.), *Nebraska Symposium on Motivation*. Lincoln, Nebraska: University of Nebraska Press, 1959, 213-229.

Katchmar, L. T., Ross, S., and Andrews, T. G., Effects of Stress and Anxiety on Performance of a Complex Verbal Task. *Journal of Experimental Psychology*, 1958, *63*, 559-563.

Lee, R. E. and Schneider, R. F., Hypertension and Arteriosclerosis in Executive and Nonexecutive Personnel. *Journal of the American Medical Association*, 1958, *167*, 1447-50.

Levinson, H., The Psychologist in Industry, *Harvard Business Review*. 1959, 37, No. 5, 93-99.

Lowe, A., Individual Differences in Reaction to Failure: Mode of Coping with Anxiety and Interference Proneness. *Journal of Abnormal and Social Psychology*, 1961, *62*, 303-308.

Mackworth, N. H., "High Incentives versus Hot and Humid Atmosphere in a Physical Effort Task." Medical Research Council of Great Britain, 1947.

Maier, N. R. F., *Frustration: The Study of Behavior Without a Goal*. New York: McGraw-Hill Book Company, Inc., 1949; reprinted as an Ann Arbor Paperback, The University of Michigan Press, 1961.

May R., *The Meaning of Anxiety*. New York: The Ronald Press Company, 1950.

McClelland, D. C. and Apicella, F., A Functional Classification of Verbal Reactions to Experimentally Induced Failure. *Journal of Abnormal and Social Psychology*, 1945, *40*, 376-390.

————, Personality. In Farnsworth, P. R. and McNemar, Q. (eds.), *The Annual Review of Psychology*, Vol. 7. Palo Alto, California: Annual Reviews, Inc., 1956, pp. 39-62.

McNeil, E. B., Psychology and Aggression. *Journal of Conflict Resolution*, 1959, *3*, 195-293.

Menzies, I. E. B., A Case Study in the Functioning of Social Systems as a Defense Against Anxiety. *Human Relations*, 1960, *13*, 95-121.

Neel, R. G., Nervous Stress in the Industrial Situation. *Personnel Psychology*, 1955, *8*, 405-415.

Otis, N. and McCandless, B., Responses to Repeated Frustrations of Young Children Differentiated According to Need Area. *Journal of Abnormal and Social Psychology*, 1955, *50*, 349-353.

Pepinsky, H., Pepinsky, P., Minor, F. J., and Robin, S. S., Team Productivity and Contradiction of Management Policy Commitments. *Journal of Applied Psychology*, 1959, *43*, 264-268.

Presthus, R., *The Organizational Society: An Analysis and a Theory*. New York: Alfred A. Knopf, Inc., 1962.

Rapoport, Anatol, *Fights, Games, and Debates*. Ann Arbor, Michigan: University of Michigan Press, 1960.

Rundquist, E. Q. and Sletto, R. F., Personality in the Depression. Minneapolis, Minn.: University of Minnesota Press, 1936.

Sarason, I., The Effects of Anxiety and Threat on the Solution of a Difficult Task. *Journal of Abnormal and Social Psychology*, 1961, *62*, 165-168.

Schacter, S., Willerman, B., Festinger, L., and Hyman, R., Emotional Disruption and Productivity. *Journal of Applied Psychology*, 1961, *45*, 211-213.

Selye, H., *The Stress of Life*. New York: McGraw-Hill Book Company, Inc., 1956.

Spector, A. J., Expectations, Fulfillment, and Morale. *Journal of Abnormal and Social Psychology*, 1956, 52, 51-56.

Sullivan, H. S., *Interpersonal Theory of Psychiatry*. H. S. Perry and M. L. Gowel (eds.), New York: W. W. Norton & Company, Inc., 1953.

Torrance, E. P., A Theory of Leadership and Interpersonal Behavior Under Stress. In Petrullo, L. and Bass, B. (eds.), *Leadership and Interpersonal Behavior*, New York: Holt, Rinehart & Winston, Inc., 1961, 100-117.

Van Buskirk, C., Performance on Complex Reasoning Tasks as a Function of Anxiety. *Journal of Abnormal and Social Psychology*, 1961, 62, 201-209.

Van Zelst, R. and Kerr, W. A., Reported Lifetime Worry Experiences of Illinois Building Trades Union Leaders. *Personnel Psychology*, 1951, 4, 151-159.

Veblen, T., as mentioned in Youmans, E. G., The Administrative Mind. *Public Personnel Review*, 1954, 15, 72-76.

Part Four: Effective Change in Human Behavior: The Learning Process

Ammons, R. B., Effects of Knowledge of Performance: A Survey and Tentative Theoretical Formulation. *Journal of General Psychology*, 1956, 54, 279-299.

Barnard, C. I., *The Functions of the Executive*. Cambridge, Mass.: Harvard University Press, 1938.

Bennis, W. G., Benne, K. D., and Chin, R., *The Planning of Change*. New York: Holt, Rinehart & Winston, Inc., 1961.

Cartwright, D., Achieving Change in People. *Human Relations*, 1951, 4, 381-392.

Christian, R. W., Guides to Programmed Learning. *Harvard Business Review*. 1962, 40, 36-44; 173-179.

Coch, L. and French, J. R. P., Jr., Overcoming Resistance to Change. *Human Relations*, 1948, 1, 512-532.

Costello, T. W., Kubis, J. F., and Shaffer, C., An Analysis of Attitudes Toward a Planned Merger. *Administrative Science Quarterly*, 1963 (in press).

Dollard, J. and Miller, N. E., *Personality and Psychotherapy*. New York: McGraw-Hill Book Company, Inc., 1950.

Duncan, C. P., Description of Learning to Learn in Human Subjects. *American Journal of Psychology*, 1960, 73, 108-114.

Edgerton, H., *The Relationship of Method of Instruction to Trained Aptitude Pattern*. Published for the Office of Naval Research, New York: Richardson, Bellows, Henry & Co., 1958.

Ericksen, S. C., Variability of Attack in Massed and Distributed Practice. *Journal of Experimental Psychology*, 1942, 31, 339-345.

Estes, W. K., An Experimental Study of Punishment. *Psychological Monographs*, 1944, 57, No. 263.

Festinger, L., The Motivating Effect of Cognitive Dissonance. In Lindzey, G. (ed.), *Assessment of Human Motives*. New York: Holt, Rinehart & Winston, Inc., 1958, 65-86.

Fryer, D. H., Feinberg, M. R., and Zalkind, S. S., *Developing People in Industry*. New York: Harper & Row, Publishers, 1956.

Ginzberg, E., The Parameters of Organizational Change. Paper presented in a symposium, *Changes in Organizational Structure: Parameters, Attitudes and Processes*. Eastern Psychological Association, 1962.

———— and Reilley, E. W., *Effecting Change in Large Organizations*. New York: Columbia University Press, 1957.

Greenspoon, J., The Reinforcing Effect of Two Spoken Sounds on the Frequency of Two Responses. *American Journal of Psychology*, 1955, 68, 409-416.

Guest, R. H., *Organizational Change: The Effect of Successful Leadership*. Homewood, Ill.: The Dorsey Press, Inc. and Richard D. Irwin, Inc., 1962.

Haire, M. (ed.), *Modern Organization Theory*. New York: John Wiley & Sons, Inc., 1959.

Hendrickson, G. and Schroeder, W. H., Transfer of Training in Learning to Hit a Submerged Target. *Journal of Educational Psychology*, 1941, 32, 205-213.

Hilgard, E. and Marquis, D., *Conditioning and Learning* (2nd ed.). Revised by G. A. Kimble, New York: Appleton-Century-Crofts, Inc., 1961, 6.

Homans, G. C., *The Human Group*. New York: Harcourt, Brace & World, Inc., 1950.

Jones, E. E. and Kohler, R., The Effects of Plausibility on the Learning of Controversial Statements. *Journal of Abnormal and Social Psychology*, 1958, 57, 315-320.

Katona, George, *Organizing and Memorizing*. New York: Columbia University Press, 1940.

Keller, F. S. and Schoenfeld, W. N., *Principles of Psychology*. New York: Appleton-Century-Crofts, Inc., 1950.

Kendler, H. H., Greenberg, A., and Richman, H., The Influence of Massed and Distributed Practice on the Development of Mental Set. *Journal of Experimental Psychology*, 1952, 43, 21-25.

Kidd, J. S., A Comparison of Two Methods of Training in a Complex Task by Means of Task Simulation. *Journal of Applied Psychology*, 1961, 45, 165-169.

Levine, J. M. and Murphy, G., The Learning and Forgetting of Controversial Material. *Journal of Abnormal and Social Psychology*, 1943, 38, 507-517.

Maier, N. R. F., *Psychology in Industry* (2nd. ed.). Boston, Mass.: Houghton Mifflin Company, 1955.

Mann, F. C. and Hoffman, L. R., *Automation and the Worker*. New York: Holt, Rinehart & Winston, Inc., 1960.

McGehee, W., Are We Using What We Know about Training?—Learning Theory and Training. *Personnel Psychology*, 1958, 11, 1-12.

McGeoch, J. A. and Irion, A. L., *The Psychology of Human Learning* (2nd ed.). New York: Longmans, Green & Co., Inc., 1952.

Merton, R. K., *Social Theory and Social Structure* (revised ed.), New York.: The Free Press of Glencoe, Inc., 1957, 123.

Miles, G. H., Achievement Drive and Habitual Modes of Task Approach as Factors in Skill Transfer. *Journal of Experimental Psychology*, 1958, 55, 156-162.

Miller, G. A. and Selfridge, J., Verbal Context and the Recall of Meaningful Material. *American Journal of Psychology*, 1950, 63, 176-185.

Miner, J. B., The Effect of a Course in Psychology on the Attitudes of Research and Development Supervisors. *Journal of Applied Psychology*, 1960, 44, 224-232.

Morison, E. E., A Case Study of Innovation. In Bennis, W. G., Benne, K. D., and Chin, R. (eds.), *The Planning of Change*. New York: Holt, Rinehart & Winston, Inc., 1961, 592-605. Reprinted from *Engineering and Science Magazine*, Pasadena, Calif., April, 1950.

Osgood, C. E., *Method and Theory in Experimental Psychology*. New York: Oxford University Press, 1953.

Postman, L. and Senders, V., Incidental Learning and Generality of Set. *Journal of Experimental Psychology*, 1946, 36, 153-165.

Pressey, S. L., Teaching Machine (and Learning Theory) Crisis. *Journal of Applied Psychology*, 1963, 47, 1-9.

Ray, W. S., Verbal Compared with Manipulative Solution of an Apparatus Problem. *American Journal of Psychology*, 1957, 70, 289-290.

Rice, A. K., *Productivity and Social Organization: The Ahmedabad Experiment*. London: Tavistock Publications, Ltd., 1958.

Riley, D. A., Rote-Learning as a Function of Distribution of Practice and the Complexity of the Situation. *Journal of Experimental Psychology*, 1952, 43, 88-95.

Rogers, E., *Diffusion of Innovations*. New York: The Free Press of Glencoe, Inc., 1962.

Ryan, T. W. and Smith, P. C., *Principles of Industrial Psychology*. New York: The Ronald Press Company, 1954.

Sanford, F. H., *Psychology*. San Francisco, California: Wadsworth Publishing Co., Inc., 1961.

Siegel, L. and Siegel, L., Personal Communication.

Skinner, B. F., *Science and Human Behavior*. New York: The Macmillan Company, 1953.

Stagner, Ross, *The Psychology of Industrial Conflict*. New York: John Wiley & Sons, Inc., 1956.

Stevenson, H. W., Weir, M. M., and Zigler, E. F., Discrimination Learning in Children as a Function of Motive-Incentive Conditions. *Psychological Reports*, 1959, 5, 95-98.

Strahm, C. L., The Influence of Instruction on Performance of a Complex Perceptual Motor Task. *Canadian Journal of Psychology*, 1955, 9, 168-172.

Thorndike, E. L., *The Fundamentals of Learning*. New York: Teachers College, Bureau of Publications, 1932.

Tiffin, J. and McCormick, E. J., *Industrial Psychology* (4th ed.). Englewood Cliffs, N.J.: Prentice-Hall, Inc., 1958.

Torrance, E. P., The Phenomenon of Resistance in Learning. *Journal of Abnormal and Social Psychology*, 1950, 45, 592-597.

Underwood, B. J., Ten Years of Massed Practice on Distributed Practice. *Psychological Review*, 1961, 68, 229-247.

Veblen, T., as mentioned in Youmans, E. G., The Administrative Mind. *Public Personnel Review*, 1954, 15, 72-76.

Verplanck, W. S., The Control of the Content of Conversation: Reinforcement of Statements of Opinion. *Journal of Abnormal and Social Psychology*, 1955, 51, 668-676.

————, The Operant Conditioning of Human Motor Behavior. *Psychological Bulletin*, 1956, 53, 70-83.

Whiting, J. M. W. and Mowrer, O. H., Habit Progression and Regression—A Laboratory Study of Some Factors Relevant to Human Socialization. *Journal of Comparative Psychology*, 1943, 36, 229-253.

Woodworth, R. S. and Schlosberg, H., *Experimental Psychology*. New York: Holt, Rinehart & Winston, Inc., 1954.

Part Five: *Attitudes and Attitude Change*

Abelson, H. I., *Persuasion*. New York: Springer Publishing Co., 1959.

Adams, J. S., The Reduction of Cognitive Dissonance by Seeking Consonant Information. *Journal of Abnormal and Social Psychology*, 1961, 62, 74-78.

Argyris, C., *Personality and Organization*. New York: Harper & Row, Publishers, 1957.

Asch, S., Effects of Group Pressure Upon the Modification and Distortion of Judgments. In Guetzkow, H. (ed.), *Groups, Leadership and Men*. Pittsburgh, Penn., Carnegie Press, 1951.

Back, K., Influence Through Social Communication. *Journal of Abnormal and Social Psychology*, 1951, 46, 9-23.

Benedict, R., *Patterns of Culture*. Boston: Houghton Mifflin Company, 1934; New York: Penguin Books, Inc., 1946.

Blake, R. R. and Mouton, J. S., The Experimental Investigation of Interpersonal Influence. In Biderman, A. D. and Zimmer, H. (eds.), *The Manipulation of Human Behavior*. New York: John Wiley & Sons, Inc., 1961.

Blau, P., The Dynamics of Bureaucracy. In Petersen, W. (ed.), *American Social Patterns*. New York: Doubleday & Company, Inc., 1956, 221.

Brehm, J. W., A Dissonance Analysis of Attitude-Discrepant Behavior. In Rosenberg, M. J., *et al.*, *Attitude Organization and Change*. New Haven, Conn.: Yale University Press, 1960, p. 193.

Bronfenbrenner, U., Socialization and Social Class through Time and Space. In Maccoby, E., Newcomb, T., and Hartley, E. (eds.), *Readings in Social Psychology*. New York: Holt, Rinehart & Winston, Inc., 1958, 400-425.

Centers, R., *The Psychology of Social Classes*. Princeton: Princeton University Press, 1949.

Charters, W. W., Jr. and Newcomb, T. M., Some Attitudinal Effects of Experimentally Increased Salience of a Membership Group. In Maccoby, E. E., Newcomb, T., and Hartley, E. (eds.), *Readings in Social Psychology* (3rd ed.). New York: Holt, Rinehart & Winston, Inc., 1958, 275-281.

Coch, L. and French, J. R. P., Jr., Overcoming Resistance to Change. *Human Relations*, 1948, 1, 512-532.

Cohen, A. R., Attitudinal Consequences of Induced Discrepancies. *Public Opinion Quarterly*, 1960, 24, No. 2, 297-318.

Converse, P. E., The Shifting Role of Class in Political Attitudes and Behavior. In Maccoby, E. E., Newcomb, T., and Hartley, E. (eds.), *Readings in Social Psychology* (3rd ed.). New York: Holt, Rinehart & Winston, Inc., 388-399.

Corsini, R. J., Shaw, M. E., Blake, R. R., *Role-Playing in Business and Industry*. New York: The Free Press of Glencoe, Inc., 1961.

Crutchfield, R. S., Conformity and Character. *American Psychologist*, 1955, 10, 191-198.

Dalton, M., The Industrial Rate-Buster: A Characterization. *Applied Anthropology*, 1948, 7, 5-18.

Deutsch, M. and Collins, M. E., The Effect of Public Policy in Housing Projects upon Interracial Attitudes. In Maccoby, E., Newcomb, T., and Hartley, E., (eds.). *Readings in Social Psychology* (3rd ed.), New York: Holt, Rinehart & Winston, Inc., 1958, pp. 612-623.

Di Vesta, F. J. and Merwin, J. C., The Effects of Need-Oriented Communications on Attitude Change. *Journal of Abnormal and Social Psychology,* 1960, *60,* 80-85.

Festinger, L., *A Theory of Cognitive Dissonance.* Stanford, Calif.: Stanford University Press, 1957.

Gerard, H., The Anchorage of Opinions in Face-to-Face Groups. *Human Relations,* 1954, *7,* 313-325.

Granick, D., *The Red Executive.* London: Macmillan & Co., Ltd., 1960.

Harding, J. and Hogrefe, R., Attitudes of White Department Store Employees Toward Negro Co-Workers. *Journal of Social Issues,* 1952, *8,* 18-28.

Harsh, H. C. and Schrickel, H. G., *Personality Development and Assessment.* New York: The Ronald Press Company, 1950.

Harvey, O. J. and Beverly, G. D., Some Personality Correlates of Concept Change Through Role-Playing. *Journal of Abnormal and Social Psychology,* 1961, *63,* No. 1, 125-130.

Heider, F., Attitudes and Cognitive Organization. *Journal of Psychology,* 1946, *21,* 107-112.

Horowitz, E. L., The Development of Attitudes Towards the Negro. *Archives of Psychology,* 1936, *28,* No. 194.

Hovland, C. I., Reconciling Conflicting Results from Experimental and Survey Studies of Attitude Change. *American Psychologist,* 1959, *14,* 8-17.

———, Janis, I. L., and Kelley, H. H., *Communication and Persuasion: Psychological Studies of Opinion Change.* New Haven, Conn.: Yale University Press, 1953.

——— and Rosenberg, M. J., Summary and Further Theoretical Issues. In Rosenberg, M. J., *et al., Attitude Organization and Change.* New Haven, Conn.: Yale University Press, 1960.

Hyman, H., *Political Socialization.* New York: The Free Press of Glencoe, Inc., 1959.

Janis, I. and King, B., The Influence of Role Playing on Opinion Change. *Journal of Abnormal and Social Psychology,* 1954, *49,* 211-218.

Kahn, R. L., Productivity and Job Satisfaction. *Personnel Psychology,* 1960, *13,* 275-278.

Katz, D., The Functional Approach to the Study of Attitudes. *Public Opinion Quarterly,* 1960, *24,* No. 2, 163-204.

——— and Stotland, E., A Preliminary Statement to a Theory of Attitude Structure and Change. In Koch, S. (ed.), *Psychology: A Study of a Science,* Vol. III: Formulations of the Person and the Social Context. New York: McGraw-Hill Book Company, Inc., 1959, 423-475.

Katz, E. and Lazarsfeld, P., *Personal Influence.* New York: The Free Press of Glencoe, Inc., 1955.

Katzell, R. A., Barrett, R. S., and Parker, T. C., Job Satisfaction, Job Performance, and Situational Characteristics. *Journal of Applied Psychology,* 1961, *45,* No. 2, 65-72.

Kelley, H. H., Salience of Membership and Resistance to Change of Group-Anchored Attitudes. *Human Relations,* 1955, *8,* 275-289.

——— and Shapiro, M. M., An Experiment on Conformity to Group Norms Where Conformity Is Detrimental to Group Achievement. *American Sociological Review,* 1954, *19,* 667-677.

——— and Volkart, E. H., The Resistance to Change of Group Anchored Attitudes. *American Sociological Review,* 1952, *17,* 453-465.

Kelman, H. C., Compliance, Identification and Internalization: Three Processes of Attitude Change. *Journal of Conflict Resolution*, 1958, *2*, 51-60.

King, B. T. and Janis, I., Comparison of the Effectiveness of Improvised vs. Non-Improvised Role Playing in Producing Opinion Changes. *Human Relations*, 1956, *9*, 177-186.

Klapper, J. T., *The Effects of Mass Communication*. New York: The Free Press of Glencoe, Inc., 1960.

Klineberg, O., *Social Psychology* (rev. ed.). New York: Holt, Rinehart & Winston, Inc., 1954.

Kornhauser, A., Sheppard, H., and Mayer A., *When Labor Votes*. New York: University Books, 1956.

Krech, D. and Crutchfield, R. S., *Elements of Psychology*. New York: Alfred A. Knopf, Inc., 1958.

Levine, J. M. and Butler, J., Lecture vs. Group Decision in Changing Behavior. *Journal of Applied Psychology*, 1952, *36*, 29-33.

Lewin, K., Frontiers in Group Dynamics: Concept, Method and Reality in Social Science; Social Equilibria and Social Change. *Human Relations*, 1947, *1*, 5-42.

Lieberman, S., The Effects of Changes in Roles on the Attitudes of the Occupants. *Human Relations*, 1956, *9*, 385-402.

Likert, R., *New Patterns of Management*. New York: McGraw-Hill Book Company, Inc., 1961, 103-104.

Maccoby, E. E., Maccoby, N., Romney, A. K., and Adams, J. S., Social Reinforcement and Attitude Change. *Journal of Abnormal and Social Psychology*, 1961, *63*, 108-114.

Maccoby, N. and Maccoby, E. E., Homeostatic Theory in Attitude Change. *Public Opinion Quarterly*, 1961, *25*, No. 4, 538-545.

McGranahan, D., A Comparison of Social Attitudes Among American and German Youth. *Journal of Abnormal and Social Psychology*, 1946, *41*, 245-257.

McNair, M. P., Thinking Ahead: What Price Human Relations? *Harvard Business Review*, 1957, *35*, 15-16; 20; 25-26; 28, 30; 32-34; 39.

Maier, N. R. F., Solem, A. R., and Maier, A. A., *Supervisory and Executive Development. A Manual for Role Playing*. New York: John Wiley & Sons, Inc., 1957.

Mann, F. C., Changing Interpersonal Relations Through Training Supervisors. In Arensberg, C. *et al.* (eds.), *Research in Industrial Human Relations*. New York: Harper & Row, Publishers, 1957, 149-157.

——— and Neff, F. W., *Managing Major Change in Organizations*. Ann Arbor, Mich.: Foundation for Research on Human Behavior, 1961.

Mann, J. H., Experimental Evaluations of Role Playing. *Psychological Bulletin*, 1956, *53*, 227-234.

Mead, M., *Coming of Age in Samoa*. New York: William Morrow & Co., Inc., 1928; reprinted, New York: Mentor Books, 1949.

Miner, J. B., Management and Development and Attitude Change. *Personnel Administration*, 1961, *24*, No. 3, 21-26.

Moreno, J. L., *Who Shall Survive?* (rev. ed.), Beacon, N. Y.: Beacon House, Inc., 1953.

Morgan, C. L., *Introduction to Psychology* (2nd ed.). New York: McGraw-Hill Book Company, Inc., 1961.

Newcomb, T., An Approach to the Study of Communicative Acts. *Psychological Review*, 1953, *60*, 393-404.

Osgood, C. and Tannenbaum, P. H., The Principle of Congruity in Attitude Change. *Psychological Review*, 1955, *62*, 42-55.

Pelz, E. B., Some Factors in "Group Decision". In Maccoby, E. *et al.* (eds.), *Readings in Social Psychology* (3rd ed.), New York: Holt, Rinehart & Winston, Inc., 1958, 212-219.

Public Opinion Quarterly, 1961, *25*, No. 2, 300-316.

Purcell, T. V., *Blue Collar Man. Patterns of Dual Allegiance in Industry*. Cambridge, Mass.: Harvard University Press, 1960.

Remmers, H. H. and Radler, D. H., *The American Teenager*. New York: Bobbs-Merrill Company, Inc., 1957.

Rim, Y., Attitudes of Israeli Executives and Trade Union Leaders to Industrial Relations. Report at the 14th International Congress of Applied Psychology, Copenhagen, August 1961.

Rokeach, M., *The Open and Closed Mind*. New York: Basic Books, Inc., 1963.

Rosenberg, M. J., Hovland, C. I., McGuire, W. J., Abelson, R. P., and Brehm, J., *Attitude Organization and Change*, Yale Studies in Attitude and Communication, Vol. 3. New Haven, Conn.: Yale University Press, 1960.

Schein, E. H., The Chinese Indoctrination Program for Prisoners of War: A Study of Attempted Brainwashing. In Maccoby, E. *et al.* (eds.), *Readings in Social Psychology* (3rd ed.), New York: Holt, Rinehart & Winston, Inc., 1958, 311-334.

————, Management Development as a Process of Influence. *Industrial Management Review of M.I.T.*, 1961, *1*, 59-77.

———— with Schneier, I. and Barker, C. H., *Coercive Persuasion*. New York: W. W. Norton Company, Inc., 1961.

Schramm, W., Book review of Rosenberg, M. J., *et al.*, *Attitude Organization and Change*, in *Public Opinion Quarterly*, 1961 (Fall), 494-496.

Shartle, C. L., *Effective Performance and Leadership*. Englewood Cliffs, N.J.: Prentice-Hall, Inc., 1956.

Sherif, M., A Study of Some Social Factors in Perception. *Archives of Psychology*, 1935, No. 187.

Smith, E. E., The Power of Dissonance Techniques to Change Attitudes. *Public Opinion Quarterly*, 1961, *25*, No. 4, 626-639.

Smith, M. B., Bruner, J. S., and White, R. W., *Opinions and Personality*. New York: John Wiley & Sons, Inc., 1956.

Staats, A. W. and Staats, C. K., Attitudes Established by Classical Conditioning. *Journal of Abnormal and Social Psychology*, 1958, *57*, 37-46.

Stagner, R., Dual Allegiance as a Problem in Modern Society. *Personnel Psychology*, 1954, 7, 41-47.

Star, S. A., Williams, R. M., and Stouffer, S., Negro Infantry Platoons in White Companies. In Maccoby, E., Newcomb, T., and Hartley, E. (eds.), *Readings in Social Psychology* (3rd ed.), 596-601.

Tannenbaum, R., Some Current Issues in Human Relations. *California Management Review*, 1959, 2, No. 1, 49-58.

Vidulich, R. N. and Kaiman, I. P., The Effects of Information Source Status and Dogmatism upon Conformity Behavior. *Journal of Abnormal and Social Psychology*, 1961, *63*, 639-642.

Walker, E. L. and Heyns, R. W., *An Anatomy for Conformity*. Englewood Cliffs, N.J.: Prentice-Hall, Inc., 1962.

Watson, J., Some Social and Psychological Situations Related to Change in Attitude. *Human Relations*, 1950, *3*, 15-56.

Worthy, J., Organizational Structure and Employee Morale. *American Sociological Review*, 1950, *15*, 169-179. Also available in Karn, H. W. and Gilmer B., *Readings in Industrial and Business Psychology*. New York: McGraw-Hill Book Company, Inc., 1952.

Zalkind, S. S. and Costello, T. W., Perception: Recent Research and Some Implications. *Administrative Science Quarterly*, 1962, *7*, No. 2, 218-235.

Part Six: Thinking: Problem Solving; Decision Making; Creativity

AC Test of Creative Ability, developed by AC Spark Plug Division, General Motors Corporation. Published by Education Industry Service, Chicago, 1960.

Adams, S. N., Status Congruence as a Variable in Small Group Performance. *Social Forces*, 1953, *32*, 16-22.

Adamson, R. E. and Taylor, D. W., Functional Fixedness as Related to Elapsed Time and to Set. *Journal of Experimental Psychology*, 1954, *47*, 122-126.

Anastasi, A., *Differential Psychology*. New York: The Macmillan Company, 1961.

Argyris, C., *Executive Leadership*. New York: Harper & Row, Publishers, 1952.

————, *Personality and Organization*. New York: Harper & Row, Publishers, 1957.

Asch, S. E., Opinions and Social Pressure. *Scientific American*, 1955, 31-35.

Bales, R. F., The Equilibrium Problem in Small Groups. In Parsons, T., Bales, R. F., and Shils, E. A., *Working Papers in the Theory of Action*. New York: The Free Press of Glencoe, Inc., 1953, pp. 111-161.

————, In Conference. *Harvard Business Review*, 1954, *32*, 44-50.

————, *Interaction Process Analysis*. Cambridge, Mass.: Addison-Wesley Publishing Co., Inc., 1950.

————, Task Roles and Social Roles in Problem-Solving Groups. In Maccoby, E. E., Newcomb, T. M., and Hartley, E. L. (eds.), *Readings in Social Psychology* (3rd ed.). New York: Holt, Rinehart & Winston, Inc., 1958, pp. 437-447.

———— and Strodtbeck, F. L., Phases in Group Problem-Solving. *Journal of Abnormal and Social Psychology*, 1951, *46*, 485-495.

Barnard, C. I., *The Functions of the Executive*. Cambridge, Mass.: Harvard University Press, 1960, p. 122.

Bass, B. M., *Leadership, Psychology, and Organizational Behavior*. New York: Harper & Row, Publishers, 1960.

Bavelas, A., A Mathematical Model for Group Structures. *Applied Anthropology*, 1948, *7*, 16-30.

Berkowitz, L., Group Standards, Cohesiveness and Productivity. *Human Relations*, 1954, *7*, 509-519.

————, Effects of Perceived Dependency Relationship upon Conformity to Group Expectations. *Journal of Abnormal and Social Psychology*, 1957, *55*, 350-354.

Bloom, B. S. and Broder, I. J., *Problem Solving Processes of College Students*. Chicago, Ill.: The University of Chicago Press, 1950.

Bourne, L. E., Jr. and Restle, E., Mathematical Theory of Concept Identification. *Psychological Review*, 1959, *66*, 278-296.

Bristow, A. P. and Gabard, E. C., *Decision Making in Police Administration*. Springfield, Ill.: Charles C Thomas, Publisher, 1961, p. 70.

Bruner, J. S., Going Beyond the Information Given. In *Contemporary Approaches to Cognition*. Cambridge, Mass.: Harvard University Press, 1957.

————, Goodnow, J. J., and Austin, G. A., *A Study of Thinking*. New York: John Wiley & Sons, Inc., 1956.

———— and Tajfel, H., Cognitive Risk and Environmental Change. *Journal of Abnormal and Social Psychology*, 1961, *62*, 231-241.

————, Wallach, M. A., and Galanter, E. H., The Identification of Recurrent Regularity. *American Journal of Psychology*, 1959, *72*, 200-209.

Buswell, G. T., *Patterns of Thinking in Solving Problems*. The University of California Public Education, 1956, *13*, 63-148.

Cartwright, D. and Zander, A., *Group Dynamics* (2nd ed.). New York: Harper & Row, Publishers, 1960.

Cook, T. W., Amount of Material and Difficulty of Problem Solving. The Disc Transfer Problem. *Journal of Experimental Psychology*, 1937, *20*, 288-296.

Cyert, R. M., Simon, H. A., and Trow, D. B., Observation of a Business Decision. *The Journal of Business*, 1956, *29*, 237-248.

Dennis, W., Age and Achievement: A Critique. *Journal of Gerontology*, 1956, *11*, 331-333; Age and Productivity Among Scientists. *Science*, 1956, *123*, 724-725; The Age Decrement in Outstanding Scientific Contributions: Fact or Artifact. *American Psychologist*, 1958, *13*, 457-460.

Detambel, M. H. and Stolurow, L. M., Stimulus Sequence and Concept Learning. *Journal of Experimental Psychology*, 1956, *51*, 31-40.

Deutsch, M., An Experimental Study of the Effects of Cooperation and Competition upon Group Process. *Human Relations*, 1949, *2*, 199-231.

Dewey, John, *How We Think*. New York: D. C. Heath & Company (revised edition), 1933; as reprinted in *Intelligence in the Modern World*, Ratner, J. (ed.). New York: The Modern Library, 1939.

Duncan, C. P., Recent Research on Human Problem Solving. *Psychological Bulletin*, 1959, *56*, 397-429.

Duncker, K., On Problem Solving. *Psychological Monographs*, 1945, *58*, No. 270.

Dunnette, M. D., Campbell, J., and Jaastad, K., The Effect of Group Participation on Brainstorming Effectiveness for Two Industrial Samples. *Journal of Applied Psychology*, 1963, *47*, 30-37.

Edwards, W., The Prediction of Decisions Among Bets. *Journal of Experimental Psychology*, 1955, *50*, 201-214.

————, The Theory of Decision Making. *Psychological Bulletin*, 1954, *51*, 380-417.

————, Behavioral Decision Theory. In Farnsworth, P. R. *et al.* (eds.), *Annual Review of Psychology*, Vol. 12. Palo Alto, Calif.: Annual Reviews, Inc., 1961, pp. 473-499.

————, Utility, Subjective Probability, Their Interaction and Variance Preferences. *Journal of Conflict Resolution*, 1962, *6*, 42-51.

Fitts, P. M. and Switzer, G., Cognitive Aspects of Information Processing: I. The Formulation of S-R Sets and Subsets. *Journal of Experimental Psychology*, 1962, *63*, 321-329.

Foa, U. G., Relation of Workers' Expectation to Satisfaction with Supervisor. *Personnel Psychology*, 1957, *10*, 161-168.

French, E. G. and Thomas, F. H., The Relation of Achievement Motivation to Problem Solving Effectiveness. *Journal of Abnormal and Social Psychology*, 1958, *56*, 45-48.

Gagne, R. M., Problem Solving and Thinking. In P. R. Farnsworth and Q. McNemar (eds.), *Annual Review of Psychology*. Palo Alto, Calif.: Annual Reviews, Inc., pp. 147-148.

———— and Smith, E., Jr., A Study of the Effects of Verbalization on Problem Solving. *Journal of Experimental Psychology*, 1962, *63*, 12-18.

Galanter, E. and Gerstenhaber, M., On Thought: The Extrinsic Theory. *Psychological Review*, 1956, *63*, 218-227.

Ghiselli, E. E. and Lodahl, T., Patterns of Managerial Traits and Group Effectiveness. *Journal of Abnormal and Social Psychology*, 1958, *57*, 61-66.

Glanzer, M. and Glaser, R., Techniques for the Study of Group Structure and Behavior: II. Empirical Studies of the Effects of Structure in Small Groups. *Psychological Bulletin*, 1961, *58*, 1-27.

Greer, F. L., Small Group Effectiveness, *Institute Report No. 6*. Philadelphia: Institute for Research on Human Relations, 1955.

Guest, R. H., *Organizational Change; The Effect of Successful Leadership*. Homewood, Ill.: Irwin-Dorsey Press, 1962.

Guetzkow, H. and Gyr, J., An Analysis of Conflict in Decision-Making Groups. *Human Relations*, 1954, *7*, 367-382.

Guilford, J. P., Traits of Creativity. In H. H. Anderson (ed.), *Creativity and Its Cultivation*. New York: Harper & Row, Publishers, 1959, pp. 142-161.

Hare, A. P., *Handbook of Small Group Research*. New York: The Free Press of Glencoe, Inc., 1962.

Harlow, H. F., The Formation of Learning Sets. *Psychological Review*, 1949, *56*, 51-65.

Heidbreder, E., An Experimental Study of Thinking. *Archives of Psychology*, 1924, *11*, No. 73.

Helmholtz, H. von, as quoted in Sanford, F. H., *Psychology*. San Francisco: Wadsworth Publishing Co., Inc., 1961, p. 368.

Hoffman, L. R., Harburg, E., and Maier, N. R. F., Difference and Disagreement as Factors in Creative Problem Solving. *Journal of Abnormal and Social Psychology*, 1962, *64*, 206-214.

Hollander, E. P., Some Effects of Perceived Status on Responses to Innovative Behavior. *Journal of Abnormal and Social Psychology*, 1961, *63*, 247-250.

Hovland, C. I., Computer Simulation of Thinking. *American Psychologist*, 1960, *15*, 687-693.

Hull, C. L., Quantitative Aspects of the Evolution of Concepts, An Experimental Study. *Psychological Monographs*, 1920, *28*, No. 123.

John, E. R., Contributions to the Study of the Problem Solving Process. *Psychological Monographs*, 1957, *71*, No. 447.

Johnson, D. M., *Psychology: A Problem Solving Approach*. New York: Harper & Row, Publishers, 1961.

Judson, A. J. and Cofer, C. N., Reasoning as an Associative Process: I. "Direction" in a Simple Verbal Problem. *Psychological Reports*, 1956, *2*, 469-476.

Kaplan, A., Skogstad, A. H., and Girshick, M. A., The Prediction of Social and Technological Events. *Public Opinion Quarterly*, 1950, *14*, 93-110.

Katona, G., Rational Behavior and Economic Behavior. *Psychological Review*, 1953, *60*, 309-311.

Katz, David, as cited in Krech, D. and Crutchfield, R. S., *Elements of Psychology*. New York: Alfred A. Knopf, Inc., 1958.

Katzell, R. A., Contrasting Systems of Work Organization. *American Psychologist*, 1962, *17*, 102-108.

Kelley, H. H. and Thibaut, J. W., Experimental Studies of Group Problem Solving and Process. In G. Lindzey (ed.), *Handbook of Social Psychology*, Vol. 2.

Cambridge, Mass.: Addison-Wesley Publishing Co., Inc., 1954, pp. 735-755.

Kendler, H. A., Greenberg, A., and Richman, H., The Influence of Massed and Distributed Practice on the Development of Mental Set. *Journal of Experimental Psychology*, 1952, *43*, 21-25.

Kendler, T. S., Concept Formation. In Farnsworth, P. R., McNemar, O., and McNemar, Q. (eds.), *Annual Review of Psychology*. Palo Alto, Calif.: Annual Reviews, Inc., 1961, pp. 447-472.

Klugman, S. F., Group Judgments for Familiar and Unfamiliar Materials. *Journal of General Psychology*, 1945, *32*, 103-110.

Korzybski, A., The Role of Language in the Perceptual Processes. In Blake, R. T., and Ramsey, G. V. (eds.), *Perception: An Approach to Personality*. New York: The Ronald Press Company, 1951, pp. 170-205.

Krech, D. and Crutchfield, R. S., *Elements of Psychology*. New York: Alfred A. Knopf, Inc., 1958.

———— and Balachey, E. L., *Individual in Society: A Textbook of Social Psychology*. New York: McGraw-Hill Book Company, Inc., 1962.

Lanzetta, J. T., Group Behavior under Stress. *Human Relations*, 1955, *8*, 552-558.

Leavitt, H. J., Some Effects of Certain Communication Patterns on Group Performance. *Journal of Abnormal and Social Psychology*, 1951, *46*, 38-50.

————, Task Ordering and Organizational Development in the Common Target Game. *Behavioral Science*, 1960, *5*, 233-239.

————, Unhuman Organizations. Prepared for the Centennial Symposium on Executive Development, School of Industrial Management, Massachusetts Institute of Technology, Cambridge, Mass., 1961; also *Harvard Business Review*, 1962, *40*, No. 4, pp. 90-98.

———— and Mueller, R. A., Some Effects of Feedback on Communication. *Human Relations*, 1951, *4*, 401-410.

Lehman, H. C., Age and Achievement. Princeton, N. J.: Princeton University Press, 1953.

Lesieur, F. G. (ed.), *The Scanlon Plan*. New York: The Technology Press of Massachusetts Institute of Technology and John Wiley & Sons, Inc., 1958.

Levy, S., Managerial Styles and Organizational Function. *The Pillsbury Management Quarterly*, Spring, 1962, Minneapolis, Minn.: Pillsbury Co., pp. 37-44.

Lewin, K., Group Decision and Social Change. In Newcomb, T. and Hartley, E. (eds.), *Readings in Social Psychology*. New York: Holt, Rinehart & Winston, Inc., 1947.

Likert, R., Effective Supervision: An Adaptive and Relative Process. *Personnel Psychology*, 1958, *11*, 317-352.

————, *New Patterns of Management*. New York: McGraw-Hill Book Company, Inc., 1961, Ch. 3.

Lippitt, R. and White, R. K., An Experimental Study of Leadership and Group Life. In Maccoby, E. E., Newcomb, T. M., and Hartley, E. L. (eds.), *Readings in Social Psychology* (3rd ed.). New York: Holt, Rinehart & Winston, Inc., 1958.

Lorge, I., Fox, D., Davitz, J., and Brenner, M., A Survey of Studies Contrasting the Quality of Group Performance and Individual Performance, 1930-1957. *Psychological Bulletin*, 1958, *55*, 337-372.

MacKinnon, D. W., The Nature and Nurture of Creative Talent. *American Psychologist*, 1962, *17*, 484-495.

————, What Makes a Person Creative? *Saturday Review*, February 10, 1962, 15-69.

Maier, N. R. F., Reasoning in Humans: I. On Direction. *Journal of Comparative Psychology*, 1930, *10*, 115-143.

———, An Aspect of Human Reasoning. *British Journal of Psychology*, 1933, *24*, 144-155.

———, An Experimental Test of the Effect of Training on Discussion Leadership. *Human Relations*, 1953, *6*, 161-173.

———, Fit Decisions to Your Needs. *Nation's Business*, 1960, *48*, 48-52.

———, *Problem-Solving Discussions and Conferences*. New York: McGraw-Hill Book Company, 1963.

——— and Hoffman, L. R., Quality of First and Second Solutions in Group Problem Solving. *Journal of Applied Psychology*, 1960, *44*, 278-283.

——— and Solem, A. R., The Contribution of a Discussion Leader to the Quality of Group Thinking: The Effective Use of Minority Opinions. *Human Relations*, 1952, *5*, 277-288.

Maltzman, I., On the Training of Originality. *Psychological Review*, 1960, *67*, 229-242.

March, J. G. and Simon, H. A., *Organizations*. New York: John Wiley & Sons, Inc., 1958.

Marquis, D. G., Guetzkow, H., and Heyns, R. W., A Social Psychological Study of the Decision Making Conference. In H. Guetzkow (ed.), *Groups, Leadership, and Men: Research in Human Relations*. Pittsburgh: Carnegie Press, 1951, pp. 55-67.

Marschak, J., Probability in the Social Sciences. Section I, Probabilities and the Norms of Behavior. In P. Lazarfeld (ed.), *Mathematical Thinking in the Social Sciences*, New York: The Free Press of Glencoe, Inc., 1954, pp. 166-169.

Mayo, E., *The Human Problems of an Industrial Civilization*. New York: The Macmillan Company, 1933.

Merrifield, P. R., Guilford, J. P., Christensen, C. R., and Frick, J. W., The Role of Intellectual Factors in Problem Solving. *Psychological Monographs*, 1962, *76*, No. 10.

Miller, G. A., The Magical Number Seven, Plus or Minus Two: Some Limits on Our Capacity for Process Information. *Psychological Review*, 1956, *63*, 81-97.

Minsky, M., A Selected Descriptor-Indexed Bibliography to the Literature on Artificial Intelligence. *IRE Transactions on Human Factors in Electronics*, March, 1961, 39-55.

Mosel, J. N., Incentives, Supervising, and Probability. *Personnel Administration*, January-February, 1962, *25*, 9-14.

Nash, D. J. and Wolfe, A. W., The Stranger in Laboratory Culture. *American Sociology Review*, 1957, *22*, 400-405.

Newcomb, T. M., *Social Psychology*. New York: Holt, Rinehart & Winston, Inc., 1950, pp. 630-650.

Newell, A., Shaw, J. C., and Simon, H. A., Elements of a Theory of Human Problem Solving. *Psychological Review*, 1958, *65*, 151-166.

——— and Simon, H. A., Computer Simulation of Human Thinking. *Science*, 1961, *134*, 2011-2017.

Olmsted, M. S., *The Small Group*. New York: Random House, 1959.

Osborn, A. F., *Applied Imagination*. New York: Charles Scribner's Sons (rev. ed.), 1957, p. 84.

Osgood, Charles E., *Method and Theory in Experimental Psychology*. New York: Oxford University Press, Inc., 1960.

Parnes, S. J. and Meadow, A., Effects of "Brain-Storming" Instructions on Creative Problem Solving by Trained and Untrained Subjects. *Journal of Educational Psychology,* 1959, *50,* 171-176. Also, *Journal of Applied Psychology,* 1959, *43,* 189-194.

Polya, G., *How to Solve It.* Princeton, N.J.: Princeton University Press, 1940. Reprinted, Garden City, N.Y.: Doubleday Anchor Book (2nd ed.), 1957, pp. 121-122.

Randall, F. D., Stimulate Your Executives to Think Creatively. *Harvard Business Review,* July-August, 1955, *33,* 121-128.

Ray, W. S., Verbal Compared with Manipulative Solution of an Apparatus-Problem. *American Journal of Psychology,* 1957, *70,* 289-290.

Roethlisberger, F. J. and Dickson, W. J., *Management and the Worker.* Cambridge, Mass.: Harvard University Press, 1939.

Ruger, H., as cited in Woodworth, R. S. and Schlosberg, H., *Experimental Psychology.* New York: Holt, Rinehart & Winston, Inc. (rev. ed.), 1954, pp. 837-838.

Sanford, F. H., *Psychology.* San Francisco: Wadsworth Publishing Co., Inc., 1961.

Saugstad, P., Problem Solving as Dependent upon Availability of Functions. *British Journal of Psychology,* 1955, *46,* 191-198.

Sayles, L. R., *Behavior of Industrial Work Groups.* New York: John Wiley & Sons, Inc., 1958.

————, New Concepts in Work Group Theory. In *Behavioral Science Research in Industrial Relations,* Industrial Relations Monograph No. 21. New York: Industrial Relations Counselors, Inc., 1962, pp. 73-99.

Schutz, W. C., *FIRO: A Three-Dimensional Theory of Interpersonal Behavior.* New York: Holt, Rinehart & Winston, Inc., 1960.

Selz, O., as cited in Woodworth, R. S. and Schlosberg, H., *Experimental Psychology.* New York: Holt, Rinehart & Winston, Inc. (rev. ed.), 1954, p. 827.

Shaw, M. E., A Comparison of Individual and Small Groups in the Rational Solution of Complex Problems. *American Journal of Psychology,* 1932, *44,* 491-504.

Simon, H. A., *Administrative Behavior.* New York: The Macmillan Company (2nd ed.), 1957.

————, *The New Science of Management Decision.* New York: Harper & Row, Publishers, 1960.

Skinner, B. F., *Science and Human Behavior.* New York: The Macmillan Company, 1953.

Smith, W. J., Albright, L. E., Glennon, J. R., and Owens, W. A., The Prediction of Research Competence and Creativity from Personal History. *Journal of Applied Psychology,* 1961, *45,* 59-62.

Stein, M. I. and Heinze, S. J., *Creativity and the Individual.* New York: The Free Press of Glencoe, Inc., 1960.

Stogdill, R. M., *Individual Behavior and Group Achievement.* New York: Oxford University Press, 1959.

Stryker, P., Can Executives Be Taught to Think. *Fortune,* May, 1953.

Tannenbaum, R. and Schmidt, W. H., How to Choose a Leadership Pattern. *Harvard Business Review,* 1958, *36,* 95-102.

Taylor, D. W., Berry, P. C., and Block, C. H., Group Participation, Brain Storming, and Creative Thinking. *Administrative Science Quarterly,* 1958, *3,* 23-47.

———— and McNemar, O., Problem Solving and Thinking. In P. R. Farnsworth and Q. McNemar (eds.). *Annual Review of Psychology.* Palo Alto, Calif.: Annual Reviews, Inc., 1955, *6*, pp. 455-482.

Thelen, H. A., Group Dynamics in Instruction: Principle of Least Group Size. *Scholastic Review*, 1959, 57, 139-148.

Thibaut, J. W. and Coules, J., The Role of Communication in the Reduction of Interpersonal Hostility. *Journal of Abnormal and Social Psychology*, 1952, 47, 770-779.

Thomson, R., *The Psychology of Thinking*. Baltimore: Penguin Books, Inc., 1959.

Thorndike, R. L., *How Children Learn the Principles and Techniques of Problem Solving*. National Society for the Study of Education, 49th Yearbook, 1950, Part I, pp. 196-216.

————, Some Methodological Issues in the Study of Creativity. *Proceedings of Educational Testing Service Meeting.* Nov., 1962.

Tillman, R., Jr., Problems in Review: Committees on Trial. *Harvard Business Review*, 1960, *38*, 6-12, 162-174.

Torrance, E. P., The Behavior of Small Groups Under the Stress of "Survival." *American Sociological Review*, 1954, *19*, 751-755.

————, Perception of Group Functioning as a Predictor of Group Performance. *Journal of Social Psychology*, 1955, *42*, 271-282.

————, Crew Performance in a Test Situation as a Predictor of Field and Combat Performance. HFORL Report No. 33, AROC, Bolling AFB, Washington (25), D.C., as cited in Hare, A. P., *Handbook of Small Group Research.* New York: The Free Press of Glencoe, Inc., 1962, p. 375.

Urwick, L., How the Organization Affects the Man. *The Management Review*, July, 1957, 59-60.

Van Zelst, R. H., An Interpersonal Relations Technique for Industry. *Personnel*, 1952, *29*, 68-76.

———— and Kerr, W. A., Some Correlates of Technical and Scientific Productivity. *Journal of Abnormal and Social Psychology*, 1951, *46*, 470-475.

————, A Further Note on Some Correlates of Scientific and Technical Productivity. *Journal of Abnormal and Social Psychology*, 1952, *49*, 129.

Vroom, V. H. and Mann, F. C., Leader Authoritarianism and Employee Attitudes. *Personnel Psychology*, 1960, *13*, 125-140.

Walker, E. L. and Heyns, R. W., *An Anatomy for Conformity*. Englewood Cliffs, N.J.: Prentice-Hall, Inc., 1962.

Wallach, M., Kogan, N., and Bem, D. J., Group Influence on Individual Risk Taking. *Journal of Abnormal and Social Psychology*, 1962, *65*, No. 2, 75-86.

Wallas, G., *The Art of Thought*. New York: Harcourt, Brace & World, Inc., 1926.

Weaver, A. E. and Madden, E. H., "Direction" in Problem Solving. *Journal of Psychology*, 1949, *27*, 331-345.

Whyte, W. F., *Man and Organization*. Homewood, Ill.: Richard D. Irwin, Inc., 1959.

Whyte, W. H., Jr., *The Organization Man*. New York: Simon and Schuster, Inc., 1956.

Wilensky, H. L., Human Relations in the Work Place: An Appraisal of Some Recent Research. In Arensberg, C. *et al.* (eds.), *Research in Industrial Human Relations*. New York: Harper & Row, Publishers, 1957, pp. 25-50.

Wispe, L. G., Evaluating Section Teaching Methods in the Introductory Course. *Journal of Educational Research*, 1951, *45*, 161-186.

Woodworth, R. S. and Schlosberg, H., *Experimental Psychology*. New York: Holt, Rinehart & Winston, Inc. (rev. ed.), 1954.

Zaleznik, A., Christiansen, C. R., and Roethlisberger, F. J., *The Motivation, Productivity, and Satisfactions of Workers*, Boston: Division of Research, Graduate School of Business Administration, Harvard University, 1958.

Zand, D. and Costello, T. W., Effect of Problem Variation on Group Problem Solving Efficiency under Constrained Communication. *Psychological Reports*, in press.

Index of Authors

This Index does not include the names mentioned within the Readings, only those in our own writing and Bibliography.

487

Subject Index

Ability, and motivation, 188-189
Absenteeism, 107, 110
  and frustration, 232
Accommodative supervision, 111 (*see also* Supervision)
Achievement (*see also* Aspirations, Need-achievement, Needs):
  group, 285
  and job satisfaction, 96
  traits of problem solvers, 375, 384-385
Acquaintance process, effect on perception, 53
Adaptation, general, syndrome, 129-130
Adjustive mechanisms to anxiety, conflict, frustration (*see also* Defense mechanisms):
  definitions of, 148-149
  illustrations of, 148-149
Adjustment, interpersonal, and perception, 52-53
Administration:
  as agent of change, 244
  and anxiety in others, 154, 156
  and attitude change, 296-297
  attitude toward frustrating stress, 131
  and change, 118, 244 (*see also* Change)
  and communication networks, 456ff.
  and concept formation, 355
  and decision making, 386
  and decision theory, 412-413
  and environmental stress, 124, 128
  knowledge of results in, 219
  and learning, 206, 221
  and need-achievement, 77
  needs, 61-63
  perception in, 3, 53-54
  and reinforcement, 217
  and risk-taking behavior, 77
  stress, implications of, 187-189
Age and creativity, 424-425
Agreement scale and perception, 52
Aggression:
  and attitudes, 269
  and defense mechanisms, 144ff.
  and frustration, 135, 139ff.
  instigation of, 142
  motivation, 141
Alienation, feelings of, 87
Allegiance, dual, 296
Anxiety, 150ff. (*see also* Stress, Conflict, Frustration):
  absence of, 153
  and attitudes, 267
  in business executives, 157-158
  characteristics of, 151
  definitions of, 127, 151-152
  effect on work attitudes, 37
  effects of, summary, 156
  and fear, differentiating factors, 151
  and frustration, distinction, 150
  as a motivating influence, 157-158
  nature of, 151ff.
  neurotic, 150, 153
  normal, 150, 152-154, 156

Anxiety (*Cont.*)
  and performance, 154ff.-159
  and problem solving, 152-153
  reduction of, 157
  and stress, 151
Apathy, 149
Appraisal interview, training for, 223
Apprehension and fear of failure, 157
Aspiration, level of:
  and anxiety, 150
  and conflict situation, 70-71
  in decision theory, 396
  defined, 73
  determinants of, 71-72
  effect of success and failure on, 67ff.
  and failure-avoiders, 155
  and frustration, 132
  and motivation, 67-73
  and self-esteem, 71-72
  and success-seekers, 154
Aspirations, job, 86
Assembly line, 94, 108
  and satisfaction, 88
Attitude change (*see also* Attitudes):
  adjustive, 265-268
  and compliance, 293, 302
  and cognitive dissonance (*see* Cognitive dissonance)
  conditions facilitating, 277ff.
  and ego defensive, 268-271, 274-275, 301
  guidelines, 291ff.
  and identification, 293, 302
  and inducements, 293-294
  and internalization, 293, 302
  and management development, 299ff.
  methods of comparison, 328-330
  model of, 299ff.
  and needs, 265
  and personal contact, 289
  procedures used in business, 298ff.
  and role, 278ff.
  and situational change, 289
  special problems in, 291
  value expressive, 271ff.
Attitudes (*see also* Perception, Job satisfaction):
  adjustive, 254, 265-268, 274-275
  and anxiety, 151
  arousal of, 265ff.
  and behavior, 254
  and change (*see* Attitude change)
  definition of, 253
  development of, 258, 260ff.
  dimensions of, 253
  and ego defensive, 255-257, 268-271, 275
  functional approach, 251, 254ff.
  information, effects of on, 288-289 (*see also* Information)
  job (*see* Job satisfaction)
  knowledge function, 255, 259, 273-274 (*see also* Cognitive dissonance)
  learning of, 222, 263 (*see also* development of)

491

DATE DUE
